VOLUME I

September 1949-December 1955

THE WRITINGS OF
MAO ZEDONG

1949-1976

Major funding for the Project on the Post-1949 Writings of Mao Zedong was provided by the Division of Research Programs of the National Endowment for the Humanities, an independent federal agency, and by Brown University.

Editors

Michael Y. M. Kau   John K. Leung

Collaborating Editors

Robert G. Lee   Helmut Martin
Richard Levy   Kimiyoshi Nakamura
Susan H. Marsh   Pierre M. Perrolle

Project Contributors

Thomas P. Bernstein   Richard Kraus
Pao-min Chang   Donna Lau
Pamela Crossley   Marjorie Lau
Christine Davey   Ellen Law
Don DeMaio   Hong Yung Lee
Lowell Dittmer   Akira Odani
Roberto A. Domenech   Suzanne Ogden
Philip E. Ginsburg   Allen Renear
Joel Glassman   Anthony Sariti
Nancy Hodes   Isabel Shen
Emily Honig   Frederic Spar
John C. S. Hsu   John Bryan Starr
Linda Jaivin   James Tong
Olga Juzyn   Byron S. J. Weng
Anna H. Kau   Jennifer Wood

VOLUME I

September 1949-December 1955

THE WRITINGS OF MAO ZEDONG

1949-1976

EDITED BY

Michael Y. M. Kau

BROWN UNIVERSITY

John K. Leung

BABSON COLLEGE and BROWN UNIVERSITY

M.E. SHARPE, INC.

ARMONK, NEW YORK/LONDON, ENGLAND

Produced in association with ⊞ **East Gate Books**,
120 Buena Vista Drive, White Plains, New York 10603.

Available in the United Kingdom and Europe from M. E. Sharpe,
Publishers, 3 Henrietta Street, London WC2E 8LU.

Library of Congress Cataloging-in-Publication Data

Mao, Tse-tung, 1893-1976.
   The writings of Mao Zedong, 1949-1976.

   Bibliography: p.
   Includes index.
   I. Kau, Michael Y. M., 1934-   . II. Leung, John
III. Title.
DS778.M3A2   1986   951.05 '092 '4   86-17910
ISBN 0-87332-391-2 (v. 1)

CONTENTS

Acknowledgments   xxi

Introduction   xxv

Introduction to Volume I   xxxiii

Editorial Conventions and Devices: A Note to the Reader   xxxvii

Opening Speech at the First Plenary Session of the CPPCC
    (September 21, 1949)   3

Speech at Banquet Celebrating Insurrection of KMT Troops
    (September 23, 1949)   7

Telegram to Xinjiang Political and Military Authorities (September 28, 1949)   8

Draft for Inscription on Monument to People's Heroes (September 30, 1949)   9

Proclamation of the Central People's Government of the PRC (October 1, 1949)   10

Telegram to the Communist Party of the United States (October 6, 1949)   12

Letter to Wang Shoudao (October 9, 1949)   13

Letter to Yang Kaizhi (October 9, 1949)   14

Telegram to the French Transportation Labor Union (October 9, 1949)   15

Telegram to General Zhao Xiguang (October 10, 1949)   15

Telegram to Insurrectionists on the "Changzhi" (October 10, 1949)   16

Telegram to Five-man Independent Group of the British Labor Party in the
    House of Commons (October 12, 1949)   16

Telegram to the United States' Committee for a Democratic Far Eastern Policy
    (October 12, 1949)   17

Letter to Feng Youlan (October 13, 1949)   17

Letter to Zhou Shizhao (October 15, 1949)   18

Reply to Ambassador of the Soviet Union (October 16, 1949)   20

Telegram to the German Democratic Republic (October 16, 1949)   21

Reply to the Hui People of Xinjiang (October 21, 1949)   22

Reply to the Provisional People's Government of Xinjiang (October 21, 1949)   22

Reply to the Xinjiang League for the Defense of Peace and Democracy and to
    People of the Tacheng-Ili-Ashan Regions (October 21, 1949)   23

Preface to *The Victory of New Democracy in China* (October 24, 1949)   23

Telegram to the Insurrectionists on the ''Hailiao'' (October 24, 1949)   24

Inscription for the Inaugural Issue of *Renmin wenxue* (People's Literature)
(October 25, 1949)   25

Telegram to Secretary of the World Federation of Trade Unions
(October 26, 1949)   26

Telegram to the Comrades of Yanan and Compatriots of the Shaanxi-Gansu-
Ningxia Border Region (October 26, 1949)   26

Telegram to the Central Committee of the Communist Party of Algeria
(October 26, 1949)   27

Telegram to the Provisional Government of Greece (October 26, 1949)   28

Telegram to the Albanian Council of Ministers (October 26, 1949)   28

Letter to Bo Yibo (October 29, 1949)   29

Telegram to the Republic of Czechoslovakia (October 29, 1949)   30

Telegram to the USSR (November 5, 1949)   31

Telegram to the Work Committee of the Communist Party of Thailand
(November 12, 1949)   31

Telegram to Managers and Staff of Two Aviation Corporations
(November 12, 1949)   32

Letter to Peng Dehuai and the Northwest Bureau (November 14, 1949)   33

Inscription on Public Morals (November 15, 1949 R)   35

Letter to Mao Xusheng (November 15, 1949)   35

Letter to Li Jiehou of Shaoshan, Hunan (November 17, 1949)   36

Telegram to the Former KMT Government Resources Committee
(November 19, 1949)   37

Telegram to the Communist Party of India (November 19, 1949)   37

Telegram to the Socialist Republican Party of India (November 19, 1949)   38

Telegram to the Central Committee of the Iranian Workers' Party
(November 19, 1949)   39

Inscription for the Third Anniversary of *Nanqiao ribao* (November 20, 1949)   39

Telegram of Condolence on the Death of Xinjiang Delegates to the CPPCC
(November 22, 1949)   40

Telegram to Panchen Gnoertehni (November 23, 1949)   41

Telegram to the Banka Federation of Labor Unions of Indonesia
(November 24, 1949)   41

Telegram to the Democratic Republic of Viet Nam (November 25, 1949)   42

Letter to Xu Beihong (November 29, 1949)   42

Telegram to the Britain-China Conference in London (November 30, 1949)   43

Letter to the People of Lushun-Dalian (December 1, 1949)   44

Letter to Liu Yazi (December 2, 1949)   44

Directive Issued at the Fourth Meeting of the CPGC (excerpts)
(December 2, 1949)   46

Instruction on the Army's Participation in Production and Construction Work
in 1950 (December 5, 1949)   47

Speech on Arrival at Moscow Train Station (December 16, 1949)   51

Telegram to Stalin (December 19, 1949)   52

Address at Birthday Celebration Meeting Held for Stalin (December 21, 1949) 52

Comment on Democratic Personages (Winter 1949)   53

Conversation with a Painter from the Soviet Union [Excerpts] (1949)   54

Inscription for First Issue of Renmin haijun (January 1, 1950)   57

Interview Given to TASS Correspondent in Moscow (January 2, 1950)   57

Inscription for Lenin's Mausoleum (January 11, 1950)   59

Telegram to Bulgaria on the Death of Vasil Kolarov (January 24, 1950)   59

Telegram to President Prasad of the Republic of India (January 28, 1950) 60

Speech on Departure from Moscow (February 17, 1950)   60

Telegram to President of the Viet Nam-China Friendship Association
(February 21, 1950)   62

Telegram to the USSR (February 23, 1950)   62

Telegram to Stalin upon Leaving the USSR (February 26, 1950)   63

Conversations During Inspection of Heilongjiang Province [Excerpts]
(February 27, 1950)   64

Inscriptions Written in Harbin (February 27, 1950)   65

Reply to Ambassador of the People's Republic of Romania (March 10, 1950) 66

Soliciting Suggestions on the Question of Strategy for Dealing with
Rich Peasants (March 12, 1950)   67

Letter to Long Bojian (March 14, 1950)   70

Letter to Liu Kuiyi (March 14, 1950)   71

Telegram to the Communist Party of France (March 31, 1950)   72

Directive on the Film Qing gong mishi (March 1950)   72

Telegram to the People's Republic of Hungary (April 1, 1950)   73

Speech at the Sixth Session of the CPGC (April 11, 1950)   74

Letter to Yang Kaizhi and Li Congde (April 13, 1950)   74

Comment on Chen Yun's Report (April 14, 1950)   75

Letter to Mao Shenpin (April 18, 1950)   76

Letter to Li Shuyi (April 18, 1950)   77

Letter to Xiang Mingqing (April 19, 1950)   78

Telegram to W. H. Andrews (April 20, 1950)   79

Telegram to Maurice Thorez (April 28, 1950)   79

Inscription Concerning the People's Education (May 1, 1950)   80

Telegram to the Republic of Czechoslovakia (May 3, 1950)   80

Inscription Commemorating the May Fourth Movement (May 4, 1950 R)   81

Letter to Wen Jianquan (May 7, 1950)   81

Letter to Zhang Ding (May 7, 1950)   82

Letter to Zhao Puzhu (May 7, 1950)   83

Letter to Mao Yimin (May 8, 1950)   84

Letter to Wen Nansong (May 12, 1950)   85

Letter to Ye Jiannong (May 12, 1950)   86

Letter to Zhou Wennan (May 12, 1950)   87

Telegram to Ho Chi Minh (May 12, 1950)   88

Letter to Mao Yuju (May 15, 1950)   89

Letter to Zou Puxun (May 15, 1950)   90

Letter to Zhou Rong (May 16, 1950)   90

Reply to Ambassador of the Republic of India (May 20, 1950)   91

Letter to Li Jinxi (May 22, 1950)   92

Telegram of Condolence to Yan Huiqing's Family (May 26, 1950)   93

Letter to Liu Yanan (May 27, 1950)   94

Letter to Liu Shaoqi (June 4, 1950)   95

Struggle for a Fundamental Turn for the Better in the Financial and
    Economic Situation in the Country (June 6, 1950)   97

Don't Attack on All Fronts (June 6, 1950)   103

Letter to Chen Mingshu (June 12, 1950)   106

Reply to Ambassador of the Republic of Poland (June 12, 1950)   107

Reply to Ambassador of the Kingdom of Sweden (June 12, 1950)   108

Opening Speech at the Second Meeting of the National Committee of
    the CPPCC (June 14, 1950)   109

Letter to Ma Xulun (June 19, 1950)   110

Closing Speech at the Second Session of the National Committee of the CPPCC
    (June 23, 1950)   111

Reply to Minister of the Kingdom of Denmark (June 24, 1950)   116

Reply to Head of Diplomatic Mission of the German Democratic Republic
    (June 24, 1950)   117

Speech at Eighth Session of the CPGC (June 28, 1950)   118

Reply to Ambassador of the People's Republic of Mongolia (July 3, 1950)   119

Telegram to the People's Republic of Mongolia (July 7, 1950)   120

Telegram to the Socialist Unity Party of Germany (July 18, 1950)   120

Letter to Wu Qirui (July 19, 1950)   121

Telegram to the Republic of Poland (July 21, 1950)   123

Telegram to the Transvaal Indian Congress (July 26, 1950) 123

Reply to Ambassador of the Union of Burma (August 7, 1950) 124

Letter to Su Yu (August 8, 1950) 125

Telegram to the People's Government of Qinghai on the Death of
Vice-chairman Ma Po (August 11, 1950) 125

Telegram to the Democratic People's Republic of Korea (August 14, 1950) 126

Telegram to the Republic of Indonesia (August 16, 1950) 126

Letter to Xu Haidong (August 20, 1950) 127

Telegram to the People's Republic of Romania (August 21, 1950) 128

Speech at Banquet Commemorating the Liberation of Romania (Excerpt)
(August 23, 1950) 128

Letter to Xu Beihong (August 26, 1950) 129

Letter to Chen Jisheng (August 29, 1950) 129

Telegram to the Democratic Republic of Viet Nam (August 29, 1950) 130

Inscription for the First National Conference on Health Care (August 1950) 131

Telegram to the People's Republic of Bulgaria (September 6, 1950) 131

Letter to Chen Yu (September 11, 1950) 132

Telegram to the South African Indian Congress (September 13, 1950) 132

Letter to Zhang Wei (September 19, 1950) 133

Telegram to the Communist Party of Great Britain (September 24, 1950) 134

Inscription for the National Conference of Representatives of Combat Heroes
(September 25, 1950) 135

Address at the Opening Session of the National Congress of Combat Heroes and
the National Congress of Worker-Peasant-Soldier Model Laborers
(September 25, 1950) 135

Comments on Suppressing and Liquidating Counterrevolutionaries
(September 27, 1950) 136

Reply to Ambassador of the People's Republic of Bulgaria (September 30, 1950) 137

Telegram to the German Democratic Republic (October 4, 1950) 138

Inscription on the Unity of the Chinese and Soviet Peoples (October 5, 1950) 138

Inscription for Display of the PLA (October 8, 1950 R) 139

Orders for the Chinese People's Volunteers (Excerpts) (October 8, 1950) 139

Letter to Wang Shoudao (October 11, 1950) 141

Telegram to the Republic of Czechoslovakia (October 26, 1950) 142

Telegram to Prince Gustaf Adolf of Sweden on the Death of King Gustaf V
(October 31, 1950) 142

In Response to Liu Yazi: A Poem (October 1950) 143

Telegram to the USSR (November 5, 1950) 144

Telegram to Harry Pollitt (November 20, 1950)   144

Letter to Hu Qiaomu (November 22, 1950)   145

Telegram to the People's Republic of Albania (November 26, 1950)   147

Comment on Hearing of Mao Anying's Death (November 1950)   147

Letter to Huang Niantian (December 2, 1950)   148

Telegram to Participants of Demonstration in Tianjin (December 2, 1950)   149

Inscription for the Air Force (December 15, 1950 R)   150

Letter to Chen Shutong (December 18, 1950)   151

Comment on Suppressing and Liquidating Counterrevolutionaries
    (December 19, 1950)   152

Telegram to the Communist Party of France (December 23, 1950)   152

Inscription for the First Normal School of Hunan (December 29, 1950)   154

Letter to Zhou Shizhao (December 29, 1950)   154

Telegram to the People's Republic of Romania (December 29, 1950)   155

Comment on "A Summary of the Relationship between the Various
    Departments of the Military and the Soviet Advisors" (January 1, 1951)   157

Telegram to the Union of Burma (January 2, 1951)   158

Telegram to Wilhelm Pieck (January 2, 1951)   158

Letter to Rao Shushi and Chen Pixian (January 10, 1951)   159

Letter to Xu Beihong (January 14, 1951)   160

Letter to Li Sian (January 14, 1951)   161

Letter to Ma Xulun (January 15, 1951)   161

Comment on Suppressing and Liquidating Counterrevolutionaries
    (January 17, 1951)   162

Directive to the Chinese People's Volunteers (January 19, 1951)   163

Letter to Zhang Lan (January 22, 1951)   164

Telegram to the Communist Party of Italy (January 22, 1951)   165

Comment on Suppressing and Liquidating Counterrevolutionaries
    (January 24, 1951)   165

Telegram to the Republic of India (January 24, 1951)   166

Toast at a Reception Given by Ambassador of India (January 26, 1951)   166

Telegram to the USSR (February 12, 1951)   167

Letter to Huang Yanpei (February 17, 1951)   168

Main Points of Resolution at a Political Bureau Meeting (February 18, 1951)   169

Telegram to the USSR (February 21, 1951)   174

Comment on Suppressing and Liquidating Counterrevolutionaries
    (February 28, 1951)   175

Inscription for Woman's Day (March 8, 1951)   175

Comment on Suppressing and Liquidating Counterrevolutionaries
    (March 9, 1951)   176

Letter to Rao Shushi and Others (March 18, 1951)   176

Comments on Suppressing and Liquidating Counterrevolutionaries
(March 24, 1951)   178

Letter to Li Da (March 27, 1951)   179

Comment on Suppressing and Liquidating Counterrevolutionaries
(March 30, 1951)   180

Comments on Suppressing and Liquidating Counterrevolutionaries
(March 30, 1951)   181

Letter to Peng Yousheng (March 31, 1951)   181

Directive on the Problem of Cultivating Cadres (March 1951)   182

Comment on Suppressing and Liquidating Counterrevolutionaries
(April 2, 1951)   183

Letter to Li Weihan (April 9, 1951)   184

Letter to Situ Meitang (April 27, 1951)   185

Letter to Chen Wenxin (April 29, 1951)   187

Letter to Zhang Zhizhong (May 5, 1951)   187

Comment on Suppressing and Liquidating Counterrevolutionaries
(May 8, 1951)   188

Directive on the Huai River (May 9, 1951)   191

Resolutions of the Third National Conference on Public Security
(May 15, 1951)   191

Comment on the ''Report of the Secretary's Office on the Handling of Letters
from the Masses'' (May 16, 1951)   195

Attention Must Be Paid to the Discussions of the Film *The Life of Wu Xun*
(May 20, 1951)   196

Speech on the Agreement on Measures for the Peaceful Liberation of Tibet
(May 24, 1951)   201

Comment on Suppressing and Liquidating Counterrevolutionaries
(June 15, 1951)   202

Letter to Li Zhuchen (June 23, 1951)   203

Inscription on the Unity of Nationalities (June 29, 1951 R)   204

Letter to Huang Yanpei (July 15, 1951)   204

Letter to Zhang Yuanji (July 30, 1951)   205

Inscription for the People of the Old Revolutionary Bases (August 5, 1951 R)   206

Telegram to the Dominion of Pakistan (August 14, 1951)   207

Telegram to the Democratic People's Republic of Korea (August 14, 1951)   207

Telegram to the Republic of Indonesia (August 14, 1951)   208

Telegram to the Democratic Republic of Viet Nam (September 1, 1951)   208

Telegram to the USSR (September 2, 1951)   209

Telegram to the People's Republic of Bulgaria (September 7, 1951)   210

Comment on Suppressing and Liquidating Counterrevolutionaries
(September 10, 1951)   210

Letter to Party Committee of Shijingshan Iron and Steel Works
(September 12, 1951)   211

Comment on Suppressing and Liquidating Counterrevolutionaries
(September 18, 1951)   211

Letter to Deng Zihui (September 25, 1951)   212

Reply to Ambassador of the Union of Burma (September 27, 1951)   213

Comment on Suppressing and Liquidating Counterrevolutionaries
(October 1, 1951)   214

Telegram to the German Democratic Republic (October 6, 1951)   214

Letter to Chen Shutong (October 14, 1951)   215

Telegram to the USSR (October 15, 1951)   216

Opening Speech of the Third Meeting of the First National Committee of
the CPPCC (October 23, 1951)   216

Telegram to the Dalai Lama (October 26, 1951)   221

Inscription for the Cultural Work Team of the Special District Party
Committee of Chu *xian* (October 1951 R)   222

Closing Speech of the Third Meeting of the First National Committee of
the CPPCC (November 1, 1951)   222

Telegram to the USSR (November 5, 1951)   223

Telegram to Gheorghiu-Dej (November 7, 1951)   224

Reply to Ambassador of Pakistan (November 12, 1951)   224

Letter to Zheng Zhenduo (December 3, 1951)   225

Letter to Dong Biwu (December 4, 1951)   226

Letter to Mao Zelian and Mao Yuanti (December 11, 1951)   227

Telegram to the Northwest Nationalities' People's Representatives' Conference
for Resisting U.S. Aggression and Aiding Korea (December 12, 1951)   228

Telegram to Panchen Gnoertehni (December 13, 1951)   229

Letter to Liu Shaoqi (December 15, 1951)   230

Take Mutual Aid and Cooperativization of Agriculture as a Major Task
(December 15, 1951)   232

Letter to Chen Yuying (December 23, 1951)   233

Telegram to William Gallacher (December 24, 1951)   233

Conversation with Zhou Shizhao (December 1951)   234

Comment Written on a Letter from Students of Chinese
People's University (1951)   234

Directive on Language Reform (1951)   235

On the "Three-Anti's" and "Five-Anti's" Struggles
(November 1951–March 1952)   235

New Year's Day Message (January 1, 1952)   243

Telegram to the Union of Burma (January 2, 1952)   244

Telegram to the Republic of India (January 24, 1952)   245

Telegram to the People's Republic of Mongolia (January 27, 1952) 245

Telegram to the Democratic Republic of Viet Nam (February 4, 1952) 246

Telegram to the USSR (February 11, 1952) 247

Imperialism's Plan for Aggression Is Bound to Be Smashed (February 14, 1952) 248

Telegram to the USSR (February 21, 1952) 248

Decree to a Division of the Xinjiang Construction Battalion (February 1952) 249

Telegram to Mátyás Rákosi (March 7, 1952) 249

Letter to Cheng Qian (March 11, 1952) 250

Instruction to Huang Yanpei (March 15, 1952) 251

Reply to Ambassador of the Democratic People's Republic of Korea
(March 18, 1952) 252

Reply to Ambassador of the Republic of Czechoslovakia (March 18, 1952) 253

Conversation with Zhai Zuojun [Excerpt] (Spring 1952) 254

Directive of the CPC Central Committee on Work in Tibet (April 6, 1952) 254

Telegram to Sa Zhenbing's Family (April 12, 1952) 259

Telegram to Boleslaw Bierut (April 16, 1952) 259

Telegram to Rajendra Prasad (May 11, 1952) 260

Letter to Tan Kah-Kee (May 16, 1952) 261

Inscription for Workers on Jing River Flood Control Project (May 19, 1952) 262

Telegram to the Dalai Lama and Panchen Gnoertehni (May 23, 1952) 262

Letter to Ye Gongzuo (May 25, 1952) 263

The Contradiction Between the Working Class and the Bourgeoisie Is the
Principal Contradiction in the Country (June 6, 1952) 265

Reply to Ambassador of the Republic of Poland (June 9, 1952) 265

Reply to Minister of the Republic of Finland (June 9, 1952) 266

Inscription on Physical Culture and Sports (June 10, 1952) 267

Letter to Huang Yanpei (June 10, 1952) 268

Letter to Zhou Enlai (June 14, 1952) 269

Inscription on Inauguration of the Chengdu-Chongqing Railway
(July 1, 1952 R) 270

Letter to Zhang Youcheng (July 7, 1952) 270

Telegram to the German Socialist Unity Party (July 8, 1952) 271

Address to the First Graduating Class of the Military Academy (July 10, 1952) 272

Inscription on the Monument to the People's Heroes (August 3, 1952 R) 274

Unite and Clearly Draw the Line Between the Enemy and Ourselves
(August 4, 1952) 274

Telegram to the Democratic People's Republic of Korea (August 13, 1952) 279

Letter to Chen Yi (August 15, 1952) 280

Letter to Li Shuqing (August 23, 1952) 280

Letter to Uighur Peasants of Xinjiang (August 30, 1952)   281

Telegram to the USSR (September 2, 1952)   282

Letter to Huang Yanpei (September 5, 1952)   283

Letter to Comrade Li Da (September 17, 1952)   285

Inscription on the Arts (September 26, 1952)   286

Reply to Ambassador of the Republic of India (September 26, 1952)   287

Inscription for Inauguration of the Tianshui-Lanzhou Railway
(September 28, 1952)   287

Toast on Third Anniversary of Founding of the PRC (September 30, 1952)   288

Letter to Mao Yuju (October 2, 1952)   289

Telegram to the Peace Conference of the Asian and Pacific Region
(October 2, 1952)   290

Letter to Qi Baishi (October 5, 1952)   290

Telegram to the German Democratic Republic (October 5, 1952)   291

Talk with Tibetan Delegates (Excerpts) (October 8, 1952)   292

Letter to Song Qingling (October 10, 1952)   294

Letter to Tan Zhenlin (October 15, 1952)   295

Letter to Li Shuqing (October 16, 1952)   296

Letter to Luo Yuankun (October 22, 1952)   297

Congratulations on the Victory of the Chinese People's Volunteers
(October 24, 1952)   298

Telegram to the Democratic People's Republic of Korea (October 28, 1952)   299

Conversation During an Inspection Tour of the Flood Prevention Works on the
Yellow River [Excerpts] (October 29–31, 1952)   300

Telegram to the USSR (November 3, 1952)   302

Inscription on Inauguration of the Kangding-Changdu Section of the
Xikang-Tibet Highway (November 19, 1952)   303

Reply to Ambassador of the Kingdom of Sweden (December 3, 1952)   304

Inscription Concerning Public Health Work (December 8, 1952)   304

Letter to the Anshan Iron and Steel Works (December 14, 1952)   305

Reply to Ambassador of the Soviet Union (December 15, 1952)   306

Letter to Yi Nanping (December 21, 1952)   307

Reply to the Ambassador of the People's Republic of Romania
(December 29, 1952)   308

Telegram to the USSR on the Transfer of the Chinese Changchun Railway
(December 31, 1952)   309

Instruction on the Arts (December 1952)   310

Directive on Education (1952)   310

Comment on a Report of the National Labor Insurance Conference (1952)   310

Telegram to the Union of Burma (January 2, 1953)   313

Intra-Party Directive on Rectification (January 5, 1953)   313

Speech to the Central People's Government Council (January 13, 1953)   316

Closing Speech at the Fourth Session of the First National Committee of
the CPPCC (Excerpts) (February 7, 1953)   317

Telegram to the USSR (February 10, 1953)   319

Instructions on the Daye Steel Plant (February 19, 1953)   320

Conversations with Naval Personnel on the Yangtze River [Excerpts]
(February 19–24, 1953)   320

Inscription Written for the Navy (February 21, 1953)   324

Telegram to the USSR (February 21, 1953)   325

Inscription Awarded to Soviet Troops in Lushun (February 22, 1953)   325

Telegram to Inquire after Stalin's Illness (March 4, 1953)   326

Telegram to the USSR on Stalin's Death (March 6, 1953)   326

Central People's Government's Decree on Stalin's Death (March 6, 1953)   328

Letter to Huang Yanpei and Chen Shutong (March 8, 1953)   328

The Greatest Friendship (March 9, 1953)   329

Telegram to Czechoslovakia on Gottwald's Death (March 15, 1953)   332

Criticize Han Chauvinism (March 16, 1953)   333

Resolve the Problem of the "Five Excesses" (March 19, 1953)   335

Telegram to Palmiro Togliatti (March 25, 1953)   338

Instruction on Leadership Work of Health Departments of Military
Commissions (April 3, 1953)   339

Reply to Ambassador of the Soviet Union (April 3, 1953)   340

Letter to Li Zhuchen (April 21, 1953)   341

Letter to Li Zhuchen (April 26, 1953)   342

Letter to Huang Yanpei and Chen Shutong (May 15, 1953)   342

Instructions on Education (May 17, 1953)   343

Criticism of Documents Issued in the Name of the Center by Liu Shaoqi and
Yang Shangkun (May 19, 1953)   344

Letter to Wang Jiaxiang (May 27, 1953)   346

Criticize the Right-Deviationist Viewpoints That Depart from the General Line
(June 15, 1953)   347

Speech on the Youth League (June 30, 1953)   351

Reply to Ambassador of the People's Republic of Mongolia (July 2, 1953)   358

Letter to Fu Dingyi (July 7, 1953)   359

On State Capitalism (July 9, 1953)   360

Letter to Huang Yanpei (July 30, 1953)   362

Telegram to the USSR (July 31, 1953)   362

Oppose the Bourgeois Ideology in the Party (August 12, 1953)   363

Telegram to the Democratic People's Republic of Korea (August 12, 1953)   375

Letter to Ye Gongzuo (August 16, 1953)   376

Telegram to the People's Republic of Albania (August 20, 1953)   376

Telegram to the Democratic People's Republic of Korea (August 25, 1953)   377

Address at the Establishment of the Institute of Military Engineering and
the Inauguration of Its First Term (August 26, 1953)   378

Letter to Li Shuqing (August 27, 1953)   379

Telegram to the Democratic Republic of Viet Nam (August 30, 1953)   380

On the General Line of the Party During the Period of Transition
(August 1953)   380

Telegram to the USSR (September 2, 1953)   381

The Path That Inevitably Must Be Followed in the Transformation of Capitalist
Industry and Commerce (September 7, 1953)   383

Speech on the Victory in Resist U.S. Aggression and Aid Korea Movement
(September 12, 1953)   386

Telegram to the Chinese People's Volunteers (September 12, 1953)   392

Telegram to the USSR (September 15, 1953)   394

Criticize the Reactionary Thought of Liang Shuming (September 16–18, 1953)   396

Telegram to the People's Republic of Mongolia on the Death of Bumatsende
(September 24, 1953)   408

Letter to Shen Junru (September 27, 1953)   409

Letter to Mao Yueqiu (October 4, 1953)   409

Letter to Ma Xulun (October 5, 1953)   411

Telegram to the German Democratic Republic (October 5, 1953)   411

Speech on Mutual Aid and Cooperativization in Agriculture (October 15, 1953)   412

Telegram to the Democratic Republic of Viet Nam (October 16, 1953)   419

Speech at Reception for Tibetan Delegation (October 18, 1953)   419

Letter to Yang Shangkun (October 22, 1953)   421

Telegram to the People's Republic of Albania (October 22, 1953)   422

Letter to Wen Jiuming (October 25, 1953)   423

Reply to Ambassador of the Republic of Indonesia (October 28, 1953)   424

Criticism of the Ministry of Public Health (October 1953)   425

Speech on Mutual Aid and Cooperativization in Agriculture
(November 4, 1953)   425

Telegram to the USSR (November 5, 1953)   432

Reply to Ambassador of the German Democratic Republic
(November 12, 1953)   433

Reply to Minister of the Republic of Finland (December 2, 1953)   434

Letter to Dai Yuben (December 9, 1953)   435

Reply to Minister of the Kingdom of Denmark (December 12, 1953)   435

Reply to Ambassador of the Democratic People's Republic of Korea
(December 12, 1953)   436

Letter to Liao Jingwen (December 13, 1953)   437

Reply to Ambassador of the Soviet Union (December 15, 1953)   438

Telegram to Anshan Workers and Staff (December 25, 1953)   439

Remark to Ke Qingshi (December 26, 1953 [?])   440

Inscription in Guest Book of the Moganshan Clinic (Winter 1953)   441

Comment on the Department of Health Care (1953)   441

Directive on Physical Culture (1953)   442

Inscription for No. 1 Automobile Manufacturing Plant of Changchun (1953) 442

Directive on the Work of the Ministry of Geology (1953)   443

Telegram to the USSR (January 4, 1954)   445

Telegram to the Democratic Republic of Viet Nam (January 29, 1954)   446

Telegram to the USSR (February 11, 1954)   446

Telegram to the USSR (February 21, 1954)   447

Letter to Tian Jiaying (March 2, 1954)   448

Letter to Huang Yanpei (March 12, 1954)   449

Telegram to Kim Du Bong (March 14, 1954)   450

Letter to Peng Shilin (March 31, 1954)   450

Letter to Party Branch and *xiang* Government of Shicheng *xiang*
(April 29, 1954)   451

Inscription on the Completion of Guanting Reservoir (May 13, 1954)   452

Telegram to the South African Indian Congress (May 28, 1954)   453

Speech on the Draft Constitution of the People's Republic of China
(June 14, 1954)   454

Beidaihe: A Poem (Summer 1954)   461

Telegram to the People's Republic of Poland (July 20, 1954)   462

Telegram to the Democratic Republic of Viet Nam (July 23, 1954)   463

Directive on Work in Traditional Chinese Medicine (July 30, 1954)   464

Letter to the Staff of the No. 320 Factory (August 1, 1954)   466

Telegram to the Democratic People's Republic of Korea (August 12, 1954) 467

Telegram to the People's Republic of Romania (August 21, 1954)   468

Telegram to the Democratic Republic of Viet Nam (August 31, 1954)   469

Reply to Ambassador of the People's Republic of Bulgaria (September 2, 1954) 470

Telegram to the USSR (September 2, 1954)   471

Telegram to the People's Republic of Bulgaria (September 7, 1954)   472

Reply to Ambassador of the People's Republic of Albania (September 13, 1954) 473

Reply to Minister of the Confederation of Switzerland (September 13, 1954) 474

Opening Speech at the First Session of the First NPC (September 15, 1954) 475

Reply to Ambassador of the People's Republic of Hungary
(September 22, 1954)   476

Toast at China's National Day Celebrations (September 29, 1954)   477

Telegram to the German Democratic Republic (October 5, 1954)   478

Letter to the Delegation of the USSR (October 12, 1954)   479

Letter to the USSR (October 12, 1954)   480

Letter on the Problems of *Hongloumeng yanjiu* (October 16, 1954)   481

Telegram to the USSR (October 16, 1954)   485

Implement the Correct Policy in Dealing with Doctors of Traditional Chinese
Medicine (October 20, 1954)   486

Toast at Reception for Prime Minister Nehru (October 21, 1954)   491

Telegram to the People's Republic of Hungary (October 22, 1954)   492

Inscription Expressing Gratitude to the Soviet Union (October 25, 1954)   492

Telegram to the Democratic People's Republic of Korea (October 25, 1954)   493

On Criticizing *Hongloumeng yanjiu* (October 1954)   494

Directive on the Film *Qing gong mishi* (October 1954)   496

Telegram to the USSR (November 6, 1954)   496

Letter to Liu Shaoqi, Zhou Enlai, et al. (November 18, 1954)   498

Telegram to the Democratic People's Republic of Korea (November 22, 1954)   499

Letter to Huang Yanpei (November 23, 1954)   500

Telegram to the People's Republic of Mongolia (November 25, 1954)   501

Telegram to the People's Republic of Albania (November 28, 1954)   502

Telegram to Petru Groza (December 1, 1954)   502

Telegram to Rajendra Prasad (December 1, 1954)   503

Toast at Dinner for Prime Minister U Nu (December 4, 1954)   503

Telegram to the Republic of Finland (December 5, 1954)   504

Telegram to Antonin Zapotocky (December 16, 1954)   504

Inscription for Workers on the Kangding-Tibet and Qinghai-Tibet Highways
(December 25, 1954)   505

Letter to Li Da (December 28, 1954)   506

Telegram to the Democratic Republic of Viet Nam (December 31, 1954)   507

On Writing Essays to Criticize Hu Shi (December 1954)   507

Speech at a Standing Committee Meeting of the Central Committee of the CPC
(Excerpts) (Winter 1954)   508

Comment on the National Budget (1954)   509

Instructions on the Work of Doctors of Traditional Chinese Medicine (1954)   510

Inscription on the Triumph of the People of Wuhan over the Flood (1954)   511

Inscription for Historical Pavilion in Caixi *xiang,* Fujian Province (1954)   511

Telegram to the Union of Burma (January 2, 1955)   513

Telegram to the Republic of India (January 24, 1955)   514

Reply to Ambassador of the Republic of Finland (January 28, 1955) 514

The Atom Bomb Cannot Scare the Chinese People (January 28, 1955) 516

Criticism of Hu Feng (January 1955) 518

Telegram to the USSR (February 12, 1955) 519

Speech at Banquet Celebrating Fifth Anniversary of Sino-Soviet Treaty
(February 14, 1955) 521

Telegram to the USSR (February 21, 1955) 522

Toast at Banquet Celebrating Tibetan New Year (February 24, 1955) 523

Letter to Lin Tie (March 5, 1955) 524

Letter to Zhou Dungu (March 6, 1955) 525

Letter to Wei Lihuang (March 17, 1955) 525

Inscription for the First Congress of Heroes and Model Soldiers of the Air Force
(March 21, 1955) 526

Opening Speech at the National Conference of the CPC (March 21, 1955) 527

Concluding Remarks at the National Conference of the CPC (March 31, 1955) 531

Speech at Meeting of the Standing Committee of the Central Committee of
the CPC (Spring 1955) 545

Telegram to the People's Republic of Hungary (April 2, 1955) 546

Order to Terminate State of War Between the PRC and Germany
(April 7, 1955) 547

Reply to Ambassador of Pakistan (April 27, 1955) 549

Inscription for Czechoslovakian Exhibition (April 28, 1955) 550

Letter to Jiang Zhuru (May 1, 1955) 551

Telegram to the German Democratic Republic (May 6, 1955) 552

Telegram to the Republic of Czechoslovakia (May 7, 1955) 553

Letter to the Party Committee of Xiangxiang *xian* (May 17, 1955) 554

Telegram to Ho Chi Minh (May 19, 1955) 555

Letter to Huang Yanpei (May 26, 1955) 556

Telegram to Afghanistan (May 26, 1955) 557

Toast at Banquet for Indonesian Prime Minister Ali Sastroamidjojo
(May 29, 1955) 558

Conversation with Security Guards on Taking Literacy Courses (May 1955) 558

Preface and Editor's Notes to Material On the Hu Feng Counterrevolutionary
Clique (May-June, 1955) 559

Letter to Tan Shiying (June 8, 1955) 583

Conversation with Soldiers (Excerpt) (June 17, 1955) 584

On Swimming [Excerpts] (June 20, 1955) 584

Telegram to Jamsarangyin Sambuu (June 27, 1955) 585

Toast to Ho Chi Minh (June 28, 1955) 586

Reply to Ambassador of the Federal People's Republic of Yugoslavia
(June 30, 1955) 586

Telegram to the People's Republic of Mongolia (July 9, 1955) 587

Telegram to the People's Republic of Poland (July 19, 1955)   588

On the Cooperativization of Agriculture (July 31, 1955)   589

Conversation with Security Guards (Mid-July 1955)   612

Telegram to the Democratic People's Republic of Korea (August 12, 1955)   613

Telegram to the Republic of Indonesia (August 15, 1955)   614

Telegram to the People's Republic of Romania (August 21, 1955)   615

Telegram to the Democratic Republic of Viet Nam (September 1, 1955)   616

Telegram to Antonin Zapotocky (September 1, 1955)   617

Intra-Party Directive on Agricultural Cooperativization (September 7, 1955) 618

Telegram to the People's Republic of Bulgaria (September 7, 1955)   620

Inscription for Tokuda Kyuichi (September 12, 1955)   621

First Preface to *Upsurge of Socialism in China's Countryside*
  (September 25, 1955)   622

Letter to Tian Jiaying (September 27, 1955)   626

Letter to Zhou Shizhao (October 4, 1955)   627

Telegram to the German Democratic Republic (October 6, 1955)   628

The Debate Over Agricultural Cooperativization and the Present Class Struggle
  (October 11, 1955)   629

A Speech at the Enlarged Sixth Plenum of the Seventh Central Committee
  [October 11, 1955]   655

Conversation with Members of the Japanese Diet (October 15, 1955)   669

Telegram to the USSR (October 24, 1955)   670

Letter to Zhang Naiqi (November 1, 1955)   671

Telegram to the USSR (November 6, 1955)   672

Letter to Huang Yanpei (November 17, 1955)   673

Remark Made to Li Kaiwen (November 20, 1955)   674

Letter to Panchen Gnoertehni (November 24, 1955)   675

Letter to Zhou Shizhao (November 24, 1955)   675

Telegram to the People's Republic of Albania (November 26, 1955)   676

Telegram to the Federal People's Republic of Yugoslavia (November 26, 1955) 677

Reply to Ambassador of the Democratic Republic of Germany
  (December 3, 1955)   678

Telegram to the Republic of Finland (December 5, 1955)   679

Talk on Opposing Right-Deviation and Conservatism (December 6, 1955)   679

Letter to Zhai Zuojun (December 12, 1955)   684

Circular Requesting Opinions on the Seventeen Articles on Agricultural Work
  (December 21, 1955)   685

Second Preface to *Upsurge of Socialism in China's Countryside*
  (December 27, 1955)   689

Editor's Notes to *Upsurge of Socialism in China's Countryside*
  (December 27, 1955)   692

Bibliography   755

ACKNOWLEDGMENTS

The task of writing this acknowledgment is a particularly pleasant one indeed, not only because it is always pleasing to express gratitude where it is due, but also because it signifies that our efforts are finally beginning to bear fruit. Searching all over the world, the Project on the Post-1949 Writings of Mao Zedong has located and collected approximately three million printed words of Mao works. It has taken a decade to translate, annotate, and edit this wealth of material for publication. A project of such scope and magnitude clearly cannot be undertaken without the devotion, hard work, and collaboration of many participants and contributors.

First, the Project wishes to acknowledge with deep gratitude the funding provided by the National Endowment for the Humanities (NEH) and by Brown University. Without their confidence and support, the initiation and execution of the project would never have been possible. The initial grant was awarded by the NEH in 1975. The support was renewed for 1977–1978 and 1980–1982. In 1983, Brown University awarded the Project a supplementary grant. Over the past decade Brown has also generously provided the Project with office space, computer facilities, and other logistical support.

While it is difficult to single out individuals from the overall superb administrative support of the NEH, we are especially appreciative of the personal concern and sympathetic support extended, beyond the call of duty, by George F. Farr, Jr., Kathy Fuller, and Helen C. Aguera, program officers of the NEH's Division of Research Grants. To Brown University's chief administrators, President Howard Swearer and Provost Maurice Glicksman, we owe our sincere gratitude and respect for their personal interest and support, which has been most valuable in the later stages of the Project's progress and in enabling us to bring the Project to fruition.

In a major undertaking like this, it is the joint dedication and collective work of all participants that makes it all possible. However, the major contributions made by John K. Leung, co-editor of these volumes, deserve special mention. Not only has he been with the Project from its inception as an energetic and hardworking translator and annotator, for the past four years he has served as the Project's operations manager, supervising and coordinating a broad range of editorial and technical activities. In addition, he is chiefly responsible for editing and standardizing the translated texts, the annotations, and the commentaries and for casting the manuscripts into final form. The Project owes a great deal to John Leung.

Of the six collaborating editors, Robert Lee, Richard Levy, Susan H. Marsh, and Pierre Perrolle were largely responsible for editing and annotating the translated texts. In the early stages of the Project, Bob Lee served for two years as associate editor. In addition to their other tasks, Susan Marsh, Rich Levy, and Pierre Perrolle were also asked to edit three thematic volumes of Mao's writings focusing on literature and art, political economy, and foreign policy, respectively. The contributions by Helmut Martin of the Ruhr University, Bochum, West Germany, and Kimiyoshi Nakamura of Sososha, Tokyo, however, were quite different in nature. Since 1975, our Project has developed a close collaborative relationship with two important research groups in Germany and Japan which are devoted to the compilation and publication of Mao writings in German and Chinese. As the respective organizers of these two groups, Helmut Martin and Kimiyoshi Nakamura have generously put their holdings at our service and provided us with a great deal of valuable bibliographic information, rare Mao texts, research notes, and other source materials. We are deeply indebted to all the collaborating editors.

Over the years, nearly forty scholars and specialists have had a role in the Project's implementation. Only the two principal editors, Michael Y. M. Kau and John K. Leung, have served continuously since its inception. Other participants have been associated with the Project for various periods of time and at different stages. Many of them worked off-location on a part-time or ad hoc basis. During the 1970s, when the project was more adequately supported, the organizational structure and operational manpower were fairly substantial. Since 1980, however, when the major tasks of bibliographic control and translation had been largely completed, and as the Project's financial resources declined, the number of participants has dwindled to a handful of editors and technical staff.

In order to properly acknowledge the effort and contribution made by every participant and to convey the sense that the Project represents a truly collective enterprise, we have listed all the contributors (on p. ii) regardless of the length and nature of their individual service.

For the search for bibliographic data and the gathering of primary material, the Project is deeply indebted to the devotion and hard work of Emily Honig, Linda Jaivin, Anna H. Kau, and Ellen Law. The arduous task of transforming the voluminous Mao texts into readable and accurate English translations was accomplished by the excellent linguistic skills and expert knowledge of our translators and editors. We extend our deep appreciation to Pao-min Chang, Philip E. Ginsburg, Nancy Hodes, John C. S. Hsu, Susan H. Marsh, Akira Odani, Suzanne Ogden, Anthony Sariti, and Frederic Spar.

In preparing source notes, editorial commentaries, and explanatory annotations, the project has sought the impressive expertise and scholarship of several China scholars, especially Pamela Crossley, Hong Yung Lee, and

James Tong. In this regard, the Project has also benefited immensely from the valuable editorial criticisms and suggestions given by such specialists as Thomas P. Bernstein, Lowell Dittmer, Joel Glassman, Richard Kraus, John Bryan Starr, and Byron S. J. Weng. We are deeply grateful to all these scholars and specialists who have contributed so generously over the years.

From the inception of the Project the technical support provided by computer programmers and assistants has played a major integral role in the Project's overall operations. To organize nearly three million words in over two thousand files for speedy and accurate storage and retrieval and for repeated editing, revision, and manuscript preparation is by no means an easy task. In this respect, we are most grateful for the competent and meticulous job performed at one time or another over the years by Christine Davey, Roberto A. Domenech, Olga Juzyn, Donna Lau, Marjorie Lau, Ellen Law, Isabel Shen, and Jennifer Wood. The Project is indebted to Allen Renear for designing the final program for the computer typesetting of the manuscript, and to Don DeMaio for the efficient execution of the program to reformat the manuscripts for publication.

During the early stage of the Project's operations, we sought and received advice and assistance from many scholars, specialists, and librarians all over the world. While it is not possible to cite and thank every individual who has given us assistance, we wish to mention at least a few whose advice and support have been vital to the Project's planning and development. We are particularly grateful to Jerome Ch'en, Wen-lin Chu, William Hsu, Chu-cheng Kan, James Lilley, John T. Ma, Takeuchi Minoru, Stuart Schram, Noriyuki Tokuda, Warren Tsuneishi, Chi Wang, Ting Wang, Eugene Wu, and P. K. Yu.

Finally, the Project owes the ultimate publication of these volumes to the publisher's unfaltering faith and enduring interest. We gratefully acknowledge the support, good humor, and patience of Doug Merwin of East Gate Books and our editor at M. E. Sharpe since the Project's inception, and of David B. Biesel, editorial director at Sharpe, and his predecessor, Arnold C. Tovell. Without their personal concern and commitment, these volumes probably would never have been published. And we thank Joan Greenfield and Angela Foote, who respectively designed the cover and the interior of these books, for the elegance and style of their work, and Susan M. Marsh, who rendered the graceful calligraphy on the cover.

Providence, R.I.   Michael Y. M. Kau
September 1986

INTRODUCTION

For nearly half a century before his death on September 9, 1976, Mao Zedong dominated the stage of China's Communist revolution and socialist experiment. The process of violent civil war and political struggle prior to 1949 and the radical political reform and economic change since then cannot be separated from Mao, the charismatic leader, or his theory and strategy of revolution and socialist development. Since his death, in spite of the purge of the "Gang of Four," the downfall of Hua Guofeng, and the growing trend toward political moderation under Deng Xiaoping, the dramatic revolutionary changes and unprecedented radical transformations in China initiated by Mao will long remain unique in human history.

In the world arena, the ebb and flow of Communist movements notwithstanding, Mao Zedong has clearly emerged as the twentieth century's most powerful symbol of political and philosophical radicalism; and "Mao Zedong Thought" has epitomized the ideals of mass mobilization, class struggle, proletarian dictatorship, people's war, and uninterrupted revolution. Today, any political forces that seek a radical alternative for political and social change are likely to turn to Mao and his vision for inspiration and strategy.

The ascendence of Mao Zedong and his thought as the dominant political and ideological force of new China can be seen vividly from the elevation of Mao to the position of indisputable chairman of the Chinese Communist Party and Mao Zedong Thought to that of official doctrine of the state. Following the Seventh Party Congress in 1945, Mao was formally exalted as the "greatest revolutionary leader" in Chinese history and the "greatest genius" of world revolution in the modern era. His thought was officially acclaimed as the "guiding principle" for all Party work and glorified as the "zenith of Marxism-Leninism" in our time. From the mid-1940s on, selected writings and speeches of Mao were compiled and published in large quantities for the entire Party to study and follow. Party doctrine held that the thought of Mao Zedong had integrated the universal truth of Marxism-Leninism with the concrete practice of revolution in China and had brought Marxism-Leninism to a new and higher stage.

The massive publication of Mao's works is indicative of the crucial role that Mao and his thought have played in China's revolutionary developments in recent decades. Prior to 1949, Mao's writings were published in a rather dispersed and unsystematic manner in various "liberated areas." After the founding of the People's Republic in October 1949, the task of editing and publishing Mao's writings and speeches was centralized under the Central Committee of the Party. The first three volumes of the official *Mao Zedong xuanji* (*Selected Works of Mao Zedong*, hereafter *Selected Works*), covering Mao's works from 1926 through 1945, were published in quick succession between December 1951 and February 1953; the fourth volume, covering the period 1945–49, appeared in September 1960.

According to the Chinese press, 10.8 million copies of the multivolume *Selected Works* were published between 1951 and 1965. In the short span of the three years between 1966 and 1968, the peak of the Cultural Revolution, a staggering 150 million copies of the *Selected Works* were printed and distributed. From 1969 to Mao's death in 1976, an additional 75.8 million copies were reported to have been published. In other words, in the twenty-five-year period during which Mao led China, the Party published as many as 236 million copies of the four-volume set of the official *Selected Works* alone.

During the 1960s and 1970s, it should be noted, the *Selected Works* was by no means the only officially sponsored Mao publication. The Party also published, just to cite a few major collections, 140 million copies of *Mao Zedong zhuzuo xuandu*, jia–yi zhong ben (*Selected Readings from the Works of Mao Zedong*, A and B editions, 1964), 96 million copies of the various versions of the poems of Chairman Mao (1958–1965), and, above all, 740 million copies of the ubiquitous *Mao zhuxi yulu* (*Quotations from Chairman Mao*, 1966–69). Soon after Mao's death, 28 million copies of Volume V of the official *Selected Works* were published in 1977–78 under the sponsorship of Mao's immediate successor, Hua Guofeng.

The massive publication of various selected works of Mao on a scale unprecedented in human history was a stunning political phenomenon. For the comprehensive and systematic scholarly study of Mao and his thought, however, the value of these officially sponsored collections is seriously limited.

First, despite the enormous volume of these publications, their contents are incomplete and extremely selective in relation to the total corpus of Mao's works. The materials that were selected for inclusion in the official collections in fact represent only a fraction of all of Mao's writings and utterances over the years. The first four volumes of the official *Selected Works*, for example, contain only 156 selections of Mao's pre-1949 works. By contrast, the two multivolume collections compiled by a group of Japanese scholars, *Mao Zedong ji* (*Collected Writings of Mao Zedong*, 10 volumes, Tokyo, 1971–72; revised edition, 1983) and *Mao Zedong ji bujuan* (*Supplements to Collected Writings of Mao Zedong*, 10 volumes, Tokyo, 1983–86), contain as many as 2,212 texts of all types for the years before 1949. When Volume V of the officially sponsored *Selected Works* was published in 1977, only 70 selections from the period between 1949 and 1957 were chosen for inclusion. By contrast, our Project files contain 750 entries of various types of Mao's works for the same period; 522 of these texts, covering the period 1949–1955, are included in the first volume of this publication.

The second limitation has to do with the criteria and methods of the selection and editing of material for the official collections. The task has always been highly sensitive politically and thus subject to political and ideological manipulation. In general, texts were invariably selected and edited by the dominant political group of the day to reflect and support its own ideological orientation and policy positions. The first four volumes of the *Selected Works* were clearly compiled and published for the purpose of exalting Mao's theory and strategy of revolution and enhancing his ideological and political leadership. The long delay in the publication of Volume V, which finally appeared in 1977, seventeen years after the appearance of Volume IV in 1960 and twenty years after the events of the period covered in the volume (1949–1957), reflects the complex factional conflict and editorial politics of the period since the mid-1950s.

Between 1956 and 1976, the control of the editorship of Mao's works changed hands at least three times: from the Liu Shaoqi–Deng Xiaoping faction (1956–1965), to the Lin Biao–Chen Boda clique (1966–1972), and then to the so-called "Gang of Four" (1973–1976). Each group tried to draft its own version of Volume V with the aim of enlisting Mao's thought for advancing its own political cause and legitimizing its own authority. The final version of Volume V (which ultimately was hastily published under the leadership of a new Committee for the Editing and Publication of the Works of Mao Zedong in March 1977, six months after Mao's death) was clearly designed by the Hua Guofeng–Wang Dongxing group to capture the prestige and influence of Mao's personality cult in order to bolster the group's own image and legitimacy.

In addition to the selections included in Volume V, the Hua-Wang leadership also released eight additional Mao works between December 1976 and July 1978, including such texts as "Speech at the Enlarged Work Conference of the Central Committee" (text January 30, 1962, in this publication), "China Will Make a Great Leap Forward" (text December 13, 1964), and "A Letter on the Mechanization of Agriculture" (text March 12, 1966). Clearly, works such as these were selected mainly to legitimatize and support the middle-to-left policy orientation pursued by Hua Guofeng at the time.

While Hua and his close associates were being ousted from their top leadership positions between 1979 and 1981, the new leadership under Deng Xiaoping disbanded, in 1980, the editorial and publishing committee for Mao works organized by Hua Guofeng and incorporated its functions into the Office of Archives and Research of the Party Central Committee. Moreover, it discarded a draft Volume VI of the *Selected Works* prepared under Wang Dongxing's editorial control.

In the years since 1979, more official collections of Mao's works have been released, notably three new thematic volumes: *Mao Zedong shuxin xuanji* (*Selections from Mao Zedong's Letters*, 1983), *Mao Zedong xinwen gongzuo wenxuan* (*Selected Writings of Mao Zedong on Newspaper Work*, 1983), and *Mao Zedong nongcun diaocha wenji* (*Collected Writings of Mao Zedong on the Investigations in the Countryside*, 1983). These new collections were all published in December 1983, ostensibly in commemoration of Mao's nineti-eth birthday. The Deng leadership has also selectively published many individual items, such as three letters to Li Da (texts March 27, 1951, September 17, 1952, and December 28, 1953) and a poem in praise of Peng Dehuai written during the Long March in 1935. An analysis of these newly compiled materials reveals without doubt that the current leadership is stressing the moderate side of Mao and deliberately shunning Mao's more radical writings. These new publications were clearly designed to support and legitimatize Deng's prag-matic reform and the pursuit of the ''four modernizations.'' In the long run, while one can expect that more Mao papers will be selected and edited for publication, one can be also sure that the kind of editorial and publishing politics described above will remain in force.

Finally, aside from the problems of extreme selectivity and heavy political editing, there is also the problem of a lack of systematic and comprehensive bibliographic control over the entire corpus of Mao's writings and speeches. Beyond the official collections, there is little systematic information about or access to the myriad of items scattered among a wide variety of Chinese newspapers, magazines, government publications, etc. For the most part buried in obscurity, they are rarely used for systematic research and analysis.

During the Cultural Revolution, many competing Red Guard organizations took advantage of the prevailing chaos to gather a wide range of Mao materials and publish them for various political purposes. At least a dozen large collec-tions of Mao papers, popularly titled *Mao Zedong sixiang wansui* (*Long Live Mao Zedong Thought*) or *Mao zhuxi wenxuan* (*Selected Writings of Chairman Mao*), were published by Red Guard factions in this period. In addition, thousands of Mao's instructions, conversations, letters, and quotations also appeared in Red Guard publications. None of these materials, however, were ever systematically checked for authenticity or accuracy; nor were they brought under a unified system of bibliographic control.

It was against this background of an urgent need to organize the massive corpus of Mao's works of all types for systematic scholarly research that the Project on the Post-1949 Writings of Mao Zedong was launched at Brown University in 1975. The primary objectives of the Project were to be achieved in three phases: (1) to gather every text available anywhere in the world of everything Mao had written or spoken between 1949 and 1976, including essays, speeches, commentaries, instructions, interviews, poems, telegrams, letters, etc. (to which we have applied the rubric ''writings''); (2) to translate, edit, annotate, and index all the materials gathered; and (3) to compile and publish these materials in a comprehensive chronological multivolume collection.

As was to be expected, the search for the texts of Mao's works and other relevant bibliographic material and information, the foundation upon which all other activities of the Project were to be carried out, received our highest priority during the initial years of the Project. Our bibliography staff checked most of China's major newspapers and journals, such as *Renmin ribao (People's Daily)*, *Guangming ribao (Guangming Daily)*, *Hongqi (Red Flag)*, *Xinhua yuebao (New China Monthly)*, and *Renmin shouce (People's Handbook)*. We also combed through large collections of news releases, newspaper clippings, and Red Guard publications, notably *New China News Agency (NCNA) News Releases*, *Youlian jianbao ziliao (Newspaper Clippings of the Union Research Institute)*, and *Hongweibing ziliao (Red Guard Publications*, 20 volumes, *Supplement*, 8 volumes, compiled by the Center for Chinese Research Materials). In addition, we also consulted hundreds of Chinese books and pamphlets that contain a wide range of Mao texts or reports on Mao. As few of these sources have adequate indexes, we undertook the time-consuming process of examining them page by page or, as in the case of microfilm, frame by frame.

In search of Mao's works the Project also systematically screened all major U.S. government translation series, such as *Survey of China Mainland Press* (SCMP), *Extracts from China Mainland Magazines* (ECMM), *Selections from China Mainland Magazines* (SCMM), *Current Background* (CB), *Foreign Broadcast Information Service* (FBIS) *Daily Report*, and *Joint Publications Research Service* (JPRS). (A detailed listing of the various sources consulted may be found in the bibliography at the end of this volume.) The Project was particularly fortunate to be able to gain access to a rich source in a special file on Mao maintained at the Foreign Broadcast Information Service. By 1982, toward the end of the major drive of material gathering, the Project's text files numbered approximately 2,300 items, totaling nearly 3 million Chinese characters of Mao's works of all types.

In the process of searching for and gathering Mao's texts, we also sought the assistance of major East Asian libraries and research centers and consulted numerous specialists and scholars throughout the world. Furthermore, the Project entered into a close collaborative relationship with two groups of China scholars in Japan (led by Minoru Takeuchi of Kyoto University and Kimiyoshi Nakamura of Sososha) and West Germany (headed by Helmut Martin of the Institute of Asian Studies in Hamburg and later of the Ruhr University of Bochum) which were dedicated to the compilation of, respectively, a Chinese and a German edition of the collected works of Mao Zedong.

Aside from gathering source material, our research staff also spent enormous amounts of time tracing the sources of the hundreds of brief instructions and quotations that, while attributed to Mao, were undocumented. Identifying textual variations among the different versions of the texts was another time-consuming task. The difficulty of these endeavors was exacerbated by the Chinese propensity to quote Mao on all occasions, but without the bibliographic niceties required by scholarly convention.

The task of translating and editing the texts was handled through the teamwork of native speakers of Chinese and native speakers of English, all with bilingual training and competence. With the former having a better grasp of the nuances of the Chinese terms and expressions, and the latter better equipped to assure readability in English, these small bilingual teams edited each draft translation with a single goal: to achieve a high standard of accuracy and readability.

Except in the few rare instances where a text is available only in an English source, the translations published in these volumes were all rendered by the Project. This policy of translating all Chinese texts, even where English translations of a text had been published previously either by Beijing or in the West, was pursued for the purpose of maintaining the independence and consistency of the Project and its publications. For the convenience of the serious researcher, the sources of all Chinese texts as well as all available English translations are cited in the source notes as fully as our bibliographic data permit. The scholarly apparatus that surrounds each text is explained in full in the technical note to the reader entitled "Editorial Conventions and Devices." The user of these volumes is advised to consult that note beforehand.

The publication of these volumes has been long delayed for many reasons. Among the major factors has been the sporadic, surprise surfacing of additional texts in the years since the Project was begun, which greatly complicated our work plan and publication schedule. To a project like ours, new discoveries of fresh materials are always a mixed blessing of excitement and frustration. On many occasions the Project has been forced to divert its energy and modify its work plan to accommodate these new discoveries. We have been constantly confronted with the dilemma of wrestling with the conflicting goals between publishing the collection according to a preset schedule or delaying it for the sake of attaining a greater comprehensiveness. For instance, when the first volume had just reached the final stage of preparation for typesetting in 1984, Beijing put out, as mentioned earlier, three new thematic collections of Mao's works. Moreover, a year later, several additional versions of unauthorized Red Guard publications, *Mao Zedong sixiang wansui* (*Long Live Mao Zedong Thought*) and *Xuexi wenxuan* (*Selected Writings for Studying*), became available for the first time outside of China. Since it was too costly and difficult to make major changes of the typeset pages without serious financial and technical complications, we were unable to integrate all of these recently unearthed texts from the 1949–1955 period into Volume I of this publication. However, these late arrivals will appear supplementarily in the final volume of this work.

The entire collection of Mao's post-1949 works is scheduled to be published

in a comprehensive set of six volumes. The first five volumes will contain the texts and annotations, arranged chronologically, with the final volume comprising supplementary texts, cumulative index, chronology of Mao's activities, and bibliography. The average length of each volume will be 800 pages, and we expect to publish all the volumes in about two and a half years following the appearance of the first volume.

For a project of the magnitude, scope, and duration of this one, it is impossible to avoid mistakes and oversights. We therefore sincerely welcome corrections or suggestions from the users of these volumes. Correspondence should be directed to: The Mao Writings Project, Department of Political Science, Brown University, Providence, Rhode Island 02912.

INTRODUCTION TO VOLUME I

The period from September 1949 to the end of 1955 was naturally crucial in Mao Zedong's political career as well as in the history of the republic of which he was leader for over two decades. In this period Mao and others in the leadership of the Chinese Communist Party developed the character of the regime that would simultaneously govern the "New China" and push toward the transition to socialism.

To identify a comprehensive and consistent perspective on the documents in this volume that reflects and underlines the developments in the People's Republic of China in this period we may take a clue from the "Three Major Movements," or campaigns, that were launched at the early stage of the PRC's history: the land reform campaign, the campaign to suppress counter-revolutionaries, and the campaign to Resist U.S. Aggression and Aid Korea. While each of these campaigns had a specific target, and operated within a specific arena, they were not isolated or insulated from one another. The land reform campaign, for instance, can be seen primarily as a socio-economic movement. Yet, at the same time, it was a reflection of the broader movement to continue to transform, in a revolutionary way, China's society and, indeed, its culture. Furthermore, the land reform campaign, particularly through the identification of and attack against elements in the government and even in the Communist Party that hindered or obstructed this process of transformation, also evolved into an issue of political struggle and "Party rectification." Similarly, the Campaign to Resist U.S. Aggression and Aid Korea had social and political ramifications that went beyond its immediate diplomatic and military substance.

In a profound sense, therefore, the campaign to suppress counterrevolutionaries (in a broader sense to do battle with the forces in Chinese society and government that were either actively opposed to the continued radical and even violent revolutionizing of China or complacent about the consolidation of the apparent fruits of the revolutionary civil war) was the underlying principle of Mao's thought and policies at this time. The fact that he fought strenuously to maintain its momentum and to prevent its suppression in the "period of recovery" from 1950 to 1953 foreshadowed many of the political struggles that emerged successively in the period covered by this volume as well as those in periods covered by later volumes, notably the ideological struggles of the late-1950s and the 1960s surrounding the emergence of what came to be hailed as Mao Zedong Thought, which itself was undergirded by the notion of "Uninterrupted Revolution."

The documents in this volume illustrate vividly the evolution of these political and yet also socio-economic, cultural, and ideological struggles. Within the period of late 1949 to 1955, these struggles emerged as, in succession, the "campaign to suppress counterrevolutionaries," from late 1950 to mid-1952; the "Three-Anti's and Five-Anti's campaigns," from late 1951 to mid-1952; the intra-Party "rectification campaign" in 1953, particularly oriented toward the eradication of the "Five Excesses" (see text Mar. 19, 1953); the early signs of the "two-line" struggle (see texts Jun. 15, 1953, and Aug. 12, 1953); the struggle over the "Gao Gang–Rao Shushi Affair" in early 1955; and a number of struggles over cultural matters and figures along the way – the criticism of *The Life of Wu Xun* (text May 20, 1951), the criticism of Liang Shuming (text Sept. 16-18, 1953), the criticism of the studies of the novel *Hongloumeng* (Dream of the Red Chamber) (text Oct. 16, 1954, etc.), and the criticism of Hu Feng (text May-Jun. 1955).

The principle of continuing revolutionary transformation within the context of socio-economic and political reform was already implicit in the two documents – texts Jun. 6, 1950(1), and Jun. 6, 1950(2) – that set the agenda for the early years of recovery and transition for the PRC. Mao's comments on May 8, 1951, outlined the specific tactics for the suppression of counterrevolutionary forces and elements, and the general implications of these were summed up in the Resolutions of the Third National Conference on Public Security (text May 15, 1951). The linkage of this issue to the Three-Anti's and Five-Anti's campaigns is made clear in text Nov. 1951-Mar. 1952. By late 1952, Mao had clearly come to the conclusion that it was necessary to assert that the continuation of the class struggle would be the chief principle of the socialist transformation of the Republic. This was expressed in the intra-Party rectification (*zhengfeng*) documents of Jan. 5, 1953, Feb. 7, 1953, and Mar. 19, 1953. In the months that followed, we see documents that forecast the two-line struggle that would later dominate PRC politics in the late 1950s and the 1960s. Although Liu Shaoqi was not yet identified as the major culprit in Mao's mind, we see, for instance, in texts May 19, 1953, Jun. 15, 1953, and Aug. 12, 1953, that Mao's difference with Liu was already, at this early stage, not merely over matters of style and personal power. We see also here that Mao was attempting to map out a steady and uncompromising road, neither wavering to the Right nor to the "Left," for revolutionary social transformation based on class struggle. Finally, in early 1955, through the struggle over the "Gao Gang–Rao Shushi Affair," this issue was brought into the immediate intra-Party political arena (text Mar. 21, 1955, and others following).

The same issue was fought over in the more directly economic arena throughout these years. Following the land reform campaign, which the PRC took to be its first major task in this sphere and which was launched in spring 1950 (texts Mar. 12, 1950, and Apr. 14, 1950), the Five-Anti's campaign brought the issue of socialist transformation into the realm of industry and handicraft industries, in other words, into the urban sector. The strategy in this realm was summed up in the notion of transforming the socio-political framework of China's industrial production through "state capitalism" (texts Jul. 9, 1953, and Sept. 7, 1953). The parallel transformation of China's rural structure was not suspended, however, and immediately on the heels of the program to socialize China's industry came the campaign to cooperativize China's agricultural economy. In addition to inaugurating programs that were intended to boost agricultural productivity, Mao clearly believed that the key to success in this sector resided with, again, the class struggle – to structurally transform China's rural economic base. And the major strategy was to over-haul, through the method of cooperativization, the system of ownership of the means of production, chiefly land. The agenda and purpose was proclaimed in several speeches in late 1953 (texts Oct. 15, 1953, and Nov. 4, 1953). In 1954 and 1955, the agricultural cooperativization program was first adopted as an experiment and then rapidly propagated and implemented. In the course of implementation, however, many problems and even abuses surfaced, lead-ing to the decision on the part of some, such as Liu Shaoqi, to curtail the pro-gram and even disband large numbers of cooperatives that were already estab-lished. Mao himself adamantly refused to abandon the program, convinced as he was that the basic principle of cooperativization was sound and, moreover, the only principle that would successfully launch the general socialization of the agricultural base of China's economy. He strenuously defended the co-operativization program against the opposition and clearly was preoccupied with this matter from late summer 1955 to the end of that year, writing copiously on the subject (texts Jul. 31, 1955, Sept. 7, 1955, Sept. 25, 1955, Oct. 11, 1955, Dec. 6, 1955, and Dec. 27, 1955).

Many documents in this volume illustrate the positioning of the PRC on the world stage. From late-1949 to the early-1970s Mao, as chairman of the Peo-ple's Republic of China and chairman of the Communist Party of China, sent many diplomatic messages – letters, telegrams and speeches – on state visits, to foreign envoys, etc. In later years, many of these became *pro forma*, but in the years covered by this volume, there are quite a few significant documents of this type. In these early years of the Republic, Mao, as representative of the Chinese government, laid the groundwork for China's revolutionary diplo-matic position through his messages to allied countries and parties or move-ments as well as to adversaries. Of special importance are the documents that trace the development of China's early friendship with the Soviet Union (especially documents produced at the time of Mao's visit to that country in early 1950 and Mao's proclamation on Stalin's death – text Mar. 19, 1953). Other documents provide evidence for the violently adversarial relationship between the PRC and the United States in these years (texts Oct. 8, 1950, and Jan. 28, 1955). Still others document the PRC's support for revolutionary movements in Southeast Asia, in Africa, and in Latin America.

The reader will also find to be of significant interest documents in this volume that reflect, in 1949-1950, the process by which the new political apparatus of the PRC assumed command of the nation's affairs (for example, letters and telegrams that Mao wrote to officials in the government, to leaders of "democratic parties," to local commanders in the field, etc.). Mao's private writings will, of course, also be of great interest to scholars, and here we have many letters, for instance, that reflect Mao's personal style. Needless to say, Mao assumed a great deal of power and responsibility in 1949-1950. These letters, many of which are published in English translation for the first time here, provide an insider's view of how Mao handled this power and responsibility in his private life.

Finally, one of the rewards of undertaking a massive editorial and publication effort such as this is the occasional serendipitous "find." We have, for instance, discovered here a poem written by Mao, in a letter to his friend Zhou Shizhao (text Oct. 4, 1955), that was overlooked by other published translations.

EDITORIAL CONVENTIONS AND DEVICES: A NOTE TO THE READER

FORMAT OF THE TEXTS

Each text by Mao is preceded by the following elements: title, date, source note, and, in some but not all instances, remarks on the source and/or an explanation of the title, and a contextual and/or critical comment. Annotative notes follow the text.

1. *TITLE*

In most cases we have created our own descriptive titles, particularly for those documents culled from news articles. They may differ from the title in the original; in many cases the original has no title. Usually the title describes the category of the document (e.g., telegram, letter, speech) and the occasion or event to which it is related (e.g., meeting, conference, anniversary). In some cases, in the interest of brevity, the title has been shortened. For example, a "speech in response" to a presentation by a foreign envoy is characterized as a "reply."

In some cases, particularly that of documents published in such well-known publications as *Xuanji* (Selected Works), Vol. 5, we have used the title from that source. For example, for Mao's speech at the Third Plenum of the Seventh Central Committee (June 6, 1950), we have foresaken the descriptive title for the more familiar "Don't Attack on All Fronts," our translation of the *Xuanji* title.

"(Excerpt)" following a title indicates that the document was excerpted from a larger document by the original publishers. (See, for example, text August 23, 1950.) When a document is clearly excerpted but is not so indicated in the original, we have not so designated it. (See, for example, text February 18, 1951.)

Where we have done our own excerpting from a larger document, presenting only the more interesting or significant portions of the original, the title is followed by "[Excerpt]." (See, for example, text Spring 1952.)

The reader should note that as a rule brackets [ ] enclose our own editorial remarks, whereas parentheses ( ) indicate editorial remarks in the original.

2. DATE

The documents are presented in chronological order. Documents for which there is a year but no month or day are placed at the end of the year, and documents for which there is a season or month but no day are placed at the end of that season or month. We have usually designated the season as a quarter (e.g., January-March for spring). Documents that overlap months or years are placed at the end of the first month or year.

The date refers to the time when the document was originally written or spoken, not when it first appeared in print. In some cases (especially many of Mao's letters) the differences between these dates can be many years; in other cases (e.g., telegrams from Mao and other Chinese leaders which generally appear in the press the day after they were written) it may be just a day or several days.

When we have no definite information about the date on which a document was produced but are fairly certain that it was not the same day it was released, we have put "R" after the date, which would then be the date of release. (See, for example, text October 8, 1950.) This is particularly true of inscriptions that Mao wrote for special occasions such as inaugurations and anniversaries.

Documents produced on the same day appear together, but the sequence is random and does not present any particular order of significance. The same is true for documents of unspecified dates put together at the end of a month, season, or year.

3. SOURCE NOTE

The source note generally occurs in three parts:

Source: This is the source from which our translation is made. When more than one source is available, we have attempted to determine which is the most complete and made our translation from that one. Significant discrepancies (not, however, minor ones such as typographical errors) are explained in the annotative notes. In several cases we have drawn our translation from several texts when each is incomplete on its own.

Other Chinese Text(s): All other versions of the Chinese document known to us. We have generally listed more complete versions ahead of less complete ones.

Available English Translation(s): Previous English translations known to us or available to us at the time when these volumes were committed to press. The order, again, is from the more complete to the less complete.

Whenever "(Excerpt)" appears in any of the above three categories, it means that that source is an excerpt in its original form. In most such cases, this indicates that the source is incomplete and we have drawn our translation from another source or combination of sources as well. Whenever "[Excerpt]" appears, we have ourselves excerpted from the source.

We have investigated as broad a range of sources as possible, including standard reference works and official yearbooks (e.g., *Renmin shouce* [People's Handbook]), document collections (e.g., *Mao Zedong xuanji* [Selected Works of Mao Zedong] and *Mao Zedong sixiang wansui* [Long Live Mao Zedong Thought]), the major Chinese newspapers, news agencies releases, the publications of the U.S. government and various official agencies and research institutes elsewhere (chiefly Hong Kong) that focus on events in the PRC, English-language monographs, and a vast number of monographs published in the PRC. We cannot, nor do we, claim to be definitive or comprehensive in our listing of sources.

When we have not been able to acquire an original Chinese text of a document – indeed, in some cases an original Chinese text may no longer exist or may never have existed (see, for example, text October 15, 1951) – we have presented it on the basis of the non-Chinese source that we have, be it English or another language. If the only source is in English, in order to preserve its integrity, we have presented it as is, without editorial corrections, even if there are discrepancies between it and our common usage; such cases are noted in the remarks that follow the source note. (For example, while it is our practice to translate the term "Zhongguo gongchandang" as "Communist Party of China," or CPC, reserving the translation "Chinese Communist Party" for the abbreviation "Zhonggong," this distinction is rarely made by other translators.) While we have not amended grammatical, typographical, or syntactical errors, we have pointed out significant discrepancies in the annotative notes.

4. REMARKS

Set in italics, this element, when it appears, follows the source note and provides information about the source or a brief explanation or identification of the context of the document.

5. COMMENT

While our main effort in these volumes is translation and not interpretation, in some important instances we have commented on the political, ideological, and historical significance of a document and its place within the context of the development of Mao's thinking. This element, when it appears, is set in italics with indented margins.

The abbreviations used in the source notes, remarks, and comments are explained in the Bibliography.

6. THE TEXT

We have rendered our translations as close to the Chinese originals as possible. While this does not mean that they are entirely literal, word-for-word translations, we have made an effort to include every element or term that appears in the original. In order to preserve the integrity of the original, we have occasionally purposely chosen not to render a given term or phrase into idiomatic English when we feel that so doing might destroy the nuance of the Chinese. Our readers must bear in mind that almost all of Mao's speeches and writings were intended primarily for a Chinese audience. His manner of speaking and his writing style are often more earthy than refined, and of course, it is just this that often lends force to his pronouncements and exclamations. In the same spirit, we have rendered Chinese aphorisms in sometimes awkward translations of the original, rather than seek an often dissimilar English aphorism that seems to make the same point. Where necessary, we explain the origin and meaning of these phrases in the annotative notes. For widely familiar but often mistranslated terms such as *xian* and *xiang* (frequently rendered as county and village) for which there is no universally agreed on English translation, we have romanized rather than translated. The titles of Chinese works are also generally romanized, with the English translation following in parentheses.

With the exception of the names of certain historical figures (e.g., Sun Yatsen and Chiang Kai-shek), we use the *pinyin* system of romanization.

Salutations in telegrams, etc., are translated as they appear in the original; where there is none in the original we have not provided one. Because the signature apparatus of telegrams is frequently very long, we have often abridged them, and provided this information in parentheses. The signature for letters is generally provided in full, with the date of the letter given as it appeared in the original source.

7. ANNOTATIVE NOTES

All textual annotations appear in notes at the end of the text.

Because there are many cross references in our annotations, the reader may trace and locate earlier and first appearances of terms and names. (Only rarely, when the meaning of a term may have changed over time, do we annotate more than once.) Cross references are keyed to the date of the earlier text (in rare cases cross references are made to a later rather than an earlier text). Many cross references will lead the reader to another volume of this work. Since more than one document may appear under any given date in these volumes, in order to assist the reader in referring to the precise document in our cross references (in the remarks, and commentaries as well as in the annotative notes) we have numbered such documents in our cross references. (For example, "text October 12, 1954(1)" refers to the first of the documents appearing under that date.)

Citations of reference and interpretive works in our notes are made by listing the name of the author (with first initial) followed by the year of publication in parentheses – e.g., "See D. Klein and A. Clark, eds. (1971), pp. 5-9." These citations are given in full in the Reference section of the Bibliography.

COMMONLY USED ABBREVIATIONS

CC	Central Committee
CPC	Communist Party of China
CPG	Central People's Government
CPGC	Central People's Government Council
CPPCC	Chinese People's Political Consultative Conference
CPSU	Communist Party of the Soviet Union
GAC	Government Administration Council
KMT	Kuomintang (Guomindang)
NPC	National People's Congress
PLA	People's Liberation Army
PRC	People's Republic of China
U.S.	United States
USA	United States of America
USSR	Union of Soviet Socialist Republics

While these abbreviations are used widely throughout the editors' comments and annotations, they are rarely used in the translated texts.

Abbreviations that do not appear on this list are spelled out at least once in any given text. Abbreviations of publications that appear frequently in our source notes and annotations are spelled out in the Bibliography.

OMISSIONS AND CHRONOLOGY

We have omitted from this collection many documents that we have found to contain interesting references to Mao's activities, but nothing significant enough for quotation. (For example, Mao may have spoken to people whom he visited on an inspection tour; the activity is notable but the conversation is insignificant.) We have reserved references of this sort for the Chronology, which will appear in the final volume.

INDEX

The index to each volume of *The Writings of Mao Zedong* will be published in a separate paperback edition and mailed to the purchaser shortly after publication. A cumulative index will appear in the final volume.

VOLUME I

September 1949-December 1955

THE WRITINGS OF MAO ZEDONG
1949-1976

1949

Opening Speech at the First Plenary Session of the CPPCC

(September 21, 1949)

Source: *XHYB*, I:1 (Nov. 15, 1949), 4-5. Other Chinese Texts: *Xuanji*, V, pp. 3-7; *Zhengxie jiniankan*; *Buyi*, pp. 1-4. Available English Translations: *SW*, V, pp. 15-18; K. Fan (1972), pp. 88-92; NCNA, *Daily Bulletin*, 634 (Oct. 2, 1952), 3-4, 5.

The preparations for the CPPCC began in June 1949 in Beijing. The First Plenary Session was held on September 21-30, 1949, in Beijing.

Fellow delegates:

The Political Consultative Conference for which the people throughout the country have been eagerly hoping is now in session.

Our conference is composed of more than six hundred delegates, representing all the democratic parties[1] and people's organizations of China, the People's Liberation Army, the various regions and localities, and the nationalities throughout China as well as the overseas Chinese. This shows that ours is a conference of great unity of the people throughout the whole country.

The achievement of this great unity among the people throughout the entire country has been made possible by our defeat of the Kuomintang reactionary government, which was aided by U.S. imperialism. In a period of just over three years, the heroic Chinese People's Liberation Army, [an army] such as the world has rarely seen, crushed the offensive of the several million troops of the U.S.-aided Kuomintang reactionary government and turned to [launching] its own counteroffensive and offensive. At present, several million troops of the field armies of the People's Liberation Army are already striking at areas close to Taiwan, Guangdong, Guangxi, Guizhou, Sichuan, and Xinjiang, and the majority of the Chinese people have already been liberated. In just over three years' time, the people all over the country have united together to aid the People's Liberation Army and oppose their own enemy, and they have won basic victory. It is on this foundation that the current People's Political Consultative Conference is convened.

Our conference is called the Political Consultative Conference because we held a Political Consultative Conference together with Chiang Kai-shek's Kuomintang three years ago.[2] The results of that conference were sabotaged by Chiang Kai-shek's Kuomintang and its accomplices; however, the conference left an indelible impression on the people. That conference proved that not a single task in the interest of the people can be resolved together with the running dogs of imperialism – Chiang Kai-shek's Kuomintang and its accomplices. Even if resolutions were reluctantly adopted, they would be useless, because [the Kuomintang and its accomplices] would tear up all the resolutions the moment the opportunity ripened and would launch a ruthless war against the people. The only gain from that conference was the profound education it gave the people, making them understand that there is absolutely no room for compromise between themselves and the running dogs of imperialism – Chiang Kai-shek's Kuomintang and their accomplices. Either overthrow these enemies or be slaughtered and oppressed by them. It must be one or the other; there is no other alternative. Within a period of just over three years, the Chinese people, led by the Communist Party of China, have quickly awakened and organized themselves into a nationwide united front to fight against imperialism, feudalism, bureaucratic capitalism, and the Kuomintang reactionary government, which represents these things in a concentrated form. They aided the People's War of Liberation, basically struck down the Kuomintang reactionary government, toppled the rule of imperialism in China, and resurrected the Political Consultative Conference.

The present Chinese People's Political Consultative Conference is convened on an entirely new foundation. It is representative of the people of the whole country and enjoys their confidence and support. Therefore, the Chinese People's Political Consultative Conference declares that it exercises the functions and powers of a National People's Congress. According to its agenda the Chinese People's Political Consultative Conference will formulate the organic law of the Chinese People's Political Consultative Conference, the organic law of the Central People's Government of the People's Republic of China, and the Common Program of the Chinese People's Political Consultative Conference.[3] It will elect the National Committee of the Chinese People's Political Consultative Conference, elect the Council of the Central People's Government of the People's Republic of China, adopt the national flag and the national emblem of the People's Republic of China, decide on the site of the capital of the People's Republic of China, and adopt the system of dating in use in the majority of countries in the world.

Fellow delegates, we all share the feeling that our work will be written down in the history of humanity; it will show that the Chinese people, forming one quarter of humanity, have now stood up. The Chinese have always been a great, courageous, and industrious nation, and it is only in modern times that they have fallen behind. This falling behind came entirely as a result of the oppression and exploitation by foreign imperialism and domestic reactionary governments. For over a century our forebears have never stopped waging tenacious struggles against domestic and foreign oppressors, including the Revolution of 1911 led by Mr. Sun Yat-sen, the great forerunner of the Chinese revolution. Our forebears have instructed us to fulfill their behest, and we have now done so accordingly. We have united and have overthrown both domestic and foreign oppressors through the People's War of Liberation and the people's great revolution, and now proclaim the establishment of the People's Republic of China. From now on our nation will join the great family of peace- and freedom-loving nations of the world. We will work with courage and diligence to create our own civilization and well-being, and at the same time promote world peace and freedom. Our nation will never again be a nation insulted by others. We have stood up. Our revolution has won the sympathy and acclamation of the broad masses of the people throughout the world. Our friends are all over the world.

Our revolutionary work has not yet been completed; the People's War of Liberation and the people's revolutionary movement are still surging forward, and we must continue our efforts. Imperialists and domestic reactionaries will certainly not take their defeat lying down; they will undertake a last-ditch struggle. After there is peace and order in the entire country, they will still engage in sabotage and cause disturbances in any and every way; they will try every day and every minute to stage a comeback in China. This is inevitable and will, without a doubt, happen; we must never relax our vigilance.

Our state system of the people's democratic dictatorship is a powerful weapon for safeguarding the fruits of the victory of the people's revolution and for thwarting the foreign and domestic enemies in their plots to stage a comeback. We must firmly grasp this weapon. Internationally, we must unite with all countries and peoples who cherish peace and freedom, first of all with the Soviet Union and the various New Democracies, so that we will not become isolated in our struggle to safeguard the fruits of the victory of the people's revolution and to thwart the plots of the foreign and domestic enemies to stage a comeback.[4] So long as we uphold the people's democratic dictatorship and unite with our international friends, we shall forever be victorious.

The people's democratic dictatorship and unity with our international friends will enable us to achieve speedy success in our work of construction. The task of nationwide economic construction already lies in front of us. Our population of 475 million people and our 9,597,000 square kilometers of territory constitute extremely favorable conditions for our endeavor.[5] There are difficulties ahead of us, a great many of them too. But we are convinced that all difficulties will be overcome by the heroic struggle of the people of the whole country. The Chinese people already have a very rich experience in overcoming difficulties. Since our forebears and we ourselves were able to weather the long, extremely difficult years and defeat the powerful domestic and foreign reactionaries, why can't we now, after victory, build a prosperous and thriving country? As long as we still maintain the work-style of plain living and hard struggle, as long as we unite as one, and as long as we uphold the people's democratic dictatorship and unite with international friends, we are sure to win swift victory on the economic front.

Following the advent of an upsurge in economic construction, there will inevitably appear an upsurge of cultural construction. The era in which the Chinese people were regarded as uncivilized is now over. We will emerge in the world as a highly civilized nation.

Our national defense will be consolidated, and no imperialist will be allowed to invade our territory again. Our people's armed forces must be preserved and developed with the heroic and tested People's Liberation Army as the foundation. We will not only have a powerful army but also a powerful air force and a powerful navy.

Let the domestic and foreign reactionaries tremble before us! Let them say that we are no good at this and no good at that, but, through indomitable effort, the Chinese people will steadily achieve their goal.

Eternal glory to the people's heroes who have given their lives to the People's War of Liberation and the people's revolution!

Hail to the victory of the People's War of Liberation and the people's revolution!

Hail to the establishment of the People's Republic of China!

Hail to the success of the Chinese People's Political Consultative Conference!

Notes

1. The term "democratic parties" often referred to in CPC literature, especially in united front work, refers specifically to a small group of political parties that were made up largely of members of the national bourgeoisie, the petty bourgeoisie, and patriotic "democratic personages." (These were distinguished from "democratic personages with no party affiliations.") These political parties were not considered to be proletarian in class identity or inherently inclined toward the socialist revolution. However, they had been developed in the period of the New Democratic Revolution, and to varying degrees of intensity, were aligned with the CPC in the struggle to bring about the socialist transformation of China, and to consolidate China's interests vis-à-vis imperialist encroachment. At this time, the democratic parties were those that fit the above description and that were represented at the CPPCC as such. This category included the following major political parties and groups (the date of their respective founding included following parentheses): Zhongguo guomindang geming weiyuanhui (the Revolutionary Committee of the Chinese Kuomintang), 1948; Zhongguo minzhu tongmeng (the Chinese Democratic League), 1941; Zhongguo minzhu jianguohui (the Chinese Democratic Association for National Construction), 1945; Zhongguo minzhu cujinhui (the Chinese Association for the Advance of Democracy), 1945; Zhongguo nonggong minzhudang (the Chinese Peasant-Worker Democratic Party), 1947; Zhongguo Zhigongdang (the Chinese Zhigong Party); Jiusan xueshe (the September Third Study Society), 1944; Taiwan minzhu zizhi tongmeng (the League for Democracy and Autonomy

for Taiwan), 1947; Zhongguo renmin jiuguohui (the Chinese People's Association for National Salvation); Sanmin zhuyi tongzhi lianhehui (the Association of Comrades of the Three People's Principles), and Zhongguo guomindang minzhu cujinhui (the Association of the Chinese Kuomintang to Promote Democracy).

2. As a result of negotiations between the CPC and the KMT a Political Consultative Conference was convened in January 1946 at Chongqing. Attended by delegates of the KMT, the CPC, and other political parties, this conference passed five resolutions concerning the peaceful reunification of the country. None of these resolutions was honored. For more on this earlier PCC, see T. Chen (1967), pp. 21-23.

3. The Common Program of the CPPCC, which served as an organic law and therefore a surrogate Constitution for the PRC, was adopted at the First Plenary Session of the CPPCC in Beijing on Sept. 29, 1949. For text in translation (English), see T. Chen (1967), pp. 34-45. The Constitution adopted by the PRC in 1954 superceded the provisions of the Common Program.

4. The countries that fell under Mao's rubric of New Democracy at this time included: Bulgaria, Romania, Czechoslovakia, Hungary, and Poland. These countries were designated as People's Democracies according to a term coined by Tito in 1945, referring to countries in Eastern Europe under the rule of Communist parties. East Germany, which also fell under the New Democracy rubric, had been designated a Democratic Republic. The People's Democracies were seen as having already begun the process of socialist construction, while the Democratic Republics, of which China was one, were seen as being in the stage of breaking away from bourgeois economic control. The term New Democracy, which applied to both sets of countries, was one which Mao began to use in the late 1930s. It designated countries that did not as yet have a dictatorship of the proletariat but were in a transitional stage before the full socialization of the society and polity and had a government in which many classes in society were represented but with a socialist leadership. For more on these terms, see Z. Brzezinski (1969), pp. 22-40.

5. Here the SW, V version reads 9,600,000 sq. kilometers.

Speech at Banquet Celebrating Insurrection of KMT Troops
(September 23, 1949)

Source: *RMRB* (Sept. 24, 1949), 1.

Owing to the insurrection of some patriotic troops among the Kuomintang armed forces, not only has the disintegration of the remnants of the Kuomintang's military forces been accelerated; moreover, it has enabled us to acquire a speedily strengthening air force and navy.

Telegram to Xinjiang Political and Military Authorities
(September 28, 1949)

Source: *RMRB* (Sept. 29, 1949), 1.

General Tao Zhiyue[1] and the officers and soldiers under his command,
Chairman Burhan[2] and the government workers under him:

Your telegrams of September 25 and 26 have been received. We believe
that your standpoint is a correct one. You have declared your severance from
the remnants of the reactionary government in Guangzhou[3] and your new orientation toward the camp of People's Democracy; you have accepted the
leadership of the People's Political Consultative Conference[4] and await and
abide by the orders and disposition of the Central People's Government and
the People's Revolutionary Military Council. This attitude conforms to the
wishes of the people of the entire nation. We are most happy. We hope that
you will unite all military and civilian governmental personnel in maintaining
the unity of the nationalities and local order and cooperate with the People's
Liberation Army, which is preparing at this movement to move northward, to
abolish the old system and implement the new one, so as to strive for the
establishment of a new Xinjiang.
(Co-signed with Zhu De and dated)

Notes

1. Tao Zhiyue (b. 1892), a Hunanese military officer who graduated from the Baoding Military
Academy in 1916 and served in various officer positions in the Hunan Army before participating
in the KMT army in the Northern Expedition period. At the beginning of the War of Resistance
against Japan, he was commander of the 36th Army, and later the commander of the First Army
and deputy commander of the 34th Army Group. At the end of the War of Resistance he became
the deputy commander of the KMT's 8th Battle Zone, and in 1946, assumed command of the
KMT's Xinjiang Garrison. In 1948, the Hexi district garrison was added to his command, and he
also became deputy director of the Northwest Communist-Suppression Bureau of the KMT. His
defection and surrender to the Communist forces at this time (Sept. 1949) was instigated by
Zhang Zhizhong, himself formerly a major military figure in the KMT, and was therefore a dou-
bly severe blow to the KMT forces. In 1949-1950, the PRC commissioned him as commander of
the 22nd Army Group and deputy commander of the Xinjiang Military District under Peng
Dehuai. In 1950 he also became a member of the Provisional People's Government of Xinjiang
and a member of the Northwest Military and Government Council. For more biographical information on Tao, see *Zhonggong renming lu*, pp. 668-669.

2. Burhan Shahidi (b. 1896), also known by the sinicized version of his name, Baoerhan, was
made governor of Xinjiang Province by the KMT government in 1948. On the eve of the Communist victory, Burhan joined the Communist side and assumed the positions of chairman of the

Provisional People's Government of Xinjiang and the president of the Xinjiang People's Court. In 1950, he became a member of the Northwest Military and Government Council, and since then he has been a prominent representative of the people of Xinjiang in various national organizations in the PRC, such as the National Committee of the CPPCC. He was de facto governor of Xinjiang until the Xinjiang Uighur Autonomous Region (XUAR) was established in October 1955, when Seypidin (Saifudin), theretofore nominally Burhan's subordinate, became chairman of the government of the XUAR. For more biographical information on Burhan, see D. Klein and A. Clark, eds. (1971), I, pp. 5-9.

3. Mao is referring here to the KMT government which had its headquarters in Guangzhou and which was nominally headed by Li Zongren since the "retirement" of Chiang Kai-shek in January 1949. In effect, however, Chiang, who had consolidated his own base in Taiwan since August 1949, was at this time still pulling the strings in KMT politics and countermanding many of Li's policies and directives, which included negotiating with the Communist Party. In November 1949, Li went to Hong Kong in frustration and from there left China to go to the United States.

4. See text Sept. 21, 1949, source note.

Draft for Inscription on Monument to People's Heroes
(September 30, 1949)

Source: *RMRB* (Oct. 1, 1949), 1.

Immortal Glory to the People's Heroes who have given their lives over the last three years in the People's War of Liberation and the People's Revolution!

Immortal Glory to the People's Heroes who have given their lives in the last thirty years in the People's War of Liberation and the People's Revolution!

Immortal Glory to the People's Heroes, who, since the year 1840, have given their lives in the many struggles to resist the enemy, domestic and foreign, to strive for the independence of the nation and the freedom of the people!

Proclamation of the Central People's Government of the PRC
(October 1, 1949)

Source: *RMRB* (Oct. 2, 1949), 1. Other Chinese Text: *XHYB*, I:1(Nov. 15, 1949), 3. Available English Translation: K. Fan (1972), pp. 79-81.

The people throughout China have been plunged into bitter suffering and tribulations since the Chiang Kai-shek Kuomintang reactionary government betrayed the fatherland, colluded with imperialists, and launched the counter-revolutionary war. Fortunately, our People's Liberation Army, backed by the whole nation, has been fighting heroically and selflessly to defend the territorial sovereignty of our homeland, to protect the people's lives and property, to relieve the people of their sufferings, and to struggle for their rights, and it eventually wiped out the reactionary troops and overthrew the reactionary rule of the Nationalist government. Now the People's War of Liberation has been basically won, and the majority of the people in the country have been liberated. On this foundation, the first session of the Chinese People's Political Consultative Conference, composed of delegates of all the democratic parties[1] and people's organizations of China,[2] the People's Liberation Army, the various regions and nationalities of the country, and the overseas Chinese and other patriotic elements, has been convened. Representing the will of the whole nation, [this session of the conference] has enacted the organic law of the Central People's Government of the People's Republic of China, elected Mao Zedong as chairman of the Central People's Government; and Zhu De, Liu Shaoqi, Song Qingling, Li Jishen, Zhang Lan, and Gao Gang as vice-chairmen [of the Central People's Government]; and Chen Yi, He Long, Li Lisan, Lin Boqu, Ye Jianying, He Xiangning, Lin Biao, Peng Dehuai, Liu Bocheng, Wu Yuzhang, Xu Xiangqian, Peng Zhen, Bo Yibo, Nie Rongzhen, Zhou Enlai, Dong Biwu, Seypidin, Rao Shushi, Tan Kah-kee [Chen Jiageng], Luo Ronghuan, Deng Zihui, Ulanhu, Xu Deli, Cai Chang, Liu Geping, Ma Yinchu, Chen Yun, Kang Sheng, Lin Feng, Ma Xulun, Guo Moruo, Zhang Yunyi, Deng Xiaoping, Gao Chongmin, Shen Junru, Shen Yanbing, Chen Shutong, Szeto Mei-tong [Situ Meitang], Li Xijiu, Huang Yanpei, Cai Ting-kai, Xi Zhongxun, Peng Zemin, Zhang Zhizhong, Fu Zuoyi, Li Zhuchen, Li Zhangda, Zhang Bojun, Cheng Qian, Zhang Xiruo, Chen Mingshu, Tan Ping-shan, Zhang Nanxian, Liu Yazi, Zhang Dongsun, and Long Yun as council members to form the Central People's Government Council, proclaimed the founding of the People's Republic of China and decided on Beijing as the capital of the People's Republic of China. The Central People's Government Council of the People's Republic of China took office today in the capital and unanimously made the following decisions: to proclaim the establishment of the Central People's Government of the People's Republic of China; to adopt the Common Program[3] of the Chinese People's Political Consultative Conference as the policy of the government; to elect Lin Boqu from among the council members as secretary general of the Central People's Government Council; to appoint Zhou Enlai as premier of the Government Administration Council of the Central People's Government and concurrently minister of Foreign Affairs, Mao Zedong as chairman of the People's Revolutionary Military Commission of the Central People's Government, Zhu De as commander-in-chief of the People's Liberation Army, Shen Junru as president of the Supreme People's Court of the Central People's Government, and Luo Ronghuan as procurator general of the Supreme People's Procuratorate of the Central People's Government, and to charge them with the task of the speedy formation of the various organs of the government to carry out the work of the government. At the same time, the Central People's Government Council decided to declare to the governments of all other countries that this government is the sole legal government representing all the people of the People's Republic of China. This government is willing to establish diplomatic relations with any foreign government that is willing to observe the principles of equality, mutual benefit, and mutual respect of territorial integrity and sovereignty.

> Mao Zedong
> Chairman
> The Central People's Government
> The People's Republic of China

Notes

1. See text Sept. 21, 1949, source note and note 1.

2. The "people's organizations" represented at the CPPCC included the All-China Federation of Trade Unions, the Federation of Literary and Artistic Circles, various peasant organizations in the liberated areas, women's organizations, youth and student organizations, trade federations, educators' associations, scientists' and social scientists' associations, journalistic associations, minority nationalities representative organizations, religious organizations, overseas Chinese representatives, and so-called federations of liberal professionals. Altogether sixteen such organizations were represented.

3. See text Sept. 21, 1949, note 3.

Telegram to the Communist Party of the United States
(October 6, 1949)

Source: *RMRB* (Oct. 8, 1949), 1. Other Chinese Text: NCNA, Supplement (n.d.), 5.

Dear Comrade Foster and Comrade Dennis,[1] and all comrades of the National Committee of the Communist Party of the United States of America:

We are extremely grateful for your enthusiastic congratulations on the founding of the People's Republic of China. Please convey our gratitude to all members of the Communist Party of the United States of America, and to all the people who love peace and justice and bear goodwill toward the Chinese people in the United States.

Indeed, as you yourselves said, the triumph of the Chinese people is a triumph over imperialism, first and foremost over United States imperialism. This victory is a part of the results of the general struggle which the working class and progressive people in the whole world are waging against the world camp of imperialism. In this struggle the Communists of the United States and all sincere advocates of democracy are fighting shoulder to shoulder with the Chinese people.

In the assistance given to the Chinese people in their cause of justice and in the heroic struggle to resist the reactionary policy of opposing China on the part of the U.S. imperialists, the Communists of the United States of America hold a place of exceptional honor. In spite of the fact that the reactionary government of the United States is savagely persecuting the Communist Party of the United States and progressive forces in the United States, and is illegally interrogating eleven leaders of the Communist Party of the United States, namely, Comrade Dennis, Comrade Williamson, Comrade Winston, Comrade Stachel, Comrade Davis, Comrade Winter, Comrade Thompson, Comrade Gates, Comrade Potash, Comrade Green, and Comrade Hall,[2] it has ultimately been demonstrated nonetheless that the Communist Party of the United States and the forces of progress in the United States of America are correct, and it is their Chinese friends who have triumphed, whereas the current imperialist government of the United States, which violates the principles of justice, has consequently gone down in shameful defeat. This fact cannot but give courage to all the forces of democracy in the world who are but temporarily in a position of being oppressed; it cannot but educate all people who are momentarily under the rule and deceptive sway of the reactionaries.

Long live the friendship of the people of China and the United States of America!

(Signed and dated)

Notes

1. William Z. Foster was national chairman of the Communist Party of the United States of America (CPUSA) and Eugene Dennis was the general secretary after the ouster of Earl Browder in July 1945.

2. In October 1949, Eugene Dennis, John Williamson (elected Labor Secretary of the CPUSA later at the 15th National Convention of the CPUSA in December 1950), Henry Winston (Organization Secretary), Jack Stachel, Benjamin Davis, Carl Winter, Robert Thompson, John Gates, Irving Potash, Gilbert Green and Gus Hall (National Secretary), all members of the National Committee of the CPUSA, were convicted for violation of the Smith Act which was passed in June 1940 and which made a crime of "teaching and advocating the overthrow of the government of the United States by force and violence." Convictions of other lesser communist leaders in the United States followed.

Letter to Wang Shoudao
(October 9, 1949)

Source: *Shuxin*, p. 342.

Wang (b. 1905), was at this time a member of the Hunan Military and Administration Committee and deputy director of the Changsha Military Control Committee. He joined the Communist Youth League in 1923 and the CPC in 1925. In 1927 he was a leader of a series of peasant uprisings (by the so-called Red Guerrillas) in northeastern Hunan. In 1928 he took part in the forming of the Southern Hunan Soviet. In 1935 he went to northern Shaanxi and worked in the following years in the Party Center, first in the Bureau of Political Security and then in the Central Secretariat. After a short sojourn in the northeast in 1947-48, he returned to Hunan in 1948 and became, under Huang Kecheng, the first deputy secretary of the Hunan Provincial Committee of the CPC. For more biographical information on Wang see Zhonggong renming lu, *pp. 47-48, and D. Klein and A. Clark, eds. (1971), II, pp. 927-931.*

Comrade Shoudao:

Yang Kaizhi[1] and company should not come to the capital. They should be given appropriate jobs in accordance with their abilities in Hunan. No unreasonable request should be approved. If his old mother is in difficulty, certain assistance can be given to her. I am sending out a separate telegram; please send someone to relay it.

Mao Zedong
The ninth

Note

1. Yang is the brother of Yang Kaihui, Mao's former wife who died in the "Great Revolution" period. (See text May 11, 1957, note 1.) For more biographical information see *Zhonggong renming lu*, appendix. p. 1136.

Letter to Yang Kaizhi
(October 9, 1949)

Source: *Shuxin*, p. 343.

See text Oct. 9, 1949 (1).

Mr. Yang Kaizhi:

I hope that you will stay in Hunan and await the Hunan Provincial Committee of the CPC to assign you to a job that is appropriate for your abilities. Do not harbor any unrealistic hopes and do not come to the capital. Whatever job the Hunan Provincial Committee assigns you, do it. Everything should be done in accordance with normal rules. Please don't put the government on the spot.

Mao Zedong
October 9

Telegram to the French Transportation Labor Union
(October 9, 1949)

Source: *RMRB* (Oct. 11, 1949), 1.

Comrades of the French Transportation Labor Union:

We express our deepest thanks for your telegram congratulating us on the birth of the People's Republic of China.
(Signed and dated in Beijing)

Telegram to General Zhao Xiguang
(October 10, 1949)

Source: *RMRB* (Oct. 12, 1949), 1.

Dear General Zhao Xiguang:[1]

Your telegram of the first instant has been received. The whole country is rejoicing at the peaceful liberation of Xinjiang. We hope that all the officers and soldiers of the troops now stationed in southern Xinjiang will unite as one and strive to transform themselves so as to become a people's army.
(Signed and dated)

Note

1. Zhao was former deputy commander of the Xinjiang Garrison and commander of the Southern Xinjiang Garrison under the KMT.

Telegram to Insurrectionists on the "Changzhi"
(October 10, 1949)

Source: *RMRB* (Oct. 12, 1949), 1.

To all the comrades who took part in the insurrection on the "Changzhi":[1]

Congratulations on your heroic insurrection. Owing to the continuing insurrections of the patriotic officers and soldiers within the Kuomintang navy, the People's Navy is already expanding rapidly. We hope that you will be industrious in learning and active in taking part in the construction of the Chinese People's Navy and in accomplishing the great task of liberating the whole of China.
(Co-signed with Zhu De and dated)

Note

1. The "Changzhi" was the flagship of the First Naval Defense Fleet of the KMT.

Telegram to Five-man Independent Group of the British Labor Party in the House of Commons
(October 12, 1949)

Source: *RMRB* (Oct. 13, 1949), 1.

Pritt, Hutchinson, Solley, Mills, and Zilliacus, Esquires:

On behalf of the Chinese people and the Central People's Government of the People's Republic of China, I express thanks for your message of congratulations. May the worthy efforts on your part and on the part of the broad masses of the people of Britain to further the friendship between the Chinese and English peoples be successful.
(Signed and dated)

Telegram to the United States' Committee
for a Democratic Far Eastern Policy[1]
(October 12, 1949)

Source: *RMRB* (Oct. 13, 1949), 1.

We are deeply grateful for your congratulations on the establishment of the People's Republic of China, and for your efforts in promoting the friendship between the Chinese and American peoples.
(Signed and dated)

Note

1. The Committee for a Democratic Far Eastern Policy was established soon after the surrender of the Japanese forces in Asia at the end of the Second World War. It was based primarily in California and the west coast of the United States. In 1948, the California Committee on Un-American Activities identified it as a "communist-front organization."

Letter to Feng Youlan
(October 13, 1949)

Source: *Shuxin*, p. 344.

Feng Youlan (b. 1905) is one of modern and contemporary China's most noted philosophers. He is the author of many historical and philosophical works on Chinese civilization, among them the renowned Zhongguo zhexue shi *(A History of Chinese Philosophy), which has been published in translation by Derk Bodde (Princeton University Press, 1953, reprinted 1969). Feng studied in the United States at Columbia University from 1919 to 1923, and received his doctorate in 1923. Throughout the 1920s Feng was in the midst and the forefront of basic philosophical debates in China over the meaning and validity of Chinese traditional culture and worldviews. Out of that debate he distilled a distinctive philosophy that was characterized by the mixture of rationalist elements of neo-Confucianist* lixue *(school of reason or principle), a daoistic transcendentalism, and Western realism. He also asserted that the economic foun-*

dations of a society determined its social values. This appeared to pave the way for his "conversion" to Marxism-Leninism later. After 1950, he announced his dedication to "remolding his ideas" and interpreting Chinese philosophy along Marxist-Leninist lines. However, in the anti-Rightist furor of 1957, he was made a target of quite strenuous criticism, and it was not until the 1960s that he was reinstated. He was never a member of the Communist Party, however. For more biographical information on Feng, see H. Boorman et al., eds. (1968), II, pp. 32-37.

Mr. Youlan:[1]

I have received your letter of October 5. We welcome people's making progress. It is very good for someone like yourself, who has committed errors in the past, to be prepared to correct them now, if this can indeed be carried out in practice. You do not need to be overly anxious about seeing results in haste; you can come around gradually. In any case, it is appropriate to adopt an attitude of honesty.

This, in reply, and with respectful regards and best wishes for your work in teaching,

Mao Zedong
October 13

Note

1. For an explanation of this usage, see text Nov. 17, 1949, note 2.

Letter to Zhou Shizhao
(October 15, 1949)

Source: *Shuxin*, pp. 345-346.

Zhou Shizhao (1897-1976) was a schoolmate of Mao's in the late 1910s when they studied together at the First Normal School of Hunan Province of which Zhou at the time of this letter was the principal. He was also a member of the Xinmin xuehui (New People's Study Society), which was formed by many of Mao's old friends, such as Cai Heshen, during the May Fourth period. (Mao was also a member.) For more biographical information on Zhou, see Zhonggong renming lu (1967 edition), p. 213. (For some unknown reason he was dropped from the 1978 expanded edition usually cited in this translation.)

My dear senior classmate Dunyuan:[1]

I have received your several telegrams as well as your long letter of September 28. Your sincere and diligent words made it possible for me to believe I was actually seeing you in person. When I was in Yanan[2] I received a letter from you. The letter you sent to Chongqing,[3] however, I did not receive. Although you did not join the revolutionary struggle of the past, my friend, teaching is itself an occupation that is beneficial to the people. The telegram from the various friends of the Chengnan xueshe [South City Study Society] has been received also. Please convey this information to them and thank them for their good wishes. I deeply applaud the fact that you are now the principal of First Normal; you are best for the job. I can also see that there is yet much life in those bones![4] If it is possible, I would like you to copy and send me some of your works and your old poems. The more the better.

With the exception of Taiwan and Tibet, in approximately a few more months we shall be able to complete the military occupation of the country as a whole. Even then, with the great calamity just over and the people's lives drained and exhausted, it will take several years' time before the people's economy can be restored to health. The tasks of completing the reforming of the land [-ownership] system and raising the level of the people's political consciousness need the cooperation of the cultural and educational work [circles].

I have received and read Mr. Chen Zetong's[5] letter of opinion, and I will forward it to the industrial [work] organs here for studying. Please convey thanks to him on my behalf. As for the question of his work, please ask him to go directly to the authorities in Hunan and ask for a solution, and do not await my reply.

Sincerely in reply, and respectfully sending my best wishes for your work in teaching,

Mao Zedong
October 15, 1949

Notes

1. Dunyuan is one of Zhou's many *zi* (i.e., an "honorific" which is not the name with which a person is born but a name acquired or adopted later on in life, usually within a scholastic context). It is customary to address one's friends by this honorific as a sign of intimacy. Mao also used the term *xuezhang xiong* in which *xuezhang* means "elder in learning" and is used customarily in addressing one's classmates or schoolmates, and *xiong* means "brother." This latter salutation is tantamount to "my dear friend" in letters.

2. This refers to the long period that Mao spent in Yanan, northern Shaanxi, from the mid-1930s to the mid-1940s. Yanan was the chief base of CPC activities from the mid-1930s onward. See text Oct. 26, 1949, note 1.

3. This probably refers to the time when Mao went to Chongqing, the wartime headquarters of Chiang Kai-shek and the KMT government, for negotiations. See text Jan. 27, 1957(1), note 5.

4. Mao used here the sentences: *jun gu wei diao, shang you sheng qi*, which translates literally as "the stallion's bones have not yet withered and there is yet the spirit of life." The classical origin of this saying could not be traced.

5. According to the source, this refers to a plan that Chen, an engineer in Changsha, Hunan, submitted to Mao in 1949 in which he proposed that a region some forty *li* along the eastern banks of the Xiangjiang River in Hunan, a region under the jurisdiction of Xiangtan *xian*, Mao's native district, should be transformed into a model "Xiangtan industrial zone."

Reply to Ambassador of the Soviet Union
(October 16, 1949)

Source: *RMRB* (Oct. 12, 1949), 1.

N. V. Roschin served as ambassador of the USSR to the PRC from October 1949 to December 1952.

Mr. Ambassador [N. V.] Roschin:

It is with great pleasure that I accept the letter of credence from the Presidium of the Supreme Soviet of the Union of Soviet Socialist Republics presented by Your Excellency, and I am sincerely grateful for Your Excellency's congratulations.

Since the very beginning of its establishment, the People's Republic of China has been honored by having the government of the Soviet Union take the lead in expressing its willingness to establish diplomatic relations with our country. We are confident that as a result of this decision on the part of your government the friendship between China and the Soviet Union will grow and become more consolidated with each passing day. I warmly welcome Your Excellency's appointment as the first ambassador extraordinary and plenipotentiary of the Soviet Union to the People's Republic of China. We believe that through Your Excellency's efforts, the cooperation between your country and ours will grow ever closer and will also be beneficial to our common quest for a lasting peace in the world. We herewith sincerely wish for the prosperity of your country and the prospering of your people, and wish for the excellent health of your head of state.

Telegram to the German Democratic Republic
(October 16, 1949)

Source: *RMRB* (Oct. 17, 1949), 1. Available English Translation: NCNA, *Weekly Bulletin*, 124 (Oct. 8, 1949), 5 (excerpt).

President Wilhelm Pieck and Premier Otto Grotewohl of the German Democratic Republic:

On behalf of the Central People's Government of the People's Republic of China and the entire Chinese people, I extend my warmest congratulations on the founding of the German Democratic Republic and warmly congratulate Herr Wilhelm Pieck and Herr Otto Grotewohl on your respective elections to the offices of president and premier of the German Democratic Republic.

The founding of the German Democratic Republic signifies a fundamental change in the history of Germany. The masses of the people have replaced the monopoly capitalists and the big landowners as the masters of Germany. Owing to the founding of the German Democratic Republic, Germany, which was the spawning ground of two world wars and the focus of militarism and fascism, has now joined the ranks of the People's Democracies in the world.[1] This is a decisive defeat for the criminal policy of the imperialist front led by the reactionary government of the United States of America of splitting Germany in the period after the Second World War and of reviving Germany as a reactionary state and a base for war. This is a great victory for the camp for world peace and democracy led by the Soviet Union.

People's Germany and People's China are both standing in the front lines of the great struggle against imperialism. We are particularly glad on this occasion of the proclamation of the founding of Democratic Germany. We extend our best wishes that under the leadership of the people's democratic forces the unification of Germany will be restored and Germany will grow in strength with each passing day. May the friendship between the Chinese and German peoples grow with each passing day.

(Signed and dated in Beijing)

Note

1. See text Sept. 21, 1949, note 4.

Reply to the Hui People of Xinjiang
(October 21, 1949)

Source: *RMRB* (Oct. 23, 1949), 1.

To Mr. Ma Liangjun[1] and, through him, to all our Hui compatriots in Xinjiang:

Thank you for your message of congratulations. We hope that you will aid the People's Liberation Army and the People's Government in uniting the people of all nationalities, carry out a true people's democracy in accordance with the Common Program,[2] and strive for the building of a new Xinjiang. (Co-signed with Zhu De and dated)

Notes

1. Ma Liangjun is described in the accompanying news release as the chief religious leader (*zongjiao zhang*) of the Hui (Moslem) people of Xinjiang. Ma was later reported to have been a member of the National Minorities Committee of the Northwest Administrative Committee during the early 1950s.
2. See text Sept. 21, 1949, note 3.

Reply to the Provisional People's Government of Xinjiang
(October 21, 1949)

Source: *RMRB* (Oct. 21, 1949), 1.

To Chairman Burhan[1] and, through him, to all committee members of the Provisional People's Government of Xinjiang Province:

Thank you for your message of congratulations. We hope that you will unite as one with the People's Liberation Army and the people of all nationalities of Xinjiang in carrying out the Common Program[2] and in striving for the building of a new Xinjiang. (Signed and dated)

120402

Notes

1. See text Sept. 28, 1949, note 2.
2. See text Sept. 21, 1949, note 3.

Reply to the Xinjiang League for the Defense of Peace and Democracy and to People of the Tacheng-Ili-Ashan Regions

(October 21, 1949)

Source: *RMRB* (Oct. 22, 1949), 1.

To Mr. Aisihaiti Itzhakov and, through him, to all comrades of the Xinjiang League for the Defense of Peace and Democracy, and to all our compatriots of the Tacheng, Ili, and Ashan Regions:

Thank you for your congratulations and good wishes. The heroic struggle of the people of the Tacheng-Ili-Ashan regions has been a major contribution to the liberation of the whole of Xinjiang and all of China. It is my sincere wish that the people of the three regions and the people of the whole of Xinjiang will unite as one and aid the People's Liberation Army in struggling for the common cause of building a people's democratic new Xinjiang. (Signed and dated)

Preface to *The Victory of New Democracy in China*

(October 24, 1949)

Source: *RMRB* (Oct. 24, 1949), 1.

According to RMRB *(Oct. 24, 1949), the book* Vitezstvi nove demokracie v Cine *(The Victory of New Democracy in China) was compiled by the editorial board of the Czechoslovakian monthly* Mezinarodni politika *(International Politics) and published in Prague on October 25, 1949. Thus the date of this document is the date of release.*

The book was edited and published under the direction of the Central Secretariat of the Communist Party of Czechoslovakia. It included, in addition to the documents of the first session of the Chinese People's Political Consultative Conference (see text Sept. 21, 1949, source note), Mao's earlier article "On the People's Democratic Dictatorship" and Zhu De's article "The Chinese People's Struggle for Liberation."

The comrades of the Communist Party of Czechoslovakia have published in the Czech language the documents of the Chinese People's Political Consultative Conference and my own essay concerning the people's democratic dictatorship of China. This is a great honor for the Communist Party of China. The struggles of the people of China and the peoples of Europe are two inseparable and mutually reinforcing parts of a common cause, despite the fact that owing to the differences in the levels of social development the stages of the development of their revolutions are different. All the readers of Europe who are concerned about the destiny of Asia will gain a basic knowledge of New China from reading these short documents and particularly from reading the Sixty Article Common Program passed by the Chinese People's Political Consultative Conference.[1] I believe that the effort which our comrades in Czechoslovakia have exerted in helping European readers to understand New China is a contribution to the international revolutionary movement for which we must be grateful.

Note

1. See text Sept. 21, 1949, note 3.

Telegram to the Insurrectionists on the "Hailiao"
(October 24, 1949)

Source: *RMRB* (Oct. 25, 1949), 1.

According to the accompanying Xinhua news release, the "Hailiao" was a 3,000-ton merchant steamer that had sailed from Hong Kong.

Captain Fang Linliu and all comrades onboard the ship "Hailiao":

Congratulations on your insurrection on the seas and on your success in

bringing the "Hailiao" to our port in the Northeast. For the sake of the people's state you have united together, overcome difficulties, and left the side of the reactionaries to stand on the side of the people. This action is applauded by the people of the entire country and should be emulated by all captains and crews who are still under the control of the Kuomintang reactionaries and bureaucratic capitalism.[1]
(Signed and dated)

Note

1. The term "bureaucratic capitalism" refers in CPC usage to capitalist structures that are tied up with the Kuomintang government and foreign imperialists who had an influence on the Chinese government prior to 1949. They are seen as people or organizations conducting economic activities and self-aggrandizement on the basis of monopolies and controls, in such areas as wartime government bonds, large-scale state-related fiscal enterprises, speculation, and foreign trade, whose advantage is granted by the KMT government. As such they are often hand-in-glove with the large landlords, the compradors and other monopolist capitalists. In China, it is often pointed out, the bureaucratic capitalists were headed by the "Four Big Families" of Chiang Kaishek, Song Ziwen (T. V. Soong), Kong Xiangxi (H. H. Kung) and the Chen brothers, Lifu and Guofu. In his December 1947 report to the Central Committee of the CPC (see "The Present Situation and Our Tasks," *SW*, IV, p. 167) Mao gave a description of "bureaucratic capitalism" in China.

Inscription for the Inaugural Issue of
Renmin wenxue (People's Literature)
(October 25, 1949)

Source: *Renmin wenxue* (Oct. 25, 1949), 8.

I hope that more good pieces of writing will be born of this.

Mao Zedong

Telegram to Secretary of the World Federation
of Trade Unions
(October 26, 1949)

Source: *RMRB* (Oct. 26, 1949), 1.

Paris
M. [Louis] Saillant, secretary of the World Federation of Trade Unions:

We are deeply grateful for your message of congratulations to the People's Republic of China. The people of China are deeply aware that their own triumph depends on the assistance given it by the international workers' movement and will strive to consolidate their mutual concern and immortal friendship with the laboring peoples of all countries of the world.
(Signed and dated in Beijing)

Telegram to the Comrades of Yanan and Compatriots
of the Shaanxi-Gansu-Ningxia Border Region
(October 26, 1949)

Source: *RMRB* (Oct. 27, 1949), 1. Other Chinese Text: *Xuanji*, V, p. 12. Available English Translation: *SW*, V, p. 23.

Comrades of Yanan and our compatriots of the Shaanxi-Gansu-Ningxia Border Region:

It made me extremely happy and grateful to receive your message of congratulations. From 1936 to 1948, Yanan and the Shaanxi-Gansu-Ningxia Border Region[1] were the location of the Party Center for the Communist Party of China and were the general rear area in the Chinese people's struggle for liberation. The people of Yanan and the Shaanxi-Gansu-Ningxia Border Region have contributed greatly to the cause of the whole nation. I congratulate the people of Yanan and the Shaanxi-Gansu-Ningxia Border Region on their continued unity, their rapid recovery from the ravages of war, and their progress in economic and cultural construction. Moreover, I hope that all people who work for the revolution throughout the country will forever maintain the work-style of hard struggle and plain living possessed by the people who worked for the last decade or longer in Yanan and the Shaanxi-Gansu-Ningxia Border Region.

(Signed and dated)

Note

1. Yanan and the Shaanxi-Gansu-Ningxia Border Region (also known as the Shaan-Gan-Ning Base Area) were the chief Communist bases in the period of the War of Resistance against Japan. Communist influence over this region existed as far back as 1934, but it was in January 1937, following the Xian (Sian) Incident in December 1936, that the Central Committee of the Communist Party, the government, and the military offices under Communist control moved to Yanan. The government of the Shaanxi-Gansu-Ningxia Border Region was formally established on September 6, 1937. Significantly, it was here, during the wartime years, that the CPC launched and consolidated its first systematic rectification campaign, streamlining the Party and leading to the consolidation of Mao's control over the Party. For more on the role of Yanan and the Shaanxi-Gansu-Ningxia Border Region in the Chinese Revolution, see M. Selden (1971), and J. Harrison (1972), ch. 15.

Telegram to the Central Committee of the Communist Party of Algeria

(October 26, 1949)

Source: *RMRB* (Oct. 27, 1949), 1. Available English Translation: S. Schram (1969), p. 378.

Comrade Larbi Buhali and the Central Committee of the Communist Party of Algeria:

Allow me to express my deepest gratitude for Comrade Larbi Buhali's message of congratulations of October 9.

The Chinese people have attained their liberation after a long period of imperialist aggression and oppression. We therefore have warm sympathy for and resolute faith in the struggle for liberation of all oppressed peoples. I believe that the Algerian people, under the leadership of the Communist Party of Algeria and with the aid of the international camp for peace and democracy, will eventually succeed in overthrowing the rule of imperialism.

Long live the victory of the Algerian people's struggle for liberation!
(Signed as Chairman of PRC and dated)

Telegram to the Provisional Government of Greece
(October 26, 1949)

Source: *RMRB* (Oct. 27, 1949), 1.

The Provisional Government of Greece,
Chairman Mitsos:

We are deeply grateful for your message of congratulations. The Chinese people express their warmest sympathy and highest respects to the people of Greece for their unyielding struggle for liberty, independence, justice, and peace under difficult conditions. May we express our best wishes for the firm maintenance of unity between the provisional government of Greece and the patriotic people of Greece to triumph over temporary difficulties and to strive for final victory.
(Signed as Chairman of CPG of PRC and dated)

Telegram to the Albanian Council of Ministers
(October 26, 1949)

Source: *RMRB* (Oct. 27, 1949), 1.

Chairman Enver Hoxha,
The Albanian Council of Ministers:

We are deeply grateful for your message of congratulations to the People's Republic of China. I hereby express my sincere wish that the friendship between the Chinese and Albanian peoples will grow closer with each passing day. I believe that the courageous Albanian people, who are advancing in the correct direction under your leadership, are bound to be able to stand shoulder to shoulder with the people of the entire world and smash the menace of imperialism and Tito's counterrevolutionary clique, and to achieve their own goals.

(Signed as Chairman of CPG of PRC and dated)

Letter to Bo Yibo

(October 29, 1949)

Source: *Shuxin*, p. 347.

Bo Yibo was at this time first secretary of the North China Bureau of the Central Committee of the CPC and political commissar of the North China Military Region of the PLA. In December 1949 he also became political commissar of the Suiyuan Military Region. For more complete biographical information on Bo, see text Aug. 12, 1953, note 5.

Comrade Yibo:

I have received your letter of October 28. The two armies and the cavalry division of Suiyuan[1] can be organized into the combat order of the People's Liberation Army and awarded registration unit numbers. The [commissioning of the] military command personnel for the two armies and the cavalry division may be approved as listed. However, they must be commissioned at the same time that the political commissars and the heads of the political departments [in those units] are; only in this way can the confidence and prestige of political work be established in the military. On this issue, please consult with Fu Yisheng.[2] If he thinks that it is somewhat inconvenient to publish [the names of] the political commissars and the heads of the political departments at this point, the military personnel can be first appointed to the job *de facto*, with their formal commissioning taking place [a bit later] when it can be done at the same time [as the commissioning of the political personnel] when the decision on the latter has been made. It is a great and arduous task to carry out the political work system earnestly in the Suiyuan armed forces. We must have beforehand full mental preparation and it must be personally led by Fu Yisheng before it can work. Otherwise chaos and troubles will be unavoidable.

Mao Zedong
October 29

Notes

1. Suiyuan is the old name of the region to the west of Liaoning Province and southwest of Heilongjiang Province. In the early years of the Chinese Republic (i.e., in the 1910s and 1920s), it was designated as a special region. In 1928 it became a province. In 1947, the region became part of the then established Inner Mongolia Autonomous Region.

2. Yisheng is the honorific name *(zi)* of Fu Zuoyi, who was governor of Suiyuan from 1931 to 1947. From the mid-1930s on he was an active opponent of the Inner Mongolian independence movement led by De Wang (Demchukdonggrub). During the War of Resistance against Japan, the Nationalist forces that defended Suiyuan were under Fu's command, and the same forces were employed by the KMT to "contain" the Communist forces in the Northwest, in this case He Long's troops which had established a base of operations in Suiyuan. For more biographical information on Fu and on Fu's surrender to the Communists, see text Sept. 16-18, 1953, note 6.

Telegram to the Republic of Czechoslovakia

(October 29, 1949)

Source: *RMRB* (Oct. 30, 1949), 1. Available English Translation: NCNA, *Weekly Bulletin*, 126 (Nov. 1, 1949), 2.

President Gottwald,
The Republic of Czechoslovakia

Your Excellency:

On the happy occasion of the thirty-first anniversary of the independence of your country, I sincerely express my warmest congratulations and my best wishes that the diplomatic relations between China and Czechoslovakia will become closer with each passing day.

(Signed as Chairman of CPG of PRC and dated)

Telegram to the USSR
(November 5, 1949)

Source: *RMRB* (Nov. 6, 1949), 1. Available English Translation: NCNA, *Weekly Bulletin*, 127 (Nov. 8, 1949), 1.

Generalissimo Stalin:

On this occasion of the thirty-second anniversary of the great socialist October Revolution, I respectfully express to Your Excellency my warmest congratulations. May the socialist construction of the Soviet Union make progress with every passing day, may the might of the camp for world peace and democracy led by the Soviet Union know no parallel, and may there always be friendship and cooperation between the two peoples of China and the Soviet Union.

(Signed as Chairman of CPG of PRC and dated)

Telegram to the Work Committee
of the Communist Party of Thailand
(November 12, 1949)

Source: *RMRB* (Nov. 13, 1949), 1.

Dear comrades of the Work Committee of the Communist Party of Thailand:

I sincerely express my deep gratitude for your congratulatory message of September 26.

(Signed and dated)

Telegram to Managers and Staff
of Two Aviation Corporations
(November 12, 1949)

Source: *RMRB* (Nov. 13, 1949), 1.

On Nov. 9, 1949, the general managers of the China National Aviation Corporation (CNAC) and the Central Air Transport Corporation (CATC) declared the separation of the two companies from the control of the KMT and "insurrected," throwing in with the new Communist government. This telegram indicates the PRC government's acceptance. Subsequently, the PRC government declared that the property of the two companies, including 71 airplanes and equipment in Hong Kong, had become the property of the Chinese people. On Nov. 24, 1949, the KMT government appealed to the Supreme Court of the Hong Kong government to freeze the two companies' assets. On Dec. 13, Premier Zhou Enlai of the PRC stated that the property of the two companies could be received only by the PRC government. Complications set in when, on Dec. 19, the Civil Air Transport Company (CAT), headed by the American general Claire Chennault, presented a case to the Hong Kong Supreme Court that the airplanes of the two companies in Hong Kong had been sold to the CAT by Yan Xishan on December 12, i.e., prior to Zhou's declaration. Litigation on the issue continued until October 1952, when finally Chennault was awarded custody and ownership of all the airplanes formerly belonging to the two companies and which had sat in Hong Kong's Kai Tak Airport for over three years.

General Manager Liu Jingyi,
China National Aviation Corporation,
General Manager Chen Zhuolin,
Central Air Transport Corporation, and
all comrades of the staff and workers of the two companies:

It is an act of greatly significant patriotism that the entire staff and workers of the China National Aviation Corporation and Central Air Transport Corporation, under the leadership of the general managers of these two companies, have resolutely separated themselves from the remnants of the Kuomintang reactionaries and have thrown themselves into the arms of the people's homeland. On this occasion I extend especially to you my congratulations, our welcome, and our regards. I hope that you will unite as one and strive for the building of the people's aviation enterprises and for the protection of the

homeland's properties that remain in Hong Kong.
(Signed and dated)

Letter to Peng Dehuai and the Northwest Bureau
(November 14, 1949)

Source: *Shuxin*, pp. 349-350.

Peng Dehuai was at this time deputy commander-in-chief of the People's Liberation Army and first secretary of the Northwest Bureau of the Central Committee of the CPC. For more complete biographical information on Peng, see text Aug. 15, 1959(2), note 3.

Comrade Dehuai and the Northwest Bureau:

1. According to the information submitted repeatedly by the Qinghai Provincial [Party] Committee, the remnants of [the forces of] Bandit Ma[1] have been fanning up fires among the masses in many places and organizing a resistance. At the imminent Lanzhou conference, please pay serious attention to this.[2] In having the various provincial, [special] district and *xian* [Party] committees focusing on the arduous job [of uniting and organizing] the masses and in all such work upholding [the principle of] equality among the nationalities, the government organs at all levels should, in accordance with the size and ratio of [minority] nationality populations, allocate quotas and absorb in large numbers those members of the Hui nationality and other minority nationalities who are capable of cooperating with us into taking part in government work. In the present period they should organize, across the board, coalition governments, i.e., united front governments. Within [the framework of] such a cooperation, minority nationality cadres will be nurtured in large numbers. Furthermore, the provincial [Party] committees of Qinghai, Gansu, Xinjiang, Ningxia and Shaanxi, and the [special] district [Party] committees of all places where there are minority nationalities ought to form training classes for minority nationality cadres, or cadre training schools. Please give this a good deal of attention. It is impossible to thoroughly resolve the problem of the minority nationalities and to totally isolate the nationalistic

reactionaries without a large number of Communist cadres who are from minority nationality backrounds.

2. Have all the comrades of the Northwest Bureau arrived in Lanzhou? On what day will your conference commence? The agenda for this conference is very full, and I am afraid that the meeting must be held for a week or so. You also need to make a decision as to where the political center of the Northwest should be located from now on – should it be in Xian? or Lanzhou? Please inform me of the major items on your agenda.

3. Please ask General Wang Zhen[3] to report to us.

Mao Zedong

November 14

Notes

1. This refers to Ma Bufang (b. 1903) who was governor of Qinghai Province under the Nationalist government in 1938-49. As governor he introduced an efficient government to that province which was predominantly populated by the Moslem (Hui) minority nationality. In 1943 he became commander-in-chief of Chiang Kai-shek's Fortieth Army Group and in 1945 deputy chairman of Chiang's northwest headquarters and a member of the KMT's Central Executive Committee. He became head of the northwest headquarters in 1949 when his erstwhile superior Zhang Zhizhong went over to the Communist side. In late July of that year, however, Ma left for Hong Kong, and soon thereafter the capital cities of Qinghai – Lanzhou and Xining – fell to the Communists. Mao was referring to the fact that in spite of his physical absence, Ma continued to have influence over the forces in Qinghai Province, mostly military leaders who had previous affiliations with the KMT and some of whom wished for Hui autonomy in the region. For more biographical information on Ma, see H. Boorman et al., eds. (1968), II, pp. 474-475.

2. According to the source, this refers to the enlarged meeting of the Northwest Bureau of the Central Committee of the CPC, held in Lanzhou in November 1949.

3. Wang Zhen (a.k.a. Wang Zhenlin, Wang Zhenting, b. 1909) was at this time the commander and political commissar of the First Army Group of the First Field Army of the PLA. Having joined the Communist Youth League in 1927, Wang rose through the CPC ranks as a labor trainer and organizer. In the early 1930s, having armed organized labor groups in the Hunan area (groups which were later absorbed into the regular armed forces of the Communist Red Army), Wang began his career as a brilliant political officer of the Communist military units. During the Long March, he reached northern Shaanxi as political commissar of the Sixth Army Corps under Xiao Ke. In the late 1930s he led his troops in productive labor in the Yanan area, and he was considered a model officer whose soldiers were equally adept at productive work as at combat duties. This apparently stemmed from his earlier experience as a labor movement organizer. At the time of this letter the First Army Group under his command was pushing into Xinjiang, and later Mao would cite his contribution to that effort, especially his ability, again, in combining productive and constructive labor and military action in the area. (See text Apr. 6, 1952, note 1, see also text Dec. 5, 1949.) Wang remained the ranking military and political officer in that region until August 1952. For more biographical information on Wang, see N. Wales (1952), pp. 90-101, and D. Klein and A. Clark, eds. (1971), II, pp. 889-894. Here Mao used the salutation *tai* for Wang Zhen, which usually is employed for a government or military official.

Inscription on Public Morals
(November 15, 1949 R)

Source: *XHYB*, I:1 (Nov. 15, 1949), 2.

Love the homeland; love the people; love labor; love and protect public property; these are the civic morals for all our citizens.

Mao Zedong

Letter to Mao Xusheng
(November 15, 1949)

Source: *Shuxin*, p. 351.

According to the source, Mao Xusheng was a native of Pingjiang, Hunan, and had been a clerk in the transportation division of the New Hunanese Army after the 1911 Revolution. Mao Zedong himself had been a clerical petty officer in that army for a very short time.

Mr. Xusheng:[1]

I have received your three letters and apologize for being so tardy in responding. It is more appropriate for you, sir, to stay and work in the village; please do not come to the capital. [As you say,] the times are difficult for maintaining a living for the family, but this may be resolved in the process of the reforming of the landownership system in the future. I can't remember accurately what position you held in the transportation division then; I would appreciate if you would let me know at your convenience. Is Mao Ziqi[2] still alive?

Respectfully I bid you good wishes and good health!

Mao Zedong
November 15, 1949

Notes

1. For an explanation of this usage, see text Nov. 17, 1949, note 2.
2. Mao Ziqi was also a native of Pingjiang, Hunan. He was the commander of the division in which Mao Xusheng served.

Letter to Li Jiehou of Shaoshan, Hunan[1]
(November 17, 1949)

Source: *Luxingjia*, 2 (Feb. 22, 1958), 3-5.

Dear Mr. Jiehou:[2]

I have respectfully read your letter and feel deeply grateful for the profound concern that you have expressed. I met my dear friend Genghou[3] once in 1928 at Ninggang *xian* on the Hunan-Jiangxi border. He then led his troops back to south Hunan, and we never met again. I've heard that he gave his life for the cause; this seems plausible, but there has been no way by which I could ascertain the date or place [of his martyrdom]. I hear that your father is well; this is something for me to be happy about, and I pray that you will convey my regards to him.

I am writing this letter in haste, but let me wish you,

Good health and progress.

Mao Zedong
November 17, 1949

Notes

1. Shaoshan Village, Xiangtan *xian*, Hunan, is Mao's native village.
2. Jiehou is Li's personal name and not his family name. It is customary in Chinese usage to address correspondence to friends by their personal names rather than their family names as a sign of intimacy. The salutation, usually *xiansheng* (Mr.), is nevertheless retained.
3. The brother of the recipient of this letter. The father mentioned in this letter was Li Shuqing, whose two sons, Genghou and Gonghou, and grandson Deshen all died in the War of Liberation as Communist troops. He was a schoolteacher and in his youth Mao often turned to him for advice. The Li family is obviously also from Mao's native village, Shaoshan. Li Shuqing died in 1957.

Telegram to the Former KMT Government Resources Committee
(November 19, 1949)

Source: *RMRB* (Nov. 20, 1949), 1.

Staff members of the Office of International Commerce of the Hong Kong Trade Office of the Former Resources Committee

Comrades:

Your telegram of the fourteenth instant has been received. I am very glad and much comforted by it. I hope that you will unite as one, uphold a patriotic position, and protect the property of the homeland in anticipation of its being received by the Central People's Government.

(Signed and dated)

Telegram to the Communist Party of India
(November 19, 1949)

Source: *RMRB* (Nov. 20, 1949), 1. Other Chinese Text: *GMRB* (Nov. 26, 1949), 2. Available English Translations: NCNA, *Weekly Bulletin*, 129 (Nov. 22, 1949), 1-5; S. Schram (1969), pp. 378-379.

This telegram was addressed to B. T. Ranadive, secretary general of the Communist Party of India.

Dear Comrade Ranadive:

Your congratulatory telegram of October 12 has been received. We are very grateful for your warm congratulations to the People's Republic of China and the Communist Party of China. The entire Chinese people will feel great joy and pride when they read the expressions of brotherly friendship and love of the revolutionary people of India in your telegram. The Indian people are one of the greatest peoples in Asia, with a long history and a large population. There are many similarities between its past fate and future path and those of China. I am deeply convinced that by relying on the unity and heroic struggle of the courageous Communist Party of India and all Indian patriots India will not remain long under the yoke of the imperialists and their collaborators. One day a free India will appear in the world as a member of the great family of socialism and People's Democracies,[1] just as free China has. That day shall end the epoch of imperialism and reaction in the history of humanity. Best wishes for the triumph of the united and heroic struggle of the patriotic people of India! Long live the brotherly unity between the Indian people and the Chinese people!

(Signed as Chairman of CPC and dated)

Note

1. See text Sept. 21, 1949, note 4.

Telegram to the Socialist Republican Party of India
(November 19, 1949)

Source: *RMRB* (Nov. 20, 1949), 1.

Mr. [Salat Chandra] Bhose:

Thank you for your congratulations to the People's Republic of China. The Chinese people welcome the establishment of extensive friendship with the people of India and with all oppressed peoples in order to oppose imperialist aggression together.

(Signed and dated)

Telegram to the Central Committee
of the Iranian Workers' Party
(November 19, 1949)

Source: *RMRB* (Nov. 20, 1949), 1.

Dear comrades of the Central Committee of the Iranian Workers' Party:

I express my deep and sincere gratitude for your congratulations.

The Chinese people are watching with respect the heroic struggle of the Iranian Workers' Party and the people of Iran against imperialism and against the reactionaries in their own country. We also firmly believe that this heroic struggle will result in their victory.

(Signed as Chairman of CPC)

Inscription for the Third Anniversary of *Nanqiao ribao*
(November 20, 1949)

Source: *RMRB* (Jan. 9, 1950), 1.

Nanqiao ribao *(Southern Overseas Chinese Daily) is a Chinese-language newspaper published in Singapore. It was founded in late 1946 by Tan Kah-Kee (see text May 16, 1952, source note), a leader of the "overseas Chinese" in Singapore, and was since then the mouthpiece of the China Democratic League, a pro-Communist organization, in Malaya.*

Serve the interests of the overseas Chinese.

Telegram of Condolence on the Death
of Xinjiang Delegates to the CPPCC
(November 22, 1949)

Source: *RMRB* (Nov. 25, 1949), 1. Available English Translation: NCNA, *Weekly Bulletin*, 131 (Dec. 6, 1949), 3.

Five delegates from Xinjiang to the First Plenary Session of the Chinese People's Political Consultative Conference died in an airplane accident en route. Their leader, Ahamaitikiang, was also chairman of the Central Committee of the Xinjiang League for the Defense of Peace and Democracy. (See text Oct. 21, 1949[3].)

Dear comrades of the Central Committee of the Xinjiang League for the Defense of Peace and Democracy:

The first group of delegates representing the people of Xinjiang in the Chinese People's Political Consultative Conference – Comrade Ahamaitikiang, vice-chairman of the Provincial Government of Xinjiang, Comrade Izhakbek, commander-in-chief of the National Army of the Tacheng-Ili-Ashan regions, Comrade Abduklimu, member of the Central Committee of the Xinjiang League for the Defense of Peace and Democracy, Comrade Dalerhan, deputy commander-in-chief of the National Army [of the Tacheng-Ili-Ashan region] and Comrade Luo Zhi of the Xinjiang Sino-Soviet Cultural Association – have unfortunately met with disaster in an airplane accident on their way to Beijing in September 1949. This is a great loss to the people of Xinjiang and to the Chinese people. For this I express my profound grief. While they lived, Comrade Ahamaitikiang and the other four comrades fought heroically for the cause of the liberation of the people of Xinjiang. In the end they gave their lives for the cause of establishing the People's Republic of China. They are worthy of the memory of the whole Chinese people forever. Eternal glory to Comrades Ahamaitikiang, Izhakbek, Abduklimu, Dalerhan, and Luo Zhi! (Signed as Chairman of CPG of PRC and dated)

Telegram to Panchen Gnoertehni
(November 23, 1949)

Source: *RMRB* (Nov. 24, 1949), 1.

Panchen Gnoertehni was the Panchen Lama of Tibet. The Panchen Lama rivaled the Dalai Lama in religious authority and political power. See also text May 24, 1951, note 2.

Panchen Gnoertehni:

We were extremely happy to receive and read your telegram of October 1. The Tibetan people love the homeland and are opposed to foreign aggression. They are dissatisfied with the policies of the reactionary government of the Kuomintang and wish to be a part of the great family of New China which is united and strong and in which all the nationalities cooperate as equals with one another. The Central People's Government and the Chinese People's Liberation Army will surely fulfill this wish of the Tibetan people. We hope that you, sir, and all the patriotic people of Tibet will strive together to fight for the liberation of Tibet and the unity of the Han and Tibetan peoples.
(Co-signed with Zhu De and dated)

Telegram to the Banka Federation of
Labor Unions of Indonesia
(November 24, 1949)

Source: *RMRB* (Nov.26,1949), 1.

The Banka Federation of Labor Unions of Indonesia:

I warmly thank you for your message of congratulations. I hope that the Indonesian people will, after their long and heroic struggle, similarly achieve the independence and freedom of their homeland.

Telegram to the Democratic Republic of Viet Nam
(November 25, 1949)

Source: *RMRB* (Nov. 26, 1949), 1. Available English Translation: NCNA, *Weekly Bulletin*, 130 (Nov. 29, 1949), 2.

The Democratic Republic of Viet Nam

President Ho Chi Minh:

We are deeply grateful for your congratulatory telegram on the founding of the Central People's Government of the People's Republic of China. Both China and Viet Nam are standing on the front line of the struggle against imperialism. With the victorious development of the struggles for liberation of the peoples of both countries, the friendship between the two peoples is bound to become closer with each passing day. Best wishes for the consolidation of the unity between the Chinese and Vietnamese peoples, and may the Democratic Republic of Viet Nam achieve complete success in its cause of independence and democracy.
(Signed as Chairman of CPG of PRC and dated)

Letter to Xu Beihong
(November 29, 1949)

Source: *Meishu fenglei*, 3 (Aug. 1967), 3.

The recipient of this letter, Xu Beihong (1895-1953), was a noted painter who, from 1946 until his death in September 1953, was the director of the Academy of Fine Arts in Beijing. On April 1, 1950, the Academy was renamed the Central Institute of Fine Arts. For more biographical information on Xu, see H. Boorman et al., eds. (1970), II, pp. 134-136.

Mr. Beihong:[1]

Your letter has been received. I have written one [inscription for the art institute] and wonder if it could be of use.[2] My best wishes to you in your teaching!

Mao Zedong
November 29, 1949

Notes

1. See text Nov. 17, 1949, note 2.

2. Mao's words here were *yi zhang*, which refers to a sheet of paper, on which he wrote the inscription for the art institute. The inscription reads *Guoli meishu xueyuan* (National Academy of Fine Arts.) It was reproduced in its original calligraphic form in the *Meishu fenglei* source.

Telegram to the Britain-China Conference in London
(November 30, 1949)

Source: *RMRB* (Dec. 6, 1949), 1. Available English Translation: NCNA, *Weekly Bulletin*, 132 (Dec. 13, 1949), 2.

The Britain-China Conference was held in Beaver Hall, London, December 3-4, 1949. The conference sent a congratulatory note to the PRC and resolved to urge the British government to establish diplomatic relations with the PRC immediately. A Britain-China Friendship Association was also formed out of this conference.

To the gentlemen sponsoring the Britain-China Conference and to all the honorable delegates through the courtesy of Mr. Jack [Deliben]:[1]

My warm and sincere congratulations on the convening of the Britain-China Conference. The Chinese people welcome all efforts to strengthen the friendship between the people of China and Britain and hope that these efforts will be successful.

(Signed and dated)

Note

1. We have not been able to identify Mao's correspondent here. This is the transliteration of the Chinese from *RMRB*.

Letter to the People of Lushun-Dalian
(December 1, 1949)

Source: *RMRB* (Dec. 26, 1949),1. Other Chinese Text: *GMRB* (Dec. 26, 1949),1.

To comrades of the Party committees of the Lushun-Dalian region and, through them, to the people of the Lushun-Dalian region:

The letter with your signatures[1] and your gifts, brought here by Comrade Kang Minzhuang, have both been received. We thank all of you as well as the people of Lushun-Dalian! We hope that you will make even greater efforts in production and construction so as to create even greater achievements!

Mao Zedong
December 1, 1949

Note

1. A letter of support for the new government on which more than 51,000 signatures appeared.

Letter to Liu Yazi
(December 2, 1949)

Source: *Shuxin*, p. 352.

Liu Yazi was an outstanding poet of the old school. He was a scholar-revolutionary in the late-Qing period and joined such associations as the Zhongguo jiaoyu hui (China Education Society) headed by Zhang Binglin and Wu Zhihui, and the Aiguo xueshe (Patriotic Study Association) headed by Cai Yuanpei, as well as Sun Yat-sen's Tongmeng hui. He was also a charter member of the influential Nan she (Southern Society) which was an association of literary and scholarly figures of the Suzhou - Shanghai - Hangzhou area. This association, while not actively espousing a particularly political ideology, included nonetheless among its members quite a few of the more radical revolutionaries of the late-Qing period such as Song Jiaoren and Huang Xing. As such it continued to have great influence in the early Republican period. During the May

Fourth period Liu became a proponent of the new-style, vernacular (baihua) literature and founded the Xin nan she (New Southern Society) to rival the Nan she, which had become devoted solely to the old style of literature. In the mid-1920s Liu became an active and moderately influential member of the KMT, but he opposed the rightward drift of the Party after Sun Yat-sen's death. Later Liu would avoid serving in the various KMT governments – both Chiang Kai-shek's Nanjing government and later Wang Jingwei's Wuhan government. Rather he dedicated himself to historical and literary pursuits and led a secluded life in Shanghai (briefly) and Hong Kong. In 1941, as a result of his reaction to the New Fourth Army Incident, Liu was expelled from the KMT. In the late-1940s Liu joined the Democratic League and formed the San min zhuyi tongzhi lianhe hui (Association of the Comrades of the Three People's Principle) and, in 1948, the Kuomintang Revolutionary Committee. He returned to Beijing in 1949 and was a member of the Government Administration Council of the new PRC government and of the standing committee of the National People's Congress until his death of pneumonia in 1958. Liu was one of the group of "democratic personages," including such figures as Ma Yinchu and Ma Xulun, who were respected by Mao and other leaders of the CPC. For more biographical information on Liu, see H. Boorman et al., eds. (1968), II, pp. 421-423.

Dear Venerable Mr. Liu:[1]

Your letter of November 4 has long been received. I apologize for the fact that, owing to my hectic schedule, I have been so tardy in responding. I have not seen the letter written in the train, but I thank you deeply for your warm and kind thoughts. At a moment of convenience I will make an inquiry on your behalf on the matter of the book for inscription.[2] Mr. Zhou[3] indeed has a very busy schedule of receiving visitors and official business, and perhaps he has forgotten it. As for the [delay in the] matter of the literary and historical organization,[4] it could perhaps be a result of the same problem. Again, at my convenience I shall ask about it.

In response, and with my regards,

Mao Zedong

December 2

Notes

1. Here Mao used the term *lao* to refer to Liu's venerated status. See text Feb. 17, 1951.

2. According to the source, this refers to a book "Commemorative Volume I on the Yi Pavilion" which Liu sent to Mao for inscription in 1949.

3. This refers to Zhou Enlai. Mao is employing a double-entendre here. The saying he used, *tu o zhi lao*, is a derivation of the aphorism *tu pu o fa*, from the "Lu Shijia" (Chronicle of the House of Lu) *Shi ji* (Historical Records), which describes the diligence of the historical figure Zhou Gong (Duke of Zhou) in ancient days, saying that he stopped in the middle of eating and had to hold his hair which had been disassembled in the middle of a bath in order to receive visitors and do business. Mao apparently placed significance in the coincidence of the "name" Zhou here. The Duke of Zhou was the chief minister of the founder of the great Zhou dynasty of ancient days, and Zhou Enlai, to whom Mao was in fact referring, was the premier of the People's Republic of China.

4. According to the source, this refers to a proposal that Liu made on the preparations for establishing a historical archive and museum under the Central Committee of the CPC.

Directive Issued at the Fourth Meeting of the CPGC
(Excerpts)
(December 2, 1949)

Source: *RMRB* (Dec. 4, 1949), 1. Other Chinese Texts: *GMRB* (Dec. 4, 1949), 1; *Mao Zedong lun caizheng*, pp. 11-12 (excerpt). Available English Translations: NCNA, *Weekly Bulletin*, 131 (Dec. 6, 1949), 2 (excerpt); *PC*, I:3 (Feb. 1, 1950), 5 (excerpt).

Although the Mao Zedong lun caizheng *source reprints these excerpts as a single paragraph, they are in fact three excerpts from the speech Mao made at this meeting. The entire speech is not reprinted in any of the sources. In the* RMRB *source, these three excerpts appeared in a news article and were preceded by colons – indicating that they were direct or verbatim quotations – but not by the Chinese equivalent of quotation marks. In our translation these three excerpts are separated by ellipses.*

[The national budget is a very important issue. The policy of the entire nation is reflected in it because it delineates the scope and orientation of the government's activities. Take, for example, the problem of providing support for all the former troops and former government and educational personnel which was raised in the draft of the rough estimate.][1] This is precisely a problem of policy. The People's Government ought to adopt a responsible attitude toward this problem. Only in this way can it be beneficial to the people. [Our situation can be summarized as follows:] There are difficulties, but there are also measures that can be taken, and there is hope. There are difficulties in our fiscal situation. We must explain to the people where our difficulties lie; we must not hide these difficulties. At the same time, however, we must also explain to the people that we do indeed have the means to overcome the difficulties. Since we have the means to overcome the difficulties, our cause is a hopeful one and our prospects are bright. Our situation will improve year by year, and we project that next year will be better than this year. Within a three-to-five-year period, our economy can be completely rehabilitated, and within eight to ten years our economy will be able to achieve a great development. . . . It is of great importance that these organizational regulations be promulgated.[2] These organizational regulations are precisely the general laws appropriate to the current period. The various local people's governments, although they may add [to these regulations] in accordance with concrete conditions [in their various localities], must implement them without exception. . . . China is a big country; only if we establish powerful local organs at such a level can things be done well. What ought to be united, must be united; and there should by no means be any separate governance, each doing what he thinks is best. However, there must be integration between [the notion of] unification and [the notion of] discretionary arrangements according to local conditions. Under the regime of the people, the historical conditions of the past, in which regional occupation by the feudalist forces has been generated, have been eliminated. The division of labor between the Center and the localities will be to our advantage and will in no way harm us.[3]

Notes

1. This section in brackets does not appear as a direct, verbatim quotation in the original *RMRB* version, but as a synopsis of what Mao said at the beginning of his speech. It has been included to provide context for the other parts which are direct quotations. The same applies to other bracketed parts in this translation.

2. These refer to the regulations governing the organization of people's representative councils for every municipality, *xian*, and province.

3. The last paragraph is in response to the suggestion of establishing military administrative councils in the various greater administrative regions.

Instruction on the Army's Participation in Production and Construction Work in 1950

(December 5, 1949)

Source: *RMRB* (Dec. 6, 1949), 1. Other Chinese Texts: *XHYB*, I:3 (Jan. 15, 1950), 669; *Wansui* (1969), pp. 1-4. Available English Translations: JPRS, *Miscellany*, I, pp. 2-5; NCNA, *Weekly Bulletin*, 132 (Dec. 13, 1949), 4 (excerpt).

According to the RMRB *and* XHYB *sources, this document was released in the name of the People's Revolutionary Military Council.*

The People's War of Liberation has basically won a nationwide victory. With the exception of [units] on a few fronts which have to devote themselves to pursuing and annihilating the remnant enemy forces so as to achieve a complete triumph, a large number of the troops of the People's Liberation Army have already engaged in, or are soon to begin to engage in, training and consolidation. The Common Program of the People's Political Consultative Conference provides that "the armed forces of the People's Republic of China shall, during peacetime, systematically take part in agricultural and industrial production in order to assist in the work of national construction, provided such work does not interfere with their military duties."[4] Here, a glorious and formidable task is given to our people's armed forces in addition to the great tasks of securing our national defense, reinforcing public order, and strengthening [their own] training and consolidation. Therefore, the People's Revolutionary Military Council is calling on the entire army, with the exception of those [units] which are still engaged in fighting and logistics service, to shoulder part of the task of production so that our People's Liberation Army will not only be an army for national defense but also an army of production, in order to cooperate with all the people in the country in overcoming the difficulties left behind by long years of war and in accelerating the economic construction of [our] New Democracy.

This production task must and can be realized.

The reason that this production task must be realized is that the long war launched against the Chinese people by reactionaries both inside and outside of our country has caused the people serious hardships and has severely damaged the economy. Today, we want to carry the revolutionary war through to the end and heal the wounds left by the long periods of war; we must undertake the work of construction in all areas of [our] economy, our culture, and [our] national defense. The state's revenue is inadequate, but its expenditure is huge. This is the one major difficulty we are facing today. The way to overcome this kind of difficulty is first to have the entire people, under the leadership of the Central People's Government, restore and develop production step by step; and as for the People's Liberation Army, it must assume the responsibility for a set [share] of the task of production. Only by doing this can it join the people of the entire country in overcoming this difficulty.

The reason that this production task can be realized is that the overwhelming majority of [the personnel in] the People's Liberation Army come from among the laboring people. They have a high degree of political consciousness and all kinds of production skills. Furthermore, during the most difficult years and months of the War of Resistance against Japan, they shouldered the tasks of production and a tradition of labor. The vast numbers of cadres and veteran fighters of the People's Liberation Army all understand that after the troops have participated in production, not only will difficulties be overcome, government expenditures decreased, and army life improved, but also, the political quality of the army will be raised through the tempering of labor, and the relations between officers and soldiers and between the army and the people will be improved. [Another] reason that this production task can be realized is that in areas where fighting has ended, in addition to assuming such tasks as securing national defense, cleaning out bandits, consolidating public order, and strengthening training, the People's Liberation Army now has spare time to take part in production and construction work. All these things are the factors which make it possible for the People's Liberation Army to carry out the task of production.

The participation of the People's Liberation Army in production is not a temporary measure; it should proceed from the perspective of long-range construction. The emphasis is on increasing the nation's wealth through labor.[2] Beginning in the spring of 1950, the heads of all military regions must therefore direct their subordinates to put into effect [a program of] participating in production and construction work in order to improve their own livelihood and to save a portion of the state's expenditure. This production and construction work ought to become a kind of movement in order to facilitate its wider adoption. A relatively long-term plan and concrete measures [for implementation] should be formulated for this type of production work. With the approval of the people's government, the categories of [such] production should stay within the confines of agriculture, animal husbandry, fishery, water conservation projects, handicraft industries, and transportation projects which [the army] is capable of undertaking. Commercial undertakings are forbidden. The leading organs of the army [unit] should carry out investigations and studies [for production] based on the conditions of the places where they are stationed and complete the preparation this winter.

Based on experience, the army's production movement must strictly prohibit the opening up of shops and engaging in commercial activities. If among the cadres there should be ideas of seeking quick profits by attempting to smuggle, hoard, and speculate, or if such activities are discovered, they must be corrected and stopped quickly, for they not only violate the correct production guidelines and disrupt economic order, but will invariably [cause] graft and corruption to occur and will destroy our own comrades. These activities are not tolerated by law. Moreover, in undertaking agricultural production, we must be careful not to cause floods as a result of reclaiming wasteland or incur the people's dissatisfaction by competing for land.

So that the army may carry out its production tasks correctly and develop its production movement, it is hereby stipulated that:

1) At levels above division, army, and military subregion, representative committees should be formed of representatives from the general headquarters, political departments, and logistic service departments. Their tasks are to take charge of the direction of production, to examine and approve production plans, to supervise the implementation of production plans, and to investigate illegal activities.

2) Producers' cooperatives are to be established in the army. Organs of leadership for these cooperatives should also be established at every level which, under the supervision and guidance of the army production committees, will control the disposition of all production funds, production activities, and fruits of production. The system of the cooperatives and the army's command system are to be parallel. They will maintain close relations with each other, but they are not to be confused with each other.

3) Implement [the principle of] taking both public and private [interests] into consideration and distributing on a fair and reasonable [basis] the net income from production. Forty per cent should go to the individual producers; the rest

should go to the production units and the state in order to establish the revolutionary way of running the affairs of one's own household as well as those of the public.[3] On the one hand, this will make the army partially self-sufficient, while on the other, it will allow the individual producer to have some income. This individual income may be kept by the individual for private use, or be sent home to the family for its use, or be deposited in the cooperative in reserve [for future use]; [the choice should be] at the discretion of the individual.

4) In areas where there is a shortage of land, in addition to participating, whenever possible, in all kinds of handicraft industries, water conservation, transportation, and construction projects, heads of army units may talk things over with the local people's governments and, on the condition that the peasants' own willingness is not violated, contribute the army's labor funds, fertilizer, and farm tools to cultivating the land jointly with the peasants in order to increase production and share the fruits equitably. However, it is necessary to make sure that this is not carried out through coercion, and that [the army] does not compete with the people for benefits.

5) The production plans of the units in all military regions must be integrated with the production plans of the people's governments of all the provinces and of all the greater administrative areas. [There should be] coordination in the use of production funds. All the production funds of the army units should be treated as investment, so interest must be computed and dates set for repayment. All the army's production enterprises should pay taxes according to the rules and observe all laws and regulations of the people's governments, and no violations will be permitted.

It is hoped that all heads of military regions will pay strict attention to the above items. They must make sure that our People's Liberation Army's production and construction work in 1950 attains remarkable results. They must, moreover, conduct check-ups all the time and rectify errors and deficiencies that may arise. On their part, the people's governments in all areas have the responsibility of providing guidance and assistance in the production work of the army units in their areas.

Notes

1. Mao is here referring to Article 24 of the Common Program. For the Common Program, see text Sept. 21, 1949, note 3.

2. The *Wansui* version only has "the nation's wealth."

3. This refers to Article 26 of the Common Program, which stipulates that the "fundamental policy for the development of economic construction of the PRC is to implement the specific policies of giving due consideration to both public and private interests, benefiting both labor and capital, practicing mutual aid between cities and villages, and allowing the interflow of commodities between home and abroad, with the purpose of developing production and promoting economic prosperity."

Speech on Arrival at Moscow Train Station
(December 16, 1949)

Source: *RMRB* (Dec. 18, 1949), 1. Other Chinese Texts: *Wansui* (1969), p. 4; *XHYB*, I:3 (Jan. 15, 1950), 579. Available English Translations: NCNA, *Weekly Bulletin*, 133 (Dec. 20, 1949), 1; *CDSP*, I:51 (Jan. 17, 1950), 27.

Dear Comrades and Friends:

For me to have the opportunity at this time to visit the capital of the Soviet Union, the first great socialist country in the world, is a very happy event in my life. A deep friendship exists between the peoples of [our] two great countries, China and the Soviet Union. After the October Socialist Revolution, the Soviet government, following the policies of Lenin and Stalin, took the lead in abrogating the unequal treaties [concluded] with China under Imperial Russia. Over a period of almost thirty years, the Soviet people and the Soviet government have, on several occasions, assisted the Chinese people in their cause of liberation. The Chinese people will never forget that in the midst of their ordeals they received such fraternal friendship of the Soviet people and the Soviet government.

The important tasks for the present are consolidating the world peace front headed by the Soviet Union and opposing those who stir up war as well as consolidating relations between our two great countries, China and and the Soviet Union, and developing the friendship of the Chinese and Soviet peoples. I am confident that with the victory of the Chinese People's Revolution and the founding of the Chinese People's Republic, with the joint efforts of the New Democracies[1] and the peace loving peoples of the world, with the common aspirations and close cooperation of [our] two great countries, China and the Soviet Union, and especially with the correct international policies of Generalissimo Stalin, these tasks will certainly be fully carried out and excellent results will be attained.

Long live the friendship and cooperation of China and the Soviet Union!

Note

1. See text Sept. 21, 1949, note 4.

Telegram to Stalin
(December 19, 1949)

Source: *RMRB* (Dec. 21, 1949), 1. Other Chinese Text: *XHYB*, I:3 (Jan. 15, 1950), 591.

Chairman Stalin,
The Council of Ministers,
The Government of the Soviet Union

Your Excellency:

On this happy occasion of Your Excellency's seventieth birthday, I sincerely extend to you my respect and my best wishes for the daily strengthening of the fortress for world peace and democracy under Your Excellency's leadership.
(Signed as Chairman of CPG of PRC and dated)

Address at Birthday Celebration Meeting Held for Stalin
(December 21, 1949)

Source: *RMRB* (Dec. 23, 1949), 1. Other Chinese Texts: *XHYB*, I:3 (Jan. 15, 1950), 579; *Wansui* (1967b), pp. 8-9; *Buyi*, p. 5. Available English Translations: NCNA, *Weekly Bulletin*, 134 (Dec. 28, 1949), 1; *CB*, 891 (Oct.8,1969), 14; J. Chen (1970), p. 19.

Dear comrades and friends:

I am genuinely pleased to have the chance to join this distinguished gathering in celebration of the seventieth birthday of Comrade Stalin.

Comrade Stalin is a teacher and friend of the people of the world as well as a teacher and friend of the Chinese people. He has further developed the revolutionary theory of Marxism-Leninism and has made extremely outstanding and extensive contributions to the cause of the world Communist movement. In the arduous struggle to resist their oppressors, the Chinese people have become deeply appreciative of the importance of Comrade Stalin's friendship.

At this distinguished gathering, on behalf of of the Chinese people and the Communist Party of China, I congratulate Comrade Stalin on his seventieth birthday and wish him health and longevity. We wish well-being, strength, and prosperity to our great friend, the Soviet Union under the leadership of Comrade Stalin. We hail the great unprecedented solidarity of the working class in the world under the leadership of Comrade Stalin.

Long live the great Stalin, leader of the world's working class and of the international Communist movement!

Long live the Soviet Union, the stronghold of world peace and democracy!

Comment on Democratic Personages[1]
(Winter 1949)

Source: *Shengping ziliao*, pp. 288-289.

This is an excerpt, reprinted in Shengping ziliao, *from Hua Ming,* San fan wu fan de poushi *(An Analytical View of the Three-Anti's and Five-Anti's), Union Research Institute, Hong Kong, November 1952.* Shengping ziliao *introduces this comment with the following: "In the winter [of 1949] certain middle-echelon cadres in Beijing felt greatly resentful at the high wages and benefits given to democratic personages in contrast to what they themselves earned. Playing on the theme that Li Jishen [a former Kuomintang general] was paid an amount equaling 5,000 catties of millet a month, they chanted the slogan: 'Better to join the revolution late than to have joined it early; better still not to have joined it at all.'" Mao's comment here is ostensibly his response to the situation.*

Let me add two more phrases for you, namely: "Better to be a counterrevolutionary than to merely keep out of the revolution."... Don't think you deserve preferential treatment because of your achievements in war. You must know that one democratic personage is possibly worth an army. By winning one Li Jishen[2] over to our side, we probably saved the lives of twenty or thirty thousand comrades and won the military victory one or two years ahead of time.... Now we will simply do it this way; this is also the only way we can do it, whether you approve of it or not.

Notes

1. See text Sept. 21, 1949, note 1.

2. Li Jishen (1886-1959) was commander of the Fourth Army of the Nationalist forces in 1925-26. Although he often held high posts in the KMT military command, his relations with the Chiang Kai-shek-dominated wing of the KMT had been strained and unstable since the Northern Expedition period. In 1929, when he attempted to mediate the dispute between Chiang and the Guangxi clique (Li Zongren, Bai Congxi), he was expelled from the KMT. After the Japanese attacked Changchun (Mukden) in 1931, and Chiang was forced from office, the Guangxi faction was restored, and Li with them. Later, when Chiang returned to power in the KMT, Li was relegated to ex-officio duties in Guangzhou. In late 1933 he became chairman of the People's Revolutionary Government in Fuzhou, which actively opposed the authority of the Nanjing KMT (Chiang) government. When that opposition was suppressed and the Fuzhou government dissolved, Li fled to Hong Kong, with a KMT arrest warrant out for him. In 1935 he and others founded the Chinese People's Revolutionary League, seeking to unite the various political factions against Japan, but also in opposition to Nanjing. This was dissolved in 1937. In 1938 he was restored to membership in the KMT and continued to hold high military advisory positions. However, he largely operated on a local level in Guangxi in organizing military opposition to the Japanese, rather than assuming his official positions in the Chongqing government. In 1947 he went to Hong Kong and on March 8 of that year issued a statement urging the KMT and the Communists to settle their differences and end the civil war. On August 6 he was expelled from the KMT for the last time, and in January 1948 he became the chairman of the newly constituted Revolutionary Committee of the KMT. (See text Sept. 21, 1949, note 1.) He went to Beijing in early 1949 and was appointed to the Preparatory Committee for the CPPCC. In September 1949 he became a vice-chairman of the Standing Committee of the CPPCC and in October, on the founding of the PRC, he became one of six vice-chairmen of the Central People's Government and vice-president of the Sino-Soviet Friendship Association. For more biographical information on Li, see H. Boorman et al., eds. (1970), II, pp. 292-295.

Conversation with a Painter from the Soviet Union [Excerpts]

(1949)

Source: *Dagong bao* (May 10, 1950).

The source does not identify the painter who had this conversation with Mao or the exact time or location at which this conversation took place. The context of this conversation is that the painter is creating a portrait of Mao. Our translation is of those passages of conversation that appeared in direct quotation in the Dagong bao *news article.*

[The Soviet painter inquires of Mao whether or not it would be too exhausting if they worked, i.e., if Mao posed for the portrait, from nine to eleven p.m. each day.]

I usually work in the nighttime as well. This is a habit cultivated through many years of working underground. Let me now accompany you for breakfast, and then we shall start. . . .

We need a portfolio of this type, of drawings about People's China, or a series of paintings. . . .

That is correct. In terms of their nature, the Chinese people are diligent, hardworking, and persevering. However, in addition [to the fact that it is in their nature,] this diligence and perseverance is also linked to the most cruel exploitation and extreme deprivation of rights suffered by the Chinese people for so many centuries. The hard life itself has forced them to pay the price, in every kind of work, of giving it their greatest labor, just so that they can feed themselves and continue to live. As for culture, we, the Chinese people, consider ourselves to be the most backward. Our culture is in this state because in the past there has not been in China an organized force or thought which has been able to unite the whole people and to direct their energy toward the correct path [of development]. Today, the Chinese Communist Party has taken this responsibility upon its shoulders. The Chinese people, under its leadership, and learning from the people of the Soviet Union, have finally discovered a correct path for themselves.

1950

Inscription for First Issue of *Renmin haijun*
(January 1, 1950)

Source: *RMRB* (Jan. 4, 1950), 1. Other Chinese Text: *JFJB* (Feb. 28, 1957).

Renmin haijun *(People's Navy) was a journal published by the political department of the East China Region headquarters of the People's Navy. Its inaugural issue was published on New Year's Day, 1950.*

We must build a navy. This navy must be able to secure our coastal defense and effectively protect us against possible aggression by the imperialists.

Interview Given to TASS Correspondent in Moscow
(January 2, 1950)

Source: *RMRB* (Jan. 3, 1950), 1. Other Chinese Text: *XHYB*, I:3 (Jan. 15, 1950), 579. Available English Translations: NCNA, *Weekly Bulletin*, 135 (Jan. 3, 1950), 1-2; *CDSP*, 2:2 (Feb. 25, 1950), 23.

In this translation, "Q" refers to the TASS correspondent, and "A" refers to Mao.

Q: What is the current situation like in China?

A: Military matters in China are going smoothly. At present, the Communist Party of China and the Central People's Government of the People's Republic of China are switching to peaceful economic construction.

Q: How long will you be staying in the Soviet Union, Mr. Mao?

A: I plan to stay for a few weeks. The length of my stay in the Soviet Union will be partly determined by the time it will take to resolve the various problems related to the interests of the People's Republic of China.

Q: Would it be possible to learn what problems you have in mind?

A: Foremost among these are the matters of the current Treaty of Friendship and Alliance between China and the Soviet Union, and of the Soviet Union's loan to the People's Republic of China and the matter of trade and of a trade agreement between our two countries.[1] There are also other questions.

Furthermore, I also plan to visit various localities and cities in the Soviet Union in order to gain a better understanding of economic and cultural construction in the Soviet state.

Note

1. The "current" Treaty of Friendship and Alliance between China and the Soviet Union to which Mao refers here is the treaty signed on August 14, 1945, between the Nationalist government and the Soviet Union. This treaty was abrogated on February 14, 1950, when a new Treaty of Friendship, Alliance, and Mutual Assistance was signed by the two countries and ratified and put into effect in April of the same year.

Aside from agreements on postal and telecommunication services, six agreements were reached during Mao's visit to the Soviet Union. The agreements, signed on February 14, 1950, were:

1) The Treaty of Friendship, Alliance, and Mutual Assistance.

2) The agreement on Joint Administration of the China-Changchun Railway and of Dalian.

3) The abrogation of the Sino-Soviet Treaty of Friendship and Alliance and of the Agreements on the Chinese Changchun Railway, Dairen (Dalian), and Port Arthur (Lushun) signed August 15, 1945; and the recognition of the Mongolian People's Republic.

4) The Soviet grant of credit to the People's Republic of China over a five-year period.

5) The gratuitous transfer by the Soviet Union to China of property acquired by Soviet organizations from Japanese owners in Manchuria in 1945.

6) The gratuitous transfer by the Soviet Union of all buildings of the Soviet military compound in Beijing.

For an English text of these agreements see NCNA, *Daily Bulletin*, 289 (Feb. 16, 1950), 80.

Inscription for Lenin's Mausoleum
(January 11, 1950)

Source: *GMRB* (Jan. 13, 1950), 1. Available English Translation: NCNA, *Weekly Bulletin*, 137 (Jan. 17, 1950), 1.

This inscription was written on a wreath placed by Mao personally on Lenin's Tomb in Moscow on January 11, 1950. In Mao's company were Wang Jiaxiang, the Chinese ambassador to the USSR, and Chen Boda. The inscription was in both Chinese and Russian.

> To Lenin – Great teacher of the revolution.
> Mao Zedong
> January 11, 1950

Telegram to Bulgaria on the Death of Vasil Kolarov
(January 24, 1950)

Source: *RMRB* (Jan. 25, 1950), 1. Available English Translation: NCNA, *Weekly Bulletin*, 139 (Jan. 31, 1950), 1.

Vasil Kolarov, one of the founders of the Communist Party of Bulgaria and a leading official in the Communist International, was at the time of his death chairman of the Council of Ministers of the People's Republic of Bulgaria and a member of the Central Committee of the Communist Party of Bulgaria.

Vice-chairman Chervenkov,
The Council of Ministers of Bulgaria

Your Excellency:

I was stunned to receive the news that Chairman Kolarov of the Council of Ministers of Bulgaria has passed away. Please allow me to respectfully

express my deepest and sincerest grief to the government and people of your country.
(Signed as Chairman of CPG of PRC and dated)

Telegram to President Prasad of the Republic of India
(January 28, 1950)

Source: *RMRB* (Jan. 29, 1950), 1. Available English Translation: NCNA, *Weekly Bulletin*, 139 (Jan. 31, 1950), 1.

President Rajendra Prasad,
The Republic of India

Your Excellency:

At this time, on Your Excellency's election as the first president of India, I express, on behalf of the Central People's Government and the people of the People's Republic of China, our sincere congratulations.
(Signed as Chairman of CPG of PRC and dated)

Speech on Departure from Moscow
(February 17, 1950)

Source: *RMRB* (Feb. 20, 1950), 1. Other Chinese Texts: *XHYB*, I:5 (Mar. 15, 1950), 1112; *XHBYK*, 22 (Nov. 1958), 7. Available English Translation: NCNA, *Weekly Bulletin*, 142 (Feb. 21, 1950), 1.

Dear comrades and friends:
    This time in Moscow, Comrade Zhou Enlai, the members of the Chinese delegation, and I met with Generalissimo Stalin and other comrades in responsible positions in the Soviet government. It is difficult for me to express in words the complete understanding and deep friendship that was established between us on the basis of the fundamental interests of the people of our two

great nations. It is plain to see that the unity of the people of the two great countries, China and the Soviet Union, solidified by treaty,[1] will be permanent and inviolable, and one which cannot be put asunder by anyone. Moreover, this unity will not only influence the prosperity of these two great countries, China and the Soviet Union, but will surely also affect the future of humanity and the triumph of peace and justice all over the world.

During our sojourn in the Soviet Union we have visited many factories and farms. We have seen the great achievements of the workers, peasants, and intellectuals of the Soviet Union in their undertaking of socialist construction; we have observed the work-style of combining a spirit of revolution with a spirit of realism and practicality which has been nurtured among the people of the Soviet Union through the teaching of Comrade Stalin and the Communist Party of the Soviet Union.[2] This has confirmed the conviction which the Chinese Communists have always held: that the experience of the Soviet Union in economic and cultural construction and its experience in construction in other major areas will serve as an example for the construction of New China.

We have received warm and enthusiastic hospitality in Moscow, the capital of the Soviet Union, and in Leningrad, birthplace of the October Revolution. As we leave this great capital of socialism, we wish particularly to express our sincerest gratitude to Generalissimo Stalin and to the government and people of the Soviet Union.

Long live the eternal friendship and the eternal cooperation between China and the Soviet Union!

Long live the people of the Soviet Union!

Long live the teacher of the world revolution and the true friend of the Chinese people – Comrade Stalin!

Notes

1. See text Jan. 2, 1950, note 1.
2. Here Mao uses the Chinese term *liangongdang*, which is commonly used to refer to the Bolshevik Party. Mao's use of the term here may be derived from the Chinese translation of Stalin's *Short Course on the History of the Communist Party of the Soviet Union (Bolshevik)* in which the term *liangongdang* is used to refer to the CPSU.

Telegram to President of the Viet Nam-China Friendship Association

(February 21, 1950)

Source: *RMRB* (Feb. 23, 1950), 1.

The president of the Provisional Executive Committee of the Viet Nam-China Friendship Association of the Democratic Republic of Viet Nam was Ho Tung Mau at this time.

Mr. Ho Tung Mau:

On receiving the joyous tidings of the establishment of the Viet Nam-China Friendship Association,[1] I sincerely extend my congratulations and best wishes for the progress of friendly relations between the two nations of China and Viet Nam.

(Signed and dated)

Note

1. This association was at the time in its organizational stage. It was proposed and sponsored on Feb. 11, 1950, by a group of thirteen leaders and officials of the government of the Democratic Republic of Viet Nam.

Telegram to the USSR

(February 23, 1950)

Source: *RMRB* (Feb. 26, 1950), 1. Available English Translation: NCNA, *Weekly Bulletin*, 143 (Feb. 28, 1950), 3.

This telegram was sent on the thirty-second anniversary of the establishment of the armed forces of the Soviet Union.

Generalissimo Stalin

Your Excellency:

On the occasion of this grand festival of the great defender of world peace, the Soviet Union's Armed Forces, we happily and sincerely express our warmest felicitations.
(Signed and dated)

Telegram to Stalin upon Leaving the USSR
(February 26, 1950)

Source: *RMRB* (Mar. 5, 1950), 1. Other Chinese Text: *XHYB*, I:61 (April 15, 1950), 1331. Available English Translations: NCNA, *Weekly Bulletin*, 144 (Mar. 7, 1950), 1; *PC*, I:6 (Mar. 16, 1950), 20.

Comrade Stalin:

Our group is now approaching the border between the Soviet Union and China. Upon leaving this great country, the Union of Soviet Socialist Republics, I would like to express to you and to all the comrades in responsible positions in the government of the Soviet Union my deep gratitude for your hospitality and my best wishes for the continuous strengthening and prospering of the Soviet Union under your leadership.
(Signed and dated)

Conversations During Inspection of Heilongjiang Province
[Excerpts]
(February 27, 1950)

Source: *Huiyi Mao zhuxi*, pp. 553-560.

These excerpts are culled from an article titled "Weida de jiaohui" (A Great Lesson) written by a reporter for Heilongjiang ribao *(Heilongjiang Daily) and which originally appeared in* Heilongjiang ribao *(Feb. 27, 1977).*

Mao visited Harbin, the capital city of Heilongjiang Province, for two days, February 27-28, 1950. These are the more important things he said in conversations during that time.

It is good to have many older workers [in the factory]; when we do not know [how to run a factory] we must rely on the older workers to manage the factories. . . .

It is also very important to cultivate new workers!

If you do not know [how to manage a factory] you must learn. We are all ignorant [in some ways] and we all have to learn.

We must transform Harbin, now a city of consumers, into a production-oriented city. . . .

After Hu Zongnan[1] attacked Yanan, I, together with Comrades Zhou Enlai and Ren Bishi,[2] directed the nationwide War of Liberation from two caves in Northern Shaanxi.

Notes

1. Hu Zongnan (1902-1962) was the deputy commander of the Eighth Battle Zone of the KMT forces during the War of Resistance against Japan and was stationed in Northern Shaanxi, responsible for the "containing" of the Communist forces in the Shaanxi-Gansu-Ningxia Border Region, and earned for himself the sobriquet of "King of the Northwest." In 1947, during the CPC-KMT civil war, when the KMT forces attacked the Shaanxi-Gansu-Ningxia Border Region, Hu's troops overran Yanan, the nerve center of the Communist forces and government, in March of that year. For more biographical information on Hu, see H. Boorman et al., eds. (1968), II, pp. 175-177.

2. Ren Bishi (1904-1950), was a veteran member of the CPC. In 1921 he joined the Communist Youth League in Shanghai and became one of its chief cadres. From 1921 to 1924 he was

studying in the Soviet Union. In 1927 he became a member of the Central Committee of the CPC. In 1931 he went to the Jiangxi Soviet and became a commissar of the Central Bureau of the Soviet. From late 1934 to 1936, as the political commissar of the Second Front Army, he was a chief organizer of the Hunan-Hubei-Sichuan-Yunnan base area. When the Red Army became the Eighth Route Army in 1937 he became the chief of the Political Department of that unit. He returned to Yanan in 1940 and became a member of the secretariat of the Central Committee of the CPC. At the First Plenum of the Seventh Central Committee of the CPC in 1945 he became a member of the Political Bureau. He remained in Yanan with Mao and Zhou, as mentioned here, in 1947, and devoted himself to the study of the problem of land reform, publishing a major tract on the question in early 1948. For more biographical information on Ren, see *Zhonggong renming lu*, appendix, pp. 31-32, and D. Klein and A. Clark, eds. (1971), I, pp. 411-416.

Inscriptions Written in Harbin
(February 27, 1950)

Source: *Huiyi Mao zhuxi*, pp. 559-560.

See source note for preceding text in this volume. The first three inscriptions here were written for the provincial Party committee, the fourth for the municipal Party committee of Harbin, and the fifth for the Second Congress of the New Democratic Youth League then being held in Harbin. Mao was then on an inspection tour of Heilongjiang Province; see preceding document.

Do not pick up a bureaucratic work-style.

Study.

Struggle.

Promote production.

Study Marxism-Leninism.

Reply to Ambassador of the People's Republic of Romania
(March 10, 1950)

Source: *RMRB* (Mar. 11, 1950), 1. Other Chinese Text: *GMRB* (Mar. 11, 1950), 1.

Teodor Rudenco served as ambassador of the People's Republic of Romania to the PRC from March 1950 to December 1952.

Mr. Ambassador:

I am very glad to accept the letter of credence from the Presidium of the Grand National Assembly of the People's Republic of Romania presented by Your Excellency and am grateful to Your Excellency for your congratulations and good wishes.

The resolute struggle against domestic and foreign reactionaries undertaken by the Romanian people since the world war against Fascism and their current industrious efforts in the work of economic construction in which glorious achievements have already been reaped have always been regarded with deep and sincere concern and admiration by the Chinese people.

Today, the governments and peoples of the two nations of China and Romania are fighting arduously and heroically for their common goal of world peace. We believe that the increasingly close cooperation of the two countries, China and Romania, in the political, economic, and cultural spheres will surely benefit the people of the two countries and will further consolidate and reinforce the strength of the camp for world democracy and peace.

I warmly welcome Your Excellency as the first ambassador extraordinary and plenipotentiary of the People's Republic of Romania to the People's Republic of China, and pledge to Your Excellency all my assistance in your work of consolidating the friendship between the two nations.

Best wishes for the prosperity of your country, the prosperity of your people, and the good health of your head of state.

Soliciting Suggestions on the Question of Strategy
for Dealing with Rich Peasants
(March 12, 1950)

Source: *Xuanji*, V, pp. 13-14. Available English Translation: *SW*, V, pp. 24-25.

This is a circular that Mao sent to the Central-South Bureau, the East China Bureau, the South China Subbureau, and the Northwest Bureau of the CPC Central Committee. In addition to specifying the conditions under which the Party could deal with the problem of the rich peasants, conditions which at this time justified restraint, this circular also illustrates the type of decision-making process that Mao favored; nevertheless this document is more important as an introduction to the issue of agricultural policy in the early 1950s.

Please report to us by telegraph the suggestions that you are soliciting at the meetings now being held by comrades in positions of responsibility in the provinces concerning the question of the strategy for dealing with the rich peasants,[1] that is, [the strategy whereby] during the land reform movement scheduled to begin this coming winter in several southern provinces and in certain areas in the northwest we are not only to refrain from dealing with the capitalistic rich peasants, but moreover, to refrain from dealing with the semifeudal rich peasants as well, and instead, to wait a few more years before we resolve the problem of the semifeudal rich peasants.[2] Please give some thought to whether or not it would be more advantageous to do things in this way. The reasons for doing this are: first, the land reform is unprecedentedly large in scale and it is easy for ultra-Left deviations to occur. If we deal only with the landlords but not the rich peasants, we can isolate the landlords even more, protect the middle peasants, and prevent indiscriminate beatings and executions; otherwise, it will be very difficult to prevent these things. Second, in the past, land reform in the north was carried out during wartime, and the atmosphere of war had overwhelmed the atmosphere of land reform. Now there is basically no more war so the land reform will be particularly conspicuous; its impact on society will appear particularly great, and the clamors of the landlords will also be particularly shrill. If we do not touch the semifeudal rich peasants for the time being but wait a few more years before we deal with them, we will be shown to be more justified. That is to say that we would have more initiative politically. Third, our united front with the national bourgeoisie[3] has already taken shape politically, economically, and organizationally, and yet the [alliance with the] national bourgeoisie is closely tied to the question of land. In order to stabilize the national bourgeoisie, it seems more appropriate not to touch the semifeudal rich peasants for the moment.

I brought up the question of not touching the rich peasants for the time being at the meeting of the Political Bureau last November,[4] but I did not make a detailed analysis; nor did I make a decision. Now it is time to make a decision. After a decision has been made, it is necessary to revise the Land Law and other documents related to land reform and promulgate them,[5] so as to facilitate the study [of them] by the cadres [responsible for] land reform from the provinces in the new [liberated] areas. Only then can we facilitate getting the land reform started after this year's autumn [harvest]. Otherwise, we would miss our opportunity and be forced into a passive position. Because of this, I am asking comrades, not only those from the Central-South Bureau, but also those from the East China Bureau, the South China Subbureau, the Southwest Bureau, and the Northwest Bureau as well, to discuss this problem. I am also asking you to transmit this telegram to your subordinate provincial and municipal [Party] committees for discussion, to collect both supporting and opposing opinions, and to report them quickly to the Central Committee by telegram, to serve as a basis for our considerations in deciding what policy to adopt. This is very important.

Notes

1. According to the class analysis of the CPC there are five main classes in China's rural society: landlords, rich peasants, middle peasants, poor peasants, and workers. The political and economic characteristics of each of these classes was outlined in Mao's 1928 article, "Analysis of Classes in Chinese Society," a substantially revised version of which is translated in *SW*, I, pp. 13-21. These classes are further defined in "How to Analyze Class Status in the Countryside" appended to the Land Reform Law of the People's Republic of China, June 1950, pp. 19-24, translated in T. Chen (1967), pp. 204-205; see also Y. Lau (1977), pp. 110-111, 565-566. In particular, see the Resolution of the Government Administration Council on the Drawing of Class Distinctions in the Countryside, passed by the 44th meeting of the GAC on August 4, 1950, and published in *RMSC* (1951), "Shen" section, pp. 48-66. Sections A(2), B(2), (3), (4), (5), (12), (13), (14) dealt specifically with the identity and variations in that identity of rich peasants. According to the Land Reform Law, rich peasants were classified on the basis of the amount and nature of their landholding and labor hiring (or even labor purchasing in some extraordinary cases). The classification of other segments of the peasant population is done on the basis of assessing their income level. Although the land reform program returned the ownership of land to the peasants, it did so on an individual basis. Consequently, rich peasants (those who held relatively larger quantities of land) had greater access to the means of agricultural production and thus continued to hold an inherent advantage over the rest of the peasant population. For more on this distinction, one should consult section 4 and footnotes 6 and 7 of Mao's article "The Present Situation and Our Tasks" (see *Xuanji*, IV, pp. 1146-1147, 1158, and *SW*, IV, pp. 164-165, 175).

2. Those rich peasants whose income were substantially derived from extracting surplus value from hired labor on their land are called capitalist rich peasants. In addition to farming their own land or hiring labor to farm their land, some rich peasants also lease out parts of their landholdings, sometimes even leasing land or making loans at exorbitant rates of interest. Those who lease out more land than they themselves farm or farm by hired labor are known as semifeudal rich peasants.

3. The term "national bourgeoisie" describes that segment of the bourgeoisie that stands in distinction from the bureaucratic bourgeoisie and the comprador bourgeoisie. It is a segment whose existence is particularly obvious in a semicolonial, semifeudal society such as modern China since the mid-nineteenth century. It is characterized by its patriotic tendencies and by its relatively insignificant ties to either foreign imperialistic capital or to comprador capital and to the forces of feudalism. The national bourgeoisie is a very important segment of Chinese society. Its character was first defined by Mao and other Communist leaders in the article "The Chinese Revolution and The Chinese Communist Party" (see SW, II, pp. 320ff). In this article, written in the Yanan days, Mao suggested that the national bourgeoisie had a dual character; it was oppressed by imperialism and the forces of feudalism, and therefore it was a revolutionary force in this respect; however, it still had ties to imperialism and feudalism, and therefore it did not have the courage to oppose imperialism and feudalism thoroughly and was therefore also a target of the revolution. Thus, at that time, Mao suggested a cautious policy toward the national bourgeoisie, deeming it a possible but at best wavering ally of the revolutionary forces.

In December 1947, in the article "The Present Situation and Our Tasks," Mao made a further differentiation within the national bourgeoisie. He claimed that there were two wings of the national bourgeoisie, a moderate pro-people patriotic wing which could become a force in the democratic nationalist revolution, and a pro-Chiang Kai-shek die-hard rightist wing which had become enemies of the people. This distinction paved the way to the formulation established in early (January to March) 1948 and expressed in Mao's articles "Several Important Problems in the Party's Policy at the Present Moment" (Jan. 18, 1948) and "On the Question of the National Bourgeoisie and the Enlightened Gentry" (March 1, 1948). In this formulation, a considerable segment of the national bourgeoisie can and should be won over to the side of the people's revolutionary forces. They will not be the leaders of the national democratic revolution, and they should eventually undergo socialist transformation. However, on the basis of the worker-peasant alliance, a further alliance between the proletariat and the national bourgeoisie and the petty bourgeoisie may be formed, an alliance whose degree of consolidation and effectiveness is crucial to the success of the revolution. This became a standard formulation for the CPC's policies regarding the socialist transformation of capitalism in the early years of the PRC.

4. Nothing appears to be known in the West about this meeting to which Mao refers.

5. This refers to the Land Law or rather an "outline program" of a land law (tudi fa dagang) adopted by the National Conference on Land Policies of the CPC on September 13, 1947. This was eventually promulgated as the "Outline of the Land Law of China" on October 10, 1947. It was primarily based on the principle of returning landownership to the individual peasants. This document and the announcement of its promulgation can be found in Mo Takuto Shu, vol. 10, pp. 87-90 and 85-86 respectively. For a synopsis see note 4 of Mao's essay or report to the Central Committee of the CPC in December 1947, entitled "The Present Situation and Our Tasks" (see Xuanji, IV, p. 1157, and SW, IV, p. 174). After Liberation, as indicated here, the new situation demanded a revision of this law and a reviewing of this principle. In June 1950, at the Second Session of the First National Committee of the Chinese People's Political Consultative Conference, the new "Land Reform Law of the People's Republic of China" was adopted. (See T. Chen [1967], pp. 196-203, for text.)

Letter to Long Bojian
(March 14, 1950)

Source: *Shuxin*, p. 353.

Long Bojian (1899-1983), a.k.a. Long Yuying, was an old acquaintance of Mao's. He was a founder of the periodical Xin Hunan *(New Hunan) and was its editor until the position was taken over by Mao himself in 1919. This student weekly, like the more famous* Xiangjiang pinglun *(Xiang River Review) which was also based in Changsha, was abruptly closed down by the Hunan warlord Zhang Jingyao shortly after Mao took over the editorship. In August 1949, shortly after the liberation of Hunan, Long was the chief of the bureau of public health of the provisional Hunan provincial government.*

Mr. Bojian:[1]

Your letter of November 11 last year has been received and read. I am extremely gratified that you, my friend,[2] are taking part in the revolution and are undertaking work in the area of public health. The name of the *Xin Hunan bao* (New Hunan Daily)[3] is coined by the comrades of Hunan. I feel just as honored, as you are elated, by the coincidence between this and the name of [our] old paper.[4] My old poetry[5] is not particularly good; there really is no need for me to write them out again. I hope that you will apply yourself to your tasks dilligently and work for the interests of the people.

With my regards,

Mao Zedong
March 14, 1950

Notes

1. For this usage of addressing friends by their personal names, see text Nov. 17, 1949, note 2.

2. Here Mao used the word *xiong*, which means "elder brother" but is a common way of addressing one's friends.

3. This refers to a daily founded by the Hunan Provincial [Party] Committee of the CPC in January 1950.

4. See source note.

5. Here Mao used the word *ci* which refers to a particular genre of poetic writing of which Mao produced quite a few specimens in his youth. For more on this genre, see text Jan. 12, 1957, note 1.

Letter to Liu Kuiyi
(March 14, 1950)

Source: *Shuxin*, p. 354

According to the source, Liu Kuiyi (1878-1950) was an early revolutionary and a founder of the Huaxing hui (China Arisen Society) and at this time was an advisor to the People's Military and Administration Committee of Hunan Province.

Honorable Mr. Linsheng:[1]

Your letter of December 27 last year has been received. I am greatly gratified. Please permit me to apologize for being tardy in responding. With regard to the bad things that have come into practice in the requisitioning of grain, the government has already issued several decrees for the purpose of correcting them; I wonder if the situation has become somewhat more relaxed lately? The trouble of the bandits must be quelled and the chief villains must be dealt with;[2] this is a fixed principle. Nonetheless, in carrying out the quelling and the dealing with [the chief villains] we must have a strategy and specific steps and measures, so that [the problem] may be resolved speedily and the situation throughout the country may be secured and stabilized. I hear that the trouble caused by the bandits has been on the whole resolved as far as Hunan is concerned. Is this true? I would be very grateful if, at your convenience, you, sir, would tell me what you know about the matter.

With best and respectful regards for your good health, and apologies for the incompleteness of this message,

Mao Zedong
March 14, 1950

Notes

1. Linsheng is Liu Kuiyi's *zi* (honorific name). For the signifigance of this term and practice see text Oct. 15, 1949, note 1.

2. See text Jan. 17, 1951, note 1.

Telegram to the Communist Party of France
(March 31, 1950)

Source: *Wenyi hongqi*, 5 (May 30, 1967), 2. Other Chinese Texts: *Shengping ziliao*, p. 290; *Wenyi yulu*, p. 93; *Mao liang*, p. 352; *HQ*, 5 (March 30, 1967), 9. Available English Translation: *SCMP*, 4000 (Aug. 14, 1967), 10.

The Twelfth Congress of the Communist Party of France (Parti Communiste Francais, PCF) was held in April 1950 at Gennevilliers, France.

The Twelfth National Congress of the Communist Party of France, in care of the Central Committee of the Communist Party of France:

We warmly congratulate you on the success of the Twelfth National Congress of the Communist Party of France and hope that the Communist Party of France, in the process of leading the French people in carrying forward the revolutionary struggle, will grow daily in strength.
(Signed as Chairman of CPC)

Directive on the Film *Qing gong mishi*
(March 1950)

Source: *Wenyi hongqi*, 5 (May 30, 1967), 2. Other Chinese Texts: *Shengping ziliao*, p. 290; *Wenyi yulu*, p. 93; *Mao liang*, p. 352; *HQ*, 5 (March 30, 1967),9. Available English Translation: *SCMP*, 4000 (Aug. 14, 1967), 10.

It appears from these sources that what is represented here are actually two different comments. The date March 1950 appears to go more accurately with the second comment, which was a retort directed at Hu Qiaomu (see text May 22, 1950, note 2). The first comment may have been made on an earlier occasion. The film Qing gong mishi *was produced in Hong Kong and was screened nationwide in the PRC in 1950. It was endorsed at the time by Lu Dingyi, director of the Department of Propaganda in the Central Committee of the CPC. Its subject dealt with the romance between the*

Guangxu Emperor (reigning 1878-1908) and his consort, Zhen Fei, with the entrance of the Yihetuan (Boxers) rebels into Beijing in June 1900 as a historical backdrop. It also exposed the conflict between the reformist movement of 1898 and the revolutionary movement of the same time represented by the Yihetuan. A key essay echoing Mao's criticism of this film is Qi Benyu's "Aiguo zhuyi haishi maiguo zhuyi – fandong yingpian Qing gong mishi de pipan" (Patriotism or Treason? A Critique of the Reactionary Film Qing gong mishi) in RMRB (April 1, 1967.)

The film *Qing gong mishi* [A Secret History of the Manchu Court] is a treasonous movie, and we should criticize it. . . .

Some say that it is patriotic: I think it is treasonous, thoroughly treasonous.

Telegram to the People's Republic of Hungary
(April 1, 1950)

Source: *RMRB* (Apr. 4, 1950), 1. Other Chinese Text: *GMRB* (Apr. 4, 1950), 1. Available English Translation: NCNA, *Daily Bulletin*, 2 (Apr. 4, 1950), 2.

Chairman [Arpad] Szakazits

Your Excellency:

On this occasion of the fifth anniversary of the liberation of Hungary, on behalf of the Central People's Government of the People's Republic of China and the Chinese people, I extend my sincerest congratulations to Your Excellency and our best wishes for the happiness and progress of the people of Hungary.

(Signed as Chairman of CPG of PRC, dated, in Beijing)

Speech at the Sixth Session of the CPGC
(April 11, 1950)

Source: *RMRB* (Apr. 13, 1950), 1.

Mao made this short address before the Sixth Session of the Central People's Government Council voted on, and ratified, the Sino-Soviet Treaty of Friendship and Alliance.

We have pointed out that implementing the people's democratic dictatorship and uniting with our international friends are two fundamental conditions for the consolidation of the victory of the revolution. The Sino-Soviet Treaty and agreements that we signed this time are to affirm the friendship between the two great countries of China and the Soviet Union in a legal fashion.[1] By gaining for us a reliable ally, they will benefit us by giving us a free hand to undertake the work of domestic construction and to deal with the possible invasion by imperialists and to strive for world peace together.

Note

1. See text Jan. 2, 1950, note 1.

Letter to Yang Kaizhi and Li Congde
(April 13, 1950)

Source: *Shuxin*, p. 355.

For more information on Yang Kaizhi, see text Oct. 9, 1949(1), note 1. Li Congde is Yang's wife.

Comrades Zizhen and Congde:[1]

I have received your letter. I am very happy that you are now working in the provincial government.[2] I hope that you will be positive and dilligent and will have much to show by way of achievements. My son Anying is returning to Hunan to celebrate the old lady's birthday[3] and visit his mother's grave. At the same time he will come and see you. Please give him the benefit of your wisdom and teach him.

With most sincere regards for your recent well-being.

Mao Zedong
April 13, 1950

Notes

1. Zizhen is Yang Kaizhi's *zi* (honorific name). See text Oct. 15, 1949, note 1, for meaning and significance. See also text Nov. 17, 1949, note 2.
2. This refers to the provincial government of Hunan. Mao, Yang, and Li were all natives of that province.
3. Mao here used the term *Lao tai tai* which is a respectful way of saying "old lady." He was referring to Yang's mother, who was Mao's mother-in-law; see text Oct. 9, 1949(1), note 1.

Comment on Chen Yun's Report
(April 14, 1950)

Source: *XHYB*, II:1 (May 15, 1950), 99. Other Chinese Text: *RMRB* (Apr. 15, 1950), 1. Available English Translation: NCNA, *Daily Bulletin*, 13 (Apr. 21, 1950), 3-4.

These comments were made at the Seventh Meeting of the Central People's Government Council, which was held on April 13, 1950. It followed the report made by Chen Yun, who was vice-premier of the GAC of the Central People's Government and chairman of the Financial and Economic Affairs Commission. Chen's report is known by the title "Report on the Financial Condition of the Nation."

The Financial and Economic Affairs Commission of the Government Administrative Council has achieved very significant results in the past six months in the work of adjusting the budget and stabilizing the prices of goods. The policies of the Financial and Economic Affairs Commission are correct, [even though] there are still some shortcomings in its work, and attention should be paid to correcting these.

The financial situation of our country has begun to change for the better. This is a very good phenomenon. However, for the financial and economic situation as a whole to take a fundamental change for the better, three conditions must be met. These are: the completion of land reform, the reasonable adjustment of existing industries and commercial concerns, and major reductions in the military and governmental expenditures of the state. We should strive to realize these step by step, and they can indeed be completely realized. Then fundamental changes for the better can take place. Within the next few months, the emphasis in the work of the organs of the government that are in charge of finance and the economy should be on the adjustment of the interrelationship between public and private enterprises and between the various departments within each public or private enterprise and on exerting as much effort as possible to overcome the state of anarchy. The stipulation in the Common Program [which states]:

> The state shall coordinate and regulate the state-owned, cooperative, individual peasant and handicraft, private capitalist, and state capitalist [sectors of the economy] in their spheres of operations, supply of raw materials, marketing, labor conditions, technical equipment, policies of public and general finance, etc. In this way all sectors of the social economy can, under the leadership of the state-owned economy, carry out division and coordination of labor and play their proper parts [in promoting the development of the social economy as a whole][1]

must be fully implemented. Only then can it serve the interests of the rehabilitation and development of the entire people's economy. Certain confused ideas that have already arisen in this area must be straightened out.

Note

1. Here we have followed Theodore Chen's translation of the corresponding paragraph in the Common Program, Article 26. See T. Chen (1967), p. 41. Parts that have not been cited by Mao here are in brackets to provide contextual meaning. For the Common Program, see text Sept. 21, 1949, note 3.

Letter to Mao Shenpin
(April 18, 1950)

Source: *Shuxin*, p. 356.

According to the source, Mao Shenpin was a classmate of Mao Zedong's.

My dear friend Shenpin:[1]
I have received your two letters and am very gratified. I apologize for the

fact that, owing to other business, I have been late in responding. I am very much saddened to be reminded of the sacrifice that my good friend Qinming made for the revolution;[2] and yet it is also an honorable and glorious thing. [In your letters you] described some shortcomings in the cadres' work; indeed there are many such cases all over, and we are redoubling our efforts to reform and rectify them, and hope that things will be improved. I greatly approve of the idea of having you come out and take up some responsibility [in government work]. The most appropriate procedure seems to be for you to demonstrate support for the interests of the masses, and when you have gained the respect of the people, you will very naturally join the government. It would not be appropriate for me to make a recommendation; that could affect your reputation adversely. Don't you think so? At your convenience, I shall be grateful to learn more of what you are doing.

Best wishes for your health and progress.

Mao Zedong

April 18, 1950

Notes

1. See text Nov. 17, 1949, note 2.

2. According to the source, this refers to Mao Shenpin's elder brother Mao Qinming, who was also at one time Mao Zedong's schoolmate and who died in 1928 as a martyr of the revolution.

Letter to Li Shuyi

(April 18, 1950)

Source: *Shuxin*, p. 357.

Li Shuyi (b. 1901) is a native of Changsha, Hunan, and the wife of Liu Zhixun, who was a good friend of Mao's and a revolutionary martyr. For information on Li, see text May 11, 1957, source note.

Comrade Shuyi:

I have received your letter. Since the sacrifice of Zhixun,[1] you have brought up his children through a great deal of hardship. You have my greatest respect for this accomplishment. For you to learn Marxism-Leninism, you can do it in your spare time from work; there is no need to come all the way to the capital to achieve this goal. Please convey my deepest regards to the two old gentlemen Mr. Xiaodan and Mr. Wuting.[2]

Best regards for your good health.
Mao Zedong
April 18, 1950

Notes

1. This refers to Li's husband Liu Zhixun. See text May 11, 1957, note 2.
2. This refers to Li's father, Li Xiaodan (1881-1953), and Liu's father, Liu Wuting (1877-1957).

———————

Letter to Xiang Mingqing

(April 19, 1950)

Source: *Shuxin*, p. 359.

According to the source, Xiang Mingqing was a native of Pingjiang, Hunan, and Yang Kaihui's (Mao's former wife) uncle. See text Oct. 9, 1949, note 1, and text May 11, 1957, note 1.

Mr. Mingqing:[1]
I have long since received your letter of October 12 last year. Permit me to apologize for the fact that, owing to [preoccupation with] other business, I have been late in responding. Your nephew Comrade Xiang Jun was a member of the Communist Party. In 1927 he was the secretary of the Hengshan *xian* [Party] Committee and was an honest and capable comrade. When the KMT betrayed us in 1927, he was arrested and gloriously gave his life for the cause. You may report all this information to the Hunan Provincial [Party] Committee. However, as for the matter of [disbursing funds for] the comforting of the bereaved, it has to be done uniformly and must not take only a few [special cases] into consideration. If the provincial committee is not yet able to handle the matter, you must understand the situation.
In reply and with respectful regards for your health.
Mao Zedong
April 19, 1950

Note

1. See text Nov. 17, 1949, note 2, for an explanation of this usage.

Telegram to W. H. Andrews
(April 20, 1950)

Source: *GMRB* (May 23, 1950), 1.

W. H. Andrews was a former chairman of the Communist Party of South Africa, of whose Central Committee he was a member at the time of this telegram.

Comrade W. H. Andrews:

My sincerest congratulations on your eightieth birthday, and best wishes for your good health.
(Signed as Chairman of CPC)

Telegram to Maurice Thorez
(April 28, 1950)

Source: *RMRB* (Apr. 28, 1950), 1. Available English Translation: NCNA, *Daily Bulletin*, 19 (May 1, 1950), 2.

Maurice Thorez (1900-1964) was secretary general of the Communist Party of France (Parti Communiste Francais, PCF), 1936-1964.

Dear Comrade Thorez:

On this occasion of your fiftieth birthday, I wish you health and longevity and pay my respects to you and to the Communist Party of France.
(Signed as Chairman of CPC)

Inscription Concerning the People's Education
(May 1, 1950)

Source: *Jiaoyu geming*, 4 (May 6, 1967), 2.

This inscription was written for the inaugural issue of Renmin jiaoyu *(People's Education), May 1, 1950.*

To rehabilitate and develop the people's education is one of the most important tasks at the present time.

Telegram to the Republic of Czechoslovakia
(May 3, 1950)

Source: *RMRB* (May 9, 1950), 1. Other Chinese Text: *XHYB*, II:3 (June 15, 1950), 288. Available English Translation: NCNA, *Daily Bulletin*, 25 (May 9, 1950), 1.

President Gottwald

Your Excellency:

On behalf of the Central People's Government of the People's Republic of China and the Chinese people, I extend to Your Excellency and the Czechoslovakian people our warmest congratulations on the occasion of the fifth anniversary of the liberation of Czechoslovakia and express our hope that the Republic of Czechoslovakia, under Your Excellency's leadership, will grow daily in prosperity and strength.
(Signed as Chairman of CPG of PRC, dated, in Beijing)

Inscription Commemorating the May Fourth Movement[1]
(May 4, 1950 R)

Source: *GMRB* (May 4, 1950), 1. Other Chinese Text: *RMRB* (May 4, 1950), 3. Available English Translation: NCNA, *Daily Bulletin*, 26 (May 10, 1950), 4.

This inscription was written for the exhibition room commemorating Li Dachao, an early Chinese Communist and leader in the May Fourth Movement at Beijing University. It was published by the Beida zhoukan *(Weekly Bulletin of Beijing University).*

Congratulations on the thirty-first anniversary of "May Fourth." Unite together to strive to build a New China.

Note

1. The May Fourth Movement, which got its name from the events on and following May 4, 1919, was a major antifeudal (antiwarlord) and anti-imperialist movement in modern Chinese history. It represents a "watershed" of sorts in twentieth century China and a turning point in the development of the social and political consciousness of the Chinese. Some identify it as a point of origin for Chinese socialism, although many socialist ideas, including early Chinese Marxist ideas, had already been introduced into China previously. Some also associate the formation of the Communist Party of China in 1920 with the May Fourth Movement. For a description and discussion of the movement see Chow Tse-tsung (1960).

Letter to Wen Jianquan
(May 7, 1950)

Source: *Shuxin*, p. 360.

Wen Jianquan and most of the people mentioned in this letter were, or are, Mao's cousins on his mother's side of the family.

Dear Cousin Jianquan:

I have received your letter of January 16, and am much gratified. How many people are still in Tangjiatuo? Can they be adequately fed? Are Tenth Cousin and Seventeenth Cousin[1] still alive? Please let me know at your convenience. It would be best for Mr. Wen Kai[2] to find a solution to his employment problem in the vicinity of Hunan; it would not do him any good to travel afar, and it is not convenient for me to recommend him either. Please understand and forgive me. Cousin Yunchang[3] wrote me several letters in succession. I wrote a reply which was sent to Baipangkou. I wonder if he has received it? I also have received Cousin Nansong's[4] second letter and am grateful for his kind thoughts.

In reply, and with best wishes for your health!

Mao Zedong
May 7, 1950

Notes

1. These refer to Wen Banxiang and Wen Meiqing, both of whom were Wen Jianquan's first cousins and also Mao's cousins. See text May 12, 1950.

2. According to the source, Wen Kai was a relative (probably a rather distant relative) and a close associate of Wen Jianquan.

3. See text May 12, 1950, note 1.

4. See text May 12, 1950, source note.

Letter to Zhang Ding

(May 7, 1950)

Source: *Shuxin*, p. 362.

According to the source, Zhang is a native of Changsha, Hunan, and had studied in a tutorial school affiliated with the "Self-Teaching University" founded in Changsha by Mao Zedong, He Shuheng, et al. in August 1921.

Mr. Zhang Ding:

I have received your letter of October 25 last year and with it the photographs of Mao Zetan[1] and company. Thank you so much for your kind thoughts. To join the Party you must do it at the local level and in accordance with the set regulations.

In reply and with best wishes for your health and good fortune,
Mao Zedong
May 7, 1950

Note

1. Mao Zetan was Mao Zedong's younger brother who died for the cause of the revolution in Hunan in 1935. See text May 12, 1950, source note.

Letter to Zhao Puzhu
(May 7, 1950)

Source: *Shuxin*, p. 363.

According to the source, Zhao was a native of Xiangxiang, Hunan, and had been a colleague of Mao's during Mao's brief sojourn in the New Hunan Army from late 1911 to spring 1912.

Mr. Puzhu:[1]

I have received and studied your letter and your writing and am very grateful. As for the problems such as that of the rent reduction and land reform in our native village, it is not convenient for me to intervene directly since I really do not know enough about the specific conditions. Please contact the comrades in the people's government in the various localities themselves and settle the problems with them with a view to a fair solution. I would also appreciate if, at your convenience, you let me know more of what you are doing. Please convey my regards to all our relatives and friends at Tangjiatuo.

In reply and with regards for your health and good fortune,
Mao Zedong
May 7, 1950

Note

1. From the salutation, in which Mao used the words *yinxiong* (not easily translatable here) Zhao would also appear to be a relative of Mao's, albeit probably a rather distant one. For the usage of personal names in salutations, see text Nov. 17, 1949, note 2.

Letter to Mao Yimin
(May 8, 1950)

Source: *HQ* (Aug. 16, 1982), 2. Other Chinese Texts: *XHYB*, 454 (Sept. 30, 1982), 76; *Shuxin*, pp. 364-365.

Comrade Yimin:[1]

Your letter of January 3 has been received. Thank you for your good wishes and for giving me so many details about the conditions in our native village.

The poor people in our home village lead a very hard life, and life is even harder for the families of [revolutionary] martyrs. For the time being, all they can do is be a bit patient, and things could become somewhat better after the land reform. By then the People's Government may also give some assistance to the people such as loans, and the people will be able to gradually make improvements in their lives.

Taking care of the families of martyrs is a national issue. There are several million households of martyrs' families throughout the country, and they all have to be taken care of. It would not be wise for us to give special and individual attention to a few places. Nonetheless, with regard to the people in the greatest difficulties, the local people's government should, during the time of rent reduction and land reform, or in the in-between-season months,[2] give them as much attention and care as possible.

It is very good that you are working in our home village. Your can write to me often and tell me what is going on in the village.

Please give my regards to the comrades in the village. I sincerely hope that everyone will work hard and make progress.

In reply, and with best wishes for your good health,

Mao Zedong
May 8, 1950

Notes

1. Mao Yimin was a native of Mao's own home village, Shaoshan of Xiangtan *xian*, Hunan Province. He joined the CPC in 1938 and, prior to Liberation, worked in the Shaoshan district committee of the CPC. Shortly after Liberation (i.e., about the time of this letter,) he worked in the Huanglong district committee of the Xiangtan *xian* committee of the CPC. He died in 1968. (Most of the above information is in a footnote in the *HQ* source.)

2. The Chinese term here is *qing huang bujie* (hiatus between green and yellow) which refers to the gap in the agricultural season between the time when the crop is still in its seedling stage (green) and the time of ripening and harvesting (yellow). It is often taken to mean a time of short-

age of means of consumption (i.e., before the crop can be harvested) and, by extension, a time of shortage of energy.

Letter to Wen Nansong
(May 12, 1950)

Source: *HQ* (Aug. 16, 1982), 2-3. Other Chinese Texts: *XHYB*, 454 (Sept. 30, 1982), 76; *Shuxin*, pp. 366-367.

Wen Nansong is Mao Zedong's cousin on his mother's side of the family.

Cousin Nansong:

Your letter of January has been received. Thank you for your good wishes. Cousin Yunchang[1] has written me many times and I have responded with one letter which was addressed to Baipangkou, Nan *xian*. Do you know if he has received it? Regarding the appointment for Cousin Yunchang, it would not be appropriate for me to make a recommendation; rather, it would be more appropriate for him to impress others with his performance among the people, and when he has gained people's confidence he will be given the opportunity to take part in the work. Are Tenth Cousin and Seventeenth Cousin still alive? I am very gratified to know that Eleventh Cousin is still alive and well.[2] He wrote a letter to me and I have sent one back to him. I wonder if he has received it? You said that there was a shortage of grain in our home village and the government was not distributing any. How are things now? Is there still a grain shortage? Has the government come up with nothing at all? When you write again, please tell me in detail.

In reply, and with concern for your recent well-being,

Mao Zedong

May 12, 1950

Notes

1. According to the footnote in the *HQ* source, this refers to Wen Yunchang, an elder cousin of Mao's. Wen died in 1961.

2. Tenth Cousin (i.e., *Shige*, or Tenth Brother in the Chinese) refers to Wen Banxiang, who died in 1949. Seventeenth Cousin (*Shiqige*) is Wen Meiqing, who is a peasant. Eleventh Cousin is Wen Jianquan. See text May 7, 1950(1).

Letter to Ye Jiannong
(May 12, 1950)

Source: *Shuxin*, p. 368.

According to the source, Ye was a native of Pingjiang, Hunan, and was a classmate of Mao's when Mao studied at the First Normal School of Hunan Province.

Dear Jianlong:[1]

I have received your various letters and telegrams. It is very good that you have such enthusiasm for the investigation of new knowledge. As for the matter of your employment, it would be best for you to be in Chongqing if it can be resolved there. If you have to come to the capital, please correspond directly with Director Shen Junru[2] of the People's Supreme Court, and ask him if there is any position that you can fill. Otherwise, you can also enter a short-term studying institution to learn more before you take part in actual work.

In reply and with best regards for you well-being,

Mao Zedong

May 12, 1950

Notes

1. Jianlong is Ye Jiannong's original name. Mao here also used the term *xuexiong* which is customarily used to address one's classmates or schoolmates. See text Oct. 15, 1949, note 1.

2. For more biographical information on Shen (1874-1963), see H. Boorman et al., eds. (1970), III, pp. 99-101.

Letter to Zhou Wennan
(May 12, 1950)

Source: *Shuxin*, p. 369.

Zhou Wennan (a.k.a. Zhou Renfang) was the wife of Mao's brother Zetan, who died in the fighting against KMT troops in Southern Fujian in late 1935. Zhou herself had stayed in Hunan to do revolutionary work. In mid-1930, when the Communists attacked Changsha, several Mao family members remaining in the region were arrested by the KMT, including Mao's first wife Yang Kaihui and his younger sister, together with Zhou. While Yang and Mao's sister were executed, Zhou was spared and subsequently released. At the time of this letter, Zhou was the chief executive officer of the criminal court of the People's Court of Shenyang Municipality. For more information on Mao Zetan and Zhou, see D. Klein and A. Clark, eds. (1971), II, p. 675, and Zhonggong renming lu, appendix, p. 18.

Comrade Wennan:

I have received your letter and am greatly gratified. As for taking your mother to the Northeast to live with you, I think it is a good thing. I can write to the authorities in Hunan to have them issue you some travel funds. Nonetheless, your mother is of an advanced age, and whether or not she will be safe along the journey if no one is there to take care of her is a question. Would you be needed to personally go to bring her with you to the Northeast? Would that not be better? Please give it some thought and let me know. If you are going [to Hunan] yourself to fetch her, than my letter to Hunan can be carried by you. The enclosed document is returned to you.[1] Jiang Qing[2] and others are all doing well.

My best wishes for your health,

Mao Zedong
May 12, 1950

Notes

1. According to the source this refers to the letter that Zhou's mother, Zhou Qian, nee Chen, wrote to Zhou in which she described her lonely conditions in Shaoshan *xian*, Hunan.

2. This refers to Mao's wife at the time. Born in 1915, Jiang began learning the Chinese traditional opera around 1929 and served her apprenticeship at the Shandong Provincial Experimental Operatic School at Jinan under the name Lian Shumeng. It was in 1932, when she joined the production of the film "Wang lao wu" (The Bachelor) in Shanghai, that she changed to the acting name of Lan Ping. In the summer of 1937, Jiang went to Yanan and enrolled at the Lu Xun School of the Arts. It was about this time that she assumed the name of Jiang Qing, which she has

used since. Around 1940 she married Mao Zedong. Jiang played almost no part in public life until the time of the Cultural Revolution. In 1963, however, she began to emerge as a somewhat influential figure in the criticism of certain orientations in literary and artistic circles, organizing with Ke Qingshi (see text Dec. 26, 1953, source note) the campaign against the film *Li Huiniang* and the article "There Is No Harm in Having Ghosts." In 1965, she promoted the "modern revolutionary operas," which she directed, *Hong deng ji* (The Red Lantern), *Zhi qu wei hu shan* (Taking Tiger Mountain by Strategy) and *Shajia bin*, as "model operas" *(yangban ju)*. In 1966 she emerged as a chief spokesperson for Mao, and when the directive (the "May 16 directive") to organize a "Cultural Revolution Group for the Central Committee" was issued by Mao at the enlarged plenum of the Political Bureau at Hangzhou that year, Jiang became a member of that group. She became one of the paramount leaders of the Cultural Revolution. In 1976, shortly after Mao's death, she and others labeled as the "Gang of Four" were toppled. Jiang has been under arrest since. For more biographical information on Jiang, see *Zhonggong renming lu*, appendix, pp. 27-31.

Telegram to Ho Chi Minh
(May 12, 1950)

Source: *XHYB*, III:2 (Jun. 15, 1950), 291. Other Chinese Text: *RMRB* (May 12, 1950), 1.

The Government of the Democratic Republic of Viet Nam,
President Ho Chi Minh

Your Excellency:

On behalf of the Central People's Government of the People's Republic of China and myself, I extend to you our warmest congratulations on this Your Excellency's sixtieth birthday. We congratulate the Democratic Republic of Viet Nam which, under your leadership and with the support of the patriotic people of all Viet Nam, has triumphed over the foreign invaders and their running dogs, and we celebrate the eternal unity of the peoples of the two countries, China and Viet Nam, and their common effort in the cause of peace in Asia.

(Signed as Chairman of CPG of PRC and dated)

Letter to Mao Yuju
(May 15, 1950)

Source: *Shuxin*, p. 370.

According to the source, Mao Yuju was Mao Zedong's older cousin and his tutor in an old-style village school when Mao was a child.

Dear Yuju:[1]

I have received your several letters in rapid succession. Thank you very much. Please let me know at your convenience more things about how conditions are in our native village. If Zou Puxun (Heng er)[2] is in dire straits and seriously ill, and if you have some extra cash on hand, please help him out a bit and let me pay you back later. Please also give the enclosed message to Zou Puxun.

My best regards for your health.

Mao Zedong
May 15, 1950

Notes

1. On the practice of using the personal name in salutation, see text Nov. 17, 1949, note 2. Here Mao used the term *Yuju xiong* in which the the latter character, meaning "elder brother," is common for addressing one's friends who are either indeed older than one is or acquaintances regardless of age as a sign of simple courtesy. Nonetheless, here Mao and his correspondent have a closer relationship, which gives this term a special meaning.

2. "Heng er," which Mao put in parentheses in the original, is a childhood nickname of Zou's. According to the source, Zou was Mao's neighbor and schoolmate in the village school.

Letter to Zou Puxun
(May 15, 1950)

Source: *Shuxin*, p. 371.

See text May 15, 1950 (1), note 2.

Dear Puxun:

I have received your letter of May 7. Thank you for your kind thoughts. I am gratified to learn that your health is improving, and I hope that you will continue, nonetheless, to pay good attention to maintaining your health. I would like to know, at your convenience, how many people there are in your family, how difficult life is for you, and whether or not you are still capable of working.

My best wishes for your health.

Mao Zedong
May 15, 1950

Letter to Zhou Rong
(May 16, 1950)

Source: *Shuxin*, p. 372.

According to the source, Zhou (a.k.a. Zhou Zanxiang) is a native of Yueyang, Hunan, and made Mao's acquaintance in the First Normal School of Hunan in 1920. The matter referred to here in Mao's response is Zhou's request that Mao recommend him for membership in the CPC.

Mr. Zanxiang:[1]

I have received your letter of August last year. I am grateful indeed for your kind thoughts. Let me apologize for being so tardy in responding. As for the matter with the organization, it is not convenient for me to recommend you in such haste. What should be done is for you to perform in the locality and make your request then to the local organization, and await its resolution.

In response, and with best wishes for your progress,

Mao Zedong

May 16, 1950

Note

1. See text Oct. 15, 1949, note 1, and text Nov. 17, 1949, note 2, for an explanation of this usage.

Reply to Ambassador of the Republic of India

(May 20, 1950)

Source: *RMRB* (May 21, 1950), 1. Other Chinese Texts: *GMRB* (May 21, 1950), 1. Available English Translation: NCNA, *Daily Bulletin*, 34 (May 22, 1950), 3.

K. M. Panikkar served as ambassador of the Republic of India to the PRC from May 1950 to September 1952.

Mr. Ambassador:

I am very happy to accept the letter of credence which has been conferred upon you by the President of the Republic of India and which Your Excellency has presented, and I am grateful for Your Excellency's congratulations and good wishes.

The two countries, China and India, share a common boundary and have had between them a long-lasting and intimate relationship historically and culturally. In the last few centuries, they both have undertaken long and heroic struggles to be liberated from the adverse destiny of their peoples. The understanding, sympathy, and concern that exist between the peoples of our two countries is profound and sincere. The establishment of formal diplomatic relations between China and India now will not only cause the friendship that already exists between the people of these two countries to grow and be consolidated with the passing of each day, but moreover, the sincere cooperation between the people of these two great Asian countries produced by this friendship will surely contribute greatly to lasting peace in Asia and the world.

I warmly welcome Your Excellency, as the first ambassador extraordinary and plenipotentiary of the Republic of India to the People's Republic of China, and pledge my assistance to Your Excellency in your work of strengthening the cooperation between the two nations.

Best wishes for the prosperity of your country, the prospering of your people, and the good health of your head of state.

Letter to Li Jinxi
(May 22, 1950)

Source: *Shuxin*, p. 373.

According to the source, Li (1890-1978), a.k.a. Shao Xi, was a native of Xiangtan, Hunan – Mao's native village. Li was a linguist and philologist who at the time of this letter was director of the Editorial Bureau for the Compilation of the Zhongguo da cidian *(A General Chinese Dictionary) and professor and chairman of the Department of Chinese Language at Beijing Normal University. For more biographical information on Li, see* Zhonggong renming lu, *p. 970.*

Mr. Shao Xi:

Your letter of May 17 has been received. I can agree with all the opinions you have expressed concerning the Dictionary Bureau,[1] and I have discussed these with Comrade Hu Qiaomu.[2] He is also in agreement with us. Please contact Comrade Hu on the telephone and discuss the matter with him.

I send best regards for your health.

Mao Zedong
May 22, 1950

Notes

1. According to the source, this refers to the opinions, expressed by Li in a letter to Mao, on the planning of a rational course of action and development in organizing the personnel at the Bureau for the Compilation of the *Zhongguo da cidian*, and on the question of under which department or branch of the government the bureau should be placed.

2. Hu Qiaomu (b. 1907) is a chief propagandist of the CPC. Known by his *nom de plume* of Qiaomu (which incidentally he shared with Qiao Guanhua in the 1930s and 1940s, thus earning for him the quaint sobriquet of Bei Qiaomu, or Qiaomu of the North, as opposed to Qiao Guanhua's Nan Qiaomu or Southern Qiaomu) Hu began his career as a writer for the Communist cause in the Shanghai area in the mid-1930s. From 1937 on, Hu worked for the Party in Yanan, largely devoting himself to youth organization. He was at this time an editor of the influential Yanan journal *Zhongguo qingnian* (China Youth), and later, in the early- to mid-1940s, became Mao Zedong's "political secretary," after serving a short stint as Zhou Enlai's secretary. In this capacity he shared with Chen Boda many responsibilities and opportunities of drafting major documents for the Central Committee of the CPC. In 1945, he accompanied Mao to the negotiations

with the KMT at Chongqing and there served as the editor of the *Xinhua ribao* (New China Daily). After Liberation, Hu became a chief organizer of the New Democratic Youth League (see text Feb. 18, 1951, note 8) and the All-China Federation of Democratic Youth, and ultimately of the influential preparatory committee of the All-China Journalists' Association. With these experiences and positions behind him, Hu very easily and naturally became a major spokesperson for the CPC in the circles of journalism and propaganda. From 1949 to 1954 he was a deputy director of the Xinhua (New China) News Agency and the managing director of *Renmin ribao* (People's Daily). Hu is also well known as the author of the book *Zhongguo gongchandang di sanshi nian* (Thirty Years of the Communist Party of China), a history, from the Marxist perspective, of the development of the CPC up to the time of the founding of the PRC. Hu was criticized and removed from his official positions during the Cultural Revolution and was rehabilitated in 1974. For more biographical information on Hu, see *Zhonggong renmin lu*, pp. 378-379, and D. Klein and A. Clark, eds. (1971), I, pp. 374-377.

The source describes Hu as being, at the time of this letter, Mao's secretary and director of the Press Administration of the Government Administration Council.

Telegram of Condolence to Yan Huiqing's Family
(May 26, 1950)

Source: *RMRB* (May 27, 1950), 1. Available English Translation: NCNA, *Daily Bulletin*, 39 (May 20, 1950), 3.

Yan was vice-chairman of the East China Military and Administrative Commission. For more information on the life and career of Yan Huiqing, see H. Boorman et al., eds. (1971), IV, pp. 50-52.

Respectfully to the family of Vice-chairman Yan Huiqing:

I am stunned to receive the news of the passing away of Mr. Yan Huiqing owing to illness. I feel extremely grieved and send this telegram expressly to extend my condolences.
(Signed with month and date, no year)

Letter to Liu Yanan
(May 27, 1950)

Source: *Shuxin*, p. 375.

According to the source, Liu Yanan (b. 1917) was at the time of this letter head of Xiangxiang xian, *Hunan Province. For more biographical information on Liu, see* Zhonggong renming lu, *p. 890.*

Comrade Yanan:

I have received the enclosed letters from four brothers of the family of Wen[1] from Dapingyao, Fengyin *xiang* of Sidu, Xiangxiang [*xian*]; and these are herewith forwarded for your perusal. They have said things that express discontent with the work of the local district and *xiang* government. I wonder what the real situation is? If it is possible, please send a comrade down to investigate a bit and let me know the results. The Wen brothers are all poor peasants, but in their letters they speak in favor of the landlords and the rich peasants. Why is this so? Please also investigate this and let me know. As far as the question of the difficulties that the Wen family (my uncle's family) has encountered and their appeal for aid and relief, you can help them relieve their problem only insofar as the normal pattern of rent reduction and land reform,[2] which is common to all peasants, will allow. You cannot give them special attention and aid, or else the people in general will be unhappy about it.

My best wishes for your health.

Mao Zedong
May 27, 1950

Notes

1. See text May 12, 1950.
2. See text Feb. 18, 1951, note 2.

Letter to Liu Shaoqi

(June 4, 1950)

Source: *Shuxin*, pp. 376-378.

The subject of this letter was the question of implementing nationwide land reform (see text Feb. 18, 1951, note 2) on which issue Liu was to make a report at the Second Session of the First National Conference of the CPPCC, held on June 14, 1950, in Beijing. (It was at this meeting that the Land Reform Law of the PRC was promulgated. See text Mar. 12, 1950, note 5.) For more biographical information on Liu Shaoqi, see text May 19, 1953, source note.

Comrade Shaoqi:

I have read [the enclosed] document.[1] I find it very well written and very useful. I am suggesting some revisions for your consideration. The part on the rich peasants is too long, so much that it is turning out to be unclear instead. In some places [this section] is not very appropriate; therefore I would, and have, deleted a major portion of it. I have added [a description of] the experience of the period from 1946 on in order to rectify a certain misunderstanding that some comrades already [appear to] have[2] – [i.e., a misunderstanding] that the "Left" deviationist errors of the past have been the result of the stipulation in the Land Reform Law Outline Program promulgated on October 10, 1947,[3] that the surplus land and property of the rich peasants is to be confiscated. Without such an explanation [as I have included] it would not be possible to correct this misunderstanding.

By the forces of production we are referring to two things – the laborers and to the material of production (also known as the means of production).[4] By the material of production, in the countryside, the first thing we mean is land, second the farming implements, draft animals, houses, and so on.[5] Grain is what the peasants produce as means of living by utilizing the material of production. It is reasonable for us to put the grain confiscated from the landlords and other confiscated things together and put them under the category of the material of production, because this type of grain contains the character of capital funds. By the relations of production, we mean the relationships of ownership which people have [with each other] with regard to the material of production, or in other words, the relations of the ownership of property. The utilization of the material of production – e.g. the utilization (renting) of the land of the landlords by the peasants – is nothing but the result of the relationship of ownership that the landlords have with regard to the land. This type of ownership relationship is expressed as the relationship of subjugation that the tenant peasant has with regard to the landlord (i.e., an interhuman relationship), and this is [what we mean by] the relations of production. In the past many comrades have committed errors on this matter of casting their thinking in a dualistic, or even a pluralistic, mode and considering the relations of production in parallel with the relations of utilization and at the same time considering the material [or means] of production in parallel with the means of living. In using this [frame of mind] as the standard for drawing class distinctions they have made the question very confusing and made mistakes in classifying the class backgrounds of many people. In the winter of 1947 I asked Qiaomu[6] to write an article entitled "Stipulations on the Various Social Classes and Their Treatment in China."[7] The first two chapters of that article were written by me, and it clarified this problem. You may consult it.

Mao Zedong
June 4, p. m.

Notes

1. According to the source, this refers to the draft of the report which Liu eventually made to the Second Session of the First National Conference of the CPPCC on the question of land reform. Liu's report is reprinted in *RMSC* (1951), "Shen" section, pp. 32-43, and translated in Liu Shaoqi (1969), II, pp. 215-233.

2. According to the source, Mao added a very long paragraph to Liu's draft here. This is the paragraph that appears toward the end of section 3 of the eventual report, i.e., the last paragraph on p. 38 of the "Shen" section of *RMSC* (1951), and paragraphs starting with "During the period" to "preserving a rich peasant economy," pp. 225-226 of Liu, *op. cit.*

3. See text Mar. 12, 1950, note 5.

4. Here Mao used the terms *shengchan ziliao* and *shengchan shouduan*; the former is translated in this document as "material of production" and the latter as "means of production" in order to preserve Mao's distinction here. It is an exception rather than the rule, since it is a general practice to render *shengchan ziliao* as "means of production," and elsewhere in this collection we will, as a rule, follow this custom.

5. According to the source, here the term "houses" refers to buildings that are used as means of production, while residential buildings were considered by Mao to be part of the means of living (*shenghuo ziliao*). The source also pointed out that in the first chapter of the "Stipulations of the Central Committee of the CPC on the Distinction of Social Classes in the Land Reform and on Their Various Treatments" (see note 7) Mao had pointed out: "In order to live people must produce the means of living, such as grain, clothing, houses, fuel, and implements. In order to produce the means of living, people must have the means of production, such as land, raw material, draft animals, implements and a workplace." We are unable to track down a published copy of this article that apparently was published under Hu Qiaomu's name.

6. This refers to Hu Qiaomu; see text May 22, 1950, note 2.

7. According to the source, this document's full title is *Zhonggong zhongyang guanyu tudi gaige zhong ge shehui jieji de huafen ji qi daiyu de guiding* (Stipulations of the Central Committee of the CPC on the Distinction of Social Classes in the Land Reform and on Their Various Treatments).

Struggle for a Fundamental Turn for the Better in the Financial and Economic Situation in the Country

(June 6, 1950)

Source: *RMRB* (June 13, 1950), 1. Other Chinese Texts: *XHYB*, II:3 (July 15, 1950), 487-488; *Xuanji*, V, pp. 15-20; *Buyi*, pp. 6-10. Available English Translations: NCNA, *Supplement*, 50 (June 16, 1950), 1-4; *SW*, V, pp. 26-32; K. Fan (1972), pp. 103-110.

This is a written report to the Third Plenum of the Seventh Central Committee of the CPC. There are minor textual discrepancies between the 1950 versions and the Xuanji, V, *version. Mao also made an oral report to the Third Plenum on June 6, entitled "Don't Attack on All Fronts," translated in* SW, *V, pp. 33-36.*

The present international situation is favorable to us. The front for world peace and democracy headed by the Soviet Union is even more powerful than it was last year. The people's movements for peace and against war in various countries throughout the world have developed. The national liberation movements that seek to throw off imperialist oppression have developed on a broad scale. Especially noteworthy are the mass movements of the Japanese and the German peoples that have already risen in opposition to U.S. occupation and the development of the people's liberation struggles of the oppressed nations in the East. At the same time, contradictions among the imperialist countries, principally between the United States and Britain, have also developed. Quarrels have also increased among the various factions within the American bourgeoisie and among the various factions within the British bourgeoisie. In contrast to this, there is strong unity in the relations among the Soviet Union and the various People's Democracies.[1] The new Sino-Soviet treaty,[2] which is of great historical significance, has consolidated the friendly relations between the two countries. On the one hand, it enables us to freely and more rapidly carry forward the work of reconstruction within our country, and on the other hand, it gives an impetus to the great struggle of peoples throughout the world in striving for peace and democracy and against war and oppression. The imperialist camp's threat of war still exists. The possibility of a third world war still exists. However, the forces fighting to check the danger of war and to avoid the outbreak of a third world war are growing rapidly. The level of consciousness of the majority of the people throughout the world is being raised. If only the Communist parties throughout the world could continue to unite all possible forces for peace and democracy and enable them to grow even stronger, a new world war could be prevented. Rumors of war spread by the Kuomintang reactionaries deceive the people and are groundless.

At present the situation of our country is this. The Central People's Government of the People's Republic of China and local people's governments at all levels have already been established. The Soviet Union, all the People's Democracies,[3] and a number of capitalist countries have successively established diplomatic relations with our country. Basically, war has been ended on the mainland; only Taiwan and Tibet still remain to be liberated, a task that still involves serious struggle. In a number of areas on the mainland, the Kuomintang reactionaries have adopted bandit-style guerrilla warfare and incited a section of the backward elements to fight against the People's Government. The Kuomintang reactionaries, furthermore, have organized many secret agents and many spies to oppose the People's Government, to spread rumors among the people in an effort to destroy the prestige of the Communist Party and the People's Government, and to undermine the unity and cooperation among the various nationalities, the democratic classes, the democratic parties, and the people's organizations. Secret agents and spies have also carried out activities to sabotage the people's economic enterprises; they adopt the method of assassinating personnel within the Communist Party and the People's Government, and they collect intelligence for the imperialists and the Kuomintang reactionaries. All these counterrevolutionary activities are engineered from behind the scenes by imperialists, particularly by the American imperialists. These bandits, secret agents, and spies are all running dogs of imperialism. In the thirteen and a half months since it began to cross the [Yangtze] River on April 21, 1949, to do battle, [which was] after it had won decisive victories in the winter of 1948 in the three great campaigns – Liaoxi-Shenyang, Huai-Hai, and Beiping-Tianjin[4] – the People's Liberation Army has occupied all of [China's] territory except for Tibet, Taiwan, and certain other islands. [The People's Liberation Army] has annihilated 1,830,000 troops of the KMT reactionaries and 980,000 bandit guerrilla troops, and the people's public security organs have uncovered and arrested large numbers of reactionary secret service organizations and secret agents. At present, the People's Liberation Army still has the task of continuing to exterminate the remaining bandits in the new liberated areas, while the people's public security organs have the task of continuing to strike against the enemy's secret service organizations. The majority of people throughout the nation enthusiastically support the Communist Party, the People's Government, and the People's Liberation Army. In recent months, the People's Government has put into effect unified mannagement and unified leadership in the financial and economic areas on a nationwide scale.[5] It has achieved a balanced budget, checked the inflation of the currency, and stabilized prices. The people throughout the country have given support to the People's Government by delivering grain, paying taxes, and buying state bonds.[6] Our country suffered widespread calamities last year with about 120 million *mu* of farmland and 40 million people stricken by flood or drought in varying degrees. The People's

Government has organized large-scale relief work for the people affected by the catastrophes and has been carrying out large-scale water conservation construction in many places. The annual crop this year is better than last year's, and the summer harvest appears to be generally good. If the autumn harvest is also good, then we can believe that next year's prospects will be better than this year's. The long period of rule by the imperialists and the KMT reactionaries has brought about an abnormal condition in our society and economy and has created a huge mass of unemployed people. Since the victory of the revolution, the old social and economic structure as a whole has been undergoing reorganization to varying degrees, and unemployment has increased. This is a serious matter, and the People's Government has already begun to adopt measures to give relief to the unemployed and jobs for them so as to solve this problem methodically. The People's Government has been carrying out widespread cultural and educational work. There are large numbers of intellectuals and young students who have joined in the study of the new knowledge or have joined in the work of the revolution. The People's Government has already done some work in rationally readjusting [the situation in] industry and commerce, has improved relations between the public and private [sectors] and between labor and capital, and is now continuing this work with great energy.

China is a large country and the situation is extremely complex. The revolution achieved victories in some areas first and then victory was achieved nationwide. Corresponding to this situation, in the old liberated areas (encompassing a population of approximately 160 million) land reform has already been completed, social order has already been established, economic construction work has already begun to proceed on course, improvements have already been made in the lives of the majority of the laboring people, and the problem of unemployed workers and intellectuals has already been solved (in the Northeast) or is nearing a solution (in North China and Shandong).[7] In the Northeast in particular, planned economic construction has already begun. On the other hand, in the new liberated areas (encompassing a population of approximately 310 million), since they were liberated only a few months – half a year or a year – ago, more than 400,000 bandits still remain scattered in various remote areas for us to annihilate. The land problem has not yet been solved. [The situation in] industry and commerce has not yet been properly adjusted, and the phenomenon of unemployment is still serious. Social order has not yet been stabilized. In a word, conditions for carrying out economic construction in a planned way have not yet been achieved. Therefore, [as] I have said, the series of victories that we have already attained on the economic front – for example, revenue and expenditure nearing a balance, the inflation of currency checked, prices tending toward stability, and so on – indicate the beginning of a turn for the better in the financial and economic situation, but not yet a fundamental turn for the better. If we want the financial and economic situation to take a fundamental turn for the better, three conditions must be met. These are: (1) the completion of land reform, (2) the proper readjustment of existing industry and commerce, and (3) large-scale reduction in necessary government expenditure. Attaining these three conditions will take some time. It will take about three years or a little longer. The entire Party and people throughout the country must struggle and strive to create these three conditions. I, along with everyone else, believe that these conditions can certainly be realized in about three years. Then we will be able to see a fundamental turn for the better in the entire financial and economic situation of our country.

To achieve this goal, the Party and all the people in the country must unite as one and thoroughly carry out the following tasks:

1) Carry out the work of land reform methodically and in an orderly manner.[8] Since the war has fundamentally ended on the mainland, and the situation is entirely different from that of the 1946-48 period (when the People's Liberation Army was locked in a life-and-death struggle with the KMT reactionaries and victory was still undecided), the state can [now] use the method of issuing loans to help poor peasants solve their difficulties, making up for the drawback that the poor peasants are receiving less land. Therefore, there should be a change in the policy regarding our treatment of the rich peasants, i.e., a change from the policy of requisitioning the surplus land and property of the rich peasants to one of preserving a rich peasant economy in order to facilitate the early restoration of rural production and the isolation of the landlords while protecting the middle peasants and protecting those who lease out small plots of lands.

2) Consolidate the unified management and unified leadership in our financial and economic work [and] consolidate the balance of revenue and expenditure in the budget and the stablization of prices. In accordance with this principle, readjust taxes and lighten the people's burden appropriately, gradually eliminate the blindness and the anarchic situation in the economy in line with the principle of unified planning and of considering the interests of all sections, and rationally readjust the existing industry and commerce; earnestly and properly improve relations between the public and private sectors and between labor and capital, so that the various components of the society and economy under the leadership of the socialist-oriented state-owned economy may establish a division of labor and cooperation and each may play its proper role in promoting the recovery and development of the economy of the entire society. Some people believe that it is possible to eliminate capitalism and implement socialism at an early date; such an idea is wrong and does not fit conditions in our country.

3) While providing for sufficient forces guaranteed for the liberation of Taiwan and Tibet, the consolidation of national defense, and the suppression of the counterrevolutionaries, the People's Liberation Army should demobilize part of its troops in 1950 while preserving its main force. We must carry out this task of demobilization carefully so that the demobilized soldiers can return to their native villages and feel secure in [particiapting in] production. Reorganization of the [PLA] administrative organizations is necessary, and

surplus personnel should be dealt with properly so that they can have the opportunity to work or study.

4) We should methodically and carefully carry out the work of reforming education in the old schools and of reforming old cultural institutions in society. We must strive to enlist all the patriotic intellectuals in the service of the people. On this question, the notion of procrastination and reluctance to reform is wrong, and excessive impatience and the idea of planning the use of violent and coercive methods to carry out reform is also incorrect.

5) We must earnestly carry out relief work for unemployed workers and unemployed intellectuals and systematically help the unemployed to find jobs. We must continue to earnestly carry out relief work for people victimized by disasters.

6) We must earnestly unite with democratic personages from all circles, help them solve the problem of work and study, and overcome the tendency toward closed-doorism[9] as well as the tendency toward making [excessive] accomodations in United Front work. We must apply our sincere efforts to convening conferences of representatives of the people from all circles, which would serve to unite people from all circles in a common effort.[10] All the important work of the People's Government ought to be submitted to the people's representative conferences to be discussed and resolved. The delegates to the people's representative conferences must be given the full right to speak. Any action that obstructs the people's representatives from speaking is wrong.

7) We must resolutely eliminate all bandits, spies, bullies and despots, and other counterrevolutionaries who menace the people. On this question we must carry out the policy of combining suppression and leniency, that is, the policy of punishing the principal culprits without fail but not those who were forced into being their accomplices, and of rewarding those who have rendered meritorious service. There must not be any bias or neglect. The whole Party and the people throughout the country must heighten their vigilance toward the conspiratorial activities of the counterrevolutionary elements.

8) We must resolutely carry out the Center's directives on consolidating and developing the Party's organization, on strengthening the links between the Party and the masses, on carrying out criticism and self-criticism, and on the rectification of the whole Party. In view of the fact that our Party has already grown to four and a half million members, from now on we must adopt a policy of carefully expanding the Party's organization. We must resolutely stop careerists from entering the Party, and careerists [already within the Party] must be properly cleaned out and expelled from the Party. We must pay attention to systematically absorbing [politically] conscious workers into the Party and expand the proportion of workers in the Party organization. The recruitment of Party members in the rural areas of the old liberated areas generally ought to stop. In the new liberated areas, in general we should not develop the Party organization in the rural areas before land reform has been completed so that we can avoid having careerists sneak into the Party. In the

summer, autumn, and winter of 1950, during these three seasons, the entire Party must carry out a large-scale rectification movement, provided that [rectification] can be intimately integrated with all of its tasks and not divorced from them. By using the methods of reading certain designated documents, summing up work, analyzing conditions, and developing criticism and self-criticism [the Party must] raise the ideological and political level of its cadres and of Party members in general, overcome mistakes committed in work, overcome feelings of pride and complacency in those who think themselves heroes, overcome bureaucratism and commandism,[11] and improve the relations between the Party and the people.

Notes

1. See text Sept. 21, 1949, note 4.

2. See text Jan. 2, 1950, note 1.

3. In using the term "People's Democracies" we follow *Xuanji*, V. Earlier versions in *RMRB* and *XHYB* have the term "new democracies." See again text Sept. 21, 1949, note 4.

4. These refer to the three major battles in the Third Revolutionary Civil War period of September 1948-February 1949. The Liaoxi-Shenyang battle was conducted by the Northeastern PLA under the command of Lin Biao and Luo Ronghuan from September 12 to November 2, 1948, in which, after a 50-day siege, Shenyang, a major city in the Jinzhou region of Western Liaoning Province, was liberated. From November 7, 1948, to January 10, 1949, the Second Field Army under the command of Liu Bocheng and Deng Xiaoping and the Third Field Army under the command of Chen Yi and Su Yu conducted a battle in the Xuzhou region in the lower Huai River basin, annihilating 57 divisions of the KMT forces. Then from December 5, 1948, to January 31, 1949, the two Communist army groups, one under Lin Biao-Luo Ronghuan and the other under Yang Dezhi-Yang Chengwu, converged on Beiping, resulting eventually in liberation of that city and of the metropolis Tianjin. These three major battles marked the completion of the military liberation of all regions north of the Yangtze River. On February 3, 1949, the Communist forces entered Beijing (then still known as Beiping) in triumph. On April 20, 1949, following the breakdown of negotiations with the Nanjing government, Mao and Zhu De issued orders for the PLA to cross the Yangtze River. This was done on April 21 in two provinces – Anhui and Jiangsu. On April 23, Nanjing was liberated.

5. The GAC of the Central People's Government issued its Resolution on the Unifying of the State's Financial and Economic Activities on March 3, 1950.

6. "This refers to the People's Victory Parity State Bonds, issued by the Central People's Government in 1950." (*Xuanji*, V, p. 20.)

7. Conventionally, before 1949, the term "old liberated areas" referred to areas that had come under Communist control after the Long March (Oct. 1934-Oct. 1935) but before the Third Revolutionary Civil War period (Aug. 1945-Oct. 1, 1949). Throughout the period of the United Front (beginning Dec. 1935) and the War of Resistance against Japan (July 1937-Sept. 1945) the CPC expanded. By the beginning of the Third Revolutionary Civil War, it controlled seven liberated areas in Central China and two small areas in South China. The old liberated areas are distinguished from the new liberated areas, which refer to areas liberated during the Third Revolutionary Civil War period. See J. Harrison (1972), p. 372. However, earlier in this article and in other places in *Xuanji*, V, the term "newly liberated areas" also appears to be used to refer specifically to areas liberated in 1949, on the verge of the nationwide military victory of the Communist forces, and in the early months of the PRC after October 1949.

8. "Beginning in the winter of 1950, large-scale reform movements were launched successively in the new liberated areas throughout the country. By the winter of 1952, except for some areas inhabited by minority nationalities, land reform was basically accomplished. In the

new and old liberated areas, approximately 300 million peasants who previously had no land or very little land received parcels of land which totaled 700 million *mu*." (*Xuanji*, V, p. 20.)

9. "Closed-doorism" *(guanmen zhuyi)* means excluding those who, for political reasons, should participate in a particular organization or activity even though their class distinction might otherwise prohibit it. Hence, it refers to the incorrect exclusion of nonproletarian and non-Party persons from the revolutionary tasks that Mao outlines here.

10. "Before the election and convocation of the local people's congress at all levels, conferences of people from all circles were convened, in accordance with the stipulations of the Common Program of the Chinese People's Political Consultative Conference of 1949, to exercise the functions and powers of the people's congresses step by step. " (*SW*, V, p. 32.) This refers to the temporary measure implemented in order to provide avenues for the people to take part in government before the local people's congresses at the various levels were convened. The people's congresses were formed by general elections at the various levels (provincial and municipal), but the representative conferences of people of all circles mentioned here (the temporary surrogate congresses) were at first formed through invitation by the democratic parties, the people's organizations, and the people's governments. This persisted until the completion of the inital stage of nationwide land reform in 1951. This arrangement was stipulated by Article 14 of the Common Program. When the people's representative conferences were not in session, their advisory function was performed by an elected consultative committee. (See text June 23, 1950, note 3.)

11. Commandism refers to an attitude in which cadres would employ the method of issuing hard and fast commands to force the masses to accept the ideology and tasks set by the Party, to coerce them into action rather than persuade them of the rationality and necessity of that ideology and those tasks. It is a work-style that proceeds from arrogance and a subjective frame of mind and from an eagerness to simply accomplish the task, without giving due consideration to the level of consciousness of the masses and without respecting the principle of voluntary participation. Mao outlined the meaning of this term and its inherent danger in the article "On Coalition Government" (April 24, 1945); see *SW*, III, p. 265.

Don't Attack on All Fronts
(June 6, 1950)

Source: *Xuanji*, V, pp. 21-24. Available English Translation: *SW*, V, pp. 33-36.

This is an excerpt from Mao's speech at the Third Plenum of the Seventh Central Committee, which was held on June 6-9, 1950, in Beijing. According to the source note in Xuanji, *this speech was an oral elaboration and extension of the written report submitted by Mao on the same day and included in this volume as the preceding text.*

Since the Second Plenum of the Seventh Central Committee,[1] the new democratic revolution led by our Party has attained victory throughout the country, and the People's Republic of China has been established. This is a great victory. It is a victory the magnitude of which is unprecedented in Chinese history. Following the October Revolution, it is also a great victory of world-wide significance. Comrade Stalin and many foreign comrades all feel that the victory of the Chinese revolution is an extremely great one. On the other hand, there are many comrades among us who do not feel this way since they have already become accustomed to this struggle, having waged it for all this time. We must yet conduct extensive propaganda within the Party and among the masses on the great significance of the victory of the Chinese revolution.

Although we are in this situation of great victory, a very complicated struggle and many difficulties still lie ahead of us.

We have already completed land reform in the North – in an area with a population of about 160 million. We should affirm this great achievement. Our War of Liberation was won primarily by relying on these 160 million people. Only after the victory in land reform were we victorious in overthrowing Chiang Kai-shek. This coming autumn we will begin to carry out land reform over a vast area with a population of about 310 million in order to overthrow the entire landlord class. In the course of this land reform, our enemies will be quite large and quite plentiful. First, the imperialists will oppose us. Second, the reactionaries in Taiwan and Tibet will oppose us. Third, the remnants of the KMT, secret agents, and bandits will oppose us. Fourth, the landlord class will oppose us. Fifth, the church schools established by the imperialists in our country, the reactionary forces in the religious circles, and the reactionary forces in the cultural and educational institutions that we have taken over from the Kuomintang will oppose us. All these are our enemies. Our struggle against these enemies to complete land reform over an area that is much larger than the area with which we had dealt in the past is bound to be a very violent struggle, a struggle unprecedented in history.

At the same time, the victory of the revolution has led to the restructuring of both the society and the economy. Such restructuring is necessary, but it has also temporarily presented us with a heavy burden. As a result of social and economic restructuring and some damage that the war has caused to industry and commerce, many people are dissatisfied with us. At present, our relationship with the national bourgeoisie[2] is very tense: they are worried day and night and extremely dissatisfied. The unemployed intellectuals and unemployed workers are not satisfied with us. In addition, there is a group of small handicraft workers who are also dissatisfied with us. In most of the rural areas, because land reform has not yet been carried out, and the grain tax is still being levied, the peasants also have complaints.

What is our general policy at the present time? It is simply to eliminate the remnants of the KMT, the secret agents, and the bandits, to overthrow the landlord class, to liberate Taiwan and Tibet, and to struggle against the imperialists to the end. In order to isolate and deal a blow to the enemies currently facing us, we must transform those among the people who are dissatisfied with us into people who support us. The work involves some difficulties at present, but we still have to work out all sorts of ways to solve them.

We should make reasonable adjustments in industry and commerce so that the factories will start running and solve the problem of unemployment. Moreover, we should set aside two billion catties of grain to solve the problem of feeding the unemployed workers, in order to get them to support us. [If] we carry out the reduction of rent and interest rates, suppress bandits and fight against the [local] tyrants, and [carry out] the land reform, the broad [masses] of the peasants will support us. We should also find a way out for the small handicraft workers and enable them to make a living. We should improve our relations with the national bourgeoisie through reasonable adjustments in industry and commerce and tax adjustments so that the relations will not be too strained. As for the intellectuals, we should organize various kinds of training classes, military-political universities, and revolutionary universities; we should make use of them and at the same time carry out education and reform among them.[3] We should let them study the history of social development, historical materialism, and several other such courses. We even have a way of making those who advocate idealism not oppose us. While they talk about the creation of human beings by God, we will talk about the evolution of human beings from the apes. Some intellectuals are advanced in age – over seventy years old. As long as they support the Party and the People's Government, we should provide for them.

The entire Party should endeavor conscientiously and carefully to make a success of United Front work. Under the leadership of the working class and on the basis of the worker-peasant alliance, we should unite with the petty bourgeoisie and the national bourgeoisie. The national bourgeoisie will be eliminated in the future, but at present we should rally them around us, rather than pushing them away. We should wage a struggle against them on the one hand and unite with them on the other. We must make this principle clear to the cadres and moreover prove with facts that it is both correct and necessary to unite with the national bourgeoisie, the democratic parties, the democratic personages, and the intellectuals. Among these people there are many who were our enemies in the past. Now they have split off from the enemy's side and have come over to our side. We should unite with those people with whom it is more or less possible for us to be united. Uniting with them would be advantageous to the laboring people. At this moment it is necessary for us to adopt this strategy.

It is very important to unite with the minority nationalities. The minority nationalities make up approximately thirty million people throughout the entire country. Social reform in the regions occupied by the minority nationalities is a very important thing and must be handled carefully. Under no circumstances should we be impatient, because impatience will lead to mistakes. Where conditions are not ripe, we cannot carry out reform. Even if one of the conditions is ripe, as long as the others are not, no major reforms should be carried out. Of course, this does not mean that we mustn't have any reform. According to the provisions of the Common Program,[4] the customs and habits of the areas inhabited by the minority nationalities can be reformed.

However, such reforms must be handled by the minority nationalities themselves. Without the element of mass [support], without the armed forces of the people, and without cadres from the minority nationalities themselves, we should not attempt any reform work of a mass nature. We have to help the minority nationalities train their own cadres and unite with the broad masses of the minority nationalities.

In sum, we should not attack on all fronts. To attack on all fronts and create a tense situation throughout the country would be very bad. We absolutely must not make too many enemies. We must make some concessions and have some moderation on one front in order to concentrate our strength to attack on the other front. We must do our work well and cause the workers, peasants, and small handicraft workers all to support us, and cause the overwhelming majority of people among both the national bourgeoisie and the intellectuals not to oppose us. In this way, the KMT remnants, the secret agents, and the bandits will be isolated, the landlord class will be isolated, the reactionaries in Taiwan and Tibet will be isolated, and the imperialists will be isolated amidst the people of our country. Such is our policy, such are our strategy, tactics, and guidelines, and such is the line of the Third Plenum of the Central Committee.

Notes

1. The Second Plenum of the Seventh Central Committee was held at Xibaibo, Hebei, Mar. 5-13, 1949. For more on the significance of this plenum, see text Mar. 22, 1958, note 23.
2. See text Mar. 12, 1950, note 3.
3. Mao appears here to be referring to the model of the Chinese People's Military and Political University in Resistance to Japan (commonly known as Kangda), which was established in Yanan on the basis of the original Red Army College in 1936, and the National Revolutionary University (Minzu geming daxue) established in Xian at about the same time. See text May-June 1955, note 20, for more detail on "Kangda."
4. See text Sept. 21, 1949, note 2.

Letter to Chen Mingshu

(June 12, 1950)

Source: *Shuxin*, p. 380.

According to the source, Chen (1889-1965) was at the time of this letter a member of the Central People's Government Council and a member of the Standing Committee of the Central Committee of the Revolutionary Committee of the KMT. (See text Sept. 21,

1949, note 1.) For more biographical information on Chen, see text June 9, 1957, note 5.

Mr. Zhenru:[1]

I have availed myself of the opportunity to briefly read your great work,[2] but since I have not studied it in great detail, I would not dare to propose any opinions of my own. I only think that certain viewpoints therein can and need to be further thought out and discussed. When I have time I shall take up the discussion with you. I have held it for some time and apologize for being so tardy in responding.

I respectfully convey my regards and best wishes for your health and well-being.

Mao Zedong
June 12

Notes

1. Zhenru is Chen's *zi* (honorific name). See text Oct. 15, 1949, note 1, for this usage. The name reflects Chen's identity as a Buddhist and is the Buddhist term (or rather, one of the Buddhist terms) for Buddha, meaning "The Truth that is as it is." It is the Chinese translation of the Sanskrit term *Bhutatathata*.

2. According to the source, this refers to a book that Chen wrote on the teaching of Buddha and that was sent to Mao for perusal and critique.

Reply to Ambassador of the Republic of Poland
(June 12, 1950)

Source: *RMRB* (June 13, 1950), 4. Other Chinese Text: *GMRB* (June 13, 1950), 1. Available English Translation: NCNA, *Daily Bulletin*, 54 (June 20, 1950), 2.

Burgin served as ambassador of the Republic of Poland to the PRC from June 1950 to June 1952.

Mr. Ambassador:

It is with great pleasure that I accept the letter of credence which has been conferred on you by the President of the Republic of Poland and which has been presented to me by Your Excellency, and I am grateful for Your Excellency's warm congratulations and good wishes.

A profound friendship has existed between the peoples of China and Poland for a long time. In the great world war against Fascism, we watched with unbounded sympathy and concern the resolute and heroic struggle of the Polish people. We furthermore bear the greatest admiration for the Polish people for their brilliant successes in the rebuilding of their homeland today.

At present, the government and peoples of both countries, China and Poland, are all continuing their efforts and struggles toward their common goal of attaining world peace. I am convinced that the increasingly close cooperation between China and Poland in the political, economic, and cultural areas will not only be beneficial to the peoples of the two countries, but furthermore will strengthen and consolidate the camp for world democracy and peace.

I warmly welcome Your Excellency as the first ambassador extraordinary and plenipotentiary of the Republic of Poland to the People's Republic of China and pledge my assistance to Your Excellency in your work of consolidating the friendship between our two countries.

Best wishes for the prosperity of your country, the prospering of your people, and the good health of your head of state.

Reply to Ambassador of the Kingdom of Sweden

(June 12, 1950)

Source: *RMRB* (June 13, 1950), 4. Other Chinese Text: *GMRB* (June 13, 1950), 1.

T. L. Hammerstrom served as ambassador of the Kingdom of Sweden to the PRC from June 1950 to July 1951.

Mr. Ambassador:

It gives me great pleasure to accept from Your Excellency the letter of credence conferred on Your Excellency by the King of Sweden, and I am grateful for Your Excellency's congratulations and good wishes.

A long friendship has existed between the peoples of China and Sweden. In their efforts in defense of world peace, the peoples of our two countries have a common wish. The establishment of diplomatic relations between China and Sweden now will not only cause the friendship that already exists between our two peoples to become more consolidated with each passing day, but will also facilitate [the growth of] a lasting peace throughout the world.

I warmly welcome Your Excellency as the first ambassador extraordinary and plenipotentiary of the Kingdom of Sweden to the People's Republic of China and pledge my assistance to Your Excellency in your work of strengthening the cooperation between our two countries.

My sincere best wishes for the prosperity of your country, the prosperity of your people, and the good health of your head of state.

Opening Speech at the Second Meeting of the National Committee of the CPPCC

(June 14, 1950)

Source: *RMRB* (June 15, 1950), 1. Other Chinese Texts: *XHYB*, 9 (July 1950), 489; *Zhengxie er ci*, pp. 1-2; *Buyi*, p. 11. Available English Translations: NCNA, *Daily Bulletin*, 51 (June 15, 1950), 1; *CDSP*, II:25 (Aug. 5, 1950), 33 (abridged).

Fellow committee members, comrades, and friends:

The Second Meeting of the National Committee of the People's Political Consultative Conference is now in session. At this meeting there will be reports on the work of the National Committee, on land reform work, on economic and fiscal work, on taxation work, on diplomatic and United Front work, on cultural and educational work, on military work, and on the work of the courts. We hope that these matters will be discussed. Of these [various issues], the central issue for this meeting is the problem of land reform. We hope that a land reform bill will be adopted at this meeting and that it might be implemented after being ratified by the Central People's Government.[1] The first thing this would do would be to enable the more than 100,000 cadres who are in the midst of preparing to carry out land reform to get an early start in studying this bill, so that after this autumn the work of reforming the land [tenure] system may be carried out smoothly throughout an area with an agricultural population of about 100 million. Naturally, all the other reports are also important. Any opinions that one may have may be voiced, and any proposal may be submitted for examination and discussion. So long as they are practicable, they ought to be adopted. We have the great and correct Common Program[2] as our standard for reviewing our work and discussing problems. The Common Program must be fully implemented, as it is presently the organic law of our country. I am convinced that through the efforts of all our comrades our meeting will be able to accomplish its tasks smoothly. At the present moment, under the leadership of the Central People's Government, the people of the entire country are in the midst of undertaking immense tasks, struggling to overcome difficulties and to strive for a turn for the better in the economic situation. All of the people's enterprises in our country are now developing in a forward direction along new paths, and with each new day we can see progress and success. No difficulty of any sort can hinder the advance of the people's cause. The People's Political Consultative Conference and the National Committee it has elected are great political organizations of the United Front that unite all nationalities, all democratic classes, all democratic parties, all people's organizations, and democratic personages from all walks of life throughout the country. They enjoy very high prestige among the people of the country. We must consolidate this type of unity, consolidate our United Front, and lead the people of the entire country in steadily attaining their own goals.

Notes

1. See text Mar. 12, 1950, note 5.
2. See text Sept. 21, 1949, note 3.

Letter to Ma Xulun
(June 19, 1950)

Source: *Shuxin*, p. 381. Other Chinese Text: *Jiaoyu geming*, 4 (May 6, 1967), 2 (excerpt).

Ma Xulun (1884-1970) was minister of education from October 1949 to November 1952. He was a philologist and a prolific scholar. Before 1911, he was an editor and publisher of many significant journals such as the Xin shijie xuebao (New World) and Guocui xuebao (National Essence) and taught at various middle and post-secondary schools. In the early years of the Republic of China he was head of the Ministry of Education and later chancellor of Beijing University. During the 1930s he held positions in the Zhejiang provincial government and taught at Beijing University. In the early 1940s he, together with Xu Guangping, Wang Juechen, et al., formed the Zhongguo minzhu cujin hui (Association for the Promotion of Democracy). In 1948 he accepted the CPC's invitation to take part in the preparations for the formation of the new CPPCC. From 1949 on, he was active in the CPPCC and in the work of uniting the "democratic parties" with the CPC. He held positions in the Association for the Promotion of Democracy (of which he became chairman in March 1953) and in the

Zhongguo minzhu tongmeng (Democratic League). For more information on Ma's life, see Zhonggong renming lu, *appendix, pp. 62-63. For another letter to Ma on the same topic see text Jan. 15, 1951.*

Minister Ma:

Your other item of correspondence is returned. This matter should be resolved as quickly as possible. Ask all schools to pay attention to health first and studies second. Where nutrition is not sufficient, operational funds should be increased. The amount of time for studying and holding meetings should be greatly reduced. People who are ill should be given special treatment. Schools throughout the country ought to be like this across the board. The conference on higher education has already been held; it would be appropriate to hold a conference each on the two [other levels:] secondary [education] and primary [education]. Please give consideration to the above and take action accordingly.

In salute,

Mao Zedong
June 19

Closing Speech at the Second Session of the National Committee of the CPPCC

(June 23, 1950)

Source: *RMRB* (June 24, 1950), 1. Other Chinese Text: *Zhengxie er ci*, pp. 91-95. Available English Translations: NCNA, *Supplement*, 55 (June 26, 1950), 1-2; *PC*, II:1 (July 1, 1950), 24-25; *CDSP*, II:26 (Aug. 12, 1950), 28; K. Fan (1972), pp. 93-95; *SW*, V, pp. 37-40.

While the RMRB *and the* Zhengxie er ci *versions are similar, the later* Xuanji *version of this text contains some variations. Where these variations are significant, they have been noted.*

The Second Session of the National Committee of the CPPCC was held on June 14-23, 1950, in Beijing. The thrust of this document is the same as that of Mao's better known talk of June 6, 1950. This document is noteworthy as an example of the position Mao took in the years just after Liberation when he viewed the

task of carrying out the socialist transformation of China as easier than the two
tasks of the New Democratic period – war and land reform.
   It is also significant in that in its last part on the method of dealing with the
people, it forecasts the specific formula of unity and criticism that Mao would
later espouse in his famous essay of 1957, "On Correctly Handling Contra-
dictions Among the People." (See text Feb. 27, 1957.)

This meeting has summed up the experience of the preceding period and
has laid down various guiding principles.

This work of summing up experience and laying down guidelines was done
by all of us together; it was done by the representatives of all the nationalities,
all the democratic classes, all the democratic parties, all the people's organizations,[1] and the democratic personages from all walks of life gathered
together. Here, we not only have the members of the National Committee of
the People's Political Consultative Conference, but we also have many personnel of the Central People's Government, of the people's governments, (the
military and administrative commissions)[2] of the various greater administrative regions, and of the people's government of the various provinces and
municipalities; [we also have] representatives from the consultative committees of the provincial and municipal conferences of people from all walks of
life,[3] as well as many specially invited patriotic personages, all sitting in on
the meeting and taking part in the discussions. In this way, we have been able
to concentrate diverse opinions, review [our] past work, and decide on principles for the future. I hope that in the future we will continue to utilize this
method, and further hope that this method will also be adopted by the people's
governments (the military and administrative commissions) of the various
greater administrative regions, and the people's governments of the various
provinces and municipalities. For the time being, the nature of our meeting is
still that of making proposals, but actually the decisions that we make in meetings of this sort will certainly be adopted by the Central People's Government
and be put into practice, as indeed they ought to be.

We have unanimously approved the report on the work of the National
Committee and the various reports on the work of the Central People's Government. These included the reports on land reform work, on political work,
on military work, on economic and financial work, on taxation work, on cultural and educational work, and on the work of the courts of law. These were
all good reports. In these reports [we] have appropriately summed up the
experience of the work of the preceeding period and have formulated the principles for work of the future. The reason that we have had so many topics for
discussion at this meeting is that since the founding of our new state work is
being initiated and developed in all areas, and the people throughout the country are in the midst of vigorously launching a great and genuine people's revolutionary struggle on all fronts. This is a tremendous struggle on the military
front, on the economic front, on the ideological front, and on the land reform
front, the likes of which has never been seen before. Every area of work has to

be summed up and given direction and guiding principles; that is why we have had so many topics for discussion. According to the law, our meeting will be held twice a year. Of these [two meetings,] one will be a meeting with many topics for discussion and the other will have fewer topics. China is a big country; our actual population is more than 475 million. Besides, we are in a great historical epoch of the people's revolution. Such circumstances demand that we do things in this particular manner, and we have been doing so. I believe that we are doing things correctly.

We have had many topics for discussion at this meeting. The central theme of our discussion has been the problem of transforming the old system of land [ownership]. We have all agreed with Vice-chairman Liu Shaoqi's report[4] and the draft land reform bill proposed by the Central Committee of the Communist Party of China.[5] We have also made certain useful amendments and supplements to the draft land reform bill. This is very good. I am filled with joy by the fact that hundreds of millions of New China's rural people have gained the opportunity to overturn their old lives and that the country has secured the basic conditions for industrialization, and I celebrate this fact. The Chinese populace consists primarily of peasants, and the revolution achieved victory only by relying on the aid of the peasants. The industrialization of the country also must rely on the help of the peasants in order to succeed. Therefore the working class should actively help the peasants carry out land reform. The urban[6] petty bourgeoisie and the national bourgeoisie[7] should also support this reform, and still more so should the democratic parties and the various people's organizations adopt this attitude. War and land reform are the two "gates"[8] that test the mettle of all people and parties in China in the historical epoch of New Democracy. Whoever stands on the side of the revolutionary people is a revolutionary; whoever stands on the side of imperialism, feudalism, and bureaucratic capitalism is a counterrevolutionary. Whoever stands on the side of the revolutionary people only in words but acts differently is a revolutionary in words only; if one not only stands on the side of the revolutionary people in words, but also in deeds, then one is a complete revolutionary. The "gate" of war has basically been passed. We have all passed this "gate" with flying colors, and the people of the whole country are satisfied with this. Now we must pass the "gate" of land reform, and I hope that we will pass it with the same flying colors as we did the "gate" of war. Let us study harder, have more discussion, clarify our thought, and march together in step to form a great antifeudal united front; then we can lead the people and help the people to pass this "gate" smoothly. When the "gates" of war and land reform have both been passed, the only remaining "gate" will be passed easily. This will be the "gate" of socialism, of carrying out socialist transformation throughout the entire country. As for those who have contributed to the revolutionary war and to the revolutionary reform of the landownership system and who in the many years to come will contribute to economic and cultural construction, they will not be forgotten by the people when the time comes in the future to implement the nationalization of [private][9] enterprises and the socialization of agriculture (this time is still in the distant future); their prospects are bright. It is in such a way that our country takes steady steps in progress; having gone through war and through the reforms of New Democracy, in the future, after the economic and cultural undertakings of the country have prospered greatly, after all sorts of conditions have been secured, and after the whole people have thoroughly considered and agreed [on the matter of the transition], we can then step into the new era of socialism in an unhurried and orderly [manner]. I believe that it is essential to make this point clear so that people can have confidence and not worry that one day they will no longer be wanted and will not be given the opportunity to serve the people even though they may want to. No, it will not be like that at all. As long as somebody is truly willing to work for the people and has indeed helped the people at the time when they were still having difficulties, has performed good deeds, and has consistently continued to do so without giving up halfway, then there will be no reason for the people or the People's Government not to want such a person, and there will be no reason not to give such a person a chance to make a living and serve [the people].

With this great aim in mind, in the international [sphere], we must firmly unite with the Soviet Union, with all the People's Democracies,[10] and with all the forces for peace and democracy throughout the world. We cannot have the slightest hesitation or wavering on this matter. Domestically, we must unite all nationalities, all democratic classes, all democratic parties, all people's organizations, and all patriotic democratic personages; we must consolidate the great and prestigious revolutionary United Front that has already been established. Whoever contributes to the work of consolidating this revolutionary United Front will be welcomed by us and will be correct; whoever harms the work of consolidating this revolutionary United Front will be opposed and will be wrong. To achieve the goal of consolidating the revolutionary united front, we must adopt the method of criticism and self-criticism. Of the standards that we must adopt in applying this method, the most important presently is our organic law, the Common Program.[11] At this meeting we have adopted the method of criticism and self-criticism based on the Common Program. This is a very good method, an excellent method that pushes all of us to uphold the truth and correct mistakes; it is the only correct method by which all the revolutionary people in a people's state can carry out self-education and self-reform. The people's dictatorship has two methods. One, which applies to the enemy, is the dictatorial method, which means that when necessary they can be forbidden to participate in political activities, forced to obey the laws of the People's Government, and forced to take part in labor and to reform themselves through labor in order to become new people. For the people it is exactly the opposite. It is not the coercive method that is applied to them, but rather the democratic method, which is to say that they must be permitted to participate in political activities. We will not force them to do this or that but will use democratic methods to carry out the work of education and persuasion among them. This type of educational work is the work of self-education among the people. The method of criticism and self-criticism is the basic method of self-education. I hope that all the nationalities, all the democratic classes, all the democratic parties, all the people's organizations, and all the patriotic democratic personages throughout the country will adopt this method.

Notes

1. See text Sept. 21, 1949, note 1, and text Oct. 1, 1949, note 3, respectively.

2. Prior to November 1952, China was divided into six "greater administrative regions," corresponding to the Northeast, North, East, Central-South, Southwest, and Northwest areas of the country. With the exception of the North, each area was overseen by a regional administrative agency; in the Northeast that was called the "people's government"; the other four were designated "military and administrative commissions." Afterward, administrative councils were established in all six regions. With the promulgation of the Constitution in 1954 the administrative councils were abolished. Also see note in *SW*, V, p. 40.

3. The *RMRB* version here has *xieyi weiyuanhui* (agreement committees), while *Xuanji* has *xieshang weiyuanhui* (consultative committees); undoubtedly the correct term is the latter. See text June 6, 1950 (1), note 9.

4. The phrase "Vice-chairman Liu Shaoqi's report and" is in the *RMRB* version but has been omitted from the *Xuanji* version of the text. On Liu's report, see K. Lieberthal (1976), p. 52. A text of Liu's report is reprinted in *RMSC* (1951), pp. 32-43, and translated in *CB*, 43 (Dec. 22, 1950).

5. See text March 12, 1950, note 5. This draft was presented to the Second Session of the First National Committee of the CPPCC on June 14, 1950; for more on this meeting see K. Lieberthal (1976), pp. 52-53. The bill was ratified and became law on June 30; thus the term *fa* (law) in the Chinese text is translated here as "bill."

6. The word "urban" occurs only in the *RMRB* text.

7. See text Mar. 12, 1950, note 3.

8. The word *guan* is commonly used as a geographic term, referring to a fortified mountain pass. Its usage has been extended to refer to a point, or grade, that one attempts to pass or a target to be achieved. In such usage it is often translated as "gate." The term *guoguan* (passing the gate) therefore has the connotation of "making the grade," or "passing the test." Here it specifically refers to critical points in the development of revolutionary consciousness and the proving of one's rectitude. For an extended illustration of the term's usage see W. Hinton (1966), especially Parts IV and V.

9. The word "private" occurs only in the *Xuanji* version.

10. The *RMRB* version has "New Democracies" here. For the definition of the terms see text Sept. 21, 1949, note 4.

11. See text Sept. 21, 1949, note 3.

Reply to Minister of the Kingdom of Denmark
(June 24, 1950)

Source: *RMRB* (June 25, 1950), 1.

A. Moerch served as minister of the Kingdom of Denmark to the PRC from June 1950 to December 1953.

Mr. Minister:

It gives me great pleasure to accept the letter of credence from His Majesty the King of Denmark presented by Your Excellency, and I am grateful for Your Excellency's congratulations and good wishes.

Friendship exists between the peoples of our two countries, China and Denmark. Moreover, in our efforts in the development of an economic relationship and in the defense of world peace, I believe that the peoples of our two countries also share common wishes. The establishment of diplomatic relations between China and Denmark today will undoubtedly further consolidate the friendship which already exists between the peoples of the two countries. I further hope that it will facilitate [the growth of] a lasting peace in the world.

I warmly welcome Your Excellency in your appointment as the first minister extraordinary and plenipotentiary of the Kingdom of Denmark to the People's Republic of China and pledge my assistance to Your Excellency in your work of strengthening the friendly relations between our two countries.

Best wishes for the prosperity of your country, the prospering of your people, and best wishes for the good health of your head of state.

Reply to Head of Diplomatic Mission
of the German Democratic Republic

(June 24, 1950)

Source: *RMRB* (June 25, 1950), 1.

Johannes Konig, as head of the diplomatic mission of the German Democratic Repub-lic to the PRC, had the rank of ambassador at this time. He was officially installed as ambassador extraordinary and plenipotentiary on Nov. 12, 1953, and served in that capacity until December 1955.

Your Excellency:

I accept with great pleasure the letter of credence from the President of the Democratic Republic of Germany which Your Excellency has presented and am grateful to Your Excellency for your warm congratulations and good wishes.

Ever since the great Soviet army crushed Hitler's reactionary state organi-zation, the Chinese people have watched with happiness the development of the democratic movement of the German people. Since the establishment of the New Germany – the Democratic Republic of Germany – under the leader-ship of the president of your country, Mr. Wilhelm Pieck, which has become the turning point of the history of Germany and of Europe, the Chinese peo-ple's happiness has multiplied. We feel that we have gained a very good and strong friend. It was at just this point that the People's Republic of China was founded and the Chinese People's Revolution won its victory throughout the entire country. Diplomatic relations were then rapidly established between our country and yours. There is no doubt that the establishment of diplomatic relations between our two countries will not only cause the friendship between our two peoples to develop and become more consolidated with each passing day, but it will also provide a strong guarantee for a lasting peace in the world.

I warmly welcome Your Excellency as the head of the diplomatic mission, with the rank of ambassador, of the Democratic Republic of Germany to the People's Republic of China, and pledge my assistance to Your Excellency in your work of strengthening the cooperation between our two nations.

Best wishes for the prosperity of your country, the prospering of your peo-ple, and the good health of your head of state.

Speech at Eighth Session of the CPGC
(June 28, 1950)

Source: *RMRB* (June 29, 1950), 1. Other Chinese Texts: *XHBYK*, 21 (Nov. 10, 1950), 7-8; *Buyi*, p. 15 (excerpts). Available English Translations: NCNA, *Daily Bulletin*, 65(July 6, 1950),1-2; *CDSP*, II:23 (July 22, 1950), 18; *CCSD*, pp. 155-156.

The Chinese people declared long ago that the affairs of all countries in the world should be managed by these countries themselves, and that the affairs of Asia should be managed by the peoples of Asia themselves, not by the United States of America. American aggression against Asia can only arouse widespread and resolute resistance by the peoples of Asia. It was only on January 5 of this year that Truman announced that the United States would not intervene in Taiwan.[1] Now he himself has proved that [statement] to be a [pack of lies], and moreover, he has torn to shreds all international agreements regarding the nonintervention of the United States in the internal affairs of China. This exposure by the United States of its own imperialist face is advantageous to the people of China and the peoples of Asia. There is absolutely no grounds for the United States' intervention in the internal affairs of countries such as Korea, the Philippines, and Viet Nam. The sympathy of the entire Chinese people and of the broad masses of the people throughout the world will be on the side of the victims of aggression and certainly not on the side of American imperialism. They will neither be enticed by the imperialists' bribes nor cowed by their threats. Imperialism is outwardly strong but inwardly feeble because it does not have the support of the people. Our people, and people all over the world, unite and be fully prepared to crush any provocation by the American imperialists!

Note

1. For the text of President Truman's statement of January 5, 1950, see U.S. Department of State, *Bulletin*, January 16, 1950, p. 79. See also Secretary of State Acheson's statement of the same day, in U.S. Department of State, *Bulletin*, January 16, 1950, p. 80.

Reply to Ambassador of the People's Republic of Mongolia
(July 3, 1950)

Source: *GMRB* (July 4, 1950), 1.

Bayaryn Jargalsaikhan served as ambassador of the People's Republic of Mongolia from July 1950 to July 1953.

Mr. Ambassador:

I accept with great pleasure the letter of credence from the Presidium of the Lesser Hural of the People's Republic of Mongolia which Your Excellency has presented and am grateful to Your Excellency for your warm congratulations and good wishes.

An intimate relationship had originally existed between the peoples of China and Mongolia. [However,] in the last few decades, owing to the seeds of discord sown among us by the imperialists and the reactionary government in China, communications between us were severed. The Mongolian people, under the influence of the October Revolution, not only had already freed themselves early of the reactionary government of China and established a true People's Democracy, but also are advancing along the road of development in economic and cultural construction. The Chinese people wholeheartedly celebrate and salute this success on the part of the Mongolian people. Now, the Chinese people's revolution has achieved a fundamental victory, and diplomatic relations between China and Mongolia have been established. I am convinced that this will not only bring about the further development and consolidation of the friendship between the peoples of our two countries, but will also facilitate [the growth of] a lasting peace in Asia and the world.

I warmly welcome Your Excellency as the first ambassador extraordinary and plenipotentiary of the People's Republic of Mongolia to the People's Republic of China and pledge to Your Excellency my assistance in your work of strengthening the cooperation between our two nations.

Best wishes for the prosperity of your country, the prospering of your people, and the good health of your head of state.

Telegram to the People's Republic of Mongolia
(July 7, 1950)

Source: *RMRB* (July 11, 1950), 1.

Bumatsende was chairman of the Presidium of the Lesser Hural of the People's Republic of Mongolia.

Chairman Bumatsende

Your Excellency:

On behalf of the Central People's Government of the People's Republic of China and the Chinese people, I sincerely express our sentiments of congratulations and good wishes to Your Excellency and to the Mongolian people on this happy occasion of the commemoration and celebration of the twenty-ninth anniversary of the founding of your country. We are deeply convinced that the Mongolian people will achieve even greater successes in the areas of economic and cultural construction.
(Signed as Chairman of CPG of PRC, dated, in Beijing)

Telegram to the Socialist Unity Party of Germany
(July 18, 1950)

Source: *RMRB* (July 19, 1950), 1. Available English Translation: NCNA, *Daily Bulletin*, 74 (July 19, 1950), 1-2.

Comrade [Wilhelm] Pieck and all comrades of the Central Committee of the Socialist Unity Party of Germany:

We are extremely honored to receive your invitation to send delegates from our Party to attend the national congress of your Party to be held from July 20 to July 23. We have now appointed Comrade Wang Jiaxiang,[1] member of the

Central Committee of our Party, to go to Berlin to attend your congress as the representative of the Communist Party of China and to convey our congratulations and good wishes.

We hereby send from afar our best wishes for the successful convening of the national congress of the Socialist Unity Party of the great German Democratic Republic, for an early end to the phenomenon of the forced division of the whole of Germany by the imperialists, for the early establishment of an integrated, unified, and democratic Germany, and for an early liberation of the entire German nation under the correct leadership of the Socialist Unity Party and the Communist Party of Germany.

Long live the great Socialist Unity Party and the Communist Party of Germany!

(Signed as Chairman of CPC, dated, in Beijing)

Note

1. Wang was also at this time the ambassador of the PRC to the USSR. For more biographical information on Wang, see D. Klein and A. Clark, eds. (1971), II, pp. 895-900, and *Zhonggong renming lu*, p. 1093.

Letter to Wu Qirui
(July 19, 1950)

Source: *Shuxin*, p. 382.

According to the source, Wu is a native of Wuxi, Jiangsu Province. She is the daughter-in-law of Wang Lian, Mao's mathematics teacher at the First Normal School of Hunan. Wu was teaching at the primary school affiliated with the Normal School of Wuxi.

Madam Qirui:[1]

I have received your letter of May. I am very concerned about your difficulties. With regard to your request that your three children be allowed to enter the school for cadres' children of southern Jiangsu in order that your difficulties may be somewhat alleviated, please bring this letter with you and discuss the matter with comrades in positions of responsibility in the appropriate local organs, and see if it can be done. It is up to you to decide which person to approach for this discussion. If necessary, you can look up Comrade Chen Pixian, secretary of the Sunan (south Jiangsu) District Party Committee.[2] I completely approve of this being done; it is just that I do not know if it would be possible for that school for cadres' children to accept more children. You are a mother of eight children, so I hope that you will take very good care of yourself. Please also convey my best regards to your children.

In response, and with my best regards for your work in teaching.

Mao Zedong
July 19

Notes

1. Mao used here the term *xiansheng*, which originally refered simply to people who are either one's elder, or whom one respects, especially in the case of teachers. Nonetheless the term has come to be commonly translated as "Mister," which conveys the sense of the masculine gender. Hence we have used the term "madam" in translation.

2. For more biographical information on Chen, see text Jan. 10, 1951, source note, and text Sept. 17, 1957, note 5.

Telegram to the Republic of Poland
(July 21, 1950)

Source: *RMRB* (July 22, 1950), 1. Available English Translation: NCNA, *Daily Bulletin*, 78 (July 25, 1950), 2-3.

President [Boleslaw] Bierut

Your Excellency:

On behalf of the Central People's Government of the People's Republic of China and the Chinese people, I sincerely extend to you and the people of Poland our congratulations and good wishes on this happy occasion of the celebration of the sixth anniversary of the founding of your country. Our best wishes for the daily growth of the Republic of Poland in prosperity and strength under Your Excellency's leadership.

(Signed as Chairman of CPG of PRC, dated, in Beijing)

Telegram to the Transvaal Indian Congress
(July 26, 1950)

Source: *RMRB* (July 17, 1950), 1. Available English Translation: NCNA, *Daily Bulletin*, 80 (July 27, 1950), 1-2.

See text Sept. 13, 1950.

Chairman,
The Transvaal Indian Congress,
The Union of South Africa

Dr. Yusuf Dadoo:

Your telegram of June 18 has been received.

On behalf of the people of China, I support you completely in your just protest against the so-called "Group Areas Bill" of the government of the Union of South Africa, which discriminates against the Chinese, against the Indians, and against other Asian peoples.

(Signed and dated in Beijing)

Reply to Ambassador of the Union of Burma
(August 7, 1950)

Source: *RMRB* (Aug. 8, 1950), 1. Other Chinese Text: *GMRB* (Aug. 8, 1950), 1. Available English Translation: NCNA, *Daily Bulletin*, 88 (August 9, 1950), 2-3.

U Myint Thein served as ambassador of the Union of Burma to the PRC from August 1950 to September 1951.

Mr. Ambassador:

I am very pleased to accept the letter of credence from the President of the Union of Burma presented by Your Excellency and am grateful to Your Excellency for your felicitations and good wishes.

The two countries, China and Burma, share a common boundary, and not only is there a close relationship between them historically and culturally, but there is also a deep fraternal friendship between the peoples of the two countries. In recent centuries, the people of both China and Burma have undertaken protracted and courageous struggles for the independence and liberty of their respective nations. Therefore, the sympathy and [mutual] understanding that exist between our peoples are also very profound. The newly established diplomatic relations between China and Burma will now undoubtedly further enhance the friendship that already exists between the peoples of the two countries. I also believe that it will facilitate the growth of a lasting peace in Asia and in the world.

I warmly welcome Your Excellency as the first ambassador extraordinary and plenipotentiary from the Union of Burma to the People's Republic of China and pledge my assistance to Your Excellency in your work of strengthening the cooperation between the two countries.

We sincerely hope for the prosperity of your country, the prospering of your people, and the good health of your head of state.

Letter to Su Yu
(August 8, 1950)

Source: *Shuxin*, p. 384.

According to the source, Su Yu (b. 1907) was at the time of this letter vice-chairman of the East China Military Region and mayor of Nanjing Municipality. Su joined the Communist Youth League in 1926 and the CPC in 1927. As an officer in the Independent Regiment of the Fourth Army (Nationalist) under Ye Ting in 1927 he took part in the Nanchang Uprising. Afterward he joined Zhu De and Mao at Jinggangshan. In the first half of the 1930s he was active in guerrilla fighting in the Fujian region. In 1937 he became a commander of a division of the New Fourth Army and in 1941, the commander of the First Division of the New Fourth Army. In 1948, after the Xuzhou-Pangfu battle, he became the deputy commander of the reorganized Second Field Army. From 1949 to 1958, he continued to hold important positions in the field commanders structure of the PLA, especially as the East China region commander with particular responsibilities for coastal defense against the KMT forces in Taiwan. He also rose to the rank of chief-of-staff of the PLA. In 1958 he became, under Lin Biao, a deputy minister of defense. For more biographical information on Su, see Zhonggong renming lu, pp. 768-769, and D. Klein and A. Clark, eds. (1971), II, pp. 774-778.

Comrade Su Yu:

Your letter brought to me by Comrade Luo Ruiqing[1] has been received. I am very much concerned about the fact that your illness is still grave. Your new post is not a very urgent one; you may devote yourself, without worrying about it, to convalescing until your health is completely restored. As for the place for resting and convalescence, if Qingdao appears to be appropriate you should stay in Qingdao; if not, then come to Beijing. Please see which you like better.

My best regards,

Mao Zedong

August 8

Note

1. According to the source, Luo (1906-1978) was at the time of this letter Minister of Public Security of the Central People's Government. Luo joined the CPC in 1926 and was with Zhu De and Mao at Jinggangshan. In 1930 he began a long career as a political officer in the communist armed forces. In 1940 he was the general director of the Political Department of the Eighth Route Army. After 1949 he served the Central People's Government mainly in the National Defense Council and in the Ministry of Public Security. During the Cultural Revolution he was arrested and publicly tried as a supporter of Liu Shaoqi. He attempted suicide in 1966, but he survived and was released in 1975. In 1977 he was rehabilitated and in September 1977 regained a high position in the Military Commission of the Central Committee of the CPC. For more biographical information on Luo, see *Zhonggong renming lu*, pp. 1059-1060 and D. Klein and A. Clark, eds. (1971), II, pp. 642-645.

Telegram to the People's Government of Qinghai on the Death of Vice-chairman Ma Po

(August 11, 1950)

Source: *RMRB* (Aug. 13, 1950), 1.

The People's Government of Qinghai Province and, through it, the family of the late Vice-chairman Ma Po:

I am deeply grieved at the passing away of Vice-chairman Ma Po and send

this telegram expressly to convey my condolences.
(Signed, with month and date, no year)

Telegram to the Democratic People's Republic of Korea
(August 14, 1950)

Source: *RMRB* (Aug. 15, 1950), 1. Available English Translation: NCNA, *Daily Bulletin*, 92 (Aug. 15, 1950), 3.

Chairman Kim Du Bong,
The Standing Committee,
The Supreme People's Assembly,
The Democratic People's Republic of Korea

Your Excellency:

On behalf of the Central People's Government of the People's Republic of China and the Chinese people, I sincerely extend to Your Excellency and the Korean people our felicitations on this happy occasion of the fifth anniversary of the liberation of Korea. The Chinese people warmly support the Korean people's just war against United States imperialist aggression and for the independence of their nation and the unity of their country. I am deeply convinced that the Korean people will certainly triumph in the end.
(Signed as Chairman of CPG of PRC, dated, in Beijing)

Telegram to the Republic of Indonesia
(August 16, 1950)

Source: *RMRB* (Aug. 17, 1950), 1. Available English Translation: NCNA, *Daily Bulletin*, 96 (Aug. 21, 1950), 4.

President Achmed Sukarno,
The Republic of the United States of Indonesia

Your Excellency:

On behalf of the Central People's Government of the People's Republic of China and the Chinese people, I sincerely extend our felicitations to Your Excellency and the people of Indonesia on this happy occasion of the anniversary of the founding of your country. We hope that the friendship between the peoples of Indonesia and China will grow with each passing day.
(Signed as Chairman of CPG of PRC, dated, in Beijing)

Letter to Xu Haidong

(August 20, 1950)

Source: *Shuxin*, p. 385.

According to the source, Xu (1900-1970) was the commander of the Twenty-fifth Army and the Fifteenth Army Group of the Red Army and commander of the Fourth Branch Regiment of the New Fourth Army and a deputy commander in the Jiangbei (North of the Yangtze) Command of that Army. He was suffering from a chronic illness and was at the time of this letter convalescing in Dalian. For more biographical information on Xu, see Zhonggong renming lu, p. 444, and D. Klein and A. Clark, eds. (1971), I, pp. 346-348.

Comrade Haidong:

I have received your letter of July 17. I am greatly comforted to understand that your health is mending. We are all very much concerned about you and hope that you will cast away all worries to devote yourself in quietude to your convalescence and recovery, so that your health may be totally restored.

In response, and my best wishes for you happiness!

Mao Zedong
August 20, 1950

Telegram to the People's Republic of Romania
(August 21, 1950)

Source: *RMRB* (Aug. 23, 1950), 1.

President Constantin Parhon,
The Presidium of the Grand National Assembly,
The People's Republic of Romania

Your Excellency:

On behalf of the Central People's Government of the People's Republic of China and the Chinese people, I sincerely extend to Your Excellency and the Romanian people our felicitations and best wishes on this occasion of the sixth anniversary of the liberation of Romania. I deeply believe that the Romanian people will achieve even greater success in their economic and cultural construction.
(Signed as Chairman of CPG of PRC, dated, in Beijing)

Speech at Banquet Commemorating the Liberation of Romania
(Excerpt)
(August 23, 1950)

Source: *RMRB* (Jan. 17, 1951), 6.

This is an excerpt of a speech that Mao made at a banquet celebrating the sixth anniversary of the liberation of Romania which was held by the Romanian embassy in Beijing on August 23, 1950. It is quoted as an excerpt in an article by Cao Xianbo, "Wo kanjian liao Mao zhuxi" (I Saw Chairman Mao) published in RMRB *(Jan. 17, 1951), 6.*

Six years ago, we too were under the oppression of Fascist bandits. Now, facts have proven that the force of the people is irresistible.

Letter to Xu Beihong
(August 26, 1950)

Source: *Meishu fenglei*, 3 (Aug. 1967), 3.

This is the second published letter from Mao to Xu Beihong since the founding of the PRC. For more on Xu, see text Nov. 20, 1949, source note.

Mr. Beihong:

Mr. X X X wrote me a letter claiming that he is a professor at the Art Institute and that life is very difficult for him. It seems he wishes me to help him. Please give the matter some thought and inform me as to what this person's condition is and how his situation should be handled. I also send you my best wishes for your work in teaching!

Enclosed is the letter from X.

Mao Zedong
August 26

Letter to Chen Jisheng
(August 29, 1950)

Source: *Shuxin*, p. 366.

According to the source, Chen Jisheng was a middle school teacher who had been studing the history of minority nationalities in China.

Mr. Jisheng:[1]

I have received and read your book and am greatly satisfied. The scholarship which you have undertaken is on a subject that I myself have not studied, so I cannot make any comments. The only thing is that I feel that unless one studies [history, in this case] Chinese history, with the methods of Marxism, one would be wasting one's energy in vain and will not achieve good results.

This is something I hope you will attend to.
In response, and with my respects,
Mao Zedong
August 29

Note

1. See text Nov. 17, 1949, note 2, for this usage.

Telegram to the Democratic Republic of Viet Nam
(August 29, 1950)

Source: *RMRB* (Sept. 9, 1950), 1. Available English Translation: NCNA, *Daily Bulletin*, 106 (Sept. 4, 1950), 4.

President Ho Chi Minh,
The Government of the Democratic Republic of Viet Nam

Your Excellency:

On this happy occasion of the fifth anniversary of the Independence of Viet Nam, on behalf of the Central People's Government of the People's Republic of China and the Chinese people, I sincerely extend to Your Excellency and to the people of Viet Nam our warmest congratulations. May the Vietnamese people win complete victory in their struggle for national liberation against imperialism and may they secure even greater successes in their cause of building an independent and democratic Viet Nam.
(Signed as Chairman of CPG of PRC, dated, in Beijing)

Inscription for the First National Conference on Health Care
(August 1950)

Source: *GMRB* (Feb. 12, 1961). Other Chinese Text: *Quanwudi* (June 26, 1967), 492. Available English Translations: *SCMM* (Suppl.), 22 (Apr. 8, 1968), 6; *CR*, 22 (July 1973), 3.

Unite the personnel in all areas of the work of medical and health care – with new medicine traditional medicine, Chinese medicine, Western medicine – to forge a consolidated united front and strive to launch the great [campaign for the] work of the health care of the people!

Telegram to the People's Republic of Bulgaria
(September 6, 1950)

Source: *RMRB* (Sept. 9, 1950), 1.

President Georgi Damyanov,
The Presidium of the National Assembly,
The People's Republic of Bulgaria

Your Excellency:

On behalf of the Central People's Government of the People's Republic of China and the Chinese people, I sincerely extend to Your Excellency and the Bulgarian people our warmest felicitations on this happy occasion of the sixth anniversary of the liberation of Bulgaria, and our wishes that the Bulgarian people will secure even greater successes in their great cause of building their homeland.
(Signed as Chairman of CPG of PRC, dated, in Beijing)

Letter to Chen Yu
(September 11, 1950)

Source: *RMRB* (Sept. 17, 1950), 1. Other Chinese Text: *Shuxin*, p. 387.

Chen Yu (1909-1974) was minister of Fuels Industry of the Central People's Government at this time. For more biographical information on Chen, see D. Klein and A. Clark, eds. (1971), I, pp. 147-149, and Zhonggong renming lu, appendix, pp. 71-72.

Comrade Chen Yu:

I have received the letter sent to me by the entire staff and workers of the Shijiazhuang[1] Bureau of Electric Works and the letter of signatures sent to me from the entire staff and workers of the Third Generator Plant of the Tianjin Bureau of Electric Works – both of which were transmitted [to me through you]. Please convey to the staff and the workers of both electric works my gratitude for their good wishes. I hope that they will unite as one and work industriously in order to strive to accomplish the tasks assigned them by the state and to better their own livelihoods.

Mao Zedong
September 11, 1950

Note

1. Shijiazhuang is the capital city of Hebei Province.

Telegram to the South African Indian Congress
(September 13, 1950)

Source: *RMRB* (Sept. 15, 1950), 1.

The South African Indian Congress held a special conference on September 15-17, 1950, in Johannesburg to discuss the intensified discriminatory attacks on nonwhite populations in the Union of South Africa. The joint secretaries of the Congress sent a letter to Mao on August 17, appealing for moral support from the PRC. At the time of this telegram its president was Dr. G. M. Naicker.

Durban,
The Union of South Africa,
Joint Secretaries of the Conference of the South African Indian Congress

Messrs. A. I. Meer and J. N. Singh:

On behalf of the Chinese people, I completely support your stand on opposing the discrimination against and oppression of the nonwhite population (including Indians and other Asian nationalities) in South Africa by the government of the Union of South Africa.[1] Best wishes for the success of your conference.
(Signed and dated in Beijing)

Note

1. At this time the most imminent issue concerning racial discrimination in the Union of South Africa was the passing of the so-called Group Areas Act, which legislated against the rights of people of non-European descent to land tenure and ownership in the Union. (See text July 26, 1950.)

Letter to Zhang Wei
(September 19, 1950)

Source: *Shuxin*, p. 388.

According to the source, Zhang (1898-1975) was a native of Liuyang, Hunan, who had a fairly close friendship with Mao in the early years. From September 1949 on Zhang taught at the Second Army Surgeons' University in Shanghai.

Dear Zhang Wei:[1]
I have received and read your letter and I am greatly comforted. I am sorry not to have anything by way of a gift for your mother's eightieth birthday; I have only written a few words to express my felicitations.[2]
Best wishes for your health!
Mao Zedong
September 19

Notes

1. Mao used here the word *xiong*, which literally means "elder brother" but is a common mode of salutation for one's friends. See text Oct. 15, 1949, note 1.

2. According to the source Mao wrote an eight-character inscription, "Ru ri zhi sheng, ru yue zhi heng" (Rising with the Splendor of the Sun, Constant as the Glory of the Moon) for Zhang's mother's birthday.

Telegram to the Communist Party of Great Britain
(September 24, 1950)

Source: *RMRB* (Sept. 24, 1950), 1. Available English Translation: NCNA, *Daily Bulletin*, 123 (Sept. 27, 1950), 4.

Dear Comrade Pollitt[1] and all comrades of the Communist Party of Great Britain:

The Communist Party of China warmly congratulates the Communist Party of Britain on the thirtieth anniversary of its founding. The staunch and unflagging struggle of the Communist Party of Britain against capitalism and imperialism for the past thirty years has demonstrated that the Communist Party of Britain is the only hope of the British working class for attaining freedom and peace. To the members of the Communist Party of Britain and to all who are fighting for social justice and international peace in Britain, our best wishes for attaining final victory.
(Signed as Chairman of CPC)

Note

1. See text Nov. 20, 1950, source note.

Inscription for the National Conference
of Representatives of Combat Heroes
(September 25, 1950)

Source: *RMRB* (Sept. 27, 1950), 1.

Combat Heroes:
    You are the models of the People's Liberation Army. We hope that you will continue to exert effort to advance even further and strive for the building of a strong national defense force.

                              Mao Zedong

Address at the Opening Session of the National Congress
of Combat Heroes and the National Congress
of Worker-Peasant-Soldier Model Laborers
(September 25, 1950)

Source: *RMRB* (Sept. 25, 1950), 1. Other Chinese Texts: *XHYB*, II:6 (Oct. 15, 1950), 1259; *Xuanji*, V, pp. 30-31. Available English Translations: *SW*, V, pp. 41-42; *CDSP*, II:39 (Nov. 11, 1950), 14.

Comrade delegates of the National Congress of Combat Heroes and of the National Congress of Worker-Peasant-Soldier Model Laborers!
    The Central Committee of the Communist Party of China extends to you its warmest congratulations on [the convening of] your congresses and expresses its gratitude and respect for your work.
    In the struggle to annihilate the enemy and to restore and develop industrial and agricultural production, you have overcome many hardships and difficulties and have demonstrated tremendous courage, wisdom, and intiative. You are models for the entire Chinese nation, the backbone pushing the various undertakings of the people forward toward triumph, the reliable pillar

of the people's government, and the bridge linking the People's Government to the broad masses.

The Central Committee of the Communist Party of China calls on all the members of the Party and all the people of the country to learn from you. At the same time, it calls on you, all dear delegates here, as well as on the combat heroes and model laborers throughout the country, to continue to learn through fighting and to learn from the broad masses of the people. Only by completely doing away with conceit and complacency and by tirelessly continuing to learn can you continue to make outstanding contributions to the great People's Republic of China, and by doing so uphold your glorious titles.

China must build a powerful national defense force and a strong economy. These are two major undertakings. In fulfilling both of these we must rely on you comrades to unite as one with all the commanders and fighters in the People's Liberation Army and with the workers, peasants, and other people of the whole country, and on all of you to make a concerted effort together. On this occasion, when the first anniversary of the founding of the People's Republic of China is approaching, the convening of your meetings here is of tremendous significance. We congratulate you on the success of your congresses and extend to you our best wishes for great victories in your work in the future.

> The Central Committee
> The Communist Party of China
> September 25, 1950

Comments on Suppressing and Liquidating Counterrevolutionaries

(September 27, 1950)

Source: *Wansui* (1969), pp. 6-7. Other Chinese Texts: *Wansui* (1967a), p. 152; *Liang Chen anjian*, 4 (1968) (excerpt). Available English Translation: JPRS, *Miscellany*, I, p. 6.

The Wansui *(1967a) version differs from the* Wansui *(1969) version in that it gives October 9, 1943, for the first paragraph and September 27, 1950, for the second paragraph here.*

[The policy of] not executing a single [secret agent] and not arresting the majority of them is a policy to which we must adhere in the current struggle against secret agents. If not a single secret agent is to be executed, they will dare to make a clean breast of things; by not arresting the majority among them, only a small number [of cases] will have to be handled by the security organs, while the majority can be handled by the various [government offices] and schools themselves. We must make the Party committees in all the localities adhere to this policy.

Party leadership should be particularly stressed in security work, which in practice should be put under the direct leadership of the Party committee; otherwise there would be danger.

Reply to Ambassador of the People's Republic of Bulgaria
(September 30, 1950)

Source: *RMRB* (Oct. 2, 1950), 4.

Petkov served as ambassador of the People's Republic of Bulgaria to the PRC from September 1950 to August 1954.

Mr. Ambassador:

I am very pleased to accept the letter of credence from the Presidium of the National Assembly of the People's Republic of Bulgaria presented by Your Excellency, and I am grateful to Your Excellency for your warm felicitations and good wishes.

There exists a profound friendship between the people of the two countries, China and Bulgaria. The deeds of the Bulgarian people, under the leadership of their great leader, Dimitrov,[1] in their heroic struggle against domestic and foreign reactionaries, and their current achievements in economic and cultural construction, have always been regarded with deep concern and admiration by the Chinese people. Now, the Chinese people's revolution has been basically won, and diplomatic relations between China and Bulgaria have been established. I believe that this will not only further promote and consolidate the friendship between the peoples of our two countries, but will also strengthen the might of the camp for world peace and democracy.

I warmly welcome Your Excellency as the first ambassador extraordinary and plenipotentiary of the People's Republic of Bulgaria to the People's Republic of China and pledge to assist Your Excellency to the best of my ability in your work.

Sincere wishes for the prosperity of your country, the prospering of your people, and the good health of your head of state.

Note

1. Georgi Dimitrov was the leader of the "Fatherland Front" government of Bulgaria established on September 9, 1944. He was the first premier of the People's Republic of Bulgaria from its establishment on Dec. 4, 1947, to his death in 1949. He was known as the father of Bulgarian Communism.

Telegram to the German Democratic Republic
(October 4, 1950)

Source: *RMRB* (Oct. 17, 1950), 1.

President Wilhelm Pieck,
The German Democratic Republic

Your Excellency:

On this happy occasion of the first anniversary of the founding of the German Democratic Republic, on behalf of the Central People's Government of the People's Republic of China and the Chinese people, I sincerely extend to Your Excellency and the people of Germany our felicitations and our best wishes to the German people for new successes in their struggle to build a united, democratic, and peace-loving Germany.
(Signed as Chairman of CPG of PRC, dated, in Beijing)

Inscription on the Unity of the Chinese and Soviet Peoples
(October 5, 1950)

Source: *RMRB* (Oct. 5, 1950), 1 Available English Translation: NCNA, *Daily Bulletin*, 130 (Oct. 6, 1950), 1.

This inscription was released on Oct. 5, 1950, as part of a message from the Chinese leadership (including Liu Shaoqi and Song Qingling) to the Sino-Soviet Friendship Association congratulating it on the first anniversary of its founding.

The unity of the Chinese and Soviet peoples is of the greatest significance. When these two peoples are united as one, it will not be difficult for the peoples of the world to be united.

Inscription for Display of the PLA
(October 8, 1950 R)

Source: *Dagong bao* (Shanghai) (Oct. 10, 1950).

Victory belongs to the People!

Orders for the Chinese People's Volunteers
(Excerpts)
(October 8, 1950)

Source: *Xuanji*, V, pp. 32-33. Available English Translations: *SW*, V, pp. 32-33; JPRS, *Selections*, p. 9.

According to Xuanji, *p. 32, these are excerpts from the orders issued to the Chinese People's Volunteers (CPV) by Mao.*

To the leading comrades at all levels of the Chinese People's Volunteers:[1]

1) In order to assist the Korean people in their war of liberation, to repel the attacks of the American imperialists and their running dogs, and to defend the interests of the Korean people, the Chinese people and the people of all Eastern countries, the Chinese People's Volunteers are hereby ordered to move immediately into the territory of Korea, to join our Korean comrades in their

fight against the invaders, and to strive for a glorious victory.

2) When the People's Volunteers of our country move into Korean territory, they must express their friendship and respect for the Korean people, for the Korean People's Army, for the Democratic Government of Korea, for the Workers' Party of Korea, for other democratic parties, and for Kim Il Sung, the leader of the Korean people. They must strictly obey military and political discipline. This is an extremely important political basis on which the fulfillment of the military task will be ensured.

3) [The People's Volunteers] must fully anticipate all sorts of difficult circumstances that they may, and inevitably will, encounter and must be prepared to exercise a high degree of enthusiasm, courage, caution, and a spirit of perseverance in overcoming these difficulties. At the present moment, in general, both the international and domestic situations are to our advantage, and to the aggressors' disadvantage. If only our comrades are resolute, brave, good at uniting with the local people and at fighting against the aggressors, the final victory will be ours.

> Mao Zedong
> Chairman
> The Chinese People's Revolutionary Military Affairs Commission
> October 8, 1950
> Beijing

Note

1. On September 30, 1950, responding to hostilities between the North and South Korean governments, which had been going on since June 1950, and to the threat of the hostilities encroaching upon China's own territorial integrity and sovereignty, Zhou Enlai, premier of the GAC of the PRC, declared in a communique that "China may no longer sit back in unconcerned observation of the invasion of a neighboring country by imperialism." On October 25, on the invitation of the Democratic People's Republic of Korea, the Chinese People's Volunteers (CPV) were dispatched to cross the Yalu River into Korea. In the beginning the CPV were commanded, in an acting capacity, by Lin Biao. Following an injury to Lin, Peng Dehuai became the commander in chief of the CPV until the conclusion of the Korean War. The CPV was made up of units of the People's Liberation Army. Volunteer status was assumed and adopted as policy in the hopes of limiting the political liabilities that might result from the intervention of the PRC on behalf of the North Korean government in the conflict, for many of the same reasons that United Nations status was conferred on an essentially United States intervention in support of the South Korean side.

Letter to Wang Shoudao
(October 11, 1950)

Source: *Shuxin*, p. 389.

See text Oct. 9, 1949. See also text Oct. 22, 1952, for an explanation of people and events mentioned by Mao here.

Comrade Shoudao:

The two old gentlemen, Mr. Zhang Cilun and Mr. Luo Yuankun, veteran members of the educational circle of Hunan, are both now in their seventies. They have been teachers their entire lives and have done nothing bad. When I studied at the First Normal [School] of Hunan, Zhang was the principal and Luo the history teacher. Now I hear that these two gentlemen have very large families to feed and are in dire straits. I hope to propose that the provincial government of Hunan consider giving each of them, each month, a certain amount of grain subsidy in order to help them out in their old age. Also, according to the letter Mr. Luo Yuankun has sent me, Mr. Yuan Zhongqian, my former teacher in the Chinese language, has died and his wife, seventy years old, is starving. I hope that the provincial authorities will also consider giving her some appropriate relief. On this matter concerning these three people, Zhang, Luo and Dai, please let me know after you have decided how things should be handled, and please send someone to convey our regards to Mr. Zhang and Mr. Luo. Their address is Miaogaofeng Middle School. Dai, on the other hand, lives in Xinhua; [as for the exact address] you may ask Mr. Luo.

With my respect,

Mao Zedong
October 11

Telegram to the Republic of Czechoslovakia
(October 26, 1950)

Source: *RMRB* (Oct. 28, 1950), 1.

President Clement Grotewohl,
The Republic of Czechoslovakia

Your Excellency:

On this happy occasion of the thirty-second anniversary of the founding of the Republic of Czechoslovakia, on behalf of the government and people of the People's Republic of China, I sincerely extend to Your Excellency and the people of Czechoslovakia our felicitations and our best wishes to the Czechoslovakian people that in the great cause of building their homeland and advancing toward socialism, they will achieve greater successes with each passing day.
(Signed and dated in Beijing)

Telegram to Prince Gustaf Adolf of Sweden
on the Death of King Gustaf V

(October 31, 1950)

Source: *RMRB* (Nov. 2, 1950), 1. Available English Translation: *SCMP*, 2 (Nov. 2, 1950), 8.

Prince Gustaf Adolf,
Kingdom of Sweden

Your Highness:

I am informed of the untimely passing away of His Majesty King Gustaf V of the Kingdom of Sweden. I hereby extend to you my deep condolences.
(Signed as Chairman of CPG of PRC, dated, in Beijing)

In Response to Liu Yazi: A Poem
(October 1950)

Source: *Poems*, p. 47. Other Chinese Texts: *Shici*, p. 27; *Mao shici,* pp. 11-12. Available English Translations: *Poems*, p. 46; *Poems of Mao Tse-tung*, p. 81.

Appended to the publication of this poem is an explanatory note that indicates that this was written in response to two poems written by Liu Yazi on the occasion of viewing theatrical performances in National Day celebrations on October 3, 1950. Both Liu's poems and Mao's own were written in the ci pattern of "Wanxisha" (Sands of the Wan Stream), which was originally a Tang dynasty song whose literary grammar had been adopted by poets as a formula or pattern ever since. For Liu's poems in translation, see Poems of Mao Tse-tung, *p. 87. For more information on Liu, see text Dec. 2, 1949, source note.*

The night is long and no dawn comes to China's sky;[1]
For a hundred years the demons have trampled it with their twisting dances,
And there is no unity among its five myriads of people.
The chanticler's clarion pierces the gloom[2] and all the world is bright;
Music resounds from all quarters, as far as Yutian.[3]
Never have so many bards and minstrels gathered in such a joyous congregation.

Notes

1. The term *chixian* which Mao uses here translates literally as "land of crimson earth," and it is an archaic term for China's self-identification, derived from the writings of Zou Yan, the Chinese philosopher of the Warring States period, in which Zou describes the geographical features of the "four major continents of the world," one of which, identified as China and its neighboring regions, was called *Chixian shenzhou.*

2. This line is derived from the poem "Zhi jiu heng" by the Tang dynasty poet Li He. For the political significance of this saying in this poem see Guo Moruo's article in *Wenyi bao* (June 11, 1958).

3. Yutian is the name given in Han dynasty times to a location in what is now southern Xinjiang. It was, and to some extent is, populated primarily by the Uighurs, a minority nationality. The reference here is appropriate particularly because the theatrical performances that prompted this literary exclamation were done by the cultural work groups of various minority nationalities, including those from Xinjiang.

Telegram to the USSR
(November 5, 1950)

Source: *RMRB* (Nov. 7, 1950), 1. Available English Translations: NCNA, *Daily Bulletin*, 152 (Nov. 7, 1950), 5 (excerpt); *SCMP*, 5 (Nov. 7, 1950), 7 (excerpt); *CDSP*, II:45 (Dec. 23, 1950), 31.

The Union of Soviet Socialist Republics

Generalissimo Stalin:

On this happy occasion of the thirty-third anniversary of the Great October Socialist Revolution, on behalf of the government and the people of the People's Republic of China, I extend to Your Excellency and the great people of the Soviet Union our warmest congratulations. We wish the Soviet Union daily progress in its cause of socialist construction. May there be close and intimate unity between the peoples of China and the Soviet Union in their struggle to defend lasting peace in the world.
(Signed and dated in Beijing)

Telegram to Harry Pollitt
(November 20, 1950)

Source: *RMRB* (Nov. 25, 1950), 1. Available English Translation: *SCMP*, 17 (Nov. 26-27, 1950), 10.

Harry Pollitt was general secretary of the Communist Party of Great Britain, 1929-1956.

Comrade Pollitt and comrades of the Central Committee of the Communist Party of Great Britain:

Please accept our warm felicitations on the sixtieth birthday of Comrade

Pollitt, the long-tested leader of the British revolutionary workers' movement. We wish Comrade Pollitt good health.
(Signed as Chairman of CPC and dated)

Letter to Hu Qiaomu
(November 22, 1950)

Source: *Shuxin*, pp. 390-391.

See text May 22, 1950, source note.

Comrade Qiaomu:

Please draft a directive in the name of the Central Committee to amend our shortcomings in the practice of sending telegram messages. For example: we should no longer use such words as *zi, chou, ren, mou, dong, dong, jiang, ji,* etc., in lieu of the month and date.[1] Instead, we should write down the complete month and date [of the telegram], as, for instance, November 22. In general, for the signature we should use our full names, and not write the last [family] name and not the first [personal] name. In only those cases where the receiver of the message is entirely aware of the person [who sent the message] would it be permissible to use the last name without the first, such as "Liu-Deng," "Chen-Rao," etc.[2] For locales and the titles of the offices or organs [from which the telegrams are sent], they should in general be written out completely, and only in extremely rare cases would it be permissible to use such [traditional] provincial designations as Jing, Jin, Hu, Han.[3] Also, in terms of syntax we must learn to be grammatical and must ban the practice of omitting the subject, or the predicate, or other indispensable nouns, and where we use adjectives and adverbs we should be able to distinguish between their usage and character. Please take the lead in this matter and write up a preliminary draft and then invite Yang Shangkun, Li Tao, Qi Yanming, Xue Muqiao,[4] and other comrades whom you believe to be necessary to be invited [to join in this endeavor], hold one or two meetings with them and revise [the draft] and give it more substance, then send it to me for my perusal.

Mao Zedong
November 22

Notes

1. *Zi, chou, ren* and *mou* are the first 4 of the 12 *di ji* (or earth branches) in the duodecimal cycle. This cycle is combined in permutation with the decimal cycle known as the *tiangan* (Heavenly Cardinals) cycle to make up the sexagenary cycle which is used in traditional China to designate the years and other elements of time. This sexagenary cycle is also known as the *jiazi* system (taking the first of each cycle) and the *ganji* system. The decimal system is also used for designating common serial things such as grades, while the duodecimal cycle is commonly used to designate hour periods in the day. *Dong, dong, jiang, ji* are the first four of the rhyme keys *(yun mu)* in the *ping* segment of the conventional rhyming patterns for Chinese traditional poetry. In the past, when the Chinese sent telegrams, they would conventionally use the duodecimal cycle's items in sequence to indicate the twelve months, and the rhyme keys to represent the dates within each month.

2. According to the source, Liu-Deng stands for Liu Bocheng and Deng Xiaoping, and Chen-Rao for Chen Yi and Rao Shushi. For more biographical information on Liu, Chen and Rao, see text Sept. 11, 1959, note 14, text Oct. 11, 1955 (1), note 53, and text Mar. 31, 1955, note 7, respectively.

3. Jing stands for Beijing, Jin for Tianjin; Hu is the common name for Shanghai, and Han refers to Hankou.

4. Yang Shangkun was at this time the director of the General Office of the Central Committee of the CPC; for more information on Yang, see text May 19, 1953, source note.

Li Tao (1905-1970) was, according to the source, a deputy director of the Combat Operations Department of the Military Council at the time of the writing of this letter. Li was a veteran of the Red Army since the late 1920s and served as a political officer in Peng Dehuai's Third Army Corps and then the First Front Army under Peng and Zhu De. During the War of Resistance, Li was in Yanan and worked in the Third Office of the Central Intelligence Department, then as chief of the Second Bureau of the Army General Staff. Later he directed the Operations Department of the Army. Shortly after the war, Li joined Lin Biao's staff in the Northeast Democratic Allied Army. In the period after Liberation he was a spokesperson for the PLA headquarters and served in various positions on the People's Revolutionary Military Council. For more biographical information on Li, see *Zhonggong renming lu*, p. 234, and D. Klein and A. Clark, eds. (1971), I, pp. 530-531.

According to the source, Qi Yanming (1907-1978) was at the time of this letter the director of the Staff Office of the CPGC. A teacher by vocation, Qi joined the CPC sometime in the early 1930s and was active in the student movement. During the time of the War of Resistance he was in Yanan, still in the capacity of a teacher. In 1949 he participated actively in the preparation of the establishment of the new government and worked with many organizations and conferences of people in the cultural, scientific, and educational circles. He became a member of the preparatory committee of the CPPCC and served later as one of the deputy secretaries-general of the Standing Committee of the National Committee of that body. At the same time that he was head of the Staff Office of the CPGC, he also served as a deputy secretary-general of the Government Administration Council, which was a cabinet-like organization under the CPGC serving as the day-to-day administrative organ for state affairs (and which was later replaced by the State Council). Qi was also a top-ranking leader in the United Front Work Department of the Central Committee of the CPC under Li Weihan. (See text Feb. 18, 1951, note 3.) For more biographical information on Qi, see *Zhonggong renming lu*, p. 867, and D. Klein and A. Clark, eds. (1971), I, pp. 168-170.

Xue Muqiao (b. 1904) is arguably the second most influential economist for the CPC in the early years of the PRC – the most influential being Chen Yun. Xue began his career in the mid-1930s lecturing on the economic problems of China's revolutionary transformation at Kangda in Yanan (see text May-June 1955, note 17). Soon after the War of Liberation he took up a position of great responsibility in organizing the circles of economists and financial planners to prepare for setting up fiscal planning and economic policy organs of the new government. At the time of the writing of this letter, Xue was secretary-general of the Finance and Economics Committee under the Government Administration Council (with Chen Yun as the chairman of the committee). Xue held this post from October 1949 to August 1952. During the 1950s, Xue's great contribution was to plan and promote the establishment of a vast network for the gathering, reporting, and studying of economic and demographic statistics throughout China. Xue is also a very productive writer of textbooks on China's new economics and the chief CPC Party spokesperson for its economic policies. For more biographical information on Xue, see *Zhonggong renming lu*, pp. 1033-1034, and D. Klein and A. Clark, eds. (1971), I, pp. 370-372.

Telegram to the People's Republic of Albania
(November 26, 1950)

Source: *RMRB* (Nov. 29, 1950), 1. Available English Translation: *SCMP*, 17 (Nov. 29, 1950), 7.

Chairman,
The Presidium,
The People's Assembly,
The People's Republic of Albania

Mr. Omer Nishani:

On this happy occasion of the sixth anniversary of Albania, on behalf of the government and the people of the People's Republic of China, I sincerely extend to Your Excellency and the Albanian people our felicitations and our wishes that the people of Albania will achieve ever greater successes in their economic and cultural construction with each passing day.
(Signed and dated in Beijing)

Comment on Hearing of Mao Anying's Death
(November 1950)

Source: Excerpt from "Xu lao tan Mao zhuxi de ji jian shi" (Venerable Old Mr. Xu Talks About a Few Things About Chairman Mao) in *Zhongguo gongren*, 8 (Apr. 27, 1959), 21-24.

While we cannot be sure that it refers to the same conversation, one Red Guard publication records a different version of Mao's reaction to this event. It quotes Mao as saying:
"In war there must be sacrifice. Without sacrifices there will be no victory. To sacrifice my son or other people's sons are just the same. There are no parents in the world who do not treasure their children. But please do not feel sad on my behalf, because this is something entirely unpredictable."
See Dong Lin, Mao zhuxi geming de yi jia *(Chairman Mao's Revolutionary Family) (n.p.: n.d.) cited in L. Pye (1976), pp. 221-222.*

We understand the hows and whys of these things. There are so many common folk whose children have shed their blood and were sacrificed for the sake of the revolution. They are in need of consolation, and we ought to pay more attention to showing them greater concern.

Letter to Huang Niantian
(December 2, 1950)

Source: *Shuxin*, p. 392.

According to the source, Huang Niantian was at the time of this letter an assistant professor of the Chinese language at Sichuan University.

Mr. Niantian:[1]
Your gracious letter and the poetry of Mr. Huang Jigang[2] as well as your own writings have been received, and I am very grateful to you. I am very gratified by the fact that you have devoted yourself to scholarly improvement and to serving the people in the cause of education. You have my great veneration for that. I hope that you will continue to apply yourself to the task and that with each day's passing improvements will come and results will be achieved. That, indeed, is our fervent hope.
    In reply and with my respects,
                        Mao Zedong
                        December 2

Notes

1. See text Nov. 17, 1949, note 2, for an explanation of this usage.

2. This refers to Huang Niantian's father, Huang Kan (Jigang is his honorific name, or *zi*), 1886-1935, who was a noted Chinese poet and philologist. Huang was a pupil of Zhang Binglin while studying in Japan in the mid-1900s, and through Zhang's influence he became an anti-Manchu revolutionary in the 1911 revolutionary movement. Later Huang taught at several major universities. As a philologist, Huang was most famous for his writing of the *Ciyun sheng lei biao* (A Table of the Phonetic Categories from the *Ciyun*) published in 1936 and his work on the famous *Wenxin diaolong* by Liu Xie, published in 1934. He also did path-breaking work in the interpretation and textual criticism of Gu Yanwu (a seventeenth century scholar)'s renowned *Ri zhi lu*. Huang's poems were also published in three collections, *Xiqiu hua shi*, *Shiqiao ji*, and *Yu Longshan shi*.

Here Mao used the word *ci*, which we translate as "poetry." This referes to a particular poetic genre. See text Jan. 12, 1957, note 1. For more biographical information on Huang, see H. Boorman et al., eds. (1968), II, pp. 197-198.

Telegram to Participants of Demonstration in Tianjin
(December 2, 1950)

Source: *RMRB* (Dec. 3, 1950), 1. Available English Translations: NCNA, *Daily Bulletin*, 173 (Dec. 6, 1950), 1; *SCMP*, 22 (Dec. 3-4, 1950), 9.

To Messrs. Li Zhuchen,[1] Bi Mingqi, and Zhu Jisheng, chairman and deputy chairmen of the Tianjin Municipal Federation of Industry and Commerce, and to our 42,989 patriotic countrymen who took part in the great demonstration, parade, and rally to Resist United States [Aggression] and Aid Korea, Protect the Home and Defend the Homeland undertaken by the industrial and commercial circles in the municipality of Tianjin:

I have read the telegram that you sent me on November 30. You have clearly recognized the reactionary nature of the aggression that the United States' imperialists have launched against China and Korea. You have not been duped by them; nor have you been cowed by their threats; instead you have taken a determined stand on the patriotic premise of resisting United States [aggression], aiding Korea, protecting your homes, and defending the homeland and have held a righteous demonstration and parade on November 30. This is worthy of our acclaim. The American imperialists have carried out a lot of deceptive propaganda among the Chinese people, and no patriot should believe in these false arguments. The American imperialists have invaded Korea, invaded China's [province of] Taiwan, bombarded the northeastern part of China, and moreover have employed all sorts of hooligan tactics to threaten the Chinese people. All patriots should be resolute in their resistance to the aggression of the American imperialists and should not succumb to their threats. The heroic deeds of the Chinese People's Volunteers to resist United States [Aggression], Aid Korea, Protect the Home, and Defend the Homeland are worthy of our praise and admiration. It is absolutely correct for all patriotic people among the workers, peasants, intellectuals, industrialists, and business people throughout the nation to unite together and resist the aggression of American imperialism. I hope that all patriotic industrialists and business people in the whole of China will join with the broad masses of the people and knit themselves into a united front against imperialist aggression that is even more consolidated than before. This will signify that the Chinese people are bound to achieve final victory in the sacred struggle against imperialist aggression.

(Signed and dated)

Note

1. See text Jun. 23, 1951, source note.

Inscription for the Air Force
(December 15, 1950 R)

Source: Released in *Jinbu ribao* (Dec. 15, 1950), 1.

Create a strong and powerful People's Air Force to wipe out the remnants of the enemy's forces and to consolidate our national defense.

Mao Zedong

Letter to Chen Shutong
(December 18, 1950)

Source: *Shuxin*, p. 393.

Chen (1876-1966) was a venerated "democratic personage." He was at this time a vice-chairman of the National Committee of the CPPCC and the head of the All-China Federation of Industry and Commerce. For more biographical information on Chen, see text Dec. 8, 1956, note 22.

Dear Venerated Mr. Shu[tong]:[1]

I have received and read your letter, and have spoken with Comrades Chen Yun and Bo Yibo[2] about the matter, asking them to think about how it can be handled. There are some five million industrial and commercial units in the country, of which approximately three million are in the commercial area. At a time when the economic enterprise [of the nation] as a whole is to be switched from the old tracks to the new track of New Democracy,[3] it is inevitable that large numbers of commercial firms and handicraft industrial units will need to be reorganized or rechanneled into other trades. The government should give good guidance in this matter.

Allow me to pay my respects and wish you good health,

Mao Zedong
December 18

Notes

1. Mao here used the term *Shu lao* in which the word *lao* (old) refers to Chen's venerated status. It is a matter of common usage to attach this term to a part of the person's personal name, without using the person's last, or family, name as a form of address to one's elders. See text Feb. 17, 1951.

2. Chen Yun was at this time a vice-premier of the Government Administration Council and the director of the the Finance and Economics Committee. Bo was a deputy-director of that committee and Minister of Finance of the PRC. For more biographical information on Chen and Bo, see text Jan. 20, 1956, note 9, and text Oct. 29, 1949, source note, and text Aug. 12, 1953, note 5, respectively.

3. For the meaning of this term, see text Jun. 15, 1953, note 2.

Comment on Suppressing and Liquidating
Counterrevolutionaries
(December 19, 1950)

Source: *Wansui* (1969), p. 7. Other Chinese Texts: *Wansui* (1967a), p. 152; *Xuanji*, V, p. 42. Available English Translations: JPRS, *Miscellany*, I, p. 6; *SW*, V, p. 52.

Both Wansui *(1967a) and* Xuanji *record only the first phrase of the comment.*

In Wansui *(1969),* Wansui *(1967a), and* Xuanji, V, *this comment here appears as the first of many comments on the subject of suppressing counterrevolutionary activity in the country. These comments span the period 1950-51 in all three cases. (In* Wansui *(1967a) there are also two comments that exist outside this time frame.) The vaulting of the issue of the suppression of counterrevolutionaries into prominence in the consciousness of the CPC leadership was partially, if not exclusively, related to the eruption of the Korean War and the imminent task of carrying out land reform programs, both of which involved CPC positions and policies particularly vulnerable to sabotage and clandestine opposition. It should be noted that in July 1950 the Organizational Regulations of the People's Courts were promulgated, in which the basic legal principles of dealing with counterrevolutionary activites were prominently featured.*

In suppressing counterrevolutionaries, please make sure that you strike firmly, accurately, and relentlessly, so that nothing [detrimental] can be said about it among the various circles in society.

Telegram to the Communist Party of France
(December 23, 1950)

Source: *RMRB* (Dec. 27, 1950), 1. Available English Translation: *SCMP*, 36 (Dec. 22-24, 1950), 20.

SCMP *cites an NCNA dispatch of December 23, 1950, while* RMRB *cites an NCNA dispatch of December 26.*

Dear Comrade Duclos[1] and all comrades of the Communist Party of France:

It is with great elation that the Central Committee of the Communist Party of China celeberates the thirtieth anniversary of the founding of the Communist Party of France.

In its thirty years of hard struggle, the Communist Party of France has proved that it is the most faithful defender of the interests of the working class of France and the entire French people.

The Communist Party of France and the working class of France are at present uniting with the entire French people to oppose resolutely the war plans of the government of the United States of America.[2] This plan is aimed at turning the French people into slaves and sacrificial victims for the monopoly capitalists of the United States.

The Communist Party of China is resolute in its conviction that the struggle of the Communist Party of France is just and that it is bound to be victorious in the end.

Long live the unity of the Chinese and French peoples in their common struggle against the aggression of American imperialism.

Long live the Communist Party of France, which is faithful to the interests of the working class of France and of the international working class, and long live its leader, Comrade Maurice Thorez.[3]

Long live Comrade Stalin, leader of the working class and progressive humanity throughout the world!

(Signed as Chairman of CPC)

Notes

1. Jacques Duclos was then acting secretary general of the Parti Communiste Francais (PCF).

2. Mao appears to be alluding to the position taken by the PCF in 1949-1950 in fierce opposition to the "imperialist aggressiveness" of the United States, and particularly its reaction to the United States' veiled threat to use atomic weapons if necessary. This French reaction was exemplified in the PCF's spearheading the Stockholm peace proposal in March 1950.

3. See text Apr. 28, 1950, source note. Thorez suffered a stroke in October 1950 and at the time of this telegram was in the Soviet Union for treatment.

Inscription for the First Normal School of Hunan
(December 29, 1950)

Source: *RMRB* (July 15, 1967), 5. Other Chinese Texts: *Jiaoyu yulu*, p. 26; *Yulu* (1964), p. 84; *Mao zai xinzhong*, p. 10.

See text Oct. 15, 1949, source note.

To be a teacher of the people, one must first be a student of the people.

Letter to Zhou Shizhao
(December 29, 1950)

Source: *Shuxin*, pp. 395-396.

See text Oct. 15, 1949, source note.

My Dear Dunyuan:[1]

I have written the words that you have told me to write; I wonder if they are usable?[2]

I have received both the letter you wrote on your departure and the one from Changsha. Thank you very much. I agree with everything you said. These are things that can be done (some of them must be done gradually). [As far as convening] a conference of [people in] normal education, let me speak about it first with Mr. Ma,[3] but I believe that in general it is possible.

I am now in the midst of correcting my fault of sleeping late. I did it for about half a month – working according to the sun's schedule and not that of the moon. Lately, however, I have reverted back to the old way. After the new year I shall try to change it around again. I am also paying more attention to getting some more rest and eating correctly. In any case, as you said, if we take these things to be big things and serious things, and not as small and insignificant things, we stand a chance of correcting them.

I wish you and your colleagues smooth success in your work and happiness for the new year.

Mao Zedong
December 29

Notes

1. See text Oct. 15, 1949, note 1.

2. According to the source, this refers to the words "Di yi shifan" (First Normal School), which Zhou asked Mao to inscribe as a billboard for the First Normal School of Hunan of which Zhou was the principal, and the inscription "Yao zuo renmin de xiansheng xian zuo renmin de xuesheng" (To be a teacher of the people one must first be a student of the people). See preceding document in this collection.

3. This refers, according to the source, to Ma Xulun. See text June 19, 1950 (1), source note.

Telegram to the People's Republic of Romania
(December 29, 1950)

Source: *RMRB* (Jan. 30, 1950), 1. Available English Translation: *SCMP*, 39 (Dec. 29-31, 1950), 17.

The President,
The Presidium,
The Grand National Assembly,
The People's Republic of Romania

Mr. Constantin Parhon:

On this happy occasion of the third anniversary of the founding of the People's Republic of Romania, on behalf of the government and people of the People's Republic of China, I sincerely extend to Your Excellency and the Romanian people our felicitations and our best wishes that the prosperity of the People's Republic of Romania will increase with the passing of each day. (Signed as Chairman of CPG of PRC, dated, in Beijing)

1951

Comment on "A Summary of the Relationship
between the Various Departments of the Military
and the Soviet Advisors"

(January 1, 1951)

Source: *Ziliao xuanbian,* p. 145.

This is from a source included in the Red Guard publications (see bibliography to this volume, introductory paragraphs) which contain no further information regarding the source itself or the context of this comment. The "summary" mentioned in the title may be a report from some military department, probably the Military Affairs Commission, or the General Political Department of the People's Liberation Army. This is, however, only our speculation.

We must never be arrogant or complacent. We must learn every bit of the advanced experiences of the Soviet Union in order to change our armed forces from their condition of backwardness and construct our armed forces into a most superior modernized military force [in the world], so as to be able to assure ourselves of the ability to defeat, in the future, the invasion of the imperialists' armies.

Telegram to the Union of Burma
(January 2, 1951)

Source: *RMRB* (Jan. 4, 1951), 1. Available English Translations: NCNA, *Daily Bulletin*, 194 (Jan. 8, 1951), 2; *SCMP*, 41 (Jan. 4, 1951), 9.

Mr. Sao Shwe Thaike,
President,
Union of Burma:

On this happy occasion of the first anniversary of the founding of your republic, on behalf of the government and people of the People's Republic of China, I sincerely extend to Your Excellency and the people of Burma our felicitations and our best wishes that the friendship between the Chinese and Burmese peoples will increase with the passing of each day.
(Signed as Chairman of CPG of PRC, dated, in Beijing)

Telegram to Wilhelm Pieck
(January 2, 1951)

Source: *RMRB* (Jan. 3, 1951), 1.

Dear President Wilhelm Pieck:

On this occasion of your seventy-fifth birthday, I extend to you on my own behalf and on the behalf of the Central People's Government of the People's Republic of China our highest esteem and warmest felicitations.
(Signed as Chairman of CPG of PRC)

Letter to Rao Shushi and Chen Pixian
(January 10, 1951)

Source: *Shuxin*, pp. 397-398.

According to the source, Rao (1903-1975) was at the time of this letter first secretary of the East China Bureau of the Central Committee of the CPC. For more biographical information on Rao, see text Mar. 31, 1955, note 7. (See also D. Klein and A. Clark, eds. [1971], I, pp. 408-411, and Zhonggong renming lu, *appendix, p. 128.) Chen was at this time secretary of the Southern Jiangsu district committee of the CPC, political commissar of the Southern Jiangsu Military Region and member of the East China Military and Administrative Committee. For more biographical information on Chen, see text Sept. 17, 1957, note 5. (See also* Zhonggong renming lu, *pp. 579-580.)*

Comrades Shushi and Pixian:

Mr. Huang Yanpei[1] has received many letters from landlords in which they have filed complaints with him. I have sent to him copies of the two directives of the East China Bureau, one issued in December of last year on rectifying the shortcomings in the work of suppressing counterrevolutionaries and the other issued on January 4 on rectifying shortcomings in the work of land reform,[2] and he has gained a better understanding of the situation. Mr. Huang is prepared to go to southern Jiangsu this month to do some inspection and investigation in the various localities. I have bidden him to contact you, and I hope that at the time you will discuss in detail the general overall situation with him.

Mao Zedong

January 10

Notes

1. See text Feb. 17, 1951, source note.

2. For these movements see text Dec. 19, 1950, source note, and text Feb. 18, 1951, note 2, respectively.

Letter to Xu Beihong

(January 14, 1951)

Source: *Shuxin*, p. 399. Other Chinese Text: *Meishu fenglei*, 3 (Aug. 1967), 4.

For more on Xu Beihong see text Nov. 29, 1949, source note. This is the third letter Mao wrote to Xu after late 1949. See also the letter of August 26, 1950.

Mr. Beihong:[1]

I have received your letter of January 13 and also the two copies of the book by Mr. Shi Yongmou[2] that you enclosed with the letter. I agree with your idea that we should take care of Mr. Shi.[3] The best thing would be to provide a position for him in the school that you are running. If this is not possible, please bring this letter to the Cultural Commission of the Party Central Committee and work out a solution with them.

In reply to your letter, and with my deep respects.

Mao Zedong

January 14

Notes

1. See text Nov. 17, 1949, note 2.

2. According to the source, Shi Yongmou was a secondary school teacher in Tianjin. The book referred to here is the book *Lun yu zheng* (Rectifying the Book *Lun yu* [Confucius' Analects]) written by Shi. In the *Meishu fenglei* source Shi's name is not given and is replaced instead by XXX.

3. Here *Meishu fenglei* has Mr. X.

Letter to Li Sian
(January 14, 1951)

Source: *Shuxin*, p. 400.

According to the source, Li Sian was an old acquaintance of Mao's, and a member of the Xinmin xuehui (New People's Study Society) that Mao and others formed in the early 1910s. He was a member of the staff at the Hunan Province Historical and Cultural Studies Institute.

Mr. Sian:

I have received your two letters and am very gratified and elated to hear from you. I agree that you should come to Beijing. If you wish to enter, with our classmates Jiang Zhuru[1] and others, the University of the Revolution to study for a period, you may enroll there. Otherwise some other plans for your work will be made. When you come you should bring this letter with you to contact Director Li Weihan of the United Front Department of the Central Committee of the Communist Party of China[2] and discuss with him the problem of your enrollment or employment.

In reply and with my respect,

Mao Zedong

January 14

Notes

1. Jiang was a classmate of Mao's when Mao studied at the First Normal School of Hunan. For more on Jiang, see text Nov. 25, 1958(2), note 12.

2. See text Feb. 18, 1951, note 3. For more biographical information on Li Weihan, see text Apr. 9, 1951, source note.

Letter to Ma Xulun
(January 15, 1951)

Source: *Shuxin*, p. 401. Other Chinese Text: *Jiaoyu geming*, 4 (May 6, 1967), 2 (excerpt).

See also Mao's letter to Ma of June 19, 1950.

Mr. Yichu:[1]

The question of student health, which I discussed with you earlier, is profoundly deserving of our attention. I suggest using administrative measures to resolve this problem concretely. I have enclosed herewith a telegram issued by the East China Bureau of the CPC; please read it. The third point deals precisely with this problem; it proposes the policy of putting health first and study second, and I believe that it is correct. Please discuss this with the comrades, the various deputy ministers [of education], and see how it can be carried out.

In salute,

Mao Zedong
January 15

Note

1. Yichu is Ma Xulun's honorific name, or *zi*. For this usage see text Mar. 27, 1951, note 1.

Comment on Suppressing and Liquidating Counterrevolutionaries
(January 17, 1951)

Source: *Xuanji*, V, p. 42. Other Chinese Texts: *Wansui* (1969), p. 7; *Wansui* (1967a), p. 152. Available English Translations: *SW*, V, p. 53; JPRS, *Miscellany*, I, p. 6.

The Wansui *versions contain only the second paragraph of this comment. The* Miscellany *translation is done on the basis of the* Wansui *versions. See text Dec. 19, 1950, source note.*

A bunch of bandit chiefs, local ruffians and petty tyrants, and secret agents[1] in the twenty-one *xian* of western Hunan [Province] have been executed, and preparations are being made to have another bunch executed by local authorities this year. I believe this arrangement is very necessary. Only in this way will we be able to quell the enemy's arrogance and give full play to the people's morale. If we are weak and indecisive, and excessively indulgent and protective of evil people, then we well bring disaster upon the people and divorce [ourselves] from the masses.

To ["]strike firmly["] means to pay attention to strategy. To ["]strike accurately["] means to avoid executing [people] by mistake. To ["]strike relentlessly["] means to execute resolutely all reactionaries who deserve to be executed. Of course, we will not execute those who do not deserve to be executed. As long as we do not kill anyone by mistake, even if there is an outcry on the part of the bourgeoisie, we will not have to be frightened by their outcry.

Note

1. This is a reference to the policy of suppressing *tu hao e ba* (local tyrants) who bullied the peasants in the past, and *fei shou* (bandit chiefs, or heads of local armed groups who had been affiliated with the KMT during the Civil War). This was considered the first stage of the land reform movement. (See text Feb. 18, 1951, note 2.) In addition, many people who gained and enjoyed special economic advantages and social privileges in the local areas prior to 1949 by way of affiliation with the KMT, and who obstructed the transformation of the Chinese economy after 1949, were considered to be *te wu* (secret agents) "left behind" by the KMT to carry out sabotage in Communist China. See text June 6, 1950(1), paragraph 2.

Directive to the Chinese People's Volunteers
(January 19, 1951)

Source: *Xuanji*, V, p. 33. Available English Translations: *SW*, V, p. 44; JPRS, *Selections*, p. 10.

For an explanation of the Chinese People's Volunteers, see text Oct. 8, 1950, note 1.

The comrades of the two countries of China and Korea must unite as brothers, stick together through thick and thin, must rely on each other in life and death, and fight heroically to the end in order to defeat the common enemy. The Chinese comrades must treat the affairs of Korea as if they were their own affairs. Our officers and soldiers must be taught to cherish every hill, every stream, every blade of grass, and every tree in Korea and not to take a single needle or thread from the Korean people; [we must act and think in Korea] just as we do inside our own country.[1] This is the political foundation for victory. If we can do this, then final victory will definitely be achieved.

Note

1. This is a reference to the second of the Three Main Points of Discipline originally issued to

the Workers-Peasants Red Army in 1928 and formulated as part of the famous Three Main Points of Discipline and Eight Cardinal Points of Observation for the People's Liberation Army issued by PLA headquarters on October 10, 1947. See text Jun. 30, 1953, note 6.

Letter to Zhang Lan
(January 22, 1951)

Source: *Shuxin*, p. 402.

Zhang Lan (1872-1955) was at the time of this letter chairman of the China Democratic League in whose establishment in 1941 he took part. (In 1941 the League of Chinese Democratic Parties and Organizations was formed and in 1944 this was reorganized as the China Democratic League. It became one of the most influential "democratic parties" in the PRC in the first decade of the republic. See text Sept. 21, 1949, note 1, and text July 1, 1957, note 10.) He was also vice-chairman of the CPGC and a deputy-chairman of the Standing Committee of the NPC. For more biographical information on Zhang, see H. Boorman et al., eds. (1967), I, pp. 82-83.

Mr. Biaofang:[1]

I am sending you a copy of a report submitted to me by Comrade Deng Xiaoping, secretary of the Southwest Bureau [of the Central Committee of the CPC]. Please read it (you may have your secretary read it to you), and you may see from it the general situation with the work in the Southwest. Please return it to me when you are done. How are you? I am very concerned about your health.

With my respect,

Mao Zedong
January 22

Note

1. Biaofang is Zhang's *zi*, or honorific name. For this usage see text Oct. 15, 1949, note 1.

Telegram to the Communist Party of Italy

(January 22, 1951)

Source: *RMRB* (Jan. 23, 1951), 1. Available English Translation: *SCMP*, 55 (Jan. 24, 1951), 3.

Comrade Longo and all comrades on the
Central Committee of the Communist Party of Italy:

On this occasion of the thirtieth anniversary of the founding of the Communist Party of Italy, I sincerely extend to you our warmest congratulations. The Communist Party of Italy has made great achievements in the past struggle against Fascism, in its present struggle against the United States' aggression and war plans, and in the struggle for a People's Democratic Italy, and has thereby made itself the nucleus of the Italian working class and of all patriotic people in Italy. We firmly believe that under the correct leadership of Comrade Togliatti[1] and the Central Committee of the Communist Party of Italy you are sure to win the final victory in your just cause.
(Signed as Chairman of CPC)

Note

1. Palmiro Togliatti (1893-1965) was at this time secretary general of the Communist Party of Italy. He was at the time of this telegram in the Soviet Union convalescing from a motor accident and thus the telegram was addressed to Longo, the deputy secretary general. See G. Bocca (1973), pp. 543-544. See also text Mar. 25, 1953, source note.

Comment on Suppressing and Liquidating Counterrevolutionaries

(January 24, 1951)

Source: *Wansui* (1969), p. 7. Other Chinese Text: *Wansui* (1967a), p. 152. Available English Translation: JPRS, *Miscellany*, I, p. 7.

With regard to secret agents[1] and leaders of secret organizations and sects against whom we have not gathered evidence, in order to avoid making a mistake and thus trapping ourselves in a passive position, we should carry out investigations in order to obtain conclusive evidence, and not arrest people or execute people arbitrarily.

Note

1. See text Jan. 17, 1951, note 1.

Telegram to the Republic of India
(January 24, 1951)

Source: *RMRB* (Jan. 26, 1951), 1. Available English Translation: *SCMP*, 57 (Jan. 26-27, 1951), 1.

Mr. Rajendra Prasad,
President,
The Republic of India:

On behalf of the government and the people of the People's Republic of China, I sincerely extend to Your Excellency and the government and people of India our felicitations on this happy occasion of the anniversary of the founding of your republic, and our best wishes that the friendship between the Chinese and Indian peoples will grow with the passing of each day.
(Signed as Chairman of CPG of PRC, dated, in Beijing)

Toast at a Reception Given by Ambassador of India
(January 26, 1951)

Source: *RMRB* (Jan. 27, 1951), 1. Other Chinese Text: *XHYB*, III:4 (Feb. 25, 1951), 777. Available English Translation: *SCMP*, 57 (Jan. 26-7, 1951), 2.

The reception was held in celebration of the first anniversary of the founding of the Republic of India, whose ambassador to the PRC at this time was K. M. Panikkar.

The Indian nation is a great nation. The people of India are a very good people. For many thousands of years, the friendship between the two nations of China and India and between the peoples of the two countries has been very good. Today, in celebrating the anniversary of the founding of the Republic of India, we hope that the Chinese and Indian nations will continue to be united and to strive for peace. People all over the world need peace. There is only a very small minority who want war. Let India, China, the Soviet Union, and all other peace-loving countries and peoples unite and strive for peace in the Far East and in the entire world. We salute and celebrate the founding of the Republic of India and congratulate the Indian people and your president.

Telegram to the USSR
(February 12, 1951)

Source: *RMRB* (Feb. 14, 1941), 1. Available English Translation: *SCMP*, 66 (Feb. 14, 1951), 1.

See text Jan. 2, 1950, note 1, for information on this treaty.

Chairman,
The Council of Ministers,
The Union of Soviet Socialist Republics

Generalissimo Stalin:

On this occasion of the anniversary of the signing of the Sino-Soviet Treaty of Friendship, Alliance, and Mutual Assistance, please accept our sincere gratitude and felicitations to Your Excellency and the government and people of the Soviet Union. The signing of the Sino-Soviet Treaty of Friendship, Alliance, and Mutual Assistance has not only been of great benefit to the construction of New China, but has also provided a strong guarantee for resisting aggression and defending the peace and security of the Far East and the entire world. We hereby send our sincere wish for the further advancement and consolidation of the friendship and cooperation between China and the Soviet Union.
(Signed as Chairman of CPG of PRC, dated, in Beijing)

Letter to Huang Yanpei
(February 17, 1951)

Source: *RMRB* (Dec. 25, 1983). Other Chinese Text: *Shuxin*, p. 403.

Huang Yanpei (1878-1965) was the chairman of the Democratic National Construction Association in 1945. A prominent educator and spokesman for vocational eduction, he was also a founding member of the China Democratic League. From 1949 to 1954 he was Minister of Light Industry for the PRC government. For more biographical information on Huang, see H. Boorman et al., eds. (1970), II, pp. 210-213.

Dear Venerable Old Mr. Huang Ren:[1]

I have just sent to you a piece of intelligence on correcting [the policy] of unlimited leniency[2] in Guangdong. Now [with this letter] I forward another set [of simliar intelligence] on Guangxi. Please read and consult them. These two places are the most typical examples. Other areas are not as extreme as they are, but in general they are not too far off; there has been a very common phenomenon of causing the dissatisfaction of the masses. If the bandit leaders and the repeat offenders are not executed, the bandits cannot be cleanly eliminated, and instead, there will be more and more bandits for us to eliminate.[3] If we do not execute the [local] tyrants, the peasant associations[4] cannot be formed and the peasants will not dare to divide up the land. If we do not execute the *chief* secret agents,[5] then we will see more and more cases of sabotage and murder. In any case, with regard to the bandit leaders, [local tyrants] and (the chief) secret agents, we have to adopt a resolute policy of suppression, and only then can the peasants turn around[6] and the people's political power be consolidated. Naturally, with regard to those people who may be executed but do not have to be executed, we should sentence them to terms of imprisonment, or turn them over to the masses to be held in probationary supervision and reform them through labor and not execute them. Just as there should be a limit to leniency, there should also be a limit to suppression; it would be wrong to not set a limit on things. In those regions where the problem has already been resolved and the masses are already satisfied, we should no longer execute anyone.

Allow me to express my regards and high respect for you.

Mao Zedong
February 17

Notes

1. The address Mao used was, in Chinese, "Huang Ren lao" in which *lao* (old) is a term of respect paid to elder people and is often translated as "venerable old." The word *Ren* is a reference to Huang Yanpei's *zi* (or honorific name) "Renzhi."

2. This is a reference to the policy of leniency in dealing with "landlords and counterrevolutionaries" who were obstructing the land reform movement either by active opposition or by the very fact that they held large landholdings and special privileges over the peasant masses. For land reform, see text Feb. 18, 1951, note 2.

3. See text Jan. 17, 1951, note 1.

4. As early as in his "Report on an Investigation of the Peasant Movement in Hunan" (*SW*, I, pp. 23-59) in 1927, Mao spoke of peasant associations (*nongmin xiehui*) as mass organizations designed to pull the peasantry together. Later, in the period of land reform, various forms of peasant associations were relied upon to carry out the programs themselves.

5. See text Jan. 17, 1951, note 1. The emphasis is in the original Chinese text.

6. The term here is *fanshen*, which literally means to turn one's body over, or right-side-up. It has come to connote the liberation of previously oppressed people, particularly the poor peasants. The description is a graphic one, alluding to the notion that for centuries the peasants had stooped and bent their backs so that the rulers and landlords could ride on their backs and whip them into submission. The term is often simply transliterated rather than translated when rendered in English, since no English aphoristic or figurative translation seems to convey the full force of the meaning of the term. See W. Hinton (1966), p. vii.

Main Points of Resolution at a Political Bureau Meeting
(February 18, 1951)

Source: *Xuanji*, V, pp. 34-38. Available English Translation: *SW*, V, pp. 45-49.

According to this source, this is an internal Party circular drafted by Mao on behalf of the Central Committee. It summarizes the main points of the major tasks of the CPC at the time (such as land reform, united front work, etc.).

The Central Committee convened a meeting of the Political Bureau in mid-February that was also attended by comrades in positions of responsibility in the various bureaus of the Central Committee. A number of important issues were discussed, and the main points of the resolution are circulated as follows:

I. Twenty-two Months for Preparatory Work:

[We must] make all the cadres from the provincial and municipal levels and above understand the idea of [having] "three years for preparation and ten years for planned economic construction." As of now, there are still twenty-two months in the period of preparation. We must proceed to intensify the work in all areas.

II. The Propaganda and Education Campaign for Resisting U.S. [Aggression] and Aiding Korea:[1]

We must continue to promote this movement throughout the entire country. We should deepen it where it has already been promoted, and spread it to where it has not yet been promoted so that every person in every place in the entire country will receive this type of education.

III. Land Reform:[2]

1. During the busy farming season, [this movement] should be suspended for a while in every place for [people]to sum up [their] experiences.

2. Strive for a bumper harvest this year.

3. Rely on the *xian* conferences of peasants' representatives and the training classes.[3]

4. Actively [work to] create [favorable] conditions. No matter where or when, if conditions are not ripe, do not force [the land reform movement] through.

5. As soon as land reform is accomplished, immediately switch over to the two major tasks of production and education.

6. We endorse the method of the East China [Bureau] of returning security money in installments.[4]

7. Persuade the peasants that it is to our advantage not to use inhuman punishment and torture.

8. After the land reform, draw up more districts and *xiang*, so as to reduce the administrative area of the district and *xiang*.

IV. Suppressing Counterrevolutionaries:[5]

1. Generally, death sentences must be passed [only in consultation] with the masses, and the opinion of the democratic personages must also be sought.

2. There should be very strict control; we must not be indiscriminate; mistakes must not be made.

3. Pay attention to the "middle 'layer'"[6] carefully weed out the counterrevolutionaries secretly hidden among the old personnel and the newly [recruited] intellectuals.

4. Pay attention to the "inner layer"; carefully clean out the counterrevolutionaries who have infiltrated the Party and strengthen to the greatest possible extent our work in guarding secret information.

5. In addition, do education work among the cadres and back up the cadres in their work.

V. Work in the Urban Areas:

1. This year, each bureau of the Central Committee, each subbureau, provincial, municipal [Party] committee, and the [Party] committee for each autonomous region must hold two meetings on urban work with agendas that are in accord with the notices issued by the [Party] Center and must submit two reports on this special topic to the Central Committee.

2. Strengthen the leadership of the Party committees over work in the urban

areas and put the resolution of the Second Plenum of the Seventh Central Committee into practice.[7]

3. Do education [work] among the cadres and [establish] clearly and firmly [in their minds] the idea that we rely on the working class.

4. In the factories, [while taking on] the fulfillment of the production plans as the central task, carry out unified [Party] leadership over the Party [organization], the political [organization], the trade unions, and the [New Democratic Youth] League.[8]

5. Strive hard to gradually improve the workers' [standard of] living on the basis of increased production.

6. In planning for municipal reconstruction we should consistently implement the viewpoint that everything must serve production and the working people.

7. The All-China Federation of Trade Unions[9] and the higher levels of each trade union should place emphasis on solving the specific problems at lower levels.

8. The Party committees and trade unions should place emphasis on the creation of model experiences, and these should be quickly spread to all other places.

VI. Rectifying the Party and Building the Party:

1. Ours is a great, glorious and correct Party. This is the primary aspect and must be affirmed and explained to the cadres at all levels. Nevertheless, the existing problems must be straightened out. Moreover, a cautious attitude should be adopted regarding Party building in new liberated areas, and this too should be clearly explained.

2. Both the rectification of the Party and Party building must come under the strict control of the Central Committee and the various bureaus of the Central Committee; the lower levels must not act as they please.

3. The rectification of the Party should be accomplished in three years' time. The steps [to be taken in this movement] should be as follows: [First,] take a year's time (1951) to carry out extensive education on how to be a member of the Communist Party, so that all the Party members will understand the standards expected of a member of the Communist Party, and to train personnel in organizational work. At the same time, we will carry out model experiments. After that, we should carry out the rectification of the Party based on [our] experiences. The cities, however, can proceed with Party rectification in 1951. In the process of rectifying the Party, the first thing to do is to clean out the "people of the fourth category."[10] Then distinctions should be drawn between "people of the second category" and "people of the third category." Those who, even after having undergone education, still fall short of the standards of a Party member should be persuaded to withdraw from the Party. We must do things in such a way that these people who withdraw from the Party do so of their own accord and without having their feelings hurt. Don't repeat the "removing rocks" experience of 1948.[11]

4. We must adopt a cautious policy toward Party building in the cities and

in the newly liberated areas.[12] In the cities, the emphasis is on building up Party organizations among the industrial workers. In the countryside, it is only after land reform has been accomplished that we can begin to build the Party branches by absorbing people who, after undergoing education, fit the standards of being Party members. In the first two years, [the size of Party] branches in the countryside generally should not exceed ten Party members. Whether in the cities or in the countryside, we should educate all those activists who are willing to accept the Party's teaching on how to be a member of the Communist Party. Then, after having had such education, those of them who truly meet the standards of being a Party member should be absorbed into the Party.

VII. United Front Work:[13]

1. The Party committees of the various bureaus of the Central Committee, sub-bureaus, and of the provinces, municipalities, and autonomous regions are asked to convene two meetings in 1951 to discuss United Front work and to submit to the Central Committee two reports on this special topic.

2. We must explain clearly to the cadres the reasons for strengthening United Front work.

3. Intellectuals, industrialists and business people, religious figures, the democratic parties,[14] and democratic personages must be united on the basis of opposition to imperialism and feudalism, and education must be conducted [among them].

4. We must carry out work among the minority nationalities in earnest. Two of the central tasks to be accomplished are the establishment of regional autonomy and the training of cadres from the minority nationalities themselves.

VIII. Rectifying Work-style:

This should be done once a year during the winter season. The duration [of rectification] should be short. The task is to inspect work and to sum up work experiences, to give recognition to achievements, and to rectify shortcomings and mistakes in order to educate the cadres.

Notes

1. Since October 1950, the Chinese government had become militarily involved in the Korean War (see text October 8, 1950, note 1). This, however, is the first official indication of mobilizing a nationwide, civilian-oriented campaign to assist and affirm the military effort.

2. In 1949, almost immediately after they took over the reins of government, the CPC began to push ahead the policy of land reform (sometimes known as "agrarian reform," and commonly known as *tugai* in China) on a nationwide scale. Since from the early 1930s onward, the CPC movement had been largely based in China's countryside, the problem of land reform had occupied the Party for two decades, and had been practiced in different forms and with different degrees of success in the CPC's base areas, such as in Jiangxi, in the 1930s. The policies followed by the CPC in the early stages of nationwide land reform were patterned after formulations suggested by people such as Ren Bishi in 1947-48. (See text Jan. 27, 1950, note 2.) The CPC saw land reform as the first and foundational step toward the socialist transformation of China's agrarian economy, and the key measure to combat and abolish China's traditional feudalistic

socio-political structure, which had been largely based on the landownership of the landlord class and its exploitation of the peasant masses. In June 1950, the Land Reform Law was promulgated and the nationwide land reform movement was fully launched. (See text Mar. 12, 1950, note 5.) It was perceived that land reform would take place in three main stages of development: (1) wiping out the remnants of bandits and local tyrants (*tu hao e ba*) – the latter category being the designation of large landlords who had an exploitative relationship with the peasants (see text Jan. 17, 1951, note 1), checking on the rental structure, forcing the returning of securities held for backrent from the peasants by the landlords (which sometimes included indenturing of young men), and establishing the boundaries of public properties; (2) drawing class distinctions, confiscation of unduly large private holdings, requisition of agrarian property other than the land itself, and redistributing the properties to the peasant households; (3) rechecking the new structures and mobilizing the peasant masses to form local organizations under Party leadership and supervision to combat any resurgence of "counterrevolutionary" landlord forces, and reforming village government. The land reform movement was seen as the means to open up the path to liberate forces of production in the countryside and pave the way to the industrialization of China.

3. The grass-roots units of democratic government under the new regime at the time were the people's representative conferences (see text June 6, 1950[1], note 10) of which the organizations mentioned by Mao here were the rural version.

4. "Before Liberation the peasants who rented land from the landlords had to pay a considerable sum of security money in advance for their tenancy. During the agrarian [land] reform the peasants demanded reimbursement of this money by the landlords, and this was known as the return of security money. Those landlords who were also running industrial and commercial enterprises or who were unable to repay the sum all at once were allowed to return it in installments." (*SW*, V, p. 49.)

The method alluded to here refers to a policy formulated by the Adminstrative Bureau of the East China Greater Administrative Region (GAR) (see text June 23, 1950, note 2), in which the most exploitative landlords who had held land in major holdings and whose landlord status was unquestionable were ordered to repay the peasants first, while others were offered a much more flexible method and schedule of repayment, ranging from postponement or reduction of repayment to total exemption, and, as indicated in the *SW* note, those whose money was tied up in commercial and industrial enterprises were allowed to repay in installments.

The East China GAR included the six provinces of Shandong, Jiangsu, Anhui, Zhejiang, Fujian, and Taiwan (not yet liberated) and the two municipalities of Shanghai and Nanjing.

5. This section should be considered in conjunction with the many comments made by Mao on the subject of suppressing counterrevolutionary activities in 1950-51. See text Dec. 19, 1950, source note. It should also be noted that, in the wake of this meeting of the Political Bureau, on February 21, 1951, the Central People's Government promulgated the "Regulations Regarding Penalty for Counterrevolutionaries." See *RMSC* (1952), pp. 39-41, and T. Chen (1967), pp. 293-296.

6. "The work of supressing counterrevolutionaries was divided into three layers: the outer, the middle, and the inner [layers]. The 'outer layer' refers to the counterrevolutionaries hidden in society. Cleaning out the 'middle layers' refers to cleaning out the counterrevolutionaries hidden in the military and government organs, cleaning out the 'inner layer' means cleaning out the counterrevolutionaries hidden in the Party." (*Xuanji*, V, p. 38, note 1.)

7. See text June 6, 1950 (2), note 1. For specifics on what Mao is referring to here, see Mao's report at this plenum, *Xuanji*, IV, pp. 1314-1329.

8. In October 1946, the Central Committee of the CPC proposed the establishment of a New Democratic Youth League. Youth organizations began to be formed in the various liberated areas. The First National Congress of the NDYL was held in Beijing (then known as Beiping) in April 1949. For more on the NDYL, see text June 30, 1953, source note.

9. The All-China Federation of Trade Unions was reinstated in August 1948. In May 1925, a national general confederation of trade unions had been formed under the name Zhonghua quanguo zong gonghui in Guangzhou (Canton). In 1927 it was banned by the KMT government. In 1948, as the Communists began to come into power, the trade union movement reemerged, and

the national body gained its current name (the Chinese remained the same as it was in 1925). With the promulgation of the Trade Union Law on June 29, 1950, by the PRC government, the legal status of trade unions in China was affirmed.

10. "During the Party rectification in 1951, Party members were divided into four categories: (1) those who met the standards of being a Party member; (2) those who did not fully meet the standards for being a Party member or those who had serious shortcomings; [such people] had to undergo transformation to raise their [political consciousness]; (3) passive and backward elements who did not meet the standards for being a Party member, and (4) alien class elements, renegades, [political] speculators, degenerates, etc., who had sneaked into the Party." (*Xuanji*, V, p. 38 note 2.)

11. "'Remove rocks' was a slogan put forward by Liu Shaoqi during land reform and Party consolidation in the new liberated areas [in 1948]. He labeled large numbers of rural cadres as 'rocks' weighing down on the peasants' heads and wanted to have them removed from their posts and purged." (*Xuanji*, V, p. 38, note 3.)

12. See text June 6, 1950(1), note 7.

13. Immediately after the founding of the PRC, the CPC proceeded to take steps to form and foster, on the basis of the worker-peasant alliance, a broader "United Front" between the proletariat and the petty bourgeoisie and the national bourgeoisie. It should be noted that this idea of a united front was based on class alliance and is not commensurate with the historical political United Fronts between the CPC and the KMT. A United Front Work Department of the Central Committee of the CPC was formed in 1950 under the leadership of Li Weihan.

14. See text Sept. 21, 1949, note 1.

Telegram to the USSR
(February 21, 1951)

Source: *RMRB* (Feb. 23, 1951), 1. Available English Translation: *SCMP*, 72 (Feb. 23-24, 1951), 9.

Chairman,
The Council of Ministers,
The Union of Soviet Socialist Republics

Generalissimo Stalin:

On this occasion of the thirty-third anniversary of the founding of the armed forces of the Union of Soviet Socialist Republics, please accept my sincere felicitations.

(Signed and dated)

Comment on Suppressing and Liquidating
Counterrevolutionaries
(February 28, 1951)

Source: *Wansui* (1969), p. 7. Other Chinese Text: *Wansui* (1967a), pp. 152-153. Available English Translation: JPRS, *Miscellany*, I, p. 1.

See text Dec. 19, 1950, source note.

In saying "unwilling followers will not be prosecuted" we refer to those who were coerced [into participating in wrongdoing] but [who themselves] did not commit any wrongdoing or did not commit any serious wrongdoing. As for those against whom there is evidence of their abetting a crime, they are accomplices and should be sentenced. If the principal culprit is given capital punishment, the accomplices should at least be given prison sentences, and some accomplices who committed serious crimes should be sentenced to death; they are not included in the category of "unwilling followers who will not be prosecuted."

Inscription for Woman's Day
(March 8, 1951)

Source: *Changjiang ribao* (Mar. 9, 1951).

Unite! Participate in production and political activities and improve women's economic and political status.
                    Mao Zedong

Comment on Suppressing and Liquidating
Counterrevolutionaries
(March 9, 1951)

Source: *Wansui* (1969), p. 8. Other Chinese Text: *Wansui* (1967a), p. 153. Available English Translation: JPRS, *Miscellany*, I, p. 7.

See text Dec. 19, 1950, source note.

Where the general policy of thorough suppression has already been carried out, [the work of suppressing counterrevolutionaries] must be suspended for a while, and no more [counterrevolutionaries] should be arrested or executed. No matter where the place is, we must have planning, pay attention to strategy, do propaganda, and not execute anyone by mistake. All this is simply a matter of course.

Letter to Rao Shushi and Others
(March 18, 1951)

Source: *Shuxin*, pp. 405-406.

The recipients of this letter were Rao Shushi, Deng Zihui, Deng Xiaoping and Xi Zhongxun. For Rao Shushi, see text Jan. 10, 1951, source note, and text Mar. 31, 1955, note 7. For Deng Zihui (1896-1972) (the source indicates that Deng was at the time of this letter second secretary of the Central-South Bureau of the Central Committee of the CPC), see text Oct. 11, 1955(1), note 34. Xi Zhongxun (b. 1903) joined the Communist Youth League in 1926 and the CPC in 1927. In the late 1920s and early 1930s Xi was active in organizing communist military forces in northern Shaanxi and subsequently joined the Twenty-sixth Army under Liu Zhidan as political commissar. In 1937 Xi became the political commissar for the Second Independent Regiment of the 120th Division of the Eighth Route Army under He Long and the commander of the Rearguard Garrison of the Eighth Route Army. In 1945 he became a deputy director of the Organization Department of the CPC and soon thereafter the deputy secretary, under Gao Gang, of the Northwest Bureau of the Central Committee of the CPC. He succeeded Gao as First Secretary of that Bureau in 1949. He was also the political commissar of the First Field Army and a member of the People's Revolutionary Military Council. At the time of this letter, he also held the position of the director of the Land Reform Committee of the Northwest Military and Administration Committee. For more information on Xi, see Zhonggong renming lu, *p. 688, and D. Klein and A. Clark, eds. (1971), I, pp. 311-314.*

Comrades Shushi, Zihui, Xiaoping, and Zhongxun:

If there are democratic personages and university professors who wish to go and see land reform [in action],[1] we should let them go and see for themselves; we must not make any preparations beforehand. Let them go and see as they wish; don't just let them see the good parts, but let them also see some of the bad things. We can educate them in this way. Wu Jingchao and Zhu Guangqian[2] and others went to the vicinity of Xian to watch the land reform; this has had a very good effect. We must use such examples to educate our cadres and dispel the ideas of closed-door-ism.[3]

Mao Zedong
March 18

Notes

1. See text Feb. 18, 1951, note 2.
2. Wu Jingchao (1901-1968) was at the time of this letter professor of sociology at Qinghua University. For more on Wu see text Oct. 13, 1957, note 51. Zhu Guangqian (b. 1898) was at the time of this letter chairman of the Foreign Languages Department of Beijing University. After graduating from Hong Kong University in 1923, he studied literature and philosophy in Britain and eventually in France where he received his D. Litt. degree. On returning to China in 1931, he taught first at Wusong Zhongguo gongxue; then in 1932 at Qinghua University and in Beijing University and the College of Arts and Science for Women at Beiping University in 1935. Zhu was in Sichuan during the years of the War of Resistance against Japan, and taught in several of the colleges and universities that were moved there from other provinces during that time. In 1945 he returned to Beiping (later Beijing) and resumed teaching there, as well as becoming engaged in the publication of literary periodicals, chiefly the *Wenxue zazhi* (Literary Gazette). Zhu is the author of many books on literature, aesthetics, and psychology, and he commanded a great deal of respect among the younger readers of the 1930s and 1940s. He was also a prolific translator, publishing in Chinese the works of Hegel, Benedetto Croce, and Plato. In 1958 he was criticized by the students of Beijing University for his "bourgeois ideological line" in aesthetic philosophy, and he quite disappeared from the political scene during the Cultural Revolution. In 1974 Hong Kong newspapers (in particular an article in *Xin wan bao* on Jan. 20) indicated that Zhu had been rehabilitated and recovered his teaching position at Beijing University.
3. See text June 6, 1950(1), note 9.

Comments on Suppressing and Liquidating Counterrevolutionaries

(March 24, 1951)

Source: *Wansui* (1967a), p. 153. Other Chinese Text: *Wansui* (1969), p. 8. Available English Translation: JPRS, *Miscellany*, I, p. 7.

In the Wansui *(1969) edition these two comments are printed separately and each dated March 24, 1950.*

The suppression of counterrevolutionaries is a great struggle. Only after this is accomplished can political power be consolidated.

The suppression of counterrevolutionaries consists of [the suppression of] (1) counterrevolutionaries in society; (2) counterrevolutionaries concealed among the old personnel and new intellectuals in the military and government systems; and (3) counterrevolutionaries concealed within the Party.[1] In order to suppress the counterrevolutionaries in these three areas, we must, of course, proceed a step at a time, and we cannot do it simultaneously. However, with regard to certain crucial departments in the Party, in the government, and in the military, and in particular, with regard to the public security department, it is necessary to clean out [counterrevolutionaries] promptly; it is absolutely essential that suspicious elements be dealt with so that these organs may be placed in the hands of reliable personnel.[2]

Notes

1. See text Feb. 18, 1951, note 4.
2. The numerals in parentheses in this paragraph appear in the *Wansui* (1967a) version only.

Letter to Li Da
(March 27, 1951)

Source: *HQ* (Jan. 1, 1979), 7. Other Chinese Text: *Shuxin*, pp. 407-408.

Li Da (1890-1966), a founding member of the Chinese Communist Party, was, in 1951, chairperson of the China Philosophical Society and president of Hunan University. For more biographical information on Li, see Zhonggong renming lu, *appendix, pp. 36-37. He is not to be confused with another CPC member of that name.*

With the exception of the last note here, the annotations and clarifications in the text itself can be found in the HQ *original source. The reference to "On Practice" is, of course, to Mao's article "Shijian lun" (On Practice); see* Xuanji, *I, pp. 259-273, and* SW, *I, pp. 295-309.*

Dear Haoming:[1]

Your two letters and the attached "Explanation of 'On Practice,' Part 2," have all been received. Thank you. I have also seen Part 1 of "Explanation" in the journal.[2] This explanation is excellent and will play a great role in disseminating materialism via popular language. When you finish writing Part 3 and have published it, you should put them into a single pamphlet so that it can be widely circulated. There are some [suggestions for] minor revisions on the two pages dealing with imperialism and dogmatic empiricism in Part 2.[3] please give them some consideration. If Part 2 has already been published, then revisions can be made when the pamphlet version is printed.

In the past, little has been done in disseminating dialectical materialism in popular language, and this is what the broad masses of working cadres and young students urgently need. I hope you will write more articles. My regards.

Mao Zedong
March 27

P.S. In "On Practice," the Taiping tianguo[4] was listed under the category of antiforeign [struggles]. This is inappropriate. I plan to revise it when *Selected Works* is published. Here I keep it as it was for the time being.[5]

Notes

1. "Haoming" is Li Da's *zi*, or scholarly honorific name – not a name a person is born with, but one he later adopts, or is given, usually in a scholarly context (e.g., when he accomplished a certain level of schooling, or is considered to have reached adulthood). It is customary in China to address friends by their *zi* rather than by their natural name. It is considered a sign of respect but

also intimacy.

2. This refers to *Xin jianshe* (New Construction), vol. 3, no. 6, 1951.

3. According to the *Shuxin* source, Mao made the following three revisions/additions to Li Da's "Explanation":

1) Mao added a paragraph of some five lines length to the part where Li Da described the Chinese people's spontaneous antiforeign struggles;

2) Mao added a comment to the part where Li Da discussed the absence of anti-imperialism in the 1911 Revolutionary Movement and in the proposals of Sun Yat-sen, its leader. Mao's comment was to the effect that although the 1911 Revolution carried within itself the effect of opposing the imperialists – in that it overthrew "the imperialists' running dogs," – the revolutionaries of the time did not consciously recognize it as a principle of anti-imperialism;

3) Mao amended a sentence that described the substance and significance of rationalism and empiricism within materialism.

For more details on these amendments, see *Shuxin*, p. 408.

4. Commonly known as the Taiping Rebellion, the Taiping tianguo (Heavenly Kingdom of Universal Peace) was a popular, largely but not exclusively peasant insurrection movement that opposed the Qing government; occupied the provinces of Hunan, Hubei, Anhui, and Jiangsu; and set up its own government in Jinling [Nanjing]. From 1850 to 1864, the Taipings ruled a large part of central and southern China. It was a nationalistic, anti-Manchu, and to a certain extent, anti-imperialist uprising. It was eventually suppressed by the Qing government with no small assistance from the foreign interests in China, particularly embodied in the formation of the "Ever Victorious Army" led by Charles George Gordon.

5. The *Shuxin* source (note 3) points out that the intended revisions were not made when volume I of *Mao Zedong xuanji* (Selected Works of Mao Zedong) was published.

Comment on Suppressing and Liquidating Counterrevolutionaries
(March 30, 1951)

Source: *Xuanji*, V, p. 43. Other Chinese Texts: *Wansui* (1969), p. 8 (excerpt); *Wansui* (1967a), p. 153 (excerpt). Available English Translations: *SW*, V, p. 54; JPRS, *Miscellany*, I, p. 7.

In some localities in Shandong there is a tendency toward insufficient fervor, and in some localities there is a tendency toward doing things carelessly. These are two kinds of tendencies that generally exist in all the provinces and municipalities in the country, and attention ought to be given to correcting them in all cases. In particular, the tendency toward doing things carelessly is the most dangerous one. [This is so] because where there is insufficient fervor, it can always be brought up to a sufficient level through education and persuasion, and whether the counterrevolutionaries are executed a few days sooner or a few days later, it does not make much difference. But if things are done carelessly, and people are arrested and executed by mistake there will be very bad repercussions. Please exercise strict control in your work of suppressing counterrevolutionaries; it is imperative for you to be cautious in doing things and to correct any tendency toward doing things carelessly. We absolutely must suppress all counterrevolutionaries, but we also must absolutely not make arrests or carry out executions by mistake.

Comments on Suppressing and Liquidating Counterrevolutionaries

(March 30, 1951)

Source: *Wansui* (1969), pp. 8-9. Other Chinese Text: *Wansui* (1967a), p. 153. Available English Translation: JPRS, *Miscellany*, I, p. 8.

At all times, the suppression of counterrevolutionaries ought to be accurate, meticulous, well-planned, and methodical. Furthermore, it ought to be controlled from above.

Whether work has been done well or poorly ought always to be determined by the masses' reaction to it.

Letter to Peng Yousheng

(March 31, 1951)

Source: *Shuxin*, pp. 409-410.

According to the source, Peng was a one-time colleague of Mao's in the New Hunan Revolutionary Army. See text Nov. 15, 1949.

Mr. Yousheng:[1]
I am very happy to receive your letter of March 14. You are too modest in your letter; please do not be so modest. If it is by the agreement of the masses that you have been classified as a poor peasant, that is very good. As for work

and employment, if you can manage in the country, it would be better if you stayed there or at least stayed in the country for a time, because I am afraid that if you ventured out it may be difficult for you to find a suitable position. If things indeed are very very difficult, you may bring this letter to Changsha and look up Mr. Cheng Xingling, Vice-chairman of the Hunan Provincial People's Government, and ask his direction and advice as to whether or not there are ways in which he may help you. I cannot guarantee that there will be results, since Mr. Cheng and the other comrades do not know you well and know nothing of your past or your recent circumstances. Even I myself am in that situation, so it would not be proper for me to suggest any concrete opinion to them. If you are willing to take the trip, you may want to give it a try. When you go, you can report to him about the fact that you had once worked in the Hunan army during the period of the Xinhai (1911) Revolution and that you were my colleague (you were the squadron second-in-command and I was a private), and give him a clear rendition of your past.

In reply and with my respect,
Mao Zedong
March 31

Note

1. See text Nov. 17, 1949, note 2, for an explanation of this usage.

Directive on the Problem of Cultivating Cadres
(March 1951)

Source: *Kexue geming*, 4 (1967), 11.

1. The older technical personnel are the legacy of the Kuomintang; they are very highly skilled, but they are, as yet, [politically] unreliable; we should strive to unite them [to our side].

2. The majority of the university and middle school students throughout the country are children of the landlords and of the bourgeoisie; they, too, are the legacy of the Kuomintang. However, we must cultivate them and transform them. One section of them is reliable, but there is another section that is unreliable.

The most important task for us at the present moment is to cultivate the backbone of the technical cadre. The most important thing is to cultivate the intellectuals who have been in our Party and our armed forces for over a decade. Another sector consists of the intellectuals who are participating in [the work of] land reform;[1] we can transfer some of them to undergo training.

Another part [of our technical cadre] can be cultivated from among [people who are at the] accelerated middle schools for industrial workers and peasants and from among the children of workers and peasants. In other words, we would like to get some people from the ranks of these two latter categories and cultivate them, after which they will be used to unite with the two other categories of people mentioned earlier.

Note

1. See text Feb. 18, 1951, note 2.

Comment on Suppressing and Liquidating Counterrevolutionaries

(April 2, 1951)

Source: *Wansui* (1969), p. 9. Other Chinese Text: *Wansui* (1967a), pp. 153-154. Available English Translation: JPRS, *Miscellany*, I, p. 8.

The suppression of counterrevolutionaries must be strictly confined to such categories as bandit chiefs, incorrigible criminals, ruffians and petty tyrants, secret agents, and chiefs of reactionary secret organizations and sects.[1] We cannot include petty thieves, drug addicts, common landlords, ordinary Kuomintang members and members of the [Sanmin zhuyi Youth] League,[2] and common officers in the Kuomintang army. Death sentences must be for those who have committed serious crimes only. It is a mistake for a light sentence to be given out for a serious crime; it is equally a mistake for a heavy sentence to be given out for a small crime.

Notes

1. See text Jan. 17, 1951, note 1.
2. The term Mao used here was *guomindang dang tuan yuan* (Party and league members of the KMT). By "league" he evidently meant the Sanmin zhuyi Youth League (or Youth Corps), which was named after Sun Yat-sen's "Three People's Principles" *(San min zhuyi)* and was formed in March 1938 as a body associated with the KMT (with an autonomous organization but also with the leader of the KMT simultaneously as its chief). The proposal to form a youth organization adjunct to the KMT was raised as early as 1930, but when it was formed, its purpose was much more specific. In 1938, as the anti-Japanese United Front among the various political parties, pri-

marily the CPC and the KMT, was formed, the Chiang Kai-shek wing of the KMT felt that at the same time that the United Front strategy was formally pursued, the internal solidarity and "purity" of the KMT must be strengthened. To counter the position of those who accepted the United Front as more than a temporary strategy, the Chiang wing, in the "Extraordinary Congress" of March 1938, pushed for the establishment of the SMZY Youth Corps, which would be constituted of younger and more energetic KMT members and affiliates who were more thoroughly indoctrinated with Chiang's political views. Chiang himself saw the institution as a means to eventually rebuild and strengthen the KMT. Until 1947, the SMZY Youth Corps maintained an autonomous existence, but in 1947, Chiang was compelled to order its amalgamation into the KMT proper. Leaders of the Youth Corps then became members of the KMT's Central Executive and Supervisory Committees, although they failed to make significant inroads into the Organization Department.

Letter to Li Weihan
(April 9, 1951)

Source: *Shuxin*, p. 411.

Li Weihan (b. 1896) was one of the earliest members of the CPC. He was a schoolmate of Mao's at the First Normal School of Hunan together with others such as Cai Hesen and He Shuheng. He became a member of the Xinmin xuehui (New People Study Society), which Cai and he organized and of which Mao also became a prominent member. In 1919 Li went to France as a participant of the qingong jianxue *(Diligent Work and Frugal Study) movement (see J. Leung [1982] for details of this movement). While in Europe, Li became a very active member of the socialist groups, which included such people as Cai Hesen, Zhou Enlai, Li Lisan, Xu Deli, Chen Yi, and Zhao Shiyan. Out of these organizations the Chinese Communist Youth League was formed. In early 1922, Li returned to China and began work with Mao Zedong in Hunan. In 1927, at the Fifth CPC Congress, Li became a member of the Political Bureau. He continued to work in Hunan and was active in planning the Nanchang Uprising of August 1927. He came under criticism by the Sixth CPC Congress in 1928, which was held in Moscow, but he held his position in the Party. From 1928 to 1931, he worked in the communist underground in Shanghai. In 1931, however, he was criticized and removed from the Central Committee for supporting Li Lisan. Wanted by the KMT police, he escaped to southern Jiangxi and joined Mao Zedong and Zhu De at Ruijin. Later he went on the Long March to nothern Shaanxi. For the next decade at Yanan he was active primarily in Party organization work, and as far as is known, was not involved in military command or action. He took on the task of organizing and managing the Party's United Front Department in 1944 and remained at the head of that department for the next two decades. He was, together with Zhou Enlai, Dong Biwu, and Ye Jianying, one of the chief CPC negotiators with the KMT in the uncertain years of 1946-1949. After 1949, he became a chief officer of the new government, serving as secretary general of the Government Administration Council until 1953, on the Political and Legal Affairs Committee of the Council, as well as heading the United Front Department. In this last position, Li was the chief CPC spokesperson to the minority nationalities and to the people's organizations, especially the industrial and commercial circles (see text Oct. 1, 1949, note 3). His influence in this area was paramount for the first decade and a half of the PRC, but he was removed in 1964. He was criticized in the Cultural Revolution but was rehabilitated in 1978. For more details on Li's life and political career, see Zhonggong renming lu, pp. 221-223, and D. Klein and A. Clark, eds. (1971), I, pp. 534-540. See also text Feb. 18, 1951, note 13. The subject of this letter is Luo Zhengwei, who, according to the source, was an acquaintance of Mao's when Mao was a student at the Higher Middle School of Hunan (later known as the First Provincial Middle School of Hunan).*

Comrade Luo Mai:[1]

This man was a member of the national assembly during the time of the Beiyang government.[2] It appears that during the period of [his association with] the KMT he didn't do any bad things. He has many children working in the People's Government. He is himself now sixty-nine years old and came to the capital, staying at the Xiangtan Guest House. He is having [financial] difficulties and has asked me to take care of him. Please send someone to speak with him and to give him some assistance.

Mao Zedong

April 9

Notes

1. Luo Mai is Li Weihan's pseudonym and a name under which he wrote many articles since the 1920s.
2. See text May-June 1955, note 54.

Letter to Situ Meitang

(April 27, 1951)

Source: *Shuxin*, p. 412.

Situ Meitang (also often translated as Szeto Mee-tong) (1868-1955) spent much of his life representing China's interests in the U.S. In 1882, as a ship's boy, Situ arrived in the United States. Several years later, he joined the Zhigongtang (The Association for Justice and Righteousness) in Boston, and began a career of opposing the Qing government of China. In 1904 he was recruited by Sun Yat-sen to work for the Chinese revolutionary movement and in 1905 he formed the On-Leong Association (Chinese Benevolent Association), a service society set up to assist Chinese-Americans in gaining a settled life and a certain measure of citizen's rights in the United States. In 1937 he organized the campaign among Chinese-Americans to raise funds to support China's struggle against Japan. In 1941, he returned to China. En route, he was captured by the Japanese in Hong Kong. Refusing to collaborate, he disguised himself and escaped to eastern Guangdong. In the summer of 1942, he went to Chongqing and returned to the United States in 1943. In 1945 he reorganized the Zhigongtang into the Hongmen zhigongdang, a Chinese political party, and became its chairman. In 1946 he again returned to China, seeking to assist in the establishment of a new democracy on the basis of a war-torn China. When this failed in 1948, he left China again, via Hong Kong, and, back in the United States, proclaimed his support for the Communists in China. In September 1949 he returned, for the last time, to China, and took up the leadership of the Zhigongdang as one of the democratic parties in the new republic (see text Sept. 21, 1949, note 1). He became a vice-chairman of the CPPCC and a member of the Central People's Government. For more on the life of Situ Meitang, see appendices to his own work, Zuguo yu huaqiao *(The Motherland and Overseas Chinese), published by* Wenhui bao, *Hong Kong, 1956.*

Mr. Meitang:[1]

I have received your letter of April 14, and am greatly gratified. I also received the gift of the peasant comrades of Haoshan.[2] Please convey my gratitude to them. It is good for you to stay for a short period in the south, but I hope that you will return to the capital in the early part of June so that I can see you and learn from you in person.

My respectful wishes for your health.

Mao Zedong
April 27

Notes

1. See text Nov. 17, 1949, note 2, for an explanation of this usage.

2. This is in Guangdong Province, where it is known in the local dialect as Hok shan, and is now known as Gaohao *xian*. According to the source, Situ Meitang was then visiting this area and inspecting the work of land reform in the region.

Letter to Chen Wenxin

(April 29, 1951)

Source: *Shuxin*, p. 413.

Chen Wenxin was, at the time of this letter, a student at the Agronomics School of Wuhan University. She is the daughter of Chen Chang, who was a member of the Xin- min xuehui (New People's Study Society) of which Mao was a prominent member. (See text Apr. 9, 1951, source note.) Chen Chang, also an early member of the CPC, died in 1930.

Comrade Wenxin:

I am very happy to have received you letter and your mother's letter. I hope that you and your sister will be diligent in your study or work, and, in the spirit of your departed father, serve the people's state in its reconstruction.

Please give my best regards to your mother.

I wish you progress.

Mao Zedong

April 29

Letter to Zhang Zhizhong

(May 5, 1951)

Source: *Shuxin*, p. 414.

Zhang Zhizhong (1890-1969) had a long and illustrious career as a military com- mander in the KMT armies. In 1946 he became the head of the KMT's Northwest Gov- ernment Headquarters and the chairman of the provincial government of Xinjiang. In 1949 he headed the KMT delegation to negotiate with the CPC in Beijing (then known as Beiping) and was detained when the negotiations fell through. He then defected to the Communists, and when the new regime was established he became a vice-chairman of the National Defense Council, a member of the Central People's Government Council, and the vice-chairman of the Northwest Military and Adminis-

trative Committee. For more biographical information on Zhang, see text Oct. 13, 1957, note 53.

Mr. Wenbai:[1]

I have received and read your letter. I am most concerned to hear of your illness. Since the inspection group has Mr. Shao to lead it,[2] it should be all right and you may put away your worries and devote yourself to convalescence and your recovery so that you may be soon restored to health.

My best wishes on your recovery!

Mao Zedong
May 5

Notes

1. Wenbai is Zhang's *zi*, or honorific name. For this usage see text Oct. 15, 1949, note 1.

2. This refers to the group delegated by the Central Committee of the CPC to inspect the flood-control work on the Huai River. Zhang was appointed its leader.

Mr. Shao refers to Shao Lizi (1882-1967), who was a journalist and teacher and became a member of Sun Yat-sen's Tongmeng hui. In the early years of the Republic of China he was a journalist and in the late 1910s began his study of Marxism with Chen Duxiu. Nonetheless, he did not join the CPC when it was formed. Instead he began his political career with the KMT government in Guangzhou. After a brief sojourn in the Soviet Union in 1927-28 he rejoined Chiang Kai-shek's government and became a member of the KMT's Central Political Council and a secretary-general for Chiang's military headquarters. In 1940-42 he became the Chinese ambassador to the Soviet Union. In 1943 he became secretary general of the People's Political Council and the secretary-general of the Committee for the Promotion of a Constitutional Government. In these positions he was influential in the KMT-CPC negotiations in the mid- to late-1940s period, during which he began to attempt to promote better understanding and new bases for cooperation between the KMT and the CPC, working with such people as Zhang Zhizhong and Yan Huiqing. Shao was a member of the KMT delegation sent to Beijing (then known as Beiping) in April 1949 (see source note above), and when those negotiations failed, he decided to stay with the Communists. After 1949, and at the time of this letter, Shao held membership in the Central People's Government Council in the new regime. For more biographical information on Shao, see H. Boorman et al., eds. (1970), III, pp. 91-92.

Comment on Suppressing and Liquidating
Counterrevolutionaries

(May 8, 1951)

Source: *Xuanji*, V, pp. 43-44. Available English Translation: *SW*, V, pp. 54-56.

The Central Committee has made the following decision regarding the counterrevolutionaries purged from within the Communist Party, and from the People's Liberation Army, the People's Government system, educational, industrial, commercial, and religious circles, and from within the various democratic parties and the various people's organizations:[1] Those people whose crimes are not so serious as to warrant their execution ought to be sentenced to limited [prison] terms or to life imprisonment, or to be placed under supervision and surveillance; apart from these, among those elements who do deserve execution, only those who have committed crimes that involved taking people's lives, and those who have committed other serious crimes that have incurred the anger of the masses, such as in cases of raping many women or stealing large amounts of property, and those who have most seriously damaged the national interest, will be executed; as to the rest, we will adopt a uniform policy of sentencing them to death but giving them a two year reprieve, during which period they will be forced to take part in labor, and [final judgment will be made] on the basis of how they behave.[2] This policy is a policy of caution that will prevent mistakes. This policy can gain extensive support among a broad range of people in society. This policy can split the counterrevolutionary forces and thus facilitate the complete extermination of the counterrevolutionaries. In addition, this policy will conserve a lot of labor power and so facilitate the task of national reconstruction. Therefore, it is a correct policy. It is estimated that among the counterrevolutionaries who, as we have mentioned above, have been purged from within the Party, the government, the military, educational and economic circles and from the [people's] organizations, and who deserve to be executed, those who have committed crimes involving the taking of lives or other crimes that have aroused the anger of the masses and those who have most seriously damaged the national interest constitute only a very small minority, generally not exceeding ten or twenty per cent, while those who should be sentenced to death but [are to be] given a reprieve probably constitute eighty or ninety per cent, which means that eighty to ninety per cent of the capital offenders will be reprieved and not executed. These people are different from the bandit chiefs, incorrigible criminals, and local ruffians and petty tyrants in the rural areas, and from local tyrants, bandit leaders, incorrigible criminals, big chiefs among hoodlums, and the big bosses of secret societies, gangs and sects in the cities; they are also different from certain secret agents who have most severely damaged the national interest in that they have not committed crimes involving the taking of people's lives or other serious crimes that have aroused the deep hatred of the masses.[3] The degree to which they have damaged the national interest is serious, but it is still not the most serious. They have committed capital offenses, but the masses were not directly harmed. If we execute these people, it will not be easily understood by the masses and public figures, and society will not give us its full support; at the same time, a large amount of labor power will be lost, and the purpose of splitting the enemy forces will not be served, and, moreover, we might make mistakes on this problem. Thus, the Central Committee has decided to adopt, with regard to this type of people, a policy of sentencing them to death but giving them a reprieve, forcing them to take part in labor, and [making the final judgment] on the basis of how they behave. If among these persons there are some who cannot be reformed and who continue to do bad deeds, we can still execute them later; the power to take action is in our hands. In disposing of counterrevolutionaries purged from within Party, government, military, educational, and economic circles, and from [people's] organizations, all local authorities are requested to handle matters in accordance with the above-stated principles. For the sake of being cautious, all [lower levels] should apply for the approval of the [authorities at the level of] the greater administrative regions or the military regions in handling all cases involving that very small minority of people whose death sentence ought to be carried out [in general constituting ten to twenty per cent of those who have committed capital crimes]. With regard to [handling cases] where important elements in the United Front[4] are involved, approval from the Central Committee must be solicited. In addition, with regard to the counterrevolutionaries in the rural areas, we must also execute only those whose execution is absolutely necessary to appease the hatred of the people and must not execute any person whose execution is not demanded by the people. Among these there will be some people to whom the policy of passing the death sentence but giving them a reprieve should also be applied. Those whose execution is demanded by the people, on the other hand, must be executed to quiet the people's anger and to promote production.

Notes

1. See text Sept. 21, 1949, note 1, and text Oct. 1, 1949, note 3.

2. This decision is reflected in the resolutions of the Third National Conference on Public Security, for which Mao wrote several paragraphs of instructions. See text May 15, 1951.

3. See text Jan. 17, 1951, note 1.

4. Mao is most likely referring to important members of the national bourgeoisie who may have engaged in counterrevolutionary activities of a sort in the past but whose cooperation was needed to consolidate the united front with the national bourgeoisie in general. See text March 12, 1950, this volume, note 3. For the nature of the "United Front" mentioned here, see text Feb. 18, 1951, note 13.

Directive on the Huai River
(May 9, 1951)

Source: *RMRB* (May 15, 1951), 1.

This is an inscription Mao wrote on a banner for the Huai River Control Project. It was first made public at a banner-awarding ceremony held in Henan on May 9, 1951.

The Huai River must be harnessed.

Resolutions of the Third National Conference on Public Security
(May 15, 1951)

Source: *Wansui* (1969), p. 506, and *Xuanji*, V, pp. 39-41. This is a combined representation of these two sources. Available English Translations: JPRS, *Miscellany*, I, pp. 9-10; and *SW*, V. pp. 50-52.

The Third National Conference on Public Security Work was held in May 1951. For more on this conference see K. Lieberthal (1976), pp. 54-55. Excerpts from the resolutions of this conference published in Wansui *(1969) are, in many instances, similar to the article "The Mass Line of the Party Must Be Implemented in the Campaign to Suppress Counterrevolutionaries" in* Xuanji, V, *which is cited as "several passages from directives written by Comrade Mao Zedong at the passing of resolutions of the Third National Conference on Public Security Work." We have therefore combined the two sources and noted differences between the two texts. Since the texts overlap each other in an intricate fashion at some points, we have eliminated the paragraph divisions in both (which are indicated in* Xuanji *by numeral headings) and, instead, indicated overlapping segments in our notes.*

The large number of prisoners who are to be sentenced to prison terms constitutes a considerable labor force. In order to reform them, to solve the difficulties of prisons, and in order not to let the counterrevolutionaries serving prison terms be fed without working for it, we must immediately take steps to organize the work of reforming people through labor.[1]

After this nationwide campaign for the suppression of counterrevolutionaries, the activities of secret agents and spies who have not yet been detected will be hidden even more deeply from view. Accordingly, public security departments must proceed to carry out even more systematic investigation work and educate the masses of the people to pay overall attention to the work of safeguarding [our nation] against the traitors.[2]

With regard to the number of executions of counterrevolutionaries, it must be kept within a certain proportion [of those arrested]. The principle here is[3] for those who have committed [crimes] involving taking human lives, or other most serious crimes for which a punishment short of the death penalty would not pacify the people's wrath, as well as for those who have most seriously injured the national interest, it is necessary that we resolutely impose the death penalty and swiftly carry out the execution. As for those who have not committed [crimes] involving taking human lives [or have committed crimes that] have not greatly aroused the people's wrath, and those who, though they have seriously injured the national interest though not to the utmost degree, but who still deserve to be sentenced to death, we should adopt the policy of sentencing them to death but staying the execution for two years and forcing them to engage in labor, [with the final judgment to be made on the basis of] how they behave in the future. [This policy applies] especially to those counterrevolutionaries who ought to be sentenced to death and who have been flushed out from [the ranks of] the Communist Party, from within the People's Government system, the People's Liberation Army system, the cultural and educational circles, the industrial and commercial circles, the religious circles, the democratic parties, and the people's organizations.[4] In general, we should, as a matter of principle, carry out executions in about ten to twenty per cent [of the cases]. In the remaining eighty to ninety per cent [we should] adopt the policy of imposing the death penalty but staying the executions, and forcing [these counterrevolutionaries] to engage in labor and see how they behave. Only in this way can we gain the sympathy of society, avoid committing mistakes on our part regarding this question, and divide and destroy our enemies. This will be helpful in the thorough destruction of the counterrevolutionary forces; furthermore, this will preserve a large labor force that will be beneficial to the nation's production and construction.[5] In addition it should be clearly stipulated that if there is a choice as to whether or not a person should be arrested, then that person should definitely not be arrested. To arrest [such a person] would be to make a mistake. If there is a choice as to whether or not a person should be executed, then that person should definitely not be executed. To execute [such a person] would be to make a mistake.[6]

The movement for the suppression of counterrevolutionaries now being carried on throughout the entire country is a great, intense, and complicated struggle. The line for [our] work that has already been carried out effectively everywhere in the country is the Party's mass line. This is simply:[7] leadership by the Party committee; mobilization of the entire Party and of the masses;

drawing on the participation of people from the democratic parties and the various circles [in society]; unified planning and unified action; strict examination of the lists of arrests and executions; paying attention to the strategy of struggle in each period; extensively carrying out the work of propaganda and education (holding all types of representative meetings, cadre meetings, forums, and mass meetings; and at these meetings, letting the plaintiffs voice their grievances and exhibit evidence of the crimes, and using films, slide shows, drama and songs, newspapers, pamphlets and leaflets, doing propaganda so that every household and every person understands and knows [what the situation is])[8] smashing closed-doorism[9] and mysticism; and steadfastly opposing the tendency to do work crudely and hastily. Wherever work is done in complete conformity to this line it is entirely correct. Wherever work is not done in conformity to this line it is totally incorrect. Where work is done in general conformity with this line, but not completely so, it is correct in the main but not completely correct. We believe that [following] this line in our work will serve to guarantee the continuous deepening of the work of suppressing the counterrevolutionaries and the achievement of complete victory. From now on we must follow this work line completely in the work of suppressing the counterrevolutionaries. The most important thing is to vigorously examine the lists of arrests and executions[10] and to do a good job of carrying out propaganda and education extensively. When we fulfill these two requirements, we will be able to avoid making mistakes.[11]

In order to prevent a "Left" deviation from occurring in the midst of the high tide of the campaign to suppress counterrevolutionaries, it is has been resolved that as of June 1 in all localities throughout the country, including those places where to date only a very few people have been executed, the power to warrant arrests will, without exception, revert to the level of the [special] district [Party] Committee and the special [district] commissioner's office, and the power to warrant executions will, also without exception, revert to the provincial level. As for cases where [a crime has been committed] far from where the provincial [authorities] are located, the provincial [authorities] will dispatch representatives to handle [these cases]. No locality may demand a reversal of these decisions.[12]

As to counterrevolutionary elements in the "middle layer" and the "inner layer,"[13] from now on we must proceed to investigate [these problems] in a planned way. It has been decided that in accord with the directives of the Central Committee, during this summer and autumn we will use the form of rectification to carry out a general preliminary investigation of personnel who have been retained [since Liberation] and intellectuals who have been recently recruited. The purpose is to clarify the situation and to dispose of the most outstanding problems. The methods are to study the documents [relating to] the suppression of counterrevolutionaries, to appeal to those who have problems among the personnel who have been retained and to recently recruited intellectuals (not all of them) to adopt an attitude of sincerity and honesty in order to give a clean account of their past and make a clean breast of their hidden problems. Such a confession movement must be put under the charge of the [unit] leaders; [we must] adopt the principle of voluntary [action], and [we must] apply no coercion. In each unit the duration [of the movement] should be short; don't stretch it out. The strategy is to win over the majority and isolate the minority in preparation for further investigation, which would come in the winter. Investigation must first be conducted in the leading organs, the public security organs, and other vital departments, so as to acquire experience that can be popularized. In carrying out this type of investigation work in the government system and in schools and factories, we must have non-Party people participate in the committees responsible for the investigation work in order to avoid [a situation where] the Communist Party members are doing the work in isolation.[14]

Everywhere in the country, in this great struggle to suppress counterrevolutionaries, there must be widespread organizing of public security and defense committees among the masses. These committees should be organized by popular elections with the *xiang* as the unit in the countryside, and in the cities, with the [governmental and Party] organs, schools, factories, and neighborhoods as units. There should be at least three and at most eleven members in each committee. [The committees] must absorb the participation of reliable patriotic people from outside the Party and become United Front organizations for public security and defense. These committees will follow the leadership of the basic-level government and public security organs and will bear the responsibility for helping the People's Government liquidate counterrevolutionaries, guard against traitors and spies,[15] protect the country, and for public order and security. In the countryside, after the completion of land reform,[16] and in the cities, after the work of suppressing counterrevolutionaries has been developed, such committees should be organized, under [strong] leadership, in order to prevent bad people from taking advantage of the situation to infiltrate them.

Notes

1. This paragraph appears only in *Wansui* (1969).

2. This paragraph appears only in *Wansui* (1969).

3. This passage, from the beginning of the paragraph to this point, appears only in *Xuanji*.

4. See text Sept. 21, 1949, note 1, and text Oct. 1, 1949, note 3.

5. The preceding passage, starting with "[This policy applies]" and up to this point, appears only in *Wansui* (1969).

6. This last section of the paragraph is an integral part of section (2) in *Xuanji* but is separated from the foregoing segments in *Wansui* (1969).

7. The phrases "is the Party's mass line" and "This is simply" are missing in *Wansui* (1969). The "mass line" (*qunzhong luxian*) method of leadership is the cardinal principle of leading the masses while also relying on the masses. It is a crucial concept in understanding Mao's political philosophy. It defines that all correct leadership stems from the masses and goes to the masses (i.e., is applied among the masses). In practice it stipulates that the leadership must first organize the ideas and opinions gathered from the masses (albeit that they are scattered and unsystematic), then turn these into systematic ideas through studying them, and then do education and propaganda work among the masses so as to transform these ideas into ones that can be generally and

popularly held by the masses themselves, and for the masses to then put the ideas thus inculcated by the leadership into action themselves. These ideas can then be tested for correctness in the crucible of practical application, and whether or not the ideas of the leadership are vindicated will depend on how usable they are for the masses. For the basic definitions of this method, see Mao's article "Some Questions Concerning Methods of Leadership" (*Xuanji*, III, pp. 117-122), where Mao called it "the Marxist theory of knowledge." For a thorough discussion of the mass line concept and practice, see J. Lewis (1963) and E. Hammond (Jan. 1978).

8. This passage in parentheses appears only in *Xuanji*.

9. See text June 6, 1950(1), note 8.

10. Here we followed the *Wansui* version. The *Xuanji* version has "lists of death sentences passed."

11. This paragraph appears as the first in *Xuanji* and the last in *Wansui* (1969).

12. This paragraph appears only in *Xuanji*.

13. See text Feb. 18, 1951, note 4.

14. This paragraph also appears only in *Xuanji*.

15. See text Jan. 17, 1951, note 1.

16. See text Feb. 18, 1951, note 2.

Comment on the "Report of the Secretary's Office on the Handling of Letters from the Masses"

(May 16, 1951)

Source: *RMRB* (Dec. 28, 1983). Other Chinese Text: *Yulu* (1969), pp. 72-73.

This was Mao's comment on the "Report to Chairman Mao on the Work of Handling Letters from the Masses in the Last Three Months" of the Work Office of the Central Committee of the CPC. The Yulu *source also cites this as part of a document of the Work Office of the Central Committee of the CPC issued on June 6, 1967.*

Attention must be paid to correspondence from the people. We must handle letters from the people properly and meet the legitimate demands of the masses. We must regard this matter as a method by which the Communist Party and the People's Government can strengthen their ties with the people. We must not adopt a bureaucratic attitude of callousness and neglect. If there are a great many letters from the people, and it is difficult for [the cadre in charge] to handle [all of] them personally, a special organ made up of an appropriate number of people should be set up or special persons assigned to deal with these letters. If there aren't too many letters, and either [the cadre in charge] or the secretary is able to handle them personally, then there won't be any need to bring in additional special personnel.

Attention Must Be Paid to the Discussions
of the Film *The Life of Wu Xun*

(May 20, 1951)

Source: *RMRB* (May 20, 1951), 1. Other Chinese Texts: *Xuanji*, V, pp. 46-47 (abridged); *Buyi*, pp. 16-21. *RMRB* (May 26, 1967), 1 (abridged); *HQ*, 9 (May 27, 1967), 3-5 (abridged); *Wansui* (1967b), p. 9 (from *RMRB* 1967); *Mao liang*, pp. 352-356 (from *RMRB* 1967); *Wenge wenjian*, pp. 231-232; *Jiaoyu yulu*, p. 8 (excerpt); *Wenge wenxuan*, pp. 231-232 (excerpt). Available English Translations: *SW*, V, pp. 57-58; *CLG*, 9:4 (Winter 1978-79), 19-21; *CB*, 891 (Oct. 8, 1969), 15 (excerpt of *RMRB*, 1951 version); *CB*, 885 (July 31, 1969), 21-22 (abridged); *CB*, 897 (Dec. 10, 1969), 20-21 (abridged); *PR*, 10:23 (June 2, 1967), 5-6 (abridged); J. Chen (1970), pp. 78-79, (abridged); S. Schram (1974), pp. 363-365, (abridged); *CR* (Aug. 1967), 20 (abridged); *SCMP* (supplement), 191 (May 26, 1967), 19 (abridged).

Wu Xun (1838-1896) was famous for his philanthropic work in the area of education. Born into a very poor family in Shandong, Wu Xun had no education himself and worked, during his boyhood, in semislavery for landlords. According to the legend, Wu later became a beggar, but diligently saved and invested his money. Through such astute and diligent management of his resources, he ultimately became a rich man and a landlord. He then invested his money in the establishment of many private schools to which poor children were admitted free of charge. His philanthropy was recognized by the Guangxu Emperor (1875-1908), and Wu Xun became a folk hero.

In 1934 the good deeds of Wu Xun were highly praised by the Nationalist government under Chiang Kai-shek, then promoting what was known as the New Life Movement, and statues of Wu Xun were erected in many primary schools throughout the country. The story of the life of Wu Xun began to be told in comic books. In 1944, at the height of the War of Resistance against Japan, gatherings of intellectuals were held in Chongqing to commemorate Wu Xun. In that year the playwright Sun Yu began work on a film script based on the story of Wu Xun's life. In 1950, with the editorial work by Xia Yan completed on this script, the movie Wu Xun zhuan *was produced in Shanghai by the Kunlun studio.*

Following the production of Wu Xun zhuan, *many articles were written and published in newspapers, heaping praise on the subject of the film for his philanthropic deeds and calling him a model for the working people.*

Mao, representing a more radical viewpoint, saw serious ideological problems with the story of Wu Xun's life. While recognizing Wu Xun's spirit of per-

severance and diligence, Mao perceived that Wu's methods of amassing his fortune was essentially one of fraud and exploitation accomplished through usury and land-grabbing. Furthermore, Mao argued that the schools that Wu Xun established were none other than institutions where fedualistic culture and education were inculcated and promulgated; thus they were nothing but training grounds for the exploiting classes.

On May 20, 1951, the editorial translated here appeared in RMRB. *It was not signed, but the attribution to Mao was, as many noted, an "open secret," and was confirmed by the annotation to the* Xuanji *version later.*

With this editorial, Mao spearheaded the campaign to criticize the film. Following its publication, a team to investigate the truth about the life of Wu Xun was dispatched by the Propaganda Department of the Central Committee of the CPC and the Cultural Ministry of the State Council to Shandong. Eventually, on July 23-28, 1951, the report of its findings, a verdict of sorts on Wu Xun and related matters, was published in RMRB. *Wu was criticized for having been a fraudulent and obsequious manipulator, a usurer, a mercilessly exploitative landlord, a "filial son of the feudal classes," and an inculcator of feudal values.*

Behind the criticism of Wu Xun's story itself lay the deeper and broader contest between bourgeois ideology represented by the intellectuals who, in 1950, were caught up in the surge of enthusiasm to heap praise on Wu Xun, and the proletarian ideology represented by Mao. The significance of this contest was particularly stark against the backdrop of the concurrent land reform movement, the movement to Resist U.S. Aggression and Aid Korea, and the movement to suppress counterrevolutionaries. It was a major component of the Patriotic Ideological Reform Campaign (see text Oct. 23, 1951, note 6) and a harbinger of the campaigns against bourgeois ideology (including the campaign against Liang Shuming, 1953; the campaign on the novel Hongloumeng, *1954; the campaign against Hu Feng and Hu Shi, 1955; and the campaign against* Wenyi bao, *1957) which would follow in the years ahead.*

As previously mentioned, the original article in RMRB *(May 20, 1951) was not signed by Mao. The* HQ *version (excerpt) in 1967 is the earliest version that bears Mao's signature.*

' When we published Comrade Yang Er's article "Is There Any Positive Significance in Tao Xingzhi's Popularization of the 'Spirit of Wu Xun?'"[1] we hoped to induce further discussion on the film *The Life of Wu Xun*. Why should we emphasize this discussion?

The questions raised by *The Life of Wu Xun* are fundamental in character. Living in the era of the Chinese people's great struggle against foreign aggressors and domestic reactionary feudal rulers in the last years of the Qing dynasty, people of Wu Xun's ilk did not attempt to disturb even the tiniest hair of the feudal economic base and its superstructure. Instead, they frantically popularized the feudal culture, and moreover, in order to obtain, for propagating feudal culture, a position which they had been denied, they did their best to slavishly flatter the reactionary feudal rulers. Can such vile conduct be the subject of our praise? Can we tolerate praising such vile conduct in front of the people's masses, praise which is even heralded by the revolutionary banner of "serving the people," praise in which the failure of the peasants' revolutionary movement is used by way of negative comparison [in order to make such conduct seem good]? To give recognition to or to tolerate such praise is to give recognition to or to tolerate the reactionary propaganda that vilifies the revolutionary struggle of the peasants, the history of China, and the Chinese nation, by regarding it as proper propaganda.

The appearance of the film *The Life of Wu Xun* and especially the many praises of Wu Xun and of the film *The Life of Wu Xun* indicate the extent of confusion the thinking of our nation's cultural circles has reached. Just check the following incomplete listing of the articles that have appeared in newspapers and periodicals in the three cities of Beijing, Tianjin, and Shanghai since the showing of the film *The Life of Wu Xun* – articles that either praise *The Life of Wu Xun* or Wu Xun himself, or which, while criticizing a certain aspect of Wu Xun, go on to praise [his] other aspects:

[1950:]

Sun Yu, "How I Wrote and Directed *The Life of Wu Xun*," *Guangming ribao*, February 26.

Chang Zhi, "The Film *The Life of Wu Xun* and the *Pictorial Biography of Wu Xun*," *Guangming ribao*, February 26.

Li Shizhao, "My View of the Film *The Life of Wu Xun*," *Guangming ribao*, February 26.

Tao Hong, "I Saw the Film *The Life of Wu Xun*," *Guangming ribao*, February 26.

Luo Wei, *"The Life of Wu Xun* – Synopsis of the Film," *Gongren ribao*, February 26.

Guan Datong, "Introducing the *Pictorial Biography of Wu Xun*," *Guangming ribao*, February 27.

Zi Guang, "The Life of Wu Xun," *Xinmin bao*, February 27.

Gu Feng, "Love Fervently Our Great Homeland – Thoughts after Seeing the Film *The Life of Wu Xun*," *Xinmin bao*, February 27.

Wang Gengrao, "About the Film *The Life of Wu Xun*," *Xinmin bao*, February 27.

Xiang Ruoyu, Wei Zhaolan, "Our Opinions on the Film *The Life of Wu Xun*," *Xinmin bao*, February 27.

Dong Weichuan, "A Review of *The Life of Wu Xun* from the Educational Viewpoint," *Guangming ribao*, February 28.

Su Juan, "After Viewing *The Life of Wu Xun*," *Xinmin bao*, March 10.

Yang Yuming, Duanmu Hongliang, "On *The Life of Wu Xun*," *Beijing wenyi*, vol. 2, no.1, March 15.

Jiang Lin, *"The Life of Wu Xun* Has Made an Ugly Representation of the Laboring People," *Xinmin bao*, March 31.

Lin, "My Opinion on *The Life of Wu Xun*," *Guangming ribao*, April 2.

Tian Jiamei, "Can *The Life of Wu Xun* express the Greatness of Our Ancestors?" *Xinmin ribao*, April 2.

Shu Ting, "Let's Clarify the Disputes with Regard to *The Life of Wu Xun*,"

Renwu zazhi, May 5.

Zhao Huan, "After Viewing *The Life of Wu Xun* – A Discussion Brought Up by Thoughts on the Two Characters – Wu Xun and Zhou Da," *Tianjin ribao*, March 19.

Yuan Ding, "Recommending *The Life of Wu Xun*," *Jinbu ribao*, March 19.

Guo Hongyuan, Bu Yunsheng, Wen Qing, Xia Wenhua, "Thoughts after Viewing *The Life of Wu Xun*," *Jinbu ribao*, March 23.

Shi Weiwen, "A Review of *The Life of Wu Xun*," *Tianjin ribao*, March 28.

Li Xin, "My View of *The Life of Wu Xun*," *Tianjin xingbao*, March 29.

Kun Yu, *"The Life of Wu Xun* Has Educated Me," *Tianjin ribao*, April 4.

Jing Zhi, "We Cannot Accept the Legacy of Wu Xun," *Jinbu ribao*, April 4.

Xun, "My View on Wu Xun," *Jinbu ribao*, April 4.

Hong Du, "Wu Xun's 'Resistance' Became Collaboration," *Jinbu ribao*, April 8.

Fang Huixian, "Some Opinions on the Problem of Selection of Subject Matter of *The Life of Wu Xun*," *Jinbu ribao*, April 8.

Lu Nanzi, "A Discourse on Whether or Not Wu Xun Is a Part of Our Good Tradition," *Jinbu ribao*, April 8.

Zhao Dan, "How I Played the Part of Wu Xun," *Dazhong dianying* (Shanghai), nos. 9-15, October 16.

Sun Yu (with illustrations by Dong Tianye), "The Life of Wu Xun," (newspaper cartoon series), *Xinwen ribao*, December 14, 1950 to January 30, 1951.

Jiang Xingyu, *"The Life of Wu Xun* and Chinese Feudal Society," *Dagong bao*, December 30.

Wang Pei, *"The Life of Wu Xun* Grows up Amidst Hardship," *Dagong bao*, December 30.

Sun Yu, "How I Expressed Wu Xun's 'Dream'," *Xinwen ribao*, December 30.

[1951:]

Sun Yu, "Before and After Writing and Directing *The Life of Wu Xun*," *Dazhong dianying*, no.14, January 1.

Dai Baitao, "Opinions after Viewing *The Life of Wu Xun*," *Xinwen ribao*, January 1; *Dazhong dianying*, no.14, January 1; *Wenhui bao*, January 3.

Ma Luxian, "Thoughts After Viewing the *The Life of Wu Xun*," *Dazhong dianying*, no.14, January.

"Teachers and Students of Yucai School Discuss *The Life of Wu Xun*," *Dazhong dianying*, no.14, January 1.

Gu Weizu, "Some Points of Understanding Gleaned from Viewing *The Life of Wu Xun*," *Wenhui bao*, January 6.

Shi Guo, "A Partial Explanation of *The Life of Wu Xun*," *Xinmin bao*, Evening Edition, January 6.

Li Xing, "My Humble Opinion on *The Life of Wu Xun*," *Dagong bao*, January 13.

Wang Dingcheng, "A Discussion Brought Up by Thoughts on *The Life of Wu Xun*," *Xinwen ribao*, January 27.

Yan Meng, "A Brief Discussion on the Problem of Portraying Historical Per-sonalities – Points Brought Up by the Film *The Life of Wu Xun*," *Wenhui bao*, March 29.

The following are a few new books on Wu Xun published in early 1951:

Sun Yu, *The Life of Wu Xun* (A Film Story), published by Xinya shudian, Shanghai;

Li Shizhao, (with illustrations by Sun Zhizhun), *A Pictorial Biography of Wu Xun*, published by Wanye shudian, Shanghai;

Bo Shui, *The Strangest Beggar of All Ages* (old-style novel),[2] published by Tonglian shudian, Shanghai.

In the view of many writers, the development of history is not the replace-ment of the old with the new, but is rather the various efforts to preserve the old from extinction; it is not motivated by class struggle to overthrow those reactionary feudal rulers who ought to be overthrown; rather it is, as in the case of Wu Xun, motivated by refuting the class struggles of oppressed people and surrendering to the reactionary feudal rulers. Our writers have not studied to find out who the enemies oppressing the Chinese people in the past were, or whether there was anything praiseworthy in those who surrendered to and served such enemies; nor have our writers studied to ascertain the new socio-economic forms, the new class forces, the new personages, and the new ideol-ogies that have emerged in the hundred or more years since the Opium War of 1840[3] to struggle against the old socio-economic forms and their superstruc-ture (politics, culture, etc.), in order to decide what is to be commended or praised, and what is not to be commended or praised, and what ought to be opposed.

Particularly noteworthy are certain Communist Party members who reput-edly have learned Marxism. They have studied the history of social develop-ment – historical materialism – and yet, when they encounter concrete histori-cal events and concrete historical characters (such as Wu Xun), and concrete anti-historical thought (such as represented by the film *The Life of Wu Xun* and other writings on Wu Xun), they lose their critical faculties. Some of them have even capitulated to these reactionary ideologies. Isn't it a fact that the reactionary ideology of the bourgeoisie has invaded the militant Communist Party? Where on earth have these Communist Party members gone to – those who have claimed to have learned Marxism?

For the various reasons stated above, we ought to launch a discussion on the film *The Life of Wu Xun* and on other writings and articles about Wu Xun, in order to seek to clarify thoroughly the confused thinking on this problem.

Notes

1. This article was published in *RMRB* on May 16, 1961, and reprinted in *Wenyi bao*, 4:2.

Tao Xingzhi (1891-1946) was an educational reformer in the Republican period. His ideas were based on the educational philosophy of John Dewey (for whom he was an interpreter during the latter's tour of China) and the epistemology of Wang Yangming, the Ming dynasty neo-Con-fucian thinker. He was a chief advocate of the mass education and rural literacy campaigns in the

1920s and the national crisis education campaign in the mid-1930s to 1940s. (See H. Boorman et al., eds. (1970), III, pp: 243-248.)

2. Here the designation is *"zhang hui xiaoshuo"* which refers to the old literary style in which a literary opus such as a novel would be divided up into chapters, known as *zhang,* and further into installments, known as *hui.*

3. This refers to the First Sino-British War, which is historically known as the "Opium War" because it was ignited by the Chinese (Qing) government's attempt to curtail the British sale of opium in China, which was draining the Chinese economy and creating many types of social problems, particularly in southern China. For more detail on this see comment on Lin Zexu in text Feb. 14, 1957, note 1.

Speech on the Agreement on Measures
for the Peaceful Liberation of Tibet
(May 24, 1951)

Source: *RMRB* (May 28, 1951), 1. Other Chinese Text: *XHYB*, IV:2 (June 25, 1951), 278. Available English Translation: NCNA, *Daily Bulletin*, 290 (May 29, 1951), 1.

According to the accompanying news account, before giving this speech at a banquet celebrating the event, Mao toasted the signing of the Agreement on the Measures for the Peaceful Liberation of Tibet by the Central People's Government and the Tibetan Regional Government, the great unity of the nationalities of China, and the internal unity of the people of Tibet. For an English translation of the Agreement on the Measures for the Peaceful Liberation of Tibet, which was signed on May 23, 1951, see, PC, III:12, Supplement.

For hundreds of years there was no unity among the various nationalities of China. In particular there was no unity between the Han people and the Tibetan people. Internally as well, the Tibetan nationality was not united. This was the result of the reactionary rule by the Manchu[1] government and the Chiang Kai-shek government, and also the result of the discord sown among us by the imperialists. Now, unity has been achieved among the forces led by the Dalai Lama,[2] those led by Panchen Gnoertehni,[3] and the Central People's Government; this was accomplished only after the Chinese people had overthrown imperialism and the domestic reactionary government. This unity is a fraternal unity and is not based on the oppression of one side by the other. This type of unity is the product of concerted efforts on all sides. From now on, on the basis of this unity, there will be development and progress among our various nationalities in all spheres, including such spheres as politics, economics, and culture.

Notes

1. Here Mao used the less common description, *manqing zhengfu*, rather than referring to the last imperial dynasty of China simply as the *qing zhengfu*, as it is officially known. The term *manqing* has ethnic connotations, thus our translation here as "Manchu."

2. Dalai is a title given to one of the "living Buddhas" of the Lama sect of the Buddhist religion of Tibet; Panchen is the title of the other. As such these two title holders are the supreme religious and cultural (and, defacto, also the supreme political and military) leaders of the Tibetan population. Mao is here referring to Dalai Danzengjiazuo (Tanzeng Gyaltzo), the fourteenth Dalai Lama (b.1933). After the establishment of the PRC in 1949, the problem of Tibet (which had declared itself independent since 1911 but has always been considered part of China by the Chinese government) remained unresolved for over a full year. In October 1950 the Chinese PLA began to move into Tibet. The Tibetan military government resisted, and the population was divided in its loyalties between those following the Dalai and those following the Panchen, who was not in Tibet at the time. In April 1951 a five-man negotiating team was sent from Tibet under the Dalai's auspices to negotiate a peace settlement with the Chinese government. Although the Dalai eventually became an important figure in China's own politics and government, he led the Tibetan rebellion against the Chinese government in 1959, after which he fled to India seeking political asylum. See text Mar. 22, 1960, note 7. See also text Apr. 6, 1952.

3. See text Nov. 23, 1949, source note.

Comment on Suppressing and Liquidating Counterrevolutionaries

(June 15, 1951)

Source: *Xuanji*, V, p. 45. Other Chinese Texts: *Wansui* (1969), p. 9; *Wansui* (1967a), p. 154. Available English Translations: *SW*, V, p. 56; JPRS, *Miscellany*, I, p. 8.

In no way should the policy of "giving two years of reprieve" be taken to mean that criminals who have committed crimes involving the shedding of people's blood or other serious crimes for which the people have demanded that they be executed are not to be executed. To do so would be a mistake. We must make it clear to the cadres and the popular masses in the districts and villages that in order to assuage the hatred of the people, those whose crimes and evil deeds are so great and who have incurred such bitter hatred of the people that unless they were executed the hatred of the people could not be assuaged must be executed. It is only with regard to those who have committed capital offense but against whom the people's anger is not deep and whose execution is not demanded by the people that we can apply [the policy of] passing the death sentence and giving them a two year reprieve, forcing them to take part in labor and [making final judgment] on the basis of how they behave.

Letter to Li Zhuchen
(June 23, 1951)

Source: *Shuxin*, p. 415.

Li Zhuchen (1881-1968) was an industrialist with enterprises in Tianjin. In 1945 he joined the Zhongguo minzhu jianguo hui (Chinese Democratic Association for National Construction) and became a member of its standing committee. (See text Sept. 21, 1949, note 1, and text Apr. 15, 1959, note 17.) Later, as a member of this organization, he became a member of the National Committee of the CPPCC. Although he never joined the CPC, Li served in several major positions in the PRC, as Minister of Food Industries, 1956-1958, and as Minister of the First Ministry of Light Industry after 1958. He was also a leader in many people's organizations, especially among industrialists and in the commercial circles. For more biographical information on Li, see Zhonggong renming lu, *pp. 234-235 and D. Klein and A. Clark, eds. (1971), I, pp. 489-490.*

Mr. Zhuchen:[1]

I have received the letter you sent me on June 13. Your suggestion is a very good one.[2] However, the timing needs to be further considered. It seems that it would be best to wait a short period before we carry it out.

In reply, and with my respect,

Mao Zedong

June 23

Notes

1. See text Nov. 17, 1949, note 2, for an explanation of this usage.

2. According to the source this refers to Li's suggestion that the propaganda campaign vis-à-vis Taiwan be launched with the participation of the various democratic parties (see text Sept. 21, 1949, note 1) and the people's organizations (see text Oct. 1, 1949, note 3) and the personages who had previously had connections with the KMT government.

Inscription on the Unity of Nationalities
(June 29, 1951 R)

Source: Released in *Changjiang ribao* (June 29, 1951).

All nationalities of the People's Republic of China, Unite!
Mao Zedong

Letter to Huang Yanpei
(July 15, 1951)

Source: *Shuxin*, p. 416.

See text Feb. 17, 1951, source note.

Mr. Renzhi:[1]

Your letter of July 14 has been received and read. I am very concerned about your illness. I fully agree that you must rest for a month to recover. If necessary, it would be proper to extend that for another month so that the restoration of your health may be complete. The times are indeed as you describe. The ancients said: "It is only when one can fight that one can make peace."[2] That is the situation with us. We took a measure yesterday that will be helpful in stripping our enemies of their excuse and facilitate the continuation of the [peace] meetings.[3]

I respectfully wish your recovery and safety.

Mao Zedong
July 15

Notes

1. See text Feb. 17, 1951, note 1.
2. We have not at this time been able to identify the original source of this saying. It appears to be a paraphrase in the way it is rendered here by Mao.
3. According to the source, this refers to the communiqué issued jointly by Kim Il Sung, the

supreme commander of the Korean People's Army, and Peng Dehuai, commander of the Chinese People's Volunteers in the Korean conflict to the command of the United States and United Nations forces in which they agreed on the neutralization and demilitarization of the Kaesong area during the period when the peace negotiations of the two sides were being held in that city and on the recognition of the U.S. press corps of twenty people as part of the working staff of the U.S. side (and therefore to be awarded diplomatic status and access to the negotiations). For more on the negotiations see text Aug. 4, 1952, note 1.

Letter to Zhang Yuanji
(July 30, 1951)

Source: *Shuxin*, p. 418.

Zhang Yuanji (a.k.a. Zhang Jusheng, Zhang Xiaozai) (1886-1969) is perhaps modern China's most famous bibliophile. A young scholar at the time of the Sino-Japanese War of 1894-95, he became imbued with the ideas of political reform, and was, with Kang Youwei, Huang Zunxian, Tan Sitong and Liang Qichao, one of the chief advisors to the Guangxu Emperor in the ill-fated "Hundred Days" Reform of 1898. After that he was banned from political or bureaucratic service and turned his attention to education and scholarship. In 1902, he became the principal of Nanyang gongxue (South Seas Public School), which was the forerunner of Jiaotong University. This academy, which emphasized foreign language education, put Zhang in touch with the subject of translation and with the concept of expanding the traditional Chinese curriculum to cover textbooks on modern subjects. Zhang became dedicated to these issues for the rest of his life. His enthusiasm carried over to his directorship of the Commercial Press, which he helped to build into the largest publishing house in China, and in which he emphasized publishing textbook series on all subjects for all levels of education, something for which that publisher has become world-famous. He also devoted himself to the collection and reprinting of rare books and such major and intimidating collections of Chinese documents as the Siku quanshu *(Complete Books of the Four Treasuries). With the aid of Cai Yuanpei, Zhang also brought together the most renowned private collection of Chinese books, known as the Hanfenlou library. After the war against Japan, Zhang, by then a senior Chinese scholar, became disillusioned with the policies of the KMT and was persuaded to take the side of the CPC. As the doyen of the Academia Sinica, of which he became a member in 1948, he had much influence on the Chinese intellectuals who remained on the mainland after 1949. At the time of this letter, Zhang was a member of the East China Military and Administrative Committee, the director of the Literature and Historical Studies Bureau of Shanghai Municipality, and a member of the National Committee of the CPPCC. For more biographical information on Zhang, see H. Boorman et al., eds. (1967), I, pp. 138-140.*

Mr. Jusheng:[1]

Your letters of December 30 last year and April 15 and May 21 [of this year] and your enclosed masterpiece and your book have all been received. Thank you for your kind thoughts. The poem "Jixue xichui" (Snow Drifts on the Western Frontier) is extremely well written. As a result of the signing of the agreements[2] our troops will be in Lhasa soon. I am greatly gratified to know that you are recovering from your illness.

In reply, and with respectful wishes for your health and well-being,

Mao Zedong
July 30, 1951

Notes

1. This is Zhang's *zi*, or honorific name. See text Oct. 15, 1949, note 1, for an explanation of this usage.

2. This refers to the Agreements on the Peaceful Liberation of Tibet. See text May 24, 1951, source note.

Inscription for the People of the Old Revolutionary Bases
(August 5, 1951 R)

Source: *Changjiang ribao* (Aug. 5, 1951), 1. Other Chinese Text: *RMRB* (Aug. 11, 1951), 1.

Both of these dates are dates of release. We have no definite knowledge of the actual date of the writing of this inscription, but we believe it to be before August 5, 1951.

Revolutionary bases (genjudi) refer to geographic areas under Communist control before 1949 in which the military and political activities and policies of the CPC were launched before Liberation. No written document may be cited to define why some of these bases were referred to as old. Generally speaking, old revolutionary bases refer to areas where the CPC operated in the 1920s and 1930s. Jinggangshan (in Jiangxi) and Yanan (in Shaanxi) are the most famous ones. See Faling huibian, 1952, pp. 45-48.

Promote the revolutionary tradition.
Strive for even greater glory.

Telegram to the Dominion of Pakistan
(August 14, 1951)

Source: *RMRB* (Aug. 14, 1951), 1. Available English Translation: *SCMP*, 155 (Aug. 14, 1951), 8.

The Governor General,
The Dominion of Pakistan

Mr. [A. K.] Nazimuddin:

On this occasion of the national day of your country, on behalf of the government and the people of the People's Republic of China I extend to Your Excellency and the people of Pakistan our felicitations and our best wishes that the friendship between the peoples of China and Pakistan will grow with each passing day.
(Signed as Chairman of CPG of PRC, dated, in Beijing)

Telegram to the Democratic People's Republic of Korea
(August 14, 1951)

Source: *RMRB* (Aug. 15, 1951), 1. Available English Translation: *SCMP* (Aug. 15, 1952), 3.

Chairman Kim Du Bong,
The Standing Committee,
The Supreme People's Assembly,
The Democratic People's Republic of Korea

Your Excellency:

On this happy occasion of the sixth anniversary of the liberation of Korea, on behalf of the government and the people of the People's Republic of China I sincerely extend to Your Excellency and the Korean people our heartfelt feli-

citations and our best wishes that in our common struggle to defend the lasting peace in Asia and in the world the fraternal friendship between the Chinese and Korean peoples will be further consolidated.
(Signed as Chairman of CPG of PRC, dated, in Beijing)

Telegram to the Republic of Indonesia
(August 14, 1951)

Source: *RMRB* (Aug. 17, 1951), 1. Available English Translation: *SCMP*, 156 (Aug. 16, 1951), 26.

Mr. Sukarno,
President,
The Republic of Indonesia:

On this happy occasion of the anniversary of the founding of your country, on behalf of the government and the people of the People's Republic of China I sincerely extend to Your Excellency and the people of Indonesia our felicitations and our best wishes for the further consolidation and development of the friendship between our two peoples with the passing of each day.
(Signed as Chairman of CPG of PRC, dated, in Beijing)

Telegram to the Democratic Republic of Viet Nam
(September 1, 1951)

Source: *RMRB* (Sept. 2, 1951), 1. Available English Translation: *SCMP*, 166 (Sept. 2-4, 1951), 28.

Chairman Ho Chi Minh,
The Government of the Democratic Republic of Viet Nam

Your Excellency:

On this happy occasion of the sixth anniversary of the founding of the Democratic Republic of Viet Nam, on behalf of the government and the people of the People's Republic of China, I sincerely extend to Your Excellency and the Vietnamese people our heartfelt felicitations and our best wishes that the struggle against imperialism by the Vietnamese people under Your Excellency's leadership for the liberation of the whole of Viet Nam will achieve new victories.

(Signed as Chairman of CPG of PRC, dated, in Beijing)

Telegram to the USSR

(September 2, 1951)

Source: *RMRB* (Sept. 3, 1951), 1. Other Chinese Text: *XHYB*, IV:5 (Sept. 25, 1951), 988. Available English Translation: *SCMP*, 166 (Sept. 24, 1951), 17.

Generalissimo Stalin:

On this occasion of the sixth anniversary of the victory in the War of Resistance Against Japan, on behalf of the Chinese People's Liberation Army and the people of all China I sincerely extend to Your Excellency, to the armed forces of the Soviet Union, and to the Soviet people our warmest felicitations and our deepest gratitude. The enormous assistance that the Soviet Union gave to the Chinese people in their War of Resistance Against Japan and the consolidated alliance between the Soviet Union and the People's Republic of China for the concerted prevention of the resurgence of Japan's aggressive forces have given the Chinese peole boundless encouragement in their struggle against aggressive forces in the Far East. Long live the great friendship of China and the Soviet Union in their just cause of resisting Japanese imperialism and defending peace in the Far East.

(Signed as Chairman of CPG of PRC and dated)

Telegram to the People's Republic of Bulgaria

(September 7, 1951)

Source: *RMRB* (Sept. 9, 1951), 1. Available English Translation: *SCMP*, 170 (Sept. 9-10, 1951), 8.

Chairman Georgi Damyanov,
Presidium of the National Assembly,
The People's Republic of Bulgaria

Your Excellency:

On the occasion of the national day of the People's Republic of Bulgaria, on behalf of the government and the people of the People's Republic of China I extend my heartfelt congratulations to Your Excellency and to the Bulgarian people and wish the People's Republic of Bulgaria ever greater successes with each passing day in its cause of construction toward socialism.
(Signed as Chairman of CPG of PRC, dated, in Beijing)

Comment on Suppressing and Liquidating Counterrevolutionaries

(September 10, 1951)

Source: *Xuanji*, V, p. 45. Available English Translation: *SW*, V, p. 56.

The work of suppressing counterrevolutionaries must be placed entirely under the unified leadership of the Party committees at each level, and the comrades in charge of all public security organs and other organs concerned with the suppression of counterrevolutionaries must, as in the past, unreservedly accept the leadership of the Party committees.

Letter to Party Committee of Shijingshan Iron and Steel Works
(September 12, 1951)

Source: *Shuxin*, p. 419.

Shijingshan is in Hebei Province within the Municipality of Beijing and located only a few km. west of Beijing city proper. It is an important iron ore mining and production area and was developed substantially during the time of the Japanese occupation by the Japanese. In 1954, however, it was identified as one of twenty-three subnormal (i.e., output being less than targeted norm) projects.

Comrades of the CPC Party Committee of the Shijingshan Iron and Steel Works:

I have read your letter of August 31. Thank you for letting me know about the situation and problems in your factory. I think that your proposals[1] are reasonable, and I have already ordered the concerned organs to resolve these problems speedily and reasonably.

In reply, and with my best wishes on your continued hard work!

Mao Zedong
September 12, 1951

Note

1. According to the source, this refers to proposals made by this Party committee on adjusting certain unreasonable features of the wage system at the factory.

Comment on Suppressing and Liquidating Counterrevolutionaries
(September 18, 1951)

Source: *Wansui* (1969), p. 9. Other Chinese Text: *Wansui* (1967a), p. 154. Available English Translation: JPRS, *Miscellany*, I, p. 8.

The dates differ in the two Wansui *sources. Here we follow the* Wansui *(1969) source.*

The Wansui *(1967a) source gives September 18, 1959 (obviously incorrect), as the date.*

[Your] view is correct; let them [i.e., the counterrevolutionaries] move, and [we will] watch carefully; then there is much to gain. They are in the palm of Tathagata[1] and are unable to jump off it. You should treat this as a major task and actively and artistically carry out observation and investigative work on it.

Note

1. Tathagata is the title for Sakyamuni (Buddha). This refers to the story in the Ming dynasty novel *Xiyou ji* (Journey to the West) of the Monkey King who is unable to jump off the palm of Tathagata in a trial of strength.

Letter to Deng Zihui
(September 25, 1951)

Source: *Shuxin*, p. 420.

See text Mar. 18, 1951, source note, and text Oct. 11, 1955(1), note 34.

Comrade Zihui:

I have received your telegram of September 25.

(1) I would like to express my condolences on the passing away of your mother.

(2) I agree with your plan on coming to the capital after the National Day celebration. It would be very good if you can arrive at the capital on October 3.

> Mao Zedong
> 24:00
> September 25

Reply to Ambassador of the Union of Burma
(September 27, 1951)

Source: *RMRB* (Sept. 28, 1951), 1. Available English Translation: NCNA, *Daily Bulletin*, 381 (Oct. 4, 1951), 3-4.

U Hla Maung became the ambassador of the Union of Burma to the PRC at this time.

Mr. Ambassador:

I am very pleased to accept the letter of credence from the President of the Union of Burma presented by Your Excellency, and I am grateful to Your Excellency for your felicitations.

Historically and culturally, China and Burma have had a long-lasting and intimate relationship. Moreover, the people of the two countries, in their protracted struggles for national independence and liberty, have gained deep sympathy for and understanding of each other. I am convinced that the development of diplomatic relations between our two countries will not only cause the friendship which already exists between the peoples of the two countries to be promoted and consolidated with the passing of each day, but will also facilitate [the growth of] peace and security in Asia.

I warmly welcome Your Excellency as the ambassador extraordinary and plenipotentiary of the Union of Burma to the People's Republic of China and pledge to Your Excellency my assistance in your work of strengthening the friendly cooperation between our two countries.

Our sincere wishes for the prosperity of your nation and of your people and for the good health of your head of state.

Comment on Suppressing and Liquidating Counterrevolutionaries

(October 1, 1951)

Source: *Wansui* (1969), p. 9. Available English Translation: JPRS, *Miscellany*, I, p. 8.

Unless we take steps to wipe out the activities of the counterrevolutionaries the people's state will be in jeopardy.

Telegram to the German Democratic Republic

(October 6, 1951)

Source: *RMRB* (Oct. 8, 1951), 1. Available English Translation: *SCMP*, 190 (Oct. 7, 1951), 8.

President Wilhelm Pieck,
The German Democratic Republic

Your Excellency:

On this happy occasion of the second anniversary of the founding of the German Democratic Republic, on behalf of the government and the people of the People's Republic of China I sincerely extend to Your Excellency and the German people our heartfelt felicitations and our best wishes that the German people will win still greater successes in their cause of striving for the unification, democracy, and independence of Germany and defending peace in Europe and the world.
(Signed as Chairman of CPG of PRC)

Letter to Chen Shutong
(October 14, 1951)

Source: *Shuxin*, p. 421.

See text Dec. 18, 1950, source note, and text Dec. 8, 1956, note 22.

Dear Venerated Mr. Shu[tong]:[1]

I have received your gracious letter of October 9. Thank you. On the subject of [going to] inspect land reform, I agree with you.[2] However, on whether or not the wintry weather would be suitable for your physical [well-being to do this], please give it some further consideration. It seems to me that it would be better [if you did it] in the spring. There will still be land reform [in progress] at that time. Furthermore, at your venerable age, it is proper for you to go and inspect the land reform, but not for you to engage in land reform [work yourself]. Besides, in inspecting it you can go to many places, but if you were to engage in the work itself, you would be limited to a district or a *xiang*. Another thing: it is not merely the land reform by itself, but if your energies would allow, such other work as [in the area of] resisting the U.S., of suppressing counterrevolutionaries, of production, of education, and of the United Front should all be within the scope of your inspection.[3]

I have here a report on the work among the minority nationalities of the Northwest. You may read it and afterward return it to me.

In salute,

Mao Zedong

October 4

Notes

1. See text Dec. 18, 1950, note 1.
2. See text Mar. 18, 1951.
3. See text Feb. 18, 1951, note 1, and text Dec. 19, 1950, source note.

Telegram to the USSR
(October 15, 1951)

Source: *CDSP*, III:42 (Dec. 1, 1951), 16.

We have no Chinese text of this telegram. This transcript, originally from the Russian newspapers Pravda *(Oct. 15, 1951), 1, and* Izvestia *(Oct. 16, 1951), is here presented in its original* CDSP *form. The telegram was evidently addressed to Stalin.*

On behalf of the government of the Chinese People's Republic and the Chinese people I express to you sincere thanks for your friendly greetings and cordial wishes on the second anniversary of the proclamation of the Chinese People's Republic.

Opening Speech of the Third Meeting
of the First National Committee of the CPPCC

(October 23, 1951)

Source: *RMRB* (Oct. 24, 1951), 1. Other Chinese Texts: *XHYB*, 11 (Nov. 25, 1951), 4-6; *Zhengxie san ci*, pp. 1-5; *RMSC* (1952), pp. 163-164; *Xuanji*, V, pp. 48-52; *XHBYK*, 22 (Nov. 1958), 2 (excerpt). Available English Translations: NCNA, *Daily Bulletin*, 395 (Oct. 24, 1941), 1-2; *CB*, 130 (Oct. 25 1951), 1-4; *SW*, V, pp. 59-63; K. Fan (1972), pp. 96-101; NCNA, *Daily Bulletin*, 442 (Jan. 2, 1952), 2 (excerpt).

The Third Meeting of the First National Committee of the CPPCC was held Oct. 23-Nov. 1, 1951, in Beijing. The main points on the agenda were (1) the movement to Resist U.S. Aggression and Aid Korea; (2) the land reform program, and (3) the suppression of counterrevolutionaries. For more on this meeting see K. Lieberthal (1976), pp. 55-56.

Committee members, comrades:

The Third Meeting of the First National Committee of our People's Political Consultative Conference is now in session. At this meeting, in addition to the members of the National Committee, we also have among us, by invitation, [members of] the Chinese People's Volunteers,[1] the People's Liberation Army, model laborers of industry, model workers of agriculture, representatives of the old [revolutionary] bases,[2] persons engaged in educational work and in literary and artistic work, industrialists and business people, experts in all fields, and representatives of the religious circles, of the minority nationalities, of the overseas Chinese,[3] of women, of youth, of the provincial and municipal consultative conferences,[4] and of [various] other circles. Besides all these, we also have with us many working personnel in the government. Among the participants and attendants there are many who have been recognized by the people as combat heroes, model laborers, and exemplary workers. The scale of our present meeting fully reflects the fact that the People's Republic of China has achieved great accomplishments and progress on every front.

In the past year, three large-scale movements were unfolded in our country – the Movement to Resist U.S. Aggression and Aid Korea, the land reform movement, and the movement to suppress counterrevolutionaries. Great victories have been achieved. The remnants of the counterrevolution on the mainland will soon be fundamentally eliminated. And as for land reform, it will be completed in 1952, except in the areas inhabited by minority nationalities. In the Movement to Resist U.S. Aggression and Aid Korea, the entire Chinese people are united on an unprecedentedly extensive scale to carry on a resolute struggle against the aggressive forces of American imperialism. The Chinese People's Volunteers, representative of the great determination of the Chinese people, have stood shoulder to shoulder with the People's Army of Korea and shattered the American imperialists' maniacal schemes of invading and occupying the Democratic People's Republic of Korea and thence invading the Chinese mainland. By doing so, they have encouraged the peace-loving people of Korea, China, Asia, and of all the world and have enhanced their confidence in defending peace and resisting aggression. We should express our congratulations and respect to the valiant Chinese People's Volunteers and the Korean People's Army.

As a result of the victories already achieved in these three aforementioned great movements and the concerted efforts at all levels of the People's Government and people of all walks of life, our country has now attained unprecedented unification. The Tibetan question has already been solved by peaceful measures,[5] and the national defense forces have been strengthened. The people's democratic dictatorship has been consolidated. Meanwhile our finances and the prices of commodities have continued to remain stable, and our work of restoring and developing our economic construction and our cultural and educational affairs has also taken a big step forward.

On the industrial and agricultural fronts, the patriotic movement for increasing production is in the process of developing.[6] This is a novel prospect in our country that is worth celebrating. Since land reform has been carried out in the rural areas and since democratic reforms have been implemented in industrial enterprises, workers and peasants have gained the opportunity to develop their tremendous initiative for a patriotic [movement to] increase production and to improve their material and cultural lives. As long as we are effective at uniting with the workers and the peasants and at educating and relying on them, our country is bound to witness a widespread and rising patriotic movement for increasing production.

On our country's cultural and educational front, and among all types of intellectuals, a movement of self-education and self-reform has been extensively developed in accordance with the policies of the Central People's Government.[7] This, too, is a novel prospect in our country that is worth celebrating. At the closing of the Second Meeting of the National Committee,[8] I proposed carrying out self-education and self-reform by means of criticism and self-criticism. Today, this proposal has been transformed step by step into reality. Ideological transformation, first and foremost the ideological transformation of all types of intellectuals, is one of the major conditions for our country to thoroughly implement democratic reforms in all areas and to gradually carry out industrialization. Therefore, let us project into the future our best wishes for even greater successes in the self-education and self-reform movement as it steadily advances.

All the facts prove that our system of people's democratic dictatorship is far superior to the political system in capitalist countries. On the basis of this sort of system, our country's people are capable of exerting their limitless and inexhaustible energies; such strength cannot be overcome by any enemy.

The great Movement to Resist U.S. Aggression and Aid Korea is still going on and must continue until the government of the United States is willing to settle the matter peacefully. We do not want to invade any country; we are simply opposing imperialist aggression against our country. Everybody knows that if American forces had not invaded our Taiwan, attacked the Democratic People's Republic of Korea, and fought their way to our northeastern frontiers, the people of China would not be fighting with American troops. Nevertheless, since the American invaders had already begun to assault us, we had no choice but to raise the banner of anti-aggression; this was absolutely necessary and entirely justified, and all the people of the country have understood this necessity and justification. In order to continue to persist in this necessary and justified struggle, we will have to continue to strengthen the work of the Movement to Resist U.S. Aggression and Aid Korea, to increase production, and to practice strict economy so as to support the Chinese People's Volunteers. This is the central task of the Chinese people today and is therefore also the central task of this meeting.

We have expressed our opinion at an early stage that the problem of Korea should be settled by peaceful means. Our opinion now is still the same. As soon as the American government is willing to settle the problem on a just and reasonable basis, and does not employ all sorts of disgraceful means to destroy and obstruct the progress of negotiations as it has done in the past, the negotiations to stop hostilities in Korea can still be successful. Otherwise there can be no success.

In the two years since the founding of the People's Republic of China, we have achieved great victories in all areas of our work. We have secured these victories only by relying on all forces with which it was possible for us to unite. At home we relied on the consolidation and unity of all the nationalities, all the democratic classes, all the democratic parties, all the people's organizations, and all the patriotic democratic personages under the leadership of the working class and the Communist Party.[9] In the international sphere we relied on the consolidation and unity of the camp for peace and democracy led by the Soviet Union and on the profound sympathy of the peace-loving people of all the countries in the world. For these reasons we have secured great victories in all areas of our work. This is something that was not foreseen by our enemies. Our enemies believed that since numerous difficulties confronted the newborn People's Republic of China and since they had launched an aggressive war against us, we would not be able to overcome our own difficulties or to deal counterblows to the aggressors. That we were actually able to overcome our own difficulties, to make counterattacks against the aggressors, and moreover to achieve great victories was beyond their expectation. Our enemies are shortsighted and shallow. They cannot perceive the strength derived from our great domestic and international unity and fail to see that the founding of the People's Republic of China proclaimed once and for all the end of the era of the Chinese people's subjugation by foreign imperialism. They also fail to see that the founding of the socialist Soviet Union, the founding of the People's Republic of China, the founding of all the People's Democracies,[10] the consolidation and unity of the two great countries, China and the Soviet Union, on the basis of the Treaty of Friendship, Mutual Assistance and Alliance,[11] the consolidation and unity of the entire camp for peace and democracy, and the profound sympathy that the broad masses of peaceful people of all countries in the world hold for this great camp have proclaimed once and for all the end of the era of imperialist hegemony over the world. Our enemies are unable to see these things; they still want to bully the People's Republic of China and to dominate the world. However, comrades, I can assure you that their ideas are fanatical, vain, and will not achieve their purpose. On the contrary, the People's Republic of China cannot be bullied, the great camp for peace led by the Soviet Union cannot be encroached upon, and the peaceful people of the world cannot be deceived. Comrades, ever since the victory of the great socialist October Revolution of the Soviet Union, [the stage has been] set for the triumph of the people in the world. Today, owing to the founding of the People's Republic of China and the founding of all the People's Democracies, this situation has been developed and consolidated. To be sure, during the historical period following the First World War and the Russian October Revolution, there was the fact that three imperialist countries, Germany, Italy and Japan, tried to establish hegemony over the world. This fact took place before the founding of the People's Republic of China and the founding of many People's Democracies. However, what were the consequences? Has it not already been proven that the designs of these three imperialist countries were maniacal and in vain? Were the results not precisely the reverse [of their designs]? [Were not] the imperialists who wished to establish a hegemony the ones who suffered the consequences of defeat? Now the situation is completely different; the great People's Republic of China has been established, and many People's Democracies have been established, the level of the consciousness of the people around the world has been raised, struggles for national liberation in the whole of Asia and North Africa are growing vigorously, and the forces of the entire imperialist system have been greatly weakened. Another crucial fact is that the strength of the Soviet Union, our closest ally, has greatly increased. At a time like this, if there are imperialist countries which attempt to tread again the old path taken by the three former aggressors, Germany, Italy and Japan, won't the consequences be absolutely predictable? In short, in one sentence, the world from now on must be a world of the people, the countries of the world must be governed by the people of the countries themselves, and it must no longer be a world tyrannized by imperialists and their running dogs. I hope that the people of our country will solidly unite among themselves as well as with our ally the Soviet Union, solidly unite with all the People's Democracies, with all the nations and peoples of the world that sympathize with us, and continue to march forward in the direction of victory in the struggle against aggression, victory in constructing our great country, and victory in the defense of lasting peace in the world. Comrades, if we do this, I believe our victory is ensured.

Notes

1. See text Oct. 8, 1950(2), note 1.

2. See text Aug. 5, 1951, source note.

3. Overseas Chinese *(huaqiao)* are people of Chinese ancestry who reside in countries other than China or Hong Kong or Macao. Overseas Chinese, regardless of their separate citizenship, were given a single bloc appointed representation in the CPPCC.

4. See text June 6, 1950(1), note 10.

5. See text May 24, 1951.

6. The Patriotic Movement to Increase Production was one of several "patriotic" movements (including the Patriotic Health Campaign, the Patriotic Ideological Education Campaign, the Patriotic Production Emulation and Competition Campaign) for which momentum had been gathering since the last quarter of 1950. These movements, and to some extent the campaign to suppress counterrevolutionaries, were all linked to the Movement to Resist U.S. Aggression and Aid Korea, since it was the fact of a war situation that placed the nation in a socially and economically vulnerable position. For much the same reason, the word patriotism also became the byword for all these campaigns. On December 29, 1951, following this meeting, the National Committee of the CPPCC issued a directive that linked the Increase Production campaign to the campaign against corruption and waste. This Increase Production campaign eventually became the model of other similar campaigns (often known as *zengchan jieyao*, or increase production and practice

economy campaigns) in subsequent years.

7. This was also known as the Patriotic Ideological Education Campaign and was the first massive ideological reform movement conducted among intellectuals in China since Liberation.

8. The second session of the National Committee of the CPPCC was held June 14-23, 1950, in Beijing. For Mao's speech at that conference, see text June 23, 1950.

9. See text Sept. 21, 1949, note 1, and text Oct. 1, 1949, note 3.

10. See text Sept. 21, 1949, note 4.

11. See text Jan. 2, 1950, note 1.

Telegram to the Dalai Lama

(October 26, 1951)

Source: *RMRB* (Oct. 27, 1951), 1. Other Chinese Text: *XHYB*, 11 (Nov. 28, 1951), 60. Available English Translation: *SCMP*, 203 (Oct. 26-27, 1951), 27.

See text May 24, 1951, note 2, for more on the Dalai Lama.

The Dalai Lama

Dear Sir:

Your telegram of October 24, 1951, has been received.[1] I am grateful for your efforts in implementing the Agreement on the Measures for the Peaceful Liberation of Tibet[2] and hereby send you my sincere congratulations. (Signed and dated)

Notes

1. For the Chinese text of this telegram, see *RMSC* (1952), p. 202.

2. See text May 24, 1951, source note.

Inscription for the Cultural Work Team
of the Special District Party Committee of Chu *xian*

(October 1951 R)

Source: Released in *RMRB* (Jan. 18, 1977), 1.

The special district of Chu xian *is located in the northeastern part of Anhui Province.*

Turn your faces toward the countryside.

Closing Speech of the Third Meeting
of the First National Committee of the CPPCC

(November 1, 1951)

Source: *RMRB* (Nov. 2, 1951), 1. Other Chinese Texts: *XHYB*, 11 (Nov. 25, 1951), 77; *RMSC* (1952), p. 164.

For more on this meeting see K. Lieberthal (1976), pp. 55-56.

Comrades:

Our meeting is drawing to a triumphant close. Let me express my congratulations on the success of this meeting. Just as we have been united in the various great struggles both internationally and domestically, so have we been united in this meeting of ours. Furthermore, our unity improves; it draws us closer to each other and grows more vigorous year after year. This is quite understandable, since the People's Democratic United Front of our country was forged, step by step, in the great revolutionary struggle. It is a united front that includes all the nationalities, all the democratic classes, all the democratic parties, all the people's organizations,[1] and all the patriotic and democratic personages in the country – a united front of several hundred million people. It is founded on the workers and peasants; it is under the leadership of the working class and the Communist Party, and it adopts the method of self-criticism. Therefore, it can solidly bind [us] together as one, and it can become more amd more vigorous, mightier and mightier. It is invincible. Comrades, we have already summed up the experience of the past year and have laid down guidelines for future work. We have also had a make-up election for eighteen additional committee members. Let us lead the people of the entire nation in continuing to march forward and in striving to win new and greater triumphs!

Note

1. See text Sept. 21, 1949, note 1, and text Oct. 1, 1949, note 3.

Telegram to the USSR
(November 5, 1951)

Source: *RMRB* (Nov. 7, 1951), 1. Other Chinese Text: *XHYB*, 11 (Nov. 25, 1951), 79. Available English Translation: *PC*, IV:10 (Nov. 16, 1962), 3.

Chairman,
The Council of Ministers,
The Union of Soviet Socialist Republics

Comrade Stalin:

On this occasion of the thirth-fourth anniversary of the great October Revolution, on behalf of the Chinese people, the government of the People's Republic of China, and on my own behalf, I extend to the people and government of the Soviet Union and to Your Excellency our sincerest congratulations.

Please allow me to congratulate the Soviet Union on its tremendous achievements in socialist construction and in the communist construction that has just begun. These achievements have instilled boundless courage in the laboring people of the whole world in their struggle for a bright future.

Please allow me to congratulate the Soviet Union on the great victory of its policy of peace. This victory has thwarted the disgraceful schemes of those who instigate war and has united the peace-loving peoples throughout the world and given them faith that peace will triumph over war.

Please allow me to express my congratulations on the great unshakeable friendship between the Soviet Union and the People's Republic of China which grows closer with each day. This friendship, which embraces one-third of the population of the entire world, is the most reliable guarantee of the certain victory of the cause of peace and progress in the world.
(Signed as Chairman of CPG of PRC, dated, in Beijing)

Telegram to Gheorghiu-Dej
(November 7, 1951)

Source: *RMRB* (Nov. 7, 1951), 1. Available English Translation: *SCMP*, 212 (Nov. 8, 1951), 8.

Gheorghiu-Dej was secretary general of the Workers' Party of Romania.

Dear Comrade Gheorghiu-Dej:

On this occasion of your fiftieth birthday, I extend to you my warmest congratulations on behalf of the Communist Party of China and myself and wish you good health.
(Signed as Chairman of CPG of PRC and dated)

Reply to Ambassador of Pakistan
(November 12, 1951)

Source: *RMRB* (Nov. 13, 1951), 1.

A. M. Raza served as ambassador of Pakistan to the PRC from November 1951 to June 1956.

Mr. Ambassador:

I am very pleased to accept the letter of credence from His Majesty the King of the United Kingdom of Great Britain, Ireland, and the Overseas Dominions presented by Your Excellency, and I am grateful to Your Excellency for your congratulations.

A long friendship has existed between the Chinese and Pakistani peoples, who share the common wish of promoting the development of economic and cultural relations between the two countries and of striving for a lasting peace in Asia and the world. The establishment of diplomatic relations between China and Pakistan will not only enable the friendship between our two peoples to steadily grow and be consolidated, but will certainly help maintain peace and security in Asia and in the world.

We warmly welcome Your Excellency as the first ambassador extraordinary and plenipotentiary from Pakistan to the People's Republic of China and pledge to Your Excellency our assistance in your work of strengthening the friendly cooperation between our two countries.

Our best wishes for the prosperity of your state, the prospering of your people, and the good health of your head of state.

Letter to Zheng Zhenduo
(December 3, 1951)

Source: *Shuxin*, p. 422.

Zheng Zhenduo (1898-1958) was a renowned writer and literary historian. In the 1920s he was the editor of several major journals on the modern Chinese literary movement, Wenxue zhoubao *(Literary Weekly) and* Xiaoshuo yuebao *(Short Story Monthly). He is most well-remembered for his work on several socially oriented collections of stories of the Ming period –* Xingshi heng yan *(Stories to Arouse the Consciousness of the Times) and* Jingshi tongyan *(Stories of Admonition for the Age), for the* Wan Qing wenxuan *(Selected Writings of the Late Qing Dynasty), and for his magnum opus,* Zhongguo wenxue shi *(History of Chinese Literature). At the time of this letter, Zheng was a vice-minister of the Cultural Ministry of the Central People's Government and the head of its Documents and Artifacts Bureau. For more biographical information on Zheng, see H. Boorman et al., eds. (1967), I, pp. 266-270.*

Mr. Zhenduo:[1]

Mr. Yao Yuqin,[2] via Mr. Chen Shutong,[3] has presented me with a gift of an original handwritten copy of a Wang Chuanshan writing.[4] I hear that such handwritten originals are extremely rare. I am sending this to your department; please preserve it for us.

With best wishes for your health and well-being.

Mao Zedong

December 3

Notes

1. See text Nov. 17, 1949, note 2, for an explanation of this usage.

2. We have not yet been able to locate accurate biographical data on Yao. The source informs us that he is a painter.

3. See text Dec 18, 1950, source note, and text Dec. 8, 1956, note 22.

4. Wang Chuanshan (a.k.a. Wang Fuzhi, 1619-1692) was a major thinker of the late-Ming-early-Qing period. He was famous for his studies on the *Zhou Yi* (Zhou Book of Changes), from which he derived the most consolidated system of thinking on the neo-Confucianist category of *qi* (spirit), his empiricist and pragmatic epistemology – he proposed, out of the earlier Wang Yangming's formulation of the unity and interpenetration of *zhi* (knowledge) and *xing* (practice), that practice forms the basis for knowledge – and for his Han nationalist thinking, which influenced late-Qing anti-Manchu thinkers. For more biographical information on Wang, see A. Hummel, ed. (1943), pp. 817-819.

According to the source, the document in question was a handwritten original (i.e., in Wang's own hand) of his *Shuang hao ruiwu fu* (Poetic Essay on the Auspicious Dance of the Brace of Cranes).

Letter to Dong Biwu

(December 4, 1951)

Source: *Shuxin*, p. 423.

Dong Biwu (1886-1975) was one of the founding members of the CPC. At the time of this letter he was a vice-premier of the Government Administration Council of the PRC and the head of the Political and Legal Committee. For more biographical information on Dong, see text May 8, 1958, note 7. According to the source, a plate original of this letter is preserved at the Documentary Office of the Central Committee of the CPC.

Comrade Biwu:

I think that the contents of your letter to Comrade Rao Shushi[1] are correct.[2] It can be copied and the copies may be sent to the comrades in positions of responsibility in all bureaus under the Central Committee other than the East China Bureau so that they may read it. I propose this so that they may be encouraged to pay attention to this matter.

Mao Zedong

December 4

Notes

1. See text Mar. 18, 1951, source note, and text Mar. 31, 1955, note 7.

2. According to the source, this refers to a letter that Dong sent to Rao on the subject of establishing government organs at the *xian* and *xiang* levels. In this letter Dong made several points, synopsized as follows: (1) While the work of establishing government organs at the lower levels should be directed by the Party, it would not be appropriate for the Party to be directly involved in day-to-day governmental matters. Instead, the Party should guide the establishment of such organs through the leadership of government organs at a higher level, and the leadership of the Party committee at all levels of government organs should be realized through the presence of Party members in these organs. For example, where there are more than three Party members, a Party group should be organized within that organ, so as to ensure the Party's leadership. (2) The establishment of government organs at the *xian* and *xiang* levels is the key. (3) There must be full organizational and ideological preparation for the endeavor.

Letter to Mao Zelian and Mao Yuanti

(December 11, 1951)

Source: *Shuxin*, p. 425.

According to the source, Mao Zelian is Mao Zedong's cousin, and Mao Yuanti is Mao Zedong's nephew.

Zelian, Yuanti:

I have received your letter.

Sixth Aunt Huisheng[1] and Zelian should not come to the capital and should not stay too long in Changsha either. After your illness[2] has been diagnosed and treated you should return to Shaoshan.[3] The People's Government is now resolved to practice streamlining and thrift and emphasizes opposition to waste and extravagance. Therefore you should not come to the capital or stay too long in Changsha.

As for difficulties that Zelian's family is having, I will try to give some measure of assistance and support at a later date; for the time being you should not expect or rely [on me] for support.

Yuanti can do some studying when he has any spare time from his work at the printing shop.

Please give my regards to Sixth Aunt.

I wish you all well!

Mao Zedong
December 11

Notes

1. According to the source, this refers to Mao Zelian's mother.
2. The illness here presumably refers to the aunt's illness and not to Mao Zelian's or Mao Yuanti's.
3. Shaoshan of Xiangtan *xian*, Hunan, is Mao's native village.

Telegram to the Northwest Nationalities' Peoples' Representatives' Conference for Resisting U.S. Aggression and Aiding Korea

(December 12, 1951)

Source: *RMRB* (Dec. 12, 1951), 1.

This conference was held at Xian, Dec. 12-15, 1951. For the nature and constituency of such conferences, see text June 6, 1950(1), note 10.

To all comrade delegates to the Northwest Nationalities' Peoples' Representatives' Conference for Resisting United States [Aggression] and Aiding Korea:

Thank you all for your telegram. During the past year or more, the people of the different nationalities in northwest China have contributed a tremendous effort to the patriotic struggle of resisting United States [aggression] and aiding Korea and have secured great results. At this conference, you have resolved to further unite the people of the various nationalities, to increase production, to practice strict economy, and to conduct patriotic propaganda and education in order to support the Chinese People's Volunteers.[1] This is very good. One of the reasons that imperialists dared to bully China in the past was that China's various nationalities were not united. However, that period in history is gone forever. From the day of the founding of the People's Republic of China, the various nationalities of China

have begun to unite as one big friendly and cooperative family that has sufficient strength to defeat any imperialist aggression and to build our homeland into a prosperous and mighty nation. Best wishes for the success of your conference!
(Signed with month and date, no year)

Note

1. For the linkage among all these movements, see text Oct. 23, 1951, notes 6 and 7.

Telegram to Panchen Gnoertehni
(December 13, 1951)

Source: *RMRB* (Dec. 15, 1951), 1. Other Chinese Text: *XHYB*, 2 (Feb. 1952), 52. Available English Translation: *SCMP*, 237 (Dec. 16-17, 1951), 12.

See text May 24, 1951, source note, and text Nov. 23, 1949, source note. Panchen Gnoertehni, the Panchen Lama of the time, who had been living in exile in Qinghai Province for over twenty years, began his return to Tibet on December 19, 1951. Before he left Qinghai, the Panchen Lama sent a telegram to Mao. For the Chinese text of this telegram, see RMSC (1952), pp. 203-204. The Panchen Lama arrived at Lhasa, the capital city of Tibet, on April 28, 1952.

Panchen Gnoertehni, through the
People's Government of Qinghai Province

Dear Sir:

Thank you for your telegram. I fully agree with your wish to unite closely with the Dalai Lama under the leadership of the Communist Party of China and the Central People's Government in order to struggle for the thorough implementation of the Agreement on the Measures for the Peaceful Liberation of Tibet,[1] expelling the influence of imperialism in Tibet, consolidating national defense, and building a New Tibet. I wish you a pleasant journey to your destination.
(Signed and dated)

Note

1. See text May 24, 1951, source note.

Letter to Liu Shaoqi
(December 15, 1951)

Source: *Shuxin*, p. 427.

See text June 4, 1950, source note, and text May, 19, 1953, source note.

Comrade Shaoqi:

How is your tour? I imagine that you should have arrived at Hangzhou by now.

According to the reports of Comrades An Ziwen and Hu Qiaomu,[1] there are still many people who, like the letter written by Yin Yigang of the Hebei Party School, are in disagreement with the idea that the semiproleteriat should also be considered a part of the leading class [in our society].[2] In the process of Party rectification in many localities, this problem has been proposed, and such a suggestion is reasonable. Now we are obliged to make some revisions on the proposal in the draft plan for Party rectification. On this matter we have already been pushed a bit to the passive side, and only by making these revisions can we capture the intiative. I am now sending for your perusal and assessment a copy of the telegram,[3] of An Ziwen's report[4] and of the letter sent to us by Yin Yigang of the Hebei Party School and asking for your opinion on the subject. Please send somebody back with your response.

Everything here is going well. Do not be concerned.

I wish you all well.

Mao Zedong
December 15

Notes

1. An Ziwen was at the time of this letter deputy director of the Organization Department of the Central Committee of the CPC. For more biographical information on An, see text Aug. 12, 1953, note 10, and text Mar. 31, 1955, note 12. For Hu Qiaomu, see text May 22, 1950, note 2.

2. According to the source, while the issue of designating the working class as the leading class in society during the period of the New Democratic Revolution (see text June 15, 1953, note 2)

and the period of socialist transition (see text June 15, 1953, note 1) is clearly defined, the issue of whether the semiproletariat should be included in this designation is a subject discussed only in several documents immediately prior to and after the founding of the People's Republic. (Note that in this letter Mao used the term *ban gongren jieji*, i.e., semi-working class. The term, however, is unclear in its meaning, and because Mao had, in similar contexts, used the term *ban wuchan jieji* – i.e., semiproletariat – we have translated the term in this way.) In February 1948, in revising the article "Stipulations of the Central Committee of the CPC on the Distinction of Social Classes in the Land Reform and on Their Various Treatments" (see text June 4, 1950, note 7), Mao wrote: "The proletariat and the semiproletariat (the poor peasants) are the leading class in the people's democratic revolution and the political regime of the new democratic state, with the proletariat being the primary leading class." In March-April 1951, at the National Conference on Organizational Work, the Central Committee stated in its Resolution on Rectifying and Reorganizing the Basic-Level Organizations of the Party (based on a report by Liu Shaoqi) that "in the past the Chinese revolution was led by the urban working class and the rural semi-working class (*ban gongren jieji*); from now on it stands in need of greater leadership by the working class." Then, in July of the same year, in a statement of Explanation of the Central Committee of the CPC on the Question of the Leadership Role of the Working Class and the Semi-working Class, this sentence was changed to read: "In the past the Chinese revolution was led by the working class and the semi-working class in the cities and in the countryside." Later, some people, such as Yin Yigang of the Hebei Party School run by the Hebei provincial committee of the CPC, wrote letters of opinion objecting to the idea of considering the semi-working class (or semiproletariat) as part of the leading class. Mao then sent these letters to An Ziwen (see note 1) for comment and suggestion on how they can be handled. An's suggestion was that the proposal that the semi-working class should be considered as part of the leading class should be amended. The implication of this letter here is that Mao agreed with An, and sent this letter to Liu Shaoqi for his opinion. Liu responded quickly with his assent, and in December 1951 the Central Committee issued an Amended Directive on the Question of the Leading Classes in the Chinese Revolution, in which it pointed out that "on the question of who leads the Chinese revolution, no matter whether with regard to the past or to the future, we should only say that it is led by the working class (through its vanguard, the Communist Party of China) and should no longer include therein the semi-working class."

3. This refers, according to the source, to the "amended directive" mentioned as the last item in note 2 and which at the time was soon to be published.

4. According to the source, this refers to An Ziwen's (see note 1) report to Mao on the question discussed here (see note 2). There is no available document of this, but the source informs us that An's report was made in November 1951.

Take Mutual Aid and Cooperativization
of Agriculture as a Major Task

(December 15, 1951)

Source: *Xuanji*, V, p. 59. Available English Translation: *SW*, V, p. 71.

According to this source, this was an intra-Party circular that Mao wrote supporting mutual aid and cooperativization and as a rebuff to Liu Shaoqi's opposition to cooperativization as expressed in a July 1951 directive that Liu issued in the name of the Party Center attacking a report of the Shaanxi Provincial Party Committee. This circular was appended to a draft resolution on cooperativization that was prepared under Mao's direction in September 1951.

Herewith we are distributing to you a copy of the Draft Resolution on Agricultural Mutual Aid and Cooperativization.[1] Please make copies of it for distribution to the *xian* and district [Party] committees. Please carry out forthwith the explanation of this draft both within and outside the Party and arrange for its implementation. This [draft resolution] is to be explained and implemented in all areas where the land reform has been completed; please take this as a major task. This draft resolution can be published in intra-Party publications, but since it is still only a draft, do not publish it in publications outside the Party.

Note

1. According to *Xuanji*, this was drafted under Mao's personal direction in September 1951. For more details on this document, see text July 31, 1955, note 8.

Letter to Chen Yuying
(December 23, 1951)

Source: *Shuxin*, p. 430.

According to the source, Chen Yuying was a nursemaid in Mao and Yang Kaihui's (his wife at the time) household from the winter of 1926 to the spring of 1931.

Comrade Chen Yuying:

I am very happy to receive your letter to me of December 18. Somebody has already told me that in the past you were very resolute in the face of [the interrogation by] counterrevolutionaries and did not surrender [to their intimidations]. This is very good. For the sake of thrift you should not come to the capital. It is very good for you to work in Changsha. If you have any difficulty, you may let me know and I'll do my best to find you some assistance.

I wish you good health!

Mao Zedong
December 23, 1951

Telegram to William Gallacher
(December 24, 1951)

Source: *RMRB* (Dec. 25, 1951), 1. Available English Translation: NCNA, *Daily Bulletin*, 439 (Dec. 28, 1951), 3.

William Gallacher was chairman of the Communist Party of Great Britain.

Dear Comrade William Gallacher:

On this happy occasion of your seventieth birthday, I extend to you my sincere congratulations on behalf of the Communist Party of China and myself and wish you excellent health.

(Signed as Chairman of CPC)

Conversation with Zhou Shizhao

(December 1951)

Source: Zhang Zizhi, "Mao zhuxi tiyu shenghuo de er san shi" (A Few Things About Physical Exercise in Chairman Mao's Life), *Tiyu bao* (Aug. 1, 1958), 12 (excerpts), reprinted in *Xian ribao* (Aug. 12, 1958).

The article from which this conversation is excerpted is the author's interview with Zhou Shizhao, principal of First Normal School, Changsha, Hunan. Zhou was Mao's former classmate and had paid a visit to the Chairman toward the end of 1951 on his way to the Northeast. See text Oct. 15, 1949, source note.

(Zhou says the weather is cold in the Northeast.)

Mao (laughing): Afraid of the cold? You two are only fifty-nine years old. Those in their fifties are still young fellows.

(Zhou asks whether the Chairman still takes cold water baths.)

Mao: I am getting older, I can no longer do it now. However, I bathe in a different way from others. Other people bathe in a bathtub and hot water. I splash a bit of somewhat colder water on my body and then take a shower.

Mao adds: I get two results from taking a bath; one is cleansing and the other is tempering.

Comment Written on a Letter from Students of Chinese People's University

(1951)

Source: *RMRB* (Sept. 8, 1977).

See also Mao's letters to Ma Xulun, June 19, 1950, and Jan. 15, 1951.

You must shorten your time for studying and protect your health.

Directive on Language Reform
(1951)

Source: This, possibly an excerpt from a lengthier and more general directive, was cited in a speech by Ma Xulun (see text June 19, 1950(1), source note) at the inaugural session of the Committee for Studying the Reform of the Chinese Language, February 5, 1952. This speech is published in *Zhongguo yuwen* (July 1952), 4.

Mao's 1951 directives on language reform are further paraphrased in PR, *16:32 (Aug. 10, 1973), 11. The July 1952 inaugural issue of* Zhongguo yuwen *also carried other articles in which Mao's concern for language reform was cited. One such is a report of a speech by Guo Moruo at the same inaugural meeting of the Committee to Study Language Reform, another was an article by Wei Yi in which an undated quotation by Mao is cited saying "the language must, under certain specific conditions, be reformed. Our language must be one that draws [us] closer to the masses."*

The written language must be reformed and oriented toward [the use of] a phonetic system as is common with the world's [other] written languages. [The reformed script] must have a national form, [its] letters and methods [of alphabetization] being formulated on the basis of Chinese characters in current use.

On the "Three-Anti's" and "Five-Anti's" Struggles
(November 1951-March 1952)

Source: *Xuanji*, V, pp. 53-58. Other Chinese Text: Point (a) of segment 5 here, dated March 5, 1952, also appears in a somewhat abbreviated version in *Wansui* (1969), p. 10, under the date of Mar. 20, 1952. Available English Translations: *SW*, V, pp. 64-70; JPRS, *Miscellany*, I, p. 11 (passage dated

Mar. 20, 1952, only).

According to the Xuanji *source, these are directives drafted by Mao on behalf of the Central Committee of the CPC.*

> *The "Three-Anti's" campaign of December 1951 to October 1952 was aimed at "opposing corruption, waste, and bureaucratism inside the Party and the state organs." The "Five-Anti's" campaign of December 1951 to June 1952 was aimed at opposing bribery, tax evasion, theft of state property, cheating on government contracts, and stealing economic information for the purpose of commercial speculation by the owners of private industrial and commercial enterprises. These campaigns had a number of effects. Economically, they contributed to the reduction of inflation and to increasing the government's knowledge of and control over important sectors of the urban economy. The "Five-Anti's" campaign led to the confiscation of some 2 billion rmb (U.S. 800 million) from capitalist elements and was a major step toward the integration of previously individually owned and managed captialist enterprises with the state-run economy (i.e., the socialist transformation of capitalism.) In addition, as noted in text August 12, 1953, the two campaigns were a severe attack on bourgeois ideology and, hence, on the authority of the bourgeoisie in the urban areas. It should be noted here that in March 1952 the Government Administration Council promulgated two documents: "Several General Regulations Regarding the Treatment of Corruption, Waste, and Overcoming the Errors of Bureaucratism" and "Standards and Methods of Differentiating between Types of Industrial and Commercial Units and Dealing with Them in the Five-Anti's Movement," and in April, the "Regulations Concerning Government Corruption" were also promulgated.*

1. The matter of opposing corruption and opposing waste is a major issue for the whole Party, and we have already told you to pay serious attention to it. We need to have a big clean up throughout the Party in order to expose thoroughly all cases of corruption, whether of major consequence or of mild or even minor significance, and to emphasize dealing heavy blows to those who have committed major offenses of corruption, while adopting a policy of education and reform toward those who have committed medium or minor offenses so as to prevent them from committing those offenses again. Only in this way can we arrest the extremely dangerous phenomenon of having many of our Party members corrupted by the bourgeoisie; only then can we overcome the situation which was foreseen at the Second Plenum of the Seventh Central Committee and carry out the policy, set forth at that Plenum, of preventing further corruption.[1] You must all be sure to give this your attention.

(November 30, 1951)

2. We must seriously note the fact that cadres have been corrupted by the bourgeoisie and that seriously corrupted behavior has occurred. We must pay attention to discovering, exposing, and punishing [such activity] and should

deal with this matter as a major struggle.

(November 30, 1951)

3. We should look on the struggle against corruption, waste, and bureaucratism as equal in importance to that of suppressing counterrevolutionaries. We should carry it out in a similar fashion, that is, by mobilizing the broad masses, including the democratic parties[2] and people from all walks of life in society, by giving it wide publicity and fanfare, by having the leading cadres take responsibility for it and take action personally, by calling on people to confess [their own wrongdoings] and to report [the wrongdoings of others], by criticizing and educating minor offenders, by removing from office the major offenders and punishing them or sentencing them to prison terms (reforming them through labor),[3] and lastly, by shooting a group of those who have committed the most serious offenses of corruption. Only thus can we solve the problem.

(December 8, 1951)

4. It is extremely necessary and extremely timely for us now to rely on the working class and unite with the law-abiding [members of the] bourgeoisie and other urban residents to launch in all cities throughout the country, and first of all in the large and medium-sized cities, a large-scale and resolute [campaign] against [members of] the bourgeoisie who violate the law–a struggle to oppose bribery, tax fraud and tax evasion, the theft of state property, cheating on labor and skimping on material [on government contracts], and the theft of economic intelligence – in order to coordinate with the struggle to oppose corruption, waste, and bureaucratism, which is [concurrently] taking place inside the Party, the government, the military, and among the people. In this struggle, Party organizations in each city must carefully deploy the class forces and the masses and must pay attention to using the strategy of utilizing contradictions, effecting splits, and uniting with the majority and isolating the minority, so as to rapidly form, through struggle, a "Five-Anti's" united front. In a large city, after the "Five-Anti's" [campaign] has been launched with intensity, such a united front can be formed in about three weeks. As soon as this united front is formed, those reactionary capitalists guilty of the most heinous crimes will be isolated and the state will be in a position to mete out to them, very reasonably and without opposition, different kinds of necessary punishment – such as arrest, imprisonment, execution by firing squad, confiscation [of their property], fines, etc. All large cities in the country (including provincial capitals) should enter the battle of the "Five-Anti's" in the first ten days of February. Please make prompt preparation for this.

(January 26, 1952)

5. (a) The basic principles in dealing with industrial and commercial units in the "Five-Anti's" movement are: leniency for past offenses and severity for offenses committed from now on (for example, payments for evaded taxes are retroactive only to 1951); leniency for the majority and severity for the minority; leniency for those who make a clean breast of their wrongdoings and

severity for those who resist; leniency for those in the industrial sector and severity for those in the commercial sector; leniency for those in general areas of the commercial sector and severity for those in the speculating areas of commerce. I hope that Party committees at all levels will maintain a firm grasp on these principles in the "Five-Anti's" [movement].

(b) In connection with the objective of the "Five-Anti's" movement, private industrial and commercial units are to be divided up into the following five types, namely, those that are law-abiding, those that are basically law-abiding, those that partly abide by the law and partly break the law, those that seriously violate the law, and those that are in complete violation of the law. For big cities, the first three types make up approximately ninety-five per cent, while the latter two types make up about five per cent. There are slight discrepancies among the large cities, but in general they do not differ greatly from one another. [The corresponding ratio] in the the medium-sized cities, however, differs rather more significantly from these percentages.

(c) These five types include bourgeois and nonbourgeois independent handicraft units and family trading units, but they do not include vendors. In the large cities, it is permissible not to deal with the vendors for the time being; it is better to deal with the independent handicraft units and the family trading units. In the medium-sized cities, it is best that the independent industrial and commercial units and the vendors be dealt with in the "Five-Anti's" movement.

There is a very large number of independent industrial and commercial units which do not hire workers or shop personnel (although some take in apprentices) in the large and medium-sized cities in our country. Many of them are law-abiding, but there are also many which are basically law-abiding but partially breaking the law (meaning that they cheat on or evade taxes in small amounts or, in other words, they have so-called minor problems), and a small number of them belong to the type that partly abides by the law and partly breaks the law or, in other words, cheats on or evades relatively larger amounts of taxes. In the current "Five-Anti's" movement, we aim to deal with a large group of small capitalists and to pass judgment on their cases, but we also ought to do our best to deal with the independent industrial and commercial units, which are more or less equal in number to the small capitalists, and to pass judgment on them. This will be beneficial not only to the present "Five-Anti's" movement but also to the economic construction of the future. There are no major problems within either of these two types of industrial and commercial units, and it will not be difficult to pass judgment on them. When this is done, we will receive the support of the broad masses. Still, if in individual cities it is believed that it is more convenient to pass judgment on other industrial and commercial units and put off for later passing judgment on the independent industrial and commercial units, it is also permissible to do so.

(d) In accordance with the actual conditions in the cities, we have decided to change the division of the industrial and commercial units from the four types of the past into five types; that is, we are changing the category of the law-abiding units into two categories – the law-abiding units and the basically law-abiding units. The other three types remain unchanged. Among the fifty thousand industrial and commercial units in Beijing (including independent industrial and commercial units, but not including vendors), law-abiding units make up about ten per cent, basically law-abiding units make up about sixty per cent, those units that partly abide by the law and partly break the law make up about twenty-five per cent, those that violate the law seriously make up about four per cent, and those that are in complete violation of the law make up about one per cent. To differentiate between the units that are completely law-abiding and those that have minor problems and are basically law-abiding, and, furthermore, to treat those among the basically law-abiding units who evade taxes in relatively small amounts differently from those who evade taxes in rather larger amounts can have a very great educational effect on them.

(e) In the large and medium-sized cities there are some municipal [Party] committees that are not at all acquainted with the situation that exists in the various types of industrial and commercial units and are very uncertain about the strategic viewpoint of differential treatment for these industrial and commercial units. In these places the organization and training of the trade union and government work teams (or investigation groups) have been done shoddily, and yet they have hastily launched the "Five-Anti's" movement; therefore some confusion has arisen. It is hoped that these municipal [Party] committees will pay attention [to this situation] and overcome it rapidly. Beyond this, the investigation of lawbreaking industrial and commercial units must be done under the strict control of the municipal [Party] committees and the municipal governments. The [other] organs are not to be allowed to send people out to make investigations on their own, much less to haul capitalists into their offices for interrogation. Furthermore, whether in the "Three-Anti's" movement or in the "Five-Anti's" movement, the method of using corporal punishment to extort confessions is not to be allowed, and strict precautions must be taken to prevent suicides. Where there have already been suicides, methods to prevent any further cases from ocurring must be formulated immediately to ensure that both the "Three-Anti's" movement and the "Five-Anti's" movement will develop soundly and on the right track, and to strive for the achievement of total victory.

(f) The "Three-Anti's" and "Five-Anti's" are not to be carried out in *xian*, districts, and *xiang* at the moment. As for when and how they will be carried out in the future, the Central Committee will issue a further notice to that effect. In individual cases, where there has already been experimentation on the "Five-Anti's" in the *xian* capitals or experimentation on the "Three-Anti's" in the districts, strict control must be exercised, and the spring farming and economic activities must not be hampered. Even in the medium-sized cities, they must not carry out the "Five-Anti's" all at the same time, but must do it in groups and only under strict control.

(March 5, 1952)

6. During and after this "Five-Anti's" struggle, we must achieve the following goals:

(a) Investigate thoroughly the situation of private industry and commerce so as to be able to unite with and control the bourgeoisie better and to carry out the country's planned economy. A planned economy cannot be carried out without a clear understanding of the situation.

(b) Draw a distinct line between the working class and the bourgeoisie, purge the trade unions of the phenomena of corruption and of bureaucratism, which alienate the masses, and weed out the running dogs of the bourgeoisie in the trade unions. Such running dogs and middle-of-the-road elements that vacillate between the workers and the capitalists can be found in trade unions everywhere. We must educate and win over the middle-of-the-road elements through struggle and expel those of the capitalist running dogs who have committed serious crimes.

(c) Reorganize the trade councils[4] and the association of industry and commerce,[5] remove from the leadership organs of these associations the people who are infected with all the "five poisons"[6] and others who have already lost all their credibility, and absorb into [these organizations] people who have deported themselves relatively well in the "Five-Anti's" movement. Except for those that are in complete violation of the law, all types of people engaged in industry and commerce ought to be represented in these associations.

(d) Help the people in responsible positions in the China Democratic National Construction Association[7] shake up that association and expel those people who are infected by all the "five poisons" and who have become seriously discredited among the people. Bring in a group of better people so that that association can become a political organization which is capable of representing the legitimate interests of the bourgeoisie, primarily the industrial bourgeoisie, and capable of educating the bourgeoisie with the principles of the Common Program[8] and the "Five-Anti's." As for the various secret organizations of different groups of capitalists, such as the "Thursday Dining Club,"[9] we ought to take steps to disband them.

(e) Eliminate the "five poisons" and wipe out commercial speculation, so that the entire bourgeoisie will obey the laws and decrees of the state and engage in industrial and commercial enterprises that are beneficial to the national economy and the livelihood of the people. Within the limits set by the state we should develop private industry (as long as the capitalists are willing and [their operation] conforms with the Common Program), and reduce the scope of private commerce gradually. The state should expand its plan to take over the sale of the products of privately owned [industry] and to contract the production of these goods[10] on a yearly basis, and to increase year by year the degree to which private industry and commerce are covered by [state] planning. We should reestablish [the limits on] the percentage of profit for private capital, so that while private capitalists will feel that they are making a profit, they will be prohibited from extracting exorbitant profits.

(f) Eliminate hidden accounts, make the economic [picture of enterprises] public, and gradually establish the system in which workers and shop personnel supervise production and management.

(g) Recover the greater part of the economic losses to the state and the people through payment of evaded taxes, restitution, fines, and confiscation.

(h) Set up Party branches among workers and shop personnel in all large and medium-sized privately owned enterprises so as to strengthen the work of the Party.

(March 23, 1952)

Notes

1. See text June 6, 1950(2), note 1.

2. See text Sept. 21, 1949, note 1.

3. The fundamental policy of dealing with civil and political criminals in the PRC involves, in many cases, not outright incarceration, but removal to labor camps where the offenders are forced to take part in labor, undergo mutual and self-criticism and political education. This practice was officially incorporated into the law of the PRC in 1954 by means of the Regulations Regarding Labor Reform in the Criminal Code promulgated that year.

4. The trade councils are guild-like labor organizations that had existed since before Liberation and that retain certain feudal characteristics. They are often exploitative vis-à-vis small capitalists.

5. This refers to the All-China Federation of Industry and Commerce which at this time was still in the planning stage and which was officially formed in 1953. See text Dec. 8, 1956, note 1.

6. The "five poisons" refer to the five targeted activities of the "Five-Anti's" campaign.

7. The China Democratic National Construction Association was formed in December 1945 in Chongqing, with capitalists in industrial and commercial enterprises as its main component. It was one of the "people's organizations" in the CPPCC. (See text Oct. 1, 1949, note 3.)

8. See text Sept. 21, 1949, note 3.

9. "The 'Thursday Dining Club' was a clandestine organization of capitalists in Chongqing which engaged in a series of serious illegal underground activities. It was exposed and disbanded during the 'Five-Anti's' movement." (*Xuanji*, V, p. 58, note 2.)

10. This plan, known as *bao xiao ding huo* (contracted marketing and contracted production, involves the establishment of contracts between the government and the privately run capitalists enterprises to have the latter's products sold to state-run enterprises according to fixed specifications, quantities, and prices, on the one hand, and for the individual enteprises to deliver such products on time according to the contracts, on the other.

1952

New Year's Day Message

(January 1, 1952)

Source: *Xuanji*, V, p. 60. Other Chinese Texts: *RMRB* (Jan. 3, 1952), 1; *XHYB*, 27 (Jan. 1, 1952), 5; *RMSC* (1952), frontispiece. Available English Translations: *SW*, V, p. 72; NCNA, *Daily Bulletin*, 445 (Jan. 7, 1952); *SCMP*, 247 (Jan. 3, 1952), 1-2.

May all of us – functionaries of the People's Government, commanders and soldiers of the People's Volunteers and the People's Liberation Army, [members of the] various democratic parties, people's organizations, minority nationalities, and people of the entire country – be victorious on all fronts in our work![1]

May we be victorious on the front to resist United States [aggression] and to aid Korea!

May we be victorious on the national defense front!

May we be victorious on the land reform front![2]

May we be victorious on the front of suppressing counterrevolutionaries!

May we win victories on the economic and financial fronts!

May we be victorious on the cultural and educational fronts!

May we be victorious on the front of the ideological transformation of the various social circles, first and foremost [the ideological transformation of the] intellectuals![3]

I would also like to wish for victory on a newly opened front, that is, a large-scale struggle against corruption, waste, and bureaucratism, which all the people in the country and functionaries [in the organizations] of our country, rising up as one, are called upon to launch with a great deal of fanfare, vigorously and resolutely, so as to cleanse away the the filth and poison left over from the old society!⁴

Comrades, in 1951 we won victories on all the above-mentioned fronts, and many of these victories were very great ones. I hope that through our concerted efforts we will be able to attain even greater victories in these areas of work in 1952.

Long live the People's Republic of China!

Notes

1. See text Oct. 8, 1950(2), note 1, text Sept. 21, 1949, note 1, and text Oct. 1, 1949, note 3.
2. See text Feb. 18, 1951, note 2.
3. See text Oct. 23, 1951, note 7.
4. See text Nov. 1951-Mar. 1952.

Telegram to the Union of Burma

(January 2, 1952)

Source: *RMRB* (Jan. 4, 1952), 1. Available English Translation: *SCMP*, 248 (Jan. 4-5, 1952), 7.

President Sao Shwe Thaike,
The Union of Burma

Your Excellency:

On this happy occasion of your country's National Day, on behalf of the government and the people of the People's Republic of China I sincerely extend to Your Excellency and to the government and people of your country our warmest congratulations. May the friendship between the Chinese and Burmese peoples grow and increase with each passing day.
(Signed as Chairman of CPG of PRC, dated, in Beijing)

Telegram to the Republic of India
(January 24, 1952)

Source: *RMRB* (Jan. 26, 1952), 1. Available English Translation: *SCMP*, 264 (Jan. 25, 1952), 8.

President,
The Republic of India

Mr. [Rajendra] Prasad:

On this occasion of your country's National Day, on behalf of the government and the people of the People's Republic of China I sincerely extend to Your Excellency and to the government and people of your country our warmest congratulations and our best wishes for the ever-growing prosperity and well-being of the Indian people.
(Signed as Chairman of CPG of PRC, dated, in Beijing)

Telegram to the People's Republic of Mongolia
(January 27, 1952)

Source: *RMRB* (Jan. 29, 1952), 1. Available English Translations: NCNA, *Daily Bulletin*, 465 (Feb. 4, 1952), 3; *SCMP*, 264 (Jan. 26-30, 1952), 7.

Chairman,
The Presidium of the Greater Hural,
The People's Republic of Mongolia

Comrade Bumatsende:

We are stunned to receive news of the passing away of Marshal Choibalsan, chairman of the Council of Ministers of the People's Republic of Mongolia.[1] On behalf of the government and the people of the People's Republic of China I extend to you and to the government and people of the

People's Republic of Mongolia our deep condolences. Marshal Choibalsan was a great leader of the Mongolian people and an outstanding leader and organizer of the Mongolian People's Revolution. His death is not only a tremendous loss to the Mongolian people, but also a loss to the camp for world peace and democracy. The assistance that Marshal Choibalsan rendered the Chinese people in the War of Resistance against Japanese imperialism will live forever in the hearts of the Chinese People.

(Signed as Chairman of CPG of PRC, dated, in Beijing)

Note

1. Marshal Khorloogiyn Choibalsan (alternately spelled Choibalsang) was the leader of the Mongolian People's Revolution and one of the co-founders of the People's Republic of Mongolia. He died in Moscow on January 26, 1952. For a biographical sketch of Choibalsan, see A. J. K. Sanders (1968), p. 172; also see C. R. Bawden (1968), chs. 6-8.

Telegram to the Democratic Republic of Viet Nam
(February 4, 1952)

Source: *RMRB* (Feb. 5, 1952), 1. Available English Translation: NCNA, *Daily Bulletin*, 469 (Feb. 8, 1952), 2.

Chairman,
The Government of the Democratic Republic of Viet Nam

Comrade Ho Chi Minh:

We are grateful for your friendly message of congratulations on the second anniversary of the establishment of diplomatic relations between the People's Republic of China and the Democratic Republic of Viet Nam. I firmly believe that the Vietnamese people, in their resolute, unyielding, and protracted struggle against imperialism and for the independence and liberty of their homeland will, under your leadership and with the sympathy of the peace-loving peoples throughout Asia and the world, eventually secure final victory.

(Signed and dated in Beijing)

Telegram to the USSR
(February 11, 1952)

Source: *RMRB* (Feb. 14, 1951), 1. Other Chinese Text: *XHYB*, 3 (Mar. 25, 1951), 45. Available English Translations: NCNA, *Daily Bulletin*, 473 (Feb. 14, 1951), 3. *SCMP*, 275 (Feb. 14, 1951), 3.

For further information on this treaty and related agreements, see text Jan. 2, 1950, note 1.

Chairman,
The Council of Ministers,
The Union of Soviet Socialist Republics

Comrade Stalin:

On behalf of the government and the people of the People's Republic of China I extend to the great people and the government of the Soviet Union and to you our deep gratitude and warm congratulations on this occasion of the second anniversary of the signing of the Sino-Soviet Treaty of Friendship, Alliance, and Mutual Assistance.

We are grateful for the enthusiastic and generous assistance which, in the last two years, the government and the people of the Soviet Union have given to the Chinese government and people in the spirit of the Sino-Soviet Treaty of Friendship, Alliance, and Mutual Assistance and its collateral agreements. This assistance has been of very great help to New China in the rehabilitation and development of its economy and in the consolidation of the state.

May the great friendship between the Chinese and Soviet peoples grow ever more intimate. The mighty alliance between China and the Soviet Union is an invincible force, a powerful guarantee against imperialist aggression and for the defense of peace and security in the Far East, and also a guarantee for the victory of the great cause of world peace.

Long live the unbreakable friendship and unity between the peoples of China and the Soviet Union!

(Signed as Chairman of CPG of PRC, dated, in Beijing)

Imperialism's Plan for Aggression Is Bound to Be Smashed
(February 14, 1952)

Source: Quoted from "Mao zhuxi lun diguo zhuyi he yiqie fandongpai dou shi zhi laohu" (Chairman Mao Discusses How the Imperialists and All Reactionaries Are Paper Tigers), in *Shijie zhishi*, 20 (1958), 5.

According to this source these comments were made by Mao at a banquet given by the Soviet ambassador to China to celebrate the second anniversary of the signing of the Sino-Soviet Treaty of Friendship, Alliance, and Mutual Assistance. They may be excerpts.

I believe that given the cooperation between the two great countries of China and the Soviet Union imperialism's plans for aggression are bound to be smashed.

It is evident to all of us that given the great cooperation between our [two countries], China and the Soviet Union, all of imperialism's plans of aggression cannot but be smashed. They are bound to be thoroughly shattered. As soon as the imperialists start a war of aggression, we and the people throughout the world will certainly wipe them from the face of the earth!

Telegram to the USSR
(February 21, 1952)

Source: *RMRB* (Feb. 2, 1951), 1. Other Chinese Text: *XHYB*, 3 (Mar. 1952), 77. Available English Translation: *SCMP*, 280 (Feb. 21-3, 1952), 14.

Chairman,
The Council of Ministers,
The Union of Soviet Socialist Republics

Comrade Stalin:

On this glorious day commemorating the thirty-fourth anniversary of the founding of the armed forces of the Union of Soviet Socialist Republics, please accept my heartfelt congratulations and best wishes.
(Signed and dated in Beijing)

Decree to a Division of the Xinjiang Construction Battalion
(February 1952)

Source: *Ziliao xuanbian*, p. 150.

According to the source, this decree was displayed in the Exhibition Hall of the First Agricultural Division of the Xinjiang Construction Battalion. The Ziliao xuanbian *text was copied from this exhibition. There is no further explanation of the circumstances under which this decree was issued.*

You are now given the glorious task of the economic construction of the homeland. In the past you have been a long-tested, highly organized and well-disciplined combat unit. We trust that, on the production and construction front, you will become a highly skilled commando troop in construction as well. You will act as heroic models, striving on a new front for the happiness of the revolutionary lives of the future, on behalf of all the people of the country, including yourselves.

You may now put your weapons of combat in reserve and take up the weapons of production and construction. If and when the homeland should have the need to call upon you, I shall once again order you to take up the weapons of combat once more to defend the homeland.

Telegram to Mátyás Rákosi
(March 7, 1952)

Source: *RMRB* (Mar. 9, 1952), 1. Available English Translation: *SCMP*, 291 (Mar. 8-10, 1952), 13.

M. Rákosi (b.1892) was general secretary of the Central Committee of the Communist Party of Hungary (Kommunisták Magyarországi Pártja, KMP) from 1945 to 1948, and general secretary of the Hungarian Workers' Party (Magyar Dolgozók Pártja, MDP) formed in 1948 by the merging of the KMP with the Hungarian Social Democratic Party (Magyar Szociál Demokrata Pártja).

The Central Committee,
The Hungarian Workers' Party

Dear Comrade Mátyás Rákosi:

On the occasion of your sixtieth birthday, on behalf of the Communist Party of China and on my own behalf, I extend to you – loyal son of the Hungarian people and outstanding fighter for the international workers' movement – our fraternal congratulations.

Respectfully, I wish you good health and further success in your cause of leading the Hungarian people on the path to socialism and of defending world peace.

(Signed as Chairman of CPC, dated, in Beijing)

Letter to Cheng Qian
(March 11, 1952)

Source: *Shuxin*, p. 431.

Cheng Qian (1881-1968) was a veteran KMT general, occupying a number of significant military and political posts in that Party and in Sun Yat-sen's government from the late 1910s through the 1940s, and by the late 1940s was one of the most powerful members of the KMT. (In 1948, he was a nearly successful candidate for the vice-presidency of the KMT national government.) He was, also in that year, governor of Hunan, his native province and in whose political affairs he had been active all his life. In August 1949 he surrendered to the Communists, who were rapidly advancing on Guangzhou, the seat of the KMT government, then nominally under the presidency of Li Zongren. His "defection" hastened the collapse of the defense of the KMT forces. After 1949, Cheng held several important political positions in the PRC. At the time of this letter he was, among other things, a deputy chairman of the Standing Committee of the NPC, and, more pertinently here, a vice-chairman of the Central-South Military and Government Administration Committee. For detailed biographical information on Cheng and particularly on his political and military career prior to 1949, see H. Boorman et al., eds. (1967), I, pp. 280-284.

Mr. Songyun:[1]

I have received your gracious letter of March 6. Your speech at the joint meeting[2] has permitted me to understand clearly the strengths and problems with [our country's] rivers and lakes and has been of great benefit to me.

In response, and with my respect,

Mao Zedong
March 11

Notes

1. "Songyun" is Cheng's *zi*, or honorific name. For explanation of this usage, see text Oct. 15, 1949, note 1.

2. According to the source, this refers to a joint meeting attended by the persons in charge of the departments of water conservation, of forestry and agriculture, and of transportation in the governments of the provinces of Hunan and Hubei and in the Central-South China Military and Government Administration Committee. This meeting, convened by the last organ mentioned above in March 1952, was held for the purpose of discussing the plans for the Jing River flood prevention project (see text May 19, 1952).

Instruction to Huang Yanpei
(March 15, 1952)

Source: *RMRB* (Sept. 14, 1952), 1.

According to this source, this is an indirect quotation of Mao's instructions transmitted by Huang Yanpei (see text Feb. 17, 1951, source note) at the fourth general meeting of the Beijing chapter of the China Democratic National Construction Association (see text Sept. 21, 1949, note 1) of which he was chairman. For more on the Association, also usually known as Minjian (for minzhu jianguo), see RMSC (1951), "Mou" section, p. 7.

1. Private capital is of value in New China's construction; it is just that we must not allow it to develop in the wrong direction.

2. The capitalists should not be allowed to seek their private interests only; they should also take the interests of the state and the workers into account.

3. Unite well with them, teach them, reform them; they should first study and carry out the Common Program.[1]

Note

1. See text Sept. 21, 1949, note 3.

Reply to Ambassador of the Democratic People's Republic of Korea (March 18, 1952)

Source: *RMRB* (Mar. 19, 1952), 1. Available English Translations: NCNA, *Daily Bulletin*, 498 (Mar. 20, 1952), 4; *SCMP*, 299 (Mar. 20, 1952), 2.

Kwon O Dik served as ambassador of the Democratic People's Republic of Korea to the PRC from March 1952 to December 1953.

Mr. Ambassador:

I am extraordinarily pleased to accept the letter of credence from the Standing Committee of the Supreme People's Assembly of the Democratic People's Republic of Korea presented by Your Excellency and am grateful for the good wishes that Your Excellency has expressed to the Chinese people on behalf of the Korean people.

In their great patriotic war of resistance against United States imperialist aggression, the heroic people of the Democratic People's Republic of Korea have displayed a noble spirit of sacrifice with which they have overcome all difficulties and have secured evident victories.

The peoples of China and Korea are engaged in a common struggle for the sake of resisting our common enemy, United States imperialist aggression, and protecting the security of our two countries and peace in the Far East. Indeed, as Your Excellency has pointed out, the long-standing friendly relations of mutual assistance between the Chinese and Korean peoples have been sealed by the noble blood of our common struggle. This struggle has already turned the consolidated unity between our peoples into an immense force for the cause of defending peace. As long as the Chinese and Korean peoples always continue to unite as one and struggle together, we will surely be able to smash the United States imperialists' plans for aggression against our two countries and to make extremely significant contributions to the defense of peace in the Far East and throughout the world.

I warmly welcome Your Excellency as the ambassador extraordinary and plenipotentiary of the Democratic People's Republic of Korea to the People's Republic of China and pledge to Your Excellency my utmost assistance in your work of consolidating and promoting the fraternal friendship between our two peoples.

My best wishes for the prosperity of your country, the prospering of your people, and the good health of your head of state.

Reply to Ambassador of the Republic of Czechoslovakia
(March 18, 1952)

Source: *RMRB* (Mar. 19, 1952), 1. Available English Translation: *SCMP*, 299 (Mar. 20, 1952), 4.

Komzala served as ambassador of the Republic of Czechoslovakia to the PRC from March 1952 to April 1955.

Mr. Ambassador:

I am extraordinarily pleased to accept the letter of credence from the President of the Republic of Czechoslovakia presented by Your Excellency and am grateful to Your Excellency for your warm congratulations.

For more than two years, the friendly relations between our two countries have achieved further development in the areas of politics, the economy, and culture. The Chinese people have paid constant attention to the brilliant achievements of the Czechoslovakian people in their work of socialist construction following liberation and are sincerely delighted with these achievements. I deeply believe that the friendly cooperation between our two countries will not only facilitate the economic prosperity of our countries and the strengthening of our friendship, but will also contribute to the consolidation of the camp for world peace and democracy led by the great Soviet Union.

I warmly welcome Your Excellency as the ambassador extraordinary and plenipotentiary from the Republic of Czechoslovakia to the People's Republic of China and pledge to Your Excellency my utmost assistance in your work of consolidating and promoting the fraternal friendship between our peoples.

Best wishes for the prosperity of your country, the prospering of your people, and the good health of your head of state.

Conversation with Zhai Zuojun
[Excerpt]
(Spring 1952)

Source: Excerpt from Zhai Zuojun, "Zai Mao zhuxi shenbian" (Being Next to Chairman Mao), *Xin guancha*, 10 (May 16, 1959), 33-38. Other Chinese Text: *Shengping ziliao*, p. 300 (excerpt).

Zhai Zuojun was a security guard for Mao in 1931. In 1952 he was working in the PLA Air Force and had been dispatched to Tianjin to gather materials on the "Three-Anti's" and "Five-Anti's" campaign. On his return to Beijing, he was invited to see Mao. The subject of the following excerpt from the ensuing conversation was the campaign.

How is the campaign going in your area?. . . (Zhai tells the Chairman that the campaign is going very well, very enthusiastically, and that workers, shop clerks, and the masses have all risen one after another to carry out struggles by reasoning with the capitalists.). . . That's good then. Without repelling the attack of the bourgeoisie, our revolutionary cause cannot develop.

Directive of the CPC Central Committee
on Work in Tibet
(April 6, 1952)

Source: *Xuanji*, V, pp. 61-64. Available English Translations: *SW*, V, pp. 75-76; JPRS, *Selections*, pp. 12-14.

According to the Xuanji *source, this is an intra-Party directive that Mao drafted for the Central Committee of the CPC that was sent to the Southwest Bureau and the Work Committee in Tibet, and further transmitted to the Northwest Bureau and the Xinjiang Sub-bureau.*

The Central Committee basically agrees with the directive of the Southwest Bureau and the Southwest Military Region cabled on April 2 to the Tibetan Work Committee[1] and the Tibetan Military Region,[2] and it considers the basic policies (except for the point about the reorganization of the Tibetan army) and the many concrete measures advocated by this telegram to be correct. Only by acting according to these [policies] can our army in Tibet stand on invincible ground.

The situation of Tibet and that of Xinjiang are not the same; both in political and in economic terms, Tibet falls far short of Xinjiang. Even when our army units under Wang Zhen entered Xinjiang, they focused all their efforts on practicing meticulous and careful budgeting, and on self-reliance and self-sufficiency in production.[3] Now they already have a firm foothold and have gained the enthusiastic support of the minority nationalities. At the present time, they are in the midst of carrying out the reduction of rents and interest; they will proceed this winter with land reform, and the masses will support us even more. Motor vehicles travel freely between Xinjiang and "China Proper,"[4] giving the minority nationalities great benefits in terms of material welfare. In Tibet it will be at least two or three years before rent reduction and land reform can be put into practice. Xinjiang has several hundred thousand Han people; Tibet, on the other hand, has almost none, and our army there is situated in the midst of a totally different nationality. We can rely only on two basic policies to win over the masses and put ourselves in an invincible position. The first policy is to practice meticulous and careful budgeting and to achieve self-sufficient production [for the army] and thereby influence the masses – this is the most basic key link. Even if the highways are built, we still must not depend on them for the transport of great quantities of grain.[5] India may agree to the exchange of food and goods with Tibet, but our foundation should be laid on the anticipation that in the event that some day in the future should India not supply food or other goods our army must still be able to survive. We must use all our efforts and any appropriate methods to win over the Dalai and the majority of his top echelon,[6] to isolate the small number of bad elements, and to attain the goal of gradually, over a number of years, revolutionizing the economy and politics of Tibet without any bloodshed. But we must also be prepared to deal with the possibility of bad elements leading the Tibetan troops in staging an uprising and attacking us, [so that] in such an event our army would be able to survive and hold out in Tibet. All this still necessarily depends on practicing meticulous and careful and self-sufficient production. Only by taking this most basic policy as the cornerstone [of our work] will we be able to attain our objective. The second policy, which can and must be followed, is to establish trade relations between India and the interior [of China], thus to move Tibet closer to a balance of imports and exports. The Tibetan people's standard of living must not experience the slightest decline as a result of our troops entering Tibet. Rather, we should strive to bring about some improvement in their lives. As long as we cannot resolve the two problems of production and trade, we will lose the material foundations for being there, the bad elements will gain capital every day that they can use to incite the backward among the masses and the Tibetan troops to oppose us, and our policy of uniting with the majority to isolate the minority will be weakened and will in no way succeed.

Of all the opinions set forth in the Southwest Bureau's telegram of April 2, only one bears [further] discussion. That is the matter of whether or not it is possible or desirable to reorganize the Tibetan army and establish a military and administrative committee fairly soon.[7] Our opinion is that at present we should not reorganize the Tibetan army and should not formally establish military subregions or a military and administrative committee. For the time being let everything remain as it has been; let things drag along and wait for a year or two until our army is really able to produce enough for itself and gain the support of the masses before discussing these matters further. Within the next one to two years, [one of] two [possible] situations may develop. One [of these possibilities] is that our united front policy toward the upper stratum, a policy of uniting with the majority to isolate the minority, will become effective and the Tibetan masses will gradually draw closer to us, and as a result, the bad elements and Tibetan troops will not dare to stage a riotous rebellion; the other is that the bad elements, assuming our weakness can be exploited, will lead the Tibetan troops into a riotous rebellion, and our army will stage a counterattack in self-defense and will strike them down. Either of these two situations would be beneficial to us. From the point of view of the Tibetan upper-stratum group, the reasons are not sufficient at this time to fully implement the Agreement[8] and reorganize the Tibetan army. After a few years, things will no longer be the same, and they may feel that the only thing to do will be to implement the Agreement in full and to reorganize the Tibetan army. If the Tibetan troops stage a rebellion, or if they stage not just one but several rebellions and are persistently knocked down by our troops' counterattacks, then we will have all the more reason for reorganizing the Tibetan army. It appears that not only the two Silons,[9] but the Dalai and the majority of his entourage as well, feel that the Agreement is being forced [on them], and they are unwilling to implement it. Not only do we not have the material base for fully implementing the Agreement at present, but we also don't have the mass base or the upper-stratum base for it. To force implementation would do more harm than good. Since they don't want to implement it, well then, let's not implement it for the time being, but just let it drag on for a while. The longer we drag it out, the more reason we will have and the less they will have. To let things drag out will not really be a great detriment to us; on the contrary, there may be some benefit. Let them do all kinds of bad things that senselessly harm people; we, in contrast, will do only good deeds in such areas as production, trade, road-building, medicine, and united front work (uniting with the majority and patiently educating [the people]). [We can] thereby win over the masses and wait until the time is ripe to resume the discussion on the matter of fully implementing the Agreement. If they feel that the setting up of primary schools is inappropriate, then even that can be stopped.[10]

The recent demonstration in Lhasa should not be seen as the work of only the two Silons and other bad individuals, but rather as an expression directed at us by the great majority of the Dalai's group. [11] The content of their petition was very tactful, not asking to break [with us], but only asking us to make concessions. One of the items hints at the restoration of a practice adopted in the Qing dynasty – [according to which they requested that] the Liberation Army not be stationed [in Tibet]; but this isn't their true intention. [12] They are well aware that this is not possible; their scheme is to use this point in exchange for other points. In their petition, they criticized the Fourteenth Dalai, absolving him of political responsibility for the current demonstration. They take on the appearance of protecting the interests of the Tibetan people, knowing that while in the area of military strength they are weaker than we are, by contrast, they are stronger in the area of social influence. We should in fact (not in form) accept this petition and postpone the full implementation of the Agreement. That they chose to stage this demonstration at a time when the Panchen[13] had not yet arrived was something to which [careful] consideration was given. After the Panchen arrives, they will probably give [him] a big pull to make him join their group. If our work is done well, and the Panchen doesn't fall into their trap and arrives safely at Shigaze,[14] the situation will then turn more to our advantage. But [we] cannot as yet change overnight the fact that our material base is inadequate or the fact that their social influence is greater than ours. Therefore, the fact that Dalai's group is unwilling to fully implement the Agreement will not be changed overnight either. We must formally take the offensive at the present time and denounce the irrationality of this demonstration and of the petition (as violating the Agreement), but in reality we must be prepared to make concessions and to wait until conditions are ripe and prepare to attack in the future (that is, implementing the Agreement).

I hope that you will ponder these matters and wire your responses.

Notes

1. The Tibetan Work Committee was a later incarnation of what was known as the Tibetan Work Team (Xizhang gongzuo dui), a team set up by the Culture and Education Commission of the State Council of the PRC to go to Tibet and do investigative studying of the local conditions with a view to "assisting in the future political, social, cultural and economic development of Tibet." This team left Beijing on June 7, 1951, and arrived at Lhasa, via Chongqing, on November 9, 1951.

2. The Tibetan Military Region was established on February 10, 1952, in accordance with Article 15 of the Agreement on Measures for the Peaceful Liberation of Tibet (see text May 24, 1951, source note). For more details, see *RMSC* (1952), p. 209.

3. In October 1949, the First Division of the First Field Army of the PLA moved into Xinjiang under Commander Wang Zhen (see text Nov. 14, 1949, note 4). It carried out Mao's directive issued in December of that year (see text Dec. 5, 1949) of having the army units actively take part in labor and production. With regard to Tibet, PLA troops under the command of Zhang Guohua

and Tan Guansan (the latter as political commissar) began to enter Tibet on the mission of "liberating" the region in the spring of 1950. Before much could be done, the Sichuan-Xikang highway had to be arduously built, and it was not until October 26, 1951, that these PLA units arrived at Lhasa, the capital city of Tibet. On December 1, 1951, they were reinforced by troops under the command of General Fan Ming. For more details on these events, see *RMSC* (1952), pp. 205-211 (a PRC description), and H. E. Richardson (1962), ch. XII (an "opposition" description).

4. Mao uses the term *guannei* here, which we have translated as "China Proper." Literally the term means "within the passes." This refers to fortified passes along the Great Wall, such as Shanhaiguan at the extreme eastern tip of Hebei Province and Yanmenguan in northern Shaanxi Province, which have traditionally been invasion routes taken by the tribes on China's northern frontiers. Consequently, the term *guannei* has traditionally meant the provinces south and southeast of the Great Wall.

5. Mao is here referring to the building of the Xikang-Tibetan and Qinghai-Tibetan highways, which were ultimately completed in December 1954. See text Dec. 25, 1954, source note.

6. See text May 24, 1951, note 2. The Dalai Lama had been titular head of the Tibetan government since the mid-eighteenth century. In the winter of 1950, the fourteenth Dalai Lama and his entourage was forced to leave Lhasa for Yadong, where in February 1951 a governmental authority under the Dalai Lama was established. On August 17, shortly after General Zhang Jingwu, representative of the PRC's Central People's Government to Tibet, arrived in Lhasa, the Dalai Lama was escorted back to Lhasa and since then a full Tibetan government, under the Dalai's rule and committed to the Agreement with the PRC on the Peaceful Liberation of Tibet was established in Lhasa.

7. This refers to the question of organizing the local Tibetan troops into regular units of the Chinese People's Liberation Army.

8. This refers to the Agreement on Measures for the Peaceful Liberation of Tibet. See text May 24, 1951, source note.

9. "The Silons are the highest administrative officials under the Dalai. At that time the two Silons were Lukhangwa and Lozang Tashi." (*Xuanji*, V, p. 64.)

10. In Article 9 of the Agreement, the Central People's Government pledged to promote, on the basis of prevalent conditions in Tibet, the culture, literacy, and education of the Tibetan people. In practice, suggestions were made to establish primary schools in Tibet. Prior to this, however, power over education in Tibet had been the private preserve of the Lama monks, and on the promulgation of the Agreement, the Lama order protested that the accompanying suggestions violated their own unique prerogatives.

11. On April 1, 1952, a People's Assembly was formed in Lhasa which demanded of the PRC Central People's Government delegation to Tibet the complete withdrawal of the PLA units from Tibet.

12. The relationship that existed between Tibet and China during China's Qing dynasty (1644-1911) was one of many changes. For the most part prior to the later part of the reign of the Kangxi Emperor (1662-1722) the Chinese emperor possessed a form of suzerainty over Tibet, which they inherited from earlier dynasties but did not exercise much actual control. Toward the end of his reign, Kangxi established a protectorate over Tibet in 1710. In 1721, after the Dsungar uprising, a Chinese garrison was stationed in Tibet. In the early years of Kangxi's successor, the Yungzheng Emperor (1723-1735), the Chinese troops were withdrawn, but toward the end of that reign, owing to the recurrence of civil strife in Tibet, the garrison was reinstated and two officials of the Chinese *Li fan yuan* (Court of Administration for Barbarian Affairs) were stationed in Tibet with no powers of intervention, but for the purpose of keeping the Chinese emperor and his court informed. These were known as ambans in Tibetan. By the mid-eighteenth century, however, these officials took on the activities of actually supervising the government of what had become in all senses a full protectorate, and in 1792 they began to participate directly in the governance of the region. This continued until the end of the Qing dynasty in 1911. For more on the subject, see L. Petech (1972) and T. T. Li (1956).

13. See text Dec. 13, 1951, source note.

14. The second largest city in Tibet next to Lhasa and approximately 120 km. southwest of Lhasa.

Telegram to Sa Zhenbing's Family
(April 12, 1952)

Source: *RMRB* (Apr. 12, 1952), 1. Available English Translation: *SCMP*, 315 (Apr. 13-15, 1952), 31.

At the time of his death, Sa Zhenbing was a member of the National Committee of the CPPCC, a member of the People's Revolutionary Military Commission, a member of the Administrative Council of the Fujian Provincial People's Government, and a senior leader in the Chinese navy. For more information on Sa's life, see H. Boorman et al., eds. (1970), III, pp. 86-87.

The Family of Mr. Sa Zhenbing:

Upon the death of Mr. Sa Zhenbing owing to illness, I feel deep sorrow and send this telegram expressly to extend my condolences. Respectfully... (Signed and dated)

Telegram to Boleslaw Bierut
(April 16, 1952)

Source: *RMRB* (Apr. 16, 1952), 1. Available English Translations: NCNA, *Daily Bulletin*, 518 (Apr. 21, 1952), 1; *SCMP*, 318 (Apr. 18-19, 1952), 12.

President,
The Republic of Poland

Comrade Bierut:

On this occasion of your sixtieth birthday, please accept the warm congratulations of the Chinese people, the government of the People's Republic of China, and myself. Under your leadership, the people of Poland have built, out of the ruins that remained after the pillage by the Nazi bandits, a country of increasing prosperity, freedom, and happiness. By their achievements in building a socialist society, the Polish people have provided powerful evidence of the shameful defeat of aggressors and have displayed the invincible, immense strength of the camp for peace and democracy.

Our best wishes to you in securing still greater achievements in your cause of socialist construction and in your struggle for world peace. We wish you good health and a long life.

(Signed as Chairman of CPG of PRC, dated, in Beijing)

Telegram to Rajendra Prasad

(May 11, 1952)

Source: *RMRB* (May 13, 1952), 1. Available English Translations: NCNA, *Daily Bulletin*, 534 (May 13, 1952), 5; *SCMP*, 334 (May 13, 1952), 5.

President Rajendra Prasad,
The Republic of India

Your Excellency:

We are happy to learn that Your Excellency has been elected President of the Republic of India. On behalf of the government and people of the People's Republic of China I sincerely extend to you our congratulations.

(Signed as Chairman of CPG of PRC, dated, in Beijing)

Letter to Tan Kah-Kee
(May 16, 1952)

Source: *Shuxin*, p. 432.

Tan Kah-Kee (alt. Chen Jiageng) (1874-1961) is an "overseas Chinese" of note. He went to Singapore in 1890 to help his father, Tan Ki Pei, who had left his family in China in the 1880s to seek his fortune. Tan became a very successful entrepreneur in rubber and, from the mid-1910s on, in shipping. He turned much of his patriotism for China into an effort to establish a university in Amoy, Fujian Province, which he single-handedly supported for fifteen years. He took frequent trips to and from China. In 1938, following the outbreak of the war between China and Japan the previous year, Tan organized the Nanyang Overseas Chinese Relief Association, which continued to be the main pillar of support for China in Southeast Asia throughout the war years. From the mid-1940s on, he became outspoken in his criticism of Chiang Kai-shek and the Nationalist government and turned to the Communists. In September 1946, Tan wrote to President Truman to appeal for an end to U.S. aid to the KMT, which he believed to be one of the causes for the prolongation of the civil war in China. In October 1949 Tan became a member of the Central People's Government Council of the PRC. He also became an influential member of the Overseas Chinese Affairs Committee. For biographical information on Tan, see under "Ch'en Chia-keng" in H. Boorman et al., eds. (1967), I, pp. 165-170, and Zhang Chukun et al. (1984).

Commissioner Tan:

Your gracious letter has long been received. I apologize for being so tardy in responding. In accordance with your bidding I have written the seven characters for the Zhimei Liberation Memorial;[1] I wonder if they are usable? How is your health of late? I am always concerned.

With my respect,

Mao Zedong
May 16, 1952

Note

1. Zhimei Village, Dongan *xian*, Fujian Province, is Tan Kah-Kee's birthplace. In 1913 Tan sponsored the building of the first of the modern primary schools in the south Fujian area here; this also marked the beginning of Tan's lifelong devotion to the enterprise of public education. Tan retired to live in Zhimei in 1951. (See Zhang Chukun et al. (1984), p. 235.)

Inscription for Workers on
Jing River Flood Control Project
(May 19, 1952)

Source: *RMRB* (May 29, 1952), 1.

See text Mar. 11, 1952, note 2.

For the benefit of the broad masses of the people, let us strive for victory in the Jing River flood control project!¹

Mao Zedong

Note

1. This project is located on the border between Hunan and Hubei provinces.

Telegram to the Dalai Lama and Panchen Gnoertehni
(May 23, 1952)

Source: *RMRB* (May 4, 1952), 1. Other Chinese Text: *RMSC* (1952), p. 203. Available English Translations: NCNA, *Daily Bulletin*, 543 (May 26, 1952), 4; *SCMP*, 343 (May 25-26, 1952), 3.

The Dalai Lama and
Panchen Gnoertehni¹

Sirs:

Thank you for your telegrams of May 23.² On this occasion of the anniversary of the peaceful liberation of Tibet, I am extremely happy that you sent telegrams to express your willingness to exert effort for the gradual and thorough implementation of the Agreement on Measures for the Peaceful Liberation of Tibet.[3] I celebrate [this act and wish that] you and all the Tibetan people will unite ever more closely together and unite with all fraternal nationalities and peoples across the country in a concerted effort to build our great homeland and build a prosperous and happy new Tibet. Furthermore I wish you success and good health.

(Signed with month and date, no year)

Notes

1. See text May 24, 1951, note 2, and text Nov. 23, 1949, source note. See also text Apr. 6, 1952.

2. For the Chinese texts of these telegrams, see *RMSC* (1952), pp. 202-203.

3. See text May 24, 1951, source note.

Letter to Ye Gongzuo
(May 25, 1952)

Source: *Shuxin*, p. 433.

Ye Gongzuo (1881-1968) was a very active political figure in the 1910s and 1920s. Previously a scholar and school teacher, he entered politics in 1906 as a protégé of Liang Shiyi. In the early years of the Chinese Republic, he was a chief official in charge of communications, in particular railway development. He became an influential member of the so-called Communications Clique in Chinese politics. In 1921, when Liang Shiyi became, for a short time, prime minister under President Xu Shichang, Ye became minister of communications. In 1925, after having served in many diverse capacities under different leaders in the chaotic politics of the period, Ye retired from politics and devoted his attention to cultural pursuits as director of classical studies at what was then Peking University. In the early 1930s, he resurfaced for a time as a minister in the Nationalist government. At the outbreak of war between China and Japan, Ye moved to Hong Kong, where he was later held in custody by the Japanese. In 1942 he returned to Shanghai and remained there until 1949. After the founding of the PRC Ye served in many cultural and educational posts in the new government and was influential in literary circles, especially in the committees on the reform of the Chinese language. In addition to his contributions to Chinese railroad-building he was also well-known as the founder of Jiaotong University, which came to be a leading center of engineering sciences in China. For more biographical information on Ye, see H. Boorman et al., eds. (1971), IV, pp. 31-33.

Mr. Yuhu:[1]

I have received and read your gracious letter of several months ago, and the poem written by Mr. Sa Zhenbing[2] which was enclosed. Soon thereafter I received and read two more poems by yourself. For all this I am very grateful. Now Mr. Sa has passed away to join the ancients, and his poem is now a part of memorabilia. I am returning it for your safekeeping. Most recently I received the letter from the four gentlemen of which you, sir, are one,[3] in which you have described the matter related to the ancestral shrine of the late-Ming patriotic leader Mr. Yuan Conghuan.[4] I have already talked with Mayor Peng Zhen[5] and, if there are no major objections, I believe it ought to be preserved. Please contact Mayor Peng and discuss this matter with him.

With my respect,

Mao Zedong
May 25

Notes

1. "Yuhu" is Ye's *zi* or honorific name. For an explanation of this usage, see text Oct. 15, 1949, note 1.

2. See text Apr. 12, 1952, source note.

3. According to the source, this refers to Ye, Liu Yazi, Li Jishen, and Zhang Shichao. For more information on Liu and Li, see text Dec. 1949, note 2, and text Winter 1949, note 2.

4. The letter written by Ye, Liu Yazi, Li Jishen and Zhang Shichao (see note 3 above) requested the preservation and repair of the ancestral shrine and tomb of the Ming dynasty general and patriot Yuan Conghuan which are in the city of Beijing. Yuan (1584-1630) and the troops under his command in northeastern China (in today's Liaoning and Heilongjiang Provinces) were the main bastion of defense for the late-Ming dynasty against the encroaching Manchu (then known as *Hou jin*, or Later Jin) armies under Nürchache. Twice, in 1626 and 1627, he won victories that repelled the Manchu forces. Yuan's political career was constantly thwarted, however, by a weak emperor and by the scheming advisors to the throne who betrayed the interests of the Ming for their own gain in power, particularly the eunuch Wei Zhongxian and his cohorts. In 1629, when the reinforced Manchu forces broke through the Longjingguan and Daankou passes and threatened the Ming capital, Yuan marshaled the latter's defense, but a ploy was used by the Manchu leaders to alienate the affection between Yuan and the emperor, and in the following year, Yuan's death was ordered by the Congjing emperor, who was the last of the Ming rulers.

5. Peng Zhen was then mayor of Beijing, in which Yuan Conghuan's tomb is located. For more on Peng, see text Nov. 26, 1957, note 1.

The Contradiction Between the Working Class and the Bourgeoisie Is the Principal Contradiction in the Country

(June 6, 1952)

Source: *Xuanji*, V, p. 65. Available English Translation: *SW*, V, p. 77.

According to this source, this comment was written by Mao on a document drafted by the United Front Work Department of the Central Committee of the CPC. See text Feb. 18, 1951, note 13. Xuanji further notes that "Chairman Mao Zedong criticized the head of this department for his error in regarding the national bourgeoisie as an intermediate class." From April 1950 to March 1965 the head of the United Front Work Department was Li Weihan.

After the landlord class and the bureaucratic bourgeoisie are toppled, the principal internal contradiction in China is the contradiction between the working class and the national bourgeoisie.[1] Therefore we should no longer call the national bourgeoisie an intermediate class.

Note

1. See text March 12, 1950, note 3.

Reply to Ambassador of the Republic of Poland

(June 9, 1952)

Source: *RMRB* (June 10, 1952), 1.

Karol Kuryluk became ambassador of the Republic of Poland to the PRC at this time.

Mr. Ambassador:

I am extremely glad to accept the letter of credence from the President of the Republic of Poland presented by Your Excellency and am grateful for Your Excellency's warm congratulations and good wishes.

For two years, the friendly relations between China and Poland in the political, economic and cultural areas have made noteworthy progress. The Chinese people have a great admiration for the inspiring cause that the Polish people have undertaken, under the leadership of President Bierut, to rebuild their homeland and march forward toward socialism, and wholeheartedly take delight in your superb achievements. I firmly believe that further close cooperation between our two peoples will not only facilitate the strengthening of the friendship between our two countries, but will also contribute to the cause of world peace for which we are in common striving.

I warmly welcome Your Excellency as the ambassador extraordinary and plenipotentiary of the Republic of Poland to the People's Republic of China and pledge to Your Excellency my utmost assistance in your work of consolidating and promoting the friendship between our two peoples.

Best wishes for the prosperity of your country, the prospering of your people, and the good health of your head of state.

Reply to Minister of the Republic of Finland
(June 9, 1952)

Source: *RMRB* (June 10, 1952), 1.

Von Knorring served as ambassador of the Republic of Finland to the PRC from June 1952 to December 1953.

Mr. Minister:

I am very glad to accept the letter of credence from the President of the Republic of Finland which Your Excellency has presented and am grateful for your president's sentiments of congratulations and wishes for the prosperity and happiness of the Chinese people which Your Excellency has conveyed to us.

The strengthening of the friendship between the peoples of China and Finland and the further development of economic and cultural relations between the two countries will contribute to the cause of world peace for which we hold a common hope.

I warmly welcome Your Excellency as the minister extraordinary and pleni-potentiary of the Republic of Finland to the People's Republic of China and pledge to Your Excellency my assistance in your work of strengthening the friendly cooperation between our two countries.

Best wishes for the prosperity of your country, the prospering of your people, and the good health of your head of state.

Inscription on Physical Culture and Sports
(June 10, 1952)

Source: *RMRB* (June 22, 1952), 1. Other Chinese Texts: *RMRB* (June 10, 1972), 1. Available English Translation: *PR*, 14:45 (Nov. 5, 1971), 19.

The date June 10, 1952, for this inscription is provided by the RMRB *(June 10, 1972)* *source. According to a news release in* RMRB *(June 22, 1952), 1, the All-China Fed-eration of Physical Culture was established on June 20, 1952, when inaugural cere-monies were held in Beijing. Mao's inscription was for this occasion. The same inscription was also written for the PLA Sports Convention in commemoration of the twenty-fifth anniversary of the "August 1" Army Day (i.e., the day of the founding of the Red Army). See* RMRB *(Aug. 2, 1952), 1.*

> Promote physical culture and sports;
> strengthen the People's physique.

Mao Zedong

Letter to Huang Yanpei
(June 10, 1952)

Source: *Shuxin*, p. 435.

See text Feb. 17, 1951, source note.

Mr. Renzhi:[1]

Your gracious letter of June 8 has been received. The year 1840 refers to the year in which Lin Zexu[2] led the people's masses of Guangzhou in resistance against the attack of the British, that is, the year of the so-called Opium War. It does not refer to Chen Sheng and Wu Guang.[3] I'm afraid your memory has failed you. China's modern revolutionary struggle has for its goal, first and foremost, the opposition against the invasion of imperialism.[4] Therefore it is possible to trace its roots to the Opium War and Lin Zexu and the Guangzhou "Battalion for the Suppression of the 'British'"[5] of its day. But it would be far too remote to trace it to over two thousand years ago to commemorate Chen Sheng and Wu Guang. That was a peasant uprising of olden times, and not a modern revolution.

In response, and with my respect,

Mao Zedong
June 10

Notes

1. "Renzhi" is Huang's *zi*. For an explanation of this usage, see text Oct. 15, 1949, note 1.

2. See text Feb. 14, 1957, note 1.

3. Chen Sheng and Wu Guang were the leaders of a rebellion at the end of the Qin dynasty circa 209 B.C. They were both among laborers being transported to Yuyang (in today's Hebei, near Beijing). En route, at Daze *xiang* (in today's Anhui Province), they were delayed by torrential rains. Fearing that according to the severe Qin laws they would be executed, Chen and Wu led an uprising that started out with the some nine hundred people in the transport and ended up involving several tens of thousands troops, over a thousand cavalry, and several hundred chariots (a fairly large-scale uprising equivalent to the size and strength of a medium-sized state of pre-Qin days). Chen was crowned by the insurrectionary troops and made his "capital" at Chen *xian* (today's Huaiyang *xian*, Henan). They were eventually defeated by the Qin general Zhang Han. Chen and Wu's uprising is known as the first popular (in Communist Chinese historiography the first peasant) rebellion in China's history.

4. See text Jul. 9, 1957, note 53.

5. This refers to the popular nickname given to the Guangdong militia that grew out of the San-yuanli Incident of late May 1841. This incident, occurring in the second year of the "Opium

War," was the culmination of severe rising tension between the Cantonese populace and the British troops stationed in and off-harbor in Guangzhou (Canton). On May 29, 1841, a British patrol violated the household of Zhang Zhaoguang in the village of Tonghua, near Sanyuanli. The local villagers armed themselves and gathered on a hill fronting the British camp. For the next two days there was prolonged fighting, and on June 1, the British troops were forced to reembark off Guangzhou harbor. This incident is known to the Chinese as the first popular movement in China's modern history against imperialism. The history and significance of this event are discussed at length in F. Wakeman (1966).

Letter to Zhou Enlai
(June 14, 1952)

Source: *Shuxin*, p. 437.

See also text 1952 on running schools for cadres' children.

Premier Zhou:

(1) If it is possible we should take over the administration of all private middle and primary schools entirely; (2) as for schools for cadres' children, the first step is to give them uniform treatment [with the others], and there should no longer be any graded differences, and the second step is to abolish such aristocratic schools so that they [the cadres' children] can be integrated with the people's children. Please think this over and see how it can be carried out.

Mao Zedong
June 14

Inscription on Inauguration of the Chengdu-Chongqing Railway

(July 1, 1952 R)

Source: *RMRB* (July 2, 1952), 1.

This inscription was given as a banner to the staff of the Railroad Engineering Office of the Southwest Bureau.

Congratulations on the opening of the Chengdu-Chongqing Railway to traffic. Continue to work hard for the construction of the Tianshui-Chengdu line.

Mao Zedong

Letter to Zhang Youcheng

(July 7, 1952)

Source: *Shuxin*, p. 438.

According to the source, Zhang Youcheng was a friend of Mao's in his youth.

My dear Youcheng:[1]
Your letters have been received. Thank you. Your letter to me of the first of the fifth month according to the lunar calendar is very good and has made it possible to learn much about the conditions in our native village. [You told me that] there is a shortage of grain and the hogs are not worth much money. Have things improved somewhat in recent months? I have also received all the letters sent to me by members of the Wen family.[2] At your convenience please tell them [that I have received their letters] and convey my regards to them. It is because of the shortage of grain that there has been a prohibition on [the consumption and manufacturing of] liquor in the villages. After the

autumn [harvest] the ban may be lifted, and you will be able to drink a little.
In response, and with my wishes for your health and safety!

Mao Zedong
July 7, 1952

Notes

1. See text Oct. 15, 1949, note 1, for an explanation of our translation of the term *xiong* used in the Chinese here.

2. See texts May 7, 1950, and May 12, 1950.

Telegram to the German Socialist Unity Party
(July 8, 1952)

Source: *RMRB* (July 11, 1952), 1. Available English Translations: NCNA, *Daily Bulletin*, 576 (July 11, 1952), 2; *SCMP*, 372 (July 11-12, 1952), 10.

The Central Committee,
The Socialist Unity Party of Germany

Dear Comrade W. Pieck, and comrade delegates to the Second Conference of the Socialist Unity Party of Germany:

On behalf of the Communist Party of China, the Chinese people and on my own behalf I extend to the Second Conference of the Socialist Unity Party of Germany our warmest congratulations. We respectfully wish the Conference success and wish the German people new triumphs in their cause of striving for unification and democracy in Germany and of defending peace in the world.

(Signed as Chairman of CPC and dated)

Address to the First Graduating Class
of the Military Academy
(July 10, 1952)

Source: *Dahai hangxing*, pp. 77-78.

President Liu, commanders, members of the Political Work Staff, members of the Rear Services Work Staff, instructors and the graduates of the First Term of the High Level Accelerated Program Department of the Military Academy, Comrades:

The first term of the high-level accelerated program department and the senior level accelerated program department of the Military Academy of the Chinese People's Liberation Army, which itself stands for a great transition in the history of the construction of the armed forces of the Chinese people, has now come to a fruitful conclusion, and we are now holding commencement exercises. I hereby extend to you my most enthusiastic congratulations.

The establishment of the Military Academy and the educational work that it has undertaken to provide in the last year or so have contributed greatly to the construction of the regularized and modernized national defense troops [of our country]. This is the result of the combined and unified efforts of President Liu, of all our comrade advisors from the Soviet Union, of all the commanders, the members of the Political Work Staff, the members of the Rear Services Work Staff, the instructors, and the students. I wish now to extend to you my gratitude and appreciation.

The Chinese people in its history of building its armed forces, has traveled through a long trek of twenty-five years. It is, in international circles, with the exception of the Soviet Union, unparalleled in its richness of revolutionary experience. Nevertheless, prior to the nationwide victory of the Chinese people, its military construction, owing to the limitations of objective material conditions, was in a relatively low stage of development. By this I mean that we were in a situation in which [our armed forces] had simple and low-quality equipment, in which there was an absence of regular organization and systematization, in which they lacked strict military discipline, and in which combat leadership was decentralized and nonunified, and often carried within it guerrilla characteristics, and so on. These were natural and inevitable conditions in the past, and were therefore correct [for the past]. Nevertheless, since the Chinese people attained nationwide victory, the objective conditions have undergone a fundamental transformation. We have now entered the higher stage in which we must be in control of modern technology. This possibility is now fully inherent in the existing objective conditions; as long as we add to it our indefatigable subjective efforts, it is bound to be realized. In step with the modernization of [our armed forces'] equipment, there is a demand that the establishment of the troops become regularized; this means the implementation of a unified command, a unified system, organization, discipline and training [for all the troops], that is, the materialization of closely knit coordinated actions on the part of all the various arms of the services. For this purpose, the decentralization, lack of unity and phenomena of lassitude and simplicity in discipline, as well as the guerrilla mentality and practices, which might have been appropriate and correct in the past but are no longer appropriate and correct today, must be overcome, and, in their place, we must strengthen the sense of organization, of planning, of precision and discipline which is to be cultivated in the full range of our work and command, and particularly first of all in terms of education and training. This is an indispensible condition in the establishment of regularized and modernized national defense troops [for our country].

At the same time, in order that we may organize [and prepare for] such complex, highly mechanized and modern battle or combat, we cannot do without a sound commanding organ that can act as the brains and is rich in scientific organization and division of labor. The type of commanding organs of the past that were unsound, low in efficiency or even far from being equal to their tasks must, from now on, be improved and strengthened by much effort. The kind of situation that in the past placed emphasis exclusively on political work and neglected staff work must be resolutely changed around (it is correct to emphasize political work, and there should still continue to be this emphasis from now on). In the past some weaker people, people who lacked organizational ability, or even people who had committed some mistakes and did not have a high level of activism, were chosen to work in the commanding organs, and this has caused some commanding officers to be reluctant to serve as staff officers or chiefs of staff. This situation must be radically turned around. From now on we must select quality commanders who are rich in organizational and commanding abilities to serve in the commanding organs at all levels, and thus create a new work-style and a new atmosphere in the commanding organs. This, too, is an indispensable condition in the establishment of regularized and modernized national defense troops [for our country].

Commanders, members of the Political Work Staff and the Rear Services Work Staff, instructors, graduates of the first term of the Military Academy, and students still in pursuit of their studies, comrades: The Military Commission hopes that you will continue to exert your efforts in the glorious cause of the building of regularized and modernized national defense troops, and also that, through your efforts, the spirit of building regularized and modernized national defense troops will be infused into all the units.

Inscription on the Monument to the People's Heroes
(August 3, 1952 R)

Source: *RMRB* (Aug. 3, 1952), 1. Available English Translation: NCNA, *Daily Bulletin*, 594 (Aug.7, 1952), 4.

The actual date of this inscription is not known. It was reported and released in RMRB *on Aug. 3, 1953. The* RMRB *news article that reported on the commencement of work on this monument, which subsequently has stood in the southern section of Tiananmen Square in Beijing, also carried a description of the shape, style, and size of the monument. It also reported that construction commenced on the day of the twenty-fifth anniversary of the founding of the Chinese Communist armed forces (i.e., August 1). This is an abbreviation of Mao's earlier inscription for the "people's heroes." (See text Sept. 30, 1949.) Work on the monument ended in late 1955. See* RMRB *(Nov. 18, 1955), 1.*

Immortal Glory to the People's Heroes.

Unite and Clearly Draw the Line
Between the Enemy and Ourselves
(August 4, 1952)

Source: *Xuanji*, V, pp. 66-69. Available English Translations: *SW*, V, pp. 78-81; JPRS, 69195 (June 3, 1977), pp. 15-17.

According to the source, the following text contains the main points of a speech made by Mao at the thirty-eighth meeting of the Standing Committee of the First National Committee of the CPPCC.

Last year we were fighting, talking, and stabilizing [the situation] at the same time.

The situation with regard to the war in Korea has been stabilized since July last year,[1] but at that time we were still not confident about stabilizing the domestic financial and economic situation. In the past we said only, "The prices of commodities have been basically stabilized, and revenue and expenditure are approaching balance." That means that the prices of commodities cannot be stabilized yet, and that revenue and expenditure have not yet been balanced. Revenue is limited and expenses are in excess [of revenue]. This is a problem. Therefore, the Central Committee of the Chinese Communist Party held a meeting in September last year and proposed increasing production and strictly practicing economy. In October, I once again proposed increasing production and practicing economy at the Third Meeting of the First National Committee of the Political Consultative Conference.[2] During the campaign to increase production and practice economy, rather serious problems of graft, waste, and bureaucratism were exposed. Then in December we launched the "Three-Anti's" campaign and subsequently the "Five-Anti's" campaign.[3] Now the "Three-Anti's" and "Five-Anti's" campaigns have been triumphantly concluded, the problems have all been made clear, and the whole country has become stable.

Last year, the cost of the War to Resist U.S. [Aggression] and Aid Korea was approximately equivalent to the cost of domestic construction; they were half and half. This year things are different, the cost of war is estimated to be only half of what it was last year. At present, [the number of] our troops has been reduced, but their equipment has been reinforced. We had been fighting wars for more than twenty years but never had any air force; it was always the other people who bombarded us. Now we have an air force, also anti-aircraft guns, cannon, and tanks. The War to Resist U.S. [Aggression] and Aid Korea has been a great school, in which we conducted large-scale maneuvers; these exercises were better than running a military academy. If we continue to fight for another year, next year we can send all our army troops by turn to be trained there.

Originally we had three question regarding this war. First, could we fight it at all? Second, could we defend [our positions]? Third, would we have enough to eat?

Could we fight? This question was answered within two or three months. The enemy had more cannons than we did, but their morale was low. They had a lot of iron but little spirit.

Could we defend [our positions]? This question was also answered last year. The method [we adopted] was to dig holes. We dug two levels of [defense] works, and whenever the enemy attacked we went into the tunnels. Sometimes the enemy occupied the upper level, but the lower level still belonged to us. Then when the enemy entered our positions, we would counterattack and inflict on them extremely heavy casualties. We just used this indigenous method to pick up Western cannons, and there was little the enemy could do to us.

The question of food, that is, the question of assuring provisions, was not solved for a long while. At the time, we didn't know to dig holes to store the grain. Now we know. Each division has three months' provisions, and each has a storage granary. We even have auditoriums, and [the troops] live very well.

Now our policies are clear, our positions are consolidated, our provisions are assured, and all our soldiers realize that they must stand firm to the end.

For just how long will the fighting go on? For how long will the negotiations go on? I say that the talks must go on, the fighting must continue, and peace will eventually be made.

Why will peace eventually be made? It is unlikely that there will be a "Thirty Years' War" or a "Hundred Years' War" because protracted war is very unfavorable to the United States.[4]

First, it costs them lives. In their struggle to detain ten thousand or so prisoners of war, more than thirty thousand of their people have been killed.[5] After all, they have many fewer people than we do.

Second, it costs money. They use up more than ten billion U.S. dollars each year. We use much less money than they do, and we have cut down our cost this year to half of what we spent last year. The money from the settling of accounts in the "Three-Anti's" and "Five-Anti's" will be enough to support the fighting for another one and a half years. Then, proceeds from the campaign to increase production and practice economy can be used totally for domestic construction.

Third, they have insurmountable contradictions both in the international and domestic arenas.

Fourth, there is a strategic problem. The strategic focus of the United States is Europe. They dispatched forces to invade Korea without anticipating that we would dispatch forces to aid Korea.

Things can be more easily handled on our side. We are in full command of domestic affairs. Nevertheless, we are not the United States' chief-of-staff. The United States has its own chief-of-staff. Therefore, whether or not the war in Korea will continue can be decided only in part by the side represented by Korea and ourselves.

In short, as far as the United States is concerned, the general tendency is that it will be unfavorable for them if peace does not come.

To say that the third world war will break out immediately is a hollow threat. We must strive to have ten years [of peace] to build our industry and to create a firm and powerful foundation.

We must all unite closely and clearly draw the distinctions between the enemy and ourselves. That we are strong today is because of the unity of the people of our entire country, and because of the cooperation from all of us present here today, the cooperation of the various democratic parties and groups, and the cooperation of the various people's organizations.[6] It is very important to be united and to draw clearly the distinctions between the enemy and ourselves. Mr. Sun Yat-sen was a good man,[7] but the Revolution of 1911 which he led failed.[8] Why? First, because it did not carry out the distribution of land, second, because it did not recognize the necessity of suppressing the counterrevolutionaries, and third, because it was not sharp in its opposition to imperialism. Besides drawing clear distinctions between the enemy and our-selves, there is still, among ourselves, distinctions between right and wrong [that must be drawn]. Comparing the two, the distinctions between right and wrong are secondary distinctions [or distinctions of a second type]. For instance, [the problems with] corrupt elements are still, for the most part, problems of right and wrong [of this type]; [the corrupt elements] can still be reformed; they are not the same as the counterrevolutionaries.[9]

We must educate the various democratic parties and the religious circles so that they cannot be tricked by the imperialists and stand on the side of the enemy. Take Buddhism, for instance. It has relatively few connections with imperialism; its basic ties are with feudalism. Because of the land problem, when we opposed feudalism we opposed the Buddhist monks. Those who came under attack were the abbots and elder monks. When this small number of people are overthrown, the "Lu Zhisen's"[10] will be liberated. I do not believe in Buddhism, but I am not opposed to the formation of a Buddhist fed-eration either.[11] Let them unite together to draw clearly the lines between the enemy and ourselves. Should the united front[12] be abolished one day? I do not approve of its abolition. We must unite with everybody, as long as they truly draw a clear distinction between the enemy and ourselves and as long as they serve the people.

Our country has a future and hope. In the past we pondered whether or not the national economy would be restored in three years. After two and a half years of hard struggle, our national economy has already been restored and, moreover, we have already begun planned construction. We must all be united and draw clear lines between the enemy and ourselves so that our coun-try can advance at a steady pace.

Notes

1. The "Fourth Battle" of the Korean War began in April 1954 and ended with the halting of the "summer offensive" of the American troops in late June of that year. The two sides remained deadlocked on the 38th parallel. On July 10, 1951, preliminary negotiations for an armistice began.

2. See text Oct. 23, 1951, and particularly note 5.

3. See text Nov. 1951-Mar. 1952, source note.

4. Mao was referring here to the historical examples of two major periods of warfare in Europe in the seventeenth century (Thirty Years' War) and the mid-fourteenth to mid-fifteenth century (Hundred Years' War.)

5. In the Korean War armistice negotiations began in July 1951; with regard to the issue of the repatriation of prisoners of war, the American side proposed the principle of "voluntary repatria-tion." In April 1952, on the basis of this unilaterally presented and accepted principle, the Ameri-can side refused the repatriation of some 10,000 captured Chinese Volunteers who, the Ameri-cans claimed, had signed letters of intent indicating that they did not wish to be repatriated. Mao is here referring to the Chinese estimate that over 30,000 U.S. troops had died in the conflict from April up to the time of this speech, i.e., early August 1952.

6. See text Sept. 21, 1949, note 1, and text Oct. 1, 1949, note 3.

7. Sun Yat-sen, a.k.a. Sun Wen, Sun Zhongshan (1866-1925). A revolutionary at the turn of

the century and ultimately a leader of the 1911 Revolution, which overthrew the Qing dynasty and established the Republic of China, Sun became, for the short period between January 1912 (when the provisional Government of the Republic was established) and the ascendency of Yuan Shikai, the provisional president of the Republic. In August 1912, on the reorganization of the revolutionary organization, the Tongmenghui, into the Kuomintang (Nationalist Party), Sun became its executive director. Sun was the chief spokesman of the principles of bourgeois democracy embodied in his nationalist principles of revolution during the early period and his "Three People's Principles" formulated in the 1910s and early 1920s. Sun was, however, deeply disillusioned by the failure of the 1911 Revolution to bring about a truly democratic society and government and the lapse of China into a period of civil war among warlords. In addition to organizing a military effort against the warlord factions and to unify China (an effort that failed in his own time and had only partial success ultimately), Sun also, in his last years, revised his Three People's Principles and introduced the strategic formulation of alliance with the Soviet Union, a united front with the Communist Party, and a sort of primitive economic and social government alliance with workers and peasants. He also directed, just before his death, the early stages of the reforming of the Kuomintang and the formation of an antifeudal (i.e., antiwarlord), anti-imperial united front between the KMT and the CPC. This did not come to complete fruition. More for reasons of his later activities than his leadership in the Revolution of 1911, Sun is respected as a pioneer revolutionary and a socialist thinker by the Chinese Communists. For more on Sun's life, see H. Boorman et al., eds. (1970), III, pp. 170-189.

8. For a more detailed analysis by Mao of the failure of the 1911 Revolution see "The Chinese Revolution and the Chinese Communist Party" (*SW*, II, pp. 305-334); and for Mao's contrast between the "Old Three People's Principle" and the "New Three People's Principle," see "On New Democracy" (*SW*, II, pp. 363-369).

9. Mao's sentence here is somewhat garbled, and there is some uncertainty as to what he means by the phrase *di er zhong jiexian*. Here, as in *SW*, we have translated it as "secondary distinction," conveying an ordinal sense. This follows the clue provided by Mao's fundamental theory, espoused in the article "On Contradictions" (August 1937, *SW*, I, pp. 311-347, especially pp. 331-334, 343-345), in which Mao says that the "principal contradiction" and the "principal aspect of a contradiction" must be distinguished from the rest. Here, however, as clearly indicated by the title of this document, Mao is moving away from the fundamentally epistemological theory of contradiction to the politically practical theory of contradiction that he would eventually put forward splendidly and in its completed form in the article "On Correctly Handling Contradictions among the People" (Feb. 1957, *SW*, V, pp. 384ff). Here Mao speaks of two categories of contradictions; contradictions "between the enemy and ourselves" and "contradictions among the people." The distinction between these two categories is not one of ordinance but of character; thus each has to be dealt with in a manner appropriate to its nature. If we were to interpret this statement here in this way, and to see this document as an important expression of Mao's progression from epistemological conviction to practical application, then the phrase *di er zhong jiexian* should not be translated as "secondary distinctions," but as "distinctions of a second type," forecasting Mao's idea of "contradiction among the people." Furthermore, even then, "right-and-wrong" distinctions, when considered in the broad sense of the term, have to transcend categories. They can be of secondary importance only when they are confined to a specific, narrower meaning; i.e., Mao is not talking of "right-wrong" distinctions in general, but of the specific "right-wrong" distinctions among the people which he delineates in the preceding sentence.

10. Lu Zhisen is one of the colorful heroes of the Ming dynasty novel *Shuihu zhuan* (variously translated as *Water Margin* or *All Men Are Brothers*). Lu was an oppressed Buddhist monk who rebelled against the hierarchy of his temple and joined the rebel-bandits at Liangshan.

11. The Chinese Buddhist Federation was eventually formed in 1953, with local branches in many provinces and municipalities and in Tibet, Inner Mongolia, and among minority nationalities in Sichuan and Yunnan. Its headquarters was in Beijing.

12. See text Feb. 18, 1951, note 13.

Telegram to the Democratic People's Republic of Korea
(August 13, 1952)

Source: *RMRB* (Aug. 15, 1952), 1. Available English Translation: *SCMP* (Aug. 15-16, 1952), 2.

The Chairman,
The Standing Committee,
The Supreme People's Assembly,
The Democratic People's Republic of Korea

Comrade Kim Du Bong:

On this occasion of the seventh anniversary of the liberation of Korea, on behalf of the Chinese people, the government of the People's Republic of China, and on my own behalf, I extend to you, to our brothers the Korean people, and to the government of the Democratic People's Republic of Korea our sincerest congratulations.

The heroic struggles undertaken by the Korean people in striving for the independence and liberation of their homeland and in resisting the United States imperialist aggressors has made a tremendous contribution to the cause of saving peace in the world.

For the sake of thwarting our common enemy and for the sake of Korea's peace and China's security, the Chinese people will forever stand firmly by the Korean people and battle for a thorough victory over the United States' imperialist aggressors.

May the friendship between China and Korea, which has grown unceasingly through the struggle and is impregnable, be forever consolidated. May the Korean people secure further and greater victories in their war of liberation.

(Signed as Chairman of CPG of PRC, dated, in Beijing)

Letter to Chen Yi
(August 15, 1952)

Source: *Shuxin*, p. 439.

See text Oct. 11, 1955(1), note 53, and text Mar. 22, 1958, note 60.

Comrade Chen Yi:

 I have received your letter. It is of the utmost necessity for you to rest for two months in order to recover your health. After you participate in another meeting of the Central Committee you may find a suitable spot to convalesce. Wait until your health is restored before you return to East China to work. For the time being it is suitable for your post to remain in East China because your role can be greater if you stay in East China.[1] There is much need for your contribution in that area.

 In response, and with regards for your daily well-being.

Mao Zedong
August 15

Note

 1. Chen was second secretary of the East China Bureau of the Central Committee of the CPC at the time of this letter.

Letter to Li Shuqing
(August 23, 1952)

Source: *Luxing jia*, 2(1958), 4.

Notably this letter is not included in Shuxin, *the recently published collection of Mao's letters.*

 For more information on Li Shuqing, see text Nov. 17, 1949, note 2.

Mr. Shuqing:

Your gracious letter has been received. I am very much in sympathy [with your situation]. I have already forwarded your letter to the people's government of Xiangtan *xian* [for its reference] so that it can handle the matter after deliberation.

In reply, and with my great respect,

Mao Zedong

August 23

Letter to Uighur Peasants of Xinjiang
(August 30, 1952)

Source: *Shuxin*, p. 440. Other Chinese text: *RMRB* (Dec. 27, 1973).

In the Shuxin *source, it is indicated that this letter was addressed specifically to the peasants of the* xiang *named here in the salutation. The* RMRB *source does not provide this information, but is simply titled "Letter to Uighur Peasants." The Uighurs are a minority nationality of Turkic origin and of the Moslem faith. They reside for the greatest part in Xinjiang Province, where they make up close to 70 per cent of the population. There are over 4 million Uighurs in the PRC.*

To the Peasant Comrades of Paihataikeli *xiang*, Suofu *xian*, Kexi Region

Comrades:

Thank you for the letter that you wrote to me in March this year at the time when you celebrated the victory of land reform.[1] You have achieved liberation from the bondage of the feudal landownership of the landlord class. I hope that you will, with the motto "Patriotism and High Yields" [as your watchwords], become even more solidly unified, strive hard for production, and make improvements in your own material [standards of] living, and, furthermore, on this basis, raise step by step, the level of your culture [and education].[2]

Notes

1. See text Feb. 18, 1951, note 2.

2. The term that Mao used here is *wenhua shuiping*, which literally translates as "level of culture." In the PRC however, the term generally also connotes education and, more precisely even, literacy. To *xue wenhua* (learn culture) is to learn to become literate, i.e., learn to recognize and

read and write characters. This sentence should not be mistaken to mean raising the level of the Uighur's own ethnic civilization.

Telegram to the USSR
(September 2, 1952)

Source: *RMRB* (Sept. 3, 1952), 1. Other Chinese Text: *XHYB*, 9 (Sept. 1952), 3. Available English Translations: NCNA, *Daily Bulletin*, 613 (Sept. 3, 1952), 1; *SCMP*, 408 (Sept. 4, 1952), 1.

Generalissimo Stalin:

On this seventh anniversary of the victory in the War of Resistance against Japan, please accept the warm congratulations and sincere gratitude that I, together with the Chinese People's Liberation Army and all the Chinese people, extend to you, to the armed forces of the Soviet Union, and to the Soviet people.

During the War of Resistance against Japan, the Soviet Union rendered the Chinese people immense assistance. The armies of the Soviet Union annihilated the Guandong Army, which was the main force of the Japanese troops. This helped the Chinese people to claim the final victory in the War of Resistance against Japan. The fraternal assistance that the Soviet Union has provided for the Chinese people while China has been undergoing the process of rehabilitation and reconstruction has also enabled the Chinese people to consolidate and increase their strength rapidly.

At this moment, when Japanese militarism is reviving and when the aggressive forces of Japan rear their heads once again, the impregnable friendship and alliance between China and the Soviet Union is a powerful guarantee that renewed aggression by Japan or by any other country that is in collusion with Japan in terms of aggressive behavior will be thwarted through our concerted effort, and that peace in the eastern hemisphere and throughout the world will be defended.

Long live the great impregnable friendship between the People's Republic of China and the Union of Soviet Socialist Republics!

(Signed as Chairman of CPG of PRC and dated)

Letter to Huang Yanpei
(September 5, 1952)

Source: *Shuxin*, pp. 441-444.

For reference on the subject discussed in this letter, see text Mar. 15, 1952. Also see text Feb. 17, 1951, source note.

Mr. Renzhi:[1]

Your letter from Beidaihe,[2] your letter of September 4, and the draft of your speech[3] have all been received. Thank you so much.

The intention of the draft of your speech is very good, but I feel that it is a bit too radical, and I am afraid that the majority of the bourgeoisie may not be able to stand it. Therefore, as according to your bidding, I have suggested certain amendments.[4] I wonder if they are suitable; please consider them and make your own decision.

To ask the bourgeoisie to accept the fundamental ideas of the working class – e.g., the elimination of exploitation, the abolition of classes, the elimination of individualism – to accept the Marxist world view, or, as you say: "Without labor there is no living; one must not seek [means of] living outside of labor or the exertion of one's own energies," is to demand of the bourgeoisie that it must accept socialism. This is possible with a small number of progressive elements. However, it is not appropriate to demand this of them as a class as a whole; at least within the period of the First Five-Year Plan[5] it would not be appropriate to engage in such propaganda.

In the present stage [of the development of socialism], we should only exhort them, as a class, to accept the leadership of the working class; i.e., to accept the Common Program.[6] It is not appropriate for us to exceed this boundary.

In the present stage we allow for the existence of the bourgeoisie, but they must be engaged in enterprises that are beneficial to the state and the people, and must not be involved with the "Five Poisons."[7] This is the *leadership* of the working class on the bourgeoisie and is stipulated by the Common Program.[8]

It is not possible, or proper, for us to step out of this line and demand that the bourgeoisie accept the working class ideology or, so to speak, [for us] to disallow such things as the bourgeoisie's making money by exploitative means and to allow them to only think, as the workers do, that "without labor there is no living" – [to allow them] to only think [in terms of] socialism and not capitalism.

In the earlier half of this year, some comrades writing articles in *Xuexi* [Study] magazine in Beijing[9] have expressed precisely these opinions; we have already instructed them to make certain revisions and corrections.

With regard to a minority among the bourgeoisie – those people with vision and foresight – I agree with your viewpoint; we can indeed propagandize socialism among them to make them interested in the socialist cause – I think this can be done and is beneficial. Under China's [present] conditions, such people may emerge, and, particularly in a few years' time, when the socialist economic sector grows stronger and larger and has further demonstrated its great contribution to the state and the people, the number of such people may grow gradually.

Of late, your ideas have made much speedy progress. For example, where you spoke in your letter from Beidaihe on the subject of the state's sovereignty and this time on the subject of socialism, this is demonstrated. Nonetheless, what you say is, at the present time, a bit premature. It is possible for a few people to think such things, but it is not possible for them to be put into action. I am expressing my humble opinions above[10] because you seem to place great trust in me. Whether or not they are proper, I would be very happy if you would examine them and teach me your thoughts.

In the near future, when I have the time, I would like very much to have a talk with you.

With my respect,

Mao Zedong
September 5, 1952

Notes

1. "Renzhi" is Huang's *zi*. For an explanation of this usage, see text Oct. 15, 1949, note 1.

2. Beidaihe, on the eastern coastal tip of Hebei Province, is a popular resort (see text Summer 1954, source note.) For its coastal climate it is often recommended by Mao to others as a suitable place for convalescence from illnesses or for relaxation and recuperation. Huang was apparently there some time in 1952 for this purpose. (See also text Jul. 15, 1951.)

3. According to the source this refers to the draft of the speech that Huang was to make in September 1952 at the general meeting of the Beijing chapter of the China Democratic National Construction Association. Its title was "How Should We Promote, On the Conclusion of the Three-Anti's and Five-Anti's Movements, the Spirit of Chairman Mao's Directive on the Policies of Democratic National Construction?" We have not been able to secure the text of this speech.

4. According to the source, Mao made the following amendments to Huang's draft: (1) Where Huang originally had: "The capitalists ought to fully accept working class ideology," Mao changed it to: "The capitalists ought to fully accept the leadership of the working class and the state-run economy." (2) Mao changed the passage reading: "working class ideology to educate and reform capitalists" to "use patriotic ideas and the ideas of the Common Program to educate and reform capitalists" and the passage reading: "help the capitalists to reform their thought" to "help the capitalists to reform those bad ideas, those ideas that do not conform to the ideas of patriotism and the Common Program, i.e., the so-called 'Five Poisons' ideas." (For the meaning of "Common Program" and "Five Poisons," see text Sept. 21, 1949, note 3, and text Nov. 1951 -

Mar. 1952, note 6, respectively). (3) To the sentence in the draft that read: "Some members of the bourgeoisie are bad, some are good" Mao added: "For the majority of the bourgeoisie, within the ideology of any individual among them, there are bad aspects, and there are good aspects; we should help them to discard the bad parts and promote the good ones." (4) At the end of the draft, Mao added the following: "This is what we demand and expect of the majority of the bourgeoisie at the present stage. However, under the current conditions in China, a minority of the bourgeoisie, consisting of people who are farsighted, may in fact exceed these expectations and come to accept the basic ideology of the working class, i.e., the ideology of socialism. They may, on the one hand, continue to run and open up factories, without seeking to be immediately reclassified [as workers] or to alter the appearance of their enterprises and, on the other hand, [however], perceive the great contribution that the socialist enterprise is making to humanity, and [thus] hope to become, in the future, socialist. It is possible that such people exist, and we ought to express to them our welcome."

5. See text Feb. 10, 1953, note 2.

6. See text Sept. 21, 1949, note 3.

7. See text Nov. 1951 - Mar. 1953, note 6.

8. The emphasis is in the Chinese original.

9. This is a periodical published by the Propaganda Department of the Central Committee of the CPC to assist Party cadres in their study of Marxist theory.

10. In the Chinese original, the wording here reads *ru you*, meaning ''as in what goes to the right of this.'' Because of the manner in which Chinese is written, this means "the above."

Letter to Comrade Li Da
(September 17, 1952)

Source: *HQ* (Jan. 1, 1979), 8. Other Chinese Text: *Shuxin*, p. 445.

See text Mar. 27, 1951, for more correspondence from Mao to Li, and for biographical information on Li. The HQ *source provides some information that we have incorporated into our notes.*

Dear Haoming:[1]

I have received your letter of September 11 and also the several previous letters. The three characters "Aiwan ting" have been written on the separate [enclosed] sheet.[2]

The third line in paragraph 10, chapter 4, of "On Contradiction" reads: "In any contradiction, and also at any time, the development of the contradictory aspects is uneven." Here the eight characters [for] "and also at any time" should be deleted. They have already been deleted in the second printing of Volume I of *Xuanji* [Selected Works].[3] Please pay attention to this when you write the explanations.[4]

Wishing you well in your teaching.

Mao Zedong
September 17, 1952

Notes

1. See text Mar. 27, 1951, note 1. See also text Nov. 17, 1949, note 2.
2. Aiwan ting is a scenic spot on Mount Yuelu, Changsha, Hunan Province, and it was completely renovated in 1952. Li Da was then president of Hunan University. At the request of Li Da, Mao inscribed in his own hand the three characters "Ai wan ting."
3. See revised version in *SW*, IV, p. 333, middle of first paragraph.
4. See text Mar. 27, 1951, note 1.

Inscription on the Arts
(September 26, 1952)

Source: *Tianjin ribao* (Sept. 26, 1952), cited in *Wenyi yulu*, p. 94. Other Chinese Texts: *Meishu fenglei*, 3 (Aug. 1967), 5; *HQ*, 6 (1967); *Mao liang*, p. 363; *Wenyi hongqi*, 5 (May 30, 1967), 2. Available English Translation: *SCMP*, 4000 (Aug. 14, 1967), 12.

This is an inscription written for the First National Operatic Exchange and Performance Festival convened by the Ministry of Culture in Beijing from October 6 to November 1, 1952. The Wenyi hongqi *source dates this inscription as Sept. 28, 1952.*

Let a hundred flowers bloom; displace the old and worn, and let new things emerge!

Reply to Ambassador of the Republic of India
(September 26, 1952)

Source: *RMRB* (Sept. 27, 1952), 1.

Shri Nedyam Raghavan served as ambassador of the Republic of India to the PRC from September 1952 to November 1955.

Mr. Ambassador:

I am very glad to accept the letter of credence from the President of the Republic of India that Your Excellency has presented and am grateful for Your Excellency's congratulations.

For more than two years, the friendly relations between China and India in the areas of economy and culture have further developed. I believe that the friendly cooperation between our two peoples will be further enhanced and consolidated in our common cause of pursuing peace in Asia and throughout the world.

I warmly welcome Your Excellency as the ambassador plenipotentiary and extraordinary of the Republic of India to the People's Republic of China and pledge to Your Excellency assistance in your work of strengthening the friendly cooperation between our two countries.

Best wishes for the prosperity of your country, the prospering of your people, and the good health of your head of state.

Inscription for Inauguration
of the Tianshui-Lanzhou Railway
(September 28, 1952)

Source: *RMRB* (Sept. 28, 1952).

The Tianshui-Lanzhou railway was opened to traffic on August 23, 1952. Tianshui and Lanzhou are both in Gansu Province.

Congratulations on the opening of the Tianshui-Lanzhou Railway to traffic. Continue to work hard for the construction of the Lanzhou-Xinjiang line.

Toast on Third Anniversary of Founding of the PRC
(September 30, 1952)

Source: *RMRB* (Oct. 1, 1952), 1. Available English Translations: NCNA, *Daily Bulletin* (Oct. 8, 1952), 8; *SCMP*, 428 (Sept. 30, 1952), 6.

Dear Friends:

The third anniversary of the founding of the great People's Republic of China has arrived!

In the past year, we have done much work for the happiness of the people and for international peace; I hope that in the coming year we will be able to accomplish even more.

Long live the People's Republic of China!

Long live the great unity among the people of China's various nationalities and the overseas Chinese!

Long live the Chinese People's Liberation Army and the Chinese People's Volunteers![1]

Long live the friendship and unity between China and the Soviet Union!

Long live the friendship and unity between China and Mongolia!

Long live the friendship and unity between China all the various New Democracies![2]

Long live the friendship and unity among the peoples of all the countries of Asia!

May the Peace Conference of the Asian and Pacific Region be successful![3]

Long live the friendship and unity of the people of the world!

To everyone's health, bottoms up!

Notes

1. See text Oct. 8, 1950(2), note 1.
2. See text Sept.21, 1949, note 4.
3. The Peace Conference of the Asian and Pacific Region was convened in Beijing, October 2-12, 1952. Thirty-seven countries were represented by 367 delegates and 37 observers. The conference condemned the United States for halting the Korean truce talks and called for the repatriation of prisoners of war in accordance with the 1949 Geneva Convention.

Letter to Mao Yuju

(October 2, 1952)

Source: *Shuxin*, pp. 446-447.

See text May 15, 1950.

My dear Yuju:[1]

Messrs. Li and Zou[2] have come to the capital. I have [therefore] received the letter you sent [through them], and I thank you for your kind gift.

Mao Zelian[3] has written a letter to me expressing his grievances. His mother is not yet buried, and the illness in his foot has not yet healed. I am hereby sending three million *rmb;*[4] one million is for Sixth Aunt's funeral costs and two million for the treatment of Zelian's illness. Please tell him not to come to the capital. He can go the Xiangya Hospital in Changsha for treatment. If they cannot cure the problem at Xiangya, nothing better can be done in Beijing.

I am also remitting another two million *rmb* for Zerong (Sunwu)[5] to help him out with household expenses. He sent me a letter to which I have not yet had the chance to respond. Please tell him on my behalf that I will not be writing a separate letter.

I thank you for spending your energy in handling the above-mentioned matters and conveying my sentiments. I wish you health and well-being.

> Mao Zedong
> October 2, 1952

[P.S.]: This money is entirely from payments for my own writings; please tell them to use it sparingly.

Notes

1. See text Oct. 15, 1949, note 1, for an explanation of the translation of the term *xiong* here.

2. This refers, according to the source, to Li Shuqing and Zou Puxun. See text Nov. 17, 1949, note 2, and text May 15, 1950, note 2.

3. See text Dec. 11, 1951, source note.

4. This figure here is for the old *renminbi* (people's currency), which was in use in the "liberated areas" prior to 1949 and throughout the country from 1950 to March 1955. The new *renminbi (rmb)* was issued by the People's Bank of China on March 1, 1955, with a conversion rate of 10,000 old *rmb yuan* (or dollars) equivalent to one new *rmb yuan*.

5. Mao Zerong is one of Mao Zedong's first cousins. Sunwu (meaning "the diminutive no. 5") is probably a family nickname for Mao Zerong.

Telegram to the Peace Conference of the Asian and Pacific Region
(October 2, 1952)

Source: *RMRB* (Oct. 3, 1952), 1. Other Chinese Text: *XHYB*, 10 (Oct. 1952), 53.

See text Sept. 30, 1952, note 3.

The Peace Conference of the Asian and Pacific Region:

The convening of the Peace Conference of the Asian and Pacific Region will be a tremendous contribution to the great common cause of the people of Asia, of the Pacific region, and of the entire world in safeguarding peace.

My sincere wishes for the success of this conference.

(Signed as Chairman of the National Committee of the CPPCC and dated)

Letter to Qi Baishi
(October 5, 1952)

Source: *Shuxin*, p. 448.

Qi (1864-1957) was perhaps modern China's most renowned and respected artist. Beginning his professional artist's career in his early thirties, Qi acquired prominence only in the latter half of his long life. His style was characteristically simple but vigorous, dedicated to the impressionistic renditions of life in its many forms and settings, always elegant and with a touch of humor. Qi's best works were done as portrayals of small living creatures such as frogs, fish, chicks, crabs, dragonflies, etc. and of fruit in abundance. He is known also for his calligraphy, seal engraving, as well as poetry. Qi was the sponsor of many national artists' organizations after the founding of the PRC, an honorary director of the Chinese Academy of Fine Arts in Beijing, and a chairman of the Association of Chinese Painters. He also served, rather inactively, as a delegate to the first National People's Congress. With his artist's reputation, he did much to foster friendly relations between foreign countries and China. On his death he willed to the Central People's Government all of his works in his possession. See also text Sept. 5, 1955, note 1. For more biographical information on Qi, see H. Boorman et al., eds. (1967), I, pp. 302-304, and T. C. Lai (1973).

Mr. Baishi:[1]

I thank you heartily for the gift of your scroll painting *Pu tian tong qing* (Joyous Celebration for All in Heaven), which I have received. I would like to express my gratitude to all your co-creators [of the masterpiece]: Messrs. Xu Shixue, Yu Feian, Wang Shensheng, Hu Peiheng, Pu Yizai, Pu Xuezai, and Guan Songfang.[2]

Mao Zedong
October 5, 1952

Notes

1. For an explanation of this usage, see text Nov. 17, 1949, note 2.

2. We have not been able to find detailed biographical information on these contemporary artists. Yu was Qi's pupil, and Hu Peiheng was Qi's contemporary. Hu once taught at the Fine Arts Institute of Beijing University. Pu Xuezai became, in 1960, vice-chairman of the Chinese Calligraphy Institute in Beijing.

Telegram to the German Democratic Republic
(October 5, 1952)

Source: *RMRB* (Oct. 2, 1952), 1. Other Chinese Text: *XHYB*, 10 (Oct. 1952), 120. Available English Translation: NCNA, *Daily Bulletin*, 639 (Oct. 9, 1952), 2.

The President,
The German Democratic Republic

Comrade Pieck:

On behalf of the Chinese people, the government of the People's Republic of China, and on my own behalf, I sincerely extend to you and to the people and government of the German Democratic Republic our heartfelt congratulations on this occasion of the third anniversary of the founding of the German Democratic Republic.

In their struggles to secure a peace treaty and to restore the unity of Germany, to develop the economy and culture, and to consolidate state power, the victories scored by the German people have had a tremendous effect on the prosperity and happiness of the German people and the cause of peace throughout the world. Our best wishes to the German people for securing even greater successes in the struggle they have undertaken to build a unified, peaceful, democratic, and socialist Germany.

(Signed as Chairman of CPG of PRC, dated, in Beijing)

Talk with Tibetan Delegates
(Excerpts)
(October 8, 1952)

Source: *RMRB* (Nov. 22, 1952), 1. Other Chinese Texts: *Ziliao xuanbian*, p. 147; *Wansui* (n.d.), p. 7. Available English Translation: NCNA, *Daily Bulletin*, 673 (Nov. 26, 1952), 1-2.

This speech was made at a reception that Mao held for the delegation of the people of the Changdu (Chambdo) region of Tibet taking part in the celebration of the anniversary of the founding of the PRC in Beijing.

The Ziliao xuanbian *and* Wansui *(n.d.) sources mistakenly date this speech as October 8, 1951.*

1. The Communist Party has adopted a policy of protecting religions.[1] Believers and nonbelievers, believers of one religion or another, are all similarly protected, and their faiths are respected. Today, we have adopted this policy of protecting religions, and in the future we will still maintain this policy of protection.

2. The problem of land redistribution is different from that of religion. In the regions inhabited by the Han people land has already been redistributed, and in these areas religions are still protected. Whether or not land should be redistributed in regions inhabited by minority nationalities will be decided by the minority nationalities themselves. At the moment, land redistribution is out of the question in Tibet. Whether or not there should be redistribution in the future will be decided by you yourselves; moreover, you yourselves

should carry out the redistribution. We will not redistribute the land for you.

3. The setting up of a military and administrative committee and the reorganization of the Tibetan army were stipulated by the Agreement.[2] [However,] because you were afraid, I have informed the comrades working in Tibet to postpone the implementation [of this].[3] The Agreement must be implemented, but since you are afraid, implementation will simply have to be postponed. If you are afraid this year, we will wait until next year to implement it. If you are still afraid next year, then [we] will wait for the year after next before implementing it.

4. Tibet is a large area with a small population. Its population must be increased from the current figure of two or three million to five or six million. Later it would be good to increase it again to more than ten million. The economy and culture also need to be developed. Culture includes such things as schools, newspapers, cinema, etc. Religion is also included. The reactionary rulers of the past, [whether] the emperors of the Qing dynasty or Chiang Kai-shek, all oppressed and exploited you, and so did the imperialists.[4] They kept your population down, weakened your economy, and obstructed the development of your culture. The Communist Party puts into practice [the principle of] the equality of nationalities; it does not wish to oppress or exploit you, but rather to assist you – to assist you in developing your population, economy, and culture. When the People's Liberation Army entered Tibet,[5] it was precisely for the purpose of carrying out the policy of helping you. In the early period of its presence there it may not be of much help, and it may not be of great help even for the next three or four years. Later, however, it will be able to help you, that is certain. If the Communist Party could not help you develop your population, economy, and culture, the Communist Party would be of no use at all. . . . [I] am happy that you have come. During the next few days you can go to Nanjing, Shanghai, Tianjin, Guangdong, and the Northeast for a visit. From now on, if more people, both ecclesiastical and lay, and from all different circles of Tibet can come out to visit the various places in the interior, it will help to strengthen the relations of unity and amity among the nationalities in China.

Notes

1. Articles 3 and 5 of the Common Program adopted September 27, 1949, respectively requisitioned rural land owned by religious institutions and guaranteed freedom of religious belief.

2. See text May 24, 1951, source note. See also text Apr. 6, 1952, notes 2 and 7.

3. See text Apr. 6, 1952, note 1.

4. See text Apr. 6, 1952, note 12.

5. See text Apr. 6, 1952, note 3.

Letter to Song Qingling
(October 10, 1952)

Source: *Shuxin*, p. 449.

Song Qingling (b.1892) was one of the most prominent women in China's modern and recent history. Born into a family that acquired very considerable wealth and influence (see text Oct. 13, 1957, note 16), she married Sun Yat-sen in 1914. For the next ten years she was also Sun's confidant in political matters, collaborating with him as a private secretary as well as wife and assistant. After Sun's death, Song Qingling's parting of ways with the rest of her own family came in 1927 when her youngest sister, Meiling, married Chiang Kai-shek. Earlier in that year, she had parted ways with the mainstream of the KMT, which Sun had founded – i.e., with both the Nanjing government and the Wuhan government – for its anti-Communist policies and purges. In 1948 she became honorary chairman of an anti-Chiang KMT splinter group, the KMT Revolutionary Committee. This organization remained active in the PRC after 1949 as one of the "democratic parties" (see text Sept. 21, 1949, note 1.) In that capacity Song remained a very active political figure in the PRC until her death, her activities being mostly in the areas of social welfare and legislation. For more biographical information on Song, see H. Boorman et al., eds. (1970), III, pp. 142-146, and D. Klein and A. Clark, eds. (1971), II, pp. 782-787.

Vice-chairman Song:

I am extremely elated by your gift of your masterpiece *Wei xin Zhongguo fendou* (Struggle for New China), and would like hereby to express my deep gratitude. Your other gifts have also been received and I thank you equally for them.

I wish you health and well-being.

Mao Zedong

October 10

Letter to Tan Zhenlin
(October 15, 1952)

Source: *Shuxin*, pp. 450-451.

Tan was, at the time of this letter, third secretary of the East China Bureau of the Central Committee of the CPC. For more information on Tan, see text May 17, 1958, note 34, and text Jul. 23, 1959, note 105.

Comrade Zhenlin:

The [information that] Comrade Chen Yun[1] has acquired on conditions in Xiaozheng *xiang*, Qingpu *xian*,[2] is quite worthy of attention. I enclose it here for your perusal; please make a copy of it and send to the Party committee of the South Jiangsu district.

According to Comrade Bo Yibo,[3] when he was in Shanghai he already knew that last year's grain requisition in the Zhejiang and South Jiangsu districts has been too heavy and that the East China Bureau has resolved to return part [of that] to the peasants. I wonder what the results have been in this matter? How much, in total, has been returned [to the peasants] in the two districts? How many people's problems have been resolved [by the action]? What is this year's harvest like? Has the quantity of the [state] grain requisition been greatly reduced?

In order to resolve this problem, I suggest that you convene at the East China Bureau a special conference of the people responsible for the two districts and the secretaries of the *xian* [Party] committees of some characteristic *xian* in the two districts. Before the meeting is held, you can dispatch two investigation teams, one to go to Zhejiang and the other to South Jiangsu; let them go directly to the villages in several *xian* and investigate [the conditions] in a dozen or so *xiang*, focusing especially on investigating the real situations with regard to the peasants' [contributions to] public grain and other burdens – this then can be the basis for discussion at the meeting.

In short, we must earnestly and solidly resolve the problem of giving relief to those peasants who in the past have had little to live on because the [public] burdens have been too heavy. The grain requisition this year must not exceed the rate stipulated by the Center.[4] [We must] greatly reduce the burden of the people.

I hope that you will notify me of your opinions.

In comrade's salute!

Mao Zedong
October 15, 1952

Notes

1. Chen was at this time a vice-premier of the Government Administration Council and director of the Financial and Economic Commission of the Central People's Government. See also text Jan. 20, 1956, note 9.

2. This locality is within the municipality of Shanghai.

3. Bo was at this time deputy director of the Financial and Economic Commission and deputy minister of Finance. See also text Aug. 12, 1953, note 5.

4. According to the source, in February 1950, when the Government Administration Council drew up regulations for the requisition of public grain in the "new liberated areas," it stipulated that such requisition "should not exceed seventeen per cent of the gross agricultural income, and the added public grain requisition done by the local people's government must not exceed fifteen per cent of the official grain requisition." In its "Directive on the Work of Agricultural Taxation and Requisition in 1952" the GAC stipulated: "In those parts of the late liberated areas where land reform has been completed, a unified system of accumulative progressive tax on the basis of a total combined rate will be followed in 1952. The accumulative progressive tax rate will start at seven per cent and end at thirty per cent. As a rule no additional surtax will be allowed." The source submits that in this way the burden of the peasants was somewhat alleviated.

Letter to Li Shuqing
(October 16, 1952)

Source: *HQ* (Aug. 16, 1982), 3. Other Chinese Texts: *XHYB*, 454 (Sept. 30, 1982), 77; *Shuxin*, p. 468.

The Shuxin *source dates this letter as October 16, 1953. For the identity of Li Shuqing, see text Nov. 17, 1949, note 2.*

Mr. Shuqing:

Your gracious letter has been received. I am very grateful for your conveying to me news of our home village. As for matters related to the localities, I wish only to collect material and information for reference purposes; I do not want to, and should not, directly handle local problems in general [because this would] make it difficult for the local Party and government [organs] to handle their affairs. Please understand my situation and forgive me.

With great respect,

Mao Zedong
October 16, 1952

Letter to Luo Yuankun
(October 22, 1952)

Source: *Shuxin*, p. 452.

See text October 11, 1950.

Mr. Hanming:[1]

Your letter of October 19 has been received. The two items sent by courtesy of Mr. Li[2] have been read, and I am extremely grateful. The autobiography is written with great spirit and is extraordinarily stimulating; the criticisms and comments [therein] are penetrating and should serve well as a model for the young people. The "characteristics" and other points described in the other item [, however,] are for the most part not particularly accurate, being the products of hearsay; please do not have these published. I now send back to you these two items. I have followed your command and have completed the inscription for Mr. Yuan's grave.[3] Please be so kind as to transmit it [to the proper people]. It is very improper for the old monasteries of Xinhua to be destroyed or damaged. Such things have occurred in many places, and [the problem is being handled by] the Government Administration Council through its centralized comprehensive measures of protecting [such historical relics]. For this reason I will not write separately [on these incidents specifically]; I hope you will forgive and understand. It is a very fair suggestion for the older people among the nuns and monks to [be permitted to] remain in the monasteries as caretakers, and the younger ones to take part in labor. I have already transmitted [this suggestion] to the government organs concerned for their consideration and handling.

In response, and with respectful wishes for your health and safety in the countryside.

Mao Zedong
October 22, 1952

Notes

1. "Hanming" is Luo's *hao* (another type of honorific besides *zi*). For an explanation of this usage, see text Oct. 15, 1949, note 1.

2. According to the source, this refers to the drafts of two articles written by Luo and which Luo had asked Li Shuqing (see text Nov. 17, 1949, note 2, and text Oct. 2, 1952) to carry to Beijing to Mao. One was an autobiographical essay and the other was titled, in translation,

"Chairman Mao in the Days of the First Normal School."
3. See text Oct. 11, 1950.

Congratulations on the Victory
of the Chinese People's Volunteers
(October 24, 1952)

Source: *Xuanji*, V, pp. 70-71. Available English Translations: *SW*, V, pp. 82-83; JPRS, *Selections* (June 3, 1977), 18.

This is a directive to the leading members of the Chinese People's Volunteers drafted by Mao for the Central Committee of the CPC and its Military Commission.

Since September 18, our Volunteers, assisting the Korean People's Army, have launched a tactical counteroffensive along the entire front of the enemy's troops. Within one month, more than thirty thousand enemy troops have been killed or wounded, and a great victory has been won.[1] The Central Committee and the Military Commission extend warm congratulations to you and to the entire body of officers and soldiers. This way of fighting involves concentrating superior forces and superior firepower at certain chosen key tactical points and employing sudden maneuvers in order to strike at entire platoons, companies, and battalions of the enemy so as to annihilate all or a large part of them. Then, at the moment that the enemy launches a counteroffensive against us, we inflict massive casualties on the enemy in repeated battles. After that, according to the circumstances of those positions that fall into our hands, we staunchly defend those that can be defended, and abandon those that cannot be defended, maintaining our initiative and preparing for further counteroffensive activities. Such methods of fighting, if continued, are bound to enable us to bring our enemies to their knees and force them to come to terms in order to end the war in Korea. Since our armies adopted solid positional warfare in July of last year, the number of casualties that we have inflicted on enemy troops is far in excess of the number of casualties that we dealt the enemy in the various mobile battles prior to that. Moreover, our own losses have been greatly reduced. Of these [losses], just taking the Volunteers as an example, casualties have been reduced in the fifteen months since July of last year by an average of more than two-thirds each month, as compared with [losses in] the preceeding eight months. These conditions are the result of implementing the method of fighting just described, relying on [fixed] battle positions. Moreover, during the period since September 18, it has been demonstrated that this method of fighting is more organized and more closely related to [the concept of] the front as a whole; therefore, it is particularly worthy of our attention.

At this moment, on the occasion of the second anniversary of the embarkation of our Volunteers for the battle abroad, I hope that you will sum up your experiences, raise your sense of organization and the level of tactics even higher, economize on ammunition, be even more intimately united with our Korean comrades and with the Korean people, and strive for even greater victories in the fighting yet to come.

Note

1. Mao is referring to the so-called "September Offensive" of the Chinese and North Korean forces. Beginning on September 18, the Chinese and North Korean forces opened up a major offensive with five main points of contact in western and central battle fronts. The fighting was particularly fierce over the control of the "bald hill" region along the banks of the Linzhong River. In the last days of September the focus of the battle moved to the eastern banks of the North Han River. According to Chinese reports, over 30,900 U.S. and South Korean troops were liquidated in September 1952.

Telegram to the Democratic People's Republic of Korea
(October 28, 1952)

Source: FBIS, *Daily Report* (Nov. 10, 1952), EEE12.

We have no Chinese text of this telegram. The FBIS transcript is therefore presented in its original form. The telegram was apparently addressed to Premier Kim Il Sung.

I humbly express my sincere thanks to the Korean people, the government of the Democratic People's Republic of Korea, and you for your greetings on the occasion of the second anniversary of the entry into the war of the Chinese People's Volunteers to resist America and aid Korea.

I am convinced, too, that our joint righteous struggle to destroy the American imperialist aggressors, with the close solidarity of the Korean and Chinese peoples and the war support of the great Soviet Union and all the peace-loving peoples of the world, will inevitably win ultimate victory.

Conversation During an Inspection Tour of the Flood Prevention Works on the Yellow River [Excerpts]

(October 29-31, 1952)

Source: Excerpts from Wang Huayun, "Mao zhuxi shicha Huang he" (Chairman Mao Inspects the Yellow River), in *Mao guanhuai*, pp. 42-50.

This article was apparently originally published in various newspapers, including Henan ribao *(Mar. 28, 1957) and* Jiefang ribao *(Apr. 6, 1957). It was also quoted in part in* Hong Qi, *"Mao zhuxi de gongzuo, xuexi he shenghuo diandi" (Bits and Pieces About Chairman Mao's Work, Study and Life) in* Gongren ribao *(Jan. 15, 1950). Another reprint of the article is in* Mao qunzhong, *pp. 1-8. The author of this article, Wang Huayun, was a worker on the Flood Prevention Works on the Yellow River at Lanfeng, Henan. He accompanied Mao on the trip, made in late October 1952, described in the article. The points on the Yellow River that Mao visited on this tour – Lanfeng, Dongbatou, Tongwaxiang – are all points on the southern bank of the Yellow River in northern Henan Province, approximately an area 25-50 km. east of the city of Kaifeng. The following represent the more significant exchanges in Mao's conversation with cadres during this tour. In some cases we have represented not only Mao's words but the cadres' responses as well. All statements, except indicated otherwise, are Mao's. The last statement here also appeared as an instruction quoted in* RMRB *(Sept. 26, 1976), 3, and* RMRB *(Oct. 8, 1976), 1, and was translated in* PR, *12:43 (Oct. 24, 1969), 18.*

The people of the old base areas[1] contributed a great deal to the revolutionary cause; we should pay attention to helping them. . . .[2]

When this enormous dam[3] is built, the flood hazards of the Yellow River, which have existed for several thousands of years, will be resolved. Moreover, we will be able to irrigate several tens of million of *mu* in the plains and generate a million kilowatts of electricity. It can also make the river navigable for steamships. All this can be studied. . . .

(At Dongbatou)

Mao: What is this place?

Wang (Huayun): Here is where the Yellow River broke through the dikes in the fifth year of the reign of the Xianfeng Emperor of the Qing dynasty[4] and changed its course. It is called Tongwaxiang.

Mao: How many main embankments and stone dikes of this kind have been built?

Wang: Along the entire river, we have built 1,800 kilometers of embankment and close to 5,000 dikes. In the past, during the rule of the Kuomintang reactionaries, the overwhelming majority of these embankments were built of hay stalks and were far from being solid. Today, they have all been rebuilt with stone.

Mao: For six years the Yellow River has not overflowed its banks and flooded. If from now on we continue to build up embankments and dikes, do you think the Yellow River could still break through?

Wang: This is not the way to bring about a fundamental solution to the problem. If there should be an extraordinarily heavy deluge, the danger would still be quite great.

Mao: And what if the Yellow River overflows to the skies?

Wang: If we do not build huge reservoirs, we will not be able to stop [the floodwaters] just by these embankments and dikes. . . .

There is a lot of water in the South and little in the North. If it were possible, it would be nice to borrow some from the South. . . .

(At Liuyuankou.)

Mao: What is this grass?

A comrade: This is called *geba* grass. The masses plant this type of grass specially on the dikes in order to protect them. The masses say that it creates an advantage, that "with *geba* grass planted on the dikes, we fear neither rain nor waves."

Mao: It is also good stuff to feed the livestock.

Mao: What is this place? Is the water level of the river here higher than [the ground] level in the city of Kaifeng?[5]

Wu Zhipu:[6] This is called Liuyuankou. Diagonally across the river is Chenqiao – the location of the Chenqiao military coup, in which Zhao Kuangyun was draped with the yellow gown.[7] This place is now a ferry crossing.

Wang: The water level is three or four meters higher than the ground level in the city of Kaifeng, and during floods it is even higher.

Mao: Then this is an elevated river. . . .

Mao: Where does this soil come from?

Wang: It is all washed down by the current from the loess plateau in the northwest.[8]

Mao: How much [is carried down]?

Wang: According to inspections made by the hydrographic station at Shen xian, an average of 1,280 million metric tons is brought past that point each year. (The revised figure is now 1,360 million metric tons.) The sedimentation of such a huge amount of silt accounts for the Yellow River's flooding and changing course. . . .

Mao: Do the work on the Yellow River well.

Notes

1. See text Aug. 15, 1951, source note.

2. This comment was made in response to Chen Zaidao, who was at the time a member of the People's Government of Henan Province. Mao had inquired of Chen how his native village was, and Chen explained that although he had not been back to his native village for some twenty-five years, he understood that things were improving since Liberation and since the land reform, even though devastation had been severe during the pre-Liberation period of KMT control. Chen, born in 1908, was a native of Macheng, Hubei. He had been the commander of the Fourth Front Army of the Communist forces in 1932 and fled to Yanan in 1936, after the defeat at Lushan. He continued to be a military commander of Communist forces (first in the Eighth Route Army and later in the Second Field Army) from 1937 to 1949. For more biographical information on Chen, see *Zhonggong renming lu*, pp. 582-583.

3. Mao is referring to the Sanmen Gorge Dam.

4. This refers to 1855 A.D.

5. Capital city of Henan Province.

6. Wu (b. 1906) was then chairman of the People's Government of Henan Province and director of the Head Office of the Yellow River Flood Prevention Committee. For more biographical information on Wu, see D. Klein and A. Clark, eds. (1971), II, pp. 944-946, and *Zhonggong renming lu*, p. 246.

7. Zhao Kuangyun (928-976) was originally a military commander of troops for the emperor of the Late Zhou dynasty (951-959). In 960 A.D., at Chenqiao, as troops under his command marched against the Khitan forces, Zhao's lieutenants staged a coup and had the troops proclaim him emperor. He then accepted the throne from the abdicating Zhou emperor and became, as Emperor Taizu, the first emperor of the Song dynasty. The draping of the yellow gown symbolizes the conferring of royal status, yellow being a royal color in China.

8. The Chinese term for loess is *huangtu*, or "yellow earth." The loess plateau encompasses parts of Inner Mongolia, the Ningxia *hui* nationality autonomous region, and Gansu, Shaanxi, and Shanxi provinces.

Telegram to the USSR
(November 3, 1952)

Source: *RMRB* (Nov. 7, 1952), 1. Other Chinese Text: *XHYB*, 37 (Nov. 1952), 38. Available English Translation: NCNA, *Daily Bulletin*, 660 (Nov. 7, 1952), 1-2;

Chairman,
The Council of Ministers,
The Union of Soviet Socialist Republics

Comrade Stalin:

On this occasion of the thirty-fifth anniversary of the great socialist October Revolution, on behalf of the Chinese people, the government of the People's Republic of China, and on my own behalf, I sincerely extend to the Soviet people, to the government of the Soviet Union, and to you our sincere congratulations.

With the greatest joy, the Chinese people congratulate the great Soviet people on the brilliant, unparalleled successes that they have achieved in the cause of building Communism. These successes are a powerful new inspiration to the Chinese people, who are about to begin economic construction on a large scale, as well as to the laboring people throughout the world.

We congratulate the Soviet people on their tremendous achievements in their unflagging struggle to safeguard and consolidate international peace. These successes have brought defeat after defeat to the plots of the instigators of war and have immeasurably strengthened the confidence of peace-loving people throughout the world in defending peace and preventing war.

May the cause of defending peace in the Far East and the world triumph, and may the great, impregnable friendship between China and the Soviet Union be ever more consolidated and developed.

(Signed as Chairman of CPG of PRC, dated, in Beijing)

Inscription on Inauguration of the Kangding-Changdu Section of the Xikang-Tibet Highway
(November 19, 1952)

Source: *RMRB* (Nov. 27, 1952), 1.

The opening of this section of the Xikang-Tibet (Kang-Zhang) Highway was held on Nov. 20, 1952. Kangding is in Sichuan Province; Changdu (Chambdo) is in the Tibetan Autonomous Region.

In order to help our brothers, the minority nationalities, let us brave any difficulty and energetically build this highway!

Reply to Ambassador of the Kingdom of Sweden
(December 3, 1952)

Source: *GMRB* (Dec. 4, 1952), 1. Available English Translation: FBIS, *Daily Report* (Dec. 4, 1952), AAA3-4 (excerpt).

Hugo Wistrand served as ambassador of the Kingdom of Sweden to the PRC from December 1952 to May 1956.

Mr. Ambassador:

I am very pleased to accept the letter of credence from the King of Sweden that Your Excellency has presented and am grateful for your congratulations.

I welcome Your Excellency's appointment as the ambassador extraordinary and plenipotentiary of the Kingdom of Sweden to the People's Republic of China.

I am also very happy to accept Your Excellency's assurance that you will strive to strengthen the friendly relations between China and Sweden. I firmly believe that your wishes and efforts in this regard will be met by the support of the government of the People's Republic of China.

I sincerely wish the King of Sweden good health, the country of Sweden prosperity, and its people well-being and happiness.

Inscription Concerning Public Health Work
(December 8, 1952)

Source: *RMRB* (Jan. 4, 1952), 1. Available English Translations: *SCMM* (suppl.), 22 (Apr. 8, 1968), 6; *CR*, 21:11 (Nov. 1972), 7 (excerpt).

According to the accompanying news item, this inscription was written by Mao for the Second National Health Conference.

Mobilize,

Pay attention to hygiene,
Cut down on disease,
Raise the standard of health,
Smash the enemy's germ warfare.[1]

Mao Zedong

Note

1. In February and March 1952, the Chinese government accused the American forces in the Korean War of waging germ warfare by dropping bombs containing viral infected bugs and other insects and bombs containing viral and bacterial culture, first on territories in Korea and then, from late February onward, also on Qingdao and other parts of northeastern China. See *RMSC* (1952), pp. 19-27.

Letter to the Anshan Iron and Steel Works
(December 14, 1952)

Source: *RMRB* (Dec. 17, 1952), 1. Other Chinese Text: *XHYB*, 1 (Jan. 25, 1953), 128.

The Anshan Iron and Steel Works, familiarly known as Angang, is one of the PRC's key industrial complexes. Located in the mineral- and coal-rich region of eastern Liaoning Province, Anshan is a natural site for steel industrial development, although the on-site iron ore is somewhat poorer in quality. During the period of Japanese occupation in the Second World War, the industry of the region (i.e., Manchuria as a whole, which served the Japanese as the chief base of operations in China) underwent special development, therefore outstripping older steel production zones such as the area of Wuhan. This emphasis was continued in the "period of national economic recovery" in the PRC, i.e., 1950-1952. By 1954, Anshan was identified as one of ten major "above-the-norm" reconstruction projects, and by 1956, the chief industrial base for steel production and machine building in the PRC. Later in the decade it would also vault into prominence in the PRC's (and Mao's personal) political-economic vocabulary because of the proposal of its "charter," known as the Angang xianfa *in 1960, which was subsequently adopted as a model of "the basic principle for running socialist enterprises." (See text Mar. 22, 1960(2).) For a brief account of the development of the Anshan Works, see T. Rawski (1980), chs. 1-2, passim.*

The staff and workers of the Smelting Plant at Anshan Iron and Steel Works

Comrades:

I am very pleased to read your letter of December 2. Congratulations on your newest success in production in open-hearth furnace smelting. With a high degree of enthusiasm in labor and in a creative spirit, aided by the Soviet specialists, you have set a new record, surpassing the level of the capitalist countries in terms of the period for turning out each heat and in terms of the coefficient of utilization of area space at the hearth bottom. This is not only an honor for you, but also a great event for our country along its path to industrialization. I hope you will continue your efforts and strive to accomplish the new task of smelting high quality steel in 1953.

Mao Zedong
December 14, 1952

Reply to Ambassador of the Soviet Union
(December 15, 1952)

Source: *RMRB* (Dec. 16, 1952), 1. Available English Translation: FBIS, *Daily Report* (Dec. 16, 1952), AAA2.

Panyushkin served as ambassador of the USSR to the PRC from December 1952 to April 1953.

Comrade Ambassador:

I am very pleased to accept the letter of credence from the Presidium of the Supreme Soviet of the Union of Soviet Socialist Republics which you have presented, and I sincerely thank you for your congratulations.

For the past three years, the friendly and cooperative relations between the People's Republic of China and the Union of Soviet Socialist Republics have been greatly consolidated and developed. As a result of unceasing efforts by the Chinese people and with the fraternal assistance of the great people and government of the Soviet Union, New China has achieved successes in every area and will soon enter into large-scale economic construction.

I firmly believe that the further development of the great friendship between our two great countries will not only be beneficial to the prosperity of China and the Soviet Union, but will also play an inestimably great role in the cause of ensuring peace in the Far East and in the world.

Comrade Ambassador, I warmly welcome you as the ambassador extraordinary and plenipotentiary of the Union of Soviet Socialist Republics to the People's Republic of China. In your work of consolidating the friendship and cooperation between China and the Soviet Union you will receive my full support and that of the government of the People's Republic of China.

I sincerely wish you complete success in your work.

Letter to Yi Nanping
(December 21, 1952)

Source: *Shuxin*, p. 454.

According to the source, Yi was a schoolmate of Mao's when Mao studied at the Higher Middle School of Hunan Province (which later changed its name to First Middle School of Hunan Province).

My dear Nanping:[1]

I have received the book and the two handcopies which you so graciously sent to me on December 6, 1952. Thank you very much! If you are weak and suffering from many illnesses, it would not be appropriate for you to leave your home, least of all to come to the capital. I am remitting [with this letter] three million *rmb* to help out with [your] medical expenses.[2] I would be grateful if from time to time you would instruct me on the situation in our home village.

In response, and with my best wishes for your health and well-being.

Mao Zedong
December 21, 1952

Notes

1. For an explanation of this translation of the term *xiong*, see text Oct. 15, 1949, note 1.
2. See text Oct. 2, 1952, note 4.

Reply to the Ambassador
of the People's Republic of Romania
(December 29, 1952)

Source: *RMRB* (Dec. 30, 1952), 1. Available English Translation: NCNA, *Daily Bulletin*, 696 (Dec. 31, 1952), 3.

Comrade Ambassador:

I am very glad to accept the letter of credence from the Presidium of the Grand National Assembly of the People's Republic of Romania presented by you, and I am sincerely grateful for your congratulations.

In the past three years, the relationship of friendship and cooperation between the People's Republic of China and the People's Republic of Romania, in all areas of politics, economy, and culture, has attained a very great development. Such a relationship of friendship and cooperation enhances the prosperity of China and Romania and the friendship of the peoples of the two countries. Moreover it strengthens the force of the camp for world peace and democracy headed by the great Soviet Union.

Under the leadership of Comrade Georghiu-Dej,[1] the Romanian people are in the midst of victoriously carrying on their socialist construction and have continuously attained brilliant achievements. These achievements have always won the deep regards and praise of the Chinese people.

Comrade Ambassador, I warmly welcome you as ambassador extraordinary and plenipotentiary of the People's Republic of Romania to the People's Republic of China. In your work of consolidating the friendship and cooperation between the two countries of China and Romania you will receive my wholehearted support and that of the government of the People's Republic of China.

I wish you complete success in your work.

Note

1. Gheorghe Gheorghiu-Dej was Secretary General of the Romanian Communist Party (Partidul Comunist Roman) from 1945 to his death in 1965.

Telegram to the USSR on the Transfer
of the Chinese Changchun Railway
(December 31, 1952)

Source: *RMRB* (Dec. 31, 1952), 1. Other Chinese Text: *XHYB* (Jan. 25, 1953), 49. Available English Translations: NCNA, *Daily Bulletin*, 699 (Jan. 5, 1952), 6; FBIS, *Daily Report* (Dec. 31, 1952), AAA3-4.

Chairman,
The Council of Ministers,
The Union of Soviet Socialist Republics

Comrade Stalin:

In the period of joint Sino-Soviet administration of the Chinese Changchun Railway, the Soviet side has made great contributions to the Chinese people's undertaking in railway construction. The Chinese people will forever remember this fraternal, friendly assistance. On this occasion when the Soviet government, in accordance with the 1950 Agreement and the 1952 Communiqué,[1] is transferring, gratis, to the government of the People's Republic of China all rights to the joint administration appertaining to the Chinese Changchun Railway and all the property of the railway, I, on behalf of the Chinese people and government, extend to the great Soviet people, the government of the Soviet Union, and to you our heartfelt gratitude. May the great friendship between the Soviet Union and China grow and become more consolidated with each passing day.

Note

1. For an English text of the agreement on the joint administration and future transfer of the Chinese Changchun Railway signed February 14, 1950, see NCNA, *Daily Bulletin*, 289 (Feb. 16, 1950), 81. For an English text of the September 15, 1952, joint communiqué on the transfer of the railroad, see *PC*, XIX:7 (1952). See also text Jan. 2, 1950, note 1.

Instruction on the Arts
(December 1952)

Source: *Meishu fenglei*, 3 (Aug. 1967). Other Chinese Text: *GMRB* (June 13, 1967) (abridged). Available English Translations: *CB*, 885 (July 31, 9169), 26; *CB*, 897 (Dec. 10, 1969), 24.

If the proletariat does not take hold of the arts such as music, chess, calligraphy, and painting, the bourgeoisie certainly will.

Directive on Education
(1952)

Source: *Jiaoyu geming*, 14 (July 29, 1967).

Don't run schools specially for children of cadres. They should become one with the masses.

Comment on a Report of the National
Labor Insurance Conference
(1952)

Source: *Quanwudi* (Aug. 8, 1967). Available English Translation: *SCMM* (supp.), 28 (Apr. 8, 1968), 6.

The comment was made on a report submitted to the Central Committee of the CPC by the National Labor Insurance Conference which was convened by the Department of

Labor on December 23-31, 1952.

The labor insurance system was a compulsory insurance system to guarantee the provision of suitable and healthy working conditions and to guarantee compensation for accidental injuries and other disabilities such as maternity. It was inaugurated by the Labor Insurance Code adopted by the seventy-third meeting of the Government Administration Council on Feb. 23, 1951. (See RMSC *[1952], pp. 227-233.)*

While taking practical steps to increase production and to practice economy,[1] we must pay attention to the workers' safety and health and to indispensable welfare undertakings.[2]

Notes

1. See text Oct. 23, 1951, note 6.
2. The *SCMM* translation of this comment includes at the end the following sentence: "If we pay attention only to the former and forget or slightly neglect the latter, that will be a mistake." This sentence does not appear in our Chinese source.

1953

Telegram to the Union of Burma
(January 2, 1953)

Source: FBIS, *Daily Report* (Jan. 19, 1953), HHH1.

We have no Chinese text of this telegram. It is referred to in RMRB *(Jan. 5, 1953), 1. The FBIS source is presented in its original form. The telegram was apparently addressed to Dr. Ba U, president of the Union of Burma.*

On this remarkable independence day of the Union of Burma, I, representing the Chinese People's Republic Government and the people of China, pray for your Excellency, the Union Government, and the people of the Union of Burma.

Intra-Party Directive on Rectification
(January 5, 1953)

Source: *Xuanji*, V, pp. 72-74. Available English Translation: *SW*, V, pp. 84-86.

This is an intra-Party directive drafted by Mao on behalf of the Central Committee. It is important to note parallels between the principles and methods suggested by Mao here and those implemented in the rectification campaign within the CPC in Yanan in 1942. This document forecasts the first major internal rectification campaign in the CPC after Liberation.

This matter of opposing bureaucratism, opposing commandism,[1] and opposing violations of law and discipline ought to arouse the attention of our leadership organs at all levels.

During the "Three-Anti's" [campaign],[2] our Party has fundamentally solved the two problems of corruption and waste among many of the personnel at the four levels of the Center, the greater administrative regions,[3] the provinces and the municipalities, and the special districts. It has also basically solved that part of the problem of bureaucratism in which many leaders are alienated from the personnel whom they lead in their organizations. However, there is still basically no solution in many places, areas, and departments as far as the other area of bureaucratism is concerned, that is, in the area that has to do with [cadres] not understanding the suffering of the masses of the people, not understanding the conditions of lower levels somewhat farther removed from the organ where they themselves work, not understanding that many bad people and bad things connected with commandism and violation of law and discipline exist among the cadres at the three levels of *xian,* district, and *xiang.* Even though they may have some knowledge of these bad people and bad things, they turn a blind eye to them, their indignation is not aroused, and they have no sense of the seriousness of the problem, and so they take no active measure to support the good people and punish the bad or to promote the good things and eliminate the bad. Take the matter of handling letters from the people, for instance. In some provinces the People's Government has piled up more than seventy thousand pieces of mail without handling them. We still don't know how many letters from the people have piled up in the Party and governmental organs at the levels below the province, but it can be imagined that the quantity is not small. Most of these letters from the people contain problems that they hope we will solve, and many of these ought to be handled promptly because they contain accusations against cadres for acts in complete disregard of the laws.[4]

In our Party and government, bureaucratism and commandism are not only a major problem at present, but will continue to be a major problem for a very long period of time. In terms of its social origins, it is a problem of the remnants of the reactionary work-style of the reactionary ruling class in its treatment of the people (a work-style that opposes the people, a Kuomintang work-style) reflected in our Party and our government. In terms of the role and method of the leadership in our Party and governmental organizations, this is a problem of the failure to connect the delegation of tasks and responsibility to giving a clear explanation of the lines of demarcation in our policies and to connect work and work-style. This is to say that it is problem of not issuing repeated instructions regarding the lines of demarcation in our policies and regarding work-style in our work to mid- and lower-level cadres at the same time that tasks and responsibilities are assigned. This is a problem of not carrying out inspections of cadres at all levels, particularly those at the three levels of *xian,* district, and *xiang,* or of doing the work of inspection poorly. This is a problem of not having yet launched the work of rectifying the Party at the three levels of *xian,* district, and *xiang,* and of not having yet launched the struggle to oppose commandism and to clear out elements who violate law and discipline in the process of the rectification of the Party. This is a problem [related to the fact] that we have not yet launched the struggle against and purged the type of bureaucratism that is [exemplified by the fact] that there still exist among our personnel in higher-level organs above the special district level a lack of understanding and concern for the suffering of the masses of the people and a lack of understanding and concern for the conditions of the basic-level organizations. If our role of leadership is strengthened and if there are improvements in our methods of leadership, then bureaucratism and commandism, which endanger and harm the masses, can be gradually reduced, and it will be possible for many of our Party and governmental organizations to break away from the Kuomintang work-style sooner. Then many bad people who have wormed their way into our Party and governmental organizations can be cleared out at an earlier date, and many of the bad things that exist at present may be eliminated sooner.

Therefore, in 1953, in coordination with Party rectification, Party building, and work in others areas, beginning with the handling of the letters from the people, please carry out an inspection of the circumstances that give rise to bureaucratism and commandism under which elements who violate law and discipline operate, and launch a resolute struggle against them. Wherever there is a typical case of bureaucratism, commandism, or violation of law and discipline it should be widely exposed in the newspapers. In cases of severe violation of the law, there should be punishment according to the law, and if it involves a Party member, then Party discipline must be applied. Party committees at all levels ought to be resolute in punishing elements who have violated law and discipline and who are deeply hated by the masses, and they should eliminate them from Party and governmental organizations. In the most serious cases, capital punishment should be applied in order to assuage the people's anger and to serve as a point of education for the cadres and the masses of the people. However, at the moment that an appropriate stage has been reached in the launching of the widespread struggle against bad people and bad things, there should be an investigation of models of good people and things everywhere, and [these should be] analyzed and publicly commended so that the entire Party can measure up to these types and the spirit of righteousness can be promoted while the spirit of evil is suppressed. We believe that there must be quite a large number of such models of good people and good things everywhere.

Notes

1. See text June 6, 1950(1), note 11.
2. See text Nov. 1951-Mar. 1952, source note.
3. See text June 23, 1950, note 2.
4. See text May 16, 1951.

Speech to the Central People's Government Council
(January 13, 1953)

Source: *RMRB* (Jan. 15, 1953), 1. Available English Translation: NCNA, *Daily Bulletin*, 708 (Jan. 16, 1953), 5.

This speech should be read in conjunction with proposals made by the CPPCC to the Central People's Government (see RMSC [1953], pp. 93ff).

Throughout the country, military activities on the mainland have already ended, land reform[1] has already been basically accomplished, and people from all walks of life have become organized. Therefore, the conditions are now ripe for convening, according to the stipulation of the Common Program of the Chinese People's Political Consultative Conference,[2] the National People's Congress[3] and people's congresses at each local level.[4] This is a great victory achieved by the Chinese people only after decades of struggling for democracy with bloodshed and sacrifice. The convening of the [National] People's Congress will further give full play to the people's democracy and strengthen national construction and the struggle to Resist U.S. Aggression and Aid Korea.[5] The government based on a system of people's congresses will remain a government based on the united front of all nationalities, all democratic classes, all democratic parties, and all people's organizations[6] throughout the country. It will serve the interests of the entire people of the country.

Notes

1. See text Mar. 1951, note 1.
2. See text Sept. 21, 1949, note 3. Mao is referring particularly to articles 2, 12, and 14 of the Common Program.
3. The First Session of the NPC was ultimately held on September 15-28, 1954, in Beijing.
4. See text June 6, 1950(1), note 10.

5. See text Feb. 18, 1951, note 1.
6. See text Sept. 21, 1949, note 1, and text Oct. 1, 1949, note 2.

Closing Speech at the Fourth Session
of the First National Committee of the CPPCC
(Excerpts)

(February 7, 1953)

Source: *RMRB* (Feb. 8, 1953), 1. Other Chinese Texts: *XHYB*, 3 (Mar. 25, 1953), 13; *Faling huibian* (1953), pp. 3-4; *Zhengxie di si ci,* pp. 1-2; *RMSC* (1953), p. 159; *XHBYK*, 22 (Nov. 1958), 6; *Ziliao xuanbian*, p. 150 (excerpt); *Wansui* (n.d.), p. 11 (excerpt); Quoted in *RMRB* (Feb. 10, 1953), editorial. Available English Translations: NCNA, *Daily Bulletin*, 725 (Feb. 10, 1953), 1 (abridged); K. Fan (1972), pp. 101-102 (abridged).

This three-point directive was given at the Fourth Session of the First National Committee of the CPPCC, held Feb. 4-7, 1953, in Beijing. For details see K. Lieberthal (1976), p. 58.

First, [we] must intensify the struggle to resist U.S. [aggression] and aid Korea. Because U.S. imperialism persists in holding Chinese and Korean prisoners-of-war[1] and undermining the cease-fire negotiations and, moreover, is vainly attempting to expand its war of aggression against Korea, the struggle to resist U.S. [aggression] and aid Korea must continue to be intensified. We desire peace, but as long as U.S. imperialism does not discard its barbaric and unreasonable demands and its plots to expand its aggression, the resolution of the Chinese people can only be to continue to fight together with the Korean people to the end. This is not because we like war; we would like to stop the war immediately and wait to resolve the remaining problems in the future, but U.S. imperialism doesn't want to do things this way. If that's the case, that's all right; we'll continue to fight. No matter how many years U.S. imperialism is willing to fight, we are prepared to fight with them for as many years, right up to the time when U.S. imperialism is willing to stop, until the time when the Chinese and Korean peoples are completely victorious.

Second, we should learn from the Soviet Union. We must carry out the great task of construction in our country. The work facing us is difficult and our experience is insufficient; therefore we must earnestly study the advanced experience of the Soviet Union. Regardless of whether they are in the Communist Party or outside the Communist Party, old cadres or new cadres, technical personnel, intellectuals, or the masses of the workers and the masses of the peasants, [our people] all must wholeheartedly learn from the Soviet Union. We should not only learn from the theories of Marx, Engels, Lenin and Stalin, but must also learn from the Soviet Union's advanced science and technology. We must whip up a high tide of learning from the Soviet Union throughout the whole country [in order] to build our country.

Third, [we] must combat bureaucratism in our leadership organs at all levels and among our leading cadres. At present among a good number of the basic-level organizations and basic-level cadres, serious commandism and breaches of law and discipline are occurring.[2] The occurrence and breeding of such phenomena cannot be separated from the bureaucratism in our leadership organs and among our leading cadres. Take, for instance, the organs at the level of the Center; a good number of leading cadres in a good number of ministries and departments are still satisfied with merely sitting in the government offices writing decisions and issuing directives, paying attention only to arranging and assigning work but not paying attention to going down to the lower levels to get an understanding of conditions and to inspect the work. They have often let their leadership become isolated from the masses and separated from reality and have caused many serious problems to come up in their work. If we want to carry out large-scale national construction we must overcome bureaucratism and link ourselves closely to the masses of the people. Leading cadres at the Center and at all the local levels must all frequently go deep down to the lower levels to inspect the work. Once the leadership organs and leading cadres have overcome bureaucratism, the bad phenomena of commandism and breaches of law and discipline at the lower levels will definitely be overcome. Once these defects have been eliminated, our planned national construction will definitely be successful, the system of the people's democracy will definitely develop, the imperialist plots will definitely be defeated, and we will definitely be able to win total victory.

Notes

1. See text Aug. 4, 1952, note 5.
2. See text Jan. 5, 1953.

Telegram to the USSR
(February 10, 1953)

Source: *RMRB* (Feb. 14, 1953), 1. Other Chinese Text: *XHYB*, 3 (Mar. 25, 1953), 38. Available English Translations: NCNA, *Daily Bulletin*, 730 (Feb. 21, 1953), 1; FBIS, *Daily Report* (Feb. 16, 1953), AA24; CDSP, V:7 (Mar. 28, 1953), 15.

Chairman,
The Council of Ministers,
The Union of Soviet Socialist Republics

Comrade Stalin:

On behalf of the Chinese people, the government of the People's Republic of China, and on my own behalf, I express sincere gratitude and warm congratulations to the great Soviet people, the government of the Soviet Union, and to you on the occasion of the third anniversary of the signing of the Sino-Soviet Treaty of Friendship, Alliance, and Mutual Assistance.[1]

In the past three years, the relations of close friendship and cooperation between the two great allies, China and the Soviet Union, have attained great consolidation and development. The truly selfless assistance that the government and people of the Soviet Union have given New China has not only accelerated China's economic recovery and development but also will have great significance for the realization of the First Five-Year Plan in China's large-scale national construction.[2]

May the great indestructible friendship between the Soviet Union and China in opposing new aggressive plots of the imperialists and in the task of safeguarding peace in the Far East and the world become more consolidated and developed with each passing day.

(Signed as Chairman of CPG of PRC, dated, in Beijing)

Notes

1. See text Jan. 2, 1950, note 1.
2. The First Five-Year Plan (FYP) covered the period 1953-57. On December 24, 1952, at the forty-third meeting of the Standing Committee of the CPPCC, Zhou Enlai declared that "the First Five-Year Plan begins in 1953." The main principles and goals were discussed and published in *RMRB* on Sept. 16, 1953. However, the draft of the plan was not finalized until February 1955. It was finally adopted at the Second Session of the First NPC in late July 1955. For a translated ver-

sion of the Plan see *First Five Year Plan for the Development of the National Economy of the People's Republic of China* (Foreign Languages Press, 1955), and for a summary see Li Fuchun's report to the Second Session of the First NPC, reprinted in R. Bowie and J. Fairbank (1962), pp. 42-91.

Instruction on the Daye Steel Plant
(February 19, 1953)

Source: Quoted in Wu Shangyin, "Mao zhuxi er ci shicha Daye gangchang" (Chairman Mao Again Inspects the Daye Steel Plant), in *Mao Hubei*, p. 26.

The Chinese version of this inscription, written after an inspection that Mao made of the Daye Steel Plant in southeastern Hubei, about 40 km. southeast of the industrial city of Wuhan, is merely a representation of the four-character slogan (or policy directive) "ban da ban hao," which is very terse. It represents a policy of maintaining the quality level of industrial management while at the same time expanding the scope of the enterprises in order to meet the increasing demands of socialist construction. The slogan has been popular since 1952.

Strive to expand the capacity of the plant
and do a good job of running it.

Conversations with Naval Personnel on the Yangtze River
[Excerpts]
(February 19-24, 1953)

Source: On February 19-21, 1953, Mao made a voyage down the Yangtze River onboard several naval vessels, which he also inspected, as a means to gauge the development of China's naval forces. While most of the trip of four days and three nights was spent aboard the "Changjiang" and the "Luoyang," he also inspected the "Nanchang," the "Guangzhou," and the "Huanghe" as well as two torpedo boats, "53-101" and "53-104." We have been able to collect four records of the conversations that Mao had with naval personnel on this trip. There is a great deal of overlapping in these four versions, and much of the conversation is not very significant. From these we have culled the following excerpts of the relatively significant pieces of conversation, and where there is overlapping we have followed one relatively complete version or created a composite rendition. The structure and source will be apparent from the notes that accompany each passage. For the sake of convenience we have given an abbreviated designation to each of the following sources:

Source A: Members of the crew, Cruiser XX, "Nan wang de hangxing" (An Unforgettable Voyage), in *Mao guanhuai,* pp. 51-65;

Source B: Zhao Laijing, "Mao zhuxi he shuibing tanhua" (Chairman Mao Converses with Sailors), in *Zhongguo qingnian bao* (Mar. 26, 1954), 1;

Source C: Correspondent for Xinhua News Agency et al., "Weida de hangcheng" (A Great Voyage), reprinted in *Mao gushi,* vol. 2, pp. 76-78;

Source D: Wei Xinwen, "Maozhuxi yongyuan huozai shuibing xinzhong" originally in *Jiefangjun wenyi,* II (1975), and reprinted in *Huiyi Mao zhuxi,* pp. 573-588.

I hear that some of you do not want to serve in the navy. Why? Do you feel that there is too much hardship in serving in the navy?. . .

You all lead a very hard life!. . .

If they [the sailors] are obedient, then things will go well. In that case you [first mates] must pay attention to being good teachers to your students!. . .(Source A, p. 56.)

You should settle down, put your worries aside, and be happy about serving in the navy. In the past, when the imperialists invaded our country, in most cases they came from the sea. Even now, the Pacific Ocean is not at all pacific. We ought to have a strong navy. . . .(Source C, p. 77.)

We ought to be very closely united with one another. Henceforth, it will be even better. When the worker and peasant elements become intellectuals and the intellectuals become workers and peasants, the distinction between intellectuals and workers and peasants will gradually disappear. . . .

In the past, we were on land, and we loved the mountains and the soil. Now we are the navy and we ought to love the ship, love the islands, and love the oceans. (Source C, p. 82; Source B; and Source D, pp. 581-582.)

We must take good care of old machines. We must cherish them and use them well. At the moment we have old machines; later on we will have new ones. . . . You must nurture your children well, and when they grow up, let them have an education so as to lay a firm foundation for the revolution, and so that they may become successors to the revolution. (Source D, pp. 576-577.)

More than twenty years ago I was fighting as a guerrilla in these areas.[1] At that time I wore a straw hat and straw sandals. The reactionaries then surrounded us and attacked us on all sides; and yet today, some twenty years later, here I am cruising along on our own naval vessel together with you. (Source A, p. 58.)

Thirty years ago I passed through at this spot. At the time the islands were over there; now they have moved over here. In the past the waterway was very narrow; now it has become much wider.... The waterway has changed; so has the world! (Source D, p. 582; Source C, p. 83.)

The imperialists take advantage of us. We must stand up for ourselves. Our country has such a long coastline, we must absolutely have a strong navy to protect our coastline. At the moment, our navy is still not sufficiently strong; we have yet to develop it in a big way.... In the past we only had infantry and artillery soldiers, now we have an air force as well as a navy. Our national defense forces are growing in strength every day, and only now can our country proceed with its national construction in peace. As long as we work together and apply our efforts, we have a very bright and pleasant future ahead of us. (Source A, p. 59; slightly different versions in Source D, p. 579 and Source C, pp. 78-79.)

The First Five-Year Plan[2] in our country has begun; do you all know about it? . . . You are all very young. (Let's see now . . .) the First Five-Year Plan, the Second Five-Year Plan, the Third Five-Year Plan . . . you will be only thirty-some years old when we arrive at a socialist society . . . and you will still be young when we achieve a communist society. (Source A, p. 59; slightly different version in Source D, p. 579.)

We must first of all pay attention to political education and enhance the political enthusiasm of the comrades.... This book is very good in its contents.[3] The language, too, is simple and very appropriate for the soldiers to read. (Source C, pp. 80-81; slightly different version in Source D, pp. 580-581.)

We have been fighting for several decades. Our country is still very poor now, but after several five-year plans it will grow powerful. At this moment, the Pacific Ocean is not pacific. When we have a powerful navy the imperialists will not dare to bully us. We must build the coastline, which is over ten thousand kilometers long, into a Great Wall on the sea. (Source D, p. 580.)

Furthermore, there's also imperialism (to be opposed)!... Our country is poor and blank,[4] we have very few factories and very little iron and steel. Our line of coastal defense is very long. The imperialists bully us precisely because we have no navy.... (Now we have a navy, a navy of our own, a navy of the people.)... You must do a good job and strive to build a powerful navy with combat capacity; then the imperialists will not dare to bully us anymore. . . . You are the navy now. If you are in the navy you mustn't be afraid of storms and waves. You simply must go out on the sea to train yourselves. . . .[5] It does not matter if one's level of education is low. Even the most illiterate person can master technology. You have a high level of class consciousness and abundant combat experience. You are the backbone cadres [of the navy.] In the past we scaled the snowcapped mountains and crossed the marshlands;[6] what difficulty can we not overcome now?. . .

(A comrade reports: Some people say that we have no experience in building a navy [and so] we must learn from other countries in a wholesale and undeviating way. They also say that fighting on the sea is different from fighting on land, and the principles employed in fighting on land are not applicable on the sea.)

We must [of course] learn from the advanced experience of other countries. However, don't think that everything is better if it is foreign. Our own things must not be discarded. The navy has its own special characteristics, and yet we cannot emphasize the pecularity of the navy. We must retain the good traditions of our military forces. . . . We can make our own [naval equipment]. In the past, in the period of the War of Resistance against Japan and the War of Liberation, we were able to manufacture our own [equipment]; now we should have even greater capacity to do so. It won't do for us to rely on others exclusively. . . .

(In a report Mao was told that the emphasis was on the technological sophistication and mobility of the navy, and that the point was made that in a sea battle the role of the people's masses was minimal.)

The navy too must rely on the people's masses and on the fishing people. It cannot become divorced from the masses. It must go among the fishing people to sink its roots. Once we have a base among the masses everything is easier to accomplish. For instance, in the past, when we fought a battle, we knew a lot about the enemy's situation, but the enemy was unable to fathom our troops' maneuvers. This is the effect of the [favorable] conditions provide [us] by the masses [in our struggle]. The army must rely on the masses in fighting a battle, so must you when you fight a battle on the sea. No matter where you go, you must rely on the masses. (Largely based on Source D, pp. 586-587, partly on Source C, pp. 86-87.)

Notes

1. Mao is referring to the part of northern Jiangxi Province on the western bank of the Yangtze River across from Xiaogushan, Anhui (Mao had boarded the vessel at Hankou and was sailing down the Yangtze). Mao appears to be stretching his point somewhat. Jinggangshan, his base of operations in the late 1920s to 1930s, was in the southwestern part of Jiangxi Province.

2. See text Feb. 10, 1953, note 2.

3. Mao is referring to a book given to him by the deputy political commissar of the cruiser

"Luoyang" as an example of books read by the crew members. The book in question apparently dealt with the heroic deeds of a commander of torpedo boat No. 414 during the War of Liberation period.

4. See text Jan. 20, 1956, note 27.

5. These three sentences appear only in Source C, p. 86.

6. Mao is here referring to what is known as the Long March, the epic trek made by the Communist forces across China in 1934-35. In the summer of 1934 the Communist armies in the central base area in Jiangxi were pressed back by KMT forces into an area of not more than five or six *xian* and were in imminent danger of destruction. The decision was made to attempt to break out of the encirclement, and the Long March began in October 1934. The Communists began the march with some 85,000 soldiers, government personnel and Party officials. They covered some 6,600 miles, crossing eighteen mountain ranges and twenty-four rivers in eleven provinces, fighting continuous skirmishes and pitched battles. The main column, led by Zhu De and Mao, arrived at its final destination in northern Shaanxi in October 1935, while a second column, under Zhang Guotao and He Long, arrived a year later; together these survivors numbered less than 40,000. Measured in strictly military terms the Long March was a costly retreat; in political and pyschological terms, however, it was a watershed that assumed heroic proportions. See also J. Harrison (1972), pp. 238-259; J. Chen (1965); and D. Wilson (1971).

Inscription Written for the Navy
(February 21, 1953)

Source: Cited in "Nan wang de hangxing" (An Unforgettable Voyage) in *Mao guanhuai*, p. 65. Other Chinese Texts: *Huiyi Mao zhuxi*, p. 588; *RMRB* (Jan. 28, 1967); *RMRB* (Dec. 3, 1967), 4; *RMRB* (Mar. 5, 1968), 1; *Mao liang*, p. 336. Available English Translation: *PR*, 11:1 (Jan.3, 1968), 40.

In order to oppose the invasion of imperialists,
we absolutely must build a strong and powerful navy.
Mao Zedong

Telegram to the USSR
(February 21, 1953)

Source: *RMRB* (Feb. 23, 1953), 1. Other Chinese Text: *XHYB*, 3 (Mar. 25, 1953), 46. Available English Translation: NCNA, *Daily Bulletin*, 739 (Mar. 2, 1953), 2.

Chairman,
The Council of Ministers,
The Union of Soviet Socialist Republics

Comrade Stalin:

On this occasion of the thirty-fifth anniversary of the founding of the armed forces of the Union of Soviet Socialist Republics, Comrade Chairman, please accept my sincere congratulations. May the powerful armed forces of the Soviet Union attain further successes in their cause of defending world peace and security.

(Signed and dated in Beijing)

Inscription Awarded to Soviet Troops in Lushun
(February 22, 1953)

Source: *RMRB* (Feb. 23, 1953), 1.

On February 22, 1953, a delegation of the PRC government, headed by Premier Zhou Enlai, visited the Soviet Union's troops stationed in the Lushun region persuant to the Sino-Soviet agreement on the joint administration of the region, which was a corollary agreement of the Sino-Soviet Treaty of Friendship, Alliance, and Mutual Assistance signed on February 14, 1950. (See text Jan. 2, 1950, note 1.) The delegation celebrated the thirty-fifth anniversary of the founding of the Soviet Union's armed forces with the Soviet troops in Lushun-Dalian. For Zhou Enlai's speech on the occasion, see RMRB *(Feb. 23, 1953), 1. Mao's inscription was embroidered on a banner which was awarded by the delegation to the Soviet troops.*

The intimate unity between the two great peoples – the Soviet People and the Chinese People – and between their armed forces is a reliable safeguard for peace in the Far East and in the world.

Telegram to Inquire after Stalin's Illness
(March 4, 1953)

Source: *RMRB* (Mar. 5, 1953), 1. Available English Translation: *SCMP*, 525 (Mar. 6, 1953), 1.

Chairman,
The Council of Ministers,
The Union of Soviet Socialist Republics

Dear Comrade J. V. Stalin:

On learning the unfortunate news that you have come down with a severe illness, the Chinese people, the Chinese government, and myself, bearing feelings of deepest concern, extend to you our sincere sympathy and wish with all our hearts that your condition will take a turn for the better, that you will be restored to health, and that the prayers of the peace-loving people of China and of the whole world may be answered.
(Signed and dated in Beijing)

Telegram to the USSR on Stalin's Death
(March 6, 1953)

Source: *RMRB* (Mar. 7, 1953), 1. Other Chinese Texts: *XHYB*, 3 (Mar. 25, 1953), 1; *RMSC* (1953), p. 10. Available English Translations: NCNA, *Daily Bulletin*, 744 (Mar. 9, 1953), 1; FBIS, *Daily Report* (Mar. 9, 1953), CC13-14; *SCMP*, 526 (Mar. 6, 1953), 13; *PC* (Mar. 16, 1953), 8.

Chairman,
The Presidium of the Supreme Soviet,
The Union of Soviet Socialist Republics

Comrade Shvernik:

It was with boundless grief that the Chinese people, the Chinese government, and I myself learned the news of the passing away of the Chinese people's closest friend and great teacher, Comrade Stalin. This is an inestimable loss, not only for the people of the Soviet Union, but for the Chinese people, for the entire camp of peace and democracy, and for peace-loving people throughout the world. On behalf of the Chinese people, the Chinese government, and on my own behalf, I extend to you and to the people and government of the Soviet Union our deepest condolences.

The victory of the Chinese people's revolution is absolutely inseparable from Comrade Stalin's unceasing care, leadership, and support of over thirty years. Since the victory of the Chinese people's revolution, Comrade Stalin and the people and government of the Soviet Union, under his leadership, have rendered generous and selfless assistance to the Chinese people's cause of construction. Such a great and profound friendship as that which Comrade Stalin had for the Chinese people will be forever remembered with gratitude by the Chinese people. The immortal beacon of Comrade Stalin will forever illuminate the path on which the Chinese people march forward.

Comrade Chairman, the glorious party of Lenin and Stalin and the great people and government of the Soviet Union will certainly have the brotherly confidence and support of the Communist Party of China, the Chinese people, and the Chinese government. With the greatest resolve, the Chinese people definitely will always and closely unite as one with the great Soviet people to consolidate and strengthen the world camp for peace and democracy headed by the Soviet Union, heighten their vigilance, redouble their efforts, strike at the provocators of war, and strive to the end for the lasting interests of the Soviet and Chinese peoples and of world peace and security. I believe that the laboring people and all progressive peace-loving people of the world will take the same path as we do, following the direction pointed out by Comrade Stalin, and take up the sacred cause of protecting world peace.

(Signed and dated in Beijing)

Central People's Government's Decree on Stalin's Death

(March 6, 1953)

Source: *RMRB* (Mar. 7, 1953), 1. Available English Translation: NCNA, *Daily Bulletin* (Supplement), 126 (Mar. 6, 1953), 3.

Generalissimo Joseph Vissarionovich Stalin, Chairman of the Council of Ministers of our great ally the Union of Soviet Socialist Republics and Secretary of the Central Committee of the Communist Party of the Soviet Union, unfortunately passed away at 9:50 p.m. (Moscow time), March 5, 1953. In order to express the Chinese people's immensely profound mourning [at the demise] of our great Comrade Stalin, the great leader of the world's laboring people and the most respected and beloved friend and mentor of the Chinese people, and in order to express the Chinese people's reverence for the leader of our great ally, it is hereby decreed that:

1. From March 7 to March 9, 1953, flags shall fly at half-mast throughout our country as a symbol of mourning;

2. In this period of mourning, all factories, mines, enterprises, units of the armed forces, government organs, schools, and people's organizations shall suspend all banquets and [other] forms of entertainment.

> Mao Zedong
> Chairman
> March 6, 1953

Letter to Huang Yanpei and Chen Shutong

(March 8, 1953)

Source: *Shuxin*, p. 455.

Dear Venerable Mr. Huang Ren and Venerable Mr. Chen Shu:[1]

Please read [the enclosed] article and, afterward, return it to me. If you have opinions [on it], please let me know.

Venerable Mr. Ren[zhi], in your letter you said that you would like to transmit what I said in our previous conversation to the industrial and commercial circles. I think that you can tell a few people those things that I said that were related to principles, such as [the words to the effect that] things should be [handled through] discussion and negotiation, that things should be fair, that people should do just as much business as they have capital for, and that they should be taxed in proportion to the amount of profit they make. As for the other [things I said], there is no need for them to be transmitted. [Also], even in the case of the words of principle, you should only talk about them in a informal way, and do not need to transmit them in any formal manner. This is because these words are indeed too common; they belong to the realm of common knowledge. It is only because there is a severe problem of bureaucratism in our government work and because many things are not done well that these words appear to be somewhat novel. As for the concrete methods of resolving [these] problems, they must be seriously and separately studied by the ministries of finance, the taxation offices and other offices before [the problems] can be appropriately and adequately resolved.

In salute,

Mao Zedong
March 8

Note

1. See text Feb. 17, 1951, source note and note 1, and text Dec. 18, 1950, source note and note 1.

The Greatest Friendship

(March 9, 1953)

Source: *RMRB* (Mar. 9, 1953), 1. Other Chinese Texts: *XHYB*, 4 (Apr. 25, 1953), 14-15; *Zui weida de youyi; RMSC* (1953), pp. 6-8. Available English Translations: NCNA, *Daily Bulletin*, 745 (Mar. 10, 1953), 1-3; K. Fan (1972), pp. 111-115; S. Schram (1969), pp. 429-431 (abridged); J. Chen (1969), pp. 119-120 (excerpt).

Comrade Joseph Vissarionovich Stalin, the greatest genius of the present age, the great teacher of the world Communist movement, and the comrade-in-arms of the immortal Lenin, has departed from the world.

Comrade Stalin's contribution to our era through his theoretical activities and practice is incalculable. Comrade Stalin represented our entire new age. His activities have led the Soviet people and the working people of all countries to turn around the whole world situation. That is to say, the cause of justice and of People's Democracy and socialism has achieved victory in an immense region of the world, a region embracing more than 800 million people – one third of the earth's population. Moreover, the influence of this victory is daily spreading to every corner of the world.

The death of Comrade Stalin has caused the laboring people of the whole world to feel unparalleled and profound grief; it has stirred the hearts of just people throughout the world. This demonstrates that Comrade Stalin's cause and his thought have gripped the broad masses of the people throughout the world and have already become an invincible force, a force that will guide those people who have already achieved victory in achieving still more fresh victories, one after another, and, at the same time, will guide all those people who are still groaning under the oppression of the evil old world of capitalism so that they can strike courageously at the enemies of the people.

After the death of Lenin, Comrade Stalin led the Soviet people in building into a magnificent socialist society the first socialist state in the world, which he, together with the great Lenin, created at the time of the October Revolution. The victory of socialist construction in the Soviet Union was not only a victory for the people of the Soviet Union, but also a common victory for the people of the whole world. First, this victory proved in the most real-life terms the infinite correctness of Marxism-Leninism and concretely educated working people throughout the world on how they should advance toward a good life. Second, this victory ensured that during the Second World War humanity would have the strength to defeat the Fascist beast. The achievement of victory in the anti-Fascist war would have been inconceivable without the victory of socialist construction in the Soviet Union. The fate of all humanity was bound up with the victory of socialist construction in the Soviet Union and victory in the anti-Fascist war, and the glory for these victories should be attributed to our great Comrade Stalin.

Comrade Stalin developed Marxist-Leninist theory in a comprehensive and epoch-making way and propelled the development of Marxism to a new stage. Comrade Stalin creatively developed Lenin's theory concerning the law of the uneven development of capitalism and the theory that it is possible for socialism to first achieve victory in one country; Comrade Stalin creatively contributed the theory of the general crisis of the capitalist system; he contributed the theory concerning the building of communism in the Soviet Union; he contributed the theory of the fundamental economic laws of present-day capitalism and of socialism; he contributed the theory of revolution in colonies and semi-colonies. Comrade Stalin also creatively developed Lenin's theory of party-building. All these creative theories of Comrade Stalin's further united the workers throughout the world, further united the oppressed classes and oppressed people throughout the world, thereby enabling the struggle of the world's working class and all oppressed people for liberation and well-being and the victories in this struggle to reach unprecedented proportions.

All of Comrade Stalin's writings are immortal documents of Marxism. His works, *The Foundations of Leninism, The History of the Communist Party of the Soviet Union [Bolshevik],* and his last great work, *Economic Problems of Socialism in the USSR,* constitute an encyclopedia of Marxism-Leninism, a synthesis of the experience of the world Communist movement of the past hundred years. His speech at the Nineteenth Congress of the Communist Party of the Soviet Union is a precious last testament bequeathed to the Communists of all the countries of the world. We Chinese Communists, like the Communists of all countries, search for our own road to victory in the great works of Comrade Stalin.

Since the death of Lenin, Comrade Stalin has always been the central figure in the world Communist movement. We rallied around him, constantly asked his advice, and constantly drew ideological strength from his works. Comrade Stalin was full of warmth for the oppressed peoples of the East. "Do not forget the East" – this was Comrade Stalin's great call after the October Revolution. Everyone knows that Comrade Stalin warmly loved the Chinese people and regarded the might of the Chinese revolution as incalculable. On the question of the Chinese revolution, he contributed his exalted wisdom. It was by following the teachings of Lenin and Stalin, along with having the support of the great Soviet state and all the revolutionary forces of other countries, that the Communist Party of China and the Chinese people achieved their historic victory a few years ago.

Now we have lost our great teacher and most sincere friend – Comrade Stalin. What a misfortune this is! The sorrow that this misfortune has brought us cannot be described in words.

Our task is to transform sorrow into strength. In memory of our great teacher Stalin, the great friendship between the Communist Party of China and the Chinese people [on the one hand] and the Communist Party of the Soviet Union and the Soviet people [on the other] formed in the name of Stalin will never cease to be strengthened. The Chinese Communists and the Chinese people will further intensify the study of Stalin's teachings and the study of Soviet science and technology in order to build our country.

The Communist Party of the Soviet Union is a party nurtured personally by Lenin and Stalin; it is the most advanced, the most experienced, and the most theoretically cultivated party in the world. This party has been our model in the past, is our model at present, and will still be our model in the future. We fully believe that the Central Committee of the Communist Party of the Soviet Union and the government of the Soviet Union headed by Comrade Malenkov will definitely be able to carry on Comrade Stalin's unfinished work and push the great cause of Communism forward and carry it to greater and more glorious development.

There is not the slightest doubt that the camp of world peace, democracy, and socialism headed by the Soviet Union will become even more united and even more powerful.

In the past thirty years, Comrade Stalin's teachings and the model of the construction of socialism in the Soviet Union have facilitated a major step forward for the world. Now that the Soviet Union has become so powerful, the Chinese people's revolution has achieved such great victories, construction in the various people's democracies has achieved such great success, the movement of the peoples of various countries throughout the world against oppression and aggression has risen to such heights, and our front of friendship and solidarity is so consolidated, we can say with complete certainty that we are not afraid of any imperialist aggression. Any imperialist aggression will be smashed by us, and all their despicable provocations will be to no avail.

The reason that the great friendship between the peoples of the two countries, China and the Soviet Union, is unbreakable is that our friendship has been built on the great principles of the internationalism of Marx, Engels, Lenin, and Stalin. The friendship between the peoples of the two countries, China and the Soviet Union, and the peoples of the various people's democracies, as well as with all the people who love peace, democracy, and justice in all the countries of the world is also built upon these great principles of internationalism and consequently is also unbreakable.

Clearly, the strength created by this kind of friendship of ours is inexhaustible and truly invincible.

Let all imperialist aggressors and warmongers tremble before our great friendship!

Long live the teachings of Marx, Engels, Lenin, and Stalin!

Immortal glory to the heroic name of the great Stalin!

Telegram to Czechoslovakia on Gottwald's Death
(March 15, 1953)

Source: *RMRB* (Mar. 15, 1953), 1. Other Chinese Text: *XHYB*, 4 (Apr. 25, 1953), 47. Available English Translations: NCNA, *Daily Bulletin*, 749 (Mar. 16, 1953), 1-2; *SCMP*, 531 (Mar. 14-16, 1953), 1.

The Presidium of the Government of the Republic of Czechoslovakia:

It was with the most profound grief that I learned the news of the passing away of Comrade Gottwald. Comrade Gottwald was not only a great leader of the Republic of Czechoslovakia, but also an outstanding fighter in the cause of world peace and democracy. His death is an irreparable loss to the Czechoslovakian people and to the entire camp for world peace and democracy. On behalf of the Chinese people, the Chinese government, and on my own behalf, I sincerely express to you and, through you, to the Czechoslovakian people our deepest sorrow.

I am confident that Comrade Gottwald's brilliant contributions will forever inspire the Chinese and Czechoslovakian peoples to march forward heroically and triumphantly in the cause of further consolidating and developing the intimate unity and friendly cooperation between the Chinese and Czechoslovakian peoples and further strengthening the camp for world peace and democracy headed by our common ally, the great Soviet Union.

(Signed and dated in Beijing)

Criticize Han Chauvinism
(March 16, 1953)

Source: *Xuanji*, V, pp. 75-76. Available English Translation: *SW*, V, pp. 87-88.

This is an intra-Party directive drafted by Mao on behalf of the Central Committee of the CPC.

According to statistics published in RMSC *(1953), pp. 153ff, the more than 60 different officially designated minority nationalities in China at the time comprised approximately 40 million people, i.e. close to 8 per cent of the total Chinese population. The vast majority of the remainder were of Han ethnicity. Traditionally, the relationship between the Han majority and the minority nationalities has been an uneven one characterized by the domination by the Han in government, the economy and most areas of social culture – except of course during the Yuan dynasty (1271-1368) and the larger part of the Qing dynasty (1644-1911) and other periods during which major geographic segments of China were ruled by non-Han peoples, such as in the time of the kingdom of Jin and the period of the Liao kingdom. Minority cultures were observed only in regions where they predominated, and even there Han culture often encroached upon minority ways of life. The dominant pattern was one of assimilation, by more or less coercive measures, of the minorites into the Han civilization, resulting often in the fostering of a Han chauvinism, or sense of cultural superiority. Although after the Revolution of 1911 the Nationalist government had accepted the principle, enunciated by Sun Yat-sen, of the equality of the ethnic groups, in practice the uneven relationship had not only not been*

reversed, but was in fact exacerbated in the period of domination by the war-
lords. The severity of this problem was felt by the PRC government and was
brought up by Liu Geping, deputy chairman of the Commission on Nationalities
Affairs of the Central People's Government in a work report in 1952. See
RMRB (Jan. 20, 1952). For more background on this issue, see J. Dreyer
(1976).

In some places, relations between nationalities are very abnormal. This sort
of situation is intolerable for Communists. We must severely criticize the serious [problem of] ideas of Han chauvinism, ideas that exist among many in our
Party. It is a reactionary ideology expressed by the landlord class and the
bourgeoisie with regard to the relations among nationalities, and it is also a
Kuomintang ideology. We must immediately take action to correct the mistakes we have made in this area. We must send visiting groups, led by comrades who understand our nationalities policy and who are filled with sympathy for those of our countrymen who belong to minority nationalities that are
still suffering from hardships and discrimination, to visit all areas in which
minority nationalities reside, to carry out earnest investigation, and to help the
local Party and government organizations discover and solve the problems,
instead of merely making a cursory visit, as if they were looking at the flowers
while riding by on horseback.[1]

In light of quite a bit of information [we have], the [Party] Center feels that
unresolved problems exist generally in all places where minority nationalities
reside. Some of these are very serious problems. On the surface everything
appears to be calm and placid, but in fact the problems are very serious. The
problems uncovered in the last two or three years are evidence that Han chauvinism exists almost everywhere. It will be very dangerous if we do not firmly
grasp this opportunity to educate [the people] and to resolutely overcome Han
chauvinism in the Party and among the people. In many places, among the
Party and among the people, the problem that exists [in the area of] relations
between nationalities is not [simply] a problem of vestiges of Han chauvinism, but rather a problem of serious Han chauvinism, that is, a problem
[resulting from the fact that] these comrades and these people are still governed by bourgeois ideology and have not as yet been educated with Marxism,
and have not yet fully grasped the nationalities policy of the Center. Therefore
it is necessary to educate them in earnest in order that this problem may gradually be resolved. Beyond that, we should write more articles in the
newspapers based on facts and thus publicly repudiate [Han chauvinism] and
educate Party members and the people.

Note

1. This is an aphorism, derived from a Tang dynasty poem, "Dengdi shi" (On Passing the
Examination) by Meng Jiao, which Mao frequently used to describe the manner of doing something hastily and perfunctorily.

Resolve the Problem of the "Five Excesses"
(March 19, 1953)

Source: *Xuanji*, V, pp. 77-79. Available English Translation: *SW*, V, pp. 89-91.

According to this source, this article was an intra-Party directive drafted by Mao and issued by the Central Committee of the CPC. The problem of the "Five Excesses" was first raised publicly in an RMRB *editorial, June 6, 1953.*

This document, like the previous one, reflects Mao's support for focusing on production and deemphasizing class struggle in the countryside at this time. It also demonstrates Mao's detailed knowledge of the work-style of the Party and government organizations in the rural areas and stands as one of his first analyses of bureaucratism and its consequences during the stage of socialism. See C. Bettelheim (1978), pp. 62-64, 71-77, for an analysis that links bureaucratism to administrative processes, i.e., reports and meetings, developed by administrative organizations in order to compensate for the lack of knowledge that they need to execute their responsibilities. Bettelheim argues that this knowledge is possessed by production units that have, however, been deprived of their decision-making responsibilities, and when the two are united, that is, when decision-making coincides with possession of knowledge, the basis for bureaucratism will be eliminated.

(1) In the work of our Party and government organizations in the rural areas there exist some serious problems of being divorced from the peasant masses and of violating the interest of the peasants and the activists among them. These constitute the so-called problem of the "Five Excesses." The "Five Excesses" refer to an excess of assignments; an excess of meetings and training courses; an excess of documents, reports, and statistical forms; an excess of organizations; and an excess of extra duties for activists. These problems have existed for a long time, and the Center, at one time, had issued directives regarding some of these problems, requesting that the Party committees at the various levels pay attention to these problems and solve them. However, not only have they not been solved, they have even become aggravated. The reason for this is that the problem has never been systematically raised as a whole. In particular, the most significant [reason for this is that] the struggle against decentralizationism[1] and bureaucratism has not been launched in the organs of Party and government leadership at the five levels of the Center, the

greater [administrative] regions, the provinces (municipalities), the special districts, and the *xian*. This is because the "Five Excesses" that exist in the districts and the *xiang* are basically not generated in the districts and *xiang* themselves but at the higher levels. [The "Five Excesses"] stem from the existence of serious decentralizationism and bureaucratism in the organs of Party and government leadership at the *xian* level and above. In some cases they are products that were left behind from the revolutionary war and the period of land reform[2] and that have not been changed up to now. In 1953, therefore, in carrying out the Center's directives with regard to opposing bureaucratism, commandism, and violation of law and order,[3] we must pay attention to overcoming bureaucratism and decentralizationism in the leadership organs, and alter those institutions and methods that were necessary in the past but are no longer necessary now. Only in this way can the problem be solved. In the leadership organs at the various levels, on the problem of assigning tasks, on the problem of calling meetings and organizing training courses, on the problem of issuing documents and statistical forms and requesting reports from the lower levels, on the problem of regulating the forms of district and *xian* organizations, and on the problem of using the activists in the rural areas, from now on it is up to the comrades in major positions of responsibility in Party committees and in governments at the levels of *xian* and above to establish appropriate regulations in accordance with practicable conditions. In some cases the Center should set out unified regulations. In the past, many work departments in the Party, government, and people's organizations at all levels had independently assigned tasks to the lower levels; arbitrarily convened meetings or held training [sessions] for lower-level personnel and the activists in the countryside; issued floods of documents, charts, and lists; or casually demanded reports from the lower levels and the rural [units]; all these bad institutions and bad methods must be resolutely abolished and should be replaced by institutions and methods for which there is leadership, that are unified, and that fit the circumstances. As for the many kinds of committees that exist in each *xiang* in the countryside and the excess of extra duties for activists, hindering production and causing people to be divorced from the masses, they should also be resolutely but gradually altered.

(2) [Regarding this problem in the] various related departments in the Party, government, and people's organizations at the Center level, the comrades in charge of the Organization Department of the Central Committee, the Central People's Government's Administration Council, and its three subsidiary committees – the Finance and Economics Committee, the Culture and Education Committee, and the Political and Judicial Affairs Committee – are respectively held responsible by the Central Committee for rapidly clearing up the various things that in the past have caused the problems of the "Five Excesses," for formulating appropriate institutions and methods [for dealing with these problems], and for reporting to the Central Committee.

(3) [Regarding this problem in] the various greater [administrative] regions and provinces and municipalities, the comrades in charge of the various

bureaus of the Central Committee, the subbureaus, the provincial and municipal [Party] committees, and the administrative organs at the corresponding levels should assume the responsiblitiy of clearing up the problems of the "Five Excesses," formulate for themselves their own method of solving them, and report to the Central Committee. In order to achieve this goal, we request that each bureau of the Central Committee, subbureau, and provincial and municipal [Party] committee send out an investigation team specifically to acquaint itself with the problems of the "Five Excesses" and to investigate the situation in one or two districts or *xiang* under its jurisdiction (in the cities they should investigate one or two districts or neighborhoods) and use [the results] as reference material for solving the problems.

(4) As for the problem of the "Five Excesses" at the special district and *xian* levels, it is up to the provincial [Party] committees to bear the responsibility of giving guidance in resolving them.

(5) Agricultural production is the predominant work in the countryside. In the countryside all other types of work revolve around agricultural production and serve its interests. All so-called work assignments and work methods that may hinder the peasants from carrying out production must be avoided. At the moment, agriculture in our country is basically still a scattered small-scale peasant economy operated with old-fashioned implements. This is vastly different from the mechanized, collectivized agriculture of the Soviet Union. Therefore in our country during the current period of transition, it is still impossible for us to put into effect unified and planned production in agriculture, except on the state farms;[4] nor is it possible to interfere too much with the peasants. We can still only use [our] pricing policy[5] and necessary and practicable economic and political work to direct agricultural production and coordinate it with industry so that it can be absorbed into the national economic plan. Any so-called agricultural "planning" and rural "assignments" that go beyond these limits will necessarily be impracticable and will necessarily incite the opposition of the peasants and cause our Party to be divorced from the peasant masses, who make up eighty per cent of the population of the entire country. This is very dangerous. The so-called problem of the "Five Excesses" in the work of the districts and the *xiang* is in large measure the expression of this type of excessive interference with the peasants. (The other part is the product of the necessities of the revolutionary war and the land reform and has been handed down [since then].) It has already aroused the dissatisfaction of the peasants, and so it must be changed.

Notes

1. The term "decentralizationism" has been used to translate the Chinese term *fensan zhuyi* which elsewhere has been variously translated as "decentralism" (as in *SW*, V), or "dispersionism," or "excessive decentralization." "Decentralizationism" preserves the connotation of Mao's usage here. Mao refers, by this term, to the practice of decentralized and uncoordinated decision-making at the various levels of the Party apparatus, a practice that in his view had

become by habit an operational principle. When we translate the term as dispersionism, as in text Mar. 21, 1955, we do so because we detect there an escalation in Mao's misgivings concerning the phenomenon, and because he seems to be describing not merely uncoordinated decision-making, but deliberate and malicious undermining of the interests of the whole by individual parts of a collective acting to their own advantage at the expense of others.

2. See text Feb. 18, 1951, note 2.

3. See text Jan. 5, 1953.

4. State farms were relatively large-scale agricultural enterprises managed directly by the state. Their establishment was explained in Article 20 of the (Twelve-Year) National Program for Agricultural Development, 1956-1967, published in Jan. 1956 (also known as the Forty Articles). The purposes of the state farms were: (1) to produce agricultural livestock products, industrial raw materials, and commodity grain directly for the state; (2) to train cadres and technicians for agricultural mechanization; and (3) to demonstrate to the peasants the advantage of collectivization (cooperativization) and large-scale mechanization. In addition, state farms provided occupations for young people and demobilized military personnel and were important to the cultivation of previously uncultivated land, particularly in border regions. State farms were usually large units of 5,000 to 10,000 *mu* each. They were also characterized by extensive cultivation and reclaimed-land areas, and a regulated wage or remuneration system. By and large, they were concentrated in north, northeast, and northwest China. The more heavily mechanized state farms were usually directly controlled by the Center through the Agricultural Exploration Department (*nongken bu*) of the State Council. Less heavily mechanized state farms were often managed by state authorities at the provincial or regional level. Although by 1962 there were close to 2,500 state farms throughout the country that together occupied about 5 per cent of the arable territory, the development of state farm enterprises had not been economically rewarding since the late 1950s and early 1960s, and in general the development of the enterprises as a whole was suspended. See J. Prybyla (1978), pp. 57-59.

5. The pricing policy to which Mao refers is the policy in which the state pays a higher price for an agricultural product for which it has a demand and thus stimulates its production and pays a lower price for products whose production it does not wish to encourage. An alternative policy is to simply assign tasks to different producers regardless of the conditions of demand and then to effect a balanced distribution of income across the board. This was not endorsed by Mao, who considered it ultraleftist.

Telegram to Palmiro Togliatti

(March 25, 1953)

Source: *RMRB* (Mar. 26, 1953), 1. Other Chinese Text: *XHYB*, 9 (Apr. 25, 1953), 75. Available English Translation: NCNA, *Daily Bulletin*, 759 (Mar. 30, 1953), 4.

Palmiro Togliatti (1893-1965) (see text Jan. 22, 1951, note 1) was secretary general of the Communist Party of Italy (PCI) from 1927 on. During the period of World War II he was in the Soviet Union. In 1944 he returned to Italy, instructing the PCI not to attempt to seize power but to surrender its military forces and support the constitu-

tional assembly. From 1945 to 1947 Togliatti himself joined the postwar Italian government, serving as minister without portfolio, then as vice-premier and minister of justice. In 1956 he joined Khrushchev in denouncing Stalin at the Twentieth Congress of the Communist Party of the Soviet Union, and subsequently became a vocal anti-Chinese partisan in the debate over that issue. In 1956, he also declared the PCI's embarkment on an "Italian road to socialism."

Secretary General,
The Central Committee,
The Communist Party of Italy

Dear Comrade Togliatti:

The Central Committee of the Communist Party of China and I convey our warmest congratulations to you and to the Central Committee of the Communist Party of Italy on the occasion of your sixtieth birthday.

Since your youth, you have devoted your life entirely to the cause of the liberation of the Italian laboring people. Relying on your heroic struggle and outstanding leadership, the Communist Party of Italy has already become a glorious banner of the Italian working class, a powerful political force in Italy, and one of the world's great bulwarks of Marxism-Leninism. Your brilliant contributions to Italy's revolutionary cause, to the international workers' movement, and to the movement for world peace have won you the respect and love, not only of the Italian people, but also of the people of China and of all countries of the world.

For victory in the cause of Italy's liberation from oppression by United States imperialism and its running dogs and victory in the cause of world peace and progress headed by the Soviet Union, I wish you good health and long life!

(Signed as Chairman of CPC and dated)

Instruction on Leadership Work
of Health Departments of Military Commissions
(April 3, 1953)

Source: *SCMM* (supplement), 22 (Apr. 8, 1968), 6-7.

We have no Chinese text of this instruction; the SCMM translation is presented here as it originally appeared. The amendments in brackets and the annotation are our own.

The disclosure by Comrade Pai X X [Bai X X][1] made me think of whether there is any major difference between the leadership work of the government health departments and that of the army's health departments. I suspect that the leadership work of the government health departments is in the same mess as that of the army's health departments. We can see neither the political leadership nor any serious professional or technical leadership. But because of the fact that there is no one else but Pai X X [Bai X X] who makes such a well-grounded disclosure, we still do not know much about this . . . .

Then the fact exists that there is no leadership, no politics, and no serious administration of the business departments. The people who run these departments are bureaucrats who just eat without working. Such a condition exists not only in the health departments of military committees but also in other departments. I ask you, in the present struggle against bureaucratism, to unmask these people and set up new organs which really do the work to replace the old ones.

Note

1. There is no definite information on who "Comrade Pai XX" is, or regarding the vehicle of his "disclosure." However, our speculation leads us in the direction of Bai Xiqing, who was at this time a member of the Northeast Administration Committee and director of the College of Medicine of Dalian. In May 1953, he became a vice-chancellor of the Chinese College of Medicine (Zhougguo yike daxue) at Shenyang. Bai was a prominent member of the Democratic League, which puts him in a likely position to have made mildly critical comments on certain aspects of CPC administration at the time. This conforms also with Mao's tone. For more biographical information on Bai Xiqing, see *Zhonggong renming lu*, pp. 113-114.

Reply to Ambassador of the Soviet Union
(April 3, 1953)

Source: *RMRB* (Apr. 4, 1980), 1. Available English Translations: NCNA, *Daily Bulletin*, 764 (Apr. 7, 1953), 5-6; FBIS, *Daily Report* (Apr. 6, 1953), AAA15.

Kuznetsov served as ambassador of the USSR to the PRC from April 1953 to December 1953.

Comrade Ambassador:

I am very happy to receive the letter of credence presented by you from the Presidium of the Supreme Soviet of the Union of Soviet Socialist Republics and am sincerely grateful for your congratulations.

Through their close mutual assistance and cooperation, the people of China and the great people of the Soviet Union have established an unbreakable friendship. All the successes attained by New China in the areas of economy and culture and the implementation of its large-scale national construction plan, which is beginning just now, are inseparable from the sincere and fraternal assistance of the people and government of the Soviet Union.

I deeply believe that with the concerted efforts of the peoples of the two countries the great friendship and unity between the Chinese and Soviet peoples is bound to continue to develop and be consolidated ceaselessly. The boundless strength generated by our friendship will definitely play an incomparably great role in the cause of peace and security throughout the Far East and in the whole world.

Comrade Ambassador, I warmly welcome you as the Ambassador Extraordinary and Plenipotentiary of the Union of Soviet Socialist Republics to the People's Republic of China. In your work of consolidating the friendship and cooperation between China and the Soviet Union, you will receive my complete support and that of the government of the People's Republic of China.

I sincerely wish you total success in your work.

Letter to Li Zhuchen
(April 21, 1953)

Source: *Shuxin*, p. 457.

See text Jun. 23, 1951, source note.

Mr. Zhuchen:

I have received and read your letters of April 19 and [April] 20. Thank you very much. You have done a lot of investigative work. Your proposals[1] will help to resolve the current problems. I have already transmitted your letter to many comrades concerned [with these problems] for their reading.

In response and with my respect,

Mao Zedong
April 21, 1953

Note

1. According to the source, Li went to do investigative studies at certain factories and, afterward, made a number of proposals to Mao concerning the resolution of problems in the relationship between the public and private sectors, between labor and capital, and in the area of tax burden, funding, etc., in industry and commerce.

Letter to Li Zhuchen
(April 26, 1953)

Source: *Shuxin*, p. 458.

See text Apr. 21, 1953.

Mr. Zhuchen:

I have received your letter of April 21.

Although one may have to do many things, one can make an [orderly] arrangement so that during any particular period one needs to be dealing with only one major problem. In that way one may not feel too busy.

In response and with my respect,

Mao Zedong

April 26, 1953

Letter to Huang Yanpei and Chen Shutong
(May 15, 1953)

Source: *Shuxin*, p. 459.

See text Mar. 8, 1953.

Messrs. Renzhi and Shutong:[1]

These two articles contain some material worth reading. Please send them back [when you are done]. The crux of the matter with the problem of privately run [enterprises], like that of [the problem of] publicly run [enterprises], lies with democratic reform and production increase and thrift. When this problem is resolved other problems, such as the problem of the relationship between labor and capital, will be easy to handle.

Mao Zedong
May 15

Note

1. See text Feb. 17, 1951, source note and note 1, and text Dec. 18, 1950, source note and note 1.

Instructions on Education
(May 17, 1953)

Source: *Jiaoyu geming*, 4 (May 6, 1967), 3. Other Chinese Text: *Jiaoyu yulu*, p. 12 (excerpt). Available English Translations: *SCMM* (supplement), 18 (Feb. 26, 1968), 7 (excerpts); P. Seybolt (1973), p. 15 (quotations); *Chinese Sociology and Anthropology*, II:1-2 (Fall/Winter 1969-70), 29 (indirect quotation).

According to our source, these instructions were issued at a Political Bureau meeting.

In order to run the schools well, we must first of all resolve the problem of the backbone of the leadership in the schools. . . .

Once you have a strong principal, good teachers will be produced. . . .

By pedagogical reform we mean the reform in the contents of education and in teaching methods. Therefore we ought to revise the teaching materials and compile [manuals on] pedagogical methodology. . . .

In primary school education, labor education ought to be emphasized. . . .

The document concerning the system of five-year primary school [curriculum] is not bad. . . .[1]

We must develop the schools with all sorts of diverse methods; we must not insist on uniformity. . . .

Primary schools that are run by the people [themselves] ought to be allowed.[2]

Notes

1. We do not know which document is referred to here. In 1951, the PRC began to restructure the education system. One argument proposed at the time was that the previously existing primary education system, which consisted of a six-year curriculum broken up into two levels (i.e., junior primary school and senior primary school), made it difficult for laboring class children to complete the curriculum. On August 10, 1951, at the 97th session of the Government Administration Council, a resolution was passed to reform the education system, and one reform had to do with reorganizing primary education into a five-year single-level *(wu nian yi guan)* curriculum. (For the resolution see *RMSC* [1952], pp. 450-453.) In 1954, however, the system reverted to the earlier six-year, two-level curriculum through the resolution passed at the 195th session of the Government Administration Council on November 26, 1953. (See *RMSC* [1955], pp. 575-577.) Later again, during the Cultural Revolution, and especially after the issuance of Mao's "supreme directives" on reforming the education system in favor of a shorter curriculum, the PRC reverted once more to the five-year system. It is possible, though by no means proven, that Mao was referring to the report made by Qian Junrui, vice-minister of Education, at the conference on the administration of primary and middle schools held on August 2-10, 1952. In this speech Qian emphasized the five-year primary school curriculum but also touched on many of the other issues mentioned by Mao here. See *RMSC* (1953), p. 406.

2. The last three comments here were directed against Xi Zhongxun, deputy director of the Committee on Culture and Education of the Government Administrative Council; Xi was generally opposed to pedagogical reform, and specifically to the items that Mao affirmed in these comments. For more on Xi, see text Mar. 18, 1951, source note.

Criticism of Documents Issued in the Name of the Center by Liu Shaoqi and Yang Shangkun

(May 19, 1953)

Source: *Xuanji*, V, p. 80. Available English Translation: *SW*, V, p. 92.

The full title of this document in Xuanji *adds the comment that these documents were issued by Liu and Yang "on their own authority in violation of [Party] discipline." A clue to Mao's criticisms expressed here can be found in his earlier directive of Dec. 15, 1951. (See source note of that text.)*

Liu Shaoqi (1898-1969) joined the CPC in 1921. In the 1920s, Liu was one of the CPC's most important labor organizers, working in the Labor Secretariat of the CPC, primarily with Zhang Guotao and Li Lisan, most notably taking part in the leadership of the Anyuan miners' strike (1922), the formation of the Shanghai General Labor Union after the May 30th Incident of 1925, the Guangzhou-Hong Kong strikes (1925-26), and the Wuhan labor union movement in 1926-27. He was vice-chairman of the All-China Federation of Labor (ACFL) from 1925 on. After the CPC was driven underground in 1927, Liu shuttled back and forth between China and the Soviet

Union. In 1927 he was elected to the CPC Central Committtee. In 1932, at Ruijin, he became chairman of the ACFL, and in April 1933 he became the vice-commissar of Labor in the Council of People's Commissars. During the period of the Long March and afterward, Liu's work was primarily focused on underground activities in the so-called "white" areas – i.e., areas controlled by the KMT. His emergence as not only a labor- and peasant-organization expert but a theoretician as well began in 1943 after the CPC intra-Party rectification movement of 1942. In 1943 he published an article "On Liquidating Menshevik Thought in the Party." In this major transition of ideological focus in the CPC, Liu was aligned with Mao, Zhou Enlai, Chen Boda, Chen Yun, etc., against Wang Ming, Zhang Wentian, and Qin Bangxian. At the founding of the PRC in 1949, Liu was elected as a vice-chairman of the Central People's Government Council and a vice-chairman of the People's Revolutionary Military Commission. When Mao resigned as the Chairman of the Republic in April 1959 at the Second NPC, Liu was elected as his replacement. In 1966, during the early stages of the Cultural Revolution, Liu was labeled "the greatest capitalist-roader among the power-holders in the CPC," and in 1968 he was removed from all his positions and offices. Information concerning his death in Nov. 1969 at a prison in Kaifeng at the age of seventy-one was not confirmed until published by the CPC in 1980. In the same year he was "rehabilitated." For more detailed biographical information on Liu, see D. Klein and A. Clark, eds. (1971), I, pp. 616-626.

Yang Shangkun (b.1905) joined the Communist Youth League in 1925 and studied in Moscow at the University of the Toilers of China from 1927 to 1930. In 1930 he returned to China as a member of the so-called "28 Bolsheviks" faction (the entourage of Pavel Mif). From 1932 on he was active in political work in the soviet areas. In 1937, he became attached with the CPC North China Bureau, working under Liu Shaoqi and Peng Zhen. For the greater part of the War of Resistance years (1940-46), Yang was in Yanan, working as the secretary general of the Eighth Route Army headquarters. On the establishment of the PRC, Yang held no government post, but his work in the CPC apparatus itself remained highly significant. In 1954-57, he was director of the Staff Office of the CPC Central Committee, in effect the highest administrative office for the Central Committee of the CPC on a day-to-day basis. He served under CPC Secretary General Deng Xiaoping in the mid-fifties and continued to be an alternate secretary under Deng in the new Party secretariat after the 1956 reform. Yang was connected with Liu Shaoqi in the Cultural Revolution period and was arrested by Red Guards in January 1967. He was labeled a revisionist and a counter-revolutionary in RMRB in May 1968. For more detailed biographical information on Yang, see D. Klein and A. Clark (1971), eds. II, pp. 984-987.

This document provides us with a clue as to the early dating of the rift between Mao and Liu Shaoqi. Although the issue here appears to be of a more technical and operational nature, it serves as evidence of Mao's uneasiness with Liu. The rift between Mao's line and that of Liu would deepen enormously in the mid-1950s over the issue of the speed and methods of cooperativization. Furthermore, this is itself an indication of the difference of opinion between the two lines over the issue of the transition from "new democracy" to socialism and of the resolving of the social and political contradictions between these two stages of development. (For more on this, see text June 15, 1953, note 2.) The inclusion of this document and the document of June 15, 1953, in successive order in

Xuanji, V, also provides us with a hint regarding the ideological line pursued by the PRC leadership at the time that volume of Xuanji was published, and which, however, was soon to be criticized by the PRC leadership that succeeded the fall of Hua Guofeng.

I. From now on, all documents and telegrams issued in the name of the [Party] Center must be inspected by me before they can be dispatched; *otherwise they will be invalid.*[1] Please pay attention to this.

II. (1) Please assume responsibility for inspecting all telegrams and documents issued in the name of the [Party] Center or the Military Commission between August 1 of last year and May 5 of this year (inspection has already been made of those [issued] prior to August 1) to see if there are any – and if so, how many – that were not inspected by myself (excluding those [issued] while I was on an inspection tour or on sick leave). Then let me know the results.

(2) It is an error, a breach of discipline, for the resolutions of the past several meetings at the Center to have been issued on [someone else's] authority without having passed my inspection.

Note

1. The emphasis is Mao's, or at least appeared in the original text.

Letter to Wang Jiaxiang
(May 27, 1953)

Source: *Shuxin*, p. 460.

For more biographical information on Wang, see text Aug. 1, 1959, note 1. According to the source, Wang was head of the Foreign Liaison Department of the Central Committee of the CPC at the time of this letter.

Comrade Wang Jiaxiang:

In the "Manual for Advisors" given to comrades working in Viet Nam,[1] in the first article, there should be, to follow the sentence: "Cherish the people of Viet Nam and each blade of grass, each tree [in their country]," the addition: "Honor Viet Nam's national independence and respect the customs of the people of Viet Nam; support the Viet Nam Workers' Party and Comrade Ho Chi

Minh, the leader of the Party and the people of Viet Nam."[2]

If that document has not yet been issued, I hope that we are in time to make the above-mentioned additions to the text.

Mao Zedong
May 27

Notes

1. According to the source, this set of regulations, rendered as *guwen shouze* in the Chinese, refers to a set of rules and work instructions formulated by the Foreign Liaison Department of the Central Committee of the CPC in May 1953 for the PRC's delegation of advisors working in Viet Nam (The Democratic Republic of Viet Nam). The sentence quoted here echoes the instructions Mao issued to the Chinese People's Volunteers in the Korean War; see text Jan. 19, 1951.

2. The Dang Lao Dong Viet Nam (Viet Nam Workers' Party, VWP) was officially formed in 1954, succeeding the Communist Party of Indochina. Therefore here, if the text is indeed accurate, Mao could only have been referring to the party apparatus within the Communist Party of Indochina, which, under Ho Chi Minh's leadership, was striving specially for Viet Nam's "liberation." This organization could have been known, even at this earlier date, to its Chinese allies as the "Viet Nam Laodong dang" (Worker's Party), even though the title was unofficial. This remained the only Communist Party apparatus in the Democratic Republic of Viet Nam (North Viet Nam) for many years. In December 1976, at its fourth congress held in Hanoi, the name of the Party was changed to Dang Cong San Viet Nam (Communist Party of Viet Nam).

Criticize the Right-Deviationist Viewpoints That Depart from the General Line

(June 15, 1953)

Source: *Xuanji*, V, pp. 81-82. Other Chinese Texts: *RMRB* (Nov. 23, 1967) 1 (excerpt); *HQ*, 16 (Nov. 23, 1967) 21 (excerpt). Available English Translations: *SW*, V, pp. 93-94; *CB*, 885 (July 31, 1969), 40-41 (excerpt); *CB*, 897 (Dec. 10, 1969), 37-38 (excerpt).

Xuanji notes that this is "part of a speech at a meeting of the Political Bureau of the Central Committee of the Communist Party of China."

This is a most significant document that provides an early indication of the formulation of the "two-line struggle" that later on would gel as the Mao-Liu (Shaoqi) struggle in the PRC in the 1960s. The main theoretical component of this struggle, as exemplified in this document, was the debate over the issue of "consolidation," i.e., whether a stage of revolution can be, and ought to be, "fully consolidated" before moving on to the next stage. In Mao's view, the attempt to fully consolidate the fruits of any stage of the revolution (e.g., the "new democratic order") would lead to the consolidation of the interests of an old set of forces or alliance of forces which would in turn stand in the way of progress in the revolution toward a further stage which liberates new forces to challenge the old ones. For example, even in the "new democratic stage" of the revolution, if there is consolidation of the "new democratic order," the interests of a multi-class alliance (in which the national bourgeouisie has a part) would be consolidated, rather than give way to further revolutionary impulse, which would pave the way to the ultimate triumph of the proletariat itself (i.e., the socialist revolution). Mao's view was that all stages of the revolution, with the exception of the final stage, i.e., communism itself, should be seen as transitional stages, i.e., stages that must, and should, give way quickly to another new stage in the struggle, rather than be consolidated. To seek consolidation of each stage before moving on to the next is therefore in Mao's view holding back the revolution rather than promoting it, and is therefore "right deviationist." In the 1960s he would call this "revisionist" (a term with which he criticized the Khrushchevist line in the Soviet Union as well as Liu Shaoqi et al. in the PRC). For Liu Shaoqi's position at this early stage, see the section "Preserve the Rich Peasant Economy" in the article "On the Agrarian Reform Law" (July 14, 1950), in Liu Shaoqi (1968), II, pp. 223-226.

The general line and the overall task of the Party during the period of transition[1] is to basically complete the nation's industrialization and the socialist transformation of agriculture, handicraft industries, and capitalist industry and commerce within a period of ten to fifteen years or a bit longer. This general line is the beacon that illuminates all our various undertakings. One must not deviate from this general line. If one deviates from it, errors either of "Left" deviation or of Right deviation will occur.

There are people who think the period of transition is too long. Consequently they have developed a mood of impatience. This will [lead them to] commit the error of "Left" deviation. After the success of the democratic revolution, some people still remained where they were. They did not understand the nature of the revolution; [they] are still continuing to carry out their "New Democracy" and have not moved [on to] carrying out socialist transformation.[2] This is liable to lead them to commit errors of Right deviation. Speaking of agriculture, the road of socialism is the only road for our country's agriculture. The heart of the Party's work in the countryside is the development of the mutual aid and cooperativization movement[3] and the continuous growth of the forces of production in agriculture.

Right deviation is manifested in these three sentences:

[1] "Firmly establish the New Democratic social order." This proposition is harmful. In the period of transition [things] are changing every day; every day, socialist elements come into being. How could this so-called "New Democratic social order" be "firmly established"? It is really difficult to have it

"firmly established"! For example, private industry and commerce are being transformed right now. If a type of order is "established" in the latter half of this year, it will no longer be "firm" next year. [The situation of the] mutual aid and cooperativization [movement] in agriculture is also changing from year to year. The period of transition is full of contradictions and struggles. Our present revolutionary struggle goes even deeper than the armed revolutionary struggle of the past. This is a revolution that will thoroughly bury the capitalist system and all other exploitative systems. The idea of "firmly establishing the New Democratic social order" does not conform to the actual situation in the struggle and impedes the development of the socialist cause.

[2] "Go from New Democracy toward socialism." This proposition is [too] vague. [All it says is] go in a certain direction and that's it. If we go in a direction year after year, in fifteen years can we still say [that we are simply] going in that direction? Going in a direction means that [the goal] has not yet been reached. At first glance this proposition looks acceptable, but after detailed analysis [one can see] it is not a sound one.

[3] "Firmly protect private property." Because the middle peasants[4] were afraid of "becoming too conspicuous"[5] and of "communization,"[6] some people put forward this slogan to calm them down. In fact, this is wrong.

We propose a gradual transition to socialism. This is better. By gradual we mean dividing [the process into] fifteen years and each year again into twelve months. Going too quickly results in being too much to the "Left," not moving results in being too much to the Right. We must oppose both "Left" and Right, make the transition gradually, and finally complete the entire transition.

Notes

1. "Here 'the transition period' refers to the period from the founding of the People's Republic of China to the basic completion of socialist transformation. The general line or the general task of the Party for this transition period was basically to accomplish the industrialization of China and the socialist transformation of agriculture, handicrafts and capitalist industry and commerce over a fairly long period of time. This transition period is different in meaning from the transition period Comrade Mao Zedong spoke of at the Tenth Plenary Session of the Party's Eighth Central Committee in September 1962 and thereafter, which denotes the entire historical period of transition from capitalism to communism." (*SW*, V, p. 94.)

This notion of setting a "general line" for the CPC to adhere to in the transitional period was in the stage of fermentation at this time – although according to a source in *RMRB* (Dec. 29, 1970), 2, the notion had already been suggested at the end of 1952 – and was apparently prompted by the realization that the Three-Anti's and Five-Anti's campaigns would end in 1953, thus setting the stage for new developments in the relationship between the Party's political leadership and the economic circles. It would be iterated by Mao in August 1953 in a comment that he wrote on Zhou Enlai's report at the Finance and Economic Work Conference (see text August 1953). The "general line" was then formally adopted as a nationwide slogan by the CPPCC on Oct. 1, 1953, and was included in the preamble to the Constitution of the PRC in 1954. (See T. Chen [1967], p. 75.)

2. The distinction that Mao makes here is one of fundamental importance. In 1940 Mao had

published his thesis on "New Democracy," suggesting that China must undergo a "new democratic revolution" in which a united front must be formed, under the leadership of the working class, of the peasants, the proletariat, the petty bourgeoisie, the national bourgeoisie, and all patriotic elements, in opposition to the forces of feudalism, imperialism, and bureaucratic capitalism. (See *SW*, II, pp. 339-384, and see also another essay of the period, "The Chinese Revoution and the Chinese Communist Party," *SW*, II pp. 305-334, especially pp. 326-327.) Thus the revolution would be moved from the national democratic stage to the new democratic stage, the former being the stage of democratic revolution wherein the bourgeoisie and not the working class played the leading role. (The democratic nature of this earlier stage of the democratic revolution is seen as essentially a "bourgeois democracy, which combats traditional and feudalistic modes of government and social order, but seeks to establish the sway of the democratic rights of the bourgeoisie" rather than liberate society fully in the interests of the broad masses of the working class. In China's case, this is seen as the stage of revolution which began in the late-nineteenth century and led up to the 1911 Revolution and slightly beyond.) This thesis was further developed in his articles, "On Coalition Government" (1945) and "On the People's Democratic Dictatorship" (1949). The "new democratic" stage of the revolution was seen, within the paradigmatic framework of Mao's thesis, as the precursor of the stage of socialist revolution. In Mao's view, the "new democratic" stage began with the May Fourth period, i.e., ca. 1919 (see text May 4, 1959, note 1,) and ended with the founding of the PRC in 1949, when the socialist stage began. The characteristics of the new democratic stage included the united front described above, formed under the leadership of the proletariat and on the basis of the worker-peasant alliance, which formed the core of the united front, but it also included the co-existence of the three main economic components – the individual economy of the peasant and the handicraft worker, privately owned capital, and the state-run economy. Enormous contradictions still existed among these three components, and these contradictions were reflected politically in the problems and inconsistencies facing the united front, as well as in many other aspects of political work and the Party's relationship to the people. Mao's view, holding that the period of socialism began in 1949, maintained that the task of the revolutionary forces would thence be to transform this "new democratic" order into a socialist order through the means of class struggle, and thus the elimination of capitalist forces. Liu Shaoqi (see text May 19, 1953, source note), on the other hand, appears to have maintained that the "new democratic" order, although having already achieved much through the period of Liberation, had yet to be consolidated. In addition, he believed that the contradictions that existed could not be resolved through class struggle alone, but that, since many of China's problems were linked to its backwardness in technology, they must be resolved through the means of major developments in the forces of production. This last notion, in Liu's view, was more compatible with the continuation of the general alliance under the new democratic order than with the notion of socialist class struggle. In effect, then, Mao's accusations of "Rightist" viewpoints were directed against Liu. See also text Aug. 12, 1953, note 24.

3. The Central Committee of the CPC issued the "First Draft Decision on Mutual Aid and Cooperation [Cooperativization] in Agriculture" on December 15, 1951 (see text Dec. 15, 1951), launching the movement toward the establishment of agricultural cooperatives throughout China. For a detailed discussion of the various types, functions, and fates of these organizations see Zheng Zhuyuan (1963), pp. 29-36.

4. See text Mar. 13, 1950, note 1, for criteria for classification of peasants. Mao is here again pointing in the direction of Liu Shaoqi, whose position was revealed in the section "Preserve the Rich Peasant Economy" in the article "On the Agrarian Reform Law" (July 14, 1950); see Liu Shaoqi (1968), II, pp. 223-226.

5. The Chinese term here is *maojian,* or literally, "stick the pointed part out," or "stick out." The term is very common in PRC usage and is variously translated, depending on syntax and context, in these volumes.

6. Mao is here referring not to the act of forming communes but to the psychological stigma then still attached to communization, i.e., the fear that it simply meant the confiscation of property. The term *gongchan* in Chinese, which translates as "communism," "communization," etc., means literally sharing or communalization of property. The goal of Marxism-Communism is

indeed, of course, the ultimate elimination of private ownership of the means of production and thus the "communalization of property," i.e., the transference of ownership to the public realm. It is a matter of difference of opinion on tactics and work method, however, as to how this can be carried out. From 1949 on, the nationwide movement to eliminate the private ownership of land by landlords was launched. This did not in itself resolve the problem of private ownership of property by other rural classes, e.g., the rich peasants. The possibility that this problem will be resolved in the same way that the landlord problem was resolved, i.e., by outright confiscation, remained a horrible prospect for the rich and middle peasants. From 1950 on, people such as Liu Shaoqi had sought to pacify these rural classes by asserting that the rich-peasant economy, i.e., their private ownership of property, would be "preserved." (See note 4.) Mao's position, on the other hand, was not that it would be "preserved," but merely temporarily tolerated, to be dealt with fully later. (See text Mar, 12, 1950.) Meanwhile steps such as promoting mutual aid and the preliminary stages of cooperativization would be taken to ease the transition so that the ultimate solution of the problem would come as a result of class struggle in the countryside (i.e., the establishment of the cooperative forces of the lower-middle and poor peasants, or, as Mao would later call it, the "upsurge of socialism" – see text Dec. 27, 1955), rather than as a result of mere fiat. Therefore, in Mao's view, to assert meanwhile that the rich peasant economy is to be preserved and to deny the purpose of *gongchan* in the interests of allaying the fears of the rich peasants would be either simply wrong, or hypocritical, or both. Nonetheless, in the long run, Mao's course proved to be a very difficult one to take to effect the orderly transition to public ownership of property. While Mao's target here was the "Rightist deviation," later "Left deviations" would also emerge (known as the "communist wind") of which Mao was also forced to be cognizant. See texts in February-March 1959.

Speech on the Youth League
(June 30, 1953)

Source: *Xuanji*, V, pp. 83-87. Other Chinese Texts: *RMRB* (July 3, 1953), 1 (excerpts); *XHYB*, 8 (Aug. 28, 1953), 33 (excerpts); *Buyi*, p. 23 (excerpts); *Wansui* (1967b), p. 14 (excerpts); *Jiaoyu yulu*, p. 6 (excerpts); *Jiaoyu geming*, p. 9 (excerpts); *Lun qingnian*, pp. 11, 21, 22, 31-32 (excerpts). Available English Translations: *SW*, V, pp. 95-100; *CLG*, X:2 (Summer 1977), 11-18; J. Chen (1970), p. 80; *SCMM* (supplement), 22 (Apr. 8, 1968), 6 (excerpt); *CB*, 888 (Aug. 22, 1969), 6 (excerpt); *CB*, 891 (Oct. 8, 1969), 16 (excerpt).

According to the Xuanji *source, this was Mao's talk at a reception given for the members of the Presidium of the Second National Congress of the Chinese New Democratic Youth League (NDYL). The title of this speech in* Xuanji *is "Qingniantuan de gongzuo yao zhaogu qingnian de tedian" (The Youth League Must Take into Consideration the Special Characteristics of the Young People in Its Work).*

The formation of the NDYL was proposed at the Central Committee of the CPC in

October 1946. After two years of experimentation, the First Congress of the NDYL was held in April 1949, and the Youth League was formally established. Its purpose was to educate progressive young people to coordinate their work and lives with the goals of the construction of the PRC and, after 1949, to bring about socialism on the basis of the gradual transformation of new democracy to socialism. (See RMSC [1951], "shu" section, pp. 14-17.) In May 1957, at the third League congress, the name was changed to the Chinese Communist Youth League. In fact, however, this name had also been adopted by the Chinese Communist Youth League which was formed in Europe in 1925. (In 1922, the Socialist Youth League was formed, heralding the formation of the European branch of the CPC, and its name was changed to the Chinese Communist Youth League in 1925.) See also text Feb. 18, 1951, note 8.

The problem of the Youth League's clamoring for independence [in its relationship] with the Party has long since passed. The problem at present is the League's lack of independent work, not its clamoring for independence.

The Youth League should coordinate [its work] with the central tasks of the Party, but while it coordinates [its work] with the central tasks of the Party it should have its own independent work and take into consideration the special needs of young people. In 1952, I talked with the comrades of the Central Committee of the League, and I brought up two topics for the League center to study; one was how the Party should lead the League in its work, and the other was how the League should go about its work.[1] [The question of] how to take into consideration the special characteristics of young people is implicit in both of these topics. All local Party committees report that they are satisfied with the work of the Youth League and that [they] are satisfied because [the League] coordinates [its efforts] with the central tasks of the Party. [But] here [I'd like to] bring up a point of dissatisfaction, which is that the work of the Youth League has not yet shaped itself to fit the special characteristics of young people and [thus has not] organized any independent activities. The leadership organs of both the Party and the League should learn how to lead the League in its work and do a good job of organizing and educating the broad masses of the young people and organizing them around the central tasks of the Party, taking into consideration the special characteristics of young people.

Under the leadership of the Party, the Youth League has actively participated in all areas of revolutionary work and has achieved very great results. Whether it be in the factories, in the rural areas, in the military, or in the schools, the revolutionary cause cannot succeed without young people. The young people of China are very disciplined; they have accomplished all the tasks that the Party has given them. Now, with the Korean conflict coming to an end and the conclusion of the land reform program,[2] the main thrust of our work within the country is right now shifting to socialist transformation and socialist construction. So we must learn. The Youth League must learn how to lead young people to work in conjunction with adults to do a good job in agriculture in the countryside, to do a good job in industry in the cities, to do a good job in studying in the schools, to do good work in the [government] organs and, in the armed forces, to train the national defense forces well [so that they may] become a modernized army.

Young people between the ages of fourteen and twenty-five must study and must work. The period of youth, however, is a period of physical growth. It would be very dangerous not to pay attention to the physical development of young people. Young people need to study even more than adults do; they have to learn many things that adults have already learned. Nevertheless, the burden of study and work placed upon them must not be too heavy. Particularly with young people from fourteen to eighteen years of age, the intensity of their labor cannot be the same as that of adults. Young people have to play a bit more and have to have a bit more recreation. They have to jump around a bit; otherwise they will be unhappy. Later on, they will fall in love and get married. In these respects they are different from adults.

Let me say a few words to young people. First, I wish them good health, second, I wish them well in their studies, and third, I wish them well in their work.

I propose that another hour be added to the sleeping time of students. [The standard] now is eight hours but in fact they only get six or seven hours, and there is a general feeling that they do not get enough sleep. Since educated youth easily suffer from nervous exhaustion, often they can't get to sleep and can't wake up. We must stipulate nine hours of sleeping time [for them]. We should issue an order; we needn't debate it, just make it obligatory. Young people must sleep well, and teachers should get enough sleep too.

Revolution brings many good things, but it also brings one bad thing, which is that everybody is too active, too enthusiastic, to a point where they become worn out. Now we must ensure that everybody is in good health; we must ensure that workers, peasants, soldiers, students, and cadres are all in good health. Of course, being in good health doesn't necessarily mean that one will study well; studying [well] requires certain methods.

Right now, the hours lower middle school students spend in class are also somewhat too long. We can consider reducing them appropriately. Activists hold too many meetings; this too should be reduced. On the one hand there is study, on the other recreation, rest, and sleep; both aspects must be taken into full consideration. Young workers, young peasants, and young soldiers study as they work; for them, too, work and study [on the one hand] and recreation, rest, and sleep [on the other] must both be taken into full consideration.

Both ends must be firmly grasped. Studying and work must be firmly grasped, but sleep, rest, and recreation must be firmly grasped also. In the past we only took hold of one end firmly, and we didn't take a firm hold on the other end, or else didn't take hold of it at all. Now we must develop some [programs for] recreation; there must be time and facilities [for recreation]. At this end too, we must take a firm hold. The Central Committee of the Party has already decided to reduce the number of meetings and the time [required] for study; you must supervise the implementation [of this decision]. If there are people who don't carry it out, [an explanation] should be demanded of them.

In short, we must make young people healthy, good in their studies, and good at their work. Some leading comrades only want the young people to work and pay no attention to the physical [well-being] of young people. [In such cases] you can use this statement [of mine] to rebuff them; the reasoning behind it is very sound. It is simply to protect the younger generation so that they may grow up better. Our generation had a bad time of it [in that] adults didn't take [good] care of children. Big people had tables to eat at, the little people didn't. Kids had no right to speak in their homes, and if they cried, they got a slap across the face. Today, New China must change its policy and be considerate of young people and teenagers.

We must elect young cadres to serve as members of the League Central Committee. In the time of the Three Kingdoms, Cao Cao led a huge army south of the Yangtze River to attack the [kingdom of] Eastern Wu. At the time, Zhou Yu was a "Youth League member" and served as marshal of Wu. The old generals such as Cheng Pu would not accept his authority, but later they were persuaded to do so and he was made marshal anyway. Consequently they won a victory.[3] Yet now, when we want Zhou Yu's to be members of the League Central Committee everybody is against it! Will it do to select only older people to be League Central Committee members and have too few young people [on it]? Naturally, we cannot go completely on this basis of age; we must consider ability as well. On the slate of candidates for the League Central Committee there were originally only nine people under thirty years of age. Now, after discussion by the Party Center, [this number] has been increased to more than sixty, which is still only a little more than one quarter [of the Committee]. Those over thirty years old still make up almost three-quarters, and some comrades still say this is too few. I say it is not too few. [As to] whether or not all these sixty-some young people are a hundred per cent suited to their positions, some comrades say that there is no certainty [about this]. We must trust young people fully; the overwhelming majority will be equal to their tasks. Some individuals may not be competent in their posts, but this is nothing to be afraid of; in the future they can be dropped in another election. Do things this way and the fundamental orientation will not be wrong. Young people are no weaker than we are. Older people have experience, and therefore are, of course, strong; their physiological capacities, however, are gradually deteriorating, their eyesight and hearing are no longer so sharp, and they are not as agile as young people are. This is a law of nature. We must persuade those comrades who disagree.

The Youth League must take into consideration the special characteristics of young people, must have work of its own [as an independent] organization, and at the same time must accept leadership from the Party committees at all levels. This isn't a new discovery; it has been so for a long time; Marxism has always said that this [should be so]. This is proceeding from reality. Young people are young people; if they weren't, why would we have to have a Youth League? Young people are different from adults; young women are also different from young men; and if we do not take these special characteristics into consideration we will become divorced from the masses. You now have nine million League members. If you do not take into consideration young people's special characteristics, perhaps only one million [of them] will support you, and eight million will not.

The work of the Youth League must take into account the [needs of the] majority, and at the same time it must pay attention to the advanced youth. Some advanced elements may not be thrilled about this; they demand that we be a bit stricter with all League members. This would not be so proper; we must persuade them of that. There are too many duties and too few rights stipulated in the draft constitution of the League.[4] It has to be made a little more lenient, so that the majority can follow [the rules]. The emphasis should be placed on the majority; we cannot focus on the minority.

Your draft constitution for the League stipulates that [if a member] fails to take part in the activities of the organization for four months, then that person is considered to have automatically dropped out of the League. This is too severe. Even the Party Constitution stipulates six months; can't you also stipulate six months? Things that can't be done or things that can be done by only one million [members] and not by [the other] eight million should not be stipulated in the League constitution. Principles must be carried out in a flexible way. There is a gap between what ought to be and what actually is. Provisions of certain laws will require a few more years before they can actually be implemented. For instance, many of the provisions in the marriage law are programmatic in nature, and it will take at least three five-year plans to implement them thoroughly.[5] The provision "do not slander people behind their backs" is correct in principle, but it is unnecessary to write it into the League constitution. The struggle against liberalism is a protracted one; there is still a lot of liberalism within the Party itself. Actually, it is impossible to forbid people to curse you even once behind your back. We must not make our circle too small; the main thing is that the boundaries between the enemy and ourselves must be distinct.

Prestige is built up gradually. In the past, there were some people inside the armed forces who made up jingles to malign people. We neither prohibited nor investigated [the practice], and yet the army did not fall apart. We just took hold of some of the major [issues], such as the Three Main Rules of Discipline and the Eight Great Points for Attention, and the troops slowly got onto the right track.[6] For the masses to truly respect their leaders, they must come to understand them through revolutionary practice. Trust comes only through true understanding. Right now the prestige of the League Center is already rather high. Some people still don't respect it, but they will slowly come to respect it. When a young person first steps onto the stage his prestige isn't high, [but] don't be anxious, it's impossible not to receive a bit of criticism and a bit of scolding. There are "small broadcasts" because the "big broadcast" is not well-developed.[7] As long as the democratic [way of] life is fully [established] and [people's] scabs are exposed openly, then, even if people were allowed to [make their] "small broadcasts," they would [turn around and] say that they didn't have the time and that they had to rest. However, there will always be problems, and we mustn't think that everything can be solved at once. There are [problems] now and there will be in the future as well.

The general task of the Party during the period of transition is to basically achieve socialist industrialization and the socialist transformation of agriculture, handicraft industries, and capitalist industry and commerce over the course of three five-year plans.[8] Three five-year plans means fifteen years. Every year is a small step, and every five years is a big step. Three big steps will just about do it. To achieve something basically is not the same as achieving it completely. To say [that we will] achieve [these things] basically is to be cautious in what we say; it is always better to be a bit cautious in matters of this world.

At present, Chinese agriculture is mainly an individual economy, and it must undergo socialist transformation step by step. In developing the mutual aid and cooperativization campaign in agriculture, we must uphold the principle of voluntary [participation]. If we don't develop [the campaign we] will [end up] following the capitalist road; that would be a Right deviation. However, it won't do to be too fierce in developing it either, that would be a "Left" deviation. It must be carried out with preparation and according to a schedule. Historically, we have refrained from fighting battles for which we were not prepared and which we were not sure [we could win]; we didn't [even] fight battles for which we were prepared but about which we were not sure [we could win]. In the past when we fought Chiang Kai-shek, at first some people committed the error of subjectivism. Later, through the rectification [campaign we] we got rid of subjectivism and we won.[9] Now we are fighting the battle of socialism, and we want to accomplish socialist industrialization and the socialist transformation of agriculture, handicraft industries, and capitalist industry and commerce. This is the general task of the people of the whole country. As to how the Youth League should carry out this general task, you should make appropriate provisions on the basis of the special characteristics of young people.

Notes

1. We have no published record of this discussion. However, it is very likely that Mao was referring here to discussions that may have preceded the issuing of the CPC Central Committee's approval of the resolutions of the Second Meeting of the Central Committee of the New Democratic Youth League. This approval was published on Jan. 4, 1952.

2. The armistice that concluded the Korean War was signed at Panmonjon on July 27, 1953. For the land reform, see text Feb. 18, 1951, note 2.

3. Cao Cao (155-220 A.D.), was a statesman, military strategist, and literary figure of the Three Kingdoms period (220-280). He amassed great military power through the suppression of the "Yellow Turban" bandits in the waning years of the Han dynasty, and in 196 A.D. he moved the Han emperor, Xiandi, within his own sphere of influence at Xudu. With that, Cao began to

issue decrees in Emperor Xiandi's name and progressively aggrandized his own power at the expense of other feudal warlords. By defeating Yuan Shao at the Battle of Guandu (199) he unified political control along the Yellow River basin. In 208 he was appointed chief minister to the emperor and marched southward across the Yangtze River against the forces of the Eastern Wu. In the same year, he was soundly defeated at the Battle of Chibi by the coalition of the forces of Eastern Wu and Shu Han. Cao was later made prince of Wei by the emperor. In 220, the year Cao Cao died, his son, Cao Pi, who succeeded him as the prince of Wei, abolished the Han dynasty and made himself Emperor Wendi of the Wei dynasty. Cao Cao was posthumously enthroned as Emperor Wudi.

Zhou Yu (175-210) was a young military strategist of the same period of the Kingdom of Wu. He was a friend of Sun Ce, the first Prince of Eastern Wu, and rose quickly to the rank of general at the age of twenty-four. Later he became marshal of the vanguard forces of the Eastern Wu. Before the battle of Chibi, he advocated the forming of the coalition with the forces of Shu-Han against the advice of many other generals, and was made marshal for the entire defensive campaign. Zhou Yu, though he led such a short life, is one of the best-known romantic figures in Chinese history and literature.

Cheng Pu was an old general of the Eastern Wu forces who had been serving the rulers of the Eastern Wu beginning with the father of Sun Ce. He was the main dissident when Zhou Yu presented his strategy for the defense against the forces of Wei in 208 A.D., and he was only won over to Zhou's side later. This episode was very dramatically described in *hui* 43-45 of the classical novel *San guo yanyi* (The Romance of the Three Kingdoms).

4. The constitution of the Chinese New Democratic Youth League remained in draft form until it was adopted at the Ninth National Congress of the League (June 29, 1964), by which time the name of the League had been changed (see source note). The issues to which Mao refers in this passage are dealt with in Chapter 1, Article 6, of the League constitution (reprinted in T. Chen [1967], pp. 166-178). It is apparent from the 1964 version that Mao's suggestions were adopted.

5. The Marriage Law of the PRC was promulgated in April 1950. See *RMSC* (1951), section "Shen," p. 1.

6. In 1928 Mao laid down the Three Rules of Discipline and Six Points for Attention for the Workers' and Peasants' Red Army in Jinggangshan, emphasizing the cultivation of congenial relations and mutual respect between the soldiers and the civilian populace. Later, slight revisions and adaptations were made. The list was standardized in 1947 as the Three Main Rules of Discipline and Eight Great Points for Attention. They include: (1) Obey orders in all actions; (2) Not a single needle or a single piece of thread is to be taken from the masses; (3) Everything captured must be turned in; and (a) Speak politely; (b) Pay a fair price for whatever you buy; (c) Return everything you borrow; (d) Pay for all damages; (e) Do not hit people or swear at people; (f) Do not damage crops; (g) Do not take any liberties with women; (h) Do not ill-treat captives.

7. By "small broadcast," Mao refers to the practice of spreading unofficial, and sometimes malicious, rumors concerning a person. Mao is saying that this practice exists only because the official channels of information are not always up to date and accurate and are unable to overcome rumors and personal slandering.

8. See text June 15, 1953, note 1. For dating of the five-year plans, see text Feb. 10, 1953, note 2. Here Mao was referring to the "general line" during the period of transition; see text June 15, 1953, and specifically note 1.

9. Mao is here referring to the major CPC rectification campaign in Yanan in 1942. The main targets of that rectification campaign were "against subjectivism, to rectify the style of studying; against sectarianism, to rectify the Party's work-style; and against eight-legged stereotyped Party writing, to rectify the Party's literary style." For more on this rectification campaign, see M. Selden (1971), pp. 188-210, 212-216, 269-275. See text Aug. 12, 1953 (1), note 24.

Reply to Ambassador of the People's Republic of Mongolia
(July 2, 1953)

Source: *RMRB* (July 3, 1953), 1. Available English Translations: NCNA, *Daily Bulletin*, 827 (July 3, 1953), 2; FBIS, *Daily Report* (July 3, 1953), AAA2-3.

Bayanbatoryn Ochirbat served as ambassador of the People's Republic of Mongolia to the PRC from July 1953 to May 1957.

Comrade Ambassador:

I am very happy to receive the letter of credence from the Presidium of the Greater Hural of the People's Republic of Mongolia which you have presented, and I am sincerely grateful for your congratulations.

In the past three years or more, the relationship of friendship and cooperation between the People's Republic of Mongolia and the People's Republic of China has achieved extremely great development and consolidation. The agreement on economic and cultural cooperation signed last year by the governments of China and Mongolia not only further strengthens this relationship of friendship and cooperation between our two countries, but also greatly promotes the friendship between and well-being of our two peoples.[1]

The Mongolian people have already obtained great successes in their work of construction. These successes have always won the deep concern and the praise of the Chinese people. I deeply believe that the unity, which grows ever more intimate between the peoples of China and Mongolia, is bound to enhance our strength for the defense of peace in the Far East and in the world and will further consolidate the world camp for peace, democracy, and socialism headed by the great Soviet Union.

Comrade Ambassador, I warmly welcome you as the Ambassador Extraordinary and Plenipotentiary from the People's Republic of Mongolia to the People's Republic of China. In your work of consolidating the friendship and cooperation between China and Mongolia you will receive my total support and that of the government of the People's Republic of China.

I wish you complete success in your work.

Note

1. An agreement on economic and cultural cooperation in the period 1952-1962 was signed by the PRC and the People's Republic of Mongolia on October 4, 1952. The text of the agreement and an accompanying joint communiqué are translated in *PC*, 20 (1952), 7.

Letter to Fu Dingyi

(July 7, 1953)

Source: *Shuxin*, p. 461

Fu was the director of the historical archives and museum of the Central Committee of the CPC at the time of this letter. For some information on the preliminary preparations for this institution, see text Dec. 2, 1949, note 3.

Mr. Yucheng:[1]

I have received your gracious letter today in which you asked me to write an inscription for the new printing of your work, *Lianmian zidian* (Dictionary of Interlocking Phrases). Since I have not had the opportunity to study your masterpiece I cannot give you my opinion. As for mentioning "The great deeds and achievements of the Emperor of Qin and the [Emperor] Wudi of the Han,"[2] perhaps you, sir, have made a mistake in what you heard. You are a writer and an analogy [between your achievements] and those of the feudal emperors and kings of ancient times would appear rather improper. I beg your forgiveness for where I cannot comply with your request, and hope that you will understand.

Mao Zedong
July 7, 1953

Notes

1. "Yucheng" is Fu's *zi*. For an explanation of this usage, see text Oct. 15, 1949, note 1.

2. Shihuangdi (First Emperor) of the Qin dynasty ruled what was China at the time from 221 to 207 B.C. Emperor Wudi of the Han dynasty ruled from 140 to 87 B.C. See text May 8, 1958, note 54, and text Mar. 22, 1958, note 10, respectively. It is perhaps notable that Mao himself mentioned these two historic rulers in his poem "On Snow" in February 1936.

On State Capitalism
(July 9, 1953)

Source: *Xuanji*, V, p. 88. Available English Translation: *SW*, V, p. 101.

According to this source, this is a comment on a document issued at the National Conference on Financial and Economic Work, which was held between June 13 and August 11, 1953. For more on this meeting see K. Lieberthal (1976), pp. 59-60.

This document and text Aug. 12, 1953, reveal Mao's understanding of the limited nature of the changes that had been brought about in China. They also illustrate his recognition of the importance of state capitalism in the transition from capitalism to Communism. However, as in the works of many other Communist leaders and Marxist theoreticians throughout the world, the exact role, nature, and duration of state capitalism remained rather ambiguous in Mao's work.[1]

"State capitalism" represents a method in the socialist transformation of previously privately owned and managed capitalist enterprises, and of their relationship to the working class represented through the state apparatus. It is, in Mao's view, a method and not a permanent and independent economic entity. The transformation of capitalist enterprises began with such measures as production and marketing contracts offered by the state and control of the profit margin and rate set by the state. (See text Nov. 1951-Mar. 1952, note 10.) For instance, the "Temporary Regulations Regarding Privately Run Enterprises" promulgated in Dec. 1950 stipulated that the highest annual profit for private capitalist enterprises should be 8 per cent. Further measures were later introduced, such as the quartering system of dividing up profits suggested in this document. However, the enterprises were still essentially privately owned and operated. By such drastic reduction of the possibilities for profits to accrue to the individual capitalist entrepreneur, however, the incentive for private capital was greatly curtailed. The next step was to set up, on a semivoluntary basis, joint state-private enterprises, with the state gradually taking up the lion's share of the funding responsibility for the enterprises as well as for staffing and technical management. When this step was accomplished, whatever remained of the capitalist economy would on the whole be already absorbed into the state's economic planning. The next step would be the paying off of capitalist entrepreneurs through the so-called "redemption policy" and the paying of "fixed interests" for enterprises bought out by the state. All of these steps would occur later, and the detailed methodology was not worked out at this point. Nevertheless, the underlying principle of using "state capitalism" to transform the economy had already been suggested and was already in practice in some

areas. The term, however, tends to be somewhat misleading, since it appears to imply that the state shall become the chief capitalist (a term that in socialist ideology innately connotes exploitation). It may perhaps be more accurately described as an integration of state interests and the existing capitalist element in the economy, with the state gradually taking over. In later years Mao made even more elaborate and reflective comments on this particular role of the state in the transformation of the economy. His final formulation, which came by way of comparing China's situation to that of the Soviet Union, is contained in his "Reading Notes on the Soviet Textbook of Political Economy" (see text 1960 Reading Notes, especially section 8 and note 42).

An overwhelmingly large portion of the capitalist economy that exists in China today is a capitalist economy that is under the management of the People's Government, which is linked in all sorts of forms to the state-owned socialist economy, and which is supervised by the workers. This type of capitalist economy is no longer an ordinary type of capitalist economy, but a particular type of capitalist economy, that is, a state capitalist economy of a new style. Its existence is not primarily for the profit of the capitalists, but to supply the needs of the people and the state. It is true that the workers still have to produce part of the profit of the capitalists, but this accounts for only a small portion of the total profits, only about one quarter; the remaining three quarters are produced for the workers (as welfare funds), for the state (as income tax), and for the expansion of production facilities (of which a small part produces profit for the capitalists).[2] Therefore, this new-style state capitalist economy carries with it a strong socialist character and is beneficial to the workers and to the state.

Notes

1. See, for example, text 1960 Reading Notes, section 8. The notion of state capitalism has been and continues to be a subject of considerable struggle within the international Communist movement. For an analysis of Lenin's treatment of the issue, see C. Bettelheim (1976), pp. 464-476.

2. Here Mao refers to the system of "dividing the spoils among the four horses" *(si ma fen fei)*. A graphic description of this system is provided in text Sept. 7, 1953. The question of the nature and significance of interest accruing to capitalists, however, remained an issue of debate through the early 1960s. There was uncertainty as to whether or not such interest constituted surplus value, and the controversy was given much attention in Chinese economic and theoretical journals.

Letter to Huang Yanpei
(July 30, 1953)

Source: *Shuxin*, p. 462.

See text Feb. 17, 1951, source note.

Mr. Renzhi:[1]

I have received and read both of your letters – the one you wrote on leaving [Beijing] and the even more recent one. The improvement in the general circumstances [in the country] is a product of the combined effort of people in all areas. I congratulate you, sir, on the insights you have reaped from reading Marx's works. The weather is hot, and it is advisable for you to spend a bit more time on the coast.[2]

With my respect,

Mao Zedong
July 30, 1953

Notes

1. "Renzhi" is Huang's *zi*. See text Oct. 15, 1949, note 1, for an explanation of this usage.
2. See text Sept. 5, 1952.

Telegram to the USSR
(July 31, 1953)

Source: *RMRB* (Aug. 1, 1953), 1. Other Chinese Text: *XHYB*, 8 (Aug. 28, 1953), 21. Available English Translations: HNA, *Daily News Release* (Aug. 1, 1953), 4; FBIS, *Daily Report* (Aug. 3, 1953), AAA13.

Comrade G. M. Malenkov, Chairman of the Council of Ministers of the Soviet Union, Comrade V. M. Molotov, Minister of Foreign Affairs of the

Soviet Union:

Our sincere thanks to the various peoples of the Soviet Union and to you for the congratulations you have expressed on the occasion of the signing of the Korean Armistice Agreement.[1]

The realization of the Korean armistice is a great victory for the camp for world peace and democracy headed by the Soviet Union. The persistent efforts that the government and people of the Soviet Union have contributed toward peacefully resolving the Korean question have played a great role in terminating the Korean war.

The Chinese people will forever unite with the great Soviet people, the heroic Korean people, and all the peace-loving people of the world and will continue to strive for the cause of strengthening and defending peace in the Far East and throughout the world.

(Co-signed as Chairman of CPG of PRC with Zhou Enlai as Premier of GAC and Foreign Minister, dated in Beijing)

Note

1. See text June 30, 1953, note 2.

Oppose the Bourgeois Ideology in the Party
(August 12, 1953)

Source: *Xuanji*, V, pp. 90-97. Available English Translation: *SW*, V, pp. 103-111.

This speech was given at the National Conference on Financial and Economic Work, held, according to K. Lieberthal (1976), p. 59, from June 13 to Aug. 11, 1953. In a speech to the Conference of People from All Circles in Shanghai in July 1957, Mao indicated that the "General Line for the Transition to Socialism" was set forth at this conference. For more on the subject of the general line, which is discussed repeatedly here, see text June 15, 1953, note 1.

Although the main focus of this document is the economic and political conse-quences of relying on incorrect ideology in developing policies, it is also impor-tant as a benchmark in the development of Mao's thought during the post-Liber-ation period. As in other documents of these early post-Liberation years, Mao continued to rely both on an unspecific notion of socialism and the various transitions associated with such a notion and on the Soviet model of development, particularly regarding the role of heavy industry.

However, this document is also important for the hints it gives about Mao's future development. It is one of the earliest indicators of Mao's increasing focus on the importance of ownership systems in the transition period. Moreover, in his characteristic analysis of class alliances and the importance of the long-term alliance of the working class with the peasantry, Mao brings up the notion of antagonistic and nonantagonistic contradictions. But in contrast to his later and more famous "On Correctly Handling Contradictions Among the People" speech (see text Feb. 27, 1957), Mao here treats the contradiction between the proletariat and the national bourgeoisie as an antagonistic one, rather than as one having both antagonistic and nonantagonistic aspects.

This document also helps to clarify Mao's position on the problem of centralization versus decentralization.[1] As is clear from evaluating this document and others dealing with that issue (texts Apr. 25, 1956, and Aug. 15, 1959), Mao held up neither centralization nor decentralization as an absolute policy. Rather, Mao argued that the two are in contradiction. Hence the specific situation must be evaluated to determine whether further centralization or decentralization is appropriate at any one time. Here Mao argued that in the specific situation in 1953 the decision-making process regarding issues of major importance should be more centralized while lesser issues could be handled in a less centralized fashion. However, by 1956, when centralization had been carried out to a much greater degree and when Mao had come to recognize some of the dangers of excessive centralization during the transition to communism, he changed his position and argued for more decentralization of decision-making.

This conference has been a very good conference, and Premier Zhou's conclusions were also very good.

We can now see that after the "Three-Anti's" and "Five-Anti's" campaigns,[2] there remain two types of errors in the Party. One type consists of general mistakes, such as the "Five Excesses,"[3] which anybody can commit and which can be committed at any time. "Five Excesses" mistakes can also turn into "Five Deficiencies" mistakes. Another type [of mistake] consists of mistakes of principle, such as the deviation toward capitalism.[4] This is a reflection of bourgeois ideology within the Party and a question of a standpoint that violates Marxism-Leninism.

The "Three-Anti's" and "Five-Anti's" campaigns were a very severe attack on bourgeois ideology in the Party. However, at that time only the bourgeois ideology related to corruption and waste was attacked at its base, while [the problem of] the bourgeois ideology reflected in the question of line was not resolved. This type of bourgeois ideology exists not only in financial and economic work but also in political and legal work, in cultural and educational work, and in other areas of work as well. It also exists both among the comrades at the Center and among the comrades at the localities.

As far as mistakes in [our] financial and economic work are concerned, since last December – when Comrade Bo Yibo proposed the new taxation system of "equality across the board for public and private [sectors]"[5] – and up to this conference, [these mistakes] have been seriously criticized. If the new tax system develops further, it will inevitably become divorced from Marxism-Leninism and from the Party's general line for the period of transition and will develop toward capitalism.

Is the period of transition to lead toward socialism or toward capitalism? According to the Party's general line, it is to be a transition to socialism. This requires a rather long period of struggle. The mistake in the new tax system is different from the problem of Zhang Zishan;[6] it is a problem of ideology, a problem of having deviated from the Party's general line. We must launch a struggle against bourgeois ideology in the Party. In terms of [its] ideological condition the Party has three types of people in it. Some comrades are steadfast and have not wavered; they have Marxist-Leninist thought. Some comrades are basically Marxist-Leninist, but they have mingled in [with their other thoughts] some non-Marxist-Leninist thought. A small number of people are no good; their thought is non-Marxist-Leninist. In the criticism of Bo Yibo's ideological mistake some people say that Bo Yibo's mistake is that of petty-bourgeois individualism. This is not appropriate. The main thing for which he ought to be criticized is his bourgeois thought, which is beneficial to capitalism and harmful to socialism. Only such a criticism is correct. We've said that "Left" opportunist mistakes are a reflection of petty-bourgeois fanaticism in the Party. Such [mistakes] occurred at times when we were splitting away from the bourgeoisie. [But] during the three periods when we cooperated with the bourgeoisie, that is, during the first period of cooperation between the Kuomintang and the Communist Party of China, the period of the War of Resistance against Japan, and the current period,[7] it was always bourgeois ideology that influenced some people in the Party and caused them to waver. Bo Yibo's mistake was committed under such circumstances.

Bo Yibo's mistake is not an isolated one. It exists not only at the Center but at two [other] levels, [the level of] the greater administrative regions and [the level of] the provinces and municipalities as well. Each of the greater administrative regions, the provinces, and the municipalities must call a meeting to inspect its own work in accordance with the resolution of the Second Plenum of the Seventh Central Committee and the conclusion of this conference in order to educate the cadres.[8]

Recently I made a trip to Wuhan and Nanjing and learned a lot about [local] conditions, which was very helpful. When I stay in Beijing I almost never hear anything [about the outside], from now on I will go out and take trips. The Central leadership organs are a factory that manufactures ideological products; if they do not understand the conditions at the lower levels, if they have no raw materials and no semifinished products, how can they manufacture [finished] products?[9] Some things have already been manufactured into finished products at the local levels; what the leadership organs at the Center can now do is to promote these [products] broadly throughout the country. For instance, the former "Three-Anti's" and the new "'Three-Anti's"[10] were both carried out in the localities first. The various departments of the Center have been very confused in issuing directives. To begin with, the things that the various departments of the Center issue ought to be quality products, but at present they are second-rate products, and what is worse, a lot of these products have no use value to speak of; big batches [of them] are rejects. The leadership organs of the greater administrative regions, the provinces, and the municipalities are the local factories that manufacture ideological products, and they too should produce quality products.

Bo Yibo's mistake is a reflection of bourgeois ideology. It is beneficial to capitalism and harmful to socialism and semisocialism;[11] it has violated the resolution of the Second Plenum of the Seventh Central Committee.

On whom do we rely? Do we rely on the working class, or do we rely on the bourgeoisie? Early on, the resolution of the Second Plenum of the Seventh Central Committee had already made it clear that "we must wholeheartedly rely on the working class." As to the problem of rehabilitating and developing production, the resolution also states that we must affirm that "production in state industries comes first, production in private industries second, and production in handicraft industries third." The emphasis is on industry, and within industry, the emphasis is on heavy industry, which is state-run. Among the five sectors of the economy in our country at present, the state-run [sector of the] economy is the leading factor.[12] Capitalist industrial and commercial enterprises must gradually be led toward state capitalism.

The resolution of the Second Plenum states that on the basis of developing production [we must] improve the living standards of the workers and the laboring people. [However,] people with bourgeois thought do not pay attention to this point, as Bo Yibo has demonstrated. Our emphasis must be placed on developing production, but we must give due consideration to both developing production and improving the people's lives. An effort must be made [to improve the people's] well-being; it cannot be too big an effort, but we cannot ignore it altogether. At present there are still quite a few cadres who disregard the people's livelihood and don't care whether they live or die. In Guizhou there was a regiment that at one time occupied a great deal of the peasants' land. This was an act of severe encroachment on the people's interests.[13] It is wrong not to be concerned with the people's livelihood, but nevertheless, the emphasis must still be put on production construction.

With regard to the problem of utilizing, restricting, and transforming the capitalist [sector of the] economy, the Second Plenum also made that very clear.[14] The resolution [it adopted] stated that the private capitalist [sector of the] economy must not be left uncurbed and unrestricted; we must restrict it in terms of its sphere of operation, the taxation policy [as it applies to this sector], market pricing, and labor conditions. The relationship between the socialist economy and the capitalist economy is one of leader and led. Restriction and opposition to restriction constitute the primary form of class struggle within the new democratic state. At present, to talk about "equality across the board for the public and private [sectors]," as the new tax system does, is at variance with the line that [accepts] the state economy as the leading sector.

As for the problem of carrying out the cooperativization of [the sector of] the agricultural economy that is based on individual [peasants' production], and the handicraft industry [sector] of the economy, the resolution of the Second Plenum stated very clearly that "these types of cooperatives are organizations of the collective economy of the masses of the laboring people that are based on the system of private ownership but are under the management of the state power led by the proletariat. The fact that the Chinese people are culturally backward and do not have a tradition of cooperativization makes expanding and developing the cooperativization campaign quite difficult for us. Nevertheless, it can still be organized, and must be organized; it must be expanded and developed. If we had only the state economy and no cooperative economy, we would not be able to lead [that sector of] the economy based on the individual [production] of the laboring people gradually onto the path of collectivization, we would not be able to develop from a new democratic country into a socialist country of the future,[15] and we would not be able to consolidate the proletariat's leadership in the state power." This resolution dates from March 1949, but quite a few comrades have not paid any attention to it; they regard it as news [when] actually it is old news. Bo Yibo wrote the article "Strengthen the Party's Political Work in the Rural Areas" in which he said that for the individual peasants to take the path [of achieving] collectivization through mutual aid and cooperativization "is pure illusion because the present mutual aid teams are based on the individual economy, and on such a basis they cannot gradually develop into collective farms, much less achieve agricultural collectivization on an overall scale by taking such a path." This is in violation of the Party's resolution.[16]

At present there are two united fronts, two alliances. One is the alliance between the working class and the peasants, which is the foundation. Another is the alliance of the working class and the national bourgeoisie.[17] The peasants are laborers and not exploiters, [so] the alliance of the working class and the peasants is a long-term one. Nevertheless there are contradictions between the working class and the peasants. In accordance with the principle of voluntary [participation] we should gradually lead the peasants from the system of individual ownership toward the system of collective ownership. In the future, there will also be contradictions between the system of state ownership and the system of collective ownership. These are all nonantagonistic contradictions.[18] [On the other hand,] the contradictions between the working class and the bourgeoisie are antagonistic contradictions.

The bourgeoisie is bound to corrupt people and bombard them with sugarcoated bullets.[19] The sugarcoated bullets of the bourgeoisie are both material ones and spiritual ones. A spiritual sugarcoated bullet has hit the mark in Bo Yibo. His mistake is [a result of] his being influenced by bourgeois thought. The bourgeoisie applauded the editorial that propagandized the new tax system,[20] and Bo Yibo was happy. He sought the opinion of the bourgeoisie regarding the new tax system beforehand and made a gentlemen's agreement with the bourgeoisie, but he did not report [this] to the Central Committee. At that time, neither the Ministry of Commerce nor the [All-China] Federation of Supply and Marketing Cooperatives approved [of the new tax system], and the Ministry of Light Industry was not satisfied either. Of the 1.1 million cadres and personnel in the financial, economic, and commercial system [of the nation], the overwhelming majority are good; a small minority are not good. These bad people can be further divided into two parts; one part consists of counterrevolutionaries who ought to be swept away; another part consists of revolutionaries who have made mistakes, including Party members and non-Party personnel. We should use the method of criticism and education in order to transform them.

In order to guarantee the success of the socialist cause throughout the whole Party, and first of all in the leading organs of the Party, the government, the military, and the people's [organizations] at these three levels – the Center, the greater administrative regions, and the provinces and municipalities – we must oppose the incorrect, Right opportunistic deviations, that is, we must oppose bourgeois thought within the Party. At an opportune moment each greater administrative region, province, and municipality should convene a meeting, which should be attended by the secretaries of special district [Party] committees and by commissioners [of the special districts],[21] to conduct criticism and discussion and explain clearly the question of the socialist road versus the capitalist road.

In order to guarantee the success of the socialist cause, we must exercise collective leadership and oppose excessive decentralism and subjectivism.

At present we must oppose subjectivism; we must oppose not only the subjectivism of blind adventurist advances,[22] but also the subjectivism of being conservative. In the past, in the period of the new democratic revolution, [our Party] made mistakes of subjectivism, some of which were "rightist" and some "leftist." [The errors of] Chen Duxiu and Zhang Guotao were "rightist"; in Wang Ming's case they were "leftist" [errors] at first and later "rightist."[23] At the time of the rectification at Yanan,[24] efforts were concentrated on opposing dogmatism, and on the side, opposing empiricism; both were [manifestations of] subjectivism. If theory is not integrated with reality, the revolution cannot be triumphant. Rectification resolved this problem. We adopted the policy of learning from past mistakes in order to avoid future ones, and curing the illness in order to save the patient.[25] This was correct. This time, when we carry out a resolute and thorough criticism of Bo Yibo, we are doing it so that people who have committed mistakes can correct them and so that the triumphant progress of socialism will be guaranteed. The present is a period of socialist revolution, but there is [still] subjectivism. Neither impetuous adventurist advance nor conservatism acts in accordance with reality; both are subjectivism. If subjectivism is not opposed and removed, the revolution and construction cannot succeed. During the period of the democratic revolution,[26] we used the method of rectification to resolve [the problem of] subjectivist mistakes throughout the whole Party, and we united those comrades who upheld the correct line and those who had made mistakes. [These comrades] proceeded on from Yanan to the various theaters of war, and the entire Party, exerting its efforts in unison, achieved victory throughout the country. Now the cadres are more mature and the level [of their political consciousness] has been raised; we hope before too long to basically rid ourselves of subjectivism in our leadership work, and strive to make the subjective correspond to the objective.

The key to resolving all these problems lies in strengthening collective leadership and in opposing decentralizationism.[27] We have always opposed decentralizationism. On February 2, 1941, the Central Committee issued a directive to the various bureaus of the Central Committee and to the various military commanders that stipulated that before they issued any circular telegrams, declarations, or intra[-Party] directives of national significance, they must ask for instructions from the Central Committee. In May, the Central Committee issued the directive on unifying [the work] of external propaganda of the various base areas.[28] On July 1 of the same year, at the time of the twentieth anniversary of the founding of the Party, the Center promulgated the resolution on strengthening the Party spirit with emphasis on opposing decentralizationism. In 1948, the Central Committee issued even more directives opposing decentralizationism. On January 7, the Center issued the directive concerning the establishment of the system of reporting, and in March a supplementary directive was issued. In September of the same year, a meeting of the Political Bureau passed the resolution concerning the system for requesting instructions from the Central Committee and reporting to the Central Committee. On September 20, the Central Committee made the decision on making the Party committee system more sound and complete.[29] On March 10, 1953, in order to avoid the danger of the various departments of the government becoming divorced from the leadership of the Party Central Committee, the Central Committee passed the resolution to strengthen the [Party] leadership over government work.

Centralization and decentralization are constantly in contradiction with each other. Since we entered the cities,[30] decentralization has developed further. In order to solve this contradiction, all major and important issues must first be discussed and decided by the Party committees before [the decisions] are carried out by the government. For instance, such major issues as erecting the Monument to the People's Heroes in Tiananmen [Square][31] and dismantling the city walls of Beijing were decided by the Center and then carried out by the government. Problems of secondary importance can be taken care of by the leading Party groups in the departments of the government. It just won't do for all problems to be monopolized by the Center. To oppose decentralizationism [is a measure] that will best win the hearts of the people because the majority of the comrades in the Party are concerned about collective leadership. In terms of their attitude toward collective leadership, people inside the Party can be classified into three types. People of the first type are concerned about the collective leadership. People of the second type are indifferent and believe that it would be best if the Party committee didn't interfere with [their affairs] but that if it did interfere, that's all right too. [The attitude that] "it's best if they do not interfere" shows a lack of Party spirit, whereas [the attitude that] "interference is all right too" [shows that they] still retain [a measure of] Party spirit. We must take hold of [their attitude that] "interference is all right" and conduct persuasion and education [to overcome] the lack of Party spirit. Otherwise, each ministry would do its own thing and the Center would not be able to exercise control over them. The ministers would not be able to manage the department and bureau heads, the division heads would not be able to manage section chiefs, and nobody would be able to manage anybody else. [Consequently] there would be a large number of kingdoms, [like the] eight hundred feudal lords.[32] The third type is made up of an extreme minority; they resolutely oppose collective leadership and believe that it is best never to interfere with anything. In the resolution on strengthening Party spirit, it was emphasized that the discipline of democratic centralism must be strictly enforced; the minority must submit to the majority, the individual must submit to the organization, the lower levels must submit to the higher levels, and the Party as a whole must submit to the Central Committee (in this case the majority must submit to the minority, [but] this minority represents the majority). If there are any opinions, please bring them up. To damage Party unity [however] is most disgraceful. Only by relying on the political experience of the collective and the wisdom of the collective can we guarantee the correct leadership of the Party and the state as well as the unshakable unity of the Party ranks as a whole.

At this conference, Liu Shaoqi said he had made some mistakes, and Comrade [Deng] Xiaoping also said he had made some mistakes. No matter who they are, people who have made mistakes must examine [their mistakes] and accept the supervision of the Party and the leadership of the Party committees at the various levels. This is a major condition for accomplishing the Party's task. Throughout the country there are a lot of people who rely on the anarchistic situation to survive. Bo Yibo is such a person. Politically and ideologically, he is somewhat corrupted, [so] it is absolutely necessary to criticize him.

One last point: we must promote the spirit of modesty, learning, and perseverance.

We must persevere. For instance, in the [War to] Resist U.S. [Aggression] and Aid Korea, we dealt United States imperialism a severe blow and made them quite scared. This was advantageous to our [task of national] construction; it was an important condition for our construction. The most important thing was that our army received tempering [in the war]; the soldiers were brave and the cadres clever. Naturally, we sacrificed some people, used some money, and paid a price. But we just weren't afraid of making sacrifices. If we did not undertake something that was one matter, but once we did embark on something we saw it through to the very end. When Hu Zonggnan attacked the Shaan-Gan-Ning Border Region,[33] we were down to our very last *xian* capital, but we did not pull out of the border region. When we had to eat leaves [off the trees] we did it. This is the type of relentlessness we should have.

We must learn; we must not be arrogant; we must not look down on people. Goose eggs look down on chicken eggs; ferrous metals look down on rare metals; such an attitude of looking down on people is unscientific. [Although] China is a great country and its Party is a great Party, there is still no reason to look down on small countries and small parties. We must always maintain an attitude of [willingness to] learn from fraternal nations, and [we] must have a true internationalist spirit. In the area of foreign trade, some people have been arrogant and self-important; this is wrong. We must conduct education within the Party as a whole, particularly among those personnel who go abroad. We must study hard and work hard in order to basically accomplish the socialist industrialization and socialist transformation [of the country] in fifteen years' time or a little longer. Even then, when our country has become big and powerful, we must still be modest and always maintain an attitude of [willingness to] learn.

There are several regulations that were adopted at the Second Plenum of the Seventh Central Committee but that were not written into the resolution. The first one is a ban on birthday celebrations. Birthday celebrations will not bring one longevity, the main thing is to do one's work well. The second one is a ban on gifts, at least within the Party itself. The third one is that we mustn't make so many toasts, [although] it is permissible on certain occasions. The fourth one is that we must not applaud so much; applause is not prohibited [however], and when the masses applaud out of enthusiasm we should not pour cold water [on them] either. The fifth one is that we mustn't name places after people. The sixth is that we mustn't list our Chinese comrades as equals of Marx, Engels, Lenin, and Stalin. The relationship [between them and us] is one of teacher to pupil and ought to be [recognized as] such. Obeying these rules is to have an attitude of modesty.

In short, we must hold fast to the spirit of modesty, [willingness to] learn, and perserverence, uphold the system of collective leadership so as to accomplish the socialist transformation [of our country] and achieve the triumph of socialism.

Notes

1. The issue of centralization-decentralization is not simply the issue of the locus of decision-making. It also affects who makes the decisions, i.e., decentralization to the level of local Party committees is different from decentralization to the level of production units' management groups. For more on this see F. Schurmann (1968), pp. 175-178, 196-199.

2. See text Nov. 1951-Mar. 1952, source note.

3. See text Mar. 19, 1953.

4. See text Jun. 15, 1953, source note.

5. In November 1952, on the eve of the promulgation of the First Five-Year Plan in January 1953, Bo Yibo, who was deputy chairman of the Finance and Economic Commission under the GAC and Minister of Finance, was appointed a member of the newly established State Planning Commission. Tax policy fell under the purview of the Commission, and Bo made a specific suggestion, which is described here by Mao. This suggestion was adopted temporarily by the Commission and superseded the tax code of 1950 governing taxation on industrial and commercial enterprises. In addition to revising the tax schedule on enterprises that are processing plants for state production and are subject to state allocation, and enterprises within the category of state-contracted production and marketing, the salient characteristics of this new tax code included also increasing the tax burden on state-run commercial enterprises, such as the supply and marketing cooperatives, and on other cooperatives, and the elimination of several key tax benefits for cooperatives, such as the exemption of cooperatives from the first year of income taxation after its establishment, and the 20 per cent reduction of taxation on sales and management costs for cooperatives.

According to *SW*, V, p. 111, note 1, "This new tax system was introduced in December 1952 and put into effect in January 1953. Though nominally entailing 'equality between public and private enterprises,' in reality it lightened the tax burdens on private industrial and commercial enterprises and increased those on state and cooperative enterprises, thus serving the interests of the capitalists at the expense of the latter. Soon after Comrade Mao Zedong made his criticism, this error was corrected."

For more biographical information concerning Bo Yibo, see D. Klein and A. Clark, eds. (1971), II, pp. 738-742.

6. According to *Xuanji*, V, 97, note 1, "Zhang Zishan was at one time secretary of the Tianjin [Special] District Committee of the CPC. Corrupted by the bourgeoisie, he became a big embezzler and, during the 'Three-Anti's' movement, he was sentenced to death."

7. These three periods were: The First United Front period from 1924 to 1927, the Second United Front period from 1937 to 1946, and the period of the Common Program from 1949 to 1953. The First United Front began with the declaration of a CPC-KMT cooperation against the forces of imperialism and against the Beiyang warlord regimes in January 1924 at the First National Congress of the KMT. In 1926 the Northern Expedition against the warlords and to unify China began. On April 12, 1927, on his way northward in this Expedition, Chiang Kai-shek ordered the liquidation of Communists in Shanghai, thus leading to the execution of hundreds of Communists and forcing the Communist movement underground. This ended the First United Front.

In July 1937, following the July 7 Lukouqiao (Marco Polo Bridge) Incident, China entered a state of war with Japan. At the same time, however, the internal conflict between the KMT and the CPC was continuing. In December 1936, following the Xian Incident, in which the need to suspend civil war in order to prepare for resisting Japanese imperialism was impressed upon Chiang Kai-shek, he made a formal commitment to take on the resistance against Japan as his main task. In September 1937 the confrontation with the national enemy forced the KMT and the CPC to once again enter a phase of cooperation. Although there was a formal declaration of cooperation, however, throughout the period of the War of Resistance the rivalry between the CPC and KMT continued, and there were many incidences of open conflict. A large portion of the KMT forces, under generals such as Hu Zongnan, were assigned the task of "containing" the Communists rather than facing the Japanese. Open civil warfare once again erupted in 1946, ending the Second United Front.

The third "united front" Mao talks about here is a very different one from the first two. It is a matter of cooperating with bourgeois elements and circles in the country "under the leadership of the proletariat" (i.e., after the CPC had come to power, and the country was already oriented, as a People's Republic, toward socialism). See text Feb. 18, 1951, note 13.

8. For the Second Plenum of the Seventh Central Committee see text June 6, 1950(2), note 1.

9. Over the years Mao has often used the analogy of the Party Center as a factory built on the basis of Marxist-Leninist theory that needs information from the lower levels to produce new

theory, lines, and policies. See Mao's speech at the Supreme State Conference, (text Jan. 28, 1958), and "Talks to the Handan Forum on the Four Clean-ups Work" (text Mar. 28, 1964).

10. The first "Three-Anti's" campaign was launched in 1952 (see text Nov. 1951-Mar. 1952, source note). In February 1953 the "Three-Anti's" slogan again appeared in a speech by An Ziwen (see text Mar. 31, 1955, note 10), in which he claimed that problems still remained from the earlier campaign. An called for a new effort against "bureaucracy, commandism, and the violation of law and discipline." See *RMSC* (1953), pp. 171-173.

11. Mao is referring to the state in which economic units are not yet fully socialized (i.e., in which the means of production are not fully publicly owned.) Although at this point he seems to be concerned more with industrial and commerical enterprises, the problem with enterprises being at and remaining at the "semisocialist" stage would have a much greater significance in the mid-1950s in the agricultural sector. Of the "five economic sectors" that Mao talks about in the next paragraph here, two sectors are classified as "semisocialist."

12. The five sectors of the economy Mao is referring to are the fully socialistic state-run economy, the semisocialistic (see note 11) cooperative economy (the vast majority of the cooperatives then in existence were as yet in the lower-level or semisocialist stage, but would eventually move toward fuller socialism, so this is a transitional category), the semisocialistic state-capitalist economy, the individual economy of peasants and handicraft workers, and the sector of private capitalism.

13. According to *Ciyu jianshi*, pp. 27-28, a certain regiment of the PLA stationed in Guizhou, in attempting to carry out exercises emulating certain practices of the Soviet Army, appropriated a considerable amount of agricultural land to build a parade ground. In this source this incident was ascribed to "the influence of the bourgeois line in the military's operations of Peng Dehuai."

14. The policy of utilizing, restricting, and transforming *(liyong, xianzhi, he gaizao)* private capital was adopted in Article 10 of the September 20, 1954, Constitution of the PRC.

15. See text June 15, 1953, note 2.

16. See *RMRB* (June 29, 1951).

17. See text Mar. 12, 1950, note 3.

18. For Mao's fundamental theory of the antagonistic nature that exists between certain types of contradictions, see section VI of his article "On Contradictions" *(SW,* I, pp. 343-345). Mao would eventually develop this into a much more sophisticated and practice-oriented theory in "On Correctly Handling Contradictions among the People" (see text Feb. 27, 1957).

19. This refers to the tactics of disguising dangerous and harmful developments or policies in enticing facades of compromise and favors, which Mao takes the tactics "used by the bourgeoisie" to "corrode the ranks of the revolutionary people" to be. He first used the term in his Report to the Second Session of the Seventh Central Committee; see *SW,* IV, p. 374.

20. See *RMRB* (Dec. 31, 1952), editorial.

21. Special districts *(zhuanqu)* were provisional administrative districts, intermediary between the province and the *xian*. There were approximately 201 such districts in 1951, but by the later 1950s all these districts had been abolished.

22. The standard definition of "adventurism," in addition to a sense of rashness, also includes the theoretical qualities of "going beyond the realm of real possibilities and beyond the level of the political consciousness of the masses or those affected by the action." The Chinese term for this is *maojin,* an abbreviation of *maoxian qianjin,* or advancing in a risky manner. It should be noted that this "label," besides connoting a psychological risk, also connotes, because of the aforementioned definition, a violation of the scientific principles of Marxist socialism – i.e., the principle that political and historical actions must be founded on the basis of possiblility and the masses form the foundation of possibility. Later, in 1955, when the "conservatives" turned this "label" against Mao and others who at the time advocated comprehensive cooperativization of agriculture, and opposed Mao under the aegis of opposing adventurist advance, Mao would turn the "label" around and oppose those who opposed adventurist advance. See text Dec. 6, 1955, note 10.

23. Chen Duxiu (1879-1942) was one of the founders of the CPC and from 1921 to 1927, its first general secretary. Mao's reference to Chen as a Rightist is in accord with the official inter-

pretation of the Party's history, which charges that Chen, while general secretary, had advocated collaboration with the KMT and deference to its leadership during the period of the First CPC-KMT United Front (1925-1927). This charge is made, for example, in the "Resolution on Some Questions in the History of Our Party" adopted by the Seventh Plenum of the Sixth Central Committee, April 20, 1945. Convincing evidence to the contrary, however, suggests that Chen was actually opposed to the United Front but was forced to acquiesce to it by the Comintern. (See, for instance, R. Kagan [1974], pp. 295-314.) Chen was purged from the CPC in 1929.

Zhang Guotao (1897-1973) was also one of the founders of the CPC and an important Party leader until 1938. Zhang was originally prominent in the Communist labor movement and later in the Oyuwan Soviet (1931-32). During the Long March of 1934-35 Zhang was in charge of the Communist Fourth Front Army, which joined the main train of the March in mid-1935. A bitter political struggle between Zhang and Mao ensued. Zhang soon led his much stronger Communist forces west toward Tibet, while Mao and his forces headed north toward Shaanxi. Zhang's army, however, suffered a series of defeats at the hands of pursuing KMT armies and in October 1936 rejoined Mao's forces, which had established their base in the Shaanxi-Gansu-Ningxia Border Region, with Yanan as its capital. With his forces severely weakened Zhang was no longer in a position to challenge Mao. In 1937, he was severely criticized and in 1938 left the movement. See J. Harrison (1972), pp. 245-259, 281-289; J. Rue (1966), and Zhang Guotao (1972).

Wang Ming (pseudonym of Chen Shaoyu, 1904-1974) was the leader of the so-called "28 Bolsheviks" or "Returned Students" faction within the CPC. This faction, consisting of students who had returned to China after studying in the Soviet Union, dominated the Party Center from 1931 to 1935. Wang Ming himself became general secretary of the CPC, succeeding Li Lisan in that post in June 1931. The "leftist" error to which Mao refers was Wang's insistence during the early 1930s that the Red Army mount attacks against key urban areas. These attacks met with defeat and resulted in major losses for the CPC in KMT controlled areas and the weakening of its bases in the countryside. Wang Ming's later Rightist error came after his faction had been defeated politically by Mao at the Zunyi Conference in 1935 when, during the debate over a second United Front policy, he advocated CPC acquiescence to the leadership of Chiang Kai-shek for the duration of the War of Resistance. For this, he was accused of class capitulationism. For a detailed study of the conflict between Wang Ming and Mao see J. Rue (1966); and T. L. Hsiao (1961). For more on the "28 Bolsheviks" see S. Schram (1967), pp. 149-150. For more biographical information on Chen, Zhang, and Wang, see D. Klein and A. Clark, eds. (1971), I, pp. 139-144, pp. 38-43, and pp. 127-134, respectively.

24. In 1942 a rectification *(zhengfeng)* movement was launched at Yanan to reform the bureaucratic work-style and streamline the military organization of the Communist base areas. It established the reading of Marxist-Leninist works, group political education, and self-criticism as precedents for later ideas of popular political participation. It was also a period of persecution for those who resisted rectification. For Mao's writings on this movement see "Rectify the Party's Style of Work," *SW*, III, pp. 35-51, and "Oppose Stereotyped Party Writing," *SW*, III, pp. 53-68; also, B. Comptom (1966). Also see text June 30, 1953, note 9.

25. This slogan encapsulates the two principles of Party rectification. The first phrase of the slogan is an aphorism derived from the poem "Jing zhi" [Respect] from the collection "Zhou song" [Paeans from Zhou] in the *Shi jing* [Book of Odes]. The second part of the slogan refers to the proper treatment of an errant Party member. The gist of this principle is that while mistakes must be corrected, if they require harsh measures, the basic purpose of the rectification is to change the situation while keeping the cadre. This became the principle under which criticism and self-criticism were to be conducted. Later the slogan was used in conjunction with the formula "unity-criticism-unity."

26. Here Mao was referring not to the traditional notion of a democratic revolution, which he described as an "old general type of bourgeois-democratic revolution," but rather to the "New Democratic Revolution." See text June 15, 1953, note 2.

27. See text Mar. 19, 1953, note 1.

28. See text Aug. 5, 1951, source note.

29. The Central Committee directives of January 7, 1948, and September 20, 1948, were

drafted by Mao. See "On Setting Up a System of Reports," *SW*, IV, pp. 177-179, and "On Strengthening the Party Committee System," *SW*, IV, pp. 267-268.

30. Here Mao may not be referring simply to the fact that Communist forces began to capture the major cities of China in late 1948 and early 1949, but rather may be referring more broadly to the period beginning with the Second Plenum of the Seventh Party Congress in March 1949. At this meeting the CPC began to focus on the problem of administering large urban areas and the transformation of those areas into the centers of social revolution. It was at this plenum that Mao declared an end to the period of "from the city to the village" and the beginning of the period of "the city leading the village." See Mao's report to the Plenum, *SW*, IV, p. 363.

31. See text Sept. 30, 1949.

32. Mao alludes here to the traditional belief that there existed eight hundred feudal lords during the Shang dynasty (ca. sixteenth-tenth centuries B.C.). Mao's general allusion is to the many small kingdoms, with their petty rulers and plethora of vassals, that existed in China prior to its primitive "unification" under the Zhou dynasty (ca. 841 B.C.). The legend of the eight hundred feudal lords is contained in *Zhou benji* (The Chronicle of Zhou) in *Shi ji* (Historical Records) by Sima Qian, and also in the popular novel *Fengshenbang*.

33. The Shaanxi-Gansu-Ningxia Border Region was the designation given in 1937, after the establishment of the Anti-Japanese United Front, to the revolutionary base area that encompassed twenty-three *xian* on the common borders of those three provinces. See text Oct. 26, 1949, note 1. See also text Feb. 27, 1950, note 1.

Telegram to the Democratic People's Republic of Korea
(August 12, 1953)

Source: *RMRB* (Aug. 15, 1953), 1. Other Chinese Text: *XHYB*, 9 (Sept. 28, 1953), 51. Available English Translations: NCNA, *Daily Bulletin*, 853 (Aug. 17, 1953), 1; FBIS, *Daily Report* (Aug. 18, 1953), EEE12-13.

The Chairman,
The Standing Committee,
The Supreme People's Assembly,
The Democratic People's Republic of Korea

Comrade Kim Du Bong:

On the occasion of the eighth anniversary of the liberation of Korea, please accept my sincere congratulations to all the Korean people and to yourself.

May the heroic Korean people who have defeated the United States imperialist aggressors achieve great success in their cause of striving to halt a resurgence of aggressive war and to establish a peaceful, unified, and independent new Korea.

(Signed as Chairman of CPG of PRC, dated, in Beijing)

Letter to Ye Gongzuo
(August 16, 1953)

Source: *Shuxin*, p. 463.

See text May 25, 1952.

Mr. Yuhu:[1]

I have received your gracious gift of the volume of portraits of Qing dynasty scholars. Thank you very much indeed! I wonder if you have access to the first volume? If you do, would it be possible for me to borrow it for a look?

With my respect,

Mao Zedong
August 16, 1953

Note

1. See text May 25, 1952, note 1.

Telegram to the People's Republic of Albania
(August 20, 1953)

Source: FBIS, *Daily Report* (Aug. 21, 1953), LL2.

We have no Chinese text of this telegram. The FBIS transcript is presented here as originally printed. It was signed by Mao as Chairman of the CPG of the PRC. The telegram was apparently addressed to Chairman Enver Hoxha of the People's Republic of Albania.

My sincere thanks to the Albanian people, to the People's Government of Albania, and to you personally for your greetings on the occasion of the signing of the Korean armistice.[1] The Chinese people will continue their relations with all the people of the world, led by the Soviet people, for a lasting peace in the Far East and in the world.

Note

1. See text June 30, 1953, note 2.

Telegram to the Democratic People's Republic of Korea
(August 25, 1953)

Source: FBIS, *Daily Report* (Aug. 26, 1953), EEE11.

We have no Chinese text of this telegram. The FBIS transcript is presented here as originally printed. It was signed by Mao as Chairman of the CPG of the PRC.

Comrade Kim Il Sung, Premier of the Cabinet of the Democratic People's Republic of Korea:

I hereby wish to express my heartfelt thanks for the congratulations extended to me on the occasion of the twenty-sixth anniversary of the founding of the Chinese People's Liberation Army by the Government of the Democratic People's Republic of Korea, the entire Korean people and you. The Chinese people will. . .(intently) good will and solidarity with the brotherly Korean people, and will jointly fight to the last for the peaceful settlement of the Korean issue and for lasting peace in the Far East and of the world.

Address at the Establishment of the Institute of Military Engineering and the Inauguration of Its First Term

(August 26, 1953)

Source: *Wansui* (n.d.), p. 253. Other Chinese Texts: *Wansui* (n.d. 2), pp. 1-2; *Xuexi wenxuan* (1967), pp. 393-394.

Information on the sources of this document, all of which are Red Guard publications, is scanty and incomplete. The date of August 26, 1953, is given by the Wansui *(n.d.) source, which we have adopted as our original source. The other sources cited above give the date of June 26, 1953, instead.*

President Chen, professors, teaching assistants, students and staff of the Institute of Military Engineering, Comrades:

At this moment of the beginning of a new term for you, I extend to you my warmest and most enthusiastic congratulations.

I take this opportunity also to express our heartfelt thanks to the government of the Soviet Union and the Soviet experts who have so enthusiastically aided us in planning and creating this institute.

The establishment of the Institute of Military Engineering of the Chinese People's Liberation Army has an extremely great significance for our country's national defense enterprise; in order to build a modernized national defense [system], our army, air force, and navy must all possess fully mechanized equipment and armaments, and none of this can be achieved without complex specialized technology. What we direly need today is a large number of people who are capable of managing and steering the direction of technological [advancement] and to see to it that our technology may improve and make progress uninterruptedly. The purpose for the creation of the Institute of Military Engineering is precisely to resolve this urgent and yet glorious task.

Learning from the Soviet Union's experts has been a fine tradition that we have followed throughout the history of the construction of our armed forces. No matter at what time or in whichever department of our work, we should [continue to] do so. This is something that has all the greater signifigance for this Institute of yours. You must learn from the Soviet Union's advanced scientific and technological knowledge, learn from the Soviet Union's rich experience in the construction of military science, and emulate the learning mentality and working attitude of our comrades, the Soviet Union's experts, and their highly developed spirit of patriotism and internationalism. In learning one must be modest and earnest; one must not become self-satisfied and arrogant as soon as one has learned a little bit.

There is something that you in this Institute, and everybody in the armed forces, must fully understand and never, not even for a single moment, forget, and that is: Maintain and develop the glorious tradition of the Chinese People's Liberation Army, and particularly the heroic spirit of dedicating oneself wholeheartedly to serve the people and of self-sacrifice!

I hope that you will unite, and be of one mind, building and running this Institute well, respecting the experts, dedicating yourselves to diligent study, and strive for the accomplishment of the glorious task that the People's Military Commission has placed on your shoulders.

Letter to Li Shuqing
(August 27, 1953)

Source: Quoted in Zhou Libo, "Shaoshan wu ri ji" (A Journal of Five Days in Shaoshan), in *Luxingjia*, 2 (Feb. 22, 1958), 35.

See text Nov. 17, 1949.

Mr. Shuqing:[1]

I have received the letter that you wrote me after we parted. Thank you very much. I hope that you will, at your convenience, tell me a few things about what's happening in our home village. Please take good care of yourself.

Allow me also to express to you my regards.

Mao Zedong
August 27, 1953

Note

1. See text Nov. 17, 1949, note 2.

Telegram to the Democratic Republic of Viet Nam
(August 30, 1953)

Source: FBIS, *Daily Report* (Sept. 2, 1953), CCC1.

We have no Chinese text of this telegram. The FBIS transcript is presented here as originally printed. The telegram was apparently addressed to President Ho Chi Minh.

On the occasion of the eighth anniversary of the establishment of the Democratic Republic of Vietnam, I sincerely extend my greetings to the Vietnam people, the Government of the Democratic Republic of Vietnam, and you, Comrade.

I wish that the Vietnam people may score many new victories in their struggle against aggression and for the independence and liberation of their Fatherland, and wish that the fraternal friendship between the peoples of Vietnam and China may consolidate day after day.

On the General Line of the Party
During the Period of Transition
(August 1953)

Source: *Xuanji*, V, p. 89. Other Chinese Texts: *RMRB* (Nov. 10, 1953), 1 (quotation); *Dang de jianshe*, p. 56 (excerpts); *Mao liang*, pp. 246-247 (excerpt), incorrectly dated June 15, 1953. Available English Translations: *SW*, V, p. 102; *PR*, 14:27 (July 2, 1971), 12.

According to Xuanji, *this is an important comment made by Mao when reviewing the draft of Zhou Enlai's concluding remarks at the National Conference on Financial and Economic Work. This conference was held June 13-Aug. 11, 1953 – see K. Lieberthal (1976), pp. 59-60, and text Aug. 12, 1953. Only the* Xuanji *source contains both paragraphs; all others have the first paragraph but not the second. Minor discrepancies in the text are noted.*

[The period] from the founding of the People's Republic of China to the fundamental completion of the socialist transformation is a period of transition. During this period of transition the general line and overall task of the Party is to basically realize,[1] over a considerably long period of time, national industrialization[2] and the socialist transformation of agriculture[3] and handicraft industries as well as of capitalist industry and commerce.[4] This general line ought to be a beacon illuminating every task we undertake. If we should depart from it in any facet of our work, we will be committing errors of either Right or "Left" deviation.

Many of the principles and policies in this general line were already proposed in the resolutions of the Second Plenum of the Party's [Seventh] Central Committee in March 1949, and solutions in the area of principles have already been reached.[5] Nevertheless, many comrades are reluctant to do their work in accordance with the stipulations of the Second Plenum and on certain problems prefer [instead] to work up another set of things that do not conform to the stipulations of the Second Plenum, or that even publicly violate the principles of the Second Plenum.

Notes

1. The *Dang de jianshe* version reads here "gradually realize" or "realize step by step. "
2. The *Dang de jianshe* version reads here "the socialist industrialization of the nation."
3. The *RMRB* quotation reads here "and to gradually realize the state's socialist transformation of. . ."
4. See text June 15, 1953, note 1.
5. See text June 6, 1950(2), note 1.

Telegram to the USSR
(September 2, 1953)

Source: *RMRB* (Sept. 3, 1953), 1. Other Chinese Text: *XHYB*, 10 (Oct. 28, 1953), 3. Available English Translations: NCNA, *Daily Bulletin*, 871 (Sept. 3, 1953), 1; FBIS, *Daily Report* (Sept. 3, 1953), AAA4-5.

Comrade G. M. Malenkov, Chairman of the Council of Ministers of the Soviet Union,
Comrade V. M. Molotov, Minister of Foreign Affairs of the Soviet Union:

On the occasion of the eighth anniversary of victory in the War of Resistance against Japan, on behalf of the Chinese people and the Chinese People's liberation Army, I extend our warm congratulations to the people and the armed forces of the Soviet Union.

From beginning to end, in the protracted and difficult war to resist Japanese imperialist aggression and in the fighting that finally crushed Japanese imperialism, the Chinese people received the support and assistance of the Soviet people. This was especially true in 1945, when, owing to the fact that the Soviet armed forces joined the war and fought alongside the Chinese people, we defeated Japanese imperialism and achieved the final victory.

Since the founding of the People's Republic of China, with the conclusion of the Sino-Soviet Treaty of Friendship, Alliance, and Mutual Assistance,[1] the unbreakable friendship between China and the Soviet Union has already been and is still being consolidated and developed with each passing day. This great friendship has now become a strong guarantee of peace in the Far East and throughout the world.

On top of this we also should point out here that the fraternal assistance that the Soviet Union has given the Chinese people is an important factor in the rapid restoration of China's economy and in its stepping onto the path to planned construction.

The recent signing of the Korean Armistice Agreement[2] is clearly a great, new achievement in the efforts of the entire camp for peace and democracy to win peace and to prevent new war. This important new achievement has contributed to the beginning of the easing of tension in the world as a whole. At the same time, it will also contribute to the efforts of the Japanese people in obtaining normalized relations with the various countries of the Far East so as to prevent the revival of Japanese imperialist aggression.

Long live the eternal cooperation between China and the Soviet Union in the just cause of defending peace in the Far East and throughout the world! (Co-signed as Chairman of CPG of PRC with Zhou Enlai as Premier of GAC and Foreign Minister, dated, in Beijing)

Notes

1. See text Jan. 2, 1950, note 1.
2. See text June 30, 1953, note 2.

The Path That Inevitably Must Be Followed in the Transformation of Capitalist Industry and Commerce

(September 7, 1953)

Source: *Xuanji*, V, pp. 98-100. Available English Translation: *SW*, V, pp. 112-114.

According to Xuanji, *this is an outline of a talk to representatives of the democratic parties and industrial and commercial circles, many of whom were gathered in Beijing for the impending enlarged meeting of the standing Committee of the CPPCC (see note 3).*

The transformation from capitalism to socialism is to be realized through [the stage of] state capitalism.[1]

1. For more than three years now, we have been doing some work [on transforming capitalist industry and commerce], but since we have been busy with other things we haven't made much of an effort. From now on, we must do more work [on this transformation].

2. Having acquired more than three years' experience, we already can say for sure that completing the socialist transformation of private industry and commerce by going through [the stage of] state capitalism is a relatively sound guideline and method.

3. The guideline set forth in Article 31 of the Common Program[2] must now be clarified and gradually made concrete. By "clarification" we mean first affirming in the minds of leadership personnel at the Center and at the local [levels] that state capitalism is a road that must inevitably be followed in the transformation of capitalist industry and commerce and in the gradual completion of the transition to socialism. This has not yet been achieved, either among Communist Party members or among the democratic personages. The purpose of this conference is to achieve this end.[3]

4. Move forward with steady steps;[4] we can't rush things too much. To basically lead the private industry and commerce of the entire country onto the track of state capitalism will take a minimum of three to five years. Therefore, there should not be repercussion or alarm.

5. The three forms of state capitalism in the sphere of private industry are: joint state-private enterprise, [the form in which] the state places orders [with private enterprises] for processing and manufacturing goods while supplying all the raw material and taking all the finished products, and [the form in which] the state receives only the bulk but not all of the products.[5]

6. In private commerce, too, we can implement state capitalism; we cannot dismiss [such commerce] simply by saying "exclude it" and leave it at that. Our experience in this area is rather limited, [so] we must still study.

7. Private industrial and commercial [enterprises] which [together employ] approximately 3.8 million workers and shop employees are a great national asset and play a large role in the national economy and the livelihood of the people. Not only do private industry and commerce supply the country with manufactured goods, but they can also accumulate funds for the state and train cadres for the state.

8. Some capitalists maintain a great distance between [themselves and] the state and still have not changed their exclusively profit-oriented thought. Some workers have advanced too quickly and won't tolerate the capitalists making any profits. We should carry out [the work of] education among these two categories of people so that they will gradually conform to the state's guidelines and policies ([although we should] strive [to achieve this] as soon as possible), which are to make China's private industry and commerce basically serve the national economy and the livelihood of the people, while serving in part [also] to earn profits for the capitalists. In this way [these enterprises] will be on the track of state capitalism.

Here is a chart of the distribution of profits of state capitalist enterprises:

Income tax	34.5%
Welfare expenses	15.0%
Public reserve funds	30.0%
Capitalist dividends	20.5%
Total	100.0%

9. We need to continue to carry out education in patriotism among the capitalists. In order to do this we must cultivate, in a planned way, a number of capitalists who are more farsighted and willing to lean close to the Communist Party and the People's Government, so that [we will be able to] persuade most of the [other] capitalists through them.

10. The implementation of state capitalism must be carried out not only in accordance with the needs and possibilities ([as specified in] the Common Program) but must also be of the capitalists' own volition, because this is a cooperative undertaking, and if it is cooperation it cannot be forced; this is different from [dealing with] the landlords.

11. Already in the past few years the various nationalities in the country, the various democratic classes, democratic parties, and people's organizations[6] have made very great progress. I am confident that in three to five years this progress will be even greater. Therefore there is the possibility that within the next three to five years [the task of] leading private industry and commerce onto the track of state capitalism will be basically completed. On the other

hand, the superiority of state-run enterprises is the guarantee, from a material standpoint, of the completion of this task.

12. As for completing the entire transition period, which includes the basic completion of the nation's industrialization and the basic completion of the socialist transformation of agriculture, handicraft industries, and capitalist industry and commerce, this is not something that can be done in three to five years. Rather, it will require a period of several five-year plans.[7] We must oppose the idea [that places this matter in] the distant and indefinite future, but we must simultaneously oppose the idea of impatient and adventurist advance.[8]

13. Leaders are one thing, those who are led are another; those not seeking private profits are one thing, those who still strive for a portion of private profits are yet another; and so forth. These are all different [elements], but under our present conditions, private industry and commerce basically serve the national economy and the livelihood of the people; (in terms of the distribution of profits, approximately three-fourths [of the profits go to the state]).[9] Therefore we can and must persuade the workers [in this sector to do the same] as in state-run enterprises, namely, to implement [a policy of] increasing production and practicing economy, to conduct labor competitions, to increase labor productivity, to reduce production costs, and to improve the quantity and quality [of the products]. All these are beneficial to both the public and private [sectors] and to both labor and capital.

Notes

1. See text July 9, 1953, particularly source note.

2. "Article 31 of the Common Program provides that 'The economy jointly operated by state and private capital is of a state-capitalist nature. Whenever necessary and possible, private capital shall be encouraged to develop in the direction of state-capitalism, in such ways as doing processing work for state-owned enterprises, jointly operating enterprises with the state, and running state enterprises in the form of concessions so as to exploit state-owned resources.'" (*Xuanji*, V, p. 100.) See text Sept. 21, 1949, note 3, and T. Chen (1967), p. 41.

3. This refers to the enlarged meeting of the Standing Committee of the CPPCC held in Beijing on Sept. 8-11, 1953.

4. The Chinese here is *wen bu qianjin*. At about this time, the term was sloganized. Later a play of words on the double entendre of the word *wen* would appear. See text Nov. 4, 1953, note 2.

5. See text Nov. 1951-Mar. 1952, note 10, and text July 9, 1953, source note and note 1.

6. See text Sept. 21, 1949, note 1, and text Oct. 1, 1949, note 3. These are the basic components of the CPPCC of which many in Mao's audience were members.

7. For the timing of the five-year plans, see text Feb. 10, 1953, note 2.

8. See text Aug. 12, 1953(1), note 22.

9. Here Mao was again referring to the system of "dividing the spoils among the four horses" *(si ma fen fei)* demonstrated in the chart above. Under this system, the first three categories would comprise approximately three-fourths of the total profits. See also text July 9, 1953, note 1.

Speech on the Victory
in Resist U.S. Aggression and Aid Korea Movement
(September 12, 1953)

Source: *Xuanji*, V, pp. 101-106. Available English Translation: *SW*, V, pp. 115-120.

This was Mao's speech at the Twenty-fourth Session of the Central People's Government Council. The full title of this speech in the Xuanji *source reads "Kang Mei yuan Chao de weida shengli he jin hou de renming" (The Great Victory in the Movement to Resist U. S. Aggression and Aid Korea, and Our Mission from This Point On).*

After three years, the [War] to Resist U.S. [Aggression] and Aid Korea has achieved a great victory, and it has already come to a halt.

On what basis has this victory in the War to Resist U.S. [Aggression] and Aid Korea been achieved? Just now, several gentlemen have said that it stems from the correctness of the leadership. Leadership, indeed, is one factor; without correct leadership, things would be done poorly. However, the major factor is that our war is a people's war; the entire people supported it, and the peoples of the two countries, China and Korea, have fought shoulder to shoulder [in it].

We fought against such a foe as U.S. imperialism, which had weapons many times more powerful than ours. Yet we were able to win and force them to make peace.[1] Why was it possible to achieve peace?

First, the U.S. aggressors were in an unfavorable situation militarily; [they were] on the receiving end in the fighting. Had they not made peace, their entire front would have been broken, and Seoul would have fallen into the hands of the Korean people. This situation had already begun to become evident in the summer of last year.

Both sides of the conflict have claimed that their front was impregnable, like a wall of bronze or iron.[2] On our side, we were indeed impregnable like a bronze or iron wall. Our soldiers and cadres were very clever, very brave, and were not afraid of death. On the other hand, the U.S. aggressor troops were afraid to die, and their officers were also rather rigid and not as flexible. Their front was not solid and was not an impregnable wall of bronze or iron.

The first question that came up on our side was whether or not we could fight, next was whether or not we could hold [our lines], and later whether or not we could guarantee supplies [to the front], and finally whether or not we could defeat germ warfare.[3] One after another these four questions were all solved. Our army grew stronger as it fought. This summer we were already able to break through enemy positions along a twenty-one kilometer front within one hour, we were able to concentrate a barrage of several hundred thousand rounds of artillery shells, and we were able to penetrate eighteen kilometers behind [the enemy's line]. Had this been kept up, after another two, or three, or four attacks, the enemy's entire line would have been broken.

Second, politically, the enemy had many unresolvable internal contradictions, and the people of the whole world demanded peace.

Third, economically, the enemy spent a fortune on its war of aggression against Korea, and its budget was not balanced.

These several reasons together forced the enemy to accept a peaceful settlement. The first of these reasons is the primary one; without this reason, it would have been difficult for us to negotiate a peace with them. The U.S. imperialists are very arrogant; wherever they can refuse to reason they will surely do so; and if they are in the least bit reasonable, it's because they are forced to be so and have no other choice.

In the Korean War, the enemy sustained 1.09 million casualties and deaths.[4] Naturally, we paid a price too.[5] But our casualty figures were much lower than anticipated, and after the tunnels were dug the casualties were even fewer.[6] The more we fought, the stronger we grew. The Americans were unable to budge us from our positions. On the contrary, they often were gobbled up by us.

Just now all of you mentioned the leadership factor, but I say that although leadership is a factor, the most important factor was that the masses thought of ways [to get things done]. Our cadres and soldiers thought of all sorts of ways to fight. Let me give you an example. In the first month of fighting, we lost many of our vehicles. What was to be done? Beyond having the leadership think of ways [to deal with this problem], the main thing was to rely on the masses to think of ways to deal with it. We posted more than ten thousand people along the sides of the roads, and whenever planes approached, they fired warning shots, so that when the drivers heard them they could dodge as they went along, or they could find places to conceal their vehicles. At the same time, we widened the roads and built many new roads so that the vehicles could go back and forth unhindered. As a result, the loss in motor vehicles was reduced from the original forty per cent to a few tenths of one percent. Later on, subterranean storage dumps were built and underground auditoriums were also constructed so that while the enemy was dropping bombs on top, we could hold meetings down below. Whenever some of us who lived in Beijing thought about the battlefield in Korea, we felt that it was very dangerous there. Of course there was danger, but as long as everybody was thinking of ways to do things, it wasn't such a big thing after all.

Our experience has been: by relying on the people and adding to that a relatively correct leadership, we could defeat the well-equipped enemy with our comparatively inferior equipment.

The victory in the War to Resist U.S. [Aggression] and Aid Korea is a great victory and is one of very great significance.

First, fighting together with the Korean people, we fought our way back to the 38th parallel and held firmly at that parallel.[7] This is very important. If we had not fought our way back to the 38th parallel and the front lines had remained at the Yalu River and the Tumen River,[8] then the people at places such as Shenyang, Anshan, and Fushun would not have been able to feel secure in carrying out production.[9]

Second, we gained some military experience. Each of the various arms of our Chinese Volunteers – the army, the air force, the navy, the infantry, the artillery corps, the engineers corps, the tank corps, the rail communications corps, the anti-aircraft defense units, the signal corps, as well as the medical corps, the logistics corps, etc. – have all gained experience in actually fighting with the U.S. aggressor troops. This time we've really felt out the U.S. armed forces. If you don't come into contact with the U.S. armed forces, you might be afraid of them. We fought with them for thirty-three months, and we've become thoroughly acquainted with them. U.S. imperialism is not such an awesome thing, it's just what it is and that's all. This is an experience that we have gained, and it is an invaluable experience.

Third, the political consciousness of the people of the entire country has been raised.

As a result of these three developments, a fourth was produced: a new invasion of China by the imperialists was delayed and a third world war was postponed.

The imperialist aggressors ought to realize that the Chinese people have now become organized and had better not be provoked. If the Chinese people are provoked, they will not be easy to deal with.

From now on, the enemy may yet fight again, and even if they do not fight, they will definitely make trouble in all sorts of ways such as sending secret agents to carry out sabotage. They have set up immense espionage organizations in such places as Taiwan, Hong Kong, and Japan. Yet, in the War to Resist U.S. [Aggression] and Aid Korea we have gained experience, so that as long as we can mobilize the masses and rely on the people we will be able to deal with them.

Our present situation is unlike that in the winter of 1950. Were the U.S. aggressors on the other side of the 38th parallel then? No, they were at the Yalu River and the Tumen River. Did we then have any experience in fighting against the U.S. aggressors? No. Were we familiar with the U.S. troops? No. But now all these situations have changed. If the U.S. imperialists refuse to postpone their new aggressive war and say that they want to fight, we'll make use of the first three [new] situations to deal with them. If they say that they will not fight any more, then for us the fourth situation would have developed. This also proves the superiority of our people's democratic dictatorship.

Are we invading any other peoples' [countries]? We are not invading any place at all. However, if others invade us we most definitely will fight and fight to the finish.

The Chinese people have this [attitude]: we approve of peace, but we're not afraid of war either. We can do either. We have the support of the people. In the War to Resist U.S. [Aggression] and Aid Korea the people enlisted in the army enthusiastically. We had to be very strict in selection; only one out of every one hundred people who volunteered was selected. Some people said that it was even stricter than selecting a son-in-law. If the U.S. imperialists want to fight some more, we'll continue to fight with them.

Fighting a war takes money. Nevertheless, the money spent on the War to Resist U.S. [Aggression] and Aid Korea was not that much. We fought for these several years, and what we spent on it was less than a year's [revenue from] commercial and industrial taxes. Naturally, it would have been better if we hadn't had to fight this war and hadn't had to spend this money, because now we need money in the area of construction, and the peasants still have some difficulties in their livelihood. The agricultural taxes levied last year and the year before that were slightly heavy, so some friends of ours complained. They demanded "a benevolent policy" as if they represented the peasants' interests.[10] Do we or do we not agree with such opinions? We do not. At the time, we had to exert all our efforts to achieve a victory in [the War to] Resist U.S. [Aggression] and Aid Korea. From the perspective of the peasants, and from the perspective of people throughout the entire country, is it more beneficial to them for life to be temporarily a little difficult and to win a victory, or is it more beneficial for them not to resist U.S. [aggression] and aid Korea, and not spend these few dollars? Naturally it is more beneficial to them to win a victory in the [War to] Resist U.S. [Aggression] and Aid Korea. The reason for our collecting a slightly larger amount of agricultural tax last year and the year before that was precisely that we needed money for [the War to] Resist U.S. [Aggression] and Aid Korea. This year things are different; the agricultural tax has not been increased; we have stabilized the tax rate.

Talking about having "benevolent policies,"[11] we are for benevolent policies. However, what was the most benevolent [policy]? It was resisting U.S. [aggression] and aiding Korea. In order to implement this benevolent policy we had to make sacrifices, to spend money, to collect some more agricultural taxes. [Because] we collected a bit more agricultural tax some people started to squeal. They even said that they represented the peasants' interests. I do not approve of such opinions.

To resist U.S. [aggression] and aid Korea was a benevolent policy; at this moment, it is also a benevolent policy to develop industrial construction.

There are two types of so-called "benevolent policies": one serves the immediate interests of the people; another serves the long-term interests of the people, such as resisting U.S. [aggression] and aiding Korea and constructing heavy industry. The first type is a policy of lesser benevolence and the second a policy of greater benevolence. Both must be considered; to ignore either is wrong. In that case, where should the emphasis be placed? The emphasis should be placed on the policy of greater benevolence. At this moment, in implementing benevolent policies our emphasis ought to be placed on the development of heavy industry. Construction takes funds. Therefore, although the people's livelihood must be improved, it cannot be improved by very much at one time. This is to say that the people's livelihood cannot remain unimproved but it cannot be improved too much either; it cannot remain uncared for but also cannot be overly cared for either. To take care of policies of lesser benevolence and [thereby] hinder the [implementation of] the policies of greater benevolence is a deviation in implementing benevolent policies.

Some friends of ours are now putting one-sided emphasis on policies of lesser benevolence; in fact they wanted us to quit the War to Resist U.S. [Aggression] and Aid Korea, and [now they want us] to stop the construction of heavy industry. We must criticize this type of incorrect thought. This type of thought exists even within the Communist Party, and we had already come across this in Yanan. In 1941, we collected two hundred thousand *shi* of public grain in the Shaan-Gan-Ning Border Region, and some people squealed and clamored, saying that the Communists were not considerate toward the peasants. Some individuals among the leading cadres of the Communist Party also raised the so-called issue of implementing benevolent policies. I criticized this type of thought at that time.[12] What was the policy of greatest benevolence at that time? It was to defeat Japanese imperialism. Had we reduced the collection of public grain, we would have had to reduce the size of the Eighth Route Army and the New Fourth Army, and that would have benefited Japanese imperialism.[13] Consequently, this sort of opinion actually represented the interests of Japanese imperialism and was helpful to it.

Now the [War] to Resist U.S. [Aggression] and Aid Korea has come to a halt; if the United States still wants to fight, we will continue to fight. To fight, we will have to collect grain and work among the peasants to persuade them to give something [to the cause]. This alone is a true representation of the interests of the peasants. To squeal and shout is in fact to represent [the interests of] U.S. imperialism.

There are major principles and there are minor principles.[14] The standard of living of the people of the entire country ought to be raised a notch each year, but not by too much. If it had been raised by too much, the War to Resist U.S. [Aggression] and Aid Korea could not have been fought, or could not have been fought with such seriousness. We fought thoroughly, earnestly, and with all our strength. So long as we had it, we would supply the front in Korea with whatever it needed. This is what we have done for the past several years.

Notes

1. See text June 30, 1953, note 2.
2. The Chinese here, *tong chang tie bi*, is an aphorism derived from *hui* 5 of the mid-Qing

novel *Er nü yingxiong zhuan* (Romance of the Young Heroes and Heroines).

3. See text Dec. 8, 1952, note 1.

4. According to Chinese estimates, the total casualties of the UN forces in the Korean War broke down as follows: U.S. troops, 397,000; South Korean troops, 667,000; others, 20,000.

5. According to Chinese estimates, about 900,000 Chinese and North Koreans were wounded, died, or were displaced. Out of these there were 180,000 dead.

6. This refers to trenches that were dug along the 38th parallel after the two sides came to a stalemate along that line in May 1951.

7. The division of the Korean peninsula at the 38th parallel had been suggested as early as the Russo-Japanese War of 1904. Following the surrender of the Japanese in August 1945, the Soviet Union occupied the northern half of the peninsula, as far as the vicinity of the 38th parallel, while American troops occupied the south. When the armistice ending the war was finally signed in July 1953, the line of division agreed upon lay just north of the 38th parallel.

8. The Yalu River and the Tumen River run westward and eastward respectively, dividing China's Jilin Province from Korea and thus serving as the boundary for the two countries.

9. All three cities are in the east-central part of Liaoning Province, all within a radius of approximately 220 km from the Korean border. Shenyang (known as Fengtian before Liberation) is China's no. 1 industrial and commerical city in the Northeastern provinces; Anshan is the steel capital of the region and Fushun the main coal producing city. For more on Anshan, see text Dec. 14, 1952, source note.

10. This is a reference to the criticism by Liang Shuming, a leader of the Democratic League, of the CPC's policies toward the peasants. See text Sept. 16-18, 1953.

11. Mao's discussion of "benevolent policies" is significant here both for its grim humor and for its theoretical importance. "Benevolent policy" is *ren zheng* in Chinese, and it is a classical Confucian term derived from the teachings of Mencius, who believed that the ethical onus on the ruler was to govern benevolently. This was the term that Liang Shuming (cited in note 10) used to criticize the CPC, asking that it carry out benevolent policies instead of revolutionary policies that disrupted people's lives. Liang is representative of the Confucianist viewpoint in politics, particularly in relating the size of taxation on the agricultural sector of society to the nature of government. (In fact, Liang has been described by one American scholar, Guy Alitto, as "The Last Confucian." See G. Alitto [1979], and text Sept. 16-18, 1953, note 1.) Mao's rebuttal here clearly contains his overall criticism of Confucianism. In a manner fraught with subtle significance, it parallels synoptically the critical views of many philosophers of the legalist school of thought in Mencius' time and in the century that followed, in particular the opinions of Han Fei, the chief Legalist philosopher of the late Warring States period (i.e. the early third century B.C.) who specifically argued against the "benevolent government" thesis of the Confucianists, claiming that in reality a "benevolent government" stemming from sentiment was a "brutal government" *(bao zheng)*. See, for example, Han Fei's article "Ba shuo" (Eight Persuasions), translated in B. Watson (1964), p. 125ff. Thus Mao's criticism here can be seen as part and parcel of the reasoning that lined up Chinese Communist social scientists and philosophers on the side of legalism in the great Legalist-Confucianist debate in Chinese scholastic circles in the 1950s.

12. See text Aug. 12, 1953, note 33, and text Oct. 26, 1949, note 1. See also text Feb. 27, 1950, note 1. In October 1940, at the height of the Japanese attack on China, the KMT forces amassed over 200,000 troops, under Hu Zongnan, to "contain" the Communist forces in this region. The CPC therefore immediately felt the economic as well as military pinch, and in response, launched a major campaign to increase production in the area. It resulted in rather heavy grain taxation to keep the base area operations alive. For details of this episode, see Mao's article, "Economic and Financial Problems in the Anti-Japanese War," *SW*, III, pp. 111-116.

13. The main force of the Red Army, which reached northern Shaanxi after the Long March (1934-1935), was reorganized into the Eighth Route Army in 1937, when the CPC and KMT negotiated a second united front to fight Japan. It was under the general command of Zhu De and Peng Dehuai, with three divisions commanded respectively by Lin Biao-Nie Rongzhen, He Long-Guan Xiangying, and Liu Bocheng-Deng Xiaoping. The Red Army guerrillas who had stayed along the Yangtze valley were likewise reorganized into the New Fourth Army of the

National Revolutionary Army, with Ye Ting and Xiang Ying in command. (Later Chen Yi and Liu Shaoqi.) At the end of the Second World War and with renewed civil war impending, these two armies were merged with others into the People's Liberation Army.

14. In Chinese usage, the term *da daoli*, which we have translated as "major principle," has the connotation of "fundamental, moral truth." Mao was playing a bit on the meaning of the words here.

Telegram to the Chinese People's Volunteers
(September 12, 1953)

Source: *Ziliao xuanbian*, pp. 154-155. Other Chinese Text: *Wansui* (n.d.), pp. 6-7.

This, according to the source, was a telegram drafted by Mao on behalf of the Central People's Government Council. Many of these points were covered in Mao's speech to the twenty-fourth session of that Council on the same day. See text Sept. 12, 1953(1).

The Twenty-fourth session of the Central People's Government Council heard the report made by XXX, XXX, on the work of the Chinese People's Volunteers in Resisting the U.S. and Aiding Korea.[1] It expresses its complete satisfaction at the glorious achievements that the Chinese People's Volunteers have attained in coordinating with the Korean People's Army in resisting aggression and defending the peace, and at the fact that they have, on this basis, persisted in their striving for negotiations for an armistice for the peaceful resolution of the Korean problem, and its glorious victory in having attained the truce in Korea. The Central People's Government thanks you for your nonpareil contribution in this war for justice and expresses to you its warm and enthusiastic felicitations and greetings.

On October 25, 1950, just when the U.S. aggressive forces invaded the Democratic People's Republic of Korea in full force, and threatened our own northeastern frontiers at the Yalu and Tumen rivers,[2] severely menacing our country's security, the Chinese People's Volunteers heroically moved toward Korea to back up the Korean People's Army in resisting the encroachment of the U.S. imperialists. In the ensuing two years and nine months, the Chinese People's Volunteers, acting in accordance with the will of the people of their homeland, stood shoulder to shoulder with the Korean People's Army and, with the full support of the Chinese and Korean peoples and the enthusiastic sympathy and support of the various countries in the democratic camp headed by the great Soviet Union and that of all peace-loving people around the world, fought unyieldingly, persisted in the efforts to attain negotiations, and finally repelled the enemy's frenetic aggression, exposing his true brutal and warlike face, inflicting on the enemy severe defeats on the military, political and moral fronts, thus forcing it to accept an armistice.[3] The achievements of the Chinese People's Volunteers and the Korean People's Army in standing and fighting together stand as shining examples of the internationalism and patriotism of the Chinese and Korean peoples, and demonstrate the firm solidarity and invincible strength of our camp for peace and democracy. They have won the respect and praises of all the progressive people of the world.

The victory represented by the Korean Armistice has totally shattered the maniacal plans of U.S. imperialism for swallowing all of Korea and invading our country's northeastern region, and protects the peace and security of China, Korea, and the Far East [as a whole]. It has put down and defeated the invader's fierce flames [of aggression] and has greatly fanned the spirit of courage and faith among the peace-loving people of the world to strive for lasting peace and against aggressive war. The Chinese people, together with the heroic Korean people and their army, have, with the example of their victory, shown the people of the world a truth: that the aggressive war conspiracy of the imperialists must and can be defeated, and as long as all peace-loving people unite as one to oppose the intervention [of their own countries] in the domestic affairs of other countries, to oppose wars of aggression, and to insist on resolving matters of international dispute by means of peaceful negotiations, peace is guaranteed.

The victory of the Korean Armistice is a triumph for the movement among the peoples of the world for the peaceful resolution of all international disputes. However, the signing of the Korean Armistice Agreement is but the first step toward the peaceful resolution of the Korean problem. The peaceful resolution of this problem with the withdrawal of all foreign troops from Korea and under the spirit of having the Korean people handle their own affairs is something that is left to the discussions and settlement of a higher level political assemblage [in the future.] The Chinese people have always advocated resolving international disputes by means of peaceful discussion, and they are willing to stand firm as a powerful back-up force for the peaceful resolution of international issues.

In view of the fact that the bellicose elements in the United States and the Syngman Rhee faction in Southern Korea[4] are still in the midst of carrying out all sorts of plots and conspiracies to forestall or sabotage [the convening of] a political assembly and further undermine the armistice, all our comrades [in] the Chinese People's Volunteers must double their vigilance and continue to strive to raise their military and political standards. They must reinforce their own combat strength, further strengthen and develop the friendship between the Chinese people and the Korean people, and hold even more fast to their battle positions together with the Korean People's Army so as to prevent any acts of aggression or provocation by the enemy.

The Chinese people themselves shall carry out economic construction with all their might, strengthen their national defense forces, and continue to develop in a more indepth manner the movement to Resist U.S. Aggression and Aid Korea, so as to back up the Chinese People's Volunteers and the Korean People's Army. The government and people of the People's Republic of China will do all they can to help the heroic Korean people heal the wounds of war and restore a life of peace.

We are convinced that with the encouragement and support of all the people of the homeland all our comrades in the Chinese People's Volunteers will live up to the hopes and expectations of the people of the homeland and continue to strive to ensure the thorough implementation of the Korean Armistice Agreement, for the peaceful resolution of the Korean people, and for the defense of peace in the Far East and throughout the world!

Long live the memory of the martyrs who gave their lives in the War to Resist U.S. Aggression and Aid Korea!

Long live the impregnable and eternal friendship between the people of China and Korea!

Notes

1. One of the XXX's here refers to Peng Dehuai, who was until about the time of this speech commander of the Chinese People's Volunteers in the Korean War (he was replaced by Deng Hua in September 1953 and became Minister of Defense of the PRC). Peng's speech is reprinted in *RMSC* (1955), pp. 310-316. For more biographical information on Peng, see text Aug. 15, 1959(2), note 3. The other XXX cannot be definitively identified, but we think that most likely it was Zhou Enlai, who was premier of the Government Administration Council.

2. See text Sept. 12 1953(1), note 8.

3. See text Jun. 30, 1953, note 1.

4. Syngman Rhee (1875-1965) was president of the Republic of Korea from its establishment in 1948 until forced to resign on May 3, 1960, by demonstrations against election fraud in his administration.

Telegram to the USSR
(September 15, 1953)

Source: *RMRB* (Sept. 16, 1953), 1. Other Chinese Text: *XHYB*, 10 (Oct. 28, 1953), 7. Available English Translations: NCNA, *Daily Bulletin*, 880 (Sept. 15, 1953), 1; FBIS, *Daily Report* (Sept. 16, 1953), AAA1; *CDSP*, V:38 (Oct. 31, 1953), 17f (excerpt).

Chairman,
The Council of Ministers,
The Union of Soviet Socialist Republics

Comrade Malenkov:

At a session on September 15, 1953, the Central People's Government Council of the People's Republic of China heard with satisfaction the report made by Comrade Li Fuchun, representative of the Delegation of the Government of the People's Republic of China, regarding its negotiations with the government of the Soviet Union over the issue of the Soviet government's aid to China's economic construction. The Central People's Government Council unanimously feels that since the great Soviet government has agreed to systematically lend economic and technical aid to China in the construction and renovation of its ninety-one new enterprises and in the fifty enterprises now under construction and renovation, the Chinese people will, with their efforts to learn from the advanced experience and latest technical achievements of the Soviet Union, be able to gradually build up their own powerful heavy industry. This plays an extremely significant role in China's industrialization in its gradual transition to socialism, and in the strengthening of the camp of peace and democracy headed by the Soviet Union.

In a single negotiation session, the two countries reached a solution on the issue of the construction of ninety-one enterprises and solved the problem of long-term aid. This is an unprecedented event in history, fully manifesting the truth of the statement made by the great Stalin: "The experience of this cooperation shows that not a single capitalist country could have rendered such genuine and technically refined and advanced assistance to the People's Democracies[1] as the Soviet Union is rendering them. The point is not only that this assistance is [rendered at] the cheapest rate possible but is technically first-rate. What is of primary importance is that at the base of this cooperation there lies a sincere desire to help one another and to seek common economic progress."

In the course of negotiations, the Soviet government, based on the more than thirty years of rich experience in its great socialist construction, has offered to us various proposals, either in principle or in concrete terms, with regard to the tasks set out in China's five-year plan.[2] These proposals will help us avoid as many mistakes and detours as possible in the course of China's economic construction.

On behalf of the Chinese government and the Chinese people, I extend my heartfelt gratitude to the government and people of the Soviet Union for this great, comprehensive, long-term, and unselfish aid. The Chinese government and people are willing to devote their unflagging efforts to strengthening the economic cooperation and friendly alliance between the Soviet Union and China so as to facilitate our common struggle for the cause of world peace.

(Signed as Chairman of CPG of PRC, dated, in Beijing)

Notes

1. See text Sept. 21, 1949, note 4.
2. See text Feb. 10, 1953, note 2.

Criticize the Reactionary Thought of Liang Shuming
(September 16-18, 1953)

Source: *Xuanji*, V, pp. 107-115. Available English Translation: *SW*, V, pp. 121-129.

These are excerpts from Mao's remarks at the Twenty-seventh Session of the Central People's Government Council, held in Beijing, September 16-18, 1953. This session, convened to discuss the "General Line on the Transition to Socialism," was attended by members of the National Committee of the CPPCC, a conference of which was convened in Beijing on September 8-11 (see text Sept. 7, 1953, note 3). Earlier in the session, Liang Shuming had leveled harsh criticism at the CPC's program for industrialization, particularly its policy toward the peasants. At that time Mao is reported to have responded with a sharp outburst of criticism. The initial criticism of Liang is said to have been mitigated by the intercession of Chen Mingshu (see text Jun. 12, 1950, source note), who argued that Liang's criticism was a problem of thought (sixiang wenti) and not a problem of politics (zhengzhi wenti). See Zhou Jingwen (1962), pp. 434-437. Zhou mistakenly identifies this meeting as an enlarged meeting of the National Committee of the CPPCC. These latter comments of Mao then, are an attempt by Mao to place his criticisms of Liang in the larger context of his view of Liang's politics. For Mao's other criticism of Liang's position made just prior to this meeting see text Sept. 12, 1953(1).

1. Is Mr. Liang Shuming a "man of integrity"?[1] What role did he play during the peace negotiations?[2]

Mr. Liang is a self-styled "man of integrity." Reactionary newspapers in Hong Kong also say that you, Mr. Liang, are "the man with the most integrity" on the mainland, and Taiwan broadcasts applaud you as well.[3] Do you really have "integrity"? If you are a man of "integrity," well then, you should be able to give everyone an account of your history, of how in the past you opposed Communism, how you opposed the people, how you used the pen to kill, and what your relations with Han Fuju, Zhang Dongsun, Chen Lifu, and Zhang Qun were.[4] What do you have to say? They are all your intimate friends. I for one don't have that many friends. They're so pleased with you; they brand me a "bandit," but they call you "sir." I simply question what Party or group you belong to. I am not the only one who has doubts; many others have doubts as well.

From the talk just delivered by Premier Zhou everyone can see that at the crucial junctures in our two peace negotiations with the Kuomintang, Mr. Liang's position was entirely supportive of Chiang Kai-shek. Chiang Kai-shek's consenting to peace negotiations was not genuine. Among those present today there are some who came to Beijing [at that time] as delegates to the peace negotiations. They all know whether Chiang Kai-shek's "peace" was genuine or false.[5]

To put it plainly, Chiang Kai-shek uses the gun to kill; Liang Shuming uses the pen to kill. There are two ways of killing people; one way is to use the gun, and one way is to use the pen. Those who disguise themselves most cleverly and kill people without shedding blood are those who use the pen to kill. You, Mr. Liang, are a murderer of this kind.

Liang Shuming is thoroughly reactionary, but he won't admit it. He paints an extremely beautiful [picture] of himself. He isn't the same as Mr. Fu Zuoyi.[6] Mr. Fu publicly admitted that he was thoroughly reactionary, but in the peaceful liberation of Beijing, Mr. Fu did something meritorious for the people. Where are your contributions, Liang Shuming? In your entire life, what have you done for the people? Not even the slightest thing. Nevertheless, you depict yourself as the most beautiful person on earth, more beautiful than Xi Shi, more beautiful than Wan Zhaojun, and even surpassing Yang the Imperial Concubine.[7]

2. In the so-called "nine levels of heaven and nine levels of hell" proposed by Liang Shuming, [he claimed that] "the workers have a place above the ninth level of heaven, and the peasants have a place below the ninth level of 'hell."[8] "The workers can depend on the trade unions, but [the peasants] can't depend on the peasant associations; [they] can't depend on the Party, the [Youth] League, or the women's associations either.[9] In terms of quality and quantity, [these organizations] are inferior and less helpful than even the industrial and commercial associations; thus the peasants have no confidence in them." Is this [kind of talk] "approval of the general line"?[10] No! This is completely and thoroughly reactionary thought. This is a reactionary proposition, not a reasonable proposition. Can the people's government adopt this kind of proposition? I don't believe it can.

3. Mr. Liang "demands to know more about the contents of certain plans." I don't approve of this either. On the contrary, people like Mr. Liang should be allowed to know less classified information; the less the better.

This guy Liang Shuming cannot be trusted. We can let others know a little more classified information, but we cannot let [him] know. When the democratic parties meet in small groups, there's no need for you, Liang Shuming, to participate.

4. Mr. Liang also demands that we don't put him in the category of nonprogressive people. On the contrary, [he says] he belongs to the progressives. How should we deal with this? I think we should be cautious; we can't con-

sent to this carelessly. If we do we'll be taken in.

5. Mr. Liang paints a beautiful portrait of himself. Even several decades ago, he had already had great dreams of a plan to reconstruct the country. According to his own account, they were *quite similar* to New Democracy and socialism.[11]

Is he indeed that beautiful? I don't think so. I have been on fairly close terms with him. There isn't a single time when I met with him that I didn't criticize his mistaken ideas.[12] I once told him to his face that I never believed in those things [he] said, such as that "China has no classes," "China's problem is one of cultural imbalance," [China should have a] "untinted, transparent" government,[13] and "the Chinese revolution had only external causes, not internal causes." This time we have heard again his esteemed views about the "nine heavens and nine hells," that "the Communist Party has lost the peasants," that "the Communist Party is not as dependable as the industrial and commercial associations," and so on. Can all these make us trust him? No. I told him that China's special characteristic was that it was semicolonial and semifeudal and that if you didn't recognize this, you would be helping imperialism and feudalism. Therefore, nobody believes what you say; the people all trust the Communist Party, no one reads your books, and no one listens to your talk except the reactionary elements or some muddleheaded people. Also, he doesn't seem to be against Chiang Kai-shek. Whether or not Mr. Liang has publicly expressed opposition to Chiang Kai-shek and his reactionary Kuomintang is something everyone should look into. I haven't read all his articles or heard all his speeches.

Is such a person qualified to ask the people's state to allow him to be in on even more of its plans and classified information? As I see it, he doesn't have such qualifications. Should we consent to this request of his? I don't think we should.

6. Mr. Liang has made another request. He wants us to include him in the category of the progressives or the revolutionaries, and he doesn't want to be placed in the nonprogressive or reactionary category. This is a matter of drawing "[class] distinctions." How should it be handled? In view of the circumstances we have discussed before, can we include him in the progressive or revolutionary category? In what ways is he progressive? When did he ever participate in the revolution? Thus, this request should not be consented to too lightly; we should wait and see.

7. For several years I have been receiving letters from a number of the people and have heard a number of discussions that raised the question: Why does the Communist Party cooperate with reactionaries? The reactionary elements to whom they refer are those people who are never willing to express, in newspapers or in public, opposition to imperialism, feudalism, or Chiang Kai-shek and his reactionary Kuomintang. They don't have even the minimal standpoint [required] of a person who works for the state. Because these people are especially unwilling to oppose Chiang Kai-shek, Taiwan broadcasts and Hong Kong newspapers express their special appreciation for them. They

never berate them! Instead, they describe them as the "people with the most integrity" on the mainland, and Liang is one of them. But they do, however, insult and berate without restraint some of [our] friends. Those who are not berated or who are praised and hailed by Taiwan are, of course, *few in number, but they do very much warrant [our] attention.*

There are some people who to this very day can express opposition only to imperialism, but would rather die than say anything against Chiang Kai-shek. In newspapers or in public discussions they don't dare mention the past; they are still somewhat nostalgic about the past. I think there are quite a few people of this kind.

There are three kinds of patriotism: one is true patriotism, one is false patriotism, and still another is half-true, half-false, a wavering patriotism. Everyone is aware [of where he or she stands]; Liang Shuming, too, knows where he stands. We'll welcome those who truly have severed relations with the imperialists and with those [people] in Taiwan, no matter how backward they might be. This type is truly patriotic. The false patriots will put on a disguise on the exterior, but underneath it's another matter. Still another kind of patriots are the wavering ones, the half-true and half-false [ones] who size up the situation and act accordingly. If World War III doesn't break out and Chiang Kai-shek does not return, then they will follow the Communist Party. If World War III should break out they will make other plans. What type [of patriots] are the majority of people? The majority are true patriots. In the past several years the number of true patriots has been increasing. The half-true, half-false patriots make up only a small part. The false patriots are very few, but they do exist. Whether this analysis is appropriate is something we can all investigate.

8. I believe Liang Shuming should perform one task. This task is not to "represent the peasants" and present the People's Government with an "appeal for liberation," but rather to give a clear account of the process of the historical development of his antipeople reactionary thought. Only after he has clearly and convincingly explained this process of change and has made people believe him – how in the past he represented the landlords and was anti-Communist and antipeople and how he has now changed from a position of representing the landlords to one "representing the peasants" – only then can we establish conclusively what group he should be placed in. My impression is that he has never considered changing his reactionary standpoint.[14] But, in order to cure the illness and save the patient,[15] I propose that we should give him some time for self-examination and then turn the matter over to the Political Consultative Conference to handle. We will not reach a conclusion at this time.

9. "All people have a sense of shame."[16] If people don't know shame, affairs will be difficult to manage. Who can believe that Mr. Liang has a greater understanding of the problems of the peasants than the Communist Party? [This is like] wielding an ax in front of Lu Ban's door.[17] Suppose I say "Mao Zedong is a better actor than Mr. Mei Lanfang,[18] a better tunnel digger

than the Volunteers, or a better pilot than the air force hero Zhao Baotong.[19] Wouldn't that be the height of shamelessness? Thus the question raised by Mr. Liang is both serious and frivolous; it has quite a touch of the comical. He says he can represent the peasants better than the Communist Party – isn't that comical?

Many "representatives of the peasants" have emerged. Whom do they really represent? Do they represent the peasants? It does not look that way to me, and the peasants don't see it that way either. They are representing the landlord class and helping the landlord class. Among them, the most outstanding, and the one who uses the most honeyed phrases while actually aiding the enemy, is Liang Shuming. Among the rest there are some people whose thinking is muddled, who have said some stupid things but who are still patriots; their hearts are still for China. These belong to one category; Liang Shuming is in another category. There are others who are about the same as Liang Shuming; they pose as "representatives of the peasants." Masquerading has always existed; now we have run into it. They have their "fox tails," and people can detect their true identity.[20] The Monkey King could transform himself into seventy-two different things,[21] but he had one difficulty; he couldn't easily disguise his tail. When he changed himself into a temple, he had to disguise his tail as a flagpole; finally Yang Erlang saw through the disguise. How did he see through it? He saw through it because the tail gave it away. There actually are such people. No matter how they disguise themselves, they can't hide their tails.

Liang Shuming is an ambitious person; he's a hypocrite. It is not true that he doesn't want to get involved in politics, and it is also not true that he does not seek official posts.[22] He promoted so-called "rural reconstruction." What kind of "rural reconstruction" did he have? It was a landlord's reconstruction. It was rural destruction and national perdition!

10. It is impossible to deal with this person in earnest. With him, we will never be able to have a fruitful discussion. He has no [sense of] logic, he can only speak nonsense. Because of this I propose turning the matter over to the biweekly forums of the People's Political Consultative Conference for discussion; at the same time, I also want to caution all of you to remember that there is no hope at all that we can truly resolve this problem. It's absolutely impossible. The result is still bound to be "discussion without resolution, resolution without action, and adjournment without reaching a conclusion." In spite of this, I still encourage you to hold the biweekly meetings and to give the matter a try. This will be better than "sending a couple of people" to listen to him preach.

11. Are we going to take this opportunity to break off relations with him and from this point on not have contact with him? That's not going to be the case either. If he himself is willing to have relations with us, we are still prepared to have relations with him. At the second People's Political Consultative Conference, I still hope he will be elected a member of the [national] committee. The reason is this: Because there are still some people

who are willing to be deceived by him and who don't understand him, he can still serve as live teaching material; as such, he is still qualified to be elected a member of the committee unless he himself is no longer interested in using the rostrum of the Political Consultative Conference to disseminate his reactionary ideas.

I have said that Liang Shuming hasn't done anything meritorious and that he has no good points. Would you say that he has the good point of providing products or paying taxes in the way that the industrial and commercial circles have? He doesn't. Does he have the good point of developing production and making the economy flourish? He doesn't. At what moment did he ever rise up in arms [on the side of the revolution]? At what moment did he ever oppose Chiang Kai-shek and oppose the imperialists? He never did. When did he cooperate with the Chinese Communists to overthrow imperialism and feudalism? He didn't.[23] Therefore, he has made no contributions. This person would not even give his approval to such a great struggle as the [War to] Resist America and to Aid Korea. He only shook his head [in disapproval].[24] Why then is it feasible for him to be a member of the National Committee of the Political Consultative Conference? Why did the Chinese Communist Party nominate him for this position? It was because he was still capable of deceiving some people that he could still perform this deceptive function. He relied on this qualification of deceiving people. All he has is this qualification of being able to deceive people.

As Liang Shuming sees it, we would be "magnaminous" if we nodded and acknowledged that he is correct. If we do not admit that he is correct we would be lacking in "magnanimity." That kind of "magnanimity" we probably do not have. But we do have a little of [our kind of] magnanimity. You, Liang Shuming, can continue to be a committee member of the Political Consultative Conference.

12. Confucius' failings, I believe, were that he was not democratic and that he lacked a spirit of self-criticism; he was a bit like Mr. Liang. [In his written statements such as] "Ever since I have had Zi Lu [as my disciple] I have never heard a hostile word," "Three times [the school] was full, and three times [the school] was deserted," and "In three months, Shaozheng Mao was executed." There is a good bit of the work-style of the bully in Confucius, and there is something of a fascistic flavor.[25] I wish that my friends, especially Mr. Liang, would not follow the ways of Confucius. I'll be most gratified if you don't.

13. If the program that has been held so highly by Mr. Liang were followed, China would not only be unable to build socialism, but the parties (the Communist Party as well as others) and the nation would also be destroyed.[26] His line is the line of the bourgeoisie. Bo Yibo's error is a reflection of bourgeois thought within the Party, [but] even Bo Yibo is better than Liang Shuming.[27]

Liang Shuming says the workers are "placed higher than the ninth level of heaven," and the peasants are "placed lower that the ninth level of hell." How are things really? Indeed, there are differences: the income of the worker is a little more than the peasant's, but since the land reform, the peasants have their land and their houses, and their lives are getting better every day.[28] There are some peasants whose livelihood is better than the workers'. There are some workers whose lives are still difficult. What method should be used to allow the peasants to receive a little more? Do you, Liang Shuming, have a solution? Your idea is that "the problem lies not in scarcity but in inequality."[29] If your ideas were put into practice, we would not be depending on the peasant's own labor and production to increase their income, but rather would be equalizing the workers' wages and the peasants' income by taking a portion [from the workers] and giving it to the peasants. Wouldn't this destroy China's industry? Doing this would destroy the country and the parties. You should not suppose that this destruction of the parties means merely destruction of the Communist Party; it means the democratic parties as well.

You said that the workers are "higher than the ninth level of heaven." If that is the case, at what level of heaven are you, Liang Shuming? You are higher than the tenth, higher than the eleventh, higher than the twelfth or thirteenth [level] because your salary is much higher than the workers' wages! You haven't suggested lowering your salary as a start, but rather that we should start by lowering the workers' wages. I think this is unjust. If we want to talk about justice, we should start by lowering your salary because you are not just "higher than the ninth level of heaven"!

Our Party has been involved in the worker-peasant alliance for over thirty years. Marxism-Leninism is all about the worker-peasant alliance and worker-peasant cooperation. There are two kinds of alliance in China today: one is that between the working class and the peasant; and the other is the alliance between the working class [on the one hand] and the capitalists, university professors, higher level technical personnel, generals who rose up in arms [against the KMT], religious leaders, and democratic parties and democratic personages without party affiliations [on the other]. Both of these alliances are necessary, and they must be continued. Which of these alliances is the fundamental one, the most important? The alliance between the working class and the peasant class is the fundamental one, the most important one. Liang Shuming says that the worker-peasant alliance has been destroyed and that national reconstruction has become hopeless. What he means by this is that if we don't adopt Liang Shuming's ideas there is no hope of carrying out the worker-peasant alliance and achieving national reconstruction, and that there will be no hope for socialism. The kind of "worker-peasant alliance" that Liang Shuming talks about is truly hopeless. Your line is the bourgeois line. To have yours put into practice would result in national destruction; China would revert to the erstwhile semicolonial, semifeudal rut, and in Beijing meetings would be held to welcome Chiang Kai-shek and Eisenhower. I repeat once again, we absolutely will not adopt your line!

Liang Shuming says that since we entered the cities we have "forgotten" the countryside, and the countryside has become "deserted." This is sowing seeds of discord. During the past three years, our major effort has been in the rural sector. Only this year have we begun to shift a large group of important cadres to urban work: even so, the majority of cadres are still engaged in work at the *xian*, district, and *xiang* levels. How can you say that we have forgotten the countryside?[30]

Liang Shuming has also charged that our rural work is "backward" and that our lower-level cadres are "lawbreakers and discipline violators." At present, in the rural areas there are indeed so-called backward *xiang*. How many are there? Only ten per cent. Why are they backward? It is mainly because the reactionaries – [former KMT] military police and secret agents, secret society bosses, local hooligans and ruffians, landlords, and rich peasants – have infiltrated the ranks of our cadres and taken over political power in the rural areas.[31] There are some who have even wormed their way into the Communist Party. These people constitute eighty to ninety per cent of the cadres who have seriously violated the law; the rest are cadres who have deteriorated. Therefore, in the backward *xiang*, the main thing is the problem of attacking counterrevolutionaries. It is also necessary to straighten out those cadres who have gone bad. In the entire country, how many of the *xiang* are good or relatively good? Ninety per cent. We must keep this situation in mind so we will not be taken in by Liang Shuming.

14. Is this a matter of resisting remonstrances and whitewashing our mistakes? If Mr. Liang's type of opinions can be called "remonstrances," then I declare: We are truly "resisting remonstrances." But we are not whitewashing our mistakes. We insist on the proletariat's right of leadership on all questions – ([concerning] the workers, peasants, industrialists, and business people, the various nationalities, the various democratic parties, the mass organizations, industry, agriculture, political matters, and military affairs – in short, everything). There must be unity and there must be struggle. If we talk about getting to the bottom of things, this is one thing on which we must get to the bottom, something which, at the bottom, is fundamental in nature. Can this be a trifling matter?

15. His question is of national scope, and it should be discussed by the entire Party and throughout the entire country as the Bo Yibo question was. [We must] grasp a typical case and [carry out] criticism and self-criticism. The general line should be discussed throughout the entire country.

There are two kinds of criticism; one is criticizing oneself, and the other is criticizing others. With regard to you, Liang Shuming, which kind of criticism should we adopt? Shall we criticize ourselves? No. We should be criticizing [you].

In criticizing Liang Shuming it is not a matter of criticizing just one individual, but of using this individual to expose the kind of reactionary thought he represents. Liang Shuming is a reactionary, but we will still put his problem in the category of thought reform.[32] Whether he can be reformed is another matter. It's quite possible that he can't be reformed. If he can't be reformed it is of no great consequence; he is just one person! Nevertheless, debating with him is useful; we shouldn't suppose that this is making a mountain out of a molehill or that it's not worth debating. Debating with him can clear up some problems. Our asking what good points he has is the one good point he does provide. What is the question we are now debating? Isn't it the question of the general line? Clearing up this question will be of benefit to all of us.

Notes

1. Liang Shuming (1894-1977) was a well-known traditionalist philosopher and educator. From 1927 to 1937, Liang was a leader of the rural reconstruction movement in China. Liang's program was based on the idea that China could be regenerated on a revived Confucian ethos. Rural reconstruction, in Liang's scheme, would have been centered on the village school, from which Confucian scholars would impart Confucian social ethics as well as promote mutual aid and cooperation. This effort would be led by a revitalized Confucian gentry devoid of the commercial values that he felt had contaminated the Chinese gentry in the twentieth century. Two of these projects were established, in Henan and in Shandong, during the 1920s and 1930s.

During the War of Resistance (1937-1945), Liang was active in "Third Force" politics in China. Between 1945 and 1946, Liang served as general secretary of the China Democratic League, a political party opposed to the domination of Chinese politics by either the KMT or the CPC. In 1950, after a brief retirement, Liang accepted nomination as a specially appointed member of the National Committee of the CPPCC. In 1951 Liang published the article "In What Ways Have I Changed Over the Last Two Years?" *(GMRB*, Oct. 5, 1951) and began to criticize the industrialization programs and agrarian policies of the CPC, which culminated in this confrontation with Mao in 1953. For an intellectual biography of Liang, see G. Alitto (1979), and for more biographical information on Liang, see H. Boorman et al., eds. (1968), II, pp. 357-359.

2. Mao is here alluding to the efforts that Liang, as leader of the Democratic League and representative of the so-called "Third Force in China," made in attempting to mediate the differences between the CPC and the KMT and to forestall civil war in China in 1945-46. In late 1945 and early 1946 the Democratic League played a major role in the Political Consultative Conference, which was convened with the original goal of working out a *modus vivendi* for Chinese politics in the postwar situation. It fell apart after three weeks of unsatisfactory negotiations (see text Sept 21, 1949, note 2). Until late 1945, Liang was a "go-between" who commanded some respect from the Communists. In February 1946, for instance, when the Marshall peace plan was undermined by Chiang Kai-shek's policy on Manchuria, Liang explained his own position in a personal letter to Mao, and in March he went to Yanan to talk with Mao. Communist confidence in Liang and in the viability of "Third Force" mediation eroded irreparably, however, when Chiang Kai-shek went on with his plans for military conquest at the same time that negotiations and mediation were taking place. When Fu Zuoyi, the KMT general, captured Kalgan on Oct. 11, 1946, and Chiang declared his plans to convene a KMT-dominated "National Assembly" on Nov. 12, hopes of averting a civil war were dashed. In the process, Liang, ever the indefatigable mediator, gained for himself, perhaps unjustifiedly, the unsavory image of one who simply stalled for time while the belligerency on Chiang Kai-shek's part grew each day. To the Communists he became a traitor, and on October 28, 1946, Zhou Enlai, the chief negotiator for the Communists, openly and stormily declared the break with Liang and the "Third Force."

3. See, for example, Hu Qiuyuan's article in *Xianggang shibao* (Hong Kong Times) (Feb. 15, 1952); Dong Shijin's letter in the same publication (Apr. 4, 1952); Hu Ying's article in *Jinri shijie* (Today's World), Hong Kong, (May 15, 1952); and *Far Eastern Economic Review*, 13:20 (Nov. 27, 1952), 679-681.

4. Han Fuju (1890-1938) was governor of Henan Province under the KMT from 1928 to 1930, and governor of Shandong Province from 1930 to 1938. While governor of these two provinces Han sponsored Liang Shuming's rural reconstruction projects. After the war against Japan broke

out, Han became the deputy commander of the Fifth Battle Zone, and commander-in-chief of the Third Army Group. He later surrendered Shandong to the Japanese and was sentenced to death by Chiang Kai-shek in 1938.

Zhang Dongsun (b. 1886) succeeded Liang as leader of the China Democratic League and the secretary of its Central Committee in 1946 and 1947. Zhang was a member of the League's delegation to the Political Consultative Conference that was convened in 1946 as a result of the Chongqing negotiations of the preceding year. In 1949, Zhang served on the preparatory committee of the new CPPCC and subsequently on the Central People's Government Council. In 1951, at the height of the Korean War, Zhang, along with three other members of the faculty of Yanjing University where he had served as chairman of the philosophy department, was criticized by the CPC. Shortly thereafter he was dismissed from both his government and academic positions.

Chen Lifu (b. 1900) was an important KMT leader. With his elder brother, Chen Guofu, he led the conservative and anti-Communist "CC" clique within the KMT. In 1928 Chen, who enjoyed the complete confidence of Chiang Kai-shek, was appointed director of the investigation division of the party's organization department. This powerful unit had as its purpose the rooting out of Communists or any who might be sympathetic to the Communist cause within the KMT. Chen later served as general secretary of the party and head of its organization department.

Zhang Qun (b. 1888) was foreign minister of the KMT government from 1935 until just after the Japanese invasion of China proper in 1937. During the war, Zhang served as governor of Sichuan Province. In the immediate postwar period Zhang was one of the principal KMT negotiators during the peace talks with the CPC. Subsequent to the Chongqing negotiations in 1945, Zhang represented the KMT on the Committee of Three (along with Zhou Enlai for the Communists, and General George Marshall for the U.S.), which had been set up to monitor the truce between the KMT and the CPC. From 1937 to 1948, Zhang held the position of president of the Executive *Yuan* (or premier) of the Nanjing government. For more biographical information on these four people, see H. Boorman et al., eds. (1967-1971), II, pp. 51-54; I, pp. 129-133; I, pp. 206-211; and I, pp. 47-52, respectively.

5. Mao refers here to peace negotiations in Chongqing in early 1946 and in Nanjing in late 1946 to avert renewed civil war and to efforts in Beijing in 1949 to end the civil war. In the first instance, as negotiations were breaking down over the issue of the convening of a National Constituent Assembly by the KMT, and as Chiang launched a new offensive against the Communist forces in Manchuria, Liang and a number of other Democratic League and "Third Force" delegates to the Political Consultative Conference of 1946 submitted a last ditch compromise proposal. This proposal called for the reorganization of the government to include all political parties, and for the reorganized government to convene the National Assembly. It also called for a ceasefire, for the stationing of Communist forces in three cities in Manchuria, and for the transfer of twenty *xian* along the China-Changchun Railroad in Manchuria to KMT control. These proposals were rejected with some vehemence by Zhou Enlai, who was then the chief Communist representative in Nanjing.

The second set of peace negotiations between the CPC and the KMT to which Mao refers took place in Beijing in April 1949. By that time the Communist forces were already victorious in North China and were preparing to cross the Yangtze River. Chiang Kai-shek had temporarily "retired" from the Nanjing government, leaving his vice-president, Li Zongren, to sue for peace. Li attempted to persuade Liang Shuming to mediate an end to the civil war but Liang refused, preferring to criticize both sides for continuing the conflict. Mao's reference to Chiang's lack of sincerity in these negotiations alludes to the fact that although he had retired as president, Chiang continued to exert control over the KMT through his position as its director general. Prior to their arrival in Beijing for the peace talks, the delegates dispatched by Li Zongren stopped in Fenghua, Zhejiang, to be briefed by Chiang. A number of Mao's commentaries on these talks are published in *SW*, IV, pp. 299-360.

6. Fu Zuoyi (1895-1974) was the chief KMT military commander in North China from 1947 to 1949. He was in command of the KMT garrison in Beijing in January 1949. On January 15-16, the CPC assault on Tianjin began, and after the fall of Tianjin, 250,000 Communist forces confronted the city of Beiping (Beijing) and its KMT defensive forces. Fu, as commander, negotiated

the surrender agreement under which the PLA took control of Beiping on February 3, 1949. For more biographical information on Fu, see H. Boorman et al., eds. (1968), II, pp. 47-51.

7. Xi Shi, Wang Zhaojun, and Yang Yuhuan were all famous beauties in Chinese history. In each case, their personal fates were tied to the fortunes of the state. Xi Shi, living in the Spring and Autumn period (ca. 722-481 B.C.), was sent by the vengeful King of Yue to the King of Wu with the mission of causing the latter to neglect his state duties. She was successful in this and the kingdom of Wu was ultimately defeated and eliminated by Yue. Wang Zhaojun was originally a junior concubine of Emperor Yuandi of the Han dynasty (reigning 48-33 B.C.), but was sent by the Han court circa 42 B.C. to wed and thereby pacify the chieftain of the Xiongnu, a nomadic tribe living on the northern frontier of China. Yang Yuhuan was a concubine of Emperor Xuanzong of the Tang dynasty (reigning 712-755 A.D.) and is more commonly known by her title Yang *guifei* (Yang The Imperial Concubine). Her beauty has sometimes been blamed for causing the Emperor Xuanzong to neglect affairs of state and for the ensuing An Lushan Rebellion (755-763 A.D.).

8. The phrase "nine levels of heaven and nine levels of hell" is taken from the book "Xingbian" of the *Sun Zi bingfa* (Sun Zi's Art of War), a fourth century B.C. military treatise written by Sun Zi. Liang Shuming borrows the term to describe the extremes of inequality in the living standards between workers and peasants.

9. By "the Party," Mao was naturally referring to the CPC. For the Youth League, or New Democratic Youth League, see text Feb. 18, 1951, note 8, and text June 30, 1953, source note. As for women's associations, they refer to the many local women's assotiations that were organized under the All-China Federation of Democratic Women's Associations. This federation was formed at the First National Congress of Delegates of Chinese Women at Beijing (then known as Beiping), March 24 - April 3, 1949.

10. See text June 15, 1953, note 1.

11. The emphasis (indicated by underlining) here and elsewhere in this translation are found in the *Xuanji* original. For the meaning of "New Democracy," see text June 15, 1953, note 2. For reference to the earlier statement in this paragraph, see note 1.

12. According to an article in *Dagong bao* (June 21, 1977), Liang was often called in by Mao for private discussions from 1950 to 1953. He attributed these meetings to "the Chairman's benevolent intentions of wanting to reform my thought."

13. "Liang advocated an untinted, transparent government (*wusi xiuming zhengfu*), that is to say, a government free of any party or factional coloration and one that transcended class interests." (*Xuanji*, V, p. 115.)

14. Here Mao appears to be responding to and expressing his dissatisfaction with Liang's review of his own development, an account of which appeared as the article "In What Ways Have I Changed Over the Last Two Years?" (see note 1). In this article, Liang acknowledged what he felt to be the CPC's achievements and his own mistakes, but while he said that "today the [ideological] distance between myself and the Communist Party has been greatly reduced," he also asserted that "there are still many things with which I cannot agree. I cannot abandon views that I have always held." Liang's position vacillated quite dramatically thereafter. While on Nov. 2, 1951, he published another article in *RMRB* in which he declared that he was prepared to work on "self-reform under the leadership of the CPC," on Jan. 10, 1952, in another *GMRB* article, he claimed that he was merely "reconciling new realities with my old theories."

15. See text Aug. 12, 1953, note 25.

16. Here Mao borrows a well-known phrase from the Chapter "Gaozi," part 1, of *Meng Zi* (Mencius).

17. Gongshu Ban (also known as Lu Ban, or Ban of the state of Lu) was renowned as the most skilled craftsman of the state of Lu during the Warring States period (ca. 403-221 B.C.). "Wielding an ax in front of Lu Ban's door" thus suggests the extreme absurdity of a person who has an inflated estimate of himself or his ability. The aphorism derives from a poem by the Tang dynasty poet Mei Zhihuan.

18. Mei Lanfang (1894-1961) was one of the most famous and celebrated actors of Beijing opera. For more detailed biographical information, see H. Boorman et al., eds. (1970), III, pp.

26-29.

19. Zhao was a famous pilot in the Korean War. His pictorial biography was included in the three-volume *Zhiyuanjun yingxiong zhuan* (Biographies of Heroes in the Chinese People's Volunteers), Beijing, 1956. He is one of the sixty-four people honored as "heroes, model soldiers, and meritorious martyrs of the Korean War."

20. In Chinese folklore, foxes were believed to be able to transform themselves into human forms in order to bewitch people. They could not, however, transform their tails, which often betrayed their true identity.

21. This alludes to the legendary monkey, Sun Wukong, the hero of the traditional novel *Xiyou ji* (Journey to the West). The story referred to by Mao here is in *hui* 6 of the novel.

22. Mao is here referring to Liang's repeated attempts to resign from his position as mediator between the KMT and the CPC in 1945-46 and in 1949. Liang had often announced his "retirement" from politics, only to become involved again later. Even in "retirement," such as in 1947-48, Liang was in fact promoting political ideas, and his pronouncements in the press, if nonpartisan, have always had political significance. It appears to be true, however, that he did not want to be nominated to the CPPCC and had written a letter to Mao to beg off.

23. In 1937, before the outbreak of war between China and Japan, Liang had, as a scholar representing the Shandong warlord Han Fuju (see note 4), gone to Japan for a study-and-observe tour on the subject of social organization. Liang came back with the verdict that Japan was a superior country because it had successfully merged industrialization with an agricultural base (thus successfully carried out "rural reconstruction"), while China had not.

24. See text Sept. 12, 1953.

25. The first quotation is taken from the section "Zhongni dizi liezhuan" (Biographies of Disciples of Confucius) *in Shi ji* (Historical Records), written by Sima Qian in the first century B.C. Zi Lu was a heroic disciple who also served as a bodyguard for Confucius and fended off hostile criticism for the master. This was an alleged lament made by Confucius on Zi Lu's death. Mao uses it here to suggest that Confucius was unwilling to accept criticism.

The second quotation is taken from *Lun heng* (On Balance), a social commentary written by Wang Chong toward the end of the Later Han dynasty (25-220 A.D.). The allusion is to the fact that Confucius ran an academy in the state of Lu where Shaozheng Mao also ran a school. Confucius' students were said to have frequently left their school to hear Shaozheng Mao.

The third quotation is taken from the section "Kongzi shijia" (Biography of Confucius and His Family) in *Shi ji*. It alludes to the fact that after Confucius became acting chief minister of the state of Lu, he had Shaozheng Mao executed. For Mao's criticism of Confucianism, linked to his criticism of Liang, see text Sept. 12, 1953, note 11.

26. See text Sept. 21, 1949, note 1, and text Feb. 18, 1951, note 13.

27. See text Aug. 12, 1953, note 5.

28. See text Feb. 18, 1951, note 2.

29. This phrase is taken from the Chapter "Ji shi," Section 16 of *Lun yu* (The Analects of Confucius). Mao's criticism here is not simply that Liang's traditionalist view is narrowly moralistic but also that it is one that denies the necessity of increasing agricultural production as a basis for industrial and national development.

30. See text Aug. 12, 1953(1), note 30.

31. See text Jan. 17, 1951, note 1.

32. "A problem of thought," as juxtaposed against "a problem of politics," is considered an internal problem, and one that calls for relatively mild measures of reprobation and reprimand. This, according to the account of this entire episode in Zhou Jingwen (1962) (see source note), is the point made by Chen Mingshu, the mediator of the clash of ideas and personalities at this meeting.

Telegram to the People's Republic of Mongolia on the Death of Bumatsende

(September 24, 1953)

Source: *RMRB* (Sept. 25, 1953), 1. Other Chinese Text: *XHYB*, 10 (Oct. 28, 1953), 31. Available English Translations: HNA, *Daily News Release* (Sept. 25, 1953), 17; FBIS, *Daily Report* (Sept. 25, 1953), AAA2.

The Presidium,
The Greater People's Hural,
The People's Republic of Mongolia:

I am deeply grieved to learn of the death of Comrade Gonchigiyn Bumatsende.[1] Comrade Gonchigiyn Bumatsende was an outstanding fighter in the revolutionary movement of the Mongolian people and a close comrade-in-arms of Marshal Choibalsan.[2] He devoted his whole life to the Mongolian people's revolutionary cause.

The passing away of Comrade Gonchigiyn Bumatsende is a great loss to the Mongolian people. On behalf of the Chinese people, the Chinese government, and on my own behalf, I express our deepest sorrow to you and, through you, to the Mongolian people.

(Signed as Chairman of CPG of PRC, dated, in Beijing)

Notes

1. Bumatsende (alternatively spelled Bumtsend) was elected by the Eighth Greater Hural of the People's Republic of Mongolia in 1940 as the head of the National Lesser Hural, and held this position until 1953. For a biographical sketch of Bumatsende, see A. J. K. Sanders (1968), p. 173.

2. See text Jan. 27, 1952, note 1.

Letter to Shen Junru
(September 27, 1953)

Source: *Shuxin*, p. 464.

See text May 12, 1950(2), note 2. Shen was the director (tantamount to chief justice) of the People's Supreme Court at this time.

Director Shen:

I have received and read your letter to me of September 16 and the enclosed documents. The damage of schistosomiasis[1] is very severe, and we must, absolutely, pay the greatest attention to its prevention and cure. I have sent your letter and the documents over to Comrade Xi Zhongxun[2] and put him in charge of handling the matter.

In reply, and with my respect,
Mao Zedong
September 27

Notes

1. See text Jul. 1, 1958, note 1.
2. See text Mar. 18, 1951, source note.

Letter to Mao Yueqiu
(October 4, 1953)

Source: *Shuxin*, p. 465-469.

According to the source, Mao Yueqiu was a receptionist at Mao Zedong's old home (which had become a sort of museum of the Communist revolution for tourists) at Shaoshan xiang, Xiangtan xian, Hunan, of which he was also a native. He had been a secretary of the CPC Party branch at Ciyue, Shaoshan, in the late 1920s and early 1930s.

Comrade Yueqiu:

I have received the letter which your sent to me.

For the purpose of understanding what is going on in our home village (not, and I must make this perfectly clear, so that you can come to celebrate my birthday – for purposes of cutting down expenses, we must not, at any time for any year, have birthday celebrations) I consent to your coming for a trip to the capital. There is also Mao Yishen[1] (I don't know his address) and Wen Dongxian[2] (of Tangjiaduo) – these two comrades have in the past written letters to me expressing their wish to come to see me. If you and other comrades in the village agree, you may arrange things with the two of them and come to the capital together. Only you three should come; all other comrades who have not made these prior arrangements must not come; no exceptions. After coming and staying for a brief spell in the capital, you will go back to the village.

When you come, first *bring this letter*[3] to the United Front Department of the Hunan Provincial Party Committee in Changsha and ask the comrades there for assistance. They will issue the three of you money for transportation to the capital. Ask them also to send one person to escort you to the capital.

Furthermore, please *bring this letter* to the *xiang* government authorities of Shaoshan and Shicheng, to the comrades in charge of the local district governments and Party organs of these two places, and discuss things with them. If they agree, ask them to prepare a written report of the conditions in those two *xiang* and districts, and the problems and difficulties which need urgently to be resolved, and you may bring this to me for reference purposes (not that we can directly and immediately resolve these problems in the *xiang*).

When you come, be sure that you *do not* bring any presents.

The time for you to come to the capital is the sooner the better; I hope you would not come any later than October 20-25.

My respects,

Mao Zedong
October 4, 1953

Notes

1. According to the source, this is a mistake for Mao Xishen, who was a distantly related great uncle of Mao Zedong's.
2. This refers to a cousin of Mao Zedong's.
3. Here and elsewhere in this letter the emphases are in the original *Shuxin* text.

Letter to Ma Xulun
(October 5, 1953)

Source: *Shuxin*, p. 467.

See text Jun. 19, 1950(1), source note.

Mr. Yichu:[1]

I hear that you are ailing, and I am very very concerned. I urge you to devote yourself entirely to the restoration of your health and to resting, and pay attention to nothing else. Take whatever time is needed – don't put a limit on your period of rest – and return to work only after your health is fully restored. If you have any needs at all, please let me know at any time.

Respectfully I wish you a rapid recovery of your health!

Mao Zedong
October 5

Note

1. "Yichu" is Ma's *zi*. See text Oct. 15, 1949, note 1, for an explanation of this usage.

Telegram to the German Democratic Republic
(October 5, 1953)

Source: *RMRB* (Oct. 7, 1953), 1. Other Chinese Text: *XHYB* 11 (Nov. 28, 1953), 77. Available English Translations: NCNA, *Daily Bulletin* (Oct. 7, 1953), 3; FBIS, *Daily Report* (Oct. 7, 1953), AAA2.

President Wilhelm Pieck,
The German Democratic Republic

Dear Comrade President:

On the occasion of the fourth anniversary of the founding of the German

Democratic Republic, on behalf of the Chinese people, the government of the People's Republic of China, and on my own behalf, I extend my most sincere congratulations to the peace-loving people of all Germany and to you personally.

The Chinese people have followed with great gladness the achievements attained by the German Democratic Republic in the past four years in all areas of politics, economy, and culture. The victories which, with the assistance of the Soviet Union, the German people have attained in the struggle against provocation by international reactionary forces, and the great results obtained in the negotiations between the government of the Soviet Union and the delegation of the government of the German Democratic Republic in Moscow, have made a tremendous contribution to the cause of consolidating peace in Europe and throughout the world.

May the German people attain even greater victories in their glorious cause of striving to establish a unified, independent, democratic, and peace-loving Germany. In this cause, the German people will always have the deep sympathy and complete support of the Chinese people and government.

(Signed as Chairman of CPG of PRC, dated, in Beijing)

Speech on Mutual Aid and Cooperativization in Agriculture
(October 15, 1953)

Source: *Xuanji*, V, pp. 116-119. (First speech.) Available English Translation: *SW*, V, pp. 131-135.

This is the first of two speeches given to members of the Rural Work Department of the CPC Central Committee before and during the Third Conference on Mutual Aid and Cooperativization in Agriculture, which was convened by the CPC Central Committee from October 26 to November 5, 1953. See also text Nov. 4, 1953.

The two talks presented here represent part of the continuing struggle over agricultural policy and collectivization in the early 1950s. In contrast to the unity the leaders shared on the issue of dealing with the rich peasants during land reform (see text Mar. 12, 1950), Mao here was clearly struggling against others in the Party over the pace of collectivization and the line to be taken toward the rich peasants. His dismissal of the argument that "life is hard in the countryside" as the ruminations of the landlords and the rich peasants for whom life actually was harder than prior to Liberation would be repeated in his more

famous speech "On the Cooperativization of Agriculture" (text July 31, 1955)
some eighteen months later, reflecting the continuity of this struggle throughout
this period.

The key issue in these documents is Mao's stress on class struggle and the
class nature of production itself. Mao insisted that the struggle to transform
social relations, to collectivize ownership in the rural areas, was the key link in
determining all agricultural policies and their eventual results – a position oth-
ers in the Party rejected.

At the time of this document, however, Mao's forces carried the day. After
the conference he called for an increase in the number of cooperatives in the
December 16, 1953, "The Central Committee's Decision on the Development of
Agricultural Producers' Cooperatives."[1] As would also be the case with Mao's
push for more rapid collectivization in 1955, the call for increasing the
number of cooperatives led to a greater increase than was called for. By May
1954 some 76,000 new cooperatives had been established, bringing the total
number to 91,000, or about four times as many as had been called for in the
December directive. By February 1955, the goal of establishing some 600,000
cooperatives throughout the country had already been accomplished. Here Mao
speaks also of the establishment of the cooperatives as a manifestation of the
implementation of the general line of the CPC during the period of transition.
This speech therefore should be studied in conjunction with text June 15, 1953.

If the agricultural producers' cooperatives are run well, they can set in motion a great development of the mutual aid teams.[2] In the new liberated areas, the *xian*, regardless of whether they are large, medium-sized or small, must set up, after adequate preparation, one or two well-run cooperatives this winter or next spring – at least one [cooperative shoud be set up], in general one or two, and at most three, contingent on the quality of the work done. The number [of cooperatives] should be apportioned [to each *xian*]. [If the quota is] too high, it is an adventurist advance;[3] [if the quota is] too low, it is a Right deviation; to consider [the quota] as something that one can have or dispense with [at will] is simply to let things drift. Can we have more than three [cooperatives in a *xian*]? As long as the conditions are suitable for it, as long as it conforms to the regulations and resolutions, as long as [they are set up] voluntarily, as long as there are capable backbone cadres in the leadership (for which there are two main requirements: fair-mindedness and capability), and as long as things are done well, then it is like Han Xin marshaling his troops, "the more the better."[4]

We must exhort all [special] district[5] and *xian* [Party] committees to exert great efforts to get [this thing] done, and they must get it done well. Rural work departments under the [regional] bureaus of the Central Committee as well as those subordinate to the provincial and municipal [Party] committees must therefore get a strong grip on this matter and focus their work on this problem.

We must have a control figure[6] and apportionment to the lower levels. Apportionment without coercion cannot be regarded as commandism.[7] After this October meeting, a period of four or five months can be used to promote this, that is, November, December, and January and February of next year, and in the North, even March. In the early part of next year let us hold a meeting to check [the work being done]. We will make it clear [to everyone] at this conference that this is what we'll do. We must check the work early next year to see how things stand with regard to the fulfillment [of this task].

In certain areas which are minority nationality areas and where land reform[8] has not yet been completed, [cooperatives] do not have to be set up. In certain *xian* where the work has been very poorly done, say, for instance, where backward *xiang* make up thirty to forty per cent of the total number of *xiang*, or where the *xian* [Party] committee secretary is very incompetent and any attempt [to set up cooperatives] would cause trouble, these *xian* can be temporarily left out [of the movement] and no quotas need be assigned to them. However, provincial and [special] district [Party] committees must take the responsibility of helping [these places] with their work of reorganization and of preparing conditions so that cooperativization can be carried out there next winter after the autumn harvest.

The general rule is to proceed toward cooperatives through the step of first [setting up] mutual aid teams; however, it is also permissible to experiment with going directly into the establishment of cooperatives. If, by taking the direct path, things can go well and we can [accomplish the goal of] establishing [cooperatives] more quickly, why can't we [try it]? We certainly can.

The rural work departments at all levels should regard this matter of [promoting] mutual aid and cooperativization as an extremely important matter. With individual peasant [production], increases in production are limited; [therefore] we must develop mutual aid and cooperativization. If socialism does not occupy [the battle] positions in the countryside, capitalism will inevitably occupy them. Can there be such a thing as following neither the capitalist road nor the socialist road? Even the capitalist road can bring about an increase in production, but it will take a long time and must go through a painful process. We are not going to engage in capitalism, that is definite; but if we do not engage in socialism, it is certain that capitalism will spill over.

The general line, the general program – industrialization and socialist transformation – will be discussed at this October conference.

Both "guaranteeing private property" and the "Four Freedoms" are beneficial to the rich peasants and the well-to-do peasants.[9] Why then do we write these into law? The law states that we will protect private property, but says nothing about "guaranteeing" [it]. At present the peasants are selling their land, and that is not good. The law does not prohibit it, but we must do some work to prevent the peasants from selling their land. The method of doing this is [to set up] cooperatives. Even mutual aid teams are not enough to prevent the peasants from selling their land; it takes the cooperatives, large cooperatives, to do the job. Large cooperatives will also make it possible for the peasants to no longer need to rent out their land. The problem can be solved with large cooperatives with [a membership of] one to two hundred households that are able to carry a few households of widows, widowers, orphans or old and childless people.[10] Whether or not small cooperatives are also capable of carrying several [such households] is a problem that remains to be studied. The mutual aid teams, too, should help such people. If it is impossible to set up large cooperatives, set up medium-sized ones; if that is impossible, set up small ones. Wherever it is possible to set up medium-sized cooperatives, however, it ought to be done, and wherever it is possible to set up large ones, we ought to do so. We mustn't be unhappy to see large cooperatives. [Cooperatives] with one or two hundred households are to be considered large, but there could even be some with three or four hundred households. We could set up a few branch cooperatives under the large cooperatives, and this, too, is an innovative measure. We do not have to disband the large cooperatives. By running [a cooperative] well we do not mean that it should be good in every aspect. We must absorb all sorts of experiences and mustn't take one pattern and apply it everywhere.

More development ought to be promoted in the old liberated areas.[11] Some new liberated areas can probably develop faster than some of the old liberated areas; for instance, the Guanzhong region[12] may develop faster than the northern Shaanxi area, and the [alluvial] plains of Chengdu may develop faster than the places at Fuping. We should dispel the notion that the new liberated areas are bound to develop more slowly. The Northeast is actually not an old liberated area; southern Manchuria is actually about the same as the areas in the Guannei region that were liberated later.[13] It is possible that [the development in] the areas around Jiangsu and Hangzhou, Jiaxing, and Huzhou will surpass that of the old liberated mountainous areas of Shandong and North China, and indeed they ought to surpass them.[14] In general we can say that the new liberated areas should move along slowly but, in certain areas where the cadres are competent, the population is concentrated, and the terrain is flat, they may develop rapidly all at once, as soon as a few models have been set up and are running well.

There are six thousand cooperatives in North China at the moment. It is [only] a matter of setting quotas to have the amount doubled, but to triple the number there must be negotiations [with those concerned]. Apportionment must be done rationally, and there should be a control figure; otherwise we will be confused and lack confidence in our work. [The number of cooperatives] in the Northeast can be doubled, or increased by 150 per cent or 200 per cent. The same can apply to North China. The control figure need not be set too high, [so that] the localities can fulfill it with surplus. Fulfillment [of tasks] in excess of the quota will give a great boost to their morale.

In developing cooperatives, we must also strive to meet [the standards of] being large in quantity, high in quality, and low in cost. By low in cost we mean that we must not produce rejects. Producing rejects means wasting the peasants' energies; the consequence will be that there will be an adverse effect [on the peasants], we will lose politically, and less grain will be produced. The final result [of cooperativization] ought to be that more grain, more cotton, more sugarcane, more vegetables, etc., is produced. If more vegetables cannot be produced, there will be no way out [in these areas] either, and this will harm the state as well as the people.

More vegetables should be produced in the suburban areas. If more vegetables cannot be produced, there will be no way out [in these areas] either, and again that will be harmful to both the state and the people. Land in the suburban areas is fertile, and the terrain is flat; besides, it is publicly owned, so we can begin with setting up large cooperatives [in these places]. Naturally we must be meticulous in doing this. Growing vegetables is unlike growing grain, and any crude [attempts] may make things worse. We should select typical examples for experimentation and must avoid adventurist advance.

As for vegetable supplies for the city, it won't do to rely on individual peasants to take vegetables into the city to sell. We must work out ways [to solve this problem] in the sphere of production; [meanwhile] the supply and marketing cooperatives[15] also should come up with some ideas. Big cities now face a very grave contradiction in terms of the supply and the demand for vegetables.

Great contradictions now exist between the supply of and demand for grain and cotton as well. Before long, contradictions will also develop in meat and edible oil. [People's] needs have grown enormously; our supply has not kept up with them.

For the purpose of resolving this contradiction between supply and demand we must [first] solve the problem of the contradiction between the system of ownership and the forces of production. Is it going to be a system of individual ownership or a system of collective ownership? Is it going to be a capitalist system of ownership or a socialist system of ownership? The relations of production in a system of individual ownership are totally in conflict with [the goal of] large-scale supply. A transition must be made from a system of individual ownership to a system of collective ownership to socialism. There are cooperatives of the lower stage where there is pooling of peasants' land as shares [which go into the cooperative]. There are also [cooperatives] of the higher stage with land being turned over to public ownership – to the public ownership of the cooperative.

The purpose of the general line, one might say, is to solve the problem of the system of ownership. The system of state ownership [must be] expanded – by establishing new state-owned enterprises or renovating and expanding existing ones. There are two kinds of systems of private ownership: [ownership] by the laboring people and [ownership] by the bourgeoisie. Only when they are transformed respectively into the system of ownership by the collective and into the system of state ownership (integrated into socialism through joint state-private ownership) can the forces of production be enhanced and industrialization of the country be realized.[16] Only when the forces of production have been developed can the contradiction between supply and demand be resolved.

Notes

1. For an English text of this document, see NCNA, *Daily Bulletin* (Jan. 8, 1954).

2. The agricultural producers' cooperatives (APC) are the basic units of the socialist transformation of agriculture and of the collective economy in China's countryside. As we see in these volumes, the first step toward socializing the agricultural economy was accomplished by the land reform, which meant taking the land from the landlords and dividing it among the peasants. (See text Feb. 18, 1951, note 2.) When this was done, however, it left China with myriads of peasants with various sizes of landholdings and control over various amounts of means of production. (Thus the various classifications of peasants.) For the poor peasants, who constitute the majority, production on an individual economy basis was not particularly successful. Productivity could be raised and the livelihood of poor peasants could be improved only by the recombination of their means of production, and in a new way, i.e., a socialist method. Accordingly, some peasants pooled their resources voluntarily to form collective units. The resources pooled first were time and labor, while other material means of production remained completely privately owned. This became a form of mutual aid and was encouraged by some local authorities before it was promoted by the central government. (For instance, see text Dec. 15, 1951, source note.) The mutual aid teams thus formed were either seasonal or year-round, with the year-round ones operating with a more permanent and sophisticated system of division of labor, and in some cases, accumulating a small amount of communal property that was not immediately divided and was reinvested in future production.

When the Resolution of the Central Committee on Agricultural Cooperativization and Mutual Aid was promulgated in December 1951, the idea was still to promote the more sophisticated forms of mutual aid, and at this time "mutual aid" and cooperativization were considered under one rubric. By 1952 and 1953, however, on the basis of the mutual aid teams, the collectivization of the agricultural economy had moved further forward. In many instances, the peasants had joined together in another form, APC's, which represented a higher stage of socialization than the mutual aid teams. In this form, the peasant economy was still based on private ownership of the means of production, but the peasants pooled their land, the large livestock – such as draft oxen – and the major farming equipment together under joint labor and joint management. This became the fundamental format of the formation of APC's at this time, and was what Mao was referring to here.

The CPC at this time generally accepted that the APC's were a more productive form of agricultural organization than for the peasants, particularly the poor peasants, to "go it on their own." Not all the people in the Rural Work Deparment, however, shared Mao's obvious and unmitigated enthusiasm. The forming of APC's in some cases did represent temporary disruption of the economic pattern, and the question was raised as to the suitability of local circumstances for cooperativization. This also led to the question of the pace of setting up cooperatives. Mao believed that given their superiority and higher level of socialization, cooperatives, even of this "primary-stage" nature, should be set up in large numbers, and rapidly – i.e., "as soon as possible wherever it is possible." Others preferred a more deliberate pace and more attention given to appeasing the richer peasants for whom the marginal returns in setting up cooperatives were obviously smaller than for the poorer peasants, whose land sometimes surrounded that of the richer peasants and whose cooperativization sometimes disrupted and affected the productive pattern of the richer peasants.

It should be noted that at this time the agricultural economy was still very diverse. There were APC's, there were rich peasants and middle peasants holding out against cooperativization, there were mutual aid teams, and there were places where there were not even mutual aid teams. Thus Mao believed that if cooperatives were set up and their productive superiority proven, it would have a positive leading influence on areas that were, so to speak, backward, and there facilitate the setting up of at least mutual aid teams. Note also that at this time the idea of cooperativization was still largely an idea of "semisocialism," i.e., of the pooling and joint usage of land, labor, and the major equipment, and based on a system of private ownership. (See text Aug. 12, 1953, note 9.) Although at the end of this speech Mao talks about "higher-stage" cooperatives being set up, his main concern at the moment was the "primary-stage" cooperative, which had to be set up on a wide scale first, and it was later that the problem of further making the transition to a yet higher level of socialization (or to what was known as the higher-stage APC's) became imminent. The latter (promoted in 1955), would mean complete socialism, with all means of production pooled and absorbed into a system of collective, and not private, ownership, and for the system of "from each according to ability, to each according to need" to be implemented, paving the way to the forming of the even larger and more intensely collectivized people's communes in 1958.

3. See text Aug. 12, 1953(1), note 22.

4. Han Xin was a military genius of the late and early second century B.C. who aided Liu Bang (first emperor of the Han dynasty) in the struggle for the throne. Han Xin was later given the title *hou* (often translated as marquis) of Huaiyin. The aphorism to which Mao refers here is drawn from a passage in "Huaiyin hou zhuan" (The Biography of the Marquis of Huaiyin) in *Shi ji* (Historical Records) in which Han was asked how large an army he was capable of controlling. His reply has become a common Chinese phrase that is the rough equivalent of the Western phrase, "the more, the merrier."

5. See text Aug. 12, 1953(1), note 21.

6. By control figures Mao meant, in this case, targeted numbers of cooperatives to be established.

7. See text June 6, 1950(1), note 11.

8. See text Feb. 18, 1951, note 2.

9. The "Four Freedoms" *(si da ziyou)* are the freedoms of usury, of selling land, of hiring labor, and of private enterprise. During the Cultural Revolution, Liu Shaoqi was accused of promoting these freedoms, which were considered to serve the interests of the rich and well-to-do middle peasants. For a more detailed description and indictment of these "freedoms," see text Oct. 11, 1955, section 3.

10. Significantly, the provision for the livelihood of these four groups of people is also a condition of the ideal state, or the "age of great harmony," as described in the classical Confucian canon. See the chapter "Li yun" in *Li ji* (Book of Rites). In modern China, the same ideal had been expressed by, among others, Kang Youwei and Sun Yat-sen. Preferential treatment for these four types of people is stipulated in Article 5 of the Land Reform Law.

11. See text June 6, 1950(1), note 7.

12. The term *guanzhong*, literally "region between the passes," refers primarily to the Wei River valley, home of China's dynastic capitals until the end of the Tang dynasty (618 to 906 A.D.). The fertility of this region stands in sharp contrast to the more arid loess soil farther north of the Wei. Chengdu is in Sichuan, while Fuping is in eastern Hebei.

13. See text Apr. 6, 1952, note 4.

14. Jiangsu is the province of China that occupies the delta region of the Yangtze River, Shanghai, now an autonomous municipality, juts into the ocean at the tip of the delta. Hangzhou and Jiaxing are districts in Zhejiang which border Jiangsu on the south. Huzhou is in the province of Anhui to the west of Zhejiang. This region as a whole has been an economic and political nerve center of East China because it is strategically located to control communications and trade throughout the entire stretch of the lower Yangtze. Furthermore, it is where much of China's premodern industry and commerce (handicraft industries and textile industries in the early stage of mechanization) became concentrated throughout the Qing dynasty (1644-1911). This region therefore possesses an advantage over other regions in terms of potential for rapid economic development. Since it is also an area where capitalism has already had greater development, it is possible that Mao might have had this factor in mind when he proclaimed here his belief that this area might develop faster (perhaps in terms of socialism as well as economically) even though it was newly liberated.

15. Supply and marketing cooperatives were originally economic units set up among the peasants, in most cases voluntarily, to streamline the processes of purchasing necessary means of production and to sell their products. In many places, these cooperatives were set up even before the APC's. In the process of promoting mutual aid teams and early cooperativization, the CPC seized

the initiative in this area as well and formularized the setting up of supply and marketing coopera-tives, establishing general offices for such cooperatives, known as *gongxiao hezuo zongshe*, at the *xian* levels. These began to set more or less uniform prices for products and for the exchange of equipment, and even to draw up contracts for supplies, which took the place of the uneven and individualized vending that had prevailed earlier in the countryside. Peasants were encouraged to join by the fact that members were given preferential prices. In July 1950 the National General Office of Supply and Marketing Cooperatives was established. See also text Mar. 19, 1953, sec-tion 5, and text Oct. 11, 1955, note 25.

16. See text July 9, 1953. See also texts, Dec. 8, 1956, Mar. 5, 1956, and Feb. 21, 1959.

Telegram to the Democratic Republic of Viet Nam
(October 16, 1953)

Source: FBIS, *Daily Report* (Oct. 26, 1953), CCC13-14.

We have no Chinese text of this telegram. The FBIS source is presented here without editing in its original form. The FBIS source does not indicate the exact manner in which this telegram was signed.

Respectfully to Comrade Ho Chi Minh, President of the Democratic Republic of Vietnam:

(On behalf of the Government) and people of China I sincerely thank the people and Government (of the Vietnam for having sent their greetings on the occasion of the anniversary of the) establishment of the People's Republic of China. I also wish that the Vietnam people may score many more victories in their glorious work to achieve national independence and freedom.

Speech at Reception for Tibetan Delegation
(October 18, 1953)

Source: *Ziliao xuanbian*, pp. 155-156. Other Chinese text: *Wansui* (n.d.), pp. 8-9.

*The Tibetan delegation was in Beijing for the National Day celebration of the PRC.
See text Apr. 6, 1952.*

We must unite with all the various nationalities; no matter whether it is a
large or small nationality, we must be united with it. For example, the Olunchun people may be no more than four thousand people, but we must be
united with them just as well.[1] As long as they are Chinese people, regardless
of national distinction, we must be united with all those who are opposed to
imperialism and who stand for patriotism and advocate unity. We should be
united [first], and [then] carry out our work [in separate ways] in accordance
with the varying conditions in the various nationalities' areas. In some places
[work] can be done a bit more quickly; in other places somewhat more slowly.
In either case, things should be discussed first before they are carried out.
Without discussion, [they] should not be forcibly carried out. When they have
been discussed and approved by the majority, then they can be carried out
with deliberation. Even good things must be discussed first before they can be
implemented. Doing things after discussion is what distinguishes the Communist Party from the Kuomintang. The Kuomintang oppresses people whenever
they hold the upper hand. Not only do they oppress the minority nationalities;
they even oppress the majority of the Han people as well. The Kuomintang
does bad things. We shouldn't do bad things; those among our cadres who
have committed mistakes ought to be criticized. Please speak up concerning
the shortcomings and mistakes in our work in Tibet; you may speak your mind
with regard to anything with which you disagree and which you believe to be
detrimental to the interests of the people, so as to help us correct [these mis-
takes]. [When we] have committed a mistake, we [seek to] correct it immediately; this is where we differ from the Kuomintang.

China as a whole is still very backward at the moment, and is in need of
being developed. This is because of the oppression by imperialism and the
Kuomintang in the past. They have now been driven away by us, and, in the
last four years, we have made great improvements. After the [period of]
national economic recovery, we have inaugurated, this year, the First Five-
Year Plan for National Construction.[2] We estimate that after three five-year
plans, our major industries will have been established. The Soviet Union
chased away imperialism and the bad people at home thirty-six years ago; and
it took them thirty-six years of construction to achieve what they have now
achieved. We are going to be a bit faster in our construction because we will
have the Soviet Union's assistance. The population in China is very large; we
have over five hundred million people and are the most populous country in
the world. We also have a very vast territory. Given three five-year plans we
shall be able to do quite well in our construction, and then we shall be able to
give greater assistance to Tibet.

If there is anything that the central [government] can do to assist you it is
bound to do so. It is in the interests of the entire country for us to aid the various minority nationalities, thus enabling them to develop and improve. The

development and improvement of the various minority nationalities is a hopeful matter.

The political, economic, cultural and religious development of Tibet must be carried out primarily on the shoulders of the leaders and people of Tibet themselves and through the discussions [among themselves]; the Center can only give assistance. This is an item written into the Agreement on the Methods for the Peaceful Liberation of Tibet.[3] However, it will be some time before [these things] can be carried out, and, moreover, [they] must be carried out on the basis of your volition, and gradually. Whatever can be done will be done; if something cannot be done [as yet,] we will wait a bit. If there is something that can be done, and on which the majority has agreed, it would not be good not to get it done. [However,] it can be done somewhat slowly, so that everyone will be happy about it, and, in that way, in reality it may actually [be done] more quickly. In any case, our policy is one of being united in our progress and further development.

Notes

1. The Olunchun people is a tribal people residing in Inner Mongolia. By the mid-1960s they have actually reached a population of only 2,400-2,500.
2. See text Feb. 10, 1953, note 2.
3. See text May 24, 1951, source note.

Letter to Yang Shangkun
(October 22, 1953)

Source: *Shuxin*, p. 469.

See text May 19, 1953, source note; see also text Nov. 22, 1950, note 4.

Comrade Shangkun:

Please take the six points in the conclusion of [the book] *Liangong dang shi* (History of the Communist Party of the Soviet Union [Bolshevik])[1] and print them as a single leaflet to be sent tonight or tomorrow to the various comrades attending the organizational meeting.[2] Please ask them to make use of the two or three days recess in the meeting to read, study, and where possible, even discuss [these points], so that when Comrade Liu Shaoqi and others reach this issue in their speeches in the conference, they [the attending comrades] may already have some understanding of this matter. When the leading group meets this afternoon, please notify Comrades Liu, Rao, and Hu Qiaomu[3] of this matter (i.e., the matter of printing and distributing the concluding points [of the book]). While you are at it, you may print some extra copies (you may print one or two thousand copies) and distribute [the surplus] to cadres in Beijing, and charge the General Party Committee[4] with notifying the various departments and Party groups, urging them to read and discuss [the subject].

Mao Zedong
2 [p. m.]
October 22

Notes

1. This probably refers to the book *Short Course on the History of the CPSU (Bolshevik)*, see text Jul. 31, 1955, note 19.
2. This refers to the Second National Organizational Work Conference convened by the Central Committee of the CPC from September to October 1953 in Beijing. For more on this conference see K. Lieberthal (1976), p. 61.
3. This refers to Liu Shaoqi and Rao Shushi, in addition to Hu Qiaomu. For more information on these people, see text May 19, 1953, source note (also text Jan. 4, 1950); text Mar. 31, 1955, note 7 (also text Nov. 22, 1950, note 2, text Jan. 10, 1951, source note, and text Mar. 18, 1951, source note), and text May 22, 1950 (also text Jan. 4, 1950), respectively.
4. This refers to the general Party (CPC) committee of the various organs directly subordinate to or affiliated with the Central Committee of the CPC at the time. It was the general Party leadership organ for the organs directly under the Central Committee, the Central People's Government, and the Military Commission as well as the people's organizations at the central level.

Telegram to the People's Republic of Albania
(October 22, 1953)

Source: FBIS, *Daily Report* (Oct. 23, 1953), LL2.

We have no Chinese text of this telegram. The FBIS source is presented here without editing in its original form.

Comrade Enver Hoxha, Chairman of the Council of Ministers of the People's Republic of Albania, Tirana:

"I extend to you on behalf of the Chinese people and their Government sincere thanks for the congratulations that the Albanian people, the Government of the People's Republic of Albania, and you personally extended to us on the occasion of the fourth anniversary of the proclamation of the People's Republic of China."

Letter to Wen Jiuming
(October 25, 1953)

Source: *Shuxin*, p. 471.

According to the source, Wen Jiuming is Mao's nephew.

Comrade Jiuming:

I have received your letter of October 2. You appear to have some opinions about the conditions in our home village to tell me; you may come to the capital for a trip [to do this]. You must furnish your own fare for the journey, and I will reimburse you for it later. Mao Zerong, whose nickname is Songwu,[1] is my brother. He lives outside the Xian gate [of Shaoshan *xiang*]. He has written me many times indicating a desire to come to the capital. Please look him up and come with him. He has never left home, so please give him whatever assistance you can. He, too, should furnish his own fare, and I will also reimburse him later. When you come, don't ask the United Front Department of the Provincial Party Committee for assistance if you can manage without them, but if you cannot raise the funds for the trip, then you may bring this letter to the comrades in the United Front Department and ask them to give you some help. It will be cold on the trip, so each of you should bring a thin cotton quilt blanket. *Don't bring any presents;*[2] this is most important. Other people must not come with you.

Mao Zedong
October 4, 1953

P.S. It would be best if you can arrive at the capital by the early part of November.

Notes

1. See text Oct. 2, 1952, note 5.
2. The emphasis is in the *Shuxin* original.

Reply to Ambassador of the Republic of Indonesia
(October 28, 1953)

Source: *RMRB* (Oct. 29, 1953), 1. Available English Translations: NCNA, *Daily Bulletin*, 916 (Nov. 5, 1953), 5-6; HNA, *Daily News Release* (Oct. 29, 1953), 15; FBIS, *Daily Report* (Oct. 29, 1953), AAA2.

A. Mononutu served as ambassador of the Republic of Indonesia to the PRC from October 1953 to July 1956.

Honorable Ambassador, Your Excellency:

I am very happy to accept the letter of credence from the President of the Republic of Indonesia presented by Your Excellency, and express my deep gratitude for the congratulations conveyed by Your Excellency from the President, government, and people of the Republic of Indonesia.

The friendship that has existed for a long time between the two peoples of China and Indonesia has been further developed over the past three years as a result of the establishment of new diplomatic relations between our two countries. I believe that from now on, with the efforts of Your Excellency, the economic and cultural relations of friendship and cooperation between China and Indonesia will grow daily ever closer, and the promotion of such friendly relations will contribute to the Asian and world peace that the people of all countries are striving to attain.

I warmly welcome Your Excellency as the Ambassador Extraordinary and Plenipotentiary of the Republic of Indonesia to the People's Republic of China. In your work of strengthening the friendship and cooperation between the two countries, you will receive my assistance and that of the government of the People's Republic of China.

I wish Your Excellency success in your work.

Criticism of the Ministry of Public Health
(October 1953)

Source: *Quanwudi*, 17 (June 25, 1967), 2.

According to this source this criticism of the Ministry of Public health was made at a meeting of the Political Bureau of the Central Committee of the CPC in October 1953. There is another 1953 criticism of the same department among documents of unspecified dates in this year (see documents at the end of 1953).

The Ministry of Public Health has been beset with many very serious short-comings during the past few years. The most serious one is that [the Ministry] is short on politics, short on political work. There is too little Marxism-Leninism and socialism there. The Party must exercise overall leadership; it must lead health work. . . . He Cheng's thinking,[1] namely, that health work is a specialized technical type of work, . . . [and that] since the Center knows nothing about technology it is uncertain whether or not the Center could solve [any problem] even if it were reported to the Center. . . is completely erroneous. The Ministry of Public Health must exert the greatest effort to solve this problem.

Note

1. See text 1953(1), source note.

Speech on Mutual Aid and Cooperativization in Agriculture
(November 4, 1953)

Source: *Xuanji*, V, pp. 120-124 (Second Speech.) Available English Translation: *SW*, V, pp. 135-140.

See text Oct. 15, 1953, source note.

Whenever we do any type of work it must be in accord with reality; not to be in accord with reality is a mistake. To be in accord with reality means observing both needs and possibilities. [The notion of] possibilities includes political conditions, economic conditions, and conditions [related to] the cadres' [abilities]. There are now both the need and the possibility of developing agricultural producers' cooperatives;[1] this has great potential. If we don't tap [this potential], we will be taking firm steps but not advancing.[2] Our feet are made for walking; it would be wrong if we just stood here and did not move. It is incorrect to forcibly dissolve cooperatives that have been established under adequate conditions. This is wrong at any time. The drive to "rectify impetuous and adventurist advance" was, after all, a gust of wind, wasn't it?[3] It has blown down to the lower levels and has blown down some agricultural producers' cooperatives that shouldn't have been blown down. Those that have been blown down mistakenly should be identified, [their cases] clarified, and the mistake admitted. Otherwise, the *xiang* cadres and the activists there will be angry and frustrated.

We must engage in socialism. "Guaranteeing private property" is a bourgeois concept. "People who stay together talking all day but never speaking to fundamentals and who like to dispense small favors are difficult to deal with."[4] By "talking but never speaking to fundamentals" we mean that they never talk about socialism; they never engage in socialism. Giving out agricultural credit, distributing food grain for relief, assessing taxation according to [fixed] rates, reducing [taxes] or exempting [people from taxes] according to law, building small-scale water-conservation projects, sinking wells and digging ditches, engaging in deep plowing and close planting, applying fertilizer in a rational way, popularizing the new type of walking plows, water-conveyance machines, sprayers, agricultural insecticides, and so on, are all good things. However, if we do not rely on socialism but rather do these things only on the basis of the small-scale peasant economy, that would be merely dispensing small favors to the peasants. But if these good things are linked up with the general line and with socialism then things will be different; it will not be merely dispensing small favors. We must engage in socialism so that all these good things can be linked up with socialism. As for "guaranteeing private property" and the "Four Freedoms,"[5] these fall even more [clearly under the category of] small favors that, moreover, benefit the rich peasants and the well-to-do middle peasants. To hope to greatly increase grain production, to resolve the grain problem, and to resolve the overall problem of the national economy and the people's livelihood without relying on socialism, [but rather] by making much of the small-scale peasant economy and dispensing small favors on the basis of [such] an individual economy – this is really "difficult to deal with."

There is an old saying, "Once the headrope of a fishing net is pulled up, all its meshes will open."[6] One must take up the headrope before the meshes can be opened. The headrope is the main theme. The contradiction between socialism and capitalism, and moreover, the step-by-step resolution of this contradiction, is the main theme; it is the headrope. Once this net is raised, then all the various particulars of the political work and economic work to help the peasants will fall into place.

There are contradictions both inside and outside the agricultural producers' cooperatives. The present agricultural producers' cooperatives are still semi-socialist,[7] while individual peasants outside the cooperatives practice a system of complete private ownership; hence there are contradictions between these two [systems]. The mutual aid team is different from an agricultural producers' cooperative; the mutual aid team involves only collective labor and not ownership systems.[8] The present agricultural producers' cooperatives are still built on the basis of private ownership: land, draft animals and large farm tools that were owned by the individual have been exchanged for shares [in the cooperatives], [so] within the cooperatives the elements of a socialist nature and the private ownership system are also in contradiction. This contradiction must be gradually resolved.[9] In the future, when the existing semipublic and semiprivate ownership [system] is transformed into a system of collective ownership, this contradiction will be resolved.[10] The steps we have chosen are steady; from the mutual aid teams [which embody] the sprouts of socialism [we will] advance to semisocialist cooperatives and then advance again to fully socialist cooperatives (which should still be called agricultural producers' cooperatives rather than collective farms). Generally speaking, the mutual aid teams are still the basis of the agricultural producers' cooperatives.

At one time, there were several documents that did not mention mutual aid and cooperativization; to all of these [documents] I added words to the effect that mutual aid and cooperativization should be developed or that we must carry out necessary and practicable political and economic work. Some people would have liked to have made something out of the small-scale peasant economy, and therefore they were particularly opposed to excessive interference in [the affairs of] the peasants. At that time, there was indeed excessive interference in some cases. There were the "Five Excesses"[11] at the top levels, and every one of these was thrust downward and created great confusion below. It won't do to have these "Five Excesses" at any time; not only won't it do [to have these] in the countryside, it won't do in the factories or in the military either. The Center issued several documents opposing excessive interference. This is good. What is excessive interference? Plans that do not take into consideration needs and possibilities, that are unrealistic and subjectivist, or that are realistic but are carried out in a commandist[12] way, such [things] are excessive interferences. Subjectivism and commandism will never do, not in ten thousand years. Not only will it not do in a scattered small-scale peasant economy, but it will not do in the cooperatives either. But we mustn't refer to those things that need to be done, that can be done, and for which the method of implementation is not commandist, as excessive interference. This standard must be the criterion in reviewing our work. Whatever is subjectivist or unrealistic is wrong. Wherever commandism is applied in carrying things out, it is wrong. To take steady steps without moving forward would be a Right [deviation]; to force the implementation [of plans] beyond the practical possibilities is a "Left" [deviation]; these are both [manifestations of] subjectivism. Adventurist advance is wrong; to refrain from doing what can be done is also wrong; to force [the cooperatives] to dissolve is an even greater error.

"Life in the rural areas is hard, things do not look very good, and our measures are not suitable for the small-scale peasant economy." There are arguments like this both inside and outside the Party. True, there is some hardship in the countryside, but we must analyze [the situation] properly. In fact, [life in] the rural areas is not all that hard. No more than ten per cent [of] households suffer a shortage of food. Of these, one half are in very great difficulty; they are widowers and widows, orphans or old people without children [to support them];[13] they lack labor power, but the mutual aid teams and the cooperatives can give them some help. At least their life is much better than the life they led under the Kuomintang; at least land has been distributed [to them]. People in disaster areas are really suffering, but they too have been given relief grain. Generally speaking, the life of the peasants is good and improving, that's why eighty to ninety per cent of the peasants are rejoicing and support the government. Approximately seven per cent of the rural population, made up of the landlords and rich peasants, are dissatisfied with the government. "There is hardship in the countryside and things are in terrible shape"; I have never viewed the situation this way. Some people, when they talk about the hardships in the countryside, also say that the countryside is decentralized, referring, that is, to the decentralized character of the small-scale peasant economy. But when they talk about this decentralized character they do not also talk about establishing cooperatives. To carry out the socialist transformation of the individual economy, to promote mutual aid and cooperativization and to establish cooperatives – this is not only the direction [in which we must proceed] but the immediate task [to be accomplished] as well.

Without the Conference on Financial and Economic [Work] held in July and August, the problem of the general line would not have been solved for many of our comrades.[14] The main [accomplishment of] the Conference on Financial and Economic [Work] in July and August was primarily the resolution of this problem. The criticism of Bo Yibo was precisely for his error in deviating from the general line.[15] In short, the general line can be summarized as follows: gradually realize the socialist industrialization of the nation and the socialist transformation of agriculture, of handicraft industries, and of capitalist industry and commerce. When we carried out the planned purchase and planned supply of grain this time, it also lent a great impetus to socialism.[16] In the wake of that, we held this Conference on Mutual Aid and Cooperativization, which also lent a great impetus [to socialism]. We must be more active at this conference, in view of the fact that for the greater part of this year the mutual aid and cooperativization movement has receded somewhat. Still, the policies should be explained clearly. It is a very important matter to make our policies known.

"[Have] active leadership [and] steady development." This is a very good statement. [The mutual aid and cooperativization movement] shrank back a bit for the larger part of this year. We took steady steps but failed to move forward; this is not quite right. Nevertheless, there are some advantages. For instance, when fighting a war, you fight a battle and then relax and reorganize, and then you launch another battle. The problem is that in some cases we have withdrawn a bit too far from our positions, and in other cases, it is not a matter of withdrawing too far, but of no development where there could have been some. People were forbidden to develop [mutual aid teams and cooperatives]; they were not given permission, so they established illegal [cooperatives]. Many newborn and correct things throughout the world are often illegal. In the past we were "illegal," and the Kuomintang was "legal"! But these illegal cooperatives have continued to persist and have been run well. Can you still refuse to acknowledge them? You have to recognize them as legal and admit that they have won.

At the conference we talked about active leadership and steady development. But we must also anticipate some possible trouble. You may talk about being active and steady, but in practice the leadership may not be active and the steps taken may not be steady development. To be active and steady means that there should be control figures,[17] and assignment of tasks, and afterward an inspection to see whether [the tasks] have been fulfilled. If things that can be accomplished are allowed to remain unaccomplished, it won't do; it shows [you are] lacking in enthusiasm for socialism. According to our survey, five to ten per cent of the cooperatives now show a decrease in production and are not well-managed; this is the result of not having active leadership. Naturally, it is unavoidable for a small number of cooperatives to reduce their production because of mismanagement; however, if twenty per cent, or even more, of the cooperatives were to reduce production, then that would present a problem.

The general line is to change the relations of production step by step. Stalin said that the basis of the relations of production is the system of ownership.[18] Our comrades must be clear about this. At the moment, the system of private ownership and the system of socialist public ownership are both legal, but the system of private ownership will gradually become illegal. If you "guarantee private property" on three *mu* of land and promote the "Four Freedoms" the result would be to promote [the interests of] the small number of rich peasants and follow the capitalist road. The work of the *xian* and district cadres must gradually turn toward mutual aid and cooperativization of agricultural production and toward promoting socialism. If they don't engage themselves in socialist undertakings, then what are they doing? Are they attending to the affairs of individual economy? The secretaries of the *xian* [Party] committees and the district [Party] committees must consider working for socialism as a major thing. We must put the responsibility on the secretaries, [and] I am the secretary for the Central Committee. The secretaries of the [regional] bureaus of the Central Committee, the provincial [Party] committee secretaries, the [special] district [Party] committee secretaries, the *xian* [Party] committee secretaries, the district [Party] committee secretaries, and the [Party] secretaries at all levels must take responsibility and personally take part in the work. At present, seventy to eighty per cent of the energy of the Central Committee is concentrated on the matter of promoting the socialist transformation of agriculture. [Similarly,] the transformation of capitalist industry and commerce is also the promotion of socialism. Our comrades of the rural work departments at all levels, and those of you present at this conference, must become experts in the socialist transformation of agriculture; [you] must become experts in understanding theory, line, policy, and method.

The supply of vegetables to the cities [should be settled] primarily through planned supply. In large municipalities and newly developed cities, the population is very concentrated. How can they do without vegetables to eat? This problem has to be solved. If it is difficult to resolve [the problem of] producing and supplying vegetables [to the cities] by establishing mutual aid teams in the suburban areas, then we can bypass the mutual aid teams and go on to establish semisocialist cooperatives, or even fully socialist cooperatives. This issue deserves some study.

The plan to develop the producers' cooperatives has already been proposed. This winter and next spring, right up to the autumn harvest next year, we will set up over 32,000 [cooperatives] and, by 1957, we can expand that to 700,000. But we must anticipate that sometimes [the number of cooperatives] may grow all of a sudden, possibly to one million, or perhaps to more than a million. In short, [we must] establish more [cooperatives] and at the same time run them well; we must exercise active leadership and develop steadily.

This conference has been very successful. If we had not held it now but had waited until next January to hold it, we would have been late. This winter would have been wasted. We will meet again on March 26 next year, to examine how the plan [drawn up] this [time] has been implemented. At this conference, we have decided the date of the next conference and we have also decided to check the implementation of the resolutions made at this conference at the next conference. This is a very good method. Next autumn we shall hold yet another conference to discuss and formulate the tasks for next year's winter.

Notes

1. See text Oct. 15, 1953, note 2.

2. Here Mao plays on the slogan *wen bu er qianjin*, which means "advance with firm steps." (See text Sept. 7, 1953, note 4.) The phrase *wen bu* has a double meaning: it can mean "to take steady steps" as in the slogan, or it can mean "to come to a halt and take a firm stance."

3. Here Mao refers to the drastic reduction of the number of cooperatives in North China, from 9,000 to 6,000, in July 1953. For "adventurist advance," see text Aug. 12, 1953(1), note 22. The term "gust of wind" (*yi gu feng*) is commonly used to describe an upsurge of certain attitudes or practices. (See, for instance, Mao's usage of the term "communist wind," text Feb. 27, 1959[1],

note 41.)

4. This sentence, *qunju zhongri, yan bu ji yi, hao xing xiao hui, nan yi zai*, is found in *Lun yu* (Analects of Confucius), section 16, chapter "Wei Ling gong" (see J. Legge (1933), pp. 226-227). The original meaning of the sentence is that nothing can be made of people who congregate all day long and gossip but never touch on the subject of moral righteousness (*yi*) and who delight in the excercise of petty shrewdness (*xiao hui*). Mao here modifies the meaning of the sentence by transferring the meaning of the character *yi* from "moral righteousness" to "socialism" (*shehui zhuyi*), and by substituting the original character *hui*, meaning "shrewdness," with a homophone meaning "favor." This comment is intended as a criticism of the Right opportunists who opposed the (socialist) cooperativization of agriculture and who instead advocated piecemeal reforms and construction on the basis of the small-scale peasant economy (by small favors). Mao is also clearly alluding to the criticisms leveled at the CPC by certain people such as Liang Shuming, who accuse the CPC of not pursuing "benevolent policies." Mao's rejoinder is that such programs as Liang suggests are nothing but "small favors." See text Sept. 16-18, 1953, and text Sept. 12, 1953, note 11.

5. See text Oct. 15, 1953, note 9.

6. This metaphor, *gang ju mu zhang*, for the relationship between principles and details, is taken from *Shi pu xu* (A Preface to the Compendium of Poetry) written by Zheng Xuan in the late second century A.D. Other *loci classicus* of this saying are Cai Cen's *Za zhuan*, and Wang Tong's *Zhong Shuo*, the later written circa 600 A.D. The allusion is to a fishnet, the individual meshes of which are hardly discernible when the net is lying in a heap. When the net is raised by its headrope (*gang*), the individual meshes become clearly perceived. This metaphor has been commonly used in Chinese political slogans, and the character (*gang*) is often translated as "key link." It may also be noted that this metaphor was prominent after the Cultural Revolution in the debate over whether the principle and defining issue (*gang*) was class struggle (as Mao and his supporters contended) or the development of the forces of production (as Deng Xiaoping and others argued). Since 1976 and the arrest of the "Gang of Four" the metaphor has slipped from prominence.

7. See text Aug. 12, 1953, note 9.

8. See text Oct. 15, 1953, note 2.

9. See text Oct. 15, 1953, note 1.

10. See text Oct. 15, 1953, last paragraph.

11. See text March 19, 1953.

12. See text June 6, 1950(1), note 11.

13. See text Oct. 15, 1953, note 10.

14. See texts July 9, 1953, and Aug. 12, 1953. Also, K. Lieberthal (1976), pp. 59-60.

15. See text Aug. 12, 1953, note 5.

16. Mao is referring to a process in effect at that time and that would be formularized in the decree of the Government Administration Council in Nov. 1953, "On the Planned Purchasing and Supplying of Grain." This policy of *tong gou tong xiao* was later based on the APC's as units, and resulted in the decree, promulgated by the State Council in Oct. 1956, on nationwide planned purchasing and marketing of grain and other foodstuffs.

17. See text Oct. 15, 1953, note 6.

18. "See Stalin, 'Dialectical and Historical Materialism.'" (*Xuanji*, V, p. 124.)

Telegram to the USSR
(November 5, 1953)

Source: *RMRB* (Nov. 7, 1953), 1. Other Chinese Texts: *XHYB*, 50 (Dec. 28, 1953), 97; Quoted in *XHBYK*, 144 (Nov. 1958), 5-6. Available English Translations: NCNA, *Supplement*, 154 (Nov. 12, 1953), 1; HNA, *Daily News Release* (Nov. 7, 1953), 1; FBIS, *Daily Report* (Nov. 9, 1953), AAA1; *CDSP*, V:45 (Dec. 23, 1953), 17-18.

Chairman,
The Council of Ministers,
The Union of Soviet Socialist Republics

Comrade Malenkov:

On the occasion of the thirty-sixth anniversary of the great October Revolution, on behalf of the Chinese people, the Chinese government, and on my own behalf, I extend to you warm and sincere congratulations.

Since the victory of the October Revolution, the Soviet state has, like a beacon, illuminated the path of forward progress for the exploited peoples and oppressed nations throughout the world. The increasingly glorious achievements of the Soviet people and the strength that they recently acquired in their cause of building communism have inspired all progressive humanity to be filled with confidence and to strive for a good future.

The stand taken by the Soviet Union to peacefully resolve all international disputes and its efforts in opposing the imperialists' policy of aggression prove that the interests of the Soviet Union and those of peace- and freedom-loving people throughout the entire world are totally in line with each other. Good and honest people of all countries are recognizing more and more clearly that the Soviet Union is a strong bulwark for defending world peace and human justice, and moreover, the anti-Soviet slander of the imperialists is only one part of their despicable scheme to enslave humanity.

Through the rich historical experiences of the past thirty-six years, the two peoples of China and the Soviet Union have knit together an unbreakable brotherly friendship. At present, as the People's Republic of China, with the generous assistance of the Soviet Union, is progressing along the glorious path of socialist industrialization and the socialist reform of its national economy – a path already traveled victoriously by the Soviet Union – people of our country sense more than ever the priceless treasure of the close ties between the Chinese and Soviet peoples and the friendship between the two countries.

In the interests of our two people's common development and in the interests of world peace and the progress of humanity, may the great friendship between China and the Soviet Union remain forever consolidated and be continuously developed!

(Signed and dated in Beijing)

Reply to Ambassador of the German Democratic Republic
(November 12, 1953)

Source: *RMRB* (Nov. 13, 1953), 1. Available English Translations: HNA, *Daily News Release* (Nov. 14, 1953), 16; FBIS, *Daily Report* (Nov. 13, 1953), AAA8.

Johannes Konig had been head of the German Democratic Republic's diplomatic mission to the PRC since June 1950 (see text Jun. 24, 1950). This speech was made on the occasion of the elevation of the diplomatic relations between the GDR and the PRC to ambassadorial level.

Comrade Ambassador:

I am very happy to receive the letter of credence from the President of the German Democratic Republic which you have presented, and I am sincerely grateful for your congratulations.

In the past four years, the relations of friendship and cooperation between the People's Republic of China and the German Democratic Republic have made tremendous progress. The transformation of the diplomatic missions between the two countries into embassies will not only further strengthen the close cooperation between the two countries in all areas of politics, economy, and culture, but will also have great significance for the consolidation of the camp for peace, democracy, and socialism headed by the great Soviet Union.

The great successes of the German people in their work of national construction and in their struggle to attain peace have already made the German Democratic Republic a strong bulwark of the forces of peace and democracy in the whole of Germany and a principal factor in the defense of peace in Europe and the world. I believe that, with the assistance of the great Soviet Union and with the sympathy and support of all the people's democracies and peace-loving people of the world, the German people are bound to attain even greater victories in their just struggle for a unified, independent, democratic, and peace-loving Germany. The German people will forever have the full support of the Chinese people in this struggle.

Comrade Ambassador, I warmly welcome you as the Ambassador Extraordinary and Plenipotentiary of the German Democratic Republic to the People's Republic of China. In your work of consolidating the friendly and cooperative relations between Germany and China, you will receive my full support and that of the government of the People's Republic of China.

I sincerely wish you complete success in your work.

Reply to Minister of the Republic of Finland
(December 2, 1953)

Source: *RMRB* (Dec. 3, 1953), 1. Available English Translations: HNA, *Daily News Release* (Dec. 3, 1953), 11-12; FBIS, *Daily Report* (Dec. 3, 1953), AAA9.

Carljohan Sundstrom replaced Von Knorring as minister of the Republic of Finland to the PRC at this time. He was installed as ambassador on January 28, 1955.

Mr. Minister:

I am very happy to receive the letter of credence from the President of the Republic of Finland presented by Your Excellency and am grateful for the congratulations to the government and people of the People's Republic of China and myself expressed by the President of the Republic of Finland through Your Excellency.

In the last three years or so, the relations of friendship and cooperation between China and Finland in terms of economy and culture have attained a remarkable development. I believe that from now on, with Your Excellency's efforts, the friendly relations between our two countries will, on the present foundation, grow closer with each passing day. The enhancement of these friendly relations will not only further consolidate the friendship between the peoples of our two countries, but will contribute to world peace which all people in the world are striving to attain.

I warmly welcome Your Excellency as the Minister Extraordinary and Plenipotentiary of the Republic of Finland to the People's Republic of China. In your work of strengthening the friendship and cooperation between China and Finland, you will have my assistance and that of the government of the People's Republic of China.

I wish Your Excellency success in your work.

Letter to Dai Yuben
(December 9, 1953)

Source: *Shuxin*, p. 472.

According to the source, Dai was a native of Hunan who studied at the Self-Teaching University founded by Mao, and who, at the time of this letter, was working at the Workers' Hospital of Tangshan.

Comrade Yuben:

I have received your letter of September. I apologize for being so tardy in responding. It is very good that you are working at the Workers' Hospital, and I hope that you can persevere in your work there. When you go to a new place, it is very likely that you will encounter some difficulties [at first]; what you should do is persevere and thereby gradually overcome the difficulties there, and after a while, things could become smoother. In this way, both yourself and the country will benefit.

In reply and with my best wishes for your continued efforts,
Mao Zedong
December 9, 1953

Reply to Minister of the Kingdom of Denmark
(December 12, 1953)

Source: *RMRB* (Dec. 12, 1953), 1. Available English Translations: HNA, *Daily News Release* (Dec. 13, 1953), 5; FBIS, *Daily Report* (Dec. 15, 1953), AAA9.

A. Gregerson served as minister of the Kingdom of Denmark to the PRC at this time and was installed as ambassador on April 10, 1956.

Mr. Minister:

I am happy to accept the letter of credence from His Majesty, the King of Denmark, presented by Your Excellency, and am grateful for your congratulations.

The Chinese people attach great importance to the development of commercial and cultural relations between the peoples of China and Denmark, and believe that the development of these relations will be of assistance in promoting friendship between the two countries and defending world peace.

I welcome Your Excellency as the Envoy Extraordinary and Minister Plenipotentiary of the Kingdom of Denmark to the People's Republic of China, and pledge to your Excellency my assistance in your work aimed at strengthening the friendly relations between our two countries.

Best wishes for the prosperity of your country, the prospering of your people, and the good health of His Majesty your King.

Reply to Ambassador
of the Democratic People's Republic of Korea
(December 12, 1953)

Source: *RMRB* (Dec. 13, 1953), 1. Available English Translations: HNA, *Daily News Release* (Dec. 14, 1953), 12; FBIS, *Daily Report* (Dec. 15, 1953), AAA12.

Choe Il served as ambassador of the Democratic People's Republic of Korea to the PRC from December 1953 to June 1957.

Comrade Ambassador:

I am very pleased to accept this letter of credence from the Standing Committee of the Supreme People's Assembly of the Democratic People's Republic of Korea which you have presented, and I sincerely thank you for your congratulations.

For over three years, the Chinese and Korean peoples have knit together a most profound friendship in the struggle to resist the United States aggressor. The recent signing of the Economic and Cultural Cooperation Agreement between our countries further consolidated and developed the already long-standing and unbreakable relations of friendship and mutual assistance between our two countries.[1] Our increasingly strong unity undoubtedly will continue to contribute to the our cause of safeguarding peace in the Far East and in the world.

I firmly believe that with the brotherly aid of countries in the camp for peace and democracy headed by the Soviet Union and with the sympathy and support of the peace-loving peoples of the world the heroic and industrious Korean people are bound to be able to attain new and glorious successes in the cause of recovering and developing their national economy and in striving for the peace and unification of their homeland.

I warmly welcome you as the Ambassador Extraordinary and Plenipotentiary of the Democratic People's Republic of Korea to the People's Republic of China. In your work of strengthening and developing the brotherly friendship, mutual assistance, and cooperation between China and Korea, you will receive my full support and that of the government of the People's Republic of China.

I sincerely wish you complete success in your work.

Note

1. A ten-year agreement on economic and cultural cooperation to take effect from December 1953 was signed between the People's Republic of China and the Democratic People's Republic of Korea on Nov. 23, 1953, in Beijing.

Letter to Liao Jingwen
(December 13, 1953)

Source: *Shuxin*, p. 473. Other Chinese Text: *Meishu fenglei*, 3 (Aug. 1967), 6.

See also texts Nov. 20, 1949, and Aug. 26, 1950. Liao Jingwen is the widow of the famed artist Xu Beihong, who died in September 1953.

Comrade Jingwen:

I have received your October letter and Mr. Xu's painting of galloping horses, and I deeply cherish the memory of him. I am now sending Comrade Tian Jiaying to find out how things are with you.[1] If you have any difficulties, please feel free to inform me.

With my regards.

Mao Zedong
December 13, 1953

Note

1. Tian was Mao's private secretary at the time of this letter. The *Meishu fenglei* source has X X X here. For more biographical information on Tian, see text Mar. 2, 1954, source note.

Reply to Ambassador of the Soviet Union
(December 15, 1953)

Source: *RMRB* (Dec. 16, 1953), 1. Available English Translation: NCNA, *Daily Bulletin*, 949 (Dec. 22, 1953), 5-6.

P. F. Yudin served as ambassador of the USSR to the PRC from December 1953 to 1960.

Comrade Ambassador:

I am very happy to accept the letter of credence from the Presidium of the Supreme Soviet of the Union of Soviet Socialist Republics which you have presented, and I sincerely thank you for your congratulations.

The brotherly friendship between the People's Republic of China and the great Union of Soviet Socialist Republics has achieved tremendous progress in the past four years and is consolidated with each passing day. The Chinese people have always esteemed the friendship of the Soviet Union. Today, in undertaking the cause of large-scale national economic construction, they recognize even more deeply the invaluable treasure of the Soviet Union's great friendship. The Chinese people will certainly, with unwavering effort, always continue to strengthen the intimate friendship, alliance, and overall cooperation between China and the Soviet Union. I am equally convinced that the unbreakable alliance and cooperation between our two great countries not only completely corresponds to the interests of our peoples, but moreover plays a great, incomparable role in the cause of consolidating the camp of peace and democracy headed by the Soviet Union and of safeguarding peace and security in the Far East and the world.

Comrade Ambassador, I welcome you with extreme warmth as the Ambassador Extraordinary and Plenipotentiary of the Union of Soviet Socialist Republics to the People's Republic of China. In your work of consolidating the friendship, mutual assistance, and cooperation between the two countries of China and the Soviet Union, you will receive my full support and that of the government of the People's Republic of China.

I wish you complete success in your work.

Telegram to Anshan Workers and Staff
(December 25, 1953)

Source: *RMRB* (Dec. 26, 1953), 1. Other Chinese Text: *Shuxin*, p. 474; *XHYB*, 1 (Jan. 28, 1954), 137. Available English Translation: NCNA, *Daily Bulletin*, 954 (Dec. 31, 1953), 3.

All workers and staff of Anshan Iron and Steel Company[1]

Comrades:

I received your letter of December 21, 1953.

The construction projects of the Anshan Seamless Tubing Mill, the Anshan Heavy Rolling Mill, and the Anshan No. 7 Blast Furnace have been completed ahead of schedule, and they have begun production. All of these are great events in our country's development of heavy industry in 1953. I convey warm congratulations and deep gratitude to all the workers and staff who were engaged in these three construction projects, all the workers and staff of the Anshan Iron and Steel Company, and all the comrades of the Soviet Union who assisted in Anshan's construction. The people of our country are now united as one in a struggle to realize the socialist industrialization of our country. Your heroic labor is a major contribution to this goal. I hope you will continue your endeavor, learn from the advanced experience of the Soviet Union, make full use of your wisdom and strength, and strive for even greater achievements.

(Signed and dated)

Note

1. See text Dec. 14, 1952, source note.

Remark to Ke Qingshi
(December 26, 1953 [?])

Source: *Pi Tan zhanbao*, 7:484 (Aug. 5, 1967).

This remark is from a Red Guard publication issued during the height of the Cultural Revolution, a publication devoted to the criticism of Tan Zhenlin (see text May 17, 1958, note 34). While the source may not be entirely reliable and there are no corroborating sources, the remark is interesting enough to warrant inclusion. The date is suggested by the contextual implication that the remark was made on or around Mao's birthday. The comment here was made in response to a letter written to Mao by Tan Zhenlin and Chen Pixian (see text May 17, 1958, note 34, and text Jan. 10, 1951, source note) and to which Ke, allegedly, had unwittingly attached his signature also. Ke Qingshi (1902-1965) was one of the earliest members of the CPC, joining the Party in 1922. For the most part of the 1920s and early 1930s Ke was an underground CPC agent in the Shanghai area. During the years of the War of Resistance against Japan, he worked in several parts of the country – in the north, in Yanan, and finally ending up in Nanjing. In 1950, he became a member of the East China Military and Administrative Committee based in Shanghai, and at the end of 1952, he became the first secretary of the Jiangsu provincial Party (CPC) committee and a vice-chairman of that province's People's Government. Later he would become the secretary of the municipal Party committee of Shanghai and mayor of Shanghai, as well as a member of the Political Bureau. For more biographical information on Ke, see D. Klein and A. Clark, eds. (1971), I, pp. 440-442.

Some people want me to go and take a rest. There are two types of resting: one is to sleep in bed; the other is to sleep in a drum.[1]

Note

1. Mao is here making a slight deviation from the aphorism *meng zhai gu li* (being sealed in a drum), which translates as "being kept in the dark about things."

Inscription in Guest Book of the Moganshan Clinic
(Winter 1953)

Source: Zhou Yurui, "Mao Zedong keneng huan you chandou mabi bing" (Mao Zedong May Be Suffering from Trembling Paralysis), *Xingdao ribao* (Hong Kong) (July 18, 1968), quoted in *Shengping ziliao*, p. 308.

No other documentation from Chinese sources has been uncovered that corroborates the information in this article by Zhou Yurui, which claims that Mao was in a clinic at Moganshan, Zhejiang Province, in the winter(?) of 1953 for treatment. The uncertainty as to season is also in the Shengping ziliao *source.*

It takes patience to recuperate from an illness, and furthermore, it requires the spirit to struggle. After striving day after day [I hope that] health will be restored to my body.

Comment on the Department of Health Care
(1953)

Source: *Quanwudi*, 17 (June 26, 1967), 2. Available English Translation: *SCMM*, IX:22 (Apr. 8, 1968), 22.

According to Quanwudi, *this criticism was made in Mao's comments on a report submitted by the Department of Health Care. It is directed against the leadership of that department under He Cheng, who was the secretary of the First Party Group of that department, and who directed its work from 1949 to 1955. In the same article, accusations were made against Liu Shaoqi for indulging He's behavior. See text Oct. 1953.*

It's a total mess. There is no visible political leadership; nor can there be seen any earnest professional or technical leadership. . . .

[It] is a department without leadership, without political [awareness], a department that does not even manage its professional [duties] in earnest. . . .

[It] is a bureaucratic office where people specialize in eating and in acting as an officer and a lord and master. . . . This is utterly intolerable. . . in the current struggle against bureaucratism, [we must] tear away [their] masks, completely overthrow these [organs], change their appearance, and establish in their place organs that are truly capable of achieving some work.

Directive on Physical Culture
(1953)

Source: *PR*, 17:36 (Sept. 6, 1974), 11.

Physical culture is of major importance, concerning as it does the health of our six hundred million people.

Inscription for No. 1 Automobile Manufacturing Plant of Changchun
(1953)

Source: *RMRB* (Sept. 22, 1976), 5.

In Memory of the Foundation-laying of No. 1 Automobile Manufacturing Plant.

Directive on the Work of the Ministry of Geology
(1953)

Source: *Keji geming*, 1 (July 1967), 4.

This is an excerpt from Dazibao xuanbian *(Selections from Big-character Posters) of the Battalion of the Revolutionary Rebels of the Offices of the Ministry of Geology, no. 14. No date for this original publication is given. It is a publication published at the height of Red Guard activities during the Cultural Revolution.*

The Ministry of Geology is a department of investigative and research work. It should [pay attention to] key issues, and [yet] also be comprehensive. . . .

At the moment you are engaged in a battle, in tactics. In the past you have done the work of [laying out] strategies; this must be strengthened step by step. . . .

Reconnaissance is the battle; prospecting is the tactic; the strategy is to conduct geological investigations on a region-by-region basis.

1954

Telegram to the USSR
(January 4, 1954)

Source: *CDSP*, VI:2 (Feb. 24, 1954), 17.

The original of this telegram is in Pravda *and* Izvestia, *both Jan. 9, 1954. We have no Chinese translation of this telegram. The* CDSP *translation is presented here as it originally appeared. The telegram was addressed to the Central Committee of the CPSU and the Council of Ministers of the USSR.*

Dear Comrades!

I thank you profoundly for your congratulations on the occasion of my birthday.

Permit me to wish that the Soviet people, under the direction of the great Communist Party of the Soviet Union, will achieve new successes in the great cause of construction of communism.

Telegram to the Democratic Republic of Viet Nam
(January 29, 1954)

Source: FBIS, *Daily Report* (Feb. 1, 1954), CCC 1.

Because we have no Chinese text of this telegram, the original FBIS transcript is presented here.

I hereby sincerely thank you, comrade, the Government, and people of the Democratic Republic of Vietnam for your New Year greetings and I hereby wish you, comrade, good health. I believe that in the new year the Viet Nam people, under your leadership, will win greater victories in the righteous struggle against imperialism.

Telegram to the USSR
(February 11, 1954)

Source: *RMRB* (Feb. 14, 1952), 1. Other Chinese Text: *XHYB*, 3 (Mar. 28, 1954), 48. Available English Translations: NCNA, *Daily Bulletin*, 986 (Feb. 15, 1954), 1; FBIS, *Daily Report* (Feb. 15, 1954), AAA 9.

See text Jan. 2, 1950, note 1.

Chairman,
The Council of Ministers,
The Union of Soviet Socialist Republics

Comrade Malenkov:

On the occasion of the fourth anniversary of the signing of the Sino-Soviet Treaty of Friendship, Alliance, and Mutual Assistance,[1] Comrade Chairman, please accept my sincere gratitude and warm congratulations.

The events that we have experienced in the past four years have clearly borne out that the great alliance between China and the Soviet Union is a dependable foundation for safeguarding peace and security in the Far East and throughout the world. The sincere and unselfish assistance given to China by the government and people of the Soviet Union has had vital significance in quickening China's socialist industrialization, ensuring China's steady transition to socialism, and expanding the strength of the camp for peace and democracy headed by the Soviet Union.

May the friendship and unity of the two peoples of China and the Soviet Union always develop and be consolidated forever.

(Signed and dated in Beijing)

Note

1. See text Jan. 2, 1950, note 1.

Telegram to the USSR
(February 21, 1954)

Source: *RMRB* (Feb. 14, 1952), 1. Other Chinese Text: *XHYB*, 3 (Mar. 1954), 51. Available English Translation: NCNA, *Daily Bulletin*, 992 (Feb. 23, 1954), 1.

Chairman,
The Council of Ministers,
The Union of Soviet Socialist Republics

Comrade Malenkov:

On the occasion of the thirty-sixth anniversary of the founding of the armed forces of the Soviet Union, I express to you, comrade chairman, our sincere congratulations. May the glorious Soviet armed forces gain daily in strength in its cause of consolidating and defending world peace.

(Signed and dated in Beijing)

Letter to Tian Jiaying
(March 2, 1954)

Source: *Shuxin*, p. 475.

Tian Jiaying (b. 1908, a.k.a. Chen Yeping) was Mao's private secretary at the time of this letter (see text Dec. 13, 1953, note 1). In October 1954, he became general secretary of the Organization Department of the Central Committee of the CPC, and in July 1955, he became the deputy director of the Office of the Chairman of the PRC, thus affirming his close contact on a daily basis with Mao and the top echelon executive leaders of the PRC. He apparently continued to hold this key position through the early 1960s. Since the Cultural Revolution he has not been active publicly. Tian is the author of the popular book Xuexi wei renmin fuwu *(Learning to Serve the People), published by* Xuexi *(a CPC journal), April 1954, Beijing. For more biographical information on Tian, see* Zhonggong renming lu, *p. 110.*

Comrade Jiaying:

(1) Please make a copy of the letter from Yang Xiusheng[1] and forward it to Mr. Yang Kaizhi in Changsha.[2] Inquire of him whether or not the things described in that letter are true. I have absolutely no recollection of these things.

(2) For this current year [our commitment] is to send, as a subsidy, 12 million *yuan (rmb)*[3] to the Yang family. The six million for the first half of the year should be sent out immediately. Please handle this matter.

(3) Madam Li Shuyi is the widow of Comrade Liu Zhixun of Changsha (a martyr).[4] Her vocation is teaching, but she is advanced in years and the teaching is becoming too much of a burden for her, and it would be difficult for her to go on much further. Someone has asked me to recommend her to a position at the Beijing Literature and History Museum. The requirements of the Literature and History Museum [in terms of the qualifications of its staff members], however, are rather high. I have indeed recommended several people, but they have not been accepted and it does not seem appropriate for me to make any more recommendations. I intend, rather, to aid her with some of the fees I receive for my writing, and thus to resolve this problem. What I do not know is whether or not she herself, on her part, would accept this type of assistance. She is a very close friend of Yang Kaihui's, so there is nothing wrong with my assisting her in some way. Please write a letter to Mr. Yang Kaizhi, asking him to relay the question to Madam Li Shuyi,[5] and ask her to express her feelings [on this].

Mao Zedong
March 2

Notes

1. According to the source, Yang Xiusheng is a cousin of Yang Kaihui, Mao's late wife (see text May 11, 1957, note 1).

2. See text Oct. 9, 1949(1), note 1.

3. See text Oct. 2, 1952, note 4.

4. See text Apr. 18, 1950(2), source note, and text May 11, 1957, source note.

5. The Chinese term that Mao used here is *xiansheng*. For an explanation of this usage, see text July 19, 1950, note 1.

Letter to Huang Yanpei
(March 12, 1954)

Source: *Shuxin*, pp. 477-478.

See text Feb. 17, 1951, source note.

Vice-premier Huang:

I have received and read your letter of March 8. I have also forwarded the appended article to Premier Zhou and Minister Li Weihan[1] for discussion and their information. [The term] "people" refers to the bourgeoisie and the democratic parties, and does not include the landlord class or the bureaucratic capitalist class; in other words, it does not "include everyone."[2] The phrase "painless labor" is best left out in the publication,[3] because, in fact, those people who do not have much [class and political] awareness would feel some pain. If we write too many checks,[4] we may cause [people to have] dreams and fantasies, and if we do not then double [our efforts] in educating [them] and studying, if we do not raise [their] levels of political consciousness, those people who do feel pain would resent us. I pray that you would give some consideration to this.

My respectful regards for your health.

Mao Zedong
March 12, 1954
Hangzhou

Notes

1. According to the source this refers to a draft of Huang's speech to Shanghai industrial and commercial circles on March 1, 1954. In this draft, Huang had planned to use the metaphor of

"painless labor" to describe the transition of industrial and commercial enterprises to the socialist stage. On Mao's suggestion, Huang eventually revised the draft and eliminated the metaphor.

Premier Zhou refers to Zhou Enlai, who was premier of the GAC at this time; for Li Weihan, see text Apr. 9, 1951, source note.

2. For the term "democratic parties," see text Sept. 21, 1949, note 1. For the term "bureaucratic capitalism," see text Oct. 24, 1949(2), note 1.

3. See note 1.

4. This is a common Chinese saying meaning "making promises."

Telegram to Kim Du Bong
(March 14, 1954)

Source: *RMRB* (Mar. 17, 1954), 1. Other Chinese Text: *XHYB*, 5 (May 1954), 15. Available English Translation: NCNA, *Daily Bulletin* (Mar. 17, 1954), 8.

Kim Du Bong was the chairman of the Standing Committee of the Supreme People's Assembly of the Democratic People's Republic of Korea. His birthday was on March 17. No form of address or signature was conveyed in the RMRB *release.*

On the occasion of your sixty-fifth birthday, I express warm greetings to you. May you have good health and attain more and greater achievements in your work of [promoting] the recovery of the national economy of your country and striving for the peaceful unification of Korea.

Letter to Peng Shilin
(March 31, 1954)

Source: *Shuxin*, pp. 479-480.

According to the source, Peng is a native of Xiangtan xian, Hunan Province (Mao's native xian. During the period of the "Great Revolution" (1925-1927, a.k.a. the First Revolutionary Civil War period), Peng was principal of the Women's Vocational

School of Qingxi xiang, *Xiangtan* xian, *and gave Mao assistance when Mao was engaging in revolutionary activities in this area.*

Mr. Shilin:

I have read with respect your letter of March 9, 1954. Since you have entrusted your matter to my friend Mao Yizhu,[1] my intervention should no longer be needed. In general I am a bit reluctant to express my thoughts and feelings on behalf of the friends of my native village and my relatives in recommendation letters; occasionally I do it, but that is extremely rare. When Mr. Li Shuqing and my friend Wen Yunchang[2] asked me [for recommendations], I had to turn them down. They resolved their problem by finding someone [else] to entrust the matters with. I know that you are encountering some financial difficulties, and you can tell me about them. It would not be difficult for me to give you some further assistance in the area of [living] expenses. I hope you will, however, forgive me for my [unsatisfying] response.

My regards,

Mao Zedong
March 31, 1954

Notes

1. This is another name for Mao Yuju; see text May 15, 1950(1), source note.
2. See text Nov. 17, 1949, note 3, and text May 12, 1950(1), note 1.

Letter to Party Branch and *xiang* Government
of Shicheng *xiang*
(April 29, 1954)

Source: *Shuxin*, pp. 481-482.

Comrades of the Shicheng *xiang* Branch [of the CPC] and of the *xiang* Government of Shicheng *xiang*:

Comrade Mao Yueqiu[1] came to Beijing with your report. I am very grateful.

Some of my relatives of the Wen family of Tangjiaduo have come to Beijing to see me in the past several years.[2] Some of them, on returning home, have become arrogant and would not accept the supervision of the government; this is wrong of them. The people of the Wen family, no matter whom, ought to be like everyone else in the village; they should obey the leadership of the Party and the government, work diligently in their farming, and observe the law; there should be nothing special about them. I ask you not to feel that because those of the Wen family are my relatives, therefore it may not be easy to control them as you wish. My attitude [toward this matter] is: First, since they are [members of] the laboring people, and are my relatives, I care about them; second, because I care about them, I hope that they will make progress, that they will work diligently in their farming and observe the law, that they will take part in the mutual aid and cooperative organizations. In all this they ought to be exactly like everyone else and may not behave at all specially. If they behave in any backward manner, they ought to be criticized. They should not be spared the criticism of their failings and errors simply because they are my relatives.

Here I have a letter from Comrade Wen Bingzhang,[3] which I enclose for your perusal. I am in agreement with Comrade Wen Bingzhang's opinion; please handle it. Please also show this letter of mine and that of Wen Bingzhang to the people of Tangjiaduo so as to help them correct their failings and mistakes. I believe that as long as both you and I take the correct attitude and as long as they are not stubborn in their opinion, their shortcomings and mistakes can be rectified and they can make progress.

In comradely salute,

Mao Zedong
April 29, 1954

Notes

1. See text Oct. 4, 1953.
2. See text May 7, 1950, text May 12, 1950, and text Oct. 25, 1953.
3. According to the source, Wen Bingzhang is Mao's nephew.

Inscription on the Completion of Guanting Reservoir
(May 13, 1954)

Source: *GMRB* (May 16, 1954), 1.

Guanting Reservoir is located west of Beijing Municipality, in Hebei Province, at the confluence of the Yongding, Yang, and Shuanggan rivers. This inscription was written for the meeting of the reservoir's builders and administrative staff celebrating the completion of the project.

In celebration of the triumphant completion of the Guanting Reservoir.
Mao Zedong

Telegram to the South African Indian Congress
(May 28, 1954)

Source: *RMRB* (May 29, 1954), 1. Other Chinese Text: *XHYB*, 6 (June 1954), 38. Available English Translations: NCNA, *Daily Bulletin* (Jun. 1, 1954), 13; FBIS, *Daily Report* (June 1, 1954), AAA 25.

The Congress was held on May 28-31, 1954. The secretaries, Yusuf Cachalia and D. Fu Mistry, had sent a letter to Mao on April 24 soliciting support for the Congress in its struggle against racial and social discrimination in South Africa. For the text of this letter see RMRB *(May 29, 1954), 1 (Chinese), and NCNA,* Daily Bulletin *(Jun. 1, 1954), 13-14 (English). See also texts July 26 and Sept. 13, 1950.*

Joint Honorary Secretaries of the South African Indian Congress

Messrs. Cachalia and Mistry:

On behalf of the Chinese people, I totally support the just stand of the non-white people of South Africa (including Indians and other Asian and African people) in struggling for democratic rights and opposing racial discrimination and oppression. May this Congress achieve success in the cause of uniting Indians and all peoples in South Africa – white and nonwhite – in striving for peace, freedom, democracy, and progress.
(Signed and dated in Beijing)

Speech on the Draft Constitution
of the People's Republic of China[1]
(June 14, 1954)

Source: *Xuanji*, V, pp. 125-131. Available English Translation: *SW*, V, pp. 141-147.

According to this source, this is a speech made by Mao at the thirtieth session of the Central People's Government Council.

This Draft Constitution appears to have won the hearts of the people. From the discussion held in Beijing among more than five hundred people and the discussions of the active elements of all circles in the provinces and municipalities – that is, the widespread discussions among the more than eight thousand people representing the country as a whole – one can see that the preliminary draft of the Draft Constitution is a rather good one and that it has won the approval and support of the public. Today, many people have spoken here and they have all said the same.

Why did we organize such widespread discussions? There were several advantages in doing so. First of all, can something that has been worked out through discussion by a few people have the approval of the general public? Through [these broader] discussions, we have verified that the basic provisions and fundamental principles in the preliminary draft of the Draft Constitution are approved by everybody. All the correct things in the preliminary draft of the Draft [Constitution] have been preserved. The opinions of a small number of leaders have gained the approval of several thousand people. This indicates that [these opinions] are reasonable, appropriate, and practicable. In this way we have gained confidence Second, in these discussions we have collected more than 5,900 opinions (not including the questions and doubts raised). These opinions can be divided into three kinds. One kind are those that are incorrect. Another kind are not really wrong but are inappropriate and are best left unadopted. If they are not going to be adopted, why bother collecting them? What's the advantage in collecting these opinions? There are some advantages; we can understand that among the ideas of these more than eight thousand people there are such points of view regarding the Constitution and we can make a comparison. The third kind [are opinions] which have been adopted. These are of course very good and quite necessary. Without these opinions, although the preliminary draft of the Draft Constitution would be basically correct, it would still be incomplete; it would have shortcomings and would not be well-thought-out. The present draft may still have shortcomings and may still be incomplete, so we must seek the opinions of the people of the entire country. Nevertheless, seen from today's perspective, this Draft [Constitution] is relatively complete, and this is the result of our having adopted reasonable opinions.

Why is it that this Draft Constitution has won the hearts of the people? As I see it, one of the reasons is that in drafting the Constitution, we adopted the method of integrating the opinions of the leadership organs with the opinions of the broad masses. This Draft Constitution integrates the opinion of the small group of leaders with those of more than eight thousand people. After it is promulgated, it will again be discussed by the people of the entire country so that the opinions of the Center can be integrated with the opinions of the people throughout the country. This is the method of integrating the leadership with the masses and, broadly, with the active elements. We adopted this method in the past; the same should be done in the future. We must adopt this method for all major legislation. This time, by adopting this method, we achieved a relatively good and complete Draft Constitution.

Why is it that all of you here and the broad masses of active elements support this Draft Constitution? Why do you feel that it is good? There are two main reasons: One is that it sums up our experiences; the other is that it integrates principle with flexibility.

First, this Draft Constitution sums up [our] historical experience, particularly the experience of revolution and of construction in the last five years. It sums up the experience of the people's revolution led by the proletariat against imperialism, feudalism, [and] bureaucratic capitalism, and the experience of social reform, economic construction, cultural construction, and government work in the last few years. This Draft Constitution also sums up the experience [the Chinese people had] with the problem of a constitution since the final years of the Qing dynasty, beginning with the "Nineteen Constitutional Articles"[2] in the last days of the Qing dynasty, to the "Provisional Constitution of the Republic of China"[3] in the first year of the Republic, to the various constitutions and draft constitutions of the Beiyang warlords' governments,[4] to the "Provisional Constitution of the Republic of China during the Period of Political Tutelage" of Chiang Kai-shek's reactionary government, up to Chiang Kai-shek's sham constitution.[5] Of these some were positive, some were negative. For instance, the "Provisional Constitution of the Republic of China" in the first year of the Republic was, at that time, a relatively good thing. Of course it was incomplete and had shortcomings and it was bourgeois in nature. However, it [also] carried in itself a revolutionary, democratic character. That constitution was very simple. It is said that it was drafted in great haste; it was only one month from the time it was being drafted to the time it was ratified. As for the other several constitutions and draft constitutions, as a whole, they were all reactionary. This Draft Constitution of ours primarily sums up the experience of revolution and construction in our country while at the same time integrating our national experience with international experiences. Our Constitution belongs to the category of social-ist constitutions. We [based it] primarily on our own experience, but we also referred to the good points in the constitutions of the Soviet Union and the var-ious People's Democracies.[6] When it comes to constitutions, the bourgeoisie was the vanguard. Whether it was in Britain, France or the United States, the bourgeoisie had its revolutionary phase and it was then that they initiated con-stitutions. We cannot write off bourgeois democracy in one stroke and assert that their constitutions have no place in history.[7] Today, however, bourgeois constitutions are no good at all; they are bad. The constitutions of the imperi-alist countries, in particular, deceive and oppress the majority of the people. Our Constitution is of the new socialist type, which is different from the bour-geois type. Our Constitution is far more progressive when compared with the constitutions of the bourgeoisie, even those in its revolutionary periods. We are superior to them.

Second, our Draft Constitution combines principle with flexibility. There are two basic principles: the principle of democracy and the principle of socialism. Our democracy is not bourgeois democracy but the people's democracy; it is the people's democratic dictatorship led by the proletariat and based on the alliance of the workers and peasants. The principle of people's democracy runs through our entire Constitution. The other principle is social-ism. There is socialism in our country today. It is stipulated in the Constitution that we must complete the socialist transformation [of our soci-ety] and realize the socialist industrialization of the nation. This is a matter of principle. If we want to carry out the principle of socialism, does that mean that early one morning socialism will be put into practice in everything throughout the country? This, in form, would be very revolutionary, but [since] it lacks flexibility, it could not be carried out; it would meet with oppo-sition and fail. Consequently,[we] must allow things that cannot be accom-plished right away to be accomplished gradually. For instance, state capitalism must be carried out gradually. State capitalism appears not only in the form of joint state-private enterprises, but in various other forms as well.[8] One word [to take into consideration] is "gradual"; another is "various." This means gradually putting various forms of state capitalism into practice in order to achieve the socialist system of ownership by the whole people. The socialist system of ownership by the whole people is the principle.[9] For this principle to be achieved, it must be integrated with flexibility. [In this case] the flexibility is [represented by] state capitalism, and what's more, it does not have just one single form, but "various" forms, and its materialization comes not in a day, but "gradually." This would be flexibility. We write [into the Constitution] what we can accomplish now and leave out what is not feasible [for the moment]. For instance, regarding the material guarantees of civil rights, later, when production has developed, they will definitely expand in comparison to their present [scope], but what we have written [into the Con-stitution] at this point is still only [that they will] "gradually expand." This, too, is flexibility. For another example, the United Front was written into the

Common Program,[10] and now it has again been written into the preamble of the Draft Constitution. We must have a "broad people's democratic united front consisting of all democratic classes, democratic parties, and people's organizations" to reassure the various strata [in society], the national bourgeoisie and the various democratic parties, the peasants, and the urban petty bourgeoisie. Then, there is also the question of the minority nationalities; here we have elements of commonality and elements of particularity. Where there is commonality, the common provisions [in the Draft Constitution] apply; where there is particularity, the particular provisions [of the Draft Constitution] apply. Politically, economically, and culturally, the minority nationalities each have their own particular characteristics. What are the particular characteristics of the minority nationalities in terms of the economy? Article 5 [of the Draft Constitution], for example, says that, at present, there are four types of systems of ownership of the means of production in the People's Republic of China, but actually, the minority nationality areas now still have other forms of ownership systems. Do we still have the system of primitive communal ownership? I'm afraid it still exists among some minority nationalities. The slave-owner ownership system and the feudal overlord ownership system, too, still exist [in some places] in our country. From a contemporary perspective, the slave system, the feudal system, and the capitalist system are all no good, but in fact, historically, they were all at one time or another more progressive than the primitive commune system. At the beginning, these systems were progressive, but subsequently they no longer worked and so other systems came on to replace them. Article 70 of the Draft Constitution provides that the minority nationality areas "may, in accordance with the particular political, economic, and cultural characteristics of the minority nationalities in a given area, work out regulations dealing with [local] autonomy and independent implementations."[11] These are all integrations of principle and flexibility.

It is precisely for these two reasons that this Draft Constitution has gained the support of the public, and that everyone says that it is good: one is that it correctly and appropriately sums up [our] experience; the other is that it correctly and appropriately combines principle with flexibility. If it were not for these, I don't think the public would approve of it or say that it is a good thing.

This Draft Constitution is fully practicable and must be put into practice. Of course, today it is still nothing but a draft, but in a few months, after it has been ratified by the National People's Congress, it will become a formal constitution. Today we must be prepared to carry it out. After it has been ratified, then everybody in the country must put it into practice. In particular, the staff personnel in the state organs must take the lead in carrying it out, [but] first and foremost you who are present should put it into practice. To fail to put it into practice will be to violate the Constitution.

After our Draft Constitution has been published, it will gain the unanimous support of the people throughout the country and will serve to promote their enthusiasm. An organization has to have a charter. A country must also have a charter. The constitution is an overall charter; it is a fundamental law. If we use such a fundamental law as the constitution to codify the principles of the people's democracy and of socialism so that the people of the whole country will have a clear track [in front of them] and so that they will feel they have a clear, precise, and correct road to follow, then we will be able to promote the enthusiasm of the people throughout the country.

Will there be international repercussions when this Draft Constitution is published? There will be repercussions in the democratic camp as well as among the capitalist countries. [People] within the democratic camp will be happy when they see that we have a clear, precise, and correct road to follow. [If] the Chinese are happy, they too will be happy. If the oppressed and exploited people in the capitalist countries see it, they too will be happy. Naturally there are some people who will be unhappy. The imperialists and Chiang Kai-shek will all be unhappy. Do you think that Chiang Kai-shek will be happy? I think that even without asking his opinion we can safely say that he will be unhappy. We are very familiar with Chiang Kai-shek, and [we know that] he absolutely will not approve of [our constitution]. President Eisenhower will not be happy either, and he'll say that it is no good. They will say that this Constitution of ours charts a clear and precise, but a very bad road, a wrong road, [and they'll say that] socialism and the people's democracy are wrong. They also disapprove of flexibility. They'd like most for us [to try] to put socialism into practice overnight and make a mess of everything; then they'd be happy. They do not approve of China promoting a united front either; they hope that we'll promote things all of "one color."[12] Our Constitution has a national character, but it also has a type of international character; it is a national phenomenon, but it is also a sort of international phenomenon. There are many countries that, like us, have suffered the oppression of imperialism and feudalism, and [the people of these countries] constitute a majority of the world's population. It would be helpful to the people in these countries for us to have a revolutionary constitution, a people's democratic constitution, and a clear, precise, and correct road to follow.

Our general objective is to strive to build a great socialist country. We are a big country with six hundred million people. In the end, how much time will be needed for us to realize socialist industrialization, realize the socialist transformation and mechanization of agriculture, and build a great socialist country? Let's not be absolutely definite now. Generally speaking, we can establish a foundation in about three five-year plans' time, that is, in about fifteen years. Will we have become very great by then? Not necessarily. As I see it, if we are able to build a great socialist country, it will take about fifty years, which means ten five-year plans. That will be about enough. Then we'll be something, and things will be quite different from what they are now. What can we make now? We can make tables, chairs, tea bowls, and teapots; we can grow grain [and even] grind it into flour, [and] we can also make paper. But we still cannot make an automobile, an airplane, a tank, or a tractor. Let's not blow our own horn too loudly or begin to get cocky. Naturally, I am not saying that we can cock our tails a bit higher if we can make one [tractor], or that we can cock it even higher if we can make ten [tractors], or that the more [tractors] we can make the higher we can cock our tails.[13] That won't do. Even when we're in good shape in fifty years we'll still have to be as modest as we are now. It won't be good if, at that time, we become arrogant and look down on everyone. We mustn't be arrogant, not even in a hundred years. We must never cock our tails.

This Constitution of ours is a constitution of a socialist type, but it still isn't a fully socialist constitution. It is a constitution for a transitional period. At present we must unite all the people in the country and unite with all forces with which we can be and ought to be united to strive for the construction of a great socialist country. The Constitution has been written for precisely this purpose.

Lastly, let me explain a problem. Some people say that certain individual provisions have been deleted from the Draft Constitution because some people were particularly modest. The matter can't be explained this way. It is not a matter of modesty but rather that, in those places, what had been written was neither proper, reasonable, nor scientific. In a People's Democracy like ours, we ought not to write such improper provisions [into the Constitution]. It is not the case that [provisions] that ought to have been written [into the Constitution] were not written in as a matter of modesty. In science there is no question of modesty or immodesty. Making a constitution is a scientific endeavor. We must not believe anything that is not scientific, that is to say, we must not be superstitious. Whether it relates to Chinese or foreigners, the dead or the living, what's right is right [and] what's wrong is wrong. To believe otherwise is to be superstitious. We must destroy superstition.[14] Whether it be something ancient or modern, we must believe what is correct and not believe anything that is incorrect. Not only will we not believe it, but we must also criticize it. This alone is a scientific attitude.

Notes

1. In the early years of the PRC, the "Common Program" served as the organic law of the state and a surrogate constitution. (See text Sept. 21, 1949, note 3.) The work of drafting and ratifying a more permanent constitution began in 1953. On January 13 of that year a resolution of the delegates of all local levels to the National People's Congress called for the establishment of a committee to produce a preliminary draft of the Draft Constitution. In March 1954, this preliminary draft was completed and was subjected to discussion (as Mao explains in this speech) in a large number of major cities from March 22 to June 11. On June 14, following Mao's speech here, the draft was adopted by the Central People's Government Council and was then subjected to two more months of nationwide discussion. On September 9, 1954, the Central People's Government Council adopted the final draft, which was submitted on September 15 to the First Session of the NPC. The Constitution was ratified unanimously by the Congress on September 20, 1954, and remained in effect, in essence, until 1975, when it was replaced by a new, revised constitution. For an English text of this constitution as finally adopted in September 1954 (but not the draft),

see T. Chen, (1967), pp. 75-92.

2. In November 1911, after the eruption of revolutionary activities in the central and southern provinces, the Qing court promulgated, with a view to stemming the insurrectionary tide, the "Xianfa zhongda xintiao shijiutiao" (Nineteen Major Articles of Good Faith on the Constitution) which in effect reaffirmed the constitutionality of the monarchy while making concessions in the areas of enlarging the powers of the national assembly and establishing a constitutional cabinet. This maneuver, however, did not succeed in forestalling the fall of the Qing or the abdication of the Xuantong Emperor in February of the following year.

3. This refers to the "Provisional Constitution" adopted by the Republic of China upon Sun Yat-sen's assumption of the position of provisional president of the Republic on March 11, 1912.

4. These refer, mainly, to four things: (1) The so-called "Tiantan xianfa caoan" (Heavenly Temple Draft Constitution) promulgated by the Yuan Shikai government in 1913. (2) The Constitution of the Republic of China, also known as the New Constitution (*Xin yaofa*) promulgated by the Yuan government in 1914. In October 1913, Yuan assumed the position of President of the Republic and proceeded to strengthen his own political advantage. This "New Constitution," therefore, reflected the ascendency and almost complete dominance of Yuan over the much weakened national constituent assembly. (3) The "constitution" promulgated by the Cao Kun government in 1923. (4) The Constitution of the Republic of China drafted by a committee in a national assembly dominated by the militarist interests of the warlord Duan Qirui in 1925. Both of the constitutions promulgated under Cao Kun and Duan Qirui included strong confederate tendencies reflecting the disintegration of the national polity under the ravaging of the warlords at the time.

5. In June 1931, the Nationalist government under Chiang Kai-shek promulgated a "constitution" (*yaofa*) to be effective for the "period of tutelage" as designated by Sun Yat-sen in his treatise *Jianguo dagang* (Outline of the Construction of the State). The fundamental principles of this "constitution" were the "Three People's Principles" (*Sanmin zhuyi*) and the recognition of the separation of the five powers of government (*wuquan fen li*). The "sham constitution" refers to the Constitution of the Republic of China ratified by a Kuomintang-dominated national assembly on November 15, 1946. This was basically an official ratification of the 1935 Draft Constitution (also known as the May 5 Draft Constitution), which was itself a derivative of the 1931 version. (For further reference, see Mao, *SW*, I, pp. 259-260.)

6. See text Sept. 21, 1949, note 4.

7. See text June 15, 1953, note 2.

8. See text July 9, 1953.

9. While Mao had spoken of various stages in the transformations of the ownership system in society (see text June 15, 1953, and text Oct.15, 1953), the system of ownership by the whole people (*quanmin suoyouzhi*), which is possible at an advanced stage of socialism, is something he did not discuss at length until quite a few years later. See text Mar. 5, 1956, note 11, and text Nov. Nov. 1958(1), note 2.

10. See text Sept. 21. 1949, note 3. Mao is here referring to the term "people's democratic united front" written into the preamble and Article 13 of the Common Program. This is distinct from the earlier "united fronts" strategically formed between political parties, notably the two CPC-Kuomintang United Fronts, once during the First Revolutionary Civil War period and the second in the War of Resistance against Japan period. See text Feb. 18, 1951, note 13.

11. This corresponds to Article 70 of the Constitution as adopted and ratified in September 1954. See T. Chen (1967), p. 88.

12. Mao's metaphor here derives from the game of *majong* in which a very high scoring value is assigned to a hand consisting of tiles of only one type, or "suit."

13. This term, *qiao weiba* in Chinese, is a common imagery frequently used by Mao to describe people's behavior when they are arrogant or cocky. In other places it has sometimes been translated as "strutting."

14. The Chinese term here is *po xu mixin*, which is sometimes translated as "dispelling blind faith." In Mao's usage *mixin* is a subjective characteristic with both a "positive" outcome and a negative outcome: one may, as a result of *mixin*, unquestioningly place one's trust in past traditions and dogmas (i.e., superstitions) or in the experience of other people and societies (e.g., that

of the Soviet Union) without regard to the realism of one's own environment. This can lead one to overestimate one's capacities. On the other hand, *mixin* can also result in one's underestimating one's own abilities, believing instead, for instance, that if other people in the past have said that a certain thing cannot be done, it cannot be done. While in the present context Mao was issuing a warning against the former type of *mixin* (and this is one of the first instances after 1949 when he did so), in subsequent years of his leadership of the PRC, Mao would combat both types of "blind faith" equally, swinging from one variation at times to the other at other times.

Beidaihe: A Poem
(Summer 1954)

Source: *Poems of Mao Tse-tung,* pp. 82-83. Other Chinese Texts: *Shici*, p. 29; *Mao shici,* pp. 12-13; *Poems,* pp. 48-49. Available English Translations: *Poems of Mao Tse-tung,* pp. 83; *Poems,* p. 48; S. Schram (1974), p. 166; J. Chen (1967), p. 345.

Beidaihe is a resort area southwest of the city of Qinhuangdao at the northeastern tip of Hebei Province, on the coast of the Bohai. This poem is set to the ci *pattern of* Lang-taosha, *which was derived from a septametric* lu *poem of the same title of the Tang dynasty, and was popularized as a modified* ci *pattern by Li Yu (Emperor Houzhu of the Southern Tang dynasty, 937-975 A.D.), and by the Song dynasty poets Liu Yong and Zhou Bangyan.*

Torrents falling upon the land of You-Yan,[1]
Foamy waves dashing toward the sky.
Beyond Qinhuangdao,[2] some fishing boats are drifting,
Screened by the vast expanse of ocean from view;
Who can tell where they are?
The story of this land reaches back beyond a thousand years,
To when Emperor Wudi of Wei brandished his whip,
And left the world his poem: I Descend Upon Jieshi.[3]
Today, as it did then, the bleak autumn wind whispers and sighs;
Nothing has changed, except in the world of Man.[4]

Notes

1. You-Yan stands for Youzhou and the state of Yan. Youzhou is the name of a Chinese administrative region whose territory had changed from the Zhou dynasty (841-221 B.C.) through the Qin (221-206 B.C.), Han (206 B.C.-220 A.D.) and subsequent dynasties until it was abolished as an administrative region designation in the Sui dynasty (589-618 A.D.) It was gener-

ally located in northeastern China, and at one time it included territory in what is today Korea. Yan was one of the many warring states in the Spring and Autumn and Warring States periods (722-481 B.C. and 403-221 B.C.). Both are archaic terms describing the northern and northeastern part of Hebei Province, where Beidaihe is located.

2. Qinhuangdao translates as "The Island of the Qin Emperor" and is named in memory of Emperor Shihuang of the Qin dynasty (221-206 B.C.). (See text May 8, 1958, note 54.) It is actually a peninsula located on the easternmost tip of Hebei Province, about 10 km. northeast of Beidaihe. It has an ice-free harbor and has been exploited as a trading port since the latter part of the nineteenth century.

3. The line "Donglin Jieshi" (I descend on my eastward journey upon Jieshi) opens the second poem in a set of five written by Cao Cao, Emperor (posthumously) Wudi of the Wei dynasty, in 207 A.D. (see text June 30, 1953, note 3), when he was making war upon the Tartars in northeastern China. The set of poems is known under the aggregate title *Buchu xiamen xing* (Ballad of a Sortee from Xiamen). Jieshi is the name of a rocky cliff near Beidaihe which has, since Wudi's time, sunk into the sea. The phrase *xiaoshi qiufeng* (shivering autumn winds) also appears in Wudi's poem.

4. This aphorism derives from the Tang dynasty poet Li Bo's poem "Shanzhong wenda" (A Dialogue in the Hills).

Telegram to the People's Republic of Poland
(July 20, 1954)

Source: *RMRB* (Jul. 22, 1954), 1. Other Chinese Text: *XHYB*, 8 (Aug. 1954), 114. Available English Translations: HNA, *Daily News Release* (Jul. 22, 1954), 17; FBIS, *Daily Report* (Jul. 23, 1954), AAA 28-29 (the date cited in this source for the telegram is Jul. 21, 1954).

Chairman,
The Council of State,
The People's Republic of Poland

Comrade Aleksander Zawadzki:

On the occasion of the tenth anniversary of the founding of the People's Republic of Poland, I extend, on behalf of the Chinese people, of the government of the People's Republic of China, and on my own behalf, sincere congratulations to the Polish people, the Government of the People's Republic of Poland, and yourself.

Over the past ten years, the Polish people, led by the Polish United Workers' Party, have achieved brilliant successes in both the consolidation of the people's democratic system and the socialist industrialization of the country. People's Poland has already become an important force in the camp for world peace, democracy, and socialism headed by the Soviet Union.

The Chinese people sincerely wish the Polish people even greater successes in continuing their efforts toward socialist construction and in the struggle of safeguarding world peace.

(Signed and dated in Beijing)

Telegram to the Democratic Republic of Viet Nam
(July 23, 1954)

Source: *RMRB* (July 24, 1954), 1. Other Chinese Text: *XHYB*, 8 (Aug. 1954), 86. Available English Translations: HNA, *Daily News Release* (July 24, 1954), 1; FBIS, *Daily Report* (July 26, 1954), AAA 25.

President,
The Government of the Democratic Republic of Viet Nam

Comrade Ho Chi Minh:

On the occasion of the reaching of an agreement on the armistice question and on the question of the political situation in Indochina, on behalf of the Chinese people and the government of the People's Republic of China, I extend the most heartfelt and warmest congratulations to our brothers, the Vietnamese people, to the government of the Democratic Republic of Viet Nam, and to you.

At the Geneva Conference[1] the delegation from the Democratic Republic of Viet Nam represented the hopes for peace of the Vietnamese people who had struggled heroically for national independence and freedom and had already attained glorious victories, and worked hard for the restoration of the peace of Indochina, and finally achieved an agreement. This is yet another great victory for the Vietnamese people. This victory is helpful in promoting collective peace and security in Asia and is beneficial to furthering the relaxation of the tension in the international situation.

All the people of China will strive together with the people of Viet Nam to assure and attain the thorough implementation of the Agreement and to preserve and consolidate the peace and security of Asia and the world.

(Signed and dated in Beijing)

Note

1. The Geneva Conference was convened from April 26 to July 21, 1954, to settle the issues of the national independence and the peace settlement of Korea and Indochina. On July 21, agreements regarding the independence of the three countries Viet Nam, Laos, and Cambodia were reached. See *RMRB* (July 22, 1954), 1.

Directive on Work in Traditional Chinese Medicine
(July 30, 1954)

Source: *Wansui* (1969), pp. 10-12. Other Chinese Text: *Dongfanghong* (May 1, 1967) (excerpts); see text 1954 Winter. Available English Translations: *SCMM* (suppl.), 22 (Apr. 8, 1968), 7-8; JPRS, *Miscellany*, I, pp. 12-13.

See also text Oct. 20, 1954.

[Traditional] Chinese medicine has made great contributions to the people of our country. With a population of six hundred million, China is the most populous country in the world. Of course, there are many factors contributing to the ability of our country's people to multiply and prosper day by day, but of these, the part played by health care must be one of the [most] important. In this respect, we must give credit first to [traditional] Chinese medicine.

If we compare Chinese and Western medicine, [traditional] Chinese medicine has a history of several thousand years, whereas Western medicine was introduced into China only a few decades ago. To this day, there are still more than 500 million people in the entire country who rely on [traditional] Chinese medicine for the diagnosis and treatment of their illnesses, while those who depend on Western medicine number only several tens of millions (and most are in big cities). Therefore, if we speak of China's health care since the beginning of history, the contributions and accomplishments of [traditional] Chinese medicine are very great.

For a number of years, not only has our homeland's medical heritage not been developed, but on the contrary, it has been slighted and repudiated. (For instance, examinations given to practitioners of traditional Chinese medicine cover the subjects of physiology and pathology. Those who fail these subjects are not given certificates. In addition, there are regulations such as those prohibiting practitioners of traditional Chinese medicine from joining hospital staffs.) The Central Committee's directive on uniting doctors of the traditional Chinese school with doctors of the Western school has not been fully carried out, and a true unity between the two sides remains unresolved. This is a mistake. This problem must be resolved; this mistake must be corrected. It requires first of all that the health care administration departments at all levels should change their way of thinking.

Henceforth, the most important thing is to first ask practitioners of Western medicine to study [traditional] Chinese medicine, and not for practitioners of [traditional] Chinese medicine to study Western medicine. First, we must transfer a hundred to two hundred graduates of medical institutes or colleges, handing them over to some well-known doctors of [traditional] Chinese medicine so that they can study their clinical experience. Furthermore, they should assume an attitude of great modesty in their studies. It is a glorious [endeavor] for practitioners of Western medicine to study [traditional] Chinese medicine, because after studying and promoting it they will be able to remove the boundary between [traditional] Chinese medicine and Western medicine and form a unified Chinese medical science as a contribution to the world. Second, all hospitals must systematically invite doctors of [traditional] Chinese medicine to come to the hospitals to give medical treatments to patients and hold consultations, and permit hospitalized patients to take [traditional] Chinese medicines. Furthermore, all sorts of regulations should be laid down to ensure systematically that respect be shown to doctors of traditional Chinese medicine so that they may not encounter difficulties or have a feeling of apprehension when they do their work of treatment in the hospitals. Third, Chinese medicine [itself] should be well-protected and developed. Our country's Chinese medicine has a history of several thousand years, and it is an extremely precious asset of our homeland. If we simply let it decline it would be a crime on our part. Therefore, we should investigate and protect the growing of medicinal herbs in the various provinces, encourage their production, facilitate their shipment, and improve their marketing. For instance, some medicinal herbs, because of their relatively long growth period, require from planting and cultivating to harvesting a period of more than two or three years. For instance, the white peony*[Peionia albiflora]*is a plant that matures in four years, and the *huanglian [Coptis japonica]* is one that matures in six years. Individual peasants often do not have the resources to plant them. Furthermore, in some herb-producing areas such as Gansu and Qinghai, the herbs produced cannot be shipped out in time because of the inconvenience in transportation, and the peasants often use them as fuel. In the past, there was a great wastage of some Chinese herbs because the processing and preserving techniques were deficient. Packaging and storage methods were not good, and losses from mildew and spoilage were severe. [The situation] should be improved. Institutions in charge of such work should henceforth adopt a joint state-private form of management. Personnel who process medicinal herbs should be classified according to their technical levels and be considered technical cadres. As for research in Chinese [herbal] medicine, it is not sufficient merely to conduct chemical analysis. We should go one step further and carry out pharmacological and clinical experiments. In particular, we should pay special attention to the compound effects of the Chinese [herb] medicines. Fourth, we should begin to sort things out and put together writings on [traditional] Chinese medicine. In the past nobody put together [such texts] because they were difficult to comprehend and were not valued. Medicinal books on [traditional] Chinese medicine will soon cease to exist if we do not collect them together. We should organize learned physicians of traditional Chinese medicine to, first of all, systematically but also selectively translate those useful [texts on traditional Chinese medicine] from ancient Chinese into modern Chinese. When the time is right we should further organize [these physicians] to summarize their own experiences and compile a set of systematic texts on [traditional] Chinese medicine.

To realize the various tasks mentioned above, we must first rectify bourgeois, individualistic, and sectarian ideology. Only when there is a change in ideology can the tasks mentioned above be carried out thoroughly.[1]

From now on, [personnel] at any level of administrative departments in public health will be dismissed if they do not do well in carrying out these tasks.

Note

1. Mao is apparently fighting certain tendencies within the leadership of the health care department that looked askance at the idea of unifying the traditional Chinese and "modern" Western schools of medicine. In 1953, Mao had berated He Cheng, the deputy minister of health care, for providing no leadership (or the wrong leadership) for the Department of Health Care. See text 1953 (1). In February 1955 the then deputy director, Yu Bin, was criticized for his opposition to the unification of the two schools, and on November 19, 1955, He Cheng's self-criticism was published.

Letter to the Staff of the No. 320 Factory
(August 1, 1954)

Source: *Shuxin*, p. 483.

According to the source, this is reprinted from an original preserved by the Ministry of Aeronautical Industry.

The workers and staff of No. 320 National Factory

Comrades:
I have read your report of July 26.[1] I congratulate you on your triumphant

success in the trial production of the first Yake 18 airplane. This is an excellent beginning for the founding of our nation's airplane building industry and for the strengthening of our national defense forces. I hope you will continue to apply your efforts, and, under the guidance and instruction of the Soviet experts, further grasp [the fine points] of the technology and improve the quality [of your product], and ensure the completion of the task of the actual production.

Mao Zedong
August 1, 1954

Note

1. According to *RMSC* (1955), p. 533, July 26, 1954, was the day on which the trial flight ceremonies of the first batch of airplanes manufactured by the PRC was held. The actual site of these ceremonies and exercises was not given.

Telegram to the Democratic People's Republic of Korea
(August 12, 1954)

Source: *RMRB* (Aug. 15, 1954), 1. Other Chinese Text: *XHYB*, 9 (Sept. 28, 1954), 53. Available English Translations: HNA, *Daily News Release* (Aug. 15, 1954), 3; FBIS, *Daily Report* (Aug. 17, 1954), FFF 18-19.

Chairman,
The Standing Committee,
The Supreme People's Assembly,
The Democratic People's Republic of Korea

Comrade Kim Du Bong:

On the occasion of the ninth anniversary of the liberation of Korea, on behalf of the government and people of China and on my own behalf, I express sincere congratulations to the government of the Democratic People's Republic of Korea, to the Korean people, and to yourself.

May the heroic Korean people attain even greater successes in their struggle to restore and develop their national economy, to consolidate peace in Korea, and to prevent the resurgence of a new war of aggression.

May the unbreakable friendship between the Chinese and Korean peoples be further consolidated and developed. This friendship is a powerful guarantee for maintaining peace in the Far East and throughout the world. (Signed and dated in Beijing)

Telegram to the People's Republic of Romania
(August 21, 1954)

Source: *RMRB* (Aug. 23, 1954), 1. Other Chinese Text: *XHYB*, 9 (Sept. 28, 1954), 101. Available English Translations: HNA, *Daily News Release* (Aug. 23, 1954), 6-7; FBIS, *Daily Report* (Aug. 24, 1954), AAA 20.

Chairman,
The Presidium,
The Grand National Assembly,
The People's Republic of Romania

Comrade [Petru] Groza:

On the occasion of the tenth anniversary of the liberation of Romania, on behalf of the government and people of the People's Republic of China and on my own behalf, I convey sincere congratulations to the Romanian people and to yourself.

Over the last ten years, the Romanian people, led by the Romanian Workers' Party, have attained brilliant successes in the area of consolidating the people's democratic political power as well as in building socialism. These successes have enabled the Romanian people to gain a life of increasing prosperity and happiness, and have strengthened the forces for world peace and democracy headed by the Soviet Union.

The Chinese people wish the Romanian people even greater successes in the cause of building socialism and defending world peace.
(Signed and dated in Beijing)

Telegram to the Democratic Republic of Viet Nam
(August 31, 1954)

Source: *RMRB* (Sept. 2, 1954), 1. Other Chinese Text: *XHYB*, 10 (Oct. 28, 1954), 198. Available English Translations: HNA, *Daily News Release* (Sept. 2, 1954), 1; FBIS, *Daily Report* (Sept. 2, 1954), AAA 4.

President,
The Democratic Republic of Viet Nam

Comrade Ho Chi Minh:

As peace is beginning to be restored in Indochina,[1] it is with great joy that I represent the government of the People's Republic of China and the Chinese people in sending warm congratulations to the government of the Democratic Republic of Viet Nam and to the Vietnamese people on this occasion of the ninth anniversary of the Democratic Republic of Viet Nam. The heroic struggle for national independence and freedom in which the Vietnamese people have been engaged for many years has already scored great achievements. I deeply believe that the Vietnamese people will win even greater victories in the cause of consolidating peace and achieving unification, independence, and democracy. In this the Vietnamese people will have the deep concern and active support of the Chinese government and all the Chinese people.
(Signed and dated in Beijing)

Note

1. See text July 23, 1954, note 1.

Reply to Ambassador of the People's Republic of Bulgaria
(September 2, 1954)

Source: *RMRB* (Sept. 3, 1954), 1. Other Chinese Text: *XHYB*, 10 (Oct. 28, 1954), 188. Available English Translation: HNA, *Daily News Release* (Sept. 3, 1954), 3.

D. Dimov served as ambassador of the People's Republic of Bulgaria to the PRC from September 1954 to April 1957.

Comrade Ambassador:

I am very happy to accept the letter of credence from the Presidium of the National Assembly of the People's Republic of Bulgaria which you have presented, and I sincerely thank you for your congratulations.

The brotherly friendship between the People's Republic of China and the People's Republic of Bulgaria and their close cooperation in the areas of politics, the economy, and culture have already developed greatly. This has not only promoted the prosperity and happiness of the two peoples, but has also strengthened the forces of world peace and democracy headed by the great Soviet Union.

The brilliant successes which the Bulgarian people, under the leadership of the Bulgarian Communist Party, have achieved in the cause of socialist construction in the ten years since liberation have stirred up the enthusiasm for labor of the Chinese people who are moving ahead with socialist construction and socialist transformation.

Comrade Ambassador, I warmly welcome you as the ambassador extraordinary and plenipotentiary from the People's Republic of Bulgaria to the People's Republic of China. In your work of consolidating and strengthening the friendship and cooperation between the two countries of China and Bulgaria, you will receive my full support and that of the government of the People's Republic of China.

I wish you complete success in your work.

Telegram to the USSR
(September 2, 1954)

Source: *RMRB* (Sept. 3, 1954), 1. Other Chinese Text: *XHYB*, 10 (Oct. 28, 1954), 180. Available English Translations: FBIS, *Daily Report* (Sept. 3, 1954), AAA 1; HNA, *Daily News Release* (Sept. 3, 1954), 1-2.

Comrade Malenkov, Chairman of the Council of Ministers of the Union of Soviet Socialist Republics,
Comrade Molotov, Minister of Foreign Affairs of the Union of Soviet Socialist Republics:

On the occasion of the ninth anniversary of the victory over Japanese militarism, we express warm congratulations and deep gratitude to the Soviet government, the Soviet armed forces, and the great Soviet people.

The agreement reached at the recent Geneva Conference[1] on restoring peace in Indochina has further eased international tension. This is an important victory for the forces of peace and a serious defeat for the forces of war. However, the United States' aggressive clique refuses to take their defeat lying down and are in the midst of actively reviving Japanese militarism, engineering the organization of war blocs in the Western Pacific and Asia, and intensifying the instigation and abetting of Chiang Kai-shek's traitorous clique in continuing its war of harassment and sabotage against the Chinese mainland and offshore islands so as to extend the threat of war throughout the Far East and the world.

The Chinese people are firmly opposed to this war policy of the United States' aggressive clique and will definitely liberate Taiwan in order to safeguard China's national sovereignty and territorial integrity and to defend the peace and security of the Far East and the world.

Restoring normal relations between the various countries of the Far East and Japan and preventing the revival of Japanese militarism have become the urgent task of all the peace-loving countries and peoples in Asia. The Chinese people are prepared to strive for the fulfillment of this task.

The friendly alliance between China and the Soviet Union is a strong guarantee for the consolidation of peace and security in the Far East and throughout the world.

Long live the great, unbreakable, and ever-growing friendship between China and the Soviet Union!

(Co-signed as Chairman of CPG of PRC with Zhou Enlai as Premier of GAC and Foreign Minister, dated in Beijing)

Note

1. See text July 23, 1954, note 1.

Telegram to the People's Republic of Bulgaria
(September 7, 1954)

Source: *RMRB* (Sept. 9, 1954), 1. Other Chinese Text: *XHYB*, 10 (Oct. 28, 1954), 210. Available English Translations: HNA, *Daily News Release* (Sept. 9, 1954), 1-2; FBIS, *Daily Report* (Sept. 10, 1954), KKK 31; FBIS, *Daily Report* (Sept. 9, 1954), AAA 6.

Chairman,
The Presidium of the National Assembly,
The People's Republic of Bulgaria

Comrade Georgi Damyanov:

On the occasion of the tenth anniversary of the liberation of Bulgaria, I convey sincere and warm congratulations to you and, through you, to the Bulgarian people and government.

Over the past ten years, the Bulgarian people, under the leadership of the Communist Party and following the teachings of Comrade Dimitrov,[1] have consolidated the people's democratic system and attained glorious achievements in the socialist construction of their country. This has not only inspired the Chinese people who are in the midst of their socialist construction, but also has strengthened the forces for world peace and democracy headed by the Soviet Union.

May the Bulgarian people achieve even greater new victories in the struggle to build socialism and to safeguard world peace.

(Signed and dated in Beijing)

Note

1. See text Sept. 30, 1950, note 1.

Reply to Ambassador of the People's Republic of Albania
(September 13, 1954)

Source: *RMRB* (Sept. 14, 1954), 1. Other Chinese Text: *XHYB*, 10 (Oct. 28, 1954), 189. Available English Translations: HNA, *Daily News Release* (Sept. 14, 1954), 14; FBIS, *Daily Report* (Sept. 14, 1954), AAA 10-11; S. Schram (1969), p. 435 (excerpt).

Nesti Nase served as ambassador of the People's Republic of Albania to the PRC from September 1954 to August 1956.

Comrade Ambassador:

I am very happy to accept this letter of credence from the Presidium of the People's Assembly of the People's Republic of Albania which you have presented and which appoints you as its first ambassador extraordinary and plenipotentiary to the People's Republic of China, and I sincerely thank you for your congratulations.

The Albanian people are an industrious and courageous people and have a glorious revolutionary historical tradition. In the ten years since their liberation, the Albanian people, under the leadership of the Albanian Party of Labor, have smashed all the schemes of both domestic and foreign enemies to carry out sabotage, are confidently building happy lives for themselves, and have achieved brilliant successes. The patriotic spirit and incomparable enthusiasm for labor demonstrated by the Albanian people in the struggle for socialist construction and for the defense of their homeland's independence and security are objects of great admiration for the Chinese people.

For the first time in history, the two peoples of China and Albania have established friendly diplomatic relations. In the last five years, our people have already knit together a brotherly friendship. I deeply believe that after the exchange of ambassadors the sincere, friendly, and cooperative relations between our two countries is bound to achieve yet further development. This not only will contribute to the enhancement of the happiness of our two peoples, but moreover will help strengthen the forces for world peace and democracy headed by the Soviet Union.

Comrade Ambassador, I warmly welcome you as the first ambassador extraordinary and plenipotentiary of the People's Republic of Albania to the People's Republic of China. In your work of consolidating the friendship and cooperation between Albania and China, you will receive my full support and that of the government of the People's Republic of China.

I wish you complete success in your work.

Reply to Minister of the Confederation of Switzerland
(September 13, 1954)

Source: *RMRB* (Sept. 14, 1954), 1. Other Chinese Text: *XHYB*, 10 (Oct. 28, 1954), 190. Available English Translations: HNA, *Daily News Release* (Sept. 14, 1954), 16; FBIS, *Daily Report* (Sept. 14, 1954), AAA 12-13.

Fernand Bernoulli became minister of the Confederation of Switzerland to the PRC at this time.

Mr. Minister:

I am very happy to accept the letter of credence presented by Your Excellency from the Federal Council of Switzerland, and express my gratitude for the greetings conveyed by you from the President of the Confederation of Switzerland to the people of the People's Republic of China and myself.

Over the last five years, the friendly relations between China and Switzerland have already been enhanced on the basis of peaceful coexistence. During the time of the Geneva Conference, the delegation from the People's Republic of China received the hospitality and assistance of the government and people of Switzerland.[1] Let me take this opportunity to express my gratitude. From now on, the economic links and cultural exchange between China and Switzerland will be further enhanced. This will not only benefit the development of the friendship between the peoples of our two countries, but will also aid the consolidation of world peace.

I warmly welcome Your Excellency as the envoy extraordinary and minister plenipotentiary of the Confederation of Switzerland to the People's Republic of China. In your work of strengthening the friendship and cooperation between China and Switzerland, you will surely have my support and that of the government of the People's Republic of China.

I wish Your Excellency success in your work, and happiness for your people, and good health for your head of state.

Note

1. See text July 23, 1954, note 1.

Opening Speech at the First Session of the First NPC
(September 15, 1954)

Source: *Xuanji*, V, pp. 152-153. Other Chinese Texts: *RMRB* (Sept. 16, 1954), 1; *XHYB*, 10 (Oct. 28, 1954), 3; *RMSC* (1955), pp. 41-42; *Wansui* (1967b), p. 10; *Buyi*, p. 24; *Rendai hui di yi ci,* pp. 3-4; *Jiaoyu yulu*, pp. 1, 11, 12 (excerpts). Available English Translations: HNA, *Daily News Release* (Sept. 16, 1954), 1-2; *CB*, 891 (Oct. 8, 1969), 17; FBIS, *Daily Report* (Sept. 15, 1954), AAA 5-6 (excerpts); NCNA, *Daily Bulletin* (Jan. 14, 1967) (excerpt); NCNA, *Daily Bulletin* (July 1, 1968) (excerpt).

For background to the convening of the National People's Congress (NPC), see text Jan. 13, 1953, note 2. The First Session of the First NPC was held on Sept. 15-28, 1954. See K. Lieberthal (1976), pp. 65-66; and RMSC (1955), pp. 33-40.

Fellow Deputies!

The First Session of the First National People's Congress of the People's Republic of China is being held today in the capital of our country, Beijing.

The number of deputies totals 1,226. Of these, 1,211 have reported their attendance; fifteen deputies have not reported and have requested leaves of absence because of illness or other matters. There are also seventy who have reported but who have taken temporary leaves today owing to illness or other matters. Therefore there are actually 1,141 deputies here at today's meeting, and this constitutes a quorum.

The First Session of the First National People's Congress of the People's Republic of China bears a very great responsibility.

The tasks of this session of the Congress are:

To formulate and adopt the Constitution;[1]

To enact several important laws;

To ratify the report on the work of the government;

To elect new personnel to do the work of the leadership of the state.

It is a milestone that signifies the new victories and new advances made by the people of our country since the founding of our Republic in 1949. The Constitution that will be adopted at the present session will greatly advance our country's socialist cause.

Our general task is to unite the people of the entire country and to win the support of all our international friends in order to strive to build a great socialist country and to struggle to defend international peace and to further the cause of human progress.

The people of our country should work hard, energetically learn from the advanced experiences of the Soviet Union and other fraternal countries, be honest and modest, be earnest and industrious, be encouraging and helpful to each other, be guarded against any vanity and arrogance, and be prepared to build our country, which is now such an economically and culturally backward one, into a great state that is industrialized and that has a high standard of modern culture within the span of several five-year plans.

Our cause is just. A just cause is unassailable by any enemy.

The core of strength that leads our cause is the Communist Party of China.

The theoretical basis that guides our thinking is Marxism-Leninism.

We are totally confident of overcoming all difficulties and hardships and of building our country into a great socialist republic.

We are now marching forward.

We are now engaged in a great and most glorious cause such as has never been undertaken by our forebears.

We must attain our goal.

We are bound to be able to attain our goal.

Let all the six hundred million people of China unite together and strive for our common cause!

Long live our great homeland!

Note

1. See text June 14, 1954, note 1.

Reply to Ambassador of the People's Republic of Hungary
(September 22, 1954)

Source: *RMRB* (Sept. 23, 1954), 1. Other Chinese Text: *XHYB*, 10 (Oct. 28, 1954), 190. Available English Translations: HNA, *Daily News Release* (Sept. 23, 1954), 5; FBIS, *Daily Report* (Sept. 23, 1954), AAA 6; FBIS, *Daily Report* (Sept. 25, 1954), II 2.

Agoston Szkladan served as ambassador of the People's Republic of Hungary to the PRC from September 1954 to 1956.

Comrade Ambassador:

I am very happy to accept the letter of credence from the Presidium of the People's Republic of Hungary which you have presented and which appoints you as the Ambassador Extraordinary and Plenipotentiary to the People's Republic of China, and sincerely thank you for your greetings.

In nine years, the Hungarian people have victoriously carried out socialist construction under the leadership of the Hungarian Worker's Party and have fundamentally changed the face of their country. The Chinese people note with gladness and admiration the tremendous successes achieved by the fraternal Hungarian people in their work of national construction.

Over the past five years, the friendly relations between the Chinese and Hungarian people and their close cooperation in the areas of politics, economy, and culture have had great success. The continuous growth of these relations of brotherly friendship will not only further enhance the prosperity of the two countries of China and Hungary and the friendship between the two peoples, but will also strengthen the forces for world peace and democracy headed by the great Soviet Union.

Comrade Ambassador, I warmly welcome you as the ambassador extraordinary and plenipotentiary of the People's Republic of Hungary to the People's Republic of China. In your work of further developing and consolidating the friendship and cooperation between China and Hungary, you will receive my total support and that of the government of the People's Republic of China.

I wish you complete success in your work.

Toast at China's National Day Celebrations
(September 29, 1954)

Source: *RMRB* (Sept. 30, 1954), 1. Available English Translations: HNA, *Daily News Release* (Sept. 30, 1954), 22; FBIS, *Daily Report* (Oct. 1, 1954), AAA 22-23.

Welcome, friends who have come to China!
We thank you for the friendship our various friends have brought!
We wish our friends good health!

May our mutual friendship be further enhanced!
May world peace be further consolidated!

Telegram to the German Democratic Republic
(October 5, 1954)

Source: *RMRB* (Oct. 7, 1954), 1. Other Chinese Text: *XHYB*, 11 (Nov. 28, 1954), 104. Available English Translation: HNA, *Daily News Release* (Oct. 7, 1954), 1.

Comrade Wilhelm Pieck,
President of the German Democratic Republic

Dear and Respected Comrade President:

On the occasion of the fifth anniversary of the founding of the German Democratic Republic, on behalf of the People's Republic of China, the Chinese people, and on my own behalf, I express sincere and warm congratulations to the German Democratic Republic, to the peace-loving people of all Germany, and to yourself.

The people of the German Democratic Republic, under the leadership of the German Socialist Unity Party and yourself, and with the sincere aid of the great Soviet Union, have already attained glorious successes in consolidating the people's democratic political power, as well as in developing the national economy and raising the people's living standards. Over the last five years the German Democratic Republic has united all the progressive patriotic forces among the German people in carrying forward an unrelenting struggle, striving for a unified, peaceful, democratic, and independent Germany, and for establishing collective security in Europe and safeguarding world peace. Thus it has won the enthusiastic support of the peace-loving peoples of Europe and throughout the world. These successes and efforts by the German Democratic Republic have inspired all the peace-loving German people and have strengthened their confidence in fighting for the peaceful unification of Germany.

The brotherly friendship and the close economic and cultural cooperation between the People's Republic of China and the German Democratic Republic are growing with each passing day. The German people have the profound sympathy of the People's Republic of China and the Chinese people in the just cause that they have undertaken in order to strive to establish a unified, peaceful, democratic, and independent Germany. The communiqué of July 25, 1954, on the discussion between our country's premier and the premier of the German Democratic Republic shows our two peoples' mutual concern and support in the great cause of peace.[1]

Comrade President, may you achieve even greater successes in leading the German people in the great struggle to realize the unification of their homeland and to defend world peace, and may you be in good health! (Signed as Chairman of PRC and dated)

Note

1. Discussions were held between Otto Grotewohl, the German representative, and Zhou Enlai, the Chinese premier, on July 25, 1954, in which the issue of Germany's peace and nonarmament principle was discussed. The text of the various agreements reached was published in *RMRB* (July 27, 1954), 1.

Letter to the Delegation of the USSR
(October 12, 1954)

Source: *RMRB* (Oct. 13, 1954), 1. Other Chinese Text: *XHYB*, 10 (Oct. 28, 1954), 35. Available English Translations: HNA, *Daily News Release* (Oct. 13, 1954), 3; FBIS, *Daily Report* (Oct. 13, 1954), AAA 4.

The delegation of the government of the USSR to the celebration of the fifth anniversary of the founding of the PRC arrived in China on September 29, 1954, and left China on October 13. A communiqué and a set of attending agreements were jointly issued by the Chinese government and the Soviet delegation headed by Khrushchev on October 12.

Dear Comrade Khrushchev and the Delegation of the Government of the Soviet Union:

The letter of October 5, 1954, from the delegation of the government of the Soviet Union has been received.

On behalf of the government of the People's Republic of China and the Chinese people I sincerely express our gratitude to the government of the Soviet Union for the gift made to us by the government of the Union of Soviet Socialist Republics of eighty-three pieces of machine tools and agricultural machinery now on display in Beijing at the exhibition of the achievements in economic and cultural construction of the Soviet Union.[1] The Chinese people see this generous gift as a concrete expression of the intimate friendship of the people of the Soviet Union toward the Chinese people.

Mao Zedong
October 12, 1954
Beijing

Note

1. An exhibition of the Soviet Union's achievements in economic and cultural construction was held beginning October 2, 1954, in the western sector of Beijing. Mao and other Chinese leaders visited the exhibition on October 25.

Letter to the USSR
(October 12, 1954)

Source: *RMRB* (Oct. 13, 1954), 1. Other Chinese Text: *XHYB*, 10 (Oct. 28, 1954), 35. Available English Translations: HNA, *Daily News Release* (Oct. 13, 1954), 2; *CDSP*, VI:41 (Nov. 24, 1954), 6; FBIS, *Daily Report* (Oct. 13, 1954), AAA 2-3.

Dear Comrade Khrushchev and the Delegation of the Government of the Soviet Union:[1]

On the occasion of the fifth anniversary of the founding of the People's Republic of China, the delegation of the government of the Soviet Union, representing the Soviet people, has given the Chinese people a gift of the machinery and equipment necessary for the organization of a grain-producing state farm with a sown acreage of twenty thousand hectares.[2] During the period of organizing this grain-producing state farm and in the first year of learning to master production on the farm, the government of the Soviet Union, in order to render China both organizational and technical assistance in establishing and managing this grain-producing state farm, is prepared to send a group of experts to the People's Republic of China as advisers so that the Chinese personnel in charge of this grain-producing state farm can, working together with the Soviet experts, master the technology and method of managing this large-scale grain-producing farm in the shortest [possible] time. On behalf of the People's Republic of China and the Chinese people, I sincerely express warm welcome and sincere gratitude to the government and people of the Soviet

Union for this important, tremendous, friendly assistance.

This state grain-producing farm will, beyond a doubt, not only play an important role as a model for the promotion of the socialist transformation of agriculture in China, but moreover, will also aid China in training technical personnel in agricultural production and learning the valuable experience of the Soviet Union in the opening of virgin soil and reclamation of idle land. With this generous aid from the people of the Soviet Union, the Chinese people have once again seen the Soviet people's deep friendship toward the Chinese people and their concern and support for the Chinese people in their cause of construction.

Long live the great brotherly friendship between China and the Soviet Union!

Mao Zedong
October 12, 1954

Notes

1. See text Oct. 12, 1954(1), source note.
2. See text Mar. 19, 1953, note 4.

Letter on the Problems of *Hongloumeng yanjiu*
(October 16, 1954)

Source: *RMRB* (May 27, 1967), 1. Other Chinese Texts: *Xuanji*, V, pp. 134-135; *HQ*, 9 (May 27, 1967), 6-7; *Buyi*, pp. 26-28; *Wuge wenjian*, pp. 5-6; *Mao liang*, pp. 356-358; quoted in *HQ*, 1 (Jan. 1, 1967), 18. Available English Translations: *PR*, 23 (June 2, 1967), 7-8; *CR* (Aug. 1967), 22; *CB*, 885 (Jul. 31, 1969), 22-23; *CB*, 897 (Dec. 10, 1969), 21-22; *SCMP* (supp.), 191 (May 26, 1967), 20; *SCMP*, 3949 (May 31,1967), 1-2; J. Chen, ed. (1970), pp. 80-81; Various quotations in *SCMP*, 4000 (Aug. 14, 1967), 12-14.

According to Xuanji, V, p. 134, this letter was addressed primarily to members of the Political Bureau of the Central Committee of the CPC. It was also sent to "other concerned comrades."

This document should be read in conjunction with text Oct. 1954(1) in this volume, with reference to the annotations there. Hongloumeng *(Dream of the Red Chamber), also known as* Shitou ji *(Story of the Stone) and* Jinyu yuan *(The Gold and Jade Romance), is a lengthy – 120* hui *or chapters – novel of the Qing dynasty. The bulk of it – the first 80* hui *– was written ca. 1790 by Cao Xueqin, a scion of a once rich and powerful textile industrialist family in the Shanghai area. (Cao Xueqin's grandfather, Cao Yin, was the founder of the Jiangnan textile enterprise, China's first semimodernized fabrics production factory in the late seventeenth century.) The substance and significance of the novel has become a matter of great controversy. For the most part, during the time of the Qing dynasty (i.e., from the time of the appearance of the novel to the late nineteenth century), the novel was dealt with as a romantic tale of sexual and familial relationships, which it was indeed on the surface. By and large, until recently, Western scholarship on the novel has continued along these lines, concentrating on textual criticism and literary exegesis. In the early twentieth century, Chinese scholars began to read beyond the surface of the novel and produce new frameworks for the studying and criticism of the novel. In general, they have agreed that the novel had deeper social meaning than previously attributed to it, but they disagreed on the exact nature of this social significance. Cai Yuanpei, a leading man of letters in the May Fourth period, proposed at first that the novel was an allegorical work, with the romantic tale disguising deeper Han nationalistic anti-Manchu sentiments. This led to more and more elaborate interpretations. One major school, represented first by Hu Shi and later by others such as Yu Pingbo, proposed that the novel was an autobiographical statement of the author Cao Xueqin and was meant to represent his critical view of a degenerating family in "late-feudal" and premodern China. This interpretation was accepted by most Chinese scholars until the 1950s, when new PRC scholarship, represented largely by young maverick critics, proposed yet another interpretation – that the novel, regardless of what the author subjectively intended it to be, was a masterful expose of the social corruptness and moral bankrupcy of the upper class in feudal society, and therefore should be studied as a topic of historical criticism rather than as a literary and artistic work alone. On, therefore, the debate waged, with dire political consequences for certain literati in the PRC. For the most part, scholars in Hong Kong and Taiwan have continued to accept the Hu Shi explanation with some variations. Scholars in the U.S. have usually taken a more detached view. (See note 9 in this document.)*

Enclosed are two articles refuting Yu Pingbo.[1] Please look them over. They are the first serious barrage in over thirty years aimed at the erroneous views of a so-called authoritative writer in the field of study of *Hongloumeng* [The Dream of the Red Chamber]. The authors [of the article] are two Youth League members.[2] They first wrote to *Wenyi bao* [Literary Gazette] to ask whether it was all right to criticize Yu Pingbo, but were ignored. Having no other alternative, they wrote to their teachers at their alma mater – Shandong University – and got support. Their article refuting *Hongloumeng jianlun* [A Brief Comment on *Hongloumeng*] was published in the university journal *Wen shi zhe* [Literature, History, and Philosophy].[3] Then the problem went back to Beijing. Some people asked to have this article reprinted in *Renmin ribao* [People's Daily] in order to stir up discussion and debate and to launch criticism. This was not done because certain persons opposed it for various reasons (the main one being that it was "an article written by nobodies" and that "the Party paper is not a forum for free debate").[4] Finally a compromise was reached, and the article was allowed to be printed in *Wenyi bao*.[5] Later the "Literary Legacy" column of *Guangming ribao* carried another article by the two young people refuting Yu Pingbo's book *Hongloumeng yanjiu* [A Study of The Dream of the Red Chamber].[6] It appears that it is now possible for the struggle against the Hu Shi school of bourgeois idealism which has been poisoning [the minds of] young people in the field of classical literature for more than thirty years to start.[7] The whole thing has been set in motion by two "nobodies." As for the "big shots," they usually ignore things or even obstruct them, and they negotiate a united front with bourgeois writers on the basis of idealism and are willing captives of the bourgeoisie. This is almost the same situation as when the films *Qing gong mishi* [Inside Story of the Qing Court] and *Wu Xun zhuan* [The Life of Wu Xun] were shown.[8] The film *Qing gong mishi*, which has been described as patriotic by [some] people but is in fact a traitorous film, has not been criticized or repudiated at any time since it was given nationwide screening. As for *Wu Xun zhuan*, although it has been criticized, up to now no lessons have been drawn from it; moreover, we have the strange situation in which Yu Pingbo's idealism is tolerated, and lively, critical essays by "nobodies" are obstructed. This deserves our attention.[9]

Toward such bourgeois intellectuals as Yu Pingbo our attitude should naturally be one of uniting with them. But we should criticize and repudiate their erroneous ideas which poison [the minds of] young people, and we should not surrender to them.

Notes

1. Yu Pingbo (b. 1899), native of Zhejiang, graduated from Beijing University in 1920. In the early 1920s, following the publication of Hu Shi's *Hongloumeng kaozheng* (A Critical Study of the Sources of the Novel *Hongloumeng*), Yu became an avid scholar of the study of the controversial novel *Hongloumeng* (Dream of the Red Chamber). In 1923 he published a collection of essays on the subject under the title *Hongloumeng bian* (Debate on *Hongloumeng*) (Yadong tushuguan, April 1923). Since 1949, he has been a *Hongloumeng* studies specialist at the Literary Studies Institute of Beijing University. In September 1952, he published the book *Hongloumeng yanjiu* (A study of *Hongloumeng*) (Tangdi chubanshe).

2. These refer to Li Xifan and Lan Ling. See text October 1954(1), note 4.

3. This refers to the article "Guanyu *Hongloumeng jianlun* ji qita" (On *Hongloumeng jianlun* and Other Writings), first published in *Wen shi zhe* (Sept. 1954). The article "Hongloumeng jianlun" (A Brief Discussion of *Hongloumeng*) was written by Yu Pingbo and published in the journal *Xin jianshe* (March 1954).

4. These objections were raised by Zhou Yang and Feng Xuefeng respectively in personal letters to Mao. Zhou was then a deputy director of the Department of Propaganda of the Central Committee of the CPC (see also text May-June 1955, note 44), and Feng was editor-in-chief of *Wenyi bao*. Since *Wenyi bao* was a publication sponsored by the Propaganda Department of the

CPC, Feng believed it to be a Party organ rather than a public forum.

5. The article by Li Xifan and Lan Ling, "Guanyu *Hongloumeng jianlun* ji qita" (see note 3) was published in *Wenyi bao* (Sept. 30, 1954). However, this publication was prefaced by a critical commentary written by Feng Xuefeng. *Wenyi bao* was a publication organized by the Wenhua gongzuozhe lianmeng (League of Cultural Workers) and later became an organ of the Zuojia xiehui (Federation of Writers). Both of its editors-in-chief up to this point, Feng Xuefeng and his predecessor Ding Ling, (see text Jan. 1957, note 16), were prominent writers who were later purged for their anti-Party views in the area of literary and artistic work. See text Oct. 1954(1), note 3.

6. This refers to the article "Ping *Hongloumeng yanjiu*" in *GMRB* (October 10, 1954). This and the other article by Li Xifan and Lan Ling, cited in note 3, are presumably the two "attached" articles referred to by Mao at the beginning of this open letter.

7. "More than thirty years" alludes to the thirty-some years between the publication of Hu Shi's *Hongloumeng kaozheng* (see note 1) – and therewith, the establishment of the so-called "Xin Hong xue," or New School on *Hongloumeng*, by Hu, Gu Jiegang, and Yu Pingbo – and the present writing by Mao. Although Mao had long held a severely critical attitude toward Hu Shi's ideas, the specific phrasing here is derived, it seems, from certain indicting sentences in the essays written by Li Xifan and Lan Ling. Hu Shi was a pioneer of the New Culture Movement and the new vernacular language movement prior to the May Fourth Movement. Many also attributed to him the leadership of the May Fourth Movement itself, although this is severely repudiated by Chinese Communists. At the height of the cultural and political controversies of the early 1920s Hu advocated that the Chinese should pay more attention to problems, and to pragmatic, "problem-solving" methodology, than to political orientations and doctrine. He engaged in an extended debate on the subject with Li Dazhao, an early Chinese Marxist. As a result of the growing tide of radicalism among many of China's young intellectuals in the 1920s and 1930s, Hu disassociated himself from the iconoclastic and revolutionary movement that he had earlier influenced. For an extensive description of the CPC indictment of and campaign against Hu Shi's "bourgeois comprador ideas," starting with the statements made by Guo Moro and Zhou Yang soon after the *Hongloumeng* controversy, see the three volume collection *Hu Shi sixiang pipan* (Criticism of Hu Shi's Thought), Sanlian shudian, 1955.

8. See text Mar. 1950, and text May 20, 1951.

9. Attention was, indeed, meted out in great measure. The controversy over the study of *Hongloumeng*, represented by Mao's writings here and elsewhere in October 1954, elicited ferocious public response against *Wenyi bao*. On October 23, Zhong Luo published an article in *RMRB* titled "Yinggai zhongshi dui *Hongluomeng yanjiu* zhong de cuowu guandian de pipan" (We Should Pay Attention to Criticizing the Erroneous Viewpoints in *Hongloumeng yanjiu*), followed by an explosive article on October 28, by Yuan Shuipai, titled "Zhiwen *Wenyi bao* bianze" (Questions for the Editors of *Wenyi bao*). As a result, not only did Yu Pingbo later publish in *Wenyi bao*, on March 15, 1955, a self-criticism, but Feng Xuefeng also published a self-criticism, titled "Jiantao wo zai *Wenyi bao* suo fan de cuowu" (Review of Mistakes I Committed in *Wenyi bao*). Feng was subsequently removed from his position as editor-in-chief of the paper. This refers to the so-called "*Wenyi bao* Affair."

That, however, was not the end of the repercussions. Not only did the *Hongloumeng* controversy play a part in the criticism campaign against Hu Shi, it was also a spark for the campaign against Hu Feng. From late October 1954 onward, several prominent writers, Hu Feng among them, criticized the part played by Zhou Yang and Yuan Shuipai in the *Hongloumeng* controversy and the "sectarian-oriented control" of the CPC over literary work. Subsequently, the Propaganda Department of the CPC directed its attack at Hu Feng and his "clique."

The controversy concerning *Hongloumeng* and its general ramifications is too broad a subject to be recounted in greater detail here. However, a commendable, relatively detached and objective essay on the subject is Yu Yingshi's "Jindai Hong xue de fazhan yu Hong xue geming" (The Development of the Modern School on *Hongloumeng* and the Revolution in the Study of *Hongloumeng*), in Yu Yingshi (1976), pp. 381-418.

Telegram to the USSR
(October 16, 1954)

Source: *CDSP*, VI: 42 (Dec. 1, 1954), 14.

We have no Chinese text for this telegram. The CDSP *translation is presented here as it originally appeared. The message was addressed to the Presidium of the Supreme Soviet of the USSR, the Council of Ministers of the USSR, and the Central Committee of the CPSU and was issued in the name of Mao himself as Head of State of the PRC, and in the name of the Standing Committee of the NPC, the State Council of the PRC, and the Central Committee of the CPC. The telegram appeared in* Pravda *and* Izvestia, *both Oct. 19, 1954, 1.*

Dear Comrades!

Permit us on behalf of the entire Chinese people to express heartfelt gratitude to you for your friendly congratulations on the fifth anniversary of the Chinese People's Republic.

The successes of our country's peoples during the last five years in social reforms, restoration of the national economy, socialist construction, and socialist reconstruction are inseparable from the sincere and unselfish aid of the great Soviet people, the Communist Party of the Soviet Union, and the Soviet government.

We ask you to convey our most sincere gratitude to all the Soviet people.

Long live the indestructible, brotherly friendship of the peoples of China and the Soviet Union!

Implement the Correct Policy in Dealing
with Doctors of Traditional Chinese Medicine
(October 20, 1954)

Source: *RMRB* (Oct. 20, 1954), 1. Other Chinese Text: *Dongfanghong* (May 1, 1967), excerpts (for publishing data see text Winter 1954, source note.)

This is an RMRB *editorial. See also text July 30, 1954.*

The medical lore of our country has a history of several thousand years. It is rich in content and contains valuable clinical experience, and it has played an immense role in the people's struggle against disease through the ages.

To inherit and to develop this cultural heritage, to study it earnestly and to research its theories and its practical experience, in order to organize and summarize it with scientific methods, and thus gradually to raise its scholarly and clinical standards so as to make it become of even more effective service to the people – this is an immensely glorious and arduous task facing the medical profession in our country. If this work is done well, it will not only greatly facilitate the development and enhancement of our people's health care and medical enterprise, but will also further enrich the contents of the medical science of the world.

The Chinese Communist Party and the People's Government have always held our homeland's cultural legacy in esteem; the policy adopted by the Party and the People's Government with regard to doctors of traditional Chinese medicine has always been clear. The Party has consistently appealed to doctors of both Chinese and Western medicine to unite and cooperate, to help and encourage each other for the general purpose of raising the standards of modern medical science and clinical capabilities and to even better serve the interests of the people and make a joint effort to study and research the medical heritage of the homeland so as to develop it unceasingly and to make it play an even greater role. Over the last several years, however, the leadership in the departments of the administration of health care has consistently failed to carry out this policy adopted by the Party and the People's Government seriously and has not concretely implemented the accurate principle of uniting doctors of Chinese and Western medicine.[1] Obviously, in the mobilization and organization of doctors of traditional Chinese medicine to take part in the hygiene and vaccination programs and in organizing clinics of Chinese doctors or joint clinics of doctors of Chinese and Western medicine, it has done some work and has had some achievements. Nevertheless, such work has not fundamentally resolved the problem of giving play to traditional Chinese medicine and certainly has not represented the adoption of an effective method in mobilizing and organizing doctors of both Chinese and Western medicine to jointly research and develop the homeland's medical heritage and to enrich the contents of modern medical science. Furthermore, the leadership in the departments of health care administration has often even violated the Party's and the People's Government's policy and adopted an attitude of disdain, discrimination, and exclusion toward doctors of traditional Chinese medicine, using all sorts of restrictive methods in dealing with them. This has been an attack on the positive attitude of the doctors of Chinese medicine in their work, has abetted the cadres in health care work and doctors of Western medicine in their erroneous mentality of despising Chinese medicine and Chinese pharmacology itself, and has adversely affected the development and improvement of the profession of traditional Chinese medicine severely. Other related work departments and public opinion in society have also shown insufficient regard or concern for Chinese medicine. These mistakes must be rectified.

The reason that the leadership cadres in health care administration are unable to implement the Party and People's Government's policy toward Chinese doctors is that they have been afflicted by the remnant poison of bourgeois ideology and consequently look down upon the medical legacy of the homeland. They do not realize the importance of inheriting and developing the homeland's cultural heritage to the construction of a new culture; they do not realize the importance of enhancing the medical legacy of the homeland to the raising of the standards of modern medical science and clinical ability and to the development of the people's cause of health care and medical treatment. Consequently they are also unaware of the importance of uniting with doctors of traditional Chinese medicine, enhancing it, and thus allowing it to take its full effect. They neglect the practical needs of the broad masses of the people for Chinese medicine and Chinese pharmacology; they ignore the traditional Chinese doctor's rich experience and obvious clinical effectiveness; they do not study or investigate in earnest; they do not carefully analyze and sum up the situation, but they jump ahead and make the generalization that Chinese medicine is "backward" and "unscientific" and negate it wholesale. Such an attitude of not recognizing facts and not emphasizing practical experience is an attitude of extremely "unscientific" arbitrariness. This erroneous attitude adopted by the leadership cadres in health care administration toward Chinese medicine and Chinese pharmacology concretely manifests gravely sectarian mentalities and sentiments. Such mentalities and sentiments of looking down upon Chinese medicine and Chinese pharmacology have not, over a long period of time, been fundamentally turned around. This has caused the situation in which there has been no apparent change in the serious and persistent backwardness in the work in traditional Chinese medicine.

Therefore, if we are to make a serious effort to improve the work in

Chinese medicine, we must first resolutely correct the serious mistake that exists within the leadership of the departments of health care administration and other related areas in that they look down upon the homeland's medical heritage and neglect the role played by Chinese medicine and Chinese pharmacology in our people's health care, and we must actively call upon and organize doctors of Western medicine to study and research Chinese medical science. This is the immediate key to the resolution of our problem.

There can be no doubt that it is necessary to appeal to and organize doctors of Western medicine to study and research Chinese medical science. This is because the enormous and arduous task of developing the homeland's legacy of medical science can be accomplished gradually only through the long-range cooperation between doctors of Chinese and Western medicine. The irrefutable clinical effectiveness of Chinese doctors and Chinese medicine has proved that Chinese medical knowledge has a rational and useful content. Its major weakness is that it has lacked a systematic scientific theory and has not yet taken hold of a reliable methodology of chemical experimentation and scientific inspection. This has greatly limited the scope of its development and enhancement. Therefore, the basic problem of developing the homeland's medical heritage is a problem of gradually integrating it with modern scientific theory through serious study, research, and practice. This means that we must, based on the theories of modern science, organize the principles of traditional Chinese medical science and summarize its clinical experience by scientific methods and absorb from it the essentials and eliminate the dross, so as to gradually channel it into modern medical science and turn it into an important component of modern medical science. Thus we should gradually establish a modern school of medicine of this nature. It should reflect the special characteristics of China's geography and climate, reflect the special characteristics of the application of pharmaceutical material produced specially in China, and reflect the particular features of the life and labor of the various peoples of China. This is the long-range and grand goal of our development of the medical legacy of the homeland. In order to attain this goal, doctors of traditional Chinese medicine will naturally have to make an arduous and sustained effort over a long period of time, but doctors of Western medicine, who are endowed with relatively rich scientific knowledge, also have their especially glorious assignment in this as well. In the current situation, in which the medical heritage of the homeland is not regarded with esteem or comprehended in general by doctors of Western medicine, the emphasis on the importance of having doctors of Western medicine study and research Chinese medical science has a particularly great practical significance. It is only through their own study and research of the medical heritage of the homeland that doctors of Western medicine can promote the role played by modern medical scientific knowledge in organizing and enhancing that heritage.

To identify the promotion of the medical heritage of the homeland with the development of modern medical science makes perfect sense. To constantly discover, by the combined effort of Chinese and Western medicine, scientific truths from this invaluable cultural legacy will surely bring about daily enrichment of the treasury of modern medical science. In the last few years, some doctors of Western medicine have achieved some success in their study and research of Chinese medicine. This is illustrated, for example, by the accomplishments in the study of Chinese acupuncture treatment on the basis of the scientific theories of neuropathology. In general, doctors of Western medicine are willing to apply methods of treatment and prevention that have a scientific foundation both in theory and in practice; this is correct as far as it goes. However, they have cast aside the several thousand years of practical experience of Chinese medicine and do not excavate new knowledge, new medicines, or new methods from the experience of Chinese medical science, and this is very wrong. In this way, certain limits have been placed on the development of modern medical science itself. For example, if we were to delve into the method of acupuncture treatment, possibly we could write a new page in the history of modern medical principles; we might therefore be obliged to revise existing theory about the mechanical mobility and neuro-adaptation of healthy and sick people alike. As long as we launch the work of studying Chinese medicine and Chinese pharmacology in a well-planned, well-organized fashion and with good leadership, we are bound to make a major contribution to modern medical science and to the cause of the people's health care. To the individual doctor of Western medicine, to study and research Chinese medicine by scientific methods not only does not pose any danger to the medical knowledge or clinical technique that he or she possessed to begin with, but indeed it can bring about enrichment and enhancement of this knowledge and technique.

In emphasizing the importance of having doctors of Western medicine study and research Chinese medical science, we have not removed in the slightest from the broad ranks of doctors of Chinese medicine the great task of promoting the medical heritage of the homeland. In the past, some doctors of Chinese medicine have carried out organization and research in the art and science of Chinese medicine by applying relatively modern viewpoints and methods, and their accomplishments have been considerable. The majority of doctors of traditional Chinese medicine, however, neglect research work. This situation should be reversed now. In order to strengthen their own research work in cooperation with doctors of Western medicine, doctors of Chinese medicine will not only have to constantly dig into the principles of Chinese medicine and have a good grasp of their clinical experience, but they must also learn the necessary fundamental scientific knowledge so as to play a greater role in organizing and summarizing the principles and experience of Chinese medicine.

In order to unite doctors of Chinese and Western medicine in a combined effort to promote effectively the medical heritage of the homeland, the leadership organs in health care ought to base themselves on the spirit of Premier Zhou Enlai's "Report on the Work of the Government"[2] and penetratingly examine the conditions of the past within their own departments regarding the issue of carrying out the policy adopted by the Party and the People's Government toward Chinese medicine and earnestly correct the erroneous attitudes toward Chinese medicine and Chinese pharmacology. At the same time they must meticulously carry out ideological work and policy education among doctors of Western medicine, remove their ideological obstacles, and on the ideological basis of their own awareness and voluntarism, stir up their enthusiasm for studying and researching the medical legacy of the homeland. Furthermore, they must adopt, in a well-planned and methodical way, a series of organizational measures and utilize necessary systems and structures to ensure an improvement in the work of Chinese medicine.

Naturally, to do this work well is very complicated. The methods of treatment are different for doctors of Chinese and Western medicine, and to make them support and complement each other, to direct them toward one goal, one result, when they begin with different paths, we must have a powerful ideological and organizational leadership, one that will guarantee that they will constantly maintain a high level of initiative and activism and will struggle for a common goal. The principle of the integration of theory and practice must be carried out; in all things we must proceed on the premise of practice and conduct research work for the purpose of resolving practical problems. The special characteristics of doctors of both Chinese and Western medicine, and particularly those of doctors of Chinese medicine, must be given attention. The preliminary experience of certain clinical units in carrying out consultations between doctors of Chinese and Western medicine must be summed up, and new experiences must be carefully planned and assigned clear priorities to serve as a basis for directing work in general. We must make realistically solid and reasonable arrangements for the cooperation between doctors of Chinese medicine and doctors of Western medicine on the basis of their practical circumstances in all areas in each locality, so that they will not have to worry, and, cooperating in a friendly and intimate atmosphere, each can fully develop his or her own special skill. Only this type of cooperation will succeed in constantly reinforcing the unity of doctors of Chinese and Western medicine, and only then can they effectively carry out the enormous task of promoting the medical heritage of the homeland.

The work of Chinese medicine covers a very broad area. Not only does it call for the positive and active effort of the departments of health care administration; it also requires the close coordination of all other related departments and the resolute support of public opinion in society. In particular, it requires the unified leadership of the Party; this is the greatest guarantee of the successful implementation of this task. Party committees in every locality must shoulder their responsibilities seriously, constantly instruct and urge all related areas to implement the Party's policy toward Chinese medicine, and actively make improvements in this major area of work that concerns the life and death as well as the general health of the people.

Notes

1. See text July 30, 1954, note 1.
2. Mao is referring to the "Report of the Work of the Government" delivered by Zhou Enlai, premier of the Government Administrative Council, on September 23, 1954, at the First Session of the First National People's Congress of the PRC. See *RMSC* (1955), pp. 129-141.

Toast at Reception for Prime Minister Nehru
(October 21, 1954)

Source: *RMRB* (Oct. 22, 1954), 1. Other Chinese Text: *XHYB*, 11 (Nov. 28, 1954), 43. Available English Translation: HNA, *Daily News Release* (Oct. 22, 1954), 3.

The reception was held by Indian Ambassador Raghavan at the Indian embassy in Beijing.

The peoples of China and India both resolutely advocate peace. Our two peoples, like people throughout the world, resolutely strive for peace.

[Let's drink]

To the cooperation between the peoples of China and India and to their prosperity,

To world peace,

To the health of President Prasad of the Republic of India,

To Prime Minister Nehru's visit to China and to his health,

To the health of the host of today's banquet, Ambassador Raghavan.

Bottoms up!

Telegram to the People's Republic of Hungary
(October 22, 1954)

Source: FBIS, *Daily Report* (Oct. 27, 1954), II 3.

We have no Chinese text for this telegram. The FBIS translation is reproduced here. The telegram was addressed to President Istvan Dobi of the People's Republic of Hungary and was signed by Mao.

On behalf of the Chinese People's Republic and the Chinese people, I have the honor of expressing my heartfelt thanks for your greetings on the occasion of the fifth anniversary of the proclamation of the Chinese People's Republic. May the indissoluble friendship between China and Hungary strengthen and develop.

Inscription Expressing Gratitude to the Soviet Union
(October 25, 1954)

Source: *RMRB* (Oct. 31, 1954), 1. Other Chinese Text: *XHYB*, 11 (Nov. 28, 1954), 110. Available English Translations: HNA, *Daily News Release* (Oct. 31, 1954), 1; FBIS, *Daily Report* (Nov. 1, 1954), AAA 16-17.

After visiting the exhibition of the Soviet Union's achievements in economic and cultural construction, we feel very gratified and happy.[1] This exhibition is concrete evidence of the swift progress of the Soviet Union's industrial and agricultural economy, the high level of development of the Soviet Union's technology and sciences, the flourishing of its undertakings in education, culture, and the arts, and the happiness in its people's lives. Through all of this, the exhibition has also vividly shown the boundless initiative and creativity of the Soviet people demonstrated in their labor, the solidarity within the Communist Party of the Soviet Union, the Soviet government, and among the people of the various nationalities in the Soviet Union. It has also demonstrated the correctness of the leadership of the Central Committee of the Communist Party of the Soviet Union. We are proud to have such a powerful ally. The might of the Soviet Union is an important factor in the general economic and cultural upsurge in the various countries in the camp striving for peace and democracy and an important factor in striving for world peace and human progress.

The glorious success of the Soviet Union in its economic and cultural construction has greatly inspired the enthusiasm of the Chinese people for building socialism and has set the best example for the Chinese people to learn from. The government and the people of the Soviet Union have consistently given us tremendous assistance in all areas of our construction work. This aid was further expanded through the recent discussions between China and the Soviet Union, and the holding of the exhibition of the achievements of the Soviet Union in economic and cultural construction is itself an expression of the enthusiastic aid given by the Soviet Union to our country. On behalf of all the Chinese people we express our gratitude for this brotherly friendship.

Mao Zedong	Lin Boqu
Liu Shaoqi	Dong Biwu
Zhou Enlai	Peng Dehuai
Zhu De	Peng Zhen
Chen Yun	Deng Xiaoping
October 25, 1954.	

Note

1. See text Oct.12, 1954(1), note 1.

Telegram to the Democratic People's Republic of Korea
(October 25, 1954)

Source: *RMRB* (Oct. 25, 1954), 1. Other Chinese Text: *XHYB*, 11 (Nov. 28, 1954), 74. Available English Translations: HNA, *Daily News Release* (Oct. 25, 1954), 3; FBIS, *Daily Report* (Oct. 25, 1954), AAA 16-17.

The English sources date this telegram October 24.

Premier,
The Democratic People's Republic of Korea

Comrade Kim Il Sung:

I have received your telegram of October 24, 1954. On behalf of the People's Republic of China, the Chinese people, and on my own behalf, I express sincere gratitude and respect to the entire Korean people, the government of the Democratic People's Republic of Korea, and yourself.

In the course of the righteous struggle against aggression and in defense of peace, the heroic Korean and Chinese peoples have already forged a friendship-in-arms that resembles a flesh and blood relationship; this is an important factor in defending peace in the Far East. In the struggle to strive for the peaceful unification of Korea and to defend peace in Asia, this friendship between our two peoples is bound to attain further consolidation and development.

May the Korean people score even greater achievements in their solemn cause of the quick recovery of the national economy of their own homeland. (Signed and dated in Beijing)

On Criticizing *Hongloumeng yanjiu*
(October 1954)

Source: *Wenyi yulu*, p. 97. Other Chinese Text: *Wenyi hongqi*, 5 (May 30, 1967), 2.

See text Oct. 16, 1954, note 1.

Hu Shi's school of thought has not undergone any substantial criticism.[1] In the area of classical literature we are still guided by the thought of the Hu Shi school.

Some people say that once a person gets criticized he can no longer lift up his head; well, there will always be one side that cannot lift up its head. If everybody raised his head it would be capitulationism.

It is not that they are not on the alert. In fact they are very alert. Their tendency is very obvious. They defend bourgeois thought, they like things that oppose Marxism, and they view Marxism with hostility.

The abominable thing is that Communist Party members do not propagate Marxism. If Communist Party members do not propagate Marxism, what is the point of their being Communist Party members? *Wenyi bao* [Literary

Gazette] must be criticized.[2] Not to do so would be unfair.

All new things are brought up by "nobodies." The young people have great aspirations and resolution to fight. We must open up paths for the young people and support "nobodies."[3]

Notes

1. The reference to Hu Shi at this point stems from the fact that since the publication of his "Hongloumeng kaozheng" in 1921, Hu Shi has dominated the study of the literary significance and sociological impact of this historical novel. See "Hongloumeng kaozheng" (A Critical Study of the Sources of *Hongloumeng*), "Kaozheng Hongloumeng de xin cailiao" (New Exegetical Material on *Hongloumeng),* and "Ba Qianlong gengshen ben zhiyanzai chongping shitouji chaoben" (Preface to the Handcopy of the Reannotated *Shitouji* – Edition of the Year of Genshen in the Reign of the Qianlong Emperor, Published by Zhiyanzai) in *Hu Shi wencun* (Collected Writings of Hu Shi) (Yuandong tushu gongsi, Taipei, 1971, third edition), vol. 1, pp. 575-620; vol. 3, pp. 373-403; vol. 4, pp. 396-407, respectively. Hu Shi (1891-1962) was one of the most influential intellectuals in twentieth-century China. For biographical details on Hu see H. Boorman et al., eds. (1968), II, pp. 167-174, and J. Grieder (1970).

Hu Shi, in these writings, is considered to have broken new paths in the investigation of the "inner logic" of the novel by affirming that the novel was written by Cao Xueqin and postulating that the novel is Cao Xueqin's autobiography, in which many of the literary devices are interpreted as derivatives of Cao's idealism. A new school of interpretation, appearing among younger scholars in the PRC and endorsed by Mao, generally adopted a combative Marxist methodology and posed a materialistic, dialectical challenge to the Hu Shi "idealistic" school of thought. At the time, Yu Pingbo was considered by these younger scholars to be a representative of the Hu Shi school, having reinforced and perpetuated Hu's "autobiographical" interpretation. Yu eventually published a "self-criticism" in *Wenyi bao* on March 15, 1955. See text Oct. 16, 1954, source note and note 7.

2. At this point, Mao perceived *Wenyi bao*, with some justification, as a publication dominated by writers and literary critics who did not totally conform to the purpose of adapting their scholarship in literature and art to the services of the socialist cause. Although *Wenyi bao* later also published such articles as Yu Pingbo's "self-criticism," it has consistently been a forum for dissident writers. See text Oct.16, 1954, note 5.

3. Mao is here referring specifically to two young literary scholars, Li Xifan and Lan Ling, who published two critical essays on Yu Pingbo's approach to *Hongloumeng* in September and October 1954. (See *Wen shi zhe*, Sept. 1954; *Wenyi bao*, Sept. 30, 1954; and *Guangming ribao*, Oct. 10, 1954; respectively.) Li Xifan also wrote the book *Cao Xueqin he ta de Hongloumeng* (Cao Xueqin and His *Hongloumeng*), published in October 1973, and the preface to the new edition of *Hongloumeng*, published by Renmin chubanshe, August 1973.

Directive on the Film *Qing gong mishi*
(October 1954)

Source: *Wenyi yulu*, pp. 93-94. Other Chinese Text: *Wenyi hongqi*, 5 (May 30, 1967), 2.

See text Mar. 1950, source note.

For five years, there has been no criticism of *Qing gong mishi*. If we do not criticize it, we would be doing ourselves a great disfavor. *Qing gong mishi* is actually a treasonous film that supports imperialism. One must not sympathize with the Guangxu Emperor indiscriminately.[1]

Note

1. A main theme in the film was the ill-fated romance between the Guangxu Emperor (the next to last emperor of the Qing Dynasty, reigning 1875-1908) and his concubine Zhen Fei, who was hated by the Empress Dowager Cixi and ultimately forced to commit suicide by plunging into a well. The emperor and Zhen Fei are cast as sympathetic characters in the film, with the empress dowager cast as the villain of the piece.

Telegram to the USSR
(November 6, 1954)

Source: *RMRB* (Nov. 7, 1954), 1. Other Chinese Text: *XHYB*, 12 (Dec. 28, 1954), 58. Available English Translations: HNA, *Daily News Release* (Nov. 7, 1954), 1; FBIS, *Daily Report* (Nov. 8, 1954), CC 43-44.

Comrade Voroshilov, Chairman of the Presidium of the Supreme Soviet of the Union of Soviet Socialist Republics,
Comrade Malenkov, Chairman of the Council of Ministers of the Union of Soviet Socialist Republics,
Comrade Molotov, First Deputy Chairman of the Council of Ministers and

Minister of Foreign Affairs of the Union of Soviet Socialist Republics:

On the occasion of the thirty-seventh anniversary of the great October Socialist Revolution, on behalf of the people and government of China we extend to you and, through you, to the great people and government of the Soviet Union our sincere and warm congratulations.

In thirty-seven years, the brilliant successes of the great Soviet people in the cause of building a communist society have played an inestimable role in furthering human progress and defending world peace. Progressive peoples of the whole world rejoice at and are inspired by the historic victory secured by the Soviet people and see the great Soviet Union as a beacon illuminating the path on which to advance.

In recent years, the forces for defending peace throughout the world, headed by the Soviet Union, have been increasingly strengthened and developed. The number of supporters of peaceful coexistence has grown larger and larger. Warlike plots to restore German and Japanese militarism have constantly met with resolute resistance from the German and Japanese peoples and from people of all countries. The struggle to oppose the creation of an aggressive military bloc; to ban atomic, hydrogen, and other types of weapons for mass extermination; and to reduce armaments in general is developing on an extensive scale. All this serves to convince us that as long as the people of all countries take up the cause of defending peace and uphold it to the end, world peace can then be preserved and consolidated.

The great alliance between China and the Soviet Union increasingly reveals its extraordinarily great role in promoting the common prosperity of the two countries and defending peace in the Far East and throughout the world. The recent discussions between the delegation of the government of the Soviet Union headed by Comrade Khrushchev and the Chinese government[1] signifies a new development in the great friendship between the two countries and have again demonstrated the unanimous aspirations and common interests of the eight hundred million Chinese and Soviet people. This friendship will accelerate the socialist construction undertaken by the Chinese people and enhance the further consolidation of peace in the Far East and throughout the world.

Long live the great Union of the Soviet Socialist Republics!

Long live the eternal and unbreakable friendship between China and the Soviet Union!

(Co-signed as Chairman of PRC with Zhou Enlai as Premier of State Council and Foreign Minister, dated in Beijing)

Note

1. See text Oct. 12, 1954, source note.

Letter to Liu Shaoqi, Zhou Enlai, et al.
(November 18, 1954)

Source: *Shuxin*, pp. 484-485.

Comrades Liu, Zhou, Li, Chen, Luo, and Tao Zhu:[1]

The November 13 and November 14 issues of *Renmin ribao* [People's Daily] carried the translation of the text of Chapter 22 of the new Soviet publication *Textbook on Political Economy*,[2] please take a look at them. I think you will find there adequate evidence that the argument that "socialist economic laws cannot exist before the construction of socialism has become complete (or [at least] for the most part complete)" is wrong.

Mao Zedong

November 18

[P.S.] Comrade Boda, please take a look at the articles that discuss the issues of economic laws in the transitional period in [the publications] *Xin jianshe* [New Construction] and *Xuexi*[3] [Study] and see if they contain any errors.

Notes

1. This letter was addressed to Liu Shaoqi, Zhou Enlai, Li Fuchun, Chen Boda, Luo Mai (Li Weihan), and Tao Zhu, all of whom, according to the source, were in Guangzhou attending a conference at the time. For Liu Shaoqi and Li Weihan, see text May 19, 1953, source note, and text Apr. 9, 1951, source note, respectively. Zhou Enlai was premier of the State Council (formerly the GAC, name changed in September 1954). For more biographical information on Zhou, see D. Klein and A. Clark, eds. (1971), I, pp. 204-219, and *Zhonggong renming lu*, appendix, pp. 51-54. Li Fuchun was a vice-premier at this time and chairman of the State Planning Commission. For more biographical information on Li, see D. Klein and A. Clark, eds. (1971), I, pp. 494-498, *Zhonggong renming lu*, appendix, pp. 35-36, and text Nov. 30, 1958, note 4. Chen Boda was deputy director of the Propaganda Department of the Central Committee of the CPC at this time. For many years he was Mao's confidant in theoretical studies. For more biographical information on Chen, see D. Klein and A. Clark, eds. (1971), I, pp. 122-125, *Zhonggong renming lu*, appendix, pp. 68-69, and text Jan. 11, 1958, note 28. Tao Zhu was secretary of the South China Sub-bureau of the Central Committee of the CPC at this time. For more biographical information on Tao, see D. Klein and A. Clark, eds. (1971), II, pp. 808-812, *Zhonggong renming lu*, appendix, pp. 87-89, and text Mar. 5, 1959, note 11.

2. Mao is apparently referring to the first edition of the Soviet publication *Political Economy, A Textbook*, which was published by the Institute of Economics of the Academy of Sciences (Academia Nauk) of the USSR in the fall of 1954. This was the product of an effort begun in 1951 by Stalin to mobilize Soviet scholars to prepare a textbook on economics based on his theses on the economic development of socialism. This edition of the textbook was, therefore, rather Stalinist in its overtones and interpretations and was quite different from the later (the third, and especially, the third revised) editions on which Mao based his later work, "Reading Notes on the

Soviet Textbook of Political Economy" (see text 1960 Reading Notes). See this later document, source note, for further information on this publication.

3. *Xin jianshe* (New Construction) was a multidisciplinary scholarly magazine published monthly in Beijing and distributed nationwide. The focus of the magazine was on philosophy and the social sciences. For the publication *Xuexi* (Study), see text Sept. 5, 1952, note 9.

Telegram to the Democratic People's Republic of Korea
(November 22, 1954)

Source: *RMRB* (Nov. 23, 1954), 1. Available English Translation: HNA, *Daily News Release* (Nov. 23, 1954), 6.

Comrade Kim Du Bong, Chairman, The Standing Committee of the Supreme People's Assembly of the Democratic People's Republic of Korea,
Comrade Kim Il Sung, Premier of the Democratic People's Republic of Korea,
Comrade Nam Il, Minister of Foreign Affairs of the Democratic People's Republic of Korea:

On the occasion of the first anniversary of the signing of the Sino-Korean Agreement on Economic and Cultural Cooperation,[1] we express warm congratulations to the Korean people, the government of the Democratic People's Republic of Korea, and yourselves.

The signing and implementation of this agreement has brought about further consolidation and development of the friendship-in-arms between the Chinese and Korean peoples formed in the war during which they stood shoulder-to-shoulder in resistance against the United States aggressors. The Chinese people greet with admiration and gladness the glorious achievements of the Korean people in carrying out the three-year plans for restoring and developing their national economy.

The Korean people and the government of the Democratic People's Republic of Korea have always enjoyed the deep concern and sympathy of the Chinese people and government in their unflagging struggle for the peaceful unification of Korea. The Korean problem must be resolved on the principle of respect for the Korean people's national rights and benefit for the safeguarding of Asian and world peace. The Chinese people will continue to give full support to the Korean people in this just cause until a final victory is won.

Long live the brotherly and ever-consolidating friendship between the Chinese and Korean peoples!

(Co-signed as Chairman of PRC with Liu Shaoqi as Chairman of Standing

Committee of NPC and Zhou Enlai as Premier of State Council and Foreign Minister, dated in Beijing)

Note

1. See text Dec. 12, 1953, note 1.

Letter to Huang Yanpei
(November 23, 1954)

Source: *Shuxin*, p. 486

See text Feb. 17, 1951, source note.

Mr. Renzhi:[1]

I have received your gracious letter of October 30. Concerning the matter of grain requisition, what I have heard in the capital is as you have described.[2] As I was on my way here to Guangzhou,[3] I made some investigations and only then found out that problems still exist; but in general things are not too bad and, according to some reports, much better than they were last year. I have asked Vice-premier Chen Yun[4] to pay attention to the lingering cases of the "Five-Anti's." I am very concerned about how you are, with your illness. I hope you will pay attention to nursing yourself back to recovery.

In reply, and with my respect,

Mao Zedong
November 23, 1954

Notes

1. "Renzhi" is Huang's *zi*, or honorific name. See text Feb. 17, 1951, note 1.
2. See text Oct. 15, 1952, note 4, and text Nov. 4, 1953, note 16.
3. See text Nov. 18, 1954, note 1.
4. Chen Yun became vice-premier of the newly established State Council (replacing the GAC) in September 1954. He was then in charge of the Fifth Office of the State Council, whose focus was on financial and commercial matters. For more biographical information on Chen, see D. Klein and A. Clark, eds. (1971), I, pp. 149-153, *Zhonggong renming lu*, pp. 598-599, and text Jan. 20, 1956, note 9.

Telegram to the People's Republic of Mongolia
(November 25, 1954)

Source: *RMRB* (Nov. 26, 1954), 1. Other Chinese Text: *XHYB*, 12 (Dec. 1954), 64. Available English Translations: HNA, *Daily News Release* (Nov. 26, 1954), 3; FBIS, *Daily Report* (Nov. 26, 1954), AAA 1.

Comrade Jamsarangiyn Sambuu, Chairman of the Presidium of the Greater People's Hural of the People's Republic of Mongolia,
Comrade Yumjaagiyn Tsedenbal, Chairman of the Council of Ministers of the People's Republic of Mongolia,
Comrade B. Jargalsaihan, Minister of Foreign Affairs of the People's Republic of Mongolia:

On the occasion of the thirtieth anniversary of the founding of the People's Republic of Mongolia, on behalf of the Chinese people and the government of the People's Republic of China, we express our sincere congratulations to all the Mongolian people, the government of the People's Republic of Mongolia, and yourselves.

Thirty years ago, the Mongolian people, under the leadership of the Mongolian People's Revolutionary Party, overthrew, by their valiant struggle, the reactionary feudal rule and established a people's democratic state. With the tireless efforts of the Mongolian people and the selfless assistance of the Soviet Union, the Mongolian people have freed themselves forever from poverty and backwardness, and they have stepped onto the glorious path of economic prosperity and cultural development. The Chinese people are joyous at and inspired by the brilliant successes of the Mongolian people.

May the Mongolian people attain still greater victories in their cause of building socialism and safeguarding world peace.

(Co-signed as Chairman of PRC with Liu Shaoqi as Chairman of Standing Committee of NPC and Zhou Enlai as Premier of State Council and Foreign Minister, dated in Beijing)

Telegram to the People's Republic of Albania
(November 28, 1954)

Source: *RMRB* (Nov. 29, 1954), 1. Other Chinese Text: *XHYB*, 12 (Dec. 1954), 78. Available English Translation: HNA, *Daily News Release* (Nov. 29, 1954), 6.

Comrade Haxhi Lleshi, Chairman of the Presidium of the People's Assembly of the People's Republic of Albania,
Comrade Mehmet Shehu, Chairman of the Council of Ministers of the People's Republic of Albania,
Comrade Behar Shtylla, Minister of Foreign Affairs of the People's Republic of Albania:

On the occasion of the tenth anniversary of the liberation of Albania, on behalf of the Chinese people and the government of the People's Republic of China, we extend our sincere and warm congratulations to you and, through you, to the Albanian people and the government of the People's Republic of Albania.

In ten years, the Albanian people, under the leadership of the Albanian Party of Labor and the government of the People's Republic of Albania, have attained tremendous successes in the areas of politics, economy, and culture. We express our best wishes to the government and people of Albania.

May the Albanian people win yet more glorious successes in their cause of struggling for the prosperity and development of their homeland and for the safeguarding of world peace.

(Co-signed as Chairman of PRC with Zhou Enlai as Premier of State Council and Foreign Minister, dated in Beijing)

Telegram to Petru Groza
(December 1, 1954)

Source: *RMRB* (Dec. 3, 1954), 4. Other Chinese Text: *XHYB*, 1 (Jan. 28, 1955), 102. Available English Translation: NCNA, *Daily Bulletin* (Dec. 3, 1954), 7.

Comrade Petru Groza, Chairman of the Presidium of the Grand National Assembly of the People's Republic of Romania:

Please accept my warm congratulations on the occasion of your seventieth birthday. May you achieve even greater successes in your activities undertaken for the prosperity and happiness of the Romanian people, and may you have good health and a long life.
(Signed and dated in Beijing)

Telegram to Rajendra Prasad
(December 1, 1954)

Source: *RMRB* (Dec. 3, 1954), 4. Other Chinese Text: *XHYB*, 1 (Jan. 28, 1954), 102. Available English Translation: NCNA, *Daily Bulletin* (Dec. 3, 1954), 7.

President Rajendra Prasad,
The Republic of India

Your Excellency:

On the occasion of your seventieth birthday, I wish to extend to you my sincere congratulations.
(Signed and dated in Beijing)

Toast at Dinner for Prime Minister U Nu
(December 4, 1954)

Source: *RMRB* (Dec. 5, 1954), 1. Other Chinese Text: *XHYB*, 1 (Jan. 28, 1955), 96. Available English Translations: HNA, *Daily News Release* (Dec. 5, 1954), 5; FBIS, *Daily Report* (Dec. 6, 1954), AAA 21.

Prime Minister U Nu of the Union of Burma arrived at Beijing on December 1, 1954, at the invitation of the PRC government.

Let us drink:
To the friendship, unity, and peaceful coexistence between the peoples of China and Burma,
To Asian peace and international peace,
To the health of Dr. Ba U, president of the Union of Burma,
To Prime Minister U Nu's visit to China and to his health,
To the host of today's dinner, Ambassador U Hla Maung, and to his health,
Bottoms up!

Telegram to the Republic of Finland
(December 5, 1954)

Source: *RMRB* (Dec. 6, 1954), 1. Other Chinese Text: *XHYB*, 1 (Jan. 28, 1955), 103. Available English Translation: HNA, *Daily News Release* (Dec. 6, 1954), 1.

President Juho Kusti Paasikivi,
The Republic of Finland

Your Excellency:

On the occasion of the Republic of Finland's National Day, please accept my sincere congratulations.
(Signed as Chairman of PRC, dated in Beijing)

Telegram to Antonin Zapotocky
(December 16, 1954)

Source: *RMRB* (Dec. 19, 1954), 1. Other Chinese Text: *XHYB*, 1 (Jan. 28, 1954), 102. Available English Translation: HNA, *Daily News Release* (Dec. 19, 1954), 4.

President,
The Republic of Czechoslovakia

Dear Comrade Zapotocky:

On the occasion of your seventieth birthday, please accept the sincere congratulations of the Chinese people and myself.

You have carried on a prolonged and heroic struggle for the cause of the liberation of the Czechoslovakian laboring people and have made outstanding contributions. Now the Czechoslovakian people, under the leadership of the Communist Party of Czechoslovakia and yourself, are in the midst of building their homeland into an increasingly prosperous and happy country and carrying out an unrelenting struggle to safeguard European peace and security. The Chinese people express profound sympathy and support for this righteous cause of the Czechoslovakian people.

May you attain even greater successes in your cause of leading the Czechoslovakian people in building socialism and defending world peace, and may you have good health and a long life.

(Signed and dated in Beijing)

Inscription for Workers on the Kangding-Tibet and Qinghai-Tibet Highways

(December 25, 1954)

Source: *Zhongguo qingnian bao* (Dec. 25, 1954), 25. Other Chinese Text: *RMRB* (Feb. 4, 1955), 1.

These sources indicate that the inscription already existed on December 25, 1954, when the ceremonies to open the two highways to traffic were held; the ceremonies held to award the inscribed banner to the workers was not held, however, until February 3, 1955, in Lhasa. See text Apr. 6, 1952, note 5.

Congratulations on the opening to traffic of the Kangding-Tibet and the Qinghai-Tibet highways. Let us consolidate the unity of the people of all nationalities and build our homeland!

Letter to Li Da
(December 28, 1954)

Source: *HQ*, 329 (Jan. 1, 1979), 10. Other Chinese Text: *Shuxin*, p. 487.

See also texts Mar. 27, 1951, and Sept. 17, 1952.

Dear Haoming:[1]
I have received and read your letter of December 20 and the two attached articles,[2] and I think they are very good; especially the article on political ideology, which is of even greater help to the readers. There seems to be some wrong words; for instance, [when you said] "the pragmatists maintain that it is matter that comes first and consciousness that comes second." Besides, when one criticizes pragmatism, a comparison and explanation is needed for [the terms] "utility" and "effects" as used by the pragmatists and broadly similar terms used by us. This is because people in general are still confused and unclear about them. "The cosmos is 'an unfinished manuscript. . .'";[3] these few sentences also need to be explicitly criticized. Your writings are in a popular language and easy to understand. This is good. When you write again, I suggest that you make use of appropriate occasions to explain certain basic concepts in philosophy so that cadres in general can read and understand them. We must use this opportunity to help the millions of cadres, both inside and outside the Party, who have no knowledge of philosophy to understand some Marxist philosophy. What do you think? My respects.

Mao Zedong
December 28, 1954

Notes

1. See text Mar. 27, 1951, note 1.
2. This refers to two articles written by Li Da to criticize Hu Shi, titled, respectively, "Hu Shi de zhengzhi sixiang pipan" (Criticism of Hu Shi's Political Thought) and "Hu Shi sixiang pipan" (Criticism of Hu Shi's Thought). The first was published in *RMRB* (Dec. 31, 1954) and the latter in *Xin jianshe* (New Construction), 1955, 1. Both can be found in *Hu Shi sixiang pipan* (Criticism of Hu Shi's Thought), Sanlian shudian, 1955.
3. See Hu Shih's *Shiyan zhuyi* (Experimentalism). Pursuant to Mao's opinion, Li Da, when compiling the book *Hu Shi fandong sixiang pipan* (Critique of Hu Shi's Reactionary Ideology) in 1955, made a comparison and explanation of the terms "utility" and "effect" as used by the pragmatists and broadly similar terms used in dialectical materialism. He also made an explicit criticism of the line "the cosmos is 'an unfinished manuscript. . .'."

Telegram to the Democratic Republic of Viet Nam
(December 31, 1954)

Source: *RMRB* (Jan. 22, 1955), 1. Other Chinese Text: *XHYB*, 2 (Feb. 28, 1955), 38. Available English Translation: NCNA, *Daily Bulletin* (Jan. 22, 1955), 16.

Comrade Ho Chi Minh, President of the Democratic Republic of Viet Nam, Comrade Pham Van Dong, Vice-Premier and Foreign Minister of the Democratic Republic of Viet Nam:

On the occasion of the ceremony of the return of the government of the Democratic Republic of Viet Nam to Hanoi, we, on behalf of the Chinese people and the government of the People's Republic of China, express warm congratulations to you and, through you, to the Vietnamese people and the government of the Democratic Republic of Viet Nam.

The return of the government of Viet Nam to Hanoi is the result of the brilliant victory scored by the heroic Vietnamese people, under the leadership of the Viet Nam Workers' Party and President Ho Chi Minh, in eight years of arduous war of resistance. It is also the result of the peace policy consistently upheld by the government of Viet Nam. May the Vietnamese people attain new successes in the coming new year in their struggles to consolidate peace and to achieve national unification, independence, and democracy, and in their cause of restoring the national economy.

(Co-signed with Zhou Enlai, dated in Beijing)

On Writing Essays to Criticize Hu Shi
(December 1954)

Source: *Wenyi hongqi*, 5 (May 30, 1967), 2. Other Chinese Text: *Xinwen zhanbao*, 4 (May 23, 1967) (Red Guards Publication 01240. For publication data on this source see text Winter 1954, source note). Available English Translation: *SCMP*, 4000 (Aug. 14, 1967), 14.

See text Oct. 1954 (1), source note, text Oct. 16, 1954, note 7, and text Dec. 28, 1954.

Essays criticizing Hu Shi's thought must be written in a vernacular and popular manner and should propagate Marxism in a direct way. Every one of Hu Shi's essays had a political purpose. We too should have targets in mind when we write.

Speech at a Standing Committee Meeting of the Central Committee of the CPC (Excerpts)

(Winter 1954)

Source: These excerpts are found in two separate sources and are combined here because they appear to be excerpts from the same speech. The long paragraph (Excerpt 1) is found in *SCMM* (suppl.) 22 (Apr. 8, 1968), 9. Because there is no available full Chinese text for this portion, we have reproduced the translation printed in this source. The other three shorter excerpts are from the Tianjin Red Guard publication *Dongfang hong* (May 1, 1967), compiled in *Hongweibing ziliao huibian* (Compilation of Red Guard Materials) (n.d: n.p), p. 371. Excerpt 3 also appears as part of Excerpt 1. However, we have translated it in a different way from the *SCMM* translation. It should be noted that this appears in many ways similiar to a speech presumably made by Mao to a Standing Committee Meeting of the CPC Central Committee in Spring 1955. See text Spring 1955.

1. I believe that China makes great contributions to the world, and one of these is Chinese medicine. Chinese medicine was born on the basis of handicraft and agricultural production. Theories regarding gold, wood, water, fire and soil may be criticized,[1] but precious experiences must be protected and promoted. Those who make criticism must understand this. What is science? Correct and systematic knowledge is called science. Isn't Western medicine a science? It is also somewhat idealistic. Mechanical materialism, for instance, must be transformed. China should have one medical service, and not two medical services, as they have existed for a long time. The term doctor of

Western medicine is improper; as materialist dialectics would have it, there should be one unified term for doctors. It is wrong for some to overexaggerate the importance of Chinese medicine. Traditional Chinese hospitals should be run experimentally at key points.[2] In regard to the question of further training of traditional doctors, it is right and proper to require them to study fundamental subjects and to exchange experiences. It may be difficult, I am afraid, for them to learn the pharmacology of Chinese medicine.

2. From now on, graduates from medical programs in the universities must study traditional Chinese medicine for two years.

3. China ought to have one [integrated school of] medicine, and not two [schools of] medicine [coexisting] over a long period of time. The terms Chinese medicine and Western medicine are inappropriate; there ought to be [only] one [integrated school of] medicine [based on] dialectical materialism. The health of the six hundred million people in China primarily relies on Chinese medicine, and not on Western medicine.

4. To look down on traditional Chinese medicine is a slavish bourgeois mentality.

Notes

1. Mao is referring here to the ancient Chinese cosmological theory that the universe is made up of these five fundamental elements or forms of matter *(wu xing)*. In the traditional sense of the words, *jin*, here translated as "gold," is more appropriately translated as "metal," and *tu* as "earth" rather than "soil." The earliest written formulation of this theory appears in the ancient book *Hongfan* (Framework of the Cosmos) in *Shangshu* (Book of History).

2. While we do not have the Chinese text, we believe that the term here is *shidian* (translatable as "spot experimenting"). This term appears often in CPC usage and in Mao's own writing in the years ahead and refers to the practice of doing experimentation in selected key areas in order to develop prototypes for emulation on a broader scale.

Comment on the National Budget

(1954)

Source: Quoted in Li Chengrui, "Liu you yudi shi yige jiji de fangzhen"(To Leave Room for Maneuvering Is a Positive Policy), in *HQ*, 16 (Aug. 31, 1964), 22, from Deng Xiaoping, "Yi jiu wu si nian guojia yusuan caoan de baogao" (Report on the Draft of the 1954 National Budget) collected in *Yi jiu wu si nian guojia yusuan* (The 1954 National Budget), Caizheng jingji chubanshe (no further publishing information cited), p. 20.

Increasing production, practicing economy, and setting aside more reserves are the three reliable defense lines to fortify the budget of the state.

Instructions on the Work of Doctors
of Traditional Chinese Medicine
(1954)

Source: *SCMM* (suppl.), 22 (Apr. 8, 1968), 8.

We have no Chinese text of this document. We are uncertain as to whether this exists as a separate document or as part of a document separate from Mao's several other pieces of writing on the subject of traditional Chinese medicine. See also texts Jul. 30, 1954, Oct. 20, 1954, and Winter 1954.

An inappropriate policy of restriction and discrimination has been adopted toward traditonal Chinese medicine in many respects, with the result that for a long time there has existed in society the situation where doctors of traditional Chinese medicine are opposed to doctors of Western medicine and are discriminated against, and this situation hasn't been changed. This is an extremely grave policy mistake of the health departments. . . . If this situation is allowed to exist for a long time, not only will our country's health protection service continue to suffer serious losses, but there is the danger of this part of the cultural legacy of our country being lost.

Inscription on the Triumph of the People
of Wuhan over the Flood.
(1954)

Source: Quoted in "Zuguo de shan shan shui shui shan yao zhuo Mao Zedong sixiang de guanghui," (The Hills and Rivers of Our Country Sparkle with the Glory of Mao Zedong Thought), in *RMRB (Oct. 2, 1976)*, 2.

In 1954, the stretch of the Yangtze River near Wuhan overflowed its banks and caused severe damage. Mao's inscription here was awarded to the people of Wuhan who took part in bringing the deluge under control.

We must still be prepared to do battle against and overcome similarly severe floods that may occur in the future.

Inscription for Historical Pavilion
in Caixi *xiang,* Fujian Province.
(1954)

Source: Reprinted in Li Shuliang, "Guangrong de Caixi xiang" (Glorious Caixi *xiang*), in *Jiefangjun huabao*, 67 (Jul. 1957).

This was an inscription written upon the rebuilding of a pavilion in Caixi xiang, Shanghang xian, Fujian, which was first built in 1933 when Caixi xiang was commended by the Central Soviet as a model village. It was intended for the display of awards, banners, and rolls of the revolutionary martyrs of Fujian Province. It was destroyed, and subsequently rebuilt in 1954.

Glory Pavilion

1955

Telegram to the Union of Burma
(January 2, 1955)

Source: *RMRB* (Jan. 4, 1955), 1. Other Chinese Text: *XHYB*, 2 (Feb. 28, 1955), 39. Available English Translation: HNA, *Daily News Release* (Jan. 4, 1955), 1.

President Dr. Ba U,
Union of Burma

Your Excellency:

On behalf of the Chinese people and on my own behalf, I extend to the Burmese people and to Your Excellency warm congratulations. On this occasion of the National Day of the Union of Burma, may the relationship of friendly cooperation between China and Burma be further consolidated and developed in the cause of defending peace in Asia and the world.
(Signed as Chairman of PRC, dated in Beijing)

Telegram to the Republic of India
(January 24, 1955)

Source: *RMRB* (Jan. 26, 1955), 1. Other Chinese Text: *XHYB*, 2 (Feb. 28, 1955), 41. Available English Translation: NCNA, *Daily Bulletin* (Jan. 26, 1955), 2.

President Rajendra Prasad,
Republic of India

Your Excellency:

On the occasion of the fifth National Day of the Republic of India, on behalf of the Chinese people and on my own behalf, I extend to the Indian people and to your Excellency warm congratulations. May the relationship of friendly cooperation between China and India grow daily firmer and develop with each passing day in the cause of defending peace in Asia and the world, and may the Republic of India prosper and the Indian people be happy. (Signed as Chairman of PRC, dated in Beijing)

Reply to Ambassador of the Republic of Finland
(January 28, 1955)

Source: *RMRB* (Jan. 29, 1955), 1. Other Chinese Text: *XHYB*, 2 (Feb. 28, 1955), 42-43. Available English Translation: HNA, *Daily News Release* (Jan. 29, 1955), 2-3.

See text Dec. 2, 1953, source note.

Mr. Ambassador:

It is with great pleasure that I accept the letter of credence from the President of the Republic of Finland which you have presented to us, and I am grateful for his friendly wishes which you have just conveyed.

In the last four years, the economic ties and cultural exchange between China and Finland have, on the foundations of equality and mutual benefit, greatly developed. It is commonly known that the friendly exchange between our two governments and our two peoples have, over the last few years, taken place in many diverse forms. Particularly satisfying has been the situation of smooth development in the trade relations and cultural ties between our two nations. There has been progress in our trade relations every year, and our trade agreements have all been satisfactorily fulfilled. The visit of the Chinese acrobatic troupe to Finland in 1952, as well as the visit to China of the Finnish cultural delegation led by Madame Kekkonen in 1953, and the visit to Finland in July 1954 of Deputy Minister Lei Renmin of the Chinese Ministry of Foreign Trade at the invitation of the Finnish government have all left lasting and good impressions on our peoples and have contributed greatly to the strengthening of the friendly feelings between the people of China and the people of Finland, and to their mutual confidence in peaceful cooperation. The friendly cooperative relationship between China and Finland provides ample evidence that nations of diverse social systems can coexist peacefully and be in friendly cooperation with one another. Now we have escalated our legations to each other to the status of embassies and we have exchanged ambassadors. This signifies that a further step has been taken in the consolidation and promotion of friendly relations between our two countries.

China and Finland share a common hope for the defense and consolidation of peace, and the enhancement of economic and cultural exchange between our two countries is bound to have a beneficial effect on the safeguarding and consolidating of world peace. We are convinced that the trade relations and the cultural interflow between China and Finland will continue to be strengthened and develop. Mr. Ambassador, I welcome your expressed wish that there be more direct contact between the representatives of our countries.

I heartily welcome your assuming the position of ambassador extraordinary and plenipotentiary of the Republic of Finland to the People's Republic of China and pledge to you my assistance and the assistance of the government of the People's Republic of China in your work of strengthening the friendly cooperation between China and Finland.

I wish you success in your mission, and I express my good wishes for the prosperity of the Republic of Finland the happiness of the people of Finland and the health of President J. K. Paasikivi of the Republic of Finland.

The Atom Bomb Cannot Scare the Chinese People
(January 28, 1955)

Source: *Xuanji*, V, pp. 136-137. Available English Translations: *SW*, V, pp. 152-153; JPRS, *Selections*, pp. 24-25.

According to Xuanji, *V, p. 136, fn., this is a summary of the main points of a conversation between Mao and Finland's first ambassador to China, Carljohan Sundstrom, on the occasion of his presentation of the letter of credence. See preceding document, source note.*

China and Finland are friendly nations. Our relations are built on the basis of the Five Principles of Peaceful Coexistence.[1]

There has never been a conflict between China and Finland. Historically, China has had wars only with England, France, Germany, tsarist Russia, Italy, the Austro-Hungarian Empire, and Holland of the European countries. In every case it was because these countries came from so far away to invade China, for example, the attacks made on China by the allied forces of England and France[2] and the allied army of the eight powers, which included the United States and Japan.[3] Sixteen countries, including ones such as Turkey and Luxemburg, participated in the war of aggression against Korea. All these aggressor countries claimed that they were peace-loving while describing Korea and China as the aggressor countries.

Today, the danger of world war and the threat to China comes primarily from the warhawks in the United States. They have invaded and occupied China's [province of] Taiwan and the Taiwan Straits and even want to launch an atomic war.[4] We have two [principles]: first, we do not want war; second, if anybody commits aggression against us, we will resolutely strike back. We have been educating the members of the Communist Party and the people of the entire country in just this way. The atomic hoax of the United States cannot scare the Chinese people. We have a population of 600 million, and a territory of 9.6 million square kilometers. That little bit of atomic weaponry that the United States has cannot annihilate the Chinese people. Even if the United States had more powerful atom bombs and used them on China, blasted a hole in the Earth, or blew it to pieces, [while] this might be a matter of great significance to the solar system, it would still be an insignificant matter as far as the universe as a whole is concerned.

We have an old saying: millet plus rifles.[5] In the United States it is airplanes plus atom bombs. But if the United States, with its airplanes plus atom bombs, launched a war of aggression against China, then China, with its millet and rifles, would definitely win. The people of the entire world would support us. As a result of the First World War, the tsar and the landlords and capitalists were swept away in Russia. As a result of the Second World War, Chiang Kai-shek and the landlords were overthrown in China, and the Eastern European countries and some Asian countries were liberated. If the United States were to launch a third world war, then even if it were to last for eight or ten years, the result would be that the ruling classes in the United States, in England, and in those other countries that were their accomplices would be completely swept away, and most places in the world would become countries led by Communist parties. The outcome of a world war would not be favorable to the warhawks, but would be favorable to the Communists and to the revolutionary people of the world. If they want to launch a war, they cannot blame us for engaging in the revolution they are constantly prating about as the "subversive activities" in which we engage. If they do not make war, they may still exist on Earth for some time. The earlier they launch a war, the earlier they will be erased from the face of the Earth.

Then a People's United Nations will be established, maybe in Shanghai, or in some place in Europe, or possibly [even] in New York if by that time the warhawks in the United States have been totally swept away.

Notes

1. Following the relinquishing of the policy of "demilitarizing and neutralizing Taiwan" by President Eisenhower in early 1953, the PRC, facing a re-armed adversary across the Taiwan Straits, began formulating a new anticolonial foreign policy. In April 1954, in the agreement between the governments of China and India concerning trade and communications between Tibet and India, this new foreign policy emerged as the Five Principles of Peaceful Coexistence, namely, (1) Mutual respect for each other's sovereignty and territorial integrity, (2) Nonaggression, (3) Noninterference in each other's domestic affairs, (4) Equality of relations and mutual benefit, and (5) Peaceful coexistence. These principles were reiterated in two subsequent joint communique as issued by the PRC in conjunction with India and with Burma respectively in June of the same year during Zhou Enlai's visit to those countries. Since then they have become the fundamental principles of the PRC's relations with countries with social systems different from its own.

2. This refers to the war of 1860, also known as the Arrow War. The British, seeking to force an imperial audience and diplomatic presence in Beijing, used the Chinese seizure of a British-owned lighter, the *Lorcha Arrow*, as a pretext to join with France, which sought greater privileges for its missionaries, in invading China. The hostilities ended with the Anglo-French force sacking Beijing and burning the Yiheyuan palace.

3. In 1900 an allied expeditionary force from Britain, France, Germany, Italy, Russia, Austria-Hungary, Japan, and the United States invaded North China on the pretext of rescuing their legations in Beijing from the Yihetuan. The Yihetuan (Righteous and Harmonious Fists), commonly known as the Boxers in the West, was a nationalistic, secret society-based mass movement that sought to expel foreign imperialism from China. Originally antidynastic, it was later coopted by the Qing court whose links with the movement then provided further justification for the destruction and looting of Beijing by the "allied" troops, including the burning of the Yuanmingyuan summer palace. The actions of the allied expeditionary forces compelled China to sign the

"Boxer Protocol" on Sept. 7, 1901.

4. Mao's statement here indicates the rationale behind the timing of the speech. On January 24, 1955, four days prior to this speech, the U.S. House of Representatives adopted the "Formosa Resolution" which authorized President Eisenhower to employ U.S. armed forces to protect the security of Taiwan and the Pescadore Islands. This resolution was adopted by the U.S. Senate on January 28, the day of the speech, and signed by the president on January 29. The issue then at stake was the "Taiwan Straits Crisis" which began when the PRC launched its campaign to militarily liberate Taiwan in September 1954. By January 18, 1955, the majority of the "offshore" islands except for the Pescadores chain and Taiwan itself were either captured or under heavy bombardment by the Communist forces.

As for U.S. threats to use nuclear weaponry to resolve the fighting in the Taiwan Straits, they were not specific. On March 8, however, following a trip to East Asia, Secretary of State John Foster Dulles warned China not to underestimate the willingness of the U.S. to counter the PRC's military challenge to Taiwan and other parts of the Southeast Asian region whose defense was considered by the U.S. to be vital to the security of non-Communist countries. In this speech, Dulles mentioned "new and powerful weapons of precision which can utterly destroy military targets without endangering unrelated civilian centers."

5. This is a term used by Mao in 1946 to describe the determination of the People's Liberation Army to attain its military revolutionary objectives in the face of overwhelming odds posed, at that time, by Chiang Kai-shek's vastly superior forces. The term derives from Mao's conversation with the American reporter Anna Louise Strong. See *Xuanji*, IV, p. 1091.

Criticism of Hu Feng
(January 1955)

Source: *Wenyi hongqi,* 5 (May 30, 1967), 2. Other Chinese Text: *Wenyi yulu*, p. 99. Available English Translation: *SCMP*, 4000 (Aug. 14, 1967), 15.

This document comes as a directive accompanying the decision to publish Hu Feng's "letter of opinions." In the source it was titled "Mao zhuxi dui wenyi gongzuo de zhongyao zhishi" (Chairman Mao's Important Directive on Literary Work). For greater detail on Hu Feng and the criticism campaign against him, see text May-June 1955.

We must never permit bourgeois idealism and thought such as Hu Feng's, which stands in opposition to the people and to the Party, to get away from us under the cover of [being merely regarded as a] "petty bourgeois viewpoint." Instead, we ought to criticize and repudiate them thoroughly.

Telegram to the USSR
(February 12, 1955)

Source: *RMRB* (Feb. 14, 1955), 1. Other Chinese Text: *XHYB*, 3 (Mar. 28, 1955), 8. Available English Translation: NCNA, *Daily Bulletin*, (Feb. 14, 1955), 19-20.

Comrade K. E. Voroshilov, Chairman of the Presidium of the Supreme Soviet of the Union of Soviet Socialist Republics,
Comrade N. A. Bulganin, Chairman of the Council of Ministers of the Union of Soviet Socialist Republics,
Comrade V. M. Molotov, First Vice-Chairman of the Council of Ministers and Minister of Foreign Affairs of the Union of Soviet Socialist Republics:

On the occasion of the fifth anniversary of the signing of the Sino-Soviet Treaty of Friendship, Alliance, and Mutual Assistance,[1] we represent the Chinese people and the government of the People's Republic of China in sincerely extending our warm congratulations to you and, through you, to the great people and government of the Soviet Union.

In the past five years, the overall political, economic, and cultural cooperation between China and the Soviet Union has developed extensively. The government and people of the Soviet Union have given all-round and systematic assistance – assistance that leaves no detail unattended – to us, the Chinese people, who are in the midst of pursuing socialist construction. The government of the Soviet Union has successively helped China build from scratch and expand 156 huge industrial enterprises, sent excellent experts in large numbers to assist China in its construction, extended to China favorable loans several times, transferred to China without cost the Sino-Soviet jointly managed China-Changchun railway and property in Northeast China acquired by Soviet organizations from Japanese owners in 1945,[2] sold to China shares owned by the Soviet Union in Sino-Soviet joint enterprises, and decided to place totally at China's disposal the naval base at Lushun and installations in that area jointly used by China and the Soviet Union. Moreover, it has also proposed to offer to China scientific, technological, and industrial assistance in promoting research in peaceful uses for atomic energy.[3] Such friendly cooperation and sincere aid have greatly promoted the development of our country's undertakings in construction and demonstrate to the world the great vitality of this new kind of international relations. The government of the People's Republic of China and the Chinese people deeply appreciate the unmatched treasure that this brotherly friendship represents. On behalf of the government of the People's Republic of China and the Chinese people, we express sincere gratitude for the tremendous assistance of the government and people of the Soviet Union.

The consolidation and development of the friendship and alliance between China and the Soviet Union has been invaluable in guaranteeing our two countries' security and maintaining peace in the Far East and in the world. The peace policy of China and the Soviet Union has promoted and brought about the Korean armistice and the restoration of peace in Indochina,[4] bringing about a certain degree of relaxation in international tensions and inspiring all peace-loving countries and peoples. The Chinese people enthusiastically support the Soviet Union's struggle for the establishment of a European collective security system and its opposition to the rearmament of West Germany.[5] China and the Soviet Union are willing to establish normalized relations with Japan and to actively support the Japanese people in taking the road of independent development and international cooperation. The sincere cooperation between China and the Soviet Union conforms to the interests not only of the people of the two countries, China and the Soviet Union, but also of all the peace-loving countries and peoples of Asia, Europe, and the rest of the world. It is a reliable guarantee for the maintenance of peace in the Far East and the world.

At this very moment, the aggressive clique of the United States and its followers are pursuing a policy of war and creating international tension everywhere, and the aggressive behavior and war provocations carried out by the United States in the Taiwan area are a grave threat to China's security.[6] It has given rise to just reprobation by peace-loving countries and peoples throughout the world. The struggle of the Chinese people to liberate their own territory of Taiwan is just. A just cause is something that no force can stop. The friendship and alliance of China and the Soviet Union, in view of the emerging international tension, will play an increasingly vital role in the cause of opposing aggression and guaranteeing peace.

The Sino-Soviet Treaty of Friendship, Alliance, and Mutual Assistance is a great peace treaty, a symbol of the great friendship between China and the Soviet Union. The events of the last five years have proved this treaty's great role in promoting world peace and human progress. From now on, in life and in practice, this treaty's great force and boundless brilliance will be further exhibited.

For the sake of the common prosperity of the two peoples of China and the Soviet Union and the consolidation of peace in the Far East and in the world, may the great friendship between China and the Soviet Union develop daily.

Long live the eternal, indestructible friendship between the Chinese and Soviet peoples!
(Co-signed as Chairman of PRC with Liu Shaoqi as Chairman of Standing Committee of NPC and Zhou Enlai as Premier of State Council and Foreign Minister, dated in Beijing)

Notes

1. See text Jan. 2, 1950, note 1.

2. See text Dec. 31, 1952, note 1.

3. In this paragraph Mao is generally referring to agreements made between China and the USSR regarding the disposition of properties held by the Soviet Union in Chinese territories prior to 1949. These agreements were published as part of a joint communiqué on October 12, 1954, which resulted from talks held in Beijing between Chinese authorities and a Soviet delegation headed by N. Khrushchev. For the texts of the communiqués see *RMRB* (Oct. 12, 1954), and also *RMSC* (1955), pp. 296-299, and text Oct. 12, 1954 (1).

4. See text June 30, 1953, note 2, and text July 23, 1954, note 1.

5. This refers to the design of the Warsaw Treaty Organization (generally known as the Warsaw Pact), which became a unified military command of the Soviet bloc at the signing of the mutual defense treaty on May 14, 1955, between the USSR, Albania, Bulgaria, Czechoslovakia, East Germany, Hungary, Romania, and Poland. The "rearmament of West Germany" refers to the induction of West Germany into NATO, which was being considered at the time of this telegram and became a reality on May 9, 1955.

6. See text Jan. 28, 1955 (2), note 4.

Speech at Banquet Celebrating Fifth Anniversary of Sino-Soviet Treaty[1]

(February 14, 1955)

Source: *RMRB* (Feb. 15, 1955), 1. Other Chinese Texts: *XHYB*, 3 (Mar. 28, 1955), 12; *XHBYK*, 22 (Nov. 25, 1958), 8; Also quoted in *XHBYK*, 21 (Nov. 10, 1958), 8. Available English Translations: HNA, *Daily News Release* (Feb. 15, 1955), 1; FBIS, *Daily Report* (Feb. 15, 1955), AAA1; Excerpts in *PR*, 1:37 (Nov. 11, 1958), 10 and in *CCSD*, p. 156.

I celebrate the great cooperation between China and the Soviet Union.

Such cooperation advances the cause of socialism, opposes imperialism's plans for aggression, and is for international peace. I believe this cooperation will be strengthened further.

Given the cooperation between our two great countries, China and the Soviet Union, I believe that imperialism's plans of aggression will be smashed.

Given the great cooperation between our two countries, we can all perceive that there are no imperialists' aggressive plans that cannot be destroyed. They are bound to be thoroughly destroyed. Should the imperialists launch an aggressive war, we, together with the people of all the world, are bound to wipe them off the face of the earth!

Let us drink to the health of Comrade Voroshilov, Chairman of the Presidium of the Supreme Soviet of the Union of Soviet Socialist Republics!

Note

1. See text Jan. 2, 1950, note 1.

Telegram to the USSR
(February 21, 1955)

Source: *RMRB* (Feb. 23, 1955), 1. Other Chinese Text: *XHYB*, 3 (Mar. 28, 1955), 15. Available English Translation: HNA, *Daily News Release* (Feb. 23, 1955), 1.

Comrade K. E. Voroshilov, Chairman of the Presidium of the Supreme Soviet of the Union of Soviet Socialist Republics,
Comrade N. A. Bulganin, Chairman of the Council of Ministers of the Union of Soviet Socialist Republics,
Comrade V. M. Molotov, First Vice-chairman of the Council of Ministers and Minister of Foreign Affairs of the Union of Soviet Socialist Republics:

On the occasion of the thirty-seventh anniversary of the founding of the armed forces of the Soviet Union, please accept our warm congratulations.

In the Second World War, the glorious armed forces of the Soviet Union, with their invincible might, devastated the forces of Fascism, defended European and world civilization, and made invaluable contributions to the cause of human progress. Now, at the very moment when the imperialist war bloc is intensifying its creation of international tension, preparing for atomic war,[1] carrying out war provocations, and gravely threatening world peace, the strong and long-tested armed forces of the Soviet Union are an invincible force for defending the peace of the world.

The armed forces of the Soviet Union that were stationed at the Lushun naval base in accordance with the Sino-Soviet agreement have played an important role in defending peace and security in the Far East and throughout the world in the last five years. They have provided powerful support to the Chinese people in their cause of socialist construction. Now, as they depart from the Lushun naval base in accordance with the Sino-Soviet communiqué of October 1954,[2] on behalf of the government and people of the People's Republic of China, we extend our heartfelt thanks to the government of the Soviet Union and to the great Soviet people and their armed forces.

May the armed forces of the Soviet Union achieve even more brilliant successes in the tasks of strengthening the national defense forces of their own homeland and defending world peace and security.

(Co-signed as Chairman of PRC with Liu Shaoqi as Chairman of Standing Committee of NPC and Zhou Enlai as Premier of State Council and Foreign Minister, dated in Beijing)

Notes

1. See text Jan. 28, 1955(2), note 4.
2. See text Feb. 12, 1955, note 3.

Toast at Banquet Celebrating Tibetan New Year
(February 24, 1955)

Source: *RMRB* (Feb. 25, 1955), 1. Available English Translations: HNA, *Daily News Release* (Feb. 25, 1955), 7; FBIS, *Daily Report* (Feb. 25, 1955), AAA7.

On the occasion of the Tibetan New Year, let us greet the Dalai Lama, Panchen Gnoerhtehni,[1] all the Tibetan personnel now in Beijing, and the Tibetan people in Tibet and all other regions! We all should strive to further strengthen and consolidate the unity among our country's various nationalities and further strengthen and consolidate the unity between the Han and Tibetan nationalities and within the Tibetan nationality itself, and together build our great homeland.

Let us [drink]:

To the health of the Dalai Lama and Panchen Gnoerhtehni, to all the Tibetan ecclesiastical and secular personnel now in Beijing, to the great unity among all nationalities of our country!

Note

1. See text May 24, 1951, note 2, and text Nov. 23, 1949, source note.

Letter to Lin Tie
(March 5, 1955)

Source: *Shuxin*, p. 489.

Lin Tie (b. circa 1905, a.k.a. Lin Guohua) was at the time of this letter chairman of the provincial government of Hebei Province and ranking Party secretary of that province. (In 1956, he became officially first secretary of the Hebei Provincial Party Committee.) In the same year he became member of the Eight Central Committee of the CPC. Lin played a significant role in promoting the cooperativization movement at this time, and, later, in the "socialist education movement in the countryside." For more biographical information on Lin, see D. Klein and A. Clark, eds. (1971), I, pp. 574-575, and Zhonggong renming lu, pp. 346-347.

Comrade Lin Tie:

Please take care of this problem.[1] This is a copy of a letter which a body-guard of mine brought back from a visit to his native village of Anping *xian*.[2] I presume that the situation [described therein] is not unique to a *xiang* in Anping *xian* – it may also be prevalent elsewhere, and is well worth our attention.

Mao Zedong
March 5

Notes

1. According to the source, this refers to the problem that was reflected in a letter written by the masses in Anping *xian*. In this letter, they reported that, in the process of promoting agricultural cooperativization, the local cadres in that *xian* simplistically used such propaganda and coercive tactics as saying "either you follow the Communist Party or you follow Lao Jiang (Old Chiang [Kai-shek])" to force the peasants into joining the cooperatives. The source also comments that such tactics had led to a serious problem of lowering the peasants' productivity and activism.

2. Anping *xian* is in Hebei Province, south of Beijing Municipality, near Baoding. The area around Anping, including such *xian* as Anguo and Ding, is an important agricultural district.

Letter to Zhou Dungu
(March 6, 1955)

Source: *Shuxin*, p. 490.

According to the source, Zhou was an acquaintance of Mao's from the early years when they were in school together in Changsha, Hunan, of which Zhou is a native. (Mao studied in Changsha over a rather lengthy period, first as a student in Xiangxiang Middle School and several vocational schools from 1910 to 1913, during which time he also briefly joined the New Hunan Army, and then, from 1913 to 1918, as a student of Hunan Normal School. We do not know in what context Zhou made Mao's acquaintance.) At the time of this letter, Zhou was an instructor at the Literary Training Institute of the Chinese Federation of Writers.

Comrade Dungu:

I have received your letter of February 28. I do not intervene directly in affairs related to the enrollment of any student in any school, and therefore, begging your understanding and forgiveness, I cannot gratify your request. It would really be up to you to decide for yourself whether or not you can wait until this summer to apply and take the examination in Beijing then.

I wish you good health.

Mao Zedong
March 6, 1955

Letter to Wei Lihuang
(March 17, 1955)

Source: *Shuxin*, p. 491.

Wei Lihuang (1896-1960) was a former KMT general who was the deputy commander of Chiang Kai-shek's Northeast Military Headquarters ("Bandit Suppression Headquarters") during the Third Revolutionary Civil War period (i.e., August 1945-October 1949). He was relieved of his command after his defeat by Communist troops at the battle of Shenyang in November 1948 (see text Jun. 6, 1950[1], note 4). Wei fled to Hong Kong in 1949, and in March 1955 returned to the mainland. He was invited to be a special delegate to the National Committee of the CPPCC and held this position from 1956 to 1959. He was also a member of the Standing Committee of the KMT and a vice-chairman of the National Defense Council. In many ways, therefore, he stood as an example of how progressive elements of the KMT could cooperate with the Communist regime after 1949. For more information on Wei, see H. Boorman et al., eds. (1970), III, pp. 405-406.

Mr. Wei Junru:[1]

I have rceived your telegram of March 16. I warmly welcome your return to China. I hope that you will come to Beijing soon, so that we may met. If you are interested, you may, of course, take a look at the conditions in [various parts of] the country along your journey, and arrive at Beijing either at the end of this month or early next month; that, too, would be excellent.

Mao Zedong

March 17

Note

1. "Junru" is Wei's *zi*, or honorific name. For an explanation of this usage, see text Oct. 15, 1949, note 1.

Inscription for the First Congress of Heroes
and Model Soldiers of the Air Force
(March 21, 1955)

Source: *RMRB* (Mar. 22, 1955), 1. Other Chinese Texts: *Mao liang*, p. 337; *RMRB* (Feb. 9, 1968), 6. Available English Translation: *CB*, 897 (Dec. 10, 1969), 55.

This inscription was written in Mao's calligraphy on a banner displayed at the First Congress of Heroes, Model Soldiers, and Meritorious Members of the Air Force of the PLA, which was convened on March 21, 1955, in Beijing.

Build a strong People's Air Force to defend the homeland and be prepared to defeat the aggressor.

Opening Speech at the National Conference of the CPC

(March 21, 1955)

Source: *Xuanji*, V, pp. 138-142. Other Chinese Text: Excerpt in *Wansui* (1967b), p. 10 (with minor differences). Available English Translation: *SW*, V, pp. 154-158.

Comrades, Delegates to the National Conference of the Communist Party of China:[1]

There are three items on the agenda for this National Conference of ours. The first concerns the First Five-Year Plan for National Economic Development and the report on this plan;[2] the second concerns the report on the Gao Gang–Rao Shushi anti-Party alliance;[3] and the third concerns the formation of a Central Control Commission.

The Central Committee, in accordance with Lenin's teachings on the period of transition, has summed up our experience since the establishment of the People's Republic of China; and when the recovery stage of our country's national economy was about to end, that is, in 1952, it proposed the Party's general line for the period of transition.[4] This general line is the gradual realization of the socialist industrialization of our country and, simultaneously, the gradual realization of the socialist transformation of agriculture, handicraft industries and capitalist industry and commerce, [to take place] within [the span of] approximately three five-year plans, so that we may achieve the goal of building a socialist society in our country. The general line of the Party and the various major policies and measures adopted by the Party in order to realize this general line have been proved, in practice, to be correct. By relying on the efforts of all the comrades in the Party and of the people throughout the whole country, our work has had great success. However, we still have some shortcomings and mistakes in our work. In many of our methods we were not able to make appropriate stipulations for all aspects; [therefore] they should be supplemented and revised on the basis of new experiences gained in implementing them.

The First Five-Year Plan for National Economic Development is a major step in the implementation of the Party's general line. This National Party Conference should discuss this draft plan earnestly and in accordance with practical experience so that its contents may become more appropriate and it may become a truly practicable plan.

In such a big country as ours, the situation is complicated, and our national economy was very backward to begin with. To build a socialist society [in our country, therefore,] is not an easy matter. We might be able to build a socialist society within the span of three five-year plans, but to build a strong country with a high degree of socialist industrialization will require several decades of strenuous effort – fifty years, let's say – which means the entire second half of this century. Our task demands that we handle the relationships among our people very well – especially the relationship between the working class and the peasants – and [that we] handle the relationships between the various nationalities in our country well; at the same time, we must do well in continuing to develop close cooperation with the great advanced socialist country – the Soviet Union – and with the various People's Democracies,[5] and also develop cooperation with all the peace-loving countries and people in the capitalist world.

We often say that we must not become conceited and self-satisfied just because we have had some success in our work, and that we should maintain a modest attitude, learn from the advanced countries, learn from the masses, and learn from each other, our own comrades, so that we may commit fewer mistakes. I feel that it is still necessary to repeat these words once again at this National Party Conference. We can see from the Gao Gang - Rao Shushi anti-Party affair that the feelings of arrogance and self-satisfaction do indeed exist in our Party. In some of our comrades, such feelings are still very serious. Unless these feelings are overcome, the completion of our great task of building a socialist society will be hindered.

[Our] comrades all know that the emergence of the Gao Gang–Rao Shushi anti-Party alliance is not an accidental phenomenon. It was an acute manifestation of the present stage of fierce class struggle in our country. The criminal purpose of this anti-Party alliance was to split our Party, to use conspiratorial means to seize the highest power in the Party and the state, and to blaze the path for the restoration of counterrevolution. The entire Party, under the united leadership of the Central Committee, has already thoroughly smashed this anti-Party alliance, and consequently our Party has become even more strongly unified and consolidated. This is a major triumph in our struggle for the cause of socialism.

The Gao Gang–Rao Shushi affair is an important lesson as far as our Party is concerned. The entire Party should take it as a warning, so as to ensure that such an affair will not be repeated within the Party. Gao Gang and Rao Shushi fooled around with conspiracies inside the Party; they engaged in clandestine activities and sowed seeds of discord and trouble behind the comrades' backs, but in public, they disguised their activities. This kind of activity of theirs is just the type of ugly activity in which, historically, the landlords and the bourgeoisie have frequently been involved. Marx and Engels said in the *Communist Manifesto*: "Communists consider it a disgraceful matter to cover up their own points of view and intentions." We are Communists, not to mention high-ranking Party cadres, [so] we should be frank and aboveboard in our politics. We should announce our political views publicly at all times and express our approval of or opposition to every major political issue. We absolutely may not fool around with conspiratorial methods the way Gao Gang and Rao

Shushi did.

In order to achieve the goal of building a socialist society, the Central Committee believes that there is a need at this time to form a Central Control Commission, in accord with the Party Constitution, to take the place of the former Discipline Inspection Commission.[6] This is to reinforce the Party's discipline in the new period of fierce class struggle, to reinforce the struggle against all occurrences of violations of law and discipline, and particularly to prevent the recurrence of an affair such as the Gao Gang–Rao Shushi anti-Party alliance, which seriously endangered the Party's interests.

In view of all kinds of historical lessons, in view of the fact that the wisdom of the individual must be integrated with the wisdom of the collective before it can be put to good use and allow us to commit fewer mistakes in our work, the Center and the Party committees of all levels must uphold the principle of collective leadership and continue to oppose the two deviations of personal dictatorship and dispersionism.[7] It is necessary to understand that the two aspects, collective leadership and personal responsibility, are not mutually opposed, but mutually integrated. Moreover, personal responsibility and personal dictatorship, [the latter] being in violation of the principle of collective leadership, are two entirely different things.

Current international conditions are advantageous to our cause of building socialism. The socialist camp headed by the Soviet Union is big and strong and united internally, while the imperialist camp is weak and has within it many irresolvable contradictions and crises. Even so, we must understand that imperialist forces are still surrounding us and we must be prepared to meet any possible emergency. In the future, if the imperialists start a war, it is quite possible that they will carry out a surprise attack, just as they did during the Second World War. Therefore we must be both psychologically and materially prepared so that when a sudden emergency occurs we will not be taken by surprise. This is one aspect. Another aspect is that the activities of the remnant forces of counterrevolution inside the country are still rampant. We must give them a few more blows in a planned, analytical, and realistic way so that the hidden forces of the counterrevolution can be weakened even further and the security of the cause of our country's socialist construction can be guaranteed. If we carry out appropriate measures in both of these two above-mentioned aspects, we will be able to avoid being severely harmed by our enemies; otherwise we may be committing a mistake.

Comrades! We are now in a new historical era. An Eastern country of six hundred million people is carrying out a socialist revolution to change the course of history and the appearance of the state in this country; to make the country basically industrialized within the span of approximately three five-year plans; furthermore, to achieve the socialist transformation of agriculture, handicraft industry and capitalist industry and commerce; to catch up to or even surpass the most powerful capitalist powers in the world within a few decades – this absolutely cannot be done without encountering difficulties, perhaps like the numerous difficulties that we encountered during the period of the democratic revolution,[8] and perhaps even greater difficulties than we encountered in the past. However, comrades, we Communists are renowned for not being afraid of difficulties. Tactically, we must take all diffculties seriously. We must adopt an attitude of treating each concrete difficulty earnestly; we must create the necessary conditions, devote particular care to the methods of dealing [with these problems], and overcome them one by one, one batch at a time. According to our experience of the last several decades, each difficulty we have encountered has been overcome in the end. All sorts of difficulties, when they meet up with Communists, can do nothing but retreat; it's truly a case of "Even the high mountains must bow, and even the rivers must yield." From this we have gained an experience that enables us to despise difficulty. All this is from the strategic point of view, from the general point of view. No matter how great the difficulty, we can perceive its nature in a single glance. By difficulties we mean those which are given to us by [our] enemies in society or by nature. We know that the imperialists, the counterrevolutionaries within the country, their agents within our Party, and so on are no more than forces in the throes of death, while we are newborn forces and truth is on our side. To them, we are, and have always been, invincible. We need but reflect a bit upon our own history to understand this. In 1921, when our Party had just been formed, we only had several dozen members. We were so very small and insignificant. Later we developed and, sure enough, we overthrew the powerful enemy within our country. There is a way of conquering even Nature as an enemy. No matter whether in Nature or in society, all newborn forces have always been by their very nature invincible. On the other hand, all old forces, no matter how great their quantitative strength may be, will inevitably be destroyed. Therefore we can, and must, despise any difficulty, however great, that we may encounter in this human world, and regard it as "nothing to speak of." This is our optimism. This kind of optimism has a scientific basis. If only we [come to] understand Marxism-Leninism more [fully], and understand natural science more [fully], in a word, if we understand the laws of the objective world more fully and commit fewer mistakes of subjectivism, our revolutionary work and our work of construction can definitely achieve their goal.

Notes

1. This National Conference of the CPC was held on March 21-31, 1955. It marked the first time that the Gao Gang–Rao Shushi "affair" was seriously discussed publicly within the CPC. Mao's "opening" speech here served as a keynote address. Chen Yun and Deng Xiaoping also made important speeches. See more in K. Lieberthal (1976), p. 68.

2. See text Feb. 10, 1953, note 2. Li Fuchun delivered the Report on the First Five-Year Plan at the Second Session of the First NPC in July 1955.

3. For details of this matter see text Mar. 31, 1955, source note and note 2.

4. See text June 15, 1953, note 1.

5. See text Sept. 21, 1949, note 4.

6. The Discipline Inspection Commission of the CPC was formed in November 1949, with

Zhu De as its secretary. Its purpose was to investigate and inspect disciplinary matters in all departments directly subsidiary to the Central Committee of the CPC and all Party units and cadres at all levels. The standard for discipline was the Party Constitution. At the present meeting it was deemed necessary to establish a new structure to replace the Discipline Inspection Commission, which was not effective in meeting the needs of disciplinary measures within the CPC in a new stage of class struggle. Together with a Central Control Commission, control committees were also established at the local levels. Dong Biwu was elected, at this conference, to be secretary of the Central Control Commission.

7. See text Mar. 19, 1953, note 1.
8. See text June 15, 1953, note 2.

Concluding Remarks at the National Conference of the CPC
(March 31, 1955)

Source: *Xuanji*, V, pp. 143-156. Other Chinese Texts: *Wansui* (1967a), p. 10 (excerpts); *Buyi*, p. 29 (excerpt). Available English Translation: *SW*, V, pp. 158-171.

Minor discrepancies in wording exist among these various versions. The National Conference of the CPC was held at Beijing from March 21 to March 31, 1955. The First Five-Year Plan was introduced at this conference, the handling of the affair of the Gao Gang–Rao Shushi anti-Party clique[1] was discussed, and central and local control committees were established. (See text Mar. 21, 1955, notes 1, 2, and 6.) For further details on this conference see K. Lieberthal (1976), pp. 68-69.

Comrades:

You have all spoken. Let me say a few words on the following topics: an evaluation of this conference, the five-year plan, the question of Gao [Gang] and Rao [Shushi], the current situation, and the Eighth Congress.

1. An Evaluation of This Conference

The overwhelming majority of the comrades believe that this present conference has been a very good one and that this has once again been a conference of rectification since the Yanan period rectification.[2] At this conference democracy has been promoted and criticism and self-criticism have been launched, enabling us to understand each other better, become more unified in our thinking, and arrive at a common understanding. We already had a common understanding to begin with, but on several problems we still held different opinions. Through this conference our understanding has become unified. On this basis, on the foundation of this common understanding of ideology, politics, and many policies, our Party can be more securely united. As Comrade [Zhou] Enlai said, if we say that it was the Seventh [Party] Congress[3] and the rectification within the entire Party in the areas of ideology and politics for a period before that Congress that established the foundations for our Party's unified thinking, that it was on this foundation that we achieved the victory of the democratic revolution against imperialism, feudalism, and bureaucratic capitalism,[4] then [we can say] that this present conference will enable us to achieve victory in [building] socialism.

This conference proves that the [political] level in our Party has been greatly raised. Not only has there been a great step forward since the time of the Seventh [Party] Congress ten years ago, but even since the time of the Second Plenum of the Central Committee in 1949 or the Third Plenum in 1950 there has been a great step forward.[5] This is a good situation; this conference proves that we are making progress.

We are entering an era, a new historical period, in which what we undertake, what we now think about, and what we probe into are socialist industrialization, socialist transformation, and the modernization of national defense and, moreover, an era in which we must begin to dig into [the study of] nuclear energy. The depth to which comrades in our Party have dug into [their jobs] differs from person to person, and the same applies to those comrades present today. Like doctors, some can operate, others cannot. In giving injections, some can give intravenous injections, some cannot and can only give hypodermic injections. Some doctors don't even dare to do anything beneath the skin, and only deal with things on the surface of the skin. Although some comrades have not yet dug into [their jobs], the majority of our comrades are digging, and it looks as if many people have dug into them and have acquired some sense of expertise. At this conference, too, we have been able to observe such a situation. This is an extremely good thing. This is because what we are faced with now are new problems: socialist industrialization, socialist transformation, new [policies of] national defense, and new tasks in the various other areas. To dig into [problems] appropriate to these new conditions and to become experts; this is our responsibility. Therefore we must carry out education among those people who are unable to dig in, who are floating on the surface, so that they can all become experts.

The struggle against the Cao Gang–Rao Shushi anti-Party alliance will enable our Party to take a big step forward.

We must carry out propaganda among the five million intellectuals inside and outside the Party and among the cadres of the various levels, so that they will acquire [an understanding of] dialectical materialism and oppose idealism. We will form a strong theoretical corps; this is something we greatly need; this, too, is a very good thing.

We must make plans to organize such a strong theoretical corps, to have several million people study the theoretical foundations of Marxism, that is, dialectical materialism and historical materialism, and oppose all sorts of idealism and mechanical materialism. We now have many cadres who are doing theoretical work, but we have not organized a theoretical corps, particularly not yet a strong one. Without this corps, the cause of our entire Party, the socialist industrialization of our country, the socialist transformation, the modernization of national defense, and the atomic energy research cannot move forward; nor can the [related] problems be resolved. Therefore, I would advise our comrades to study philosophy. Quite a few people are uninterested in philosophy; they do not have the habit of studying philosophy. They can start with reading pamphlets and short articles and acquire an interest through those things. Then they can read things seventy, eighty thousand characters in length, and later go on to read books several hundred thousand characters long. There are a number of subjects in Marxism: Marxist philosophy, Marxist economics, Marxist socialism – the theory of class struggle; but the basic thing is Marxist philosophy. Unless this thing is studied and understood, we will not have a common language or a common method among us; we could argue back and forth, but things still would not be clear. But if we have dialectical materialist thought, we will save ourselves a lot of trouble and commit many fewer mistakes.

2. Concerning the First Five-Year Plan[6]

Our comrades feel that when we were discussing the five-year plan most of the speeches made by the comrades were very good and satisfactory to everybody. Some were particularly good, ones that penetrated the problem and conveyed a sense of expertise. However, some of the speeches made by the [comrades from the] various departments at the Center were poorer in content and were lacking in analysis and criticism. Some of the speeches made by comrades from the localities were also somewhat poorer and lacking in analysis and criticism. There is another situation; in their speeches some comrades, in dealing with the problem of serious waste and other mistakes, only exposed the situations but did not show how to deal with them. Some comrades are dissatisfied with these speeches. I believe there is reason for such dissatisfaction.

I hope that all the provincial [Party] committee secretaries, municipal [Party] committee secretaries, [special] district [Party] committee secretaries and comrades in positions of responsibility in the departments at the Center will stir themselves to exert their utmost effort to turn themselves into experts proficient in political and economic work on the basis of the raising of their level of Marxism-Leninism. On the one hand, we must do political and ideological work well; on the other hand, we must carry out economic construction well. With regard to economic construction, we really must study and understand it.

At this conference the localities have asked the Center to solve many problems; active steps should be taken to quickly solve those for which the Center has already set forth guidelines. As for the other problems, the secretariat [of the conference] should consult with the comrades who raised the issues to work out solutions and report them to the Center for approval.

The various departments at the Center have also asked for the cooperation of the localities on quite a few matters. The enterprises established by the departments of the Center in the various localities ought to solicit the supervision and assistance of the local Party committees, especially in the areas of political and ideological work. The local Party Committees have the responsibility of helping the enterprises founded by the Center in the localities to accomplish their tasks. Therefore, not only do the localities make demands on the Center, but the Center also makes demands on the localities. Only if the various departments of the Center and the local Party committees are of a single mind and effort and divide up the work and cooperate can the First Five-Year Plan be fully and satisfactorily accomplished.

3. Concerning the Gao Gang–Rao Shushi Anti-Party Alliance[7]

The first point: Some people ask: Is there, after all, such an alliance? Or perhaps it is not really an alliance, but rather two separate independent kingdoms, two go-it-aloners? Some comrades say that they have not seen any documents, and that if they were an alliance, they should have had an agreement of some sort and with the agreement there would be documents. Indeed, there were no written agreements; we were not able to discover any. We say [however] that Gao Gang and Rao Shushi did form an alliance. From what can we see this? It can be seen, first, in the joint activities of Gao Gang and Rao Shushi at the time of the Conference on Finance and Economic work,[8] second, from the collaboration between Rao Shushi and Zhang Xiushan[9] in carrying out anti-Party activities at the time of the Conference on Organization Work;[10] and third, from Rao Shushi's own words. Rao Shushi said, "From now on the Center's Organization Department should have Guo Feng[11] as its core." The Organization Department had Rao Shushi as its director, and [then] Guo Feng, Gao Gang's confidant, was made its core. Now isn't that just fine! What solid unity! Fourth, we can see it from the fact that Gao Gang and Rao Shushi distributed everywhere a slate of candidates for the Political Bureau, privately put together by An Ziwen. An Ziwen was given a disciplinary warning for this.[12] Gao Gang, Rao Shushi, and their people distributed this list of names to everybody who attended the Conference on Organization Work and to each of the southern provinces. What was their motive for distributing this thing everywhere? Fifth, [we can see it] from Gao Gang's expression to me on two occasions of his [desire to] protect Rao Shushi and Rao Shushi's insistence on protecting Gao Gang to the very last. Gao Gang told me that Rao Shushi was in big trouble and asked me to bail him out. I said to him, why are you speaking on Rao Shushi's behalf? I'm in Beijing, so is Rao Shushi; why should he want you to represent him and not come directly to me [himself]? Even if he were in Tibet he could send a telegram, but he is in Beijing! He has legs, doesn't he? The second time was on the day before Gao Gang was exposed. Gao Gang was still expressing his desire to protect Rao Shushi. To the very last, Rao Shushi wanted to protect Gao Gang; he wanted to redress the injustice against Gao Gang. At the meeting of the Central Committee at which Gao Gang was exposed,[13] I said that there were two headquarters in Beijing; one was a headquarters led by myself; we blew a *yang* wind and set a *yang* fire.[14] The other was a headquarters commanded by someone else; it blew a *yin* wind, set a *yin* fire, and was a subterranean stream. After all, should government come from one source, or should it come from many sources? From the many things mentioned above, it can be seen that they [Gao and Rao] had an anti-Party alliance and were not two unrelated independent kingdoms[15] or "go-it-aloners."

As for the doubts that some comrades have because there are no written agreements, and the question that it may not have been an alliance, this would be to equate anti-Party alliances formed by conspirators with other usual open and formal political and economic alliances, and to see them as similar things. These people were engaging in a conspiracy! Do you need a written agreement when you are forming a conspiracy? If you say that it was not an alliance because it did not have any written agreements, then how about the internal [structure] of each of the two anti-Party cliques of Gao Gang and Rao Shushi? Gao Gang did not have any agreements with Zhang Xiushan, Zhang Mingyuan, Zhao Dezun, Ma Hong, and Guo Feng either. We haven't seen their written agreements either. Then, does that also negate [the existence of] this anti-Party clique of theirs? Then again, we haven't seen any pact between Rao Shushi and people like Xiang Ming and Yang Fan.[16] Therefore, the idea that you cannot consider something an alliance if you have not found a written agreement for it is wrong.

The second point: What attitude should be adopted by comrades who have been influenced by Gao and Rao and by those who were able to avoid their influence? Among those who have been influenced, some were more deeply influenced and some less so. Some have been influenced generally and have merely been brushed by their wings. A few comrades have been more deeply influenced; they have talked with them about many questions, and were active down below, doing propaganda for them. These two [groups] are different. Nevertheless, at this conference, regardless of whether the influence on them was slight or deep, most of these comrades have already indicated their attitudes. Some gave a very clear expression [of their attitudes] and were welcomed by the entire audience. Others were adequate and were welcomed by the majority of the comrades, but there were still some shortcomings [in what they said]. Some did not make an adequate expression [of their attitudes] and have made supplementary [remarks] today. Some delivered speeches that were on the whole quite good, but were not quite right in certain parts. No matter how they did it, these types of people all have already made some expression [of their attitudes]. We ought to welcome them one and all; after all, they have each made some sort of a statement! There were also some individuals who requested to speak but who were not given the floor because of the lack of time; they can submit a written report to the [Party] Center. The problem with those who have not yet spoken is not a serious one. They were just brushed by [the conspirators'] wings; they know something but did not speak out about it. As for those who spoke, aren't there some who still retain a tail? Therefore, we have now decided that all speeches and reports, whether they concern the Five-Year Plan or the problem of the Gao-Rao anti-Party alliance, can be taken back and revised. Pay attention to each word, phrase, and sentence, and within five days revise all those parts that are incomplete or incorrect. We must not grab people's little queues[17] just because they did not give a correct account of themselves at this Conference, and then make it difficult for them to acquit themselves in the future. You can make revisions, and only the revised final draft will count.

With regard to these comrades, we should adopt this type of attitude, that is, hoping that they will correct their mistakes. We must not only observe but should also help. That is to say, we must not only observe to see whether or not they change, but must also help them to make the change. People need help. Even though the lotus flower is pretty, it needs green leaves to enhance its beauty.[18] A fence has to be propped up by three stakes; a stouthearted man needs the help of three other people. It's not good for people to go it alone; help is always needed, especially with problems of this nature. Observing is necessary; observe to see if they change or not; but merely watching is passive; we must also help them. We welcome the reform of all those who were influenced [by Gao and Rao], no matter whether deeply or slightly influenced; we must not only observe, but must also help. This is the positive attitude that we must take toward comrades who have made mistakes.

Comrades who have not been influenced must not be arrogant and should take serious precautions to guard against [this] disease. This is an extremely important matter. Some of the comrades we mentioned above may have been duped, some others have been more deeply entrapped, but because they have committed a mistake their vigilance may have been heightened so that they will not commit mistakes of this sort again in the future. After being sick once, one becomes immune; getting a vaccination has a preventive effect. Nevertheless, nothing can be guaranteed; it's still possible to catch smallpox. Therefore, it would be best to have another vaccination in three or five years' time, that is, to hold a meeting like this one. Other comrades should not be arrogant, and should be very cautious to avoid committing mistakes. Why did Gao Gang and Rao Shushi not touch people like these? There are various possibilities. The first is that they are people whom they [Gao and Rao] considered enemies; naturally, therefore, they did not go among them to propagandize [their cause]. The second type are those they looked down on and considered to be people of no major consequence. They thought that it was not necessary to propagandize among these people then [and] that later, when "the major affair of state was settled," [these people] would naturally go over to their side. The third type are people they did not dare touch. These people probably had stronger immunity, and one look told [Gao and Rao] that they were not [people whom they could easily influence]. Although these comrades were not considered to be their enemies, nor were they people of no major consequence, [Gao and Rao] did not dare touch [them]. The fourth type are those whom they did not have time [to reach]. It took time even for this epidemic to spread. If it had not been exposed for another year, it would be hard to say where some people would stand. Therefore let us not thumb our noses, [or say:] "Look, weren't you contaminated all over? I am clean!" If it had not been exposed, I am sure that in another year many people would have been influenced.

I think that what we've just said are precisely the things to which both those comrades who have been influenced by Gao and Rao, as well as those who have not been influenced by them, should pay attention.

The third point: Over issues of principle, we should always carefully keep our distance from the comrades whose arguments and activities are in violation of the Party's principles. If what they say and what they do do not conform to the Party's principles and are unacceptable to us, then, with regard to these questions and under these conditions, we should not identify ourselves with them. With regard to other questions on which they do conform to the Party's principles, such as the Five-Year Plan, the resolution and the report on the Gao-Rao anti-Party alliance, various correct policies, and the correct internal Party rules and regulations – [with regard to] these arguments and activities we should of course actively support them and identify ourselves with them. However, we should keep those who do not conform to the Party's principles at a distance, which is to say we should draw the distinctions clearly and repulse them at once. You must not fail to keep a distance [between yourselves and these people] just because they are old friends, old bosses, old subordinates, old colleagues, old schoolmates, or because they are from your native village. In this Gao-Rao anti-Party affair, as well as in two-line struggles within the Party in the past, we've often had the experience in which people found it difficult to speak [frankly] and could not maintain a distance because they felt that the [personal] relationship was too longstanding and too deep, and so they did not repulse them or draw clear distinctions. Consequently they were trapped more and more deeply, and they got tangled up with those "ghosts" [who violate Party principles]. Therefore we should make our attitudes public and should adhere to the principles.

The fourth point: Some comrades say, "We know some bad things about Gao and Rao, but we can't see that they have a conspiracy." I say that there are two types of situations. One type is where people heard Gao Gang and Rao Shushi say many things that were in violation of the Party's principles, or even [some cases] in which Gao Gang and Rao Shushi discussed some matters of anti-Party activity with them. In these cases [our comrades] should have been able to see [that there was a conspiracy]. The other type [of situation] is where people knew some bad things in general about them but did not recognize [the existence of] the conspiracy. This is understandable because [the conspiracy] was difficult to see. Even the Party Center did not discover their anti-Party conspiracy until 1953. It was through [the events at] the Finance and Economy Work Conference, the Conference on Organizational Work and the various problems prior to the Finance and Economic Conference that one could see that they were abnormal. At the time of the Finance and Economy Work Conference their abnormal activities were discovered, and each time [they did something abnormal] they were rebuffed. Therefore they later turned completely to secret activities. We didn't discover this conspiracy, these conspirators, and the conspiratorial cliques until the autumn and winter of 1953. For a long time, we didn't see that Gao Gang and Rao Shushi were bad people. Such things have happened before. During the Jinggangshan period,[19] there were a few traitors whom we never thought would have become traitors. I believe every one of you must have had this experience.

We should derive a [lesson from this] experience, which is that we should not become confused by false appearances. Some of our comrades are easily confused by false appearances. Contradictions exist between the appearance and the essence of all things. People can understand the essence of a thing only through the analysis and study of its appearance. That is why there is need for science. Otherwise, if we could see by intuition the essence of a thing at a glance, what would be the purpose of science? What would be the purpose of studying? It is precisely because there is a contradiction between appearance and essence that we need to study. However, there is a difference between a false appearance and appearances in general because [the former] is a false appearance. Therefore we should derive a [lesson from this] experience, which is that, as far as possible, we must not be confused by false appearances.

The fifth point: The danger of having an arrogant attitude. Don't play the hero. Things are achieved by the majority. The role of the minority is limited. We ought to recognize the role played by the minority, that is, the role of the leaders and the cadres. Yet this role is not that tremendous; the tremendous role is still that of the masses! The correct relationship between the cadres and the masses is such that while we cannot do without the cadres, things are accomplished by the broad masses; the cadres have a leadership role, but this role ought not to be exaggerated. Will things be terrible without you? History proves, and all sorts of facts prove, that things would still be all right without you. Would things be in terrible shape, for instance, without Gao Gang and Rao Shushi? Wouldn't things be all right anyway? Without Trotsky, without Zhang Guotao, without Chen Duxiu,[20] wouldn't things have been all right just the same? These were all bad people. Confucius is long gone and now China has a Communist Party, it's at least slightly more capable than Confucius, isn't it? We can see therefore that without Confucius things can be done even better! As for you good people, things can be done even without you. Will the earth stop rotating without you? The earth will rotate just the same; the cause will continue just the same, and perhaps would continue even better.

There are two types of people. One type are people of long standing [in the Party]. Many of us here today are people with a lot of seniority. Another type is newborn strength. These are young people. Of these two types, which has the greater hope? Comrade [Zhou] Enlai also spoke about this subject today. Of course, it is the newborn strength that has greater hope. Some comrades are arrogant because they are old revolutionaries; this is very inappropriate. By comparison, if we were to permit people to take pride in themselves, it is the young people who would have cause to be proud. Those people over forty, over fifty, should have gained more experience as they have grown older and therefore should be even more modest. We should let the young people see that we truly do have experience. [Let them say,] "These older folks really do have experience; don't look down on them. See, they are so modest." But if you are forty, fifty years old, and you become arrogant because you have accumulated a lot of experience, then isn't it a bit unseemly? The young people will say, "Your experience means nothing; you are just like a kid." It's a little more reasonable for kids to have a bit of a feeling of pride. But for elderly people with so much experience to still be arrogant and to strut with their tails so high in the air is truly unnecessary. The saying goes: "Behave yourself and tuck your tail tightly [between your legs]." Human beings do not really have tails; why should we tuck our tails tightly? It is like a dog, who sometimes cocks its tail and sometimes has its tail between its legs. Generally speaking, after it has been beaten with a stick a few times it will clench its tail tightly between its legs; if it's made some achievements its tail will be cocked. I hope that all our comrades, especially old comrades, will not cock their tails, but rather tuck their tails firmly, refrain from being arrogant, refrain from being impatient, and always maintain a modest and energetic spirit.[21]

The sixth point: Refrain from being "Left," and refrain from being Right. Some people say, "It's better to be 'Left' than to be Right." Many comrades also say this. In fact many people may say in their hearts, "It's better to be Right than 'Left'," but they just don't say it aloud. Only honest people would say it aloud. There are two kinds of opinions. What is "Left"? Running ahead of the times and running ahead of the present circumstances, being an adventurist in orientation, policy, and action, and engaging in undisciplined struggle on questions that are being struggled over and on controversial matters is "Left." This is not good. To be Right is to lag behind the times and behind the present circumstances and to lack the spirit of struggle. This is no good either. In our Party there are not only people who like to be "Left," but also quite a few people who like to be Right or right-of-center. All these are no good. We must struggle on both fronts and oppose both "Left" and Right.

I'll say only this much about the question of the Gao Gang–Rao Shushi anti-Party alliance.

4. On the Current Situation

How are things with these three situations: the international situation, the domestic situation, and the situation within the Party? Is the bright side dominant or is the dark side dominant? It should be affirmed that no matter whether it is the international situation, the domestic situation, or the situation within the Party, it is the bright side that is dominant and the dark side that is at a disadvantage. The same is true in this assembly hall of ours. Don't think that things are black just because many people made self-criticisms here. These comrades emphasized their shortcomings and mistakes and did not talk about their strengths; they didn't tell us which year they joined the revolution, or where they had won a victory, or where they had made some achievements in their work. If we look at nothing but their self-criticism then things are black. Actually this is only one side, and for many comrades only the secondary side. This is different from [the cases of] Gao Gang, Rao Shushi, and their five "tiger" generals, Zhang, Zhang, Zhao, Ma, Guo.[22] The estimation that the bright side is dominant does not apply in their cases. In Gao Gang's case, is the bright side at all dominant in any area? With him everything is dark; the skies are dark and the earth is black; there is no sunshine or any moonlight. But things are different with our comrades; there is some slight darkness, but these things can be cleaned out, so let's use soap to clean them a few more times.

Why do we suggest that preparations be made for dealing with sudden emergencies, with a counterrevolutionary restoration and a repetition of the Gao-Rao affair? This simply means that [we have to] consider things from the worst possible [angle] so that we'll never be at a disadvantage. No matter what kind of work we are doing, we should think in terms of and prepare for the worst possibilities. [These possibilities] are none other than such terrible contingencies as: the imperialists launching a new world war; Chiang Kai-shek coming back to reign in Beijing; or an incident such as the Gao-Rao anti-Party alliance repeating itself; and, what is more, not just one, but ten, or a hundred [of these things can happen]. Nevertheless, even if there are so many [bad things], we will have nothing to fear if we are prepared beforehand. If you have ten [bad things], that's only five pairs; that's no big problem; we've anticipated it all. The atom bombs and the hydrogen bombs which the imperialists use to scare us are not all that terrifying either.[23] For everything on earth there's something else to beat it back. If you read *Fengshenbang* you would know that.[24] There's no "magic weapon" that cannot be defeated. Many "magic weapons" have already been defeated. We believe that as long as we rely on the people, there will be no "magic weapon" on earth that cannot be defeated.

5. Struggle to Victoriously Convene the Eighth Party Congress

The Center has decided to convene the Eighth Party Congress during the second half of 1956.[25] There will be three items on the agenda: (1) the work report of the Central Committee, (2) the revision of the Party Constitution,[26] (3) the election of a new Central Committee. We must complete the work of electing delegates and preparing the documents [for the Congress] by July of next year. We hope that within a little more than one year's time, our work in all areas, in the economy, in culture and education, in the military, in the Party, in politics and ideology, in the mass organizations, in the united front[27] and in minority nationality work, will take a big step forward.

Let me take this opportunity to talk a little about problems in minority nationality work. We must oppose Han chauvinism.[28] Don't believe that it's just the Han people who have helped the minority nationalities, the minority nationalities have also helped the Han people greatly. Some comrades are always boasting that we helped you [the minority nationalities] and ignoring the fact that we couldn't do without the minority nationalities. Who inhabits fifty to sixty per cent of the territory in our country? Is it the Han people? Is it other peoples? Fifty to sixty per cent of the territory is inhabited by the minority nationalities. Products from these places are very abundant, and there are abundant precious [natural resources]. At the moment, we are giving very little help to the minority nationalities, and in some areas we still haven't helped them at all. The minority nationalities, on the other hand, have helped the Han people. There are some minority nationalities that needed our help before they could help us. Politically, the minority nationalities have given the Han people great help. Their joining the great family of the Chinese nation is itself a help to the Han people politically. The minority nationalities have united with the Han people; [consequently] the people of the entire country are glad. Therefore, in terms of politics, economics, and national defense, the minority nationalities have rendered great help to the entire country and to the entire Chinese nation. The idea that only the Han people have helped the minority nationalities while the minority nationalities have not helped the Han people and the point of view that makes one very proud of oneself just because one has given a bit of help to the minority nationalities are wrong.

By saying that we want to take a great step forward in all areas of our work during this coming year we mean that we will correct the shortcomings and mistakes that already have been exposed. Let's not make a lot of promises at this conference and then have the same number of shortcomings and mistakes untouched by the time we hold the "Eighth Congress" next year. By struggling to hold the "Eighth Congress" we mean to rectify our shortcomings and mistakes; for instance, extravagance and waste and such things as the big roofs [in architecture] should be earnestly and responsibly corrected. Let us not make promises here and then, as soon as we get home, just stretch our legs and go to sleep.

Some people suggest that such conferences ought to be held once a year or once every two years, so that there can mutual supervision among comrades. I think the idea merits consideration. Who will supervise people like us? Mutual supervision is a good method. That will promote greater and faster progress in Party and state affairs. This will mean rapid progress and not slow progress. The Party has not held a Congress for ten years. Of course, it was right for us not to have held any during the first five years, because the country was in great turmoil, a great armed conflict was going on at that time, and also because the "Seventh Congress" was [already] held. During the last five years, we could have held a Congress but we didn't. There was some good in not holding it then too, in that we waited until the Gao-Rao problem was cleared up before we held [the Congress]; otherwise they would have used the "Eighth Congress" to serve their purposes. At the same time, our Five-Year Plan has gotten on track, and the general line for the period of transition has been proposed. And through this conference we have made everybody more unified ideologically and have prepared the conditions for holding the Eighth Party Congress. At the Eighth Party Congress, we do not have to have everybody make a self-examination, but we still have to make public criticisms and self-criticisms of the shortcomings and mistakes in our work. We can't do without observing this tenet of Marxism.

Criticism must be sharp. I feel that some of the criticisms made this time were not that sharp, [it was] always as if they were afraid of offending people. If you are not sharp, and the thrust does not hit home, the person will not feel the pain and will not take notice. We must identify the person and the department involved by name. If you do not do things well, I won't be satisfied with it, and if I offend you, I offend you, and that's that. To be afraid of offending people is nothing more than being afraid of losing votes and being afraid of having difficult relations in one's work with one's co-workers. Will I starve if you don't vote for me? Nothing of the sort. Actually, relations will be smoother if you speak out and put the problem clearly on the table. Don't polish away the sharp angles. Why does a bull have two horns? A bull has two horns because it has to fight. One purpose is for defense and another purpose is for offence. I have often asked comrades, "Have you grown any 'horns' on your head?" You comrades can feel your heads and see. As I see it, some comrades have grown "horns," some have grown "horns" but they are not very sharp, and some other comrades have not grown "horns" at all. I think that it's better to grow two "horns," because that conforms to Marxism. There's a tenet in Marxism called criticism and self-criticism.

Therefore, holding conferences regularly to carry out criticism and self-criticism is a good method for our comrades to supervise each other and to promote the rapid progress of the affairs of the Party and state. I propose that the comrades of the provincial and municipal [Party] committees think about it, and see whether or not you can do the same. Aren't you [speaking of] emulating the Center? I think this is one thing that you can emulate.

Finally, I ask you, comrades, and the comrades of the entire Party, to pay attention to this:

Struggle to convene the Eighth Party Congress in 1956!

Struggle to victoriously accomplish the First Five-Year Plan!

Notes

1. The Gao Gang–Rao Shushi affair refers to the expulsion of Gao Gang, former vice-premier and chairman of the Administrative Committee of the Northeast China Bureau, and Rao Shushi, a political commissar heading the Party Organization Bureau and chairman of the Administrative Committee of the East China Bureau, from the Party for anti-Party activities. Gao was charged with attempting to turn the Northeast into an "independent kingdom" while Rao was charged with being his chief ally, especially after his transfer to the Party Center in 1953. There is considerable evidence to suggest also that Gao's purge was linked to his connections with the Soviet Union.

2. See text June 30, 1953, note 9, and text Aug. 12, 1953, note 24.

3. Held in April 1945 in Yanan, although it had originally been scheduled for 1938. For a summary of the Congress, see J. Harrison (1972), pp. 357-362.

4. See text June 15, 1953, note 2, and text July 9, 1957, note 53.

5. This refers to the Second and Third Plenum of the Seventh Central Committee of the CPC. See text June 6, 1950(2), note 1, and text Apr. 25, 1956, note 15.

6. See text Feb. 10, 1953, note 2.

7. Gao Gang (1905-1954) was one of the earliest CPC members in Shaanxi Province and played a key role in developing the Shaanxi-Gansu-Ningxia Border Region, which served as

Mao's base of operations after the Long March in 1935. Gao became the senior CPC official in Manchuria in the late 1940s and early 1950s. In 1952 he was a Political Bureau member and the chairman of the State Planning commission.

Rao Shushi (1903-?) was the political commissar of the New Fourth Army in 1943, the first Party secretary of the CPC East China Bureau and the Shanghai Municipal Committee in 1951 and, in 1952, the director of the CPC's Organizational Department.

At this National Conference of the CPC, Gao and Rao were accused of having formed an anti-Party clique at the National Conference on Finance and Economic Work in the summer of 1953 and at the Conference on Organizational Work of the Central Committee in September 1953. This clique allegedly inflated the role of Gao Gang in the Northeast; advocated the appointment of Guo Feng, a protégé of Gao Gang, to the directorship of the Organization Department of the Central Committee; and circulated a membership list of the Political Bureau, secretly made up by An Ziwen, in an attempt to control the Political Bureau. Furthermore, Gao and Rao were charged with lobbying for Gao to become first Party secretary, vice-chairman of the PRC, and premier of the State Council when Mao was on inspection tours outside the capital. Another charge was that the two had instigated a group of people to write a joint letter asking Mao to relinquish power. Both were expelled from the Party in 1955; Gao Gang is reported to have committed suicide in 1954, Rao Shushi has not been heard of. For more details on the life of Gao and Rao, see D. Klein and A. Clark, eds. (1971) I, pp. 430-436, 408-411, respectively.

8. The National Conference on Financial and Economic Work was convened by the CPC Central Committee, June 13-August 11, 1953, and set forth the "General Line on the Transition to Socialism." For a synopsis of this meeting see K. Lieberthal (1976), pp. 59-60; see also text June 15, 1953.

9. Zhang, like Gao Gang, was a native of Shaanxi Province, and graduated from the Party middle school at Yanan. In the early 1950s he held several posts in the Northeast administration then under Gao's direction. In 1955 he was second secretary of the Northeastern Bureau of the Central Committtee of the CPC. For more biographical information on Zhang, see *Zhonggong renming lu*, p. 528.

10. The First National Conference on Organizational Work was held March-April 1951 and was presided over by An Ziwen. See K. Lieberthal (1976), pp. 53-54.

11. Guo, a native of Jiangxi, participated in the occupation of the Northeast under the command of Gao Gang in 1947 and returned to the region in 1951 as director of the Northeast People's Administrative Affairs Office.

12. An Ziwen was acting director of the Central Committee's Organization Department from 1950 to 1952, when his duties were suspended. He returned to the post in early 1954 and served until September 1956. See also text Aug. 12, 1953, note 10. For more biographical information on An, see D. Klein and A. Clark, eds. (1970), I, pp. 3-5.

13. Mao is here referring to the Fourth Plenum of the Seventh Central Committee, held February 6-10, 1954, in Beijing.

14. The terms *yang* wind and *yang* fire are used by Mao to refer to an active or creative role as opposed to a passive role, which would be described as *yin*. *Yin* and *yang* are the two polar forces in traditional Chinese cosmology; supposedly, *yang* represents the male, light, positive force while *yin* represents the female, dark, passive force.

15. Here Mao is using the term "independent kingdom" (*duli wangguo*) in a slightly different sense from the normal meaning of the phrase. For the latter, see text Oct. 11, 1955 (1), note 51. See also text Apr. 1956, note 16.

16. Both Xiang and Yang were associates of Rao Shushi and were alleged co-conspirators of Rao and Gao. Xiang Ming was deputy governor of Shandong Province from 1951 to 1953, and second secretary of the Party's Shandong sub-bureau. Yang was chief of the Bureau of Public Security of Shanghai. Zhang Mingyuan was general secretary of the Administrative Council of the Northeast People's Government and, from January 1953 to September 1954, vice-chairman of that Administrative Council. He was third deputy secretary of the Northeast Bureau of the Central Committee of the CPC. Zhao Dezun was director of the Rural Work Department of the Northeast Bureau and chairman of the People's Government of Heilongjiang Province. Ma Hong was dep-

uty secretary general of the Northeast Bureau and a member of the State Planning Council. They, together with Zhang Xiushan and Guo Feng, were all associates of Gao Gang.

17. The queue, or braid, refers to the popular mandated hairstyle for males in the Qing dynasty, deriving from a Manchu custom. At the turn of the century, in a spirit of anti-Qing revolution, many Han Chinese cut off their queues. The retention of the queue around and after the Revolution of 1911 thus became a sign of a reactionary, loyalist frame of mind. To grab someone's queue was therefore to attack their outdated mode of thinking.

18. This aphorism, in whose original version the lotus is replaced by the peony, is derived from the 110th *hui* of the classical novel *Hongloumeng*, and was spoken by Mao's favorite character in this novel, Wang Xifeng. Mao provides a further, more elaborate explanation of how he interprets this adage in the article ''Dangnei tuanjie de bianzheng fangfa'' (The Dialectical Method to Forge a Unity Within the Party); see text Nov. 18, 1957.

19. Jinggangshan was the mountainous region in western Jiangxi to which Mao withdrew after the fall of 1927. Mao and his troops were joined there by Zhu De and his followers in the spring of 1928. Mao and Zhu formally founded the CPC's Red Army at Jinggangshan in 1928, but by the beginning of 1929 they had been driven into southern Jiangxi by the KMT. It was there in 1930 that the Communists established the Jiangxi Soviet with its capital at Ruijin. For Mao's commentaries on this period see *SW*, I, pp. 63-104.

20. See text Aug. 12, 1953, note 23.

21. See text June 14, 1954, note 13.

22. The term ''five tiger generals'' (*wu hu zhang*) emerged out of the folklore related to the five famous warriors in the service of the Kingdom of Shu-Han in the Three Kingdoms period of Chinese history (ca. 220-265 A.D.), and their exploits were dramatically described in the popular novel *San guo yanyi* (Romance of the Three Kingdoms). These original ''five tiger generals'' were Guan Yu, Zhang Fei, Zhao Yun, Huang Zhong, and Ma Chao. Other sets of ''five tiger generals'' emerged at later periods of Chinese history (such as during the mid-Song dynasty), continuing to feed the charisma of the term. Here it is obvious that Mao was playing on the term, perhaps because there were coincidences between the list of people he was describing and the original ''five tigers.''

23. See text Jan. 28, 1955(2), note 4.

24. *Fengshen zhuan* (The Apotheosis of Heroes), together with *Shuihu zhuan* (Water Margin) and *Xiyou ji* (Journey to the West), is one of the three great novels of the early Ming period. It was originally compiled by Xu Zhonglin and was later revised by Li Yuncheng. It dramatizes the combat between the Zhou dynasty's (841-221 B.C.) founder, King Wu, and the last Shang emperor, King Zhou, in which the former represented the forces of good and the latter the forces of evil. King Wu became the first Zhou emperor while his companion in arms, Jiang Taigong (Duke Jiang), achieved deification, together with a myriad heroes of the campaign – hence the title of the novel. The reference here is also to the many *fabao*, or "magic weapons," that the heroes possessed and employed.

25. See text Aug. 20, 1956, note 1.

26. See text June 14, 1954, note 1, and text April 1956, note 17.

27. See text Feb. 18, 1951, note 13.

28. See text Mar. 16, 1953, source note.

Speech at Meeting of the Standing Committee of the Central Committee of the CPC

(Spring 1955)

Source: *SCMM*, (supplement), 22 (Apr. 8, 1968), 9.

The SCMM *information that this document was a speech delivered by Mao at a meeting of the Standing Committee of the Central Committee of the CPC is accepted by one authority, the Japanese scholar Nakamura Kimiyoshi (see Kyoto Daigaku [1980], vol. 1, p. 76), although there does not seem to be an available Chinese document and the contents of the following appear to indicate that it was only partly Mao's speech, or a very garbled transcript of a speech, with many indirect quotations interspersed between what Mao actually said. We have chosen to represent the transcript here as it was in the* SCMM *original. Where the transliterations of Chinese terms and names differ from our usual convention, however, we have provided our own transliterations in brackets. The annotations are also ours.*

> *This document repeats much of what had been said by Mao in 1954 on the subject of traditional Chinese medicine. See texts July 30, 1954, and Oct. 20, 1954 and Winter 1954. It should be noted that the text of Winter 1954 is also identified, rather confusingly, as a speech at a Standing Committee of the Central Committee.*

Last year Comrade X X X[1] was instructed to sum up and examine the work of traditional Chinese doctors. This year, it has been found that people at the lower level are aginst [sic] traditional doctors and medicinal herbs. The Chairman has instructed Comrade X X[2] to see that good results are produced in respect of the work of traditional doctors and medicinal herbs within a time limit. For the past several years almost everything has been liberated. Operas, too, have been liberated. Yet traditional Chinese medicine has not been liberated. The health of six hundred million people in China depends primarily on traditional Chinese medicine, and not on Western medicine.[3] This is because the number of Western doctors is small. Doctors of traditional Chinese medicine play a very significant role in the health of people, but this fact is seldom reflected in the leadership because doctors of traditional Chinese medicine are out of power while doctors of Western medicine are in power.

Chinese medicine has a long history, and this very fact proves that it has made great contributions to the people. It is necessary to set up institutions to study Chinese medicine. Some doctors of Chinese medicine are so influenced by Western medicine in their advanced studies that they say Chinese medicine is unscientific. While it is unscientific for them to say so, they must not be criticized too early, and should be treated in the same manner as national minorities are treated. They should play a part in various institutions. To look down upon Chinese medicine is a slavish bourgeois idea, and something must be wrong that no good results have been produced for the past several years. . . .

In the future graduates of medical universities shall be required to study Chinese medicine for two years.

It should be admitted that doctors of Chinese medicine are capable and should be treated as specialists and received and paid as specialists. Haven't they performed great merits? We must oppose sectarianism among doctors of Chinese medicine and step up research of Chinese medicine. (Turning to Ho Ch'eng [He Cheng])[4] Isn't there a Ch'ichow [Qizhou] in Hopei [Hebei]? That is the place for concentration and dispersal of medicinal herbs. Commercial departments must study it.

Notes

1. We have found no conclusive evidence to show who X X X might be. A thorough search of 1954 published documents on the work of traditional Chinese medicine has not revealed to us any specific charge such as Mao described here.

2. There is no conclusive information on who X X might be. We feel that it is possible to make a suggestion here that this might have been a reference to He Cheng, although we would not venture to explain why He Cheng would be mentioned by name later in this speech if his name was to be substituted by X X here.

3. This statement is an exact duplicate of one made in point 3 of text Winter 1954. In the opening paragraphs of text July 20, 1954, Mao made a similar argument.

4. See text 1953 (1), source note, and text July 20, 1954, note 1.

Telegram to the People's Republic of Hungary
(April 2, 1955)

Source: *RMRB* (Apr. 4, 1955), 1. Other Chinese Text: *XHYB*, 5 (May 28, 1955), 130. Available English Translation: NCNA, *Daily Bulletin* (Apr. 15, 1955), 6-7.

Comrade Istvan Dobi, Chairman of the Presidium of the People's Republic of Hungary,

Comrade Andras Hegedus, Acting Chairman of the Council of the People's Republic of Hungary,

Comrade Janos Boldoczki, Minister of Foreign Affairs of the People's Republic of Hungary:

On the occasion of the tenth anniversary of Hungary's liberation, we convey to you and, through you, to the Hungarian people and the government of the People's Republic of Hungary sincere and warm congratulations on behalf of the Chinese people and the People's Republic of China.

In the last ten years, the Hungarian people, under the leadership of their own Hungarian Workers' Party and the government of the People's Republic of Hungary, have victoriously consolidated the people's democratic system and have achieved brilliant successes in the socialist construction of their country. These successes have strengthened the socialist camp for peace and democracy headed by the Soviet Union, and have inspired the Chinese people who are in the midst of pursuing their socialist construction. The Chinese people greet the victories of our brothers the Hungarian people with very joyful feelings.

We wish the Hungarian people new victories in the cause of socialist construction in their own homeland and in the struggles to smash the new war plans of the imperialist aggressive bloc and to ensure peace in Europe and throughout the world.

(Co-signed as Chairman of PRC with Liu Shaoqi as Chairman of Standing Committee of NPC and Zhou Enlai as Premier of State Council and Foreign Minister, dated in Beijing)

Order to Terminate State of War Between the PRC and Germany

(April 7, 1955)

Source: *RMRB* (Apr. 9, 1955), 1. Other Chinese Texts: HNA, *Daily News Release* (Apr. 9, 1955), 1; FBIS, *Daily Report* (Apr. 8, 1955), AAA15.

The following resolution was passed by the Ninth Meeting of the Standing Committee of the First NPC.

Owing to the fact that Hitler's Germany had unleashed a fascist war of aggression that undermined world peace and had supported Japan's war of aggression against China, China proclaimed itself to be in a state of war with Germany on December 9, 1941. After the Hitlerian aggressors were wiped out, the Potsdam Conference of 1945[1] resolved that Germany ought to develop into a peaceful, democratic, and unified state and also decided on the approach to concluding a peace treaty with Germany.

However, because of the policy consistently pursued by the United States, Britain, and France of dividing Germany, reviving militarism in West Germany in order to bring it into aggressive military blocs, Germany is still divided and it is still impossible to conclude a peace treaty with Germany. Now the three countries, the United States, Britain, and France, are all actively plotting by implementing the Paris agreements[2] to further obstruct the peaceful unification of Germany and the conclusion of a peace treaty with Germany, thus posing a serious threat to peace and security in Europe.

The People's Republic of China resolutely supports the German Democratic Republic and the people of all of Germany, as well as the Soviet Union and all peace-loving countries and peoples, in their struggle to attain the peaceful unification of Germany, the promotion of the conclusion of a peace treaty with Germany, the safeguarding of European collective security, and the defense of world peace. At the same time, [the People's Republic of China,] in the interests of the Chinese people and the people of all Germany, and based on the resolution adopted by the Ninth Meeting of the Standing Committee of the First National People's Congress of the People's Republic of China on April 7, 1955, proclaims:

1. The state of war between the People's Republic of China and Germany shall end forthwith. Peaceful relations between the two countries shall be established.

2. The termination of the state of war between the People's Republic of China and Germany does not in any way change Germany's international obligations. At the same time it also does not in any way affect the rights or commitments of the People's Republic of China under international agreements relating to Germany.

> Mao Zedong
> Chairman
> The People's Republic of China
> April 7, 1955

Notes

1. The Potsdam Conference was the last summit conference held among the heads of the governments of the so-called Big Three – the U.S., Britain, and the USSR – during the Second World War. It took place July 17 to August 2, 1945. One of its resolutions was to create a foreign ministers' council consisting of the U.S., Britain, the USSR, France, and eventually China, to draft the peace treaties with Germany and the other Axis powers.

2. The Paris Conference, a crucial prelude to the formation of the North Atlantic Treaty

Organization (NATO), was held October 20-23, 1954. It resulted in the signing of the Protocol on the Termination of the Occupational Regime in the Federal Republic of Germany (FDR) on October 23, 1954, and on May 5, 1955, the formal accession of the FDR to NATO was ratified. For more see text Feb. 12, 1955, note 5.

Reply to Ambassador of Pakistan
(April 27, 1955)

Source: *RMRB* (Apr. 28, 1955), 1. Available English Translation: HNA, *Daily News Release* (Apr. 28, 1955), 23.

Pakistan was one of five initiatory countries for the Afro-Asian Conference held at Bandung, Indonesia, on April 18-24, 1955, at which the basic principles of intra-Asia and Asian-African international relations and a general anticolonial anti-imperialist diplomatic united front were formulated. The Chinese delegation to this conference was headed by Zhou Enlai. The RMRB *source does not provide the entire text of this speech.*

Sultanuddin Ahmad became ambassador of Pakistan to the PRC at this time. When the Islamic Republic of Pakistan was established on March 23, 1956, he was re-installed as ambassador of the new republic to the PRC on June 13, 1956.

Over the past four years, the friendly and cooperative relations between China and Pakistan in the areas of the economy and culture have made progress. With the efforts of Your Excellency, I believe the friendly relations between our two countries will, on the existing basis, grow even more intimate with each passing day. The advancement of such friendly relations will not only further consolidate the friendship between the peoples of our two countries but will also contribute to the peace in Asia and in the world for which the people of all nations are striving.

The government of the People's Republic of China and myself welcome Your Excellency's appointment as the ambassador extraordinary and plenipotentiary of Pakistan to the People's Republic of China and pledge our full assistance in your work to strengthen the friendly cooperation between our two countries and to safeguard international peace.

Inscription for Czechoslovakian Exhibition
(April 28, 1955)

Source: *RMRB* (May 15, 1955), 1. Other Chinese Text: *XHYB*, 6 (June 28, 1955) 103. Available English Translation: HNA, *Daily News Release* (May 15, 1955), 5.

The Exhibition of Czechoslovakia's Achievements in Socialist Construction was held in Beijing from late April through mid-May 1955. This inscription, written for the exhibition on April 28, was not released in the Chinese press until May 15.

The exhibition on the achievements of ten years of socialist construction in Czechoslovakia has made a deep impression on us. Over the past ten years, socialist Czechoslovakia has made rapid progress in the areas of the economy and culture. This comes as a result of the correct leadership of the Communist Party and the government of Czechoslovakia and the efforts of all the laboring people of Czechoslovakia in striving for a happy life for themselves. The fact that Czechoslovakia has made rapid progress in the area of industry, especially in the machine-building industry, greatly strengthens the confidence of the Chinese people in their undertaking of industrialization which has just begun. It also projects an ever broadening vista for future trade development and scientific and technical cooperation between China and Czechoslovakia. May Czechoslovakia become more prosperous and powerful with each passing day. May the friendship between the people of Czechoslovakia and the people of the People's Republic of China always continue to grow and be consolidated.

Mao Zedong, Liu Shaoqi, Zhu De, Chen Yun, Peng Zhen, Lin Boqu, Dong Biwu, Kang Sheng, Zhang Wentian, Deng Xiaoping
April 28, 1955

Letter to Jiang Zhuru
(May 1, 1955)

Source: *Shuxin*, p. 492.

According to the source, Jiang Zhuru was a fellow native of Mao's of Xiangtan xian, Hunan. He was Mao's schoolmate at the First Normal School of Hunan in Changsha, and an early member of the Xinmin xuehui (New People's Study Society) founded by Mao, Cai Hesen et al. He was engaged in education work. See also text Jan. 14, 1951, note 1.

My dear Zhuru:

Your gracious letter of February has been received; thank you very much. You are engaged in linguistic studies, and have proposed some unconventional opinions. Although I cannot agree with you [on these views], I am sure that the debate would be beneficial [to all of us]. Your letter has been sent to the Committee for Language Reform for studying. A phonetic language is by and large a form of language that is more convenient and easy to handle. Chinese characters are too complicated and difficult. At the moment we are only engaged in reforming [the language] by simplifying them; in the future, there will come the day when we have to carry out some basic reforms.[1]

In response, and with best regards for your work in teaching,

Mao Zedong
May 1, 1955

Note

1. The plans for reforming (mainly simplifying and thereby popularizing) the Chinese language went back as far as mid-1951. (See text 1951, source note and text.) For a general study of this subject, see J. DeFrancis (1984), J. DeFrancis (1972), W. Lehman (1975), and P. Seybolt and G. Chiang, eds. (1979).

Telegram to the German Democratic Republic
(May 6, 1955)

Source: *RMRB* (May 8, 1955), 1. Other Chinese Text: *XHYB*, 6 (June 28, 1955), 85-86. Available English Translation: HNA, *Daily News Release* (May 8, 1955), 2.

Comrade Wilhelm Pieck, President of the German Democratic Republic,
Comrade Johannes Dieckmann, Chairman of the Presidium of the People's Chamber of the German Democratic Republic,
Comrade Otto Grotewohl, Premier of the Council of Ministers of the German Democratic Republic:

On the occasion of the tenth anniversary of the German people's achievement of liberation, the Chinese people and the government of the People's Republic of China express warm congratulations to you and, through you, to our brothers the German people and the government of the German Democratic Republic.

After the army of the Soviet Union smashed Hitler's fascist rule, the German people, under the leadership of the Socialist Unity Party of Germany, carried out all sorts of democratic reforms and established their own German Democratic Republic. In the past five years, the people of the German Democratic Republic have triumphantly built a new life with their own creative labor and have made gigantic achievements in the areas of politics, the economy, and culture. The German Democratic Republic has become the strong bulwark of the German people in their struggle to attain unification, peace, democracy, and independence.

Ignoring the national interests of the German people, the ruling cliques of the United States and Britain have actively revived German militarism and deepened the division of Germany in an attempt to convert West Germany into the hotbed of a new war. The recent ratification of the Paris Agreements[1] has greatly increased the danger of war and posed a serious threat to peace in Europe and the world. The Chinese people fully support all the necessary measures that the Soviet Union, the German Democratic Republic, and other peace-loving European countries have taken to ensure their own security and to safeguard European and world peace. They also deeply believe that the powerful unity of the countries within the socialist camp of peace and democracy headed by the Soviet Union is bound to thoroughly smash all the imperialist plans for war and that the righteous cause of the German people is bound to achieve success.

We sincerely wish the German people new successes in their struggle to oppose the implementation of the Paris Agreement and in their cause of building the German Democratic Republic.

(Co-signed as Chairman of PRC with Liu Shaoqi as Chairman of Standing Committee of NPC and Zhou Enlai as Premier of State Council and Foreign Minister, dated in Beijing)

Note

1. See text Apr. 7, 1955, note 1.

Telegram to the Republic of Czechoslovakia
(May 7, 1955)

Source: *RMRB* (May 9, 1955), 1. Other Chinese Text: *XHYB*, 6 (June 28, 1955), 94. Available English Translation: HNA, *Daily News Release* (May 9, 1955), 5.

Comrade Antonin Zapotocky, President of the Republic of Czechoslovakia, Comrade Zdenek Fierlinger, Chairman of the National Assembly of the Republic of Czechoslovakia, Comrade Viliam Siroky, Prime Minister of the Republic of Czechoslovakia:

On the occasion of the tenth anniversary of the achievement of liberation by the Czechoslovakian people, the government of the People's Republic of China and the Chinese people extend to the government of the Republic of Czechoslovakia and the Czechoslovakian people their warm and heartfelt congratulations.

Over the past ten years, the Czechoslovakian people, under the correct leadership of the Communist Party of Czechoslovakia and the government of the Republic of Czechoslovakia and with the selfless help rendered by the Soviet Union, have made brilliant achievements in the area of consolidating the political power of the people's democracy and laying the foundation for the construction of socialism. These achievements add to the strength of the world camp of peace, democracy, and socialism headed by the Soviet Union and lend great encouragement to the Chinese people who are in the midst of pursuing socialist construction.

Currently the imperialist aggressive bloc is sparing no effort to carry into effect the Paris Agreement[1] and is actively reviving German militarism, thus forcing the people of Europe and of the entire world to confront the threat of a new war. The Chinese people fully support all necessary measures taken by the Soviet Union, Czechoslovakia, and other peace-loving countries and peoples in Europe to safeguard their own security and European peace. We are deeply convinced that with the sympathy and support of the people all over the world, the powerful camp of peace, democracy, and socialism headed by the Soviet Union is bound to smash the imperialists' war plans.

We wish the Czechoslovakian people still greater triumphs in their cause of building socialism and defending peace.

(Co-signed as Chairman of PRC with Liu Shaoqi as Chairman of Standing Committee of NPC and Zhou Enlai as Premier of State Council and Foreign Minister, dated in Beijing)

Note

1. See text April 7, 1955, note 1.

Letter to the Party Committee of Xiangxiang *xian*
(May 17, 1955)

Source: *Shuxin*, p. 493.

Xiangxiang xian *is adjacent to Xiangtan in the province of Hunan (Xiangtan is Mao's native village). Shidong* xian, *presumably also in the area, is not identified in our map.*

Comrades of the CPC Party Committee of Xiangxiang *xian* and, through them, comrades of the Second District Committee and the Party Branch of Shidong *xiang*:

Tan Shiying of Shidong *xiang* was a classmate of mine some forty years ago at the Dongshan School of Xiangxiang. Since Liberation, he has sent me several letters and I sent several letters in reply. Because he claimed and complained that he is in [financial] difficulty, recently I sent him some money. Lately, he came down with an eye ailment and went to Hankou to look up Comrade Tan Zheng for help in getting treatment.[1] When he couldn't find Tan there, he came to Beijing to look me up. At the moment he is interned at a hospital for the treatment of his eye and will be on his way back to the village in two or three weeks. I have bade him to listen well to the teaching and discipline of the Party and government cadres of the local district and the *xiang*. According to what he told me, two of his sons were executed some three years ago in the struggle to suppress counterrevolutionaries. One of them was a battalion commander and the other a squad commander. Allegedly they were executed because they had committed crimes involving the shedding of other people's blood. He himself was deprived of his civilian rights and was subjected to control and surveillance for a year. At the present moment that has been lifted but he still cannot join the peasants' association.[2] His wife and two other sons, meanwhile, retained their civilian rights and have joined the peasants' association. He claims that his background is that of a poor peasant. He also claims that he had been a schoolteacher for several decades, and that except for the fact that twenty-seven years ago he had been, for five months, a member of the staff in the Kuomintang Shaoyang *xian* government, he has never done anything criminal or bad. I know absolutely nothing about this person's past. Please investigate and let me know.

I wish you smooth success in your work.

Mao Zedong

May 17, 1955

Notes

1. Tan Zheng (b. 1903) is a veteran political officer of the Communist military forces. According to the source, he was, at the time of this letter, a deputy minister of Defense and a deputy secretary of the Control Commission of the Central Committee of the CPC. He was also a member of the National Defense Council and a director of the General Political Department of the PLA. In 1956 he became a member of the Central Committee of the CPC and a member of the secretariat of that body. For more biographical information on Tan, see D. Klein and A. Clark, eds. (1971), II, pp. 802-805, and *Zhonggong renming lu*, pp. 1063-1064.

2. See text Feb. 17, 1951, note 4.

Telegram to Ho Chi Minh

(May 19, 1955)

Source: *RMRB* (May 20, 1955), 1. Other Chinese Text: *XHYB*, 6 (June 28, 1955), 31. Available English Translation: HNA, *Daily News Release* (May 20, 1955), 1.

Dear Comrade Ho Chi Minh:

On the occasion of your sixty-fifth birthday, please accept the warm congratulations of the Chinese people and of myself.

Under the outstanding leadership of the Viet Nam Workers' Party and yourself, the Vietnamese people have carried on a heroic struggle in striving for the independence and freedom of their homeland, and they have already achieved a major victory. The brilliant contributions you have made in the past decades command the respect and admiration, not only of the Vietnamese people, but also of the Chinese people.

May you achieve even greater success in the glorious cause of fighting for Viet Nam's peace, independence, unity, and democracy and for the restoration and development of its national economy.

(Signed and dated in Beijing)

Letter to Huang Yanpei
(May 26, 1955)

Source: *Shuxin*, p. 495.

See text Feb. 17, 1951, source note.

Mr. Renzhi:

I have received and read your gracious letter of May 25. It is always to our advantage to patiently and painstakingly ask for [people's] opinions on critical problems. Recently I contacted the comrades in positions of responsibility in fifteen provinces and municipalities and solicited their opinions on the various issues regarding grain [production and requisition], the suppression of counterrevolutionaries, and the [establishment of agricultural producers'] cooperatives.[1] I managed to get [from them] even more material, confirming what I said at the Supreme State Conference.[2] Nevertheless, a further investigation and study is needed to ascertain whether or not things are truly as we have thought. When you, dear sir, go down [to the lower levels] to make your inspection and investigation, I hope you will use a method of comprehensive, all-round analysis. I have seen the material of the Association for Democratic National Construction, and I am very much interested. I suggest that it may be distributed to the other parties for their reference.[3]

With my respect,

Mao Zedong
May 26, 1955

Notes

1. See text Sept. 25, 1955, source note and text.

2. We have no information regarding this Supreme State Conference. In fact, K. Lieberthal (1976), the most comprehensive list of national and CPC meetings, does not contain any reference to any Supreme State Conference prior to the one in January of 1956.

3. According to the source, this refers to material that Huang Yanpei sent to Mao reporting on a forum held by the Association for Democratic National Construction (of which Huang was chairman) on the subjects of suppressing counterrevolutionaries and a general amnesty. We have no specific information on this forum, but, according to *RMSC* (1957), p. 252, the Association for Democratic National Construction held its First National Congress in Beijing in April 1955. The forum mentioned here may be a byproduct of that congress. For more information on the Association, see text Apr. 15, 1959, note 17; also see *RMSC* (1955), pp. 374-376, and *RMSC* (1957), pp. 252-254.

Telegram to Afghanistan
(May 26, 1955)

Source: *RMRB* (May 28, 1955), 1. Other Chinese Text: *XHYB*, 6 (June 28, 1955), 31. Available English Translation: HNA, *Daily News Release* (May 28, 1955), 4.

Mohammed Zahir Shah,
King of Afghanistan

Your Majesty:

On the occasion of the Independence Day of the Kingdom of Afghanistan, I send warm congratulations to the people of Afghanistan and to you on behalf of the Chinese people and on my own behalf and wish the Kingdom of Afghanistan prosperity and the people of Afghanistan all happiness.
(Signed as Chairman of PRC, dated in Beijing)

Toast at Banquet for Indonesian
Prime Minister Ali Sastroamidjojo
(May 29, 1955)

Source: *RMRB* (May 30, 1955), 1. Available English Translation: HNA, *Daily News Release* (May 30, 1955), 2.

I propose that we drink:
To the ever-growing friendship and cooperation between the People's Republic of China and the Republic of Indonesia,
To peace in Asia and throughout the world,
To the health of President Sukarno of the Republic of Indonesia,
To Prime Minister Ali Sastroamidjojo's visit to China and to his health and that of his wife,
To the health of the host of today's banquet, Ambassador Mononutu.
Bottoms up!

Conversation with Security Guards
on Taking Literacy Courses
(May 1955)

Source: Quoted in "Mao zhuxi guanhuai jingwei zhanshi xue wenhua" (Chairman Mao Cares About the Security Guards' Studying to Become Literate), in *RMRB* (May 23, 1960), 3. Other Chinese Text: *Mao jingwei*, p. 2. Available English Translation: *SCMP*, 2271 (June 3, 1960), 3.

This short conversation with security guards is one of many reported in the cited RMRB *article, written by a reporter for* Jiefangjun bao *(Liberation Army Daily), and reprinted in* Jiefangjun wenyi *(Liberation Army Literature), and subsequently in the book whose title is abbreviated here as* Mao jingwei *(see bibliography). We have elected to separate the conversations from one another, and they will each appear under the date(s) on which they respectively took place.*

Mao: What is the purpose of our work?

The troops: For Communism! To serve the people!

Mao: You are all engaged in security work. Now I'd like to give you the extra assignment of taking literacy courses.[1] Do you accept it?

The troops: Yes!

Note

1. The Chinese term here is *xue wenhua*, which literally translates into "learn some culture." However, it is a colloquialism in the PRC for "learning to become literate." See text Aug. 30, 1952, note 2.

Preface and Editor's Notes to Material on the Hu Feng Counterrevolutionary Clique

(May-June, 1955)

Source: *Hu Feng cailiao*. Other Chinese Texts: *RMRB* (May 13, 1955), 2-3; *RMRB* (May 24, 1955), 2-3; *RMRB* (June 10, 1955), 2-3; *Xuanji*, V, pp. 157-159, 160-167 (selections); *Buyi*, pp. 30-35, 36-41 (selections); *Xuexi wenjian*, pp. 28-30, 40-51 (selections); *Wansui* (1967b), pp. 11-12 (selections); *Wenyi yulu*, passim (selections). Available English Translations: *SW*, V. pp. 172-175, 176-183 (selections); J. Chen, ed. (1970), pp. 51-55.

The comments represented here have also been quoted in many articles and essays not written by Mao since their initial appearances, and excerpts have appeared in many articles contained in periodicals such as Current Background. *These are too numerous to be cited here. These comments made by Mao are scattered throughout the book titled* Guanyu Hu Feng fan geming jituan de cailiao *(hereafter abbreviated as* Hu Feng cailiao*) which is cited here as the principal source. In the* RMRB *source as well as in* Xuanji, V, *which are cited here as alternate sources, they are also scattered. To list the pages on which they appear in these sources in the source note here would therefore be cumbersome. We have, instead, written an explanatory note to go with each section in which the exact location in the various sources of that particular section is indicated. In these explanatory notes, the citation "Book" refers to the book* Hu Feng cailiao, *and "RMRB version" refers to the respective issues of* RMRB *(i.e., May 13, 1955, for the first editor's comment, May 24, 1955, for the editor's comment and sectional commentaries for the "Second Collection," and June 10, 1955, for the editor's comment and sectional commentaries for the "Third Collection").*

Since the Preface *to* Hu Feng cailiao *is included in* Xuanji, *we have conclusive evi-*

dence that it was written by Mao. At the same time, since some of the sectional commentaries for both the "Second" and "Third Collections" were collected in Xuanji, *in which they were known under the title "selections," we have reason to believe that these sectional commentaries, which stand out against the remainder of the text in both* Hu Feng cailiao *and in* RMRB *by a different typeface, may all have been Mao's writing. Evidence for attributing to Mao the "editor's comments" to the "Second" and "Third" collections, on the other hand, is mostly circumstantial; in many auxilliary sources small excerpts or phrases from them have been attributed either directly or indirectly to Mao. For instance, in PRC newspapers in the late 1960s, many such quotations appeared in the bold typeface that usually, in those days, indicated attribution to Mao.*

The book Hu Feng cailiao *was published by Renmin chubanshe in 1955. The Preface is dated June 15, 1955. It contains an* RMRB *editorial comment (May 13, 1955), an article by Shu Wu, reprints of the "Second" and "Third" "Collection of Materials on the Hu Feng Counterrevolutionary Clique" from* RMRB *(May 24 and June 10, 1955), and the editorial of the June 10, 1955, issue of* RMRB. *The "Second Collection" includes sixty-eight items altogether, divided into five sections. The "Third Collection" includes sixty-seven items, divided under six headings. There are three passages of comment to the "Second Collection," the first two of which did not appear in the original* RMRB *version. The first of these two appears separately in* Xuanji, V. *There are altogether nineteen sectional comments to the "Third Collection."*

This is the single largest batch of materials gathered in a political campaign against a target in PRC literary and artistic circles. This and Mao's personal participation in the campaign indicate the significance of the "Hu Feng Affair." It was particularly intense because, as the comments to the collection here indicate, the controversy involved the exposure of a conspiratorial clique of writers who not only criticized the Communist Party's line on literature and art, but allegedly stole secret Party documents as well. The timing was also significant. As many of our notes herein indicate, the Hu Feng Affair has to be considered historically in conjunction with the campaigns to criticize several "counterrevolutionary" literary studies and productions, principally Yu Pingbo's study of Hongloumeng, and the movie Qing gong mishi *(The Secret History of the Qing Court) (see texts October 1954 (1) and (2)), as well as with the campaign against "the bourgeois thought of Hu Shi" (see text Dec. 1954).*

The campaign against Hu Feng, therefore, had very broad ramifications. It represented one of the two major political "purging" campaigns in the mid-1950s, the other one being the campaign against Gao Gang and Rao Shushi. This latter campaign was largely an intra-Party matter, dealing with factions within the CPC that sought to split political power off from the Party Center and from the Mao-influenced central government apparatus. The Hu Feng Affair, on the other hand, represented the deep current of antagonism between the CPC and a significant sector of China's intellectuals, which had rebelled and continued to rebel against Mao's (and the CPC's) insistence that instead of "art for art's sake," people in literary and artistic work must adapt themselves to a Marxist-Leninist revolutionary purpose in their areas of work. The issues of principle at stake in the Hu Feng Affair therefore broadly underlined the CPC's ongoing relations and struggles with intellectuals.

Zhang Gufei (a.k.a. Zhang Guangren), alias Hu Feng (b. 1903), was a literary critic, essayist, and poet. He was generally Marxist in his literary orientation and was a disciple of Lu Xun (see text Apr. 25, 1956, note 10). In 1925 he joined the "Socialist Youth League" led then by Chen Shaoyu (Wang Ming), and in 1928, when he went to Keio University in Japan, he joined the Japanese Communist Party. In the mid-1930s, back in China, he joined the League of Left-wing Writers. In 1936, he became a controversial figure in a debate with Zhou Yang, who advocated "National defense literature" (guofang wenyi). Hu at the time coined the slogan "Popular Literature in the Nationalist Revolutionary War" (guomin geming zhanzheng zhong de dazong wenxue). This debate continued, though in a somewhat abated fashion, through the years of the War of Resistance against Japan and the civil war that followed. In 1945 he returned to Shanghai from Chongqing and in 1948 was escorted by the CPC to the liberated area in the North (his life being endangered at the time because of his leftist identity) on the eve of the CPC's crossing of the Yangtze River (see text Jan. 27, 1957 (1), note 12). In 1954 he was named as a delegate for Sichuan to the First National People's Congress. In July of that year, he attacked the CPC line on literary work, blaming the Party authorities in that area for the failure of literary development in China, and as a result of the controversy over the study made of the novel Hongloumeng *by Yu Pingbo, whom he defended, became himself a target of intense criticism by the "Party-liners" in the Chinese Association of Writers and the Chinese Federation of Literary and Artistic Circles, especially Zhou Yang and Guo Moruo. On May 25, 1955, he was removed from the membership of these two federations and stripped of his position as delegate to the NPC. For a more detailed biography of Hu Feng, see D. Klein and A. Clark, eds.(1971), I, pp. 377-379, and Li Liming (1977), pp. 233-234, and H. Boorman et al., eds. (1968), II, pp. 155-158.*

Preface

In response to the needs of the broad masses of readers, we have put together and turned over to the People's Publishing House for publication the three batches of materials on the Hu Feng counterrevolutionary clique published in *Renmin ribao* [People's Daily] during the period from May 13, 1955, to June 10, 1955, along with the *Renmin ribao* editorial of June 10, 1955. The title of the volume is *Guanyu Hu Feng fan geming jituan de cailiao* [A Collection of Materials on the Hu Feng Counterrevolutionary Clique.] In this volume we have included Hu Feng's "My Self-Criticism,"[1] as a piece of source material through which the readers may study this counterrevolutionary double-dealer faction. However, we have treated it only as an appendix and have placed it after Shu Wu's article "Materials."[2] We have made a few changes in wording in the comments on and notes to these three [batches of] "materials." In the second [batch of] "materials" we have revised a few of the notes, made some additional notes, and added two comments. For the sake of uniformity, the phrase "anti-Party clique" in the titles of the first two articles has been changed to "counterrevolutionary clique" to conform to [the phrasing of] the third article. Everything else remains as it was originally.

We estimate that the publication of this book, like the publication of these materials in *Renmin ribao*, will attract attention from two groups of people. On the one hand, the counterrevolutionary elements will pay attention to it. On the other hand, the broad masses of the people will give it even more attention.

Counterrevolutionary elements and persons with a certain counterrevolutionary sentiment will find [themselves] in sympathy with [what is expressed in] the correspondence among the Hu Feng elements. Hu Feng and the Hu Feng elements are, indeed, mouthpieces for all counterrevolutionary classes, cliques, and individuals. Counterrevolutionary elements who get hold of this book will delight in the words with which they revile the revolution, as well as in their activities and plans; [this volume] will also provide them with some education of a counterrevolutionary nature about the class struggle. No matter what the circumstances, however, it will not save them from destruction. These documents of the Hu Feng elements, like all those documents of their protectors – the imperialists and Chiang Kai-shek's Kuomintang – documents that oppose the Chinese people and are counterrevolutionary, are not records of successes; they are records of defeats. They have not saved their own clique from destruction.

The broad masses of the people have a great need for a set of materials of this kind. How did the counterrevolutionary elements play their double-dealing tricks? How did they deceive us with false images and surreptitiously carry out activities unsuspected by us? All this was unknown to thousands upon thousands of good people. It is precisely for this reason that a great many counterrevolutionary elements have wormed their way into our ranks. Our eyesight has not been very keen; we haven't been very good at distinguishing good people from bad ones. We may be good at distinguishing good people from bad people when they are carrying out activities under normal conditions, but we are not good at distinguishing certain people who carry out activities under unusual circumstances. The Hu Feng elements were counterrevolutionary elements who appeared in disguise; they gave people a false image and hid their true face. However, since their purpose was counterrevolutionary, they could not conceal their true face thoroughly. Being representatives of a clique, they disputed with us on many occasions, both before and after Liberation. Their [public] pronouncements and actions not only differed from those of Communist Party members, but also from those of the broad masses of revolutionaries and democratic personages outside the Party. The recent big exposé is nothing more than [our] getting hold of a large amount of incontestable evidence against them. With regard to quite a few individuals among the Hu Feng elements, the reason we were deceived by them is that our Party organization, state organs, people's organizations, cultural and educational organizations, as well as business organizations, failed [to carry out] strict investigation procedures at the time they took in [these people]. It is also because in the past we were in a period of great revolutionary storm, and we were the victors, so all sorts of people came over to our side. It was unavoidable to have sand mixed with mud and fish mingled with dragons,[3] and we did not as yet have the time to sift them out thoroughly. Furthermore, the task of distinguishing and purging bad persons can be done only by relying on the integration of correct leadership on the part of the leading organs and a high degree of consciousness among the broad masses, and this aspect of our work has been deficient in the past. All these things are lessons for us.

We are taking the Hu Feng affair seriously because we want to use it to educate the broad masses of the people, first of all those literate working cadres and the intellectuals. We recommend these "materials" to them in order to raise their level of consciousness. These "materials" have an enormous incisiveness and lucidity which will command people's attention. The counterrevolutionaries will certainly pay attention to them, and revolutionaries will especially give them attention. As long as the broad masses of the revolutionary people learn something from this affair and these materials, thus having their revolutionary enthusiasm stirred up and their ability to distinguish [good from bad persons] enhanced, we will gradually uncover the various kinds of covert counterrevolutionaries.

The Editorial Department,
Renmin ribao
June 15, 1955

Renmin ribao's Editor's Comment (May 13, 1955)

The reason for our publishing only now Hu Feng's "My Self-Criticism," which he first wrote in January, revised in February, and to which he added an "afterword" in March, along with Shu Wu's "Material on the Hu Feng Counterrevolutionary Clique," is to prevent Hu Feng from making use of our newspapers to continue to deceive the readers. From the materials brought to light in Shu Wu's article, the readers can see how early Hu Feng and the anti-Communist, antipeople, counterrevolutionary clique[4] he led showed their hostility, enmity, and hatred for the Communist and non-Communist progressive writers. Can the readers possibly detect even the slightest revolutionary flavor in Hu Feng's letters to Shu Wu? Isn't the odor emanating from these letters exactly the same as the one we used to detect in such journals as *Shehui xinwen* [Social News] and *Xinwen tiandi* [The World of News] published by the Kuomintang secret service organs? He talks about "a petty-bourgeois revolutionary character and standpoint," "realistic literature and art based on democratic demands and the various antifeudal, antitraditional tendencies," "the standpoint of sharing the fate of the people," "a spirit of revolutionary humanitarianism," "an anti-imperialist, antifeudal revolutionary ideology of people's liberation," "in accordance with the Party's political program," and "if it had not been for the revolution and the Chinese Communist Party I personally would not have been able to find a secure spot in which to make a living for the past twenty or more years." Are all these statements believable? If he were not putting up a false signpost but were an intellectual who truly had a "petty-bourgeois revolutionary character and standpoint" (there are thousands upon thousands of such people in China, and they cooperate with the Communist Party and are willing to accept the Party's leadership), could he have adopted such a hostile, inimical, and hateful attitude toward the Party and progressive writers?[5] What is false is false; the disguise must be peeled off. It is possible that there are still people among the Hu Feng counterrevolutionary clique who, like Shu Wu, were deceived and now do not wish to forever run along with Hu Feng. They should hand over to the government still more materials exposing Hu Feng. Concealment cannot last long; the day will inevitably come when the truth is exposed. Even the strategy of shifting from attack to retreat (that is, self-criticism) cannot deceive people. Self-criticism must be like that of Shu Wu; phony self-criticism won't do. Lu Ling[6] must have received even more secret letters from Hu feng. We hope he will turn them in. Everyone who was mixed up with Hu Feng and who has received secret letters from him should hand them over. Turning [the letters] in is much better than holding on to them or destroying them. Hu Feng should undertake the task of peeling off his mask and not make deceitful self-criticism. The only way out for Hu Feng and everyone in the Hu Feng faction is to peel off their mask, expose the real situation, help the government to thoroughly clarify the whole picture on Hu Feng and his counterrevolutionary clique, and become people from now on.

Editor's Comment to the Second Collection of Materials on the Hu Feng Counterrevolutionary Clique
[May 24, 1955]

Since the publication of Shu Wu's "Some Materials on the Hu Feng Counterrevolutionary Clique," people have become incensed about Hu Feng's anti-Communist, antipeople, and counterrevolutionary evildoings. This newspaper has already received from readers in every part of the country and from all circles a large quantity of essays and letters. They unanimously demand that the evils of Hu Feng and his clique be fully exposed. This feeling of indignation cannot be suppressed. However, some people who sympathize with Hu Feng, or who say they are against Hu Feng but in their hearts sympathize with him, are saying that those materials were mostly from before Liberation and cannot be the basis for conviction. Well, then, now take a look at a second collection of materials.

The materials we are now publishing have been excerpted from sixty-eight secret letters Hu Feng sent to the members of his reactionary clique. All these letters were written by Hu Feng since the time the entire country was liberated. In these letters Hu Feng viciously reviles the Chinese Communist Party, smears the Party's guidelines in literature and art, slanders comrades in positions of responsibility in the Party, and curses Party-member and non-Party writers in literary and artistic circles. In these letters Hu Feng orders the members of his reactionary clique to carry out sinister anti-Communist, antipeople activities and organizes them secretly and in a planned way to launch frenzied attacks against the Chinese Communist Party and the literary and artistic front led by the Party. In these letters, Hu Feng urges his adherents to make their way into the Communist Party and revolutionary organizations in order to establish a base, to expand their "power," to do intelligence work, and to steal internal Party documents. From these letters, people can clearly see that after Liberation Hu Feng went even further with his double-dealing tricks: Publicly [his position] was "don't clash with them," "go along with the Party and the people," but covertly he intensified "sharpening [his] sword and maintaining a lookout," and "used the Monkey King's strategem of crawling into the belly" [infiltration] to carry out counterrevolutionary activities.[7] After his reckless attacks against the Party failed, he quickly directed his adherents to plan a retreat, to "find a second life in patient endurance." Everyone was to prepare a false self-examination in order to lay low for a while, awaiting an opportunity to rise up again. This is evidence of the extremely serious nature of the counterrevolutionary conspiracy of Hu Feng and his clique. We must redouble our vigilance and certainly not be taken in by their trick of feigning surrender.

In most of the letters between Hu Feng and the members of his clique, devious and covert devices were used. Hu Feng made arrangements with them for the use of codes and secret allusions in their letters. Whenever comrades in positions of responsibility in the Chinese Communist Party and in literary and artistic circles and Party-member writers were referred to in the letters, code names were used for them. The names of the addressees and Hu Feng's own signature were also very inconsistent; the name on the envelope was often that of the wife of the person who was supposed to receive the letter, or someone else entirely; the signature at the end of the letter was often changed or absent altogether. Many of Hu Feng's letters were written on *Renmin ribao* or *Jiefang ribao* stationery. Many of the envelopes carried return addresses such as "Luo of the Shanghai New Literature and Art Publishing House," or "Luo of *Qingnian bao,* Shanghai," or "Zhang of the Beijing Central Drama School," or the names of some other organizations.

The following are materials excerpted from these secret letters. They are divided into three categories according to content. Within each category they are arranged, on the whole, chronologically, with necessary explanations added. All the underscoring in the letters is in the originals.

* * *

The so-called "regimentation of public opinion" mentioned by Hu Feng refers to the prohibition imposed on counterrevolutionaries against publishing their counterrevolutionary views. Indeed, this is true. Our system does deprive all counterrevolutionaries of freedom of speech, and it allows such freedom only among the people. Among the people we allow divergence of public opinion. This is the freedom of criticism, the freedom to publish all kinds of views, and the freedom to propagate either theism or atheism (i.e., materialism). In any society, at any time, there are always two kinds of people and two kinds of opinions, the advanced and the backward, that exist in mutual conflict and are struggling with each other. Advanced opinion always conquers backward opinion; it is impossible to "regiment public opinion"; nor should its regimentation be attempted. Only by bringing progressive things into full play to subdue backward things can society move forward. However, at a time when internationally and domestically there is still the existence of classes and class struggle, the working class and the masses of the people, having obtained state power, must suppress all resistance to revolution put up by counterrevolutionary classes, cliques, and individuals, prohibit their activities for restoration, and forbid all counterrevolutionary elements from utilizing the freedom of speech to reach their counterrevolutionary goals. This has made counterrevolutionary elements such as Hu Feng feel that "regimentation of public opinion" is inconvenient to them. That they feel inconvenienced is exactly our purpose. It is exactly what is convenient to us. Our public opinion is regimented, but it is also unregimented. Among the people we allow both the progressive people and the backward people to freely utilize our newspapers, periodicals, lecture platforms, and so forth to compete, in the hope that the progressive people may educate the backward people with the methods of democracy and persuasion and conquer backward ideology and institutions. When a certain contradiction is resolved, new contradictions will arise. We then use the same methods to compete. Thus society will advance continuously. When contradictions exist, there is no uniformity. When a contradiction is resolved there is temporary uniformity; soon, however, new contradictions will arise, and there is again divergence, which needs to be overcome. The contradiction between the people and the counterrevolutionaries is [exemplified in] the dictatorship of the people under the leadership of the working class and the Communist Party over the counterrevolutionaries. In this case what is used is not the democratic method; rather, the method is authoritarian, or dictatorial. It permits [the counterrevolutionaries] only to behave themselves according to rules, but not to be unruly in words and deeds. In this regard, not only is public opinion regimented, but the law, too, is regimented. On this question, counterrevolutionaries such as Hu Feng seem to have a lot of persuasive arguments; some muddleheaded people, after listening to these counterrevolutionary arguments, also seem to find themselves short of reason. Look, isn't "regimentation of public opinion," or "no public opinion," or "suppression of liberty" unpleasant to the ears? They cannot distinguish between the two realms: that among the people and that external to the realm of the people. Internally, it is criminal activity to suppress liberty, to suppress people's criticism of the mistakes and shortcomings of the Party and the government, and to suppress freedom of discussion in the academic world. This is our system. In capitalist countries, however, these are legal activities. Externally, it is criminal behavior [here] to let counterrevolutionaries indulge in unruly words and deeds, whereas it is legal to exercise dictatorship [over them]. This is our system. In capitalist countries, it is just the opposite. There, they have the dictatorship of the bourgeoisie, and revolutionary people are not allowed to say and do what they want and are made to observe rigid rules of behavior. Exploiters and counterrevolutionaries are always in the minority at any time and any place; the exploited and the revolutionaries are always in the majority. Therefore, the latter's dictatorship is fully justified and the former's dictatorship always lacks justification. Hu

Feng also said, "The great majority of readers take part in some kind of organizational [way] of life there; the atmosphere is oppressive." Among the people, we are opposed to the method of commandism;[8] we uphold the democratic method of persuasion. The atmosphere there ought to be free. [To say that it is] "oppressive" is incorrect. That "the great majority of the readers take part in some sort of organizational [way of] life" is an immensely good thing, unprecedented in the past several thousand years. Only after long and difficult struggle under the leadership of the Communist Party have the people won the possibility of changing themselves from the state of being a [pan of] loose sand,[9] which lends itself to the exploitation and oppression of the reactionaries, to a state of unity; moreover this kind of great unity among the people has been realized several years after the victory of the revolution. What Hu Feng means by "coercing the people" is simply oppression against counterrevolutionaries. They are indeed scared out of their wits and feel like "a daughter-in-law, always afraid she will be beaten" or feel that "every little cough will be recorded." We regard this as a very good thing also. This good thing is also unprecedented over several thousand years. It is only after the protracted and difficult struggle of the people under the leadership of the Communist Party that these rotten eggs have been made to feel uncomfortable. In a word, the day of rejoicing for the great masses of the people is the day of grief for the counterrevolutionary elements. On every National Day we celebrate, above all, this very thing. Hu Feng also said, "the problem of literature can be handled most effortlessly with the theory of mechanism." What he called "the theory of mechanism" is [his way of twisting] the meaning of dialectical materialism into its opposite; that "it can be handled most effortlessly" is his nonsense. In this world only idealism and metaphysics are the most effortless because they allow people to talk nonsense, without the need to base themselves on objective reality, and without being subject to examination according to objective reality. On the other hand, materialism and dialectics demand effort. They have to be based on objective reality, and they are subject to examination based on objective reality. If one makes no effort, one will slide into idealism and metaphysics. In this letter, Hu Feng raised three questions of principle which we deem necessary to refute in detail.[10] In that letter, he also said, "At present, there is everywhere sentiment for rebellion, and there is everywhere the demand to go one step forward." He said this in 1950. At that time, on the mainland we had just wiped out Chiang Kai-shek's main military forces. We had yet to eliminate many counterrevolutionary armed forces that had turned into bandits. Large-scale land reform and the movement to suppress the counterrevolutionaries had not yet begun.[11] The cultural and educational sectors had not yet begun their rectification work. What Hu Feng said indeed reflected the contemporary situation. But his statement was incomplete. A complete picture would be as follows: "At present there are counterrevolutionary sentiments everywhere, sentiments that resist the revolution; and everywhere there are counterrevolutionaries making further demands on the revolution through their sabotage of the revolution."[12]

* * *

Factions, which were called "cliques"[13] by our forebears, are called "rings" or stalls[14] by people today. We hear of them a great deal. Those who engage in this kind of activity, in order to attain their political goals, often charge that others are sectarian and that sectarians are the bad guys while they themselves are the good guys; the good guys have no factions. The bunch of people led by Hu Feng allegedly were "youth writers" and "revolutionary writers," "hated" and "persecuted" by a Communist faction that was upholding "bourgeois theories" and "building an independent kingdom"; they therefore wanted revenge. [They regarded] the *Wenyi bao* affair[15] as "no more than a chink in the armor to be seized and taken advantage of," and [that] this "problem was not an isolated one"; [they believed] it was necessary to proceed from there to "broaden [their] focus to include the whole situation," and "to show that the problem [was] one of sectarian domination"; moreover "[it was a problem of] sectarian and warlord rule." The problem was so serious [to them] that in order to get to the root of the matter they "exposed" quite a few things. In this way Hu Feng and his bunch attracted people's attention. Many people made a careful investigation and found out that they were a group of considerable size. In the past it was said they were a "small group. " This was incorrect; they had quite a few people. In the past it was said they were purely cultural people. This was incorrect; their people have wormed their way into every political, military, economic, cultural, and educational sector. In the past it was said that they looked like a revolutionary party in open rebellion. This was incorrect; most of their people had serious problems. Their basic ranks were made up of secret agents for the imperialists and the Kuomintang Trotskyists, reactionary military officers, and Communist Party renegades. With these people as the backbone, a counterrevolutionary splinter group, hidden within the camp of the revolutionaries, an underground independent kingdom,[16] has been formed. This counterrevolutionary splinter group and underground kingdom takes the overthrow of the People's Republic of China and the restoration of imperialist and Kuomintang rule as its mission. They are everywhere and at all times probing for our weaknesses so that they may have a pretext for carrying out their destructive activities. Wherever they gather, some strange problems are sure to arise. This counterrevolutionary clique has expanded since Liberation, and if we don't put a stop to it, it will expand still further. Now that we have gotten to the bottom of Hu Feng and company, we have found a rational explanation for many phenomena, and their activities can be stopped.[17]

* * *

From the above materials we can see that: (1) Since Liberation the anti-Communist, antipeople, conspiratorial activities of the Hu Feng clique have become better organized and have further expanded. Their attacks on the Communist Party and on the battlefront of literature and art under the Party's leadership have been increasingly frenzied. (2) Like all counterrevolutionary cliques, they always adopt covert or double-dealing tactics to carry out their destructive activities. (3) Because their plot has been exposed, the Hu Feng clique cannot avoid being forced to turn from attack to retreat; but this reactionary clique whose hatred for the Communist Party, hatred for the people, and hatred for the revolution has reached insane proportions is by no means really putting down its weapons. Rather, they are planning to continue to use double-dealing tactics to preserve their "strength" and await opportunities to make a comeback. Hu Feng's use of such expressions as "find a second life in patient suffering," "all is for the cause, for an even brighter future," to encourage the members of his clique is clear proof [of this]. The counterrevolutionary Hu Feng elements are the same as other open or hidden counterrevolutionaries. They place their hopes in a restoration of counterrevolutionary political power and in the collapse of the people's revolutionary political power. They believe this is the opportunity they are waiting for.

We must learn a thorough lesson from this experience with the conspiratorial activities of the Hu Feng clique. We must maintain a high level of vigilance in every sector of our work. We must be adept at recognizing elements who feign support for the revolution but are actually opposed to the revolution and purge them on all fronts so as to preserve the great victories we have already won and those still to come.[18]

Editor's Comments to The Third Collection of Materials on the Hu Feng Counterrevolutionary Clique
[June 10, 1955]

The publication of the first and second collections of materials on the Hu Feng counterrevolutionary clique stirred up the extreme anger of the broad masses of the people all over the country toward the counterrevolutionary elements. The people demand to investigate the political background of the Hu Feng clique. They ask: Who is really behind Hu Feng? With regard to this question, the People's Government has already obtained a great deal of material. We are now publishing part of it in this "Third Collection of Materials." Hu Feng and the many backbone elements in the Hu Feng clique have, since long ago, been loyal running dogs of imperialism and Chiang Kai-shek's Kuomintang.[19] They have intimate connections with the imperialist and the Kuomintang secret services. For a long period they disguised themselves as revolutionaries and concealed themselves among the progressive people to carry out counterrevolutionary schemes.

In the following materials, the people can see the true face of A Long, who was touted by Hu Feng as "a revolutionary writer in pursuit of [the interests of] the revolution for a dozen or more years," and of Hu Feng himself, who also claimed to have pursued the revolution for some twenty years. A Long, in a letter to Hu Feng, said he was "full of optimism" about the nationwide [campaign of] counterrevolutionary civil war launched by Chiang Kai-shek in July 1946. He thought that the "main force" of the Chinese People's Liberation Army "could be defeated in three months," and "would be wiped out in one year." Moreover, he shamelessly exaggerated the importance of the bandit Chiang's "instructions," and talked about "[Chiang's] self-confidence which is inspiring to everyone." A Long regarded the revolutionary strength of the people as "pus" that "has to be squeezed out" and felt that the attack on the people's revolutionary forces had to be determined and thorough: "A thing once begun will not be put off until done!"

Why were they so determined? The truth is that Hu Feng, A Long, and others were people with a particular history behind them. A Long, who is in fact Chen Yimen, also known as Chen Shoumei, is from Zhejiang.[20] Originally he was a Kuomintang military officer. At the start of the War of Resistance against Japan he "wormed his way" into the Yanan Anti-Japanese Military and Political University, where he studied for a few months.[21] He didn't go to the front; instead he went to Hu Zongnan's "Wartime Cadres Fourth Corps"[22] to serve as a military instructor with the rank of major. One of the letters published here was written by him in July 1946 from the Army College in Shandong in Chongqing[23] to which he had already been transferred from Hu Zongnan's [staff] for training.[24] After graduation, he became an instructor in military tactics. Shandong was the site of Chiang Kai-shek's Army College and was also Chiang Kai-shek's personal home during the Chongqing period.

Hu Feng, who is in fact Zhang Guangren, also known as Gu Fei, is from Hubei. During the period of the First Revolutionary Civil War he joined the Communist Youth League. In 1925 he was in Beijing; the white terror of Duan Qirui rule[25] at that time scared him out of his wits, and he determinedly sought the Party's permission to withdraw from the League. Later, he did anti-Communist political work with the Jiangxi Army "to exterminate the Communists." Afterward, he went to Japan where he muddled around for a time and engaged in some shady "deals." After he returned to China, he found his way into the left-wing cultural group in Shanghai and from the inside carried on all kinds of splitist and destructive activities. During the Fuhan and Chongqing periods he had contact with many bigshots in the Kuomintang secret service. From one of Hu Feng's letters to A Long published here, one can see Hu Feng's relationship with one of the head men in the Kuomintang secret service, Chen Zuo.[26] This brief history of Hu Feng has been brought to light only recently. Because he covered things up so skillfully, everyone was deceived by him.

Before Liberation in the country as a whole was achieved, the Hu Feng clique fervently placed its hopes on a victory for Chiang Kai-shek in the anti-people civil war, and a defeat for the people's revolutionary forces. After Chiang Kai-shek was defeated and the whole country liberated, they took cover on the mainland and used even more insidious double-dealing tactics to continue to carry on counterrevolutionary activities.

They expressed their deeply ingrained hatred for the new post-Liberation society and for the people's revolutionary political power. They said, "I despise this social order." They cursed the people's revolutionary political power, [predicting its] "doom" and "its perdition."

After this newspaper published the first and second collections of materials exposing [the Hu Feng clique], there were still a number of people who said that the Hu Feng clique was nothing but a small clique made up of a handful of power-hungry elements in literary circles, and that they don't necessarily have any reactionary political background. Those who say this sort of thing may do so either because their class instincts put them in wholehearted sympathy with them, or perhaps because their political senses are not very sharp and they look at things too innocently. There is also a group who are secret reactionaries or who are actually inside the Hu Feng clique, Lu Ying in Beijing, for example.

Now the time has come when the face of Hu Feng's black gang of counterrevolutionaries is to be thoroughly exposed. The Chinese people will no longer permit them to continue to play their deceitful tricks! The entire people must heighten their vigilance! All secret counterrevolutionary elements must be exposed. They must receive the punishment that they deserve for their counterrevolutionary crimes![27]

Editor's Notes

From letters of this sort it can be seen that the Hu Feng clique is not simply a "literature and art" clique, but is a counterrevolutionary political clique using the signpost of "literature and art." They hate all the people's revolutionary forces. Zhang Zhongxiao of the Hu Feng clique said he "hated almost everyone." Many people think "Hu Feng is no more than a literary figure, and the Hu Feng affair is no more than an affair of the cultural circle, with no connection to other circles." After reading this sort of material they should be awakened![28]

* * *

From the above two letters the true face of Lu Yuan, a backbone member of the Hu Feng clique, can be seen. The backbone of the Hu Feng clique was composed of just this sort of person. In May 1944, Lu Yuan "was transferred" "to work" "in the Sino-American Cooperation Organization." The "Sino-American Cooperation Organization" is the abbreviated name for "Sino-American Special Technical Services Cooperation Organization." This was a black and sinister secret service organization jointly run by the American imperialists and Chiang Kai-shek's Kuomintang in which the Americans trained and dispatched secret service agents as well as engaged directly in terrorist activities both for the Americans themselves and for Chiang Kai-shek. It was notorious for its brutal torture and murder of Communist Party members and progressive elements. Who could have had Lu Yuan "transferred to" this secret service organization? And who could be "transferred" by the secret service to do its "work"? The answer goes without saying. In the second letter, written in September 1947, Lu Yuan was still cursing the Chinese Communist Party and the people's revolutionary forces as "the damnable evil Communist bandits." And yet, in the beginning of 1948 he was recommended to be a member of the Communist Party by Zeng Zuo, another backbone member of the Hu Feng elements, and he sneaked into an underground Party organization. Later Lu Yuan suddenly took off in secret. At the time of the liberation of Wuhan he unexpectedly returned to Wuhan and, together with Zeng Zhuo, claimed to "represent the Communist Party" and took us over.[29] In 1950 he once again wormed his way into the Party (see number 28 of this collection of material). This, then, was the way the Hu Feng elements "pursued the revolution" and wormed their way into the Communist Party.[30]

* * *

From these letters of A Long's we can see that the Hu Feng elements understood quite well some of the tactics of underground counterrevolutionary work. He said: "Don't fire before our battle position is secured." Furthermore, [he said] "The important thing is to prepare [favorable] conditions, then make a few more preparations and, again, still more preparations!" "[We] must work intensely, and make sure that the work among the masses is done well," "establish a firm mass base," and then "find a big target," which is to take aim at a vital area of the revolution and launch an attack. [He said] when they are about to attack, they must first have "consulted" a good deal with their "friends," and "must first have organized and thought through their arguments even more meticulously; it is best to ignore trivial matters." The counterrevolutionary elements are not so slow-witted; those tactics of theirs are very cunning and ruthless. All members of the revolutionary parties must absolutely not take them lightly, must not be insensitive and careless. We must greatly elevate the people's political vigilance; only then can we deal with [these counterrevolutionaries] and get rid of them.[31]

* * *

Lu Dian's[32] strategy of mounting an offensive for purposes of defense was, sure enough, practiced by Hu Feng later. This was [the strategy demonstrated by] Hu Feng's going to Beijing to request a work assignment, his request for a discussion of his case, his 300,000-word written presentation [on literature and art],[33] and finally his catching on to the issue of *Wenyi bao* and setting off a barrage.[34] Representatives of the various exploiting classes, when they find themselves in unfavorable circumstances, often adopt the strategy of mounting an offensive for purposes of defense to protect themselves for the time being and to abet their future expansion. They may make something out of nothing, spreading rumors right in front of your face; they may latch on to some superficial phenomena to attack the substance of the issue; they may laud one group to attack another; they may make use of some pretext to "break through a chink in our armor" and place us in a difficult position. In any case, they are always studying strategies for dealing with us; they are "on the lookout" for a chance to further their ambitions. Sometimes they will "lie low and play dead" while waiting for an opportunity to "counterattack." They have long experience in class struggle. They will use all different forms of struggle – legal struggle as well as illegal struggle. We members of the revolutionary party must understand these tricks of theirs. We must study their tactics in order to defeat them. We must not be so completely bookish and oversimplify what is in fact a complex class struggle.[35]

* * *

Because the members of our revolutionary Party have been arrogant, self-satisfied, insensitive, and careless, or have been preoccupied with daily routine business and have forgotten about politics, many counterrevolutionary elements have "penetrated deeply" into our "vital organs." This certainly is not limited to the Hu Feng elements; many other secret agents or bad elements have also crept in.[36]

* * *

The members of the Hu Feng clique and many other hidden counterrevolutionary elements have in general adopted the double-dealing tactics discussed by Fang Ran in this letter, especially the second and third of the tactics. These can trick a great many people. But there is always some slip-up that people can spot; the exposure of the Hu Feng clique is proof of this. Especially after the level of consciousness and vigilance of the majority of people was raised, their double-dealing tactics were much more easily exposed.[37]

* * *

From these [letters] we can also see the importance and the necessity of our struggle to criticize the Hu Shih[38] brand of bourgeois idealism. There are some people who profess their belief in Marxism-Leninism but who do not take seriously the struggle to criticize idealism. They say that they themselves are not idealists or that they have nothing to do with Hu Shi, and thus the best way for them is to avoid the subject. But the Hu Feng clique in fact pays much attention [to struggle], and they searched for a way of dealing with it. [They concluded:] "There are contradictions and difficulties." Criticism of idealism has indeed presented the Hu Feng clique with "contradictions and difficulties" – this shows that our criticism was correct. Is it possible that among the revolutionary ranks of the people there are also "contradictions and difficulties"?[39]

* * *

That a large group of Hu Feng elements were able to force their way into the Chinese Communist Party and obtain Party membership is a matter that should draw the attention of all Party organizations. Lu Yuan had once wormed his way into our underground Party organizations before Liberation, but later, because he took off secretly, he lost his Party membership. In 1950 this counterrevolutionary character presented to our Party organizations "three reports with the utmost sincerity, each one more thorough and sincere than the previous one"; except for his thinking on literature and art, he was [considered] "on the whole qualified in other respects," and indeed, later he was again accepted as a "Party member." Shouldn't this matter draw the attention of Party organizations? It was after these counterrevolutionary elements had put their heart and soul into deceiving us that they were able to crawl their way into the Party. They treated this as a "round of struggle," and they beat us; they came into [the Party]!⁴⁰

* * *

Whenever a Communist Party member's liberal tendencies were subjected to criticism, it was regarded as a "setback" by the Hu Feng elements. If such a person "lacked fighting spirit," or, in other words, if he did not persist in his liberal standpoint and was willing to accept the Party's criticism and switch over to the correct standpoint, to the Hu Feng clique he was a hopeless case because he could not be pulled over to their side. [But] if this person had a "relatively good," rather than "a lack" of, "fighting spirit" in insisting on his liberal position, then such a person would be susceptible to being pulled over. The Hu Feng elements will certainly "give it a try," and they already addressed such a person as "comrade." Shouldn't this kind of situation be instructive to us? What attitude should Communist Party members take when they receive criticism for ideological or political errors they have committed? There are two paths from which to choose : one is to correct the mistakes and become a good Party member; the other is to continue to backslide, or even to fall into the pit of the counterrevolutionaries. The latter path really exists, and it is possible that the counterrevolutionaries are there beckoning.⁴¹

* * *

These kinds of letters ought to arouse our vigilance. We cannot let them "slip by."⁴²

* * *

From letters of this sort it can be seen that the counterrevolutionaries hidden among the ranks of the revolutionaries are very afraid of rectification, so it is evident that rectification is beneficial. Those who fear rectification are not all counterrevolutionaries. An overwhelming majority (over ninety per cent) are people who have committed certain ideological or political errors, and our policy is to help them correct their mistakes. But toward the counterrevolutionaries, who are very afraid of rectification, our policy is to go a bit further and dig out their counterrevolutionary roots. The face of the Hu Feng counterrevolutionary clique was exposed step by step during several rectification [campaigns] before and after Liberation, that is, in several ideological struggles in the past. It is these several rectification [campaigns] that produced splits within the Hu Feng clique, and only then was the Hu Feng clique forced to adopt the strategy of taking the offense for purposes of defense – writing the 300,000-word written presentation [on literature and art],⁴³ and only then was there the last big disclosure.⁴⁴

* * *

From letters of this sort, it can be seen that [when counterrevolutionary cliques are] confronted with the powerful people's revolutionary forces, that is, the people's democratic dictatorship, if this dictatorship raises the consciousness of the masses and adopts correct policies, then no matter how many secret counterrevolutionary cliques there are, no matter how strict the discipline within each counterrevolutionary clique, and no matter how strong their military alliance with each other, it is always possible to split off a number of people [from the cliques]. This splitting off is beneficial to the people. Shu Wu's splitting off from the Hu Feng clique, which caused the Hu Feng clique great anxiety, is an example. Recently, in every locality, many Hu Feng elements have made confessions. Either voluntarily or under pressure, they are turning over secret documents and exposing the situation within [the group.] This is a continuing development in this struggle.[45]

* * *

From letters of this sort it can be seen that there are people in our [Party and government] organs, military units, enterprises, and other organizations who steal state secrets. These people are counterrevolutionary elements who have infiltrated these organs, military units, enterprises, or organizations. Some liberal elements are the good friends of these counterrevolutionaries. Shouldn't this situation draw the serious attention of all work personnel and all the people?[46]

* * *

From this letter it can be seen that the Hu Feng clique firmly opposed the direction for literature and art set by the Chinese Communist Party and had extreme loathing for Comrade Mao Zedong's *Talks at the Yanan Forum on Literature and Art*.[47] Because the Party and Comrade Mao Zedong called on workers in literature and art to praise the workers, peasants, and soldiers and to expose the enemies of the workers, peasants, and soldiers, and [because] the Hu Feng clique was precisely the mortal enemy of the workers, peasants, and soldiers, they sensed that to expose the enemies of the workers, peasants, and soldiers would mean that they would not be able to continue to lead their deceptive way of life. They felt [this policy] would "slaughter" what this counterrevolutionary band referred to as their "human lives" and would "stifle" what they called "innovations." They didn't dare, however, to oppose these speeches publicly. In fact Hu Feng instructed his accomplices to "go along with them" on the surface and occasionally even to quote a few lines from them. These were all masks with which the Hu Feng elements disguised themselves. In this secret letter, however, the Hu Feng elements' loathing for these speeches and their true anti-Party complexion are completely exposed. Zhang Zhongxiao said: "This book (referring to Mao's *Talks at the Yanan Forum on Literature and Art)* may have been of some use during the Yanan period, but now I think it's no longer relevant." Are there not a few others in literary and artistic circles who have also said, "now it is no longer relevant"? People who have said this kind of thing, please read Zhang Zhongxiao's letter carefully! Of course, some of those who say this sort of thing are merely still holding a bourgeois viewpoint on literature and art and therefore are unable to recognize the importance of this speech. Zhang Zhongxiao, on the other hand, this member of the Hu Feng clique, understands profoundly on the basis of his counterrevolutionary sensitivity that after the Liberation of the entire country the *Talks* would influence the masses on an even larger scale and would be useful in destroying all sorts of reactionary thought in literature and art. Therefore, they urgently wanted to obstruct and sabotage the spreading influence of these speeches. This is the reason for their saying "now it is no longer relevant."[48]

* * *

From letters of this sort it can be seen that the attack on a small number of people by the counterrevolutionary elements was no more than a pretext, a strategy of theirs. Their actual feeling was that there was "hardly a single clean piece of ground." Owing to this situation they "prescribed a bitter and protracted struggle." Ever since Liu Bi, Prince Wu in the Han dynasty, discovered the famous strategy of requesting the execution of Chao Cuo (the principal adviser of Emperor Jingdi of the Han dynasty) to "purify the ranks of the emperor's closest counsellors," many ambitious careerists have held this up as an extremely valuable [strategem].[49] The Hu Feng clique has also fallen heir to this bag of tricks. In the 300,000-word presentation, they attacked only several people, Comrades Lin Mohan, He Qifang, and Zhou Yang.[50] They said these people were messing everything up. Some people, who in their basic class instincts sympathize with Hu Feng, also accordingly aided his cause by making a lot of nonsensical noises, saying "this is no more that an interpersonal struggle between Zhou Yang and Hu Feng for leadership. " This is something to which we should pay attention in the struggle to purge the Hu Feng elements and other counterrevolutionary elements.[51]

* * *

In the 300,000-word presentation and in other public pronouncements,[52] the Hu Feng clique appears to be primarily opposed only to Communist Party writers and not to others. Of course they have never opposed Chiang Kai-shek and other persons in the Kuomintang (except that on occasion, they have scolded them lightly in a few sentences so as to put up a front, but this is truly what is meant by "small scoldings, but big help"). It is not true, however, that they did not oppose others. We have proof of this from the numerous secret letters of the Hu Feng group. In fact, they despised, cursed, and opposed without exception such revolutionaries and democratic personages as Lu Xun, Wen Yiduo, Guo Moruo, Mao Dun, Ba Jin, Huang Yaomian, Cao Yu, and Lao She.[53] Is not this kind of work-style of rejecting anyone outside one's own clique the work-style of Chiang Kai-shek's fascist Kuomintang?[54]

* * *

Just as we regularly estimate the trends of the balance of forces in the international and domestic class struggles, the enemy also regularly makes estimates of these trends. But our enemies are backward, decadent reactionaries, and they are destined to be destroyed. They do not understand the laws of the objective world. They think about things with subjective and metaphysical methods, and thus their estimates are always incorrect. Their basic class instincts lead them to think all the time of themselves as really extraordinary and the forces of revolution as invariably no good. They always overestimate their own strength and underestimate our strength. We have seen with our own eyes many counterrevolutionaries such as the Qing government, the Beiyang warlords, the Japanese militarists, Mussolini, Hitler, and Chiang Kai-shek[55] falling [from power] one after another. They made and could not have avoided making mistakes in thought and action. At present, all the imperialists are also bound to commit this kind of mistake. Isn't this ridiculous? According to the Hu Feng elements, the Chinese people's revolutionary forces led by the Communist Party are "taking their last gasp," and these forces are no more than "withered leaves" or "rotting corpses." And what about the counterrevolutionary forces represented by the Hu Feng elements? Although "some of the fragile buds will be crushed," [they think] most of these buds are "bursting open" and "will grow up strong and healthy." If in the bourgeois national assembly of France there are even today representatives of the monarchist party, then it is quite possible that years after the exploiting classes all over the earth have been thoroughly eliminated there will still be representatives of the Chiang Kai-shek dynasty active everywhere. The most stubborn elements among those people will never acknowledge their defeat. This is because they not only need to deceive others, but also to deceive themselves; otherwise they could not go on living.[56] Why are the Hu Feng elements so ridiculously and insanely arrogant? It is because they in fact march to the tune of their own class instincts.[57]

* * *

This Hu Feng element[58] is somewhat more pessimistic. He says "perhaps" "it will take a few decades" to "bring about a situation where there are no contradictions among people." That is to say, it will take decades for Chiang Kai-shek's dynasty to have hope of a restoration. After several decades, when the Chiang Kai-shek dynasty returns, when all the people's revolutionary forces are crushed – that is what [he] meant by "no contradictions among people" – [he said] "then, a person's dignity and integrity will not be impaired." This "person" here refers to all counterrevolutionaries, including the Hu Feng elements, but it doesn't include a single revolutionary. "In today's China, people still don't respect other people. . . ." The former "people" refers to the revolutionaries, and the latter "people" refers to the counterrevolutionaries. The Hu Feng elements do not express themselves clearly in their writing, not even in secret letters. This, too, is determined by their basic class nature. They are unable to put forward their ideas clearly the way we do when we make annotations for them.[59]

* * *

The statement in this letter that "the latent forces of feudalism are now insanely killing people" is a manifestation of the feeling of horror the Hu Feng counterrevolutionary clique has for the great struggle in which the people's revolutionary forces in our country are suppressing the counterrevolutionary forces. This kind of feeling is representative of all counterrevolutionary classes, cliques, and individuals. What they feel frightened about is precisely what the masses feel happy about. They were right when they said, "This is without precedent in history." Previous revolutions, except for that in which the slave system replaced the system of primitive communism – which was a case of a system of exploitation replacing a nonexploitative system – all have resulted in one kind of system of exploitation replacing another. They had neither the need to nor the possibility of carrying out the thorough suppression of counterrevolutionaries. Only ours, only the revolution of the broad [masses of the] people under the leadership of the proletariat and the Communist Party, is a revolution for which the final eradication of all exploitative systems and all classes have been set as the goal. No matter what, the exploiting classes which are being destroyed will offer resistance through their counterrevolutionary political parties, cliques, or individuals, and the broad [masses of the] people will have to unite together to suppress these totally. Only at this time do we have this need and this possibility. [When they said] "the struggle must be deepened" they were also entirely correct. Only the phrase "the latent forces of feudalism" is wrong. This is just their [negative] way of saying "the people's democratic dictatorship, which is based on the alliance of the workers and peasants and is under the leadership of the proletariat and the Communist Party"; just as "mechanistic theory" is their ironic phrase for "dialectical materialism."[60]

* * *

This Zhang Zhongxiao again. His counterrevolutionary sensitivities are quite keen. His level of class awareness is much higher and his political senses are far more acute than [those of] a great many people in our revolutionary ranks, including some Communist Party members. By comparison in this regard, many of our people don't come close to the people in the Hu Feng clique. Our people must study, raise their class consciousness and vigilance, and sharpen their political senses. If there is anything positive the Hu Feng clique can give us, it is that this soul-wrenching struggle can greatly raise our political consciousness and political sensitivity and enable us to firmly suppress all counterrevolutionary elements. This will greatly consolidate our revolutionary dictatorship so that we may carry the revolution through to the end and reach the goal of constructing a great socialist country.[61]

Notes

1. Hu Feng's "self criticism" was published on May 13, 1955, in *RMRB*.

2. Shu Wu was a writer whose works were published in the journal *Xiwang* (Hope), edited by Hu Feng, in 1945. His "article" here refers to the article "Guanyu Hu Feng fandang jituan de yixie cailiao" (Some Materials on the Hu Feng Counterrevolutionary Clique), published in *RMRB* on May 13, 1955, and represented the first collection of incriminating evidence against Hu Feng. This article is collected in *Hu Feng cailiao*, pp. 7-22.

3. The first half of the saying here, *ni sha ju xia*, cannot be traced and may be of Mao's own coinage. The second half, *yu long hunzha*, is derived from the poem "Zui yan shi" (Poem on a Drinking Banquet) by Li Longji, Emperor Xuanzhong of the Tang dynasty (reigning 712-756). It

refers originally to the mingling of people of different statuses and identities.

4. The *RMRB* version here has "literary" instead of "counterrevolutionary."

5. This refers to a criticism made by Guo Moruo in 1947 in his article in *Wenyi bao* "Xiang qi liao zhuo yingtao shu de gushi" (Reminded of the Story of Chopping Down the Cherry Tree), in which Guo described the indiscriminate attacks made by the critics associated with Hu Feng on the works of "progressive writers" such as Ba Jin as comparable to the story of George Washington's chopping down the cherry tree. On April 3, 1947, Lu Ling discussed the Guo article in a letter to Hu Feng. (Excerpt in section 50 of the third batch of Hu Feng materials here.)

6. Lu Ling, a playwright whose dramatic writing, especially "Yun Que" (The Lark) which was produced in Nanjing in 1947, was highly praised by Hu Feng.

7. This metaphor derives from the 59th *hui* of the classical novel *Xiyou ji* (Journey to the West), in which Sun Wukong, the Monkey King, who is a chief character in the novel, transforms himself into a bug and creeps into the belly of his adversary, the Princess with the Iron Fan.

8. See text June 6, 1950(1), note 11.

9. This description of the tendency for the Chinese people to be in disunity is attributed to Sun Yat-sen.

10. Mao is here referring to the letter written by Hu Feng to Zhang Zhongxiao on August 13, 1950, excerpted and presented as section 43 in this second collection of materials (p. 67 in the book).

11. See text Feb. 18, 1951, note 2, and texts in Dec. 1950 and Jan. 1951.

12. (*Book*, pp. 67-68; *Xuanji*, V, pp. 157-159; not in *RMRB*.) This section is Mao's commentary on Hu Feng's letter to Zhang Zhongxiao on August 13, 1950 (see previous note). English translations of this section are available in *SW*, V, pp. 172-175, and J. Chen (1970), pp. 51-54.

13. The Chinese here is *pengdang*, which refers to political coalitions that were formed, in traditional China, among officials who shared a common background or political viewpoint. The term derives from *Zhanguo ce* (The Book of the Warring States), in the section on the state of Zhao.

14. The term "stalls," originally *tanzi* in Chinese, is used in the CPC to indicate the appearance of factions in public. The term originates from the practice of hawkers displaying their merchandise on the ground along much-traveled pedestrian thoroughfares and is used, in this way, usually with a derogatory connotation.

15. The *Wenyi bao* affair refers to the uproar that was caused by the role played by the editorial board of that paper, particularly Feng Xuefeng, in defending Yu Pingbo in the earlier controversy over the interpretation of the novel *Hongloumeng*, and the critique of both the novel and that paper that ensued among literary circles after October 1954. This affair was the fuse for the eruption of the campaign against Hu Feng. See notes for text Oct. 16, 1954.

16. See text Mar. 31, 1955, note 15.

17. (*Book*, pp. 82-83; *Xuanji*, V, pp. 162-163; not in *RMRB*.) This section is Mao's comment on Hu Feng's letters to Zhang Zhongxiao on October 27, 1954, November 2, 1954, November 14, 1954, to Fang Ran and Qi Fang on November 7, 1954, and to Fang Ran on November 14, 1954.

18. (*Book*, p. 87; *RMRB* (May 24 1955); excerpt in *Jiaoyu yulu*, p. 9; not in *Xuanji*.) This is Mao's commentary on letters written by Hu Feng to Zhang Zhongxiao and Fang Ran in February 1955. The sentences "find a second life in patient suffering," etc., are contained in Hu's letter to Zhang on February 8, 1955.

19. The *RMRB* (June 10, 1955), 2-3, version does not include "imperialism" here.

20. According to Li Liming (1977), p. 347, Chen was actually a native of Shaanxi Province. He was born in 1915. Chen was a member of the League of Left-wing Writers. He was referred to as "Mei *xiong* (Brother Mei)" in Hu Feng's correspondence.

21. This refers to the central training institute for CPC cadres and military officers in the Red Army, established at Yanan from 1936 to 1945. Originally known as the Resist Japan Red Army University (Kangri hongjun daxue), it changed its name to the Chinese People's Anti-Japanese Military and Political University (Zhongguo renmin kangri junzheng daxue) in July 1937. Throughout it was also known as "Kangda." In July 1939 its headquarters was moved out of

Yanan to North China, and branches were set up in southeast Shanxi, in the Shanxi-Chahar-Hebei Border Region, and in Shandong Province. See text June 6, 1950(2), note 3.

22. The reference here is to the Wartime Political Cadres Training Corps of the KMT for which Hu Zongnan was responsible. See text Feb. 27, 1950, note 1.

23. This is an abbreviation for the Army Staff College, which was an institute for the training of army officers and military cadres of the KMT. It was originally located at Taoyuan in northern Hunan, and when the KMT government abandoned Hankou for Chongqing in late 1938, it was transferred first to Zunyi in Guizhou then subsequently (in name more than in physical structure) to Chongqing itself which served as Chiang Kai-shek and the KMT government's headquarters for the remainder of the war years. Shandong (referring, in this case, not to the province, but meaning "the cave") is the name of a location in the vicinity of Chongqing.

24. According to Li Liming (1977), p. 347, A Long (Chen Yimen) did not go from the Wartime Political Cadres Training Corps to the Army College, but rather joined the instructor staff of the Corps after graduating fom the Army College in 1939. Also, he studied at the Yanan "Kangda" in 1936.

25. Duan Qirui (1863-1936). A leader of the Anfu clique of the Beiyang warlords who dominated Chinese politics for two decades after the Revolution and the establishment of the Republic in 1911, Duan began as a close and faithful follower of Yuan Shikai and was appointed prime minister of the Beiyang government by Yuan before his death. During the ineffectual regimes under presidents Li Yuanhong, Feng Guozhang and Xu Shichang, Duan continued to aggrandize his own military power, and by the early 1920s had emerged, with Zhang Zuolin and Feng Yuxiang, as one of the three most powerful warlords in North China and became a dominant figure in the warlords politics throughout the 1920s. For more biographical information on Duan, see H. Boorman et al., eds. (1970), III, pp. 330-335.

26. According to Hu Feng's letter to A Long (Chen Yimen) on September 26, 1947, presented in excerpt here (p. 90 of book of materials) as the first piece of material in the third collection, Chen Zuo was the chief of police of Beijing under the KMT in 1946. The argument that Hu was connected with Chen Zuo, and hence with the KMT secret service, is based on this letter in which Hu asked A Long to go to Chen Zuo to argue for the release of Jin Zhifang, a friend of Hu's who had been arrested by the KMT for association with the Communist movement.

27. Book, pp. 88-90; RMRB (June 10, 1955), but not in Xuanji.

28. (Book, pp. 91-92; RMRB; not in Xuanji.) This is Mao's commentary on the first four "selections" in the third collection of materials, which were letters between Hu and A Long on September 26 and 28, 1957, October 1, 1947, and July 15, 1946. (Book, pp. 90-91).

29. The identity of Lu Yuan has never been fully disclosed. Dagang bao was a civilian-sponsored and -managed newspaper with no ostensible government or political affiliations. It was connected systematically to Daguang bao in Guangzhou and Li bao of Changsha, Hengyang, and Guilin. At the time described here, Dagang bao was located both in Hankou (cited as Wuhan here) and Nanjing. The Hankou Dagang bao was under the general editorship of Liu Renxi when Zeng Zuo took over in 1949. Later, Lu Yuan, who apparently aided Zeng Zuo in the takeover, was assigned to Changjiang ribao (Yangtze River Daily).

30. (Book, pp. 92-93; RMRB; not in Xuanji.) This is Mao's commentary on two letters written by Lu Yuan to Hu Feng from Chongqing on May 13, 1944, and to A Long and Liu Deqing on September 23, 1947, from Wuhan. ("Selections" 5 and 6 in "Third Collection.")

31. (Book, pp. 96-97; RMRB; not in Xuanji.) This is Mao's comment on A Long's letters cited as sections 15-18 in the book at this point. These were letters to Luo Lo (July 31, 195?, and August 30, 195?), to Hu Feng (August 16, 1951), and to Mei Zhi (August 24, 1951). Here the RMRB version omits seven characters, represented here by "must not be insensitive and careless."

32. According to Ciyu jianshi, p. 102, Lu was originally a military officer in the KMT forces and an instructor of the KMT "Communism-liquidation" corps. He joined the KMT in 1937 and became a Communist cadre in 1945. According to the material gathered here in these collections, Lu was active as a "Hu Feng element" in Tianjin. In his letter to Hu Feng on May 7, 1952, he suggested to Hu that "you must adopt the tactical method of attacking, which is not to wait for them to raise questions about you, but first to go to the higher levels of authority and bring out

your views about the current literary movement; in other words, to give them a blow on the head."

33. This refers to a "report" made by Hu Feng to the Central Committee of the CPC in 1954, in which he criticized the Party line on literature and art, especially the "principles" laid down by Mao in the Yanan Forum of May 1942. In this report Hu said that the Party line imposed unduly on artists and writers the "three clubs" (of workers, peasants, and soldiers) and the "five swords" (of "the forced coordinations between literary and artistic work and the worker-peasant-soldier alliance," "the need for artists and writers to undergo thought reform," "the Communist world-view," "the nationalist form," and "serving the interests of politics"). He described Mao's speech at the Yanan forum as "totemism." According to the notes to selection 52 in the second collection of materials here, Hu was accused of having gathered many of his collaborators in Beijing to discuss and draft this report. (See *Book*, p. 77.)

34. This refers to Hu's speeches at the Enlarged Joint Meetings of the Presidium of the Chinese Federation of Literary and Artistic Circles and the Presidium of the Chinese Association of Writers. Hu made speeches at the second and third of these meetings, of which there were eight in all from October 31 to December 8, 1954. This speech was published in issue no. 22 of *Wenyi bao* in 1954. The meeting was convened to review the issue of *Wenyi bao*, triggered by the *Honglou-meng* affair. (See notes to text October 16, 1954.)

35. (*Book*, pp. 99-100, and *Xuanji*, V, pp. 163-164.) This is Mao's commentary on Lu Dian's letter to Hu Feng on May 7, 1952.

36. (*Book*, p. 100; *RMRB*; and *Xuanji*, V, p. 164.) This is Mao's commentary on Lu Yuan's letter to Hu Feng on May 18, 1952.

37. (*Book*, p. 101; *RMRB*; not in *Xuanji*.) This is Mao's commentary on Fang Ran's letter to Hu Feng on May 5, 1954. In this letter Fang suggested three ways to pose an attitude of being close to the Communist Party: (1) Submit theoretical essays and opinions and submit applications for membership to the Party; (2) Actively take part in literary as well as social activities; do not decline invitations to forums and such; and (3) Do not make complaints to anyone.

38. See texts October 1954 and October 16, 1954.

39. (*Book*, p. 102; *RMRB*; not in *Xuanji*.) This is a commentary to A Long's letter to Hu Feng on November 15, 1954.

40. (*Book*, pp. 103-104; *RMRB*; not in *Xuanji*.) This is a commentary to Lu Yuan's letter to Hu Feng on July 23, 1950, in which he talked about the impending expiration of the term of probation on his CPC membership application.

41. (*Book*, p. 104; *RMRB*; and *Xuanji*, V, pp. 164-165.) This is a Mao commentary on Ouyang Zhuang's letter to Hu Feng on June 24, 1951, in which he described a prospective "comrade" in Suzhou.

42. (*Book*, p. 105; *RMRB*.) This commentary is in response to Lu Ling's letter to Hu Feng on January 30, 1952.

43. See note 33.

44. (*Book*, p. 106; *RMRB*; not in *Xuanji*.) This is a commentary on Lu Dian's letters to Hu Feng on April 4, April 7, and April 18, 1952.

45. (*Book*, p. 107; *RMRB*; not in *Xuanji*.) This is a commentary on more of Lu Dian's letters (May 7 and June 9, 1952) to Hu Feng.

46. *Book*, p. 110; *RMRB*; not in *Xuanji*.

47. See note 33. Also see Mao, *SW*, III, pp. 69 ff.

48. This is a commentary on Zhang Zhongxiao's letter to Hu Feng on August 22, 1951. (*Book*, pp. 111-112; *RMRB*; not in *Xuanji*.)

49. Chao Cuo was a legal scholar who became a confidant of the Emperor Jingdi of the Han dynasty (reigning 156-141 B.C.) He counselled the reduction of the size of the fiefdoms held by the feudal lords of the realm and thereby triggered a rebellion of the nobility led by the princes of Wu and Chu. He was subsequently executed. The term for "purifying the ranks of the emeperor's counsellors" is *qing jun ze* (literally, to clean up that which stands next to the sovereign.) It is indeed a common slogan for insurrectionary forces during China's imperial period.

50. Lin was, at the time, deputy director of the Office of the Literary and Education Council of

the State Council and member of the executive committee (and Presidium) of the Chinese Association of Writers. He Qifang was a member of both the Presidium of the Chinese Association of Writers and the Chinese Federation of Literary and Artistic Circles. Zhou was vice-chairman of both organizations, and at the same time deputy director of the Propaganda Department of the CPC. All three played a role in the active criticism of Yu Pingbo in the *Hongloumeng* Affair and in the convening of the joint meeting of the two federations, at which Hu Feng announced his criticism of the Party line on literature. (See notes to text October 16, 1954, and note 12 here.) For more detailed biographies of these people, see *Zhonggong renming lu*, Li Liming (1977), and text Oct. 16, 1954, note 4.

51. (*Book*, p. 115; *RMRB*; not in *Xuanji*.) This is a commentary on Lu Dian's letters to Lu Yuan on December 27, 1951.

52. See note 33.

53. With the exception of Wen Yiduo, short literary biographies of these famed writers of modern China are found in Li Liming (1977). For Mao Dun see under Shen Yanbing.

54. (*Book*, p. 119; *RMRB*; not in *Xuanji*.) This is a commentary on letters received by Hu Feng from Lu Yuan (April 1, 1952), Qi Fang (March 24, 1947), Lu Ling (April 3 and May 7, 1947), and Lu Dengtai (undated), in which the works of Guo Moruo and Lao She were specifically criticized.

55. The Qing dynasty in China existed from 1644 to 1911, when it was overthrown by the Republican Revolution. In 1912, Yuan Shikai, who had been governor of Zhili Province and grand minister of Beiyang, became provisional president of the Republic of China and established a government in Beijing known as the Beiyang government. (The term Beiyang, or Northern Seas, refers, in the late Qing, to the area of northern China encompassing the several northern coastal provinces such as Liaoning, Hebei, and Shandong.)

After Yuan's death, the political system he had created fell apart, with his erstwhile lieutenants split up into various factions: the Anhui clique controlled largely by Duan Qirui (see note 25) and supported by the Japanese; the Fengtian clique, also supported by Japan, controlled by Zhang Zuolin; and the Zhili clique controlled by Feng Guozhang, Cao Kun and Wu Peifu were the major cliques. Since these warlords were mostly formerly affiliated with Yuan Shikai and derived their military power from his "Beiyang" Army, they were known as Beiyang warlords. It should be noted that these were only the bigger warlords, and there were many others, some aligned with the Beiyang cliques and others independent of them. The Beiyang cliques, however, contended against each other for power and influence mostly in North and Central China, and for control of the government in Beijing, which constantly changed hands in the most sporadic fashion. This plunged China into intermittent civil war and total disintegration, a situation that continued until 1927, when the Northern Expedition of the Republican Army controlled by the KMT and warlords of south and western China aligned with the KMT succeeded in ousting at long last the Beiyang government and "unifying" China. For more details on this period of Chinese history, see J. Sheridan (1975), particularly Ch. 3.

By Japanese militarism Mao refers to the phenomenon of Japanese militarist imperialist expansion beginning in the late-1920s in Korea and extending over northern China in the early and mid-1930s, which in turn led to Japan's occupation of most of China in the late 1930s, all of which occurred before Pearl Harbor and Japan's involvment in the Pacific War with the United States during the period of the Second World War. For more details on this see J. Crowley, ed. (1970), pp. 235 ff., R. Butow (1961), and Y. Maxon (1957).

56. (*Book*, pp. 121-122; *RMRB*; and *Xuanji*, V, pp. 165-166.) This is Mao's comment on Lu Dian's letter to Hu Feng on June 20, 195?. The various descriptions quoted in this comment are verbatim from the letter.

57. These last two sentences here appear only in the *RMRB* version.

58. This refers to Niu Han, whose letter to Hu Feng on February 3, 1952, preceded this comment.

59. *Book*, pp. 122-123; *RMRB*; not in *Xuanji*.

60. (*Book*, pp. 124-125; *RMRB*; and *Xuanji*, V, pp. 166-167.) This is Mao's comment on a letter written by Zhang Zhongxiao to Hu Feng on May 25, 1951.

61. (*Book*, p. 125; *RMRB*; and *Xuanji*, V, p. 167.) This is Mao's comment on a letter from Zhang Zhongxiao to Hu Feng on July 27, 1950.

Letter to Tan Shiying

(June 8, 1955)

Source: *Shuxin*, pp. 496-497.

See text May 17, 1955.

Dear Shiying:[1]

I have received your letter of June 4 and your masterpiece. Thank you very much. I approve of your idea of returning to your native village soon.

The *xian* committee of the Chinese Communist Party of Xiangxiang [*xian*] sent me a letter (I also received one from the Party branch of the *xiang*) which clarified a few things concerning your family's circumstances. According [to these reports]: your two sons are indeed guilty; this is because, even after having been forgiven and released several times, they kept returning to their criminal ways, and because they have committed serious crimes. Therefore it is only their just deserts that the government and the people have dealt with them in accordance with the law. On your part, [it was decided that] you only have some of the shortcomings brought over from the old society and a few improprieties regarding the attitude with which you have treated your two sons. For that reason you have been subjected to a year of probationary control and surveillance; now that has been lifted. The letter of the *xian* [Party] committee indicates that they have not found you guilty of anything else. I think that the comments that the *xian* [Party] committee made regarding you are fair and just.

You ought to [learn to] look at problems from the perspective of the fundamental changes between the old and the new societies, and gradually change around your own thoughts and temperament. In this way you can become more open-minded, and you can change and get rid of some of your faults and lead your entire family in promoting diligence and hard work at production. The most important thing is for you to obey the laws and ordinances of the government and listen to the cadres. In this way, in a few years, people's attitude toward you will change even more for the better.

If you feel the need to do so, you may show this letter to the comrades in positions of responsibility in the *xian*, or district, or *xiang*.

I wish you peace.

Mao Zedong
June 8, 1955.

Note

1. Mao used the salutation *xiong* here. For an explanation of this usage, see text Mar. 14, 1950, note 2.

Conversation with Soldiers
(Excerpt)

(June 17, 1955)

Source: Quoted in Lin Jinlai, "Zai Mao zhuxi jia li zuo ke" (As a Guest at Chairman Mao's Home), in *Zhongguo qingnian*, 1 (Jan. 1, 1959), 28.

We whose job is to make revolution must be prepared to be maligned. As a matter of fact, being maligned by [our] enemies is something for us to be happy about.

On Swimming
[Excerpts]

(June 20, 1955)

Source: "Mao zhuxi youyong de gushi" (Stories of Chairman Mao Swimming) in *Tiyu bao* (May 31, 1965). Other Chinese Text: *Xin tiyu*, 3 (Feb. 6, 1959), 3-4.

These are our own excerpts from the source, which is a news story on Mao's experience in swimming and using the practice of swimming in public to touch base with the common people and cadres. The article contains reports of many such incidences; the excerpts here are of the more important pronouncements Mao made on one such an occasion on this day.

Whether the water is clean or muddy is not the main criterion for determining whether or not the water is suitable for swimming. The point you raise here does not merit concern. Did Zhuang Zi not say: "Unless water is accumulated to a great depth it is powerless to carry big boats"?[1] The deeper the water, the greater its buoyancy, and the more convenient it makes for swimming. How can you say that it is not suitable [for swimming]? I need no rest unless I am tired. I'll not board the boat until I get to my destination.

Note

1. This is a sentence from the book *Zhuang Zi* in the chapter "Xiao yao you" (On Free Roaming). The book is a collection of essays attributed for the most part to Zhuang Zhou, a philosopher of the Warring States period (ca. fifth to third century B.C.).

Telegram to Jamsarangyin Sambuu
(June 27, 1955)

Source: *RMRB* (June 29, 1955), 1. Other Chinese Text: *XHYB*, 7 (July 28, 1955), 89. Available English Translation: HNA, *Daily News Release* (June 29, 1955), 3.

Chairman,
The Presidium of the Greater People's Hural,
The Mongolian People's Republic

Comrade J. Sambuu:

On the occasion of your sixtieth birthday, I extend to you sincere and warm congratulations on behalf of the People's Republic of China and on my own behalf.
(Signed as Chairman of PRC, dated in Beijing)

Toast to Ho Chi Minh

(June 28, 1955)

Source: *RMRB* (June 29, 1955), 1. Other Chinese Text: *XHYB*, 7 (July 28, 1955), 3. Available English Translations: HNA, *Daily News Release* (June 29, 1955), 1-2; FBIS, *Daily Report* (June 29, 1955), AAA8.

I propose that we drink:
To the intimate friendship between the Chinese and Vietnamese peoples,
To peace in Asia and the world,
To the visit to China of President Ho Chi Minh and the delegation of the government of the Democratic Republic of Viet Nam led by him,
To President Ho Chi Minh's health,
To the health of the host of today's banquet – Ambassador Hoang Van Hoan,
Bottoms up!

Reply to Ambassador of the Federal People's Republic of Yugoslavia

(June 30, 1955)

Source: *RMRB* (July 1, 1955), 1. Other Chinese Text: *XHYB*, 7(July 28, 1955), 89-90. Available English Translation: HNA, *Daily News Release*, (July 1, 1955), 5.

Popovic became ambassador of the Federal People's Republic of Yugoslavia to the PRC at this time.

Mr. Ambassador:
I am very glad to accept the letter of credence from the President of the Federal People's Republic of Yugoslavia which you have presented, and thank you for your greetings.
The various peoples of Yugoslavia have a glorious revolutionary tradition.

The Chinese people express sincere congratulations to the Yugoslavian people for their efforts in achieving independence for their homeland and building happy lives [for their people]. The recent discussions carried on between the governments of Yugoslavia and the Soviet Union and its results were important contributions to world peace and the cause of human progress.[1]

Now, the two countries of Yugoslavia and China have already established diplomatic relations. Our two countries have a common desire to develop mutual friendship and cooperation in the areas of politics, economy, and culture. I deeply believe that the strengthening of the friendly relations between our two peoples and governments not only conforms to the interests of the two countries of China and Yugoslavia, but also has great significance in the cause of promoting world peace and cooperation.

Mr. Ambassador, I warmly welcome you as the ambassador extraordinary and plenipotentiary of the Federal People's Republic of Yugoslavia to the People's Republic of China. In your work of developing the friendship and cooperation between China and Yugoslavia, you will receive my assistance and support and that of the government of the People's Republic of China.

I wish you success in your work.

Note

1. Talks between the USSR and Yugoslavia, with the purpose of improving relations between the two countries, began on May 27, 1955, and concluded with an agreement on June 2, 1955. The agreement did not completely resolve the ideological differences between the Communist parties of the two countries, but was rather a declaration of resumption of diplomatic relations between the two states. The USSR delegation was headed by Khrushchev.

Telegram to the People's Republic of Mongolia
(July 9, 1955)

Source: *RMRB* (July 11, 1955), 1. Other Chinese Text: *XHYB*, 8 (Aug. 8, 1955), 260. Available English Translation: HNA, *Daily News Release* (July 11, 1955), 1.

Comrade Jamsarangyin Sambuu, Chairman of the Presidium of the Greater People's Hural of the Mongolian People's Republic,
Comrade Yumjaagiyn Tsedenbal, Prime Minster of the Mongolian People's Republic,
Comrade S. Lavdan, Acting Minister of Foreign Affairs of the Mongolian

People's Republic:

On the occasion of the thirty-fourth anniversary of the victory of the Mongolian people's revolution, on behalf of the government and people of the People's Republic of China, I express sincere congratulations to the government and people of the Mongolian People's Republic.

The government and people of the People's Republic of China note with happiness and excitement the brilliant successes achieved in the past thirty-four years by the Mongolian People's Republic in its cause of construction in advancing toward socialism. We wish the Mongolian people, under the leadership of the long-tested Mongolian People's Revolutionary Party, even greater victories in triumphantly carrying out the second five-year plan for the development of the national economy and culture and in the struggle to defend world peace.

(Co-signed as Chairman of PRC with Liu Shaoqi as Chairman of Standing Committee of NPC and Zhou Enlai as Premier of State Council and Foreign Minister, dated in Beijing)

Telegram to the People's Republic of Poland

(July 19, 1955)

Source: *RMRB* (July 22, 1955), 1. Other Chinese Text: *XHYB*, 8 (Aug. 28, 1955), 260. Available English Translations: HNA, *Daily News Release* (July 22, 1955), 22; FBIS, *Daily Report* (July 22, 1955), AAA10-11.

Comrade Aleksander Zawadzki, Chairman of the Council of State of the People's Republic of Poland,
Comrade Jozef Cyrankiewicz, Chairman of the Council of Ministers of the People's Republic of Poland,
Comrade Stanislaw Skrzeszewski, Minister of Foreign Affairs of the People's Republic of Poland:

On the occasion of the eleventh anniversary of the National Day of the People's Republic of Poland, on behalf of the government and people of the People's Republic of China we express sincere congratulations to you and, through you, to the government and people of the People's Republic of Poland.

In the last eleven years, under the correct leadership of the Polish United Workers' Party and with the Soviet Union's unselfish assistance, the Polish people have attained tremendous successes in the area of socialist construction. As a result of the successful implementation of the six-year plan, which laid the economic foundation of socialism, the People's Republic of Poland has already become a socialist industrialized country with a tremendous economic potential.

The prosperity and wealth of the People's Republic of Poland greatly adds to the strength of the socialist camp for world peace and democracy headed by the Soviet Union and to the forces defending world peace. For this the Chinese people are joyful and encouraged.

The Chinese people wish our brothers the Polish people even greater success in the cause of building socialism. May the friendship between the two peoples of China and Poland be consolidated and developed with each passing day in their continuous struggle to ease international tension and safeguard world peace.

(Co-signed as Chairman of PRC with Liu Shaoqi as Chairman of Standing Committee of NPC and Zhou Enlai as Premier of State Council and Foreign Minister, dated in Beijing)

On the Cooperativization of Agriculture
(July 31, 1955)

Source: *Xuanji*, V, pp. 168-191. Other Chinese Texts: *RMRB* (Oct. 17, 1955), 1-2; *Xuandu* A, pp. 295-317; *Guanyu nongye huozuohua wenti*, pp. 1-38; *Buyi*, pp. 42-62; *Gaizao wenji*, III, pp. 9-30. *XHYB*, 11 (Nov. 28, 1955), 1-13; *ZFYJ*, 6 (Dec. 1955), 1-10. Available English Translations: *SW*, V, pp. 184-207; *SR* (1971), pp. 289-420.

Minor variations exist among the various Chinese versions listed here, particularly between the Xuanji *and the* RMRB *versions.*

Mao's speech on the cooperativization of agriculture marked a decisive intervention in the struggle over agricultural collectivization. Although the struggle had been going on within the CPC since land reform had been basically completed in 1953, the lagging agricultural growth rates through 1956 – the midpoint of the First Five-Year Plan – forced the issue of agricultural policy to the forefront. During this struggle, many within the CPC national leadership, including Liu Shaoqi, had argued that in this period the need for accumulation from agricultural production to finance industrial development could best be

*met by relying primarily on consolidating the rich peasant economy, i.e., pro-
viding the conditions that would allow the most skilled and best equipped peasants to increase production most rapidly, and only secondarily on collectivization. Thus in line with the position of the Soviet Union at that time, they argued
that collectivization must be postponed until mechanization of agriculture had
at least been begun.*

*Mao, to the contrary, argued that such a policy could lead to increased polar-
ization in the countryside. Thus, although these policies might allow for rapid
accumulation, they would do so in such a way as to develop the conditions for
the reemergence of classes in the countryside. Therefore, he argued for primary
reliance on a rapid cooperativization of agriculture[1] and for the first time chal-
lenged the prevailing Soviet model of socialist development.*

*In July 1955 the opposition to Mao had the upper hand. The plan adopted by
the NPC in July called for postponing collectivization until the economy was
capable of producing sufficient machinery and the other requisite factors to
allow for full-scale mechanization of agriculture, and until 70 to 80 per cent of
the peasantry had become rich peasants.*

*Mao strongly opposed this approach and the consequences to which he feared
it would lead. Therefore, on the day following the NPC, he addressed a conference of secretaries of provincial, municipal, and autonomous region Party committees – who, he felt, would be more supportive of his position than the Central
Committee – with his position on agricultural cooperativization. He argued that
immediate and rapid collectivization would not only increase accumulation, but
would do so in a way favorable to the development of the further revolutioniza-
tion of China's economy.[2] Subsequently, in October 1955, at an enlarged meeting of the Central Committee – which was attended by 338 regional Party secretaries, as opposed to only 38 Central Committee members and 25 Central
Committee alternative members – the "Resolution on the Question of Agricultural Cooperativization," which was based largely on Mao's position, was
passed. But victory in the struggle for acceptance of this position did not mean
that Mao's suggestions were carried out as planned. Once the country got
caught up in the struggle for rapid collectivization, the pace of collectivization
far outstripped anything suggested either by Mao himself or by the Resolution.[3]
Mao's preoccupation with the problem of agricultural cooperativization for the
remainder of 1955 and 1956 is evident in the many speeches and writings on the
subject in this period. As we shall see, the issue was not merely a major
program of the transformation of the agricultural base of the Chinese economy,
which it was, but also a problem of ideological and policy struggle in Chinese
society at large (with "conservative" intellectuals such as Liang Shuming) and
within the Party (with, for example, Liu Shaoqi and the Rural Work Department). On this issue, the CPC published two major sets of documents:*

1) Shi Jingtang, Zhang Lin, Zhou Qinghe, Bi Zhongjie, eds. Zhongguo nongye
hezuohua yundong shiliao *(Materials on the History of the Movement for the
Cooperativization of Agriculture in China) (1957, Sanlian chubanshe, Beijing),
2 volumes, with vol. 1 concentrating on pre-Liberation conditions and vol. 2 on
the situation from 1953 to 1955;*

2) Nongye shehui zhuyi gaizao wenji *(Documents on the Socialist Transformation
of Agriculture) (1955, Caizheng jingji chubanshe, Shanghai), 3 volumes.
(Herein abbreviated as* Gaizao wenji.*) This article is contained in vol. 3 of this
latter set, pp. 9-30.*

I

A high tide in the new socialist mass movement will soon sweep across the rural areas throughout the country. Some of our comrades, however, are tottering along like a woman with bound feet,[4] complaining all the time about others, saying: [You're] going too fast, [you're] going too fast. [They are given to] excessive nitpicking, unwarranted complaints, endless worries, and countless taboos and take this to be the correct policy for guiding the socialist mass movement in the rural areas.

No, this is not the correct policy; it is a wrong policy.

At present, the high tide of the social transformation of cooperativization in the countryside is already evident in some areas and will soon engulf the whole country. This is a large-scale socialist revolutionary movement involving a rural population of over five hundred million and has tremendous worldwide significance. We should give this movement active, enthusiastic, and well-planned leadership, rather than dragging it back by all sorts of means. That there are some deviations in the movement is unavoidable. It is understandable and also not hard to rectify. Shortcomings and errors that exist among cadres and peasants can be overcome or corrected provided we actively help them. The cadres and peasants are advancing under the leadership of the Party, and the movement is basically sound. In some places, they have made mistakes in their work. For example, on the one hand, [some] poor peasants have been prevented from joining the cooperatives in disregard of their difficulties; on the other hand, [some] well-to-do middle peasants have been forced to join the cooperatives in violation of their interests.[5] On all of these things people should be educated and corrected instead of simply being reprimanded. Blunt reprimands cannot solve problems. We must guide the movement boldly and not fear dragons ahead and tigers behind. Both cadres and peasants will remold themselves through their own experience in struggle. We should let them get down to doing the work, and they will draw lessons and enhance their talents while doing it. In this way, large numbers of outstanding people will come to the fore. The attitude of fearing dragons ahead and tigers behind is not conducive to the making of [good] cadres. Large numbers of cadres with short-term training must be sent to the countryside from the higher levels to guide and assist the cooperativization movement, but even cadres sent down from higher levels can only learn how to do their work by being in the movement [themselves]. They may not necessarily know how to do their work just by attending a training class and listening to an instructor lecture on several dozen points.

In short, the leadership should not fall behind the mass movement. Yet, as things stand now, it is the mass movement that is running ahead of the leadership, and the leadership is unable to catch up with the movement. This situation must be changed.

II

The nationwide cooperativization movement is now moving forward on a giant scale, and yet we still have to argue such questions as whether the cooperatives can develop and whether they can be consolidated. As far as certain comrades are concerned, the crux of the matter seems to be their worry about whether the several hundred thousand existing semisocialist and generally rather small cooperatives (averaging twenty-odd households each) can be consolidated.[6] If they cannot be consolidated, their development is, of course, out of the question. Despite the record of the development of [agricultural] cooperativization in the last few years, certain comrades still remain skeptical; they still want to see how things develop during this year, 1955. They may even want to wait and see for another year in 1956. Only if more cooperatives are consoilidated will they be truly convinced that agricultural cooperativization is feasible and that the policy of the Central Committee of our Party is correct. Therefore, the work in these two years is of crucial importance.

In order to prove the feasibility of agricultural cooperativization and the correctness of our Party Center's policy regarding agricultural cooperativization, it is perhaps not without benefit for us to review the history of the agricultural cooperativization movement in our country.

During the twenty-two years of revolutionary wars prior to the founding of the People's Republic of China, our Party had already had the experience of guiding the peasants, after the land reform, in forming agricultural producers' mutual aid organizations containing the rudiments of socialism. At that time [these organizations included] the mutual aid labor groups and plowing teams in Jiangxi Province, labor-exchange teams in northern Shaanxi, and mutual aid teams in northern, eastern, and northeastern China.[7] At that time, organizations of semisocialist or socialist agricultural producers' cooperatives had also come into existence already in isolated cases. For example, an agricultural producers' cooperative of a socialist nature came into being in Ansai *xian* in northern Shaanxi during the time of the War of Resistance against Japan.[8] But this type of cooperative was not popularized at that time.

It was after the founding of the People's Republic of China that our Party led the peasants in setting up agricultural producers' mutual-aid teams on a more extensive scale and in starting to organize agricultural producers' cooperatives in large numbers on the basis of [these] mutual aid teams. Nearly six more years has since been added to the history of this work.

By December 15, 1951, when our Party Center adopted the first Draft Resolution on Mutual Aid and Cooperativization in Agricultural Production[9] which had first been issued to local Party organizations and carried out on an experimental basis in various areas (this document was not published in the press in the form of a formal resolution until March 1953),[10] more than 300 agricultural producers' cooperatives had already come into being. Two years later, when our Party Center issued its Resolution on Agricultural Producers' Cooperatives on December 16, 1953,[11] the number of agricultural cooperatives had grown to more than 14,000, a 46-fold increase in the course of two years.

This resolution pointed out that between the winter of 1953 and the autumn harvest season of 1954, the number of agricultural producers' cooperatives was to increase from more than 14,000 to over 35,800; that is to say, an increase of only 150 per cent was contemplated. As it turned out, the number of cooperatives actually rose to 100,000 during this one year, representing more than seven times [the figure of] over 14,000 cooperatives.

In October 1954, the Central Committee of our Party decided on an increase of a further 500 per cent, from 100,000 to 600,000 cooperatives; as it turned out, 670,000 cooperatives were established. By June 1955, after a preliminary readjustment, the number decreased by 20,000 to 650,000, or 50,000 cooperatives more than the planned figure. A total of 16,900,000 peasant households joined the cooperatives, with an average of 26 households in each cooperative.

These cooperatives are to be found mostly in the several northern provinces that were liberated early. As for most of the provinces in the country that were liberated later, a number of agricultural producers' cooperatives have been set up in each of them. More cooperatives have been set up in Anhui and Zhejiang provinces, but there are not many in other provinces.

These cooperatives are generally small, but there are also a few large ones among them, some with 70 to 80 households, others with over a hundred and still others with several hundred.

These cooperatives are generally semisocialist [in nature], but there are a few among them that have developed into higher-stage cooperatives of a socialist nature.[12]

Simultaneous with the development of the cooperativization movement in agricultural production among peasants, a small number of socialist state farms have already come into being in our country.[13] By 1957, the number of state farms will reach 3,038, with a total of 16,870,000 *mu* of cultivated land. Of these, the number of mechanized farms will reach 141 (including those already in existence in 1952 and those to be set up during the period of the First Five-Year Plan), with a total of 7,580,000 *mu* of cultivated land, and the number of nonmechanized state farms [under] local [administration will reach] 2,897, with a total of 9,290,000 *mu* of land under cultivation. State-operated agriculture will undergo a large-scale development during the period of the second and third five-year plans.

In the spring of 1955, our Party Center decided that the number of agricultural producers' cooperatives should increase to one million. This figure, compared to the original [number] of 650,000 cooperatives, [represents] an increase of only 350,000, or only a little over 50 per cent. It seems to me that the increase may be a bit too small. Probably the figure of 650,000 existing cooperatives should be roughly doubled, that is, increase the number of cooperatives to approximately 1.3 million so that the 200,000-odd *xiang* in the country, except in some of the border regions, may each have one or several small agricultural producers' cooperatives of a semisocialist nature to serve as models. These cooperatives will have experience and become old cooperatives after a year or two, and other people will [strive to] learn from them. There are still fourteen months to go between now and the autumn harvest of October 1956; the realization of this plan for establishing cooperatives should be possible. I hope that the comrades responsible for this in the various provinces and autonomous regions will go back and study this matter, make appropriate plans in accordance with concrete circumstances, and report to the Central Committee within two months. We will then discuss the matter again and make a final decision.

The question is whether [the cooperatives] can be consolidated. Some people say that last year's plan to establish 500,000 cooperatives was too big and was adventurist and that this year's plan to establish 350,000 cooperatives is also too big and adventurist. They suspect that so many cooperatives, once established, cannot be consolidated.

Can they be consolidated or not?

Of course neither socialist industrialization nor socialist transformation is an easy job. There are indeed many difficulties involved in getting some 110 million peasant households to switch from individual farming to collective farming and then to proceed to accomplish the technological transformation of agriculture. Nevertheless, we must have confidence that our Party is capable of guiding the masses in overcoming these difficulties.

As far as the question of agricultural cooperativization is concerned, I think we should be confident, first, that the poor peasants and the lower-middle peasants among both the new and old middle peasants[14] who, either because they are in a difficult economic position (as in the case of the poor peasants) or because, even though their economic position has been improved in comparison with that before Liberation, are still not well-off (as in the case of the lower-middle peasants), have a certain enthusiasm about taking the socialist road and are enthusiastic in responding to the Party's call for cooperativization. In particular, those among them who have a higher level of political consciousness have even more of this kind of enthusiasm.

Second, I think we should be confident that the Party is capable of leading the people of the whole country into socialist society. Since our Party has successfully led a great people's democratic revolution[15] and established a people's democratic dictatorship led by the working class, it can certainly lead the people of the whole country in basically accomplishing socialist industrialization and the socialist transformation of agriculture, handicraft industries, and capitalist industry and commerce in the course of roughly three five-year plans. We already have powerful and convincing proof of this in agriculture, as in other fields. Witness [the fact that] the first batch of 300 cooperatives, the second batch of 13,700, and the third batch of 86,000, three batches totaling 100,000 cooperatives, were all established before the autumn of 1954 and have all been consolidated. Why, then, should it not be possible for the fourth batch of cooperatives (550,000) established between 1954 and 1955 and the fifth batch of cooperatives [to be established] between 1955 and 1956 (the tentative control figure is 350,000, yet to be finally determined) to be consolidated as well?

We must have faith in the masses, and we must have faith in the Party. These are two fundamental principles. If we doubt these two principles, we won't be able to accomplish anything.

III

In order to accomplish, step by step, cooperativization throughout the rural areas of the country, we must conscientiously reorganize the existing cooperatives.

We must stress paying attention to the quality of cooperatives and oppose the tendency to pursue only [the increase in] the numbers of cooperatives and of the peasant households [in them] without regard to quality. We must therefore pay attention to the work of reorganizing cooperatives.

Reorganization of cooperatives is not to be done once a year, but rather two or three times a year. A certain number of cooperatives went through a reorganization in the first half of this year (in certain places, the reorganization seems to have been very cursory, conducted without vigorous effort); I suggest that a second reorganization be carried out in the autumn and winter of this year, and a third in the spring and summer of next year. Of the 650,000 cooperatives now in existence, there are 550,000 that are new ones established last winter and this spring, including a batch of so-called "first category cooperatives"[16] that are more consolidated. If we add to these the previous 100,000 old cooperatives that are already consolidated, the number of cooperatives already consolidated is by no means small. Can these cooperatives that are already consolidated lead those yet to be consolidated to achieve gradual consolidation? The answer should definitely be that it is possible.

We should treasure and not thwart any small bit of socialist enthusiasm on the part of the peasants and cadres. We should throw in our lot with the members and cadres of the cooperatives and the cadres of the *xian,* districts, and *xiang* and not thwart their enthusiasm.

Cooperatives that are determined to dissolve are only those in which all, or nearly all, the members are determined not to carry on. In a cooperative, if only some members are determined to quit, let those people withdraw while the majority stay in and carry on. If the majority are determined to quit while only a minority want to carry on, let the majority withdraw and the minority stay in and carry on. Even if this should happen, it will still be a good thing. There is a very small cooperative of only six households in Hebei Province in which three households, [made up of] former old middle peasants, were determined to quit and were consequently allowed to withdraw, while the three households of poor peasants[17] showed that they wanted to continue on no matter what. As a result, they stayed in, and consequently the organization of the cooperative was preserved. Actually, the direction indicated by these three households of poor peasants represents the direction that the five hundred million peasants of the country [will follow]. All peasants [now] operating individually will eventually take the road resolutely chosen by these three households of poor peasants.

The policy of so-called "resolute reduction" adopted in Zhejiang[18] (not a decision made by the Zhejiang Provincial Party Committee) resulted in the dissolution at one stroke of 15,000 cooperatives, comprising 400,000 peasant households, out of 53,000 cooperatives, causing great dissatisfaction among the masses and cadres. This was very unsound. This policy of "resolute reduction" was decided on when they were gripped by a mood of panic. It was also unsound to make such a major move without the approval of the Central Committee. Moreover, in April 1955 the Central Committee had already issued a warning: "Don't repeat the error of dissolving large numbers of cooperatives as committed in 1953 or you will have to make self-criticism again."[19] But some comrades turned a deaf ear [to the warning].

It seems to me that there are two undesirable [tendencies] in the face of victory. First, that victory makes one dizzy and makes one's head swell so much that one commits "leftist" mistakes. This, of course, is bad. Second, that victory scares one silly so as to cause one to call for a "resolute reduction" and commit rightist mistakes. This is also bad. The present situation belongs in the latter category; some comrades have been scared silly by several hundred thousand small cooperatives.

IV

Good preparatory work must be done seriously before cooperatives are established.

The quality of cooperatives must be emphasized from the very beginning, and the tendency to solely seek [the increase of] their numbers must be opposed.

Fight no battle without making preparations for it; fight no battle without being sure of [winning] it. This was the well-known slogan of our Party in the past during the period of the Revolutionary War. This slogan can also be applied to the work of building socialism. To be sure of success, one must be prepared, and be adequately prepared. A great deal of preparatory work must be done before a new batch of agricultural producers' cooperatives can be established in a province, a special district, or a *xian*. Such work, in the main, consists of [the following]: (1) criticizing erroneous ideas and summing up work experience; (2) systematically and repeatedly publicizing among the peasant masses our Party's principles, policies, and measures on agricultural cooperativization; in doing so, we should not only explain [to the peasants] the advantages of cooperativization, but should also point out the difficulties likely to be encountered in the course of cooperativization so that the peasants can be well-prepared mentally; (3) drawing up a comprehensive plan for developing agricultural cooperativization throughout each province, [special] district, *xian*, district, or *xiang* in light of the actual situation and formulating an annual plan out of it; (4) training cadres for running cooperatives through short-term [courses]; (5) developing agricultural mutual aid teams on a wide scale and in large numbers, and wherever possible prevailing upon many teams to join together in organizations of united mutual aid teams so as to lay a good foundation for uniting them further into cooperatives.

If these requirements are met, it will be possible to basically solve the problem of uniting quantity and quality in the development of cooperatives; however, it is still necessary to follow the establishment of each batch of cooperatives by going immediately into the work of reorganization.

Whether a batch of cooperatives, once established, can be consolidated or not depends first on whether the preparatory work before their establishment is done well and second on whether the reorganization work after their establishment is done well.

We must rely on the *xiang* branches of the Party and Youth League[20] for the work of establishing and reorganizing cooperatives. Therefore, the work of establishing and reorganizing cooperatives must be done in close coordination with that of building and rectifying the Party and Youth League organizations in the rural areas.

Whether in establishing cooperatives or in reorganizing them, the local cadres in the rural areas should be the main force. They should be given encouragement and be held responsible for the work. The cadres sent from above should be the auxiliary force, whose function is to provide guidance and assistance and not to take everything into their own hands.

V

In production, the agricultural producers' cooperatives must achieve higher crop yields than "going-it-alone" households and mutual aid teams. On no account should [the cooperatives'] output remain at the same level as that of "going-it-alone" households or mutual aid teams. Otherwise it would mean failure, and then what would be the point in having cooperatives at all? Still less should crop yields be allowed to fall. Over eighty per cent of the 650,000 agricultural producers' cooperatives that have already been established have increased crop yields. This is an excellent situation; it proves that members of agricultural producers' cooperatives have great enthusiasm for production and that cooperatives are superior to mutual aid teams and even more superior to peasant households farming on their own.

To increase crop yields it is necessary: (1) to adhere to the principles of voluntary [participation] and mutual benefit; (2) to improve management (planning of production, management of production, organization of labor, etc.); (3) to improve farming techniques (deep plowing and intensive cultivation, close planting in small clusters, increase in the area of multiple cropping, introduction of improved seed strains, popularization of new types of farming implements, the fight against plant diseases and insect damage, etc.); and (4) to increase the means of production (land, fertilizer, water conservation facilities, draft animals, farming implements, etc.). These are the few indispensable conditions for consolidating the cooperatives and ensuring growth in production.

In adhering to the principles of voluntary [participation] and mutual benefit, attention must now be paid to solving the following problems: (1) whether or not it is proper to delay for a year or two the turning over of draft animals and large farming implements to the cooperatives [as shares], whether or not they are fairly priced when they are turned over to the cooperatives, and whether or not the payment period is too long; (2) whether or not the ratio between the payment for land [shares] and the payment for labor is appropriate; (3) how the funds needed by the cooperatives are to be raised; (4) whether or not certain members of the cooperatives may use part of their labor in certain types of sideline occupations (since the agricultural producers' cooperatives we are now establishing are generally still semisocialist in nature, care must be taken to solve the above-mentioned four problems properly so that the principle of mutual benefit between the poor peasants and the middle peasants is not violated, and voluntary [participation] can only be realized on the basis of mutual benefit); (5) how much [land] members of the cooperatives should retain as private plots;[21] and (6) the question of the class composition of cooperative membership, and so on.

Let's take up the question of the class composition of the cooperatives' membership. I think that, in the next year or two, wherever popularization of cooperatives has just begun or has taken place recently, as in the case of most areas of the country at present, [the cooperatives] should be [made up of] the active elements among the following sectors: (1) poor peasants, (2) lower-middle peasants among the new middle peasants, and (3) lower-middle peasants among the old middle peasants. We should get them to organize first. Those among the members of these sectors who are not yet active elements for the time being should not be dragged in against their will. The cooperatives can admit them in groups when their level of [political] consciousness has risen and they have become interested in cooperatives. People in these sectors have a rather similar economic status. They either are still living a hard life ([as in the case of] poor peasants who have been given land and are much better off than before Liberation, but whose lives are still difficult owing to a shortage of human resources, draft animals, and farming implements) or are still not well-off ([as in the case of] lower-middle peasants). Therefore, they have the enthusiasm to form cooperatives. Even so, their enthusiasm varies in degree for a variety of reasons; some of them are very enthusiastic, others are not so enthusiastic yet, and still others prefer to wait and see. Therefore, we must take a period of time to educate all those who do not want to join cooperatives yet, even though they may be poor or lower-middle peasants; we must patiently wait for them to become [politically] conscious, and we must not violate the principle of voluntary [participation] and drag them in against their will.

As for the upper-middle peasants among the new and old middle peasants, that is, all the middle peasants who are economically relatively well-off, except for some who already have the [political] consciousness to take the socialist road and are really willing to join the cooperatives, and can be admitted, the rest should not be admitted into the cooperatives for the time being, and we certainly should not drag them in against their will. This is because they do not yet have the [political] consciousness to take the socialist road; they will make up their minds to join the cooperatives only when the majority of people in the rural areas have joined, when the per *mu* yield of the cooperatives has reached or even surpassed that of these well-to-do middle peasants and they feel that it is to their disadvantage in all respects to continue to go it alone and that it is in their interest to join the cooperatives.

So those who are economically poor or not well-off (approximately sixty to seventy per cent of the rural population) should first be grouped according to their level of [political] consciousness and should form cooperatives in various batches within a few years, and then the well-off middle peasants will be drawn in. In this way we can avoid commandism.[22]

For the next few years, in all areas where cooperativization has not been basically completed, landlords and rich peasants should resolutely not be accepted into the cooperatives. In areas where cooperativization has basically been completed, those cooperatives that are already consolidated may, under certain conditions, admit by stages and in groups former landlord and rich peasant elements who have long since given up exploitation and who engage in labor and abide by the laws and decrees of the government, and may allow them to participate in collective labor while continuing to reform them through labor.

VI

As far as the development [of cooperativization] is concerned, the question at present is not that of criticizing adventurist advance. It is wrong to say that the present development of cooperatives has "surpassed what is practically possible" and "overtaken the level of [political] consciousness of the masses." This is how things stand in China: [the country has] a vast population, insufficient cultivated land (there are only three *mu* per capita on the average in the country, and one *mu* or even less in many areas of the southern provinces), frequent natural calamities (every year large areas of farmland suffer to varying degrees from flood, drought, windstorm, frost, hail, or insect pests) and backward methods of management. Consequently, though the life of the broad masses of peasants has improved or greatly improved since the land reform, the life of many of them is still difficult; many are still not well-off, and well-off peasants are, relatively speaking, in the minority. Therefore, the majority of the peasants are enthusiastic about taking the socialist road. Their enthusiasm is being daily heightened by our country's socialist industrialization and its achievements. For them there is no way out other than socialism. Peasants in this situation make up sixty to seventy per cent of the country's rural population. In other words, the only way for the majority of the peasants in the country to attain the goal of shaking off poverty, improving their livelihood, and resisting natural calamities is to unite and advance along the high road of socialism. This feeling is rapidly growing among the broad masses of poor peasants and peasants who are not well-off. Well-to-do or fairly well-to-do peasants, who make up only twenty to thirty per cent of the country's rural population, are wavering, and some [of them] are bent on following the capitalist road. As I said earlier, many among the poor peasants and those not well-off, because of their low [political] consciousness, still take a wait-and-see attitude for the time being, and they, too, are wavering. Nevertheless, compared with the well-to-do peasants, it is relatively easy for them to accept socialism. This is the actual existing situation. Yet some of our comrades ignore this situation and choose to believe that the several hundred thousand newly formed small and semisocialist agricultural producers' cooperatives have already "surpassed what is actually possible" and "overtaken the level of the masses' [political] consciousness." This is [because they] are looking only at the comparatively small number of well-to-do peasants while neglecting the overwhelming majority – the poor peasants and those peasants who are not well-off. This is the first kind of wrong thinking.

These comrades also underestimate the strength of the Communist Party's leadership in the countryside and the wholehearted support of the broad masses of peasants for the Communist Party. In their view, since it is difficult enough as it is for our Party to consolidate the several hundred thousand small-scale cooperatives, big expansion is inconceivable. They pessimistically describe the present state of the Party's work of leading agricultural cooperativization as having "outstripped the level of the cadres' experience." True, socialist revolution is a new revolution. In the past we only had experience in bourgeois democratic revolution but not in socialist revolution. Yet how can we gain such experience? Will we gain it by sitting back and doing nothing or will we gain it by plunging into the struggles of socialist revolution and learning amidst the struggles? How can we gain experience in industrialization if we do not carry out the Five-Year Plan and do not engage in undertaking the work of socialist industrialization? Agricultural cooperativization is incorporated in the Five-Year Plan. If we do not guide the peasants in forming one or a few agricultural cooperatives in every *xiang* or village, let me ask you, where will "the level of the cadres' experience" come from and how will it be raised? Evidently, the idea that the present development of the agricultural producers' cooperatives has "outstripped the level of the cadres' experience" is a wrong one. This is the second kind of wrong thinking.

The way these comrades look at problems is wrong. They do not look at the essential or principal aspects of the problems but emphasize things that are not essential or principal in nature. It should be pointed out that problems that are not essential or principal are not to be overlooked but they must be resolved one by one. However, we should not take them to be [something of] essential or principal [importance] and thereby get our bearings confused.

We must have faith, first, that the broad masses of peasants are willing to take, step by step, the socialist road under the leadership of the Party and, second, that the Party is capable of leading the peasants in taking the socialist road. These two points are the essential and principal aspects of the matter. Without this faith we would be unable to basically accomplish the building of socialism in a period of about three five-year plans.

VII

The Soviet Union's great historical experience of completing the construction of socialism inspires the people of our country and gives us full confidence in building socialism in our country. However, there are divergent views even on this question of international experience. Some comrades disapprove of the Party Center's policy of keeping the steps taken toward our country's agricultural cooperativization at pace with those taken toward the country's socialist industrialization, even though this policy has been proven to be a correct one in the Soviet Union.[23] They believe that as far as industrialization is concerned, the speed set at present may be adopted, but that agricultural cooperativization should proceed at a particularly slow pace and need not keep in step with industrialization. This is to ignore the experience of the Soviet Union. These comrades do not realize that socialist industrialization cannot proceed in isolation from the cooperativization of agriculture. In the first place, [as] we all know, the present level of production of commodity grain[24] and industrial raw materials is very low, whereas the state's need for these materials grows year by year. This is a sharp contradiction. If within the period of roughly three five-year plans we cannot basically accomplish the solution of the problem of the cooperativization of agriculture, that is to say, [if we cannot bring about] a leap in agriculture from small-scale farming with animal-drawn farming implements to large-scale mechanized farming, including large-scale state-organized [projects for] migration and resettlement of the [peasant] population and land reclamation involving the use of machinery (the plan is to reclaim 400 to 500 million *mu* of wasteland in the course of three five-year plans), we will not be able to resolve the contradiction between the annually increasing need for commodity grain and industrial raw materials and the generally very low output of staple crops at present, and we will encounter extremely great difficulties in our cause of socialist industrialization and will be unable to accomplish it. The Soviet Union once faced the same problem in the course of building socialism and solved it by guiding and developing agricultural cooperativization in a planned way, and we can only solve the problem by the same method. In the second place, some of our comrades have not considered the following two matters in connection with each other; namely, heavy industry, the most important branch of socialist industrialization,[25] with its production of tractors and other farm machinery, its production of chemical fertilizer, its production of modern means of transportation, oil, electric power for agricultural use, etc., all of this can be utilized, or utilized extensively, only on the basis that agriculture has achieved large-scale cooperativization. We are now engaged not only in a revolution in the social system to transform private ownership into public ownership, but also in a revolution in technology to change from handicraft production to large-scale modern mechanized production, and these two revolutions are interrelated. Under the conditions that prevail in our country, agriculture must go through cooperativization before it can adopt the usage of large machines (in capitalist countries, [this is attained] through the development of agriculture in a capitalist way). Therefore, we should on no account separate industry and agriculture or socialist industrialization and socialist transformation of agriculture, or regard them as two matters isolated from each other, and on no account should we emphasize the one at the expense of the other. On this issue, the Soviet experience has also indicated the direction for us, and yet some of our comrades pay no attention and always see these matters as isolated and unconnected. In the third place, some of our comrades have also not considered the following two matters in connection with each other; namely, large amounts of funds are needed to accomplish national industrialization and the transformation of technology in agriculture, and a considerable portion of them must be accumulated in the area of agriculture. Apart from directly levying taxes on agriculture, this is [to be achieved by] developing production in light industry [to produce] in large quantities consumer goods needed by the peasants, and exchanging them for the peasants' commodity grain and raw materials for light industry, so that the material needs of both the peasants and the state can be met and funds can also be accumulated for the state. Furthermore, large-scale development of light industry requires not only the development of heavy industry, but of agriculture as well. This is because large-scale development of light industry cannot be realized on the basis of a small peasant economy, but depends on large-scale agricultural [operations], which in our country means socialist cooperativized agriculture. This is because only this type of agriculture can give the peasants a purchasing power I don't know how many times greater than the present [level]. The Soviet Union has also furnished us with experience in this matter, but some of our comrades pay no attention [to it]. They always take the stand of the bourgeoisie, the rich peasants, or the well-to-do middle peasants with spontaneous tendencies toward capitalism and look after the interests of the comparatively few. They never take the stand of the working class and look out for the interests of the whole country and people.

VIII

Some comrades have also found a rationale from the history of the Communist Party of the Soviet Union for their criticism of what they call impetuosity and adventurist advance in the present work of agricultural cooperativization in our country. Does not *A Short Course on the History of the Communist Party of the Soviet Union (Bolsheviks)*[26] tell us that during a certain period of time many of the [Soviet Union's] local Party organizations committed the error of impetuosity and adventurist advance[27] on the question of the pace of cooperativization? Should we not pay attention to this international experience?

I think we should pay attention to this Soviet experience and must oppose any impetuous and adventurist thinking that foregoes preparation and disregards the level of political consciousness of the peasant masses, but we should not allow some of our comrades to use this Soviet experience as a smoke screen to cover up their idea of moving at a snail's pace.

What is our Party Center's decision on how to carry out agricultural cooperativization in China?

First, it is prepared to basically accomplish this plan in eighteen years. The period of a little over three years from the founding of the People's Republic of China in October 1949 to 1952 was devoted to accomplishing the task of restoring the economy of our country. In the sphere of agriculture during this period, in addition to carrying out such tasks as the land reform[28] and the restoration of agricultural production, we greatly expanded the organization of agricultural producers' mutual aid teams in all the old liberated areas[29] and also began to organize agricultural producers' cooperatives of a semisocialist nature and gained some experience. This was followed by the First Five-Year Plan, which began in 1953 and has been in operation for nearly three years now, [during which time] our agricultural cooperativization movement has been spreading on a nationwide scale and our experience has likewise increased. The period from the founding of the People's Republic of China to the completion of the Third Five-Year Plan covers eighteen years, during which time we plan to basically accomplish the socialist transformation of agriculture together with the basic completion of socialist industrialization and of socialist transformation of handicraft industry and capitalist industry and commerce. Is this possible? Soviet experience tells us that this is entirely possible. In the Soviet Union the civil war came to an end in 1920; the seventeen years from 1921 to 1937 brought the cooperativization of agriculture to completion, and the main part of the work of cooperativization in their case was accomplished in the six years from 1929 to 1934. Although, as stated in *A Short Course on the History of the Communist Party of the Soviet Union (Bolshevik)*, when some local Party organizations in the Soviet Union once committed the so-called error of being "dizzy with success,"[30] it was quickly corrected. By a great effort the Soviet Union eventually accomplished the socialist transformation of its entire agriculture successfully and at the same time brought about a tremendous technological transformation in agriculture. This road traveled by the Soviet Union is our very model.

Second, we have adopted the method of step-by-step advance in the socialist transformation of agriculture. As the first step, we called on the peasants, in accordance with the principles of voluntary [participation] and mutual benefit, to organize in the countryside agricultural producers' mutual aid teams that had only certain rudimentary elements of socialism and comprised a few to a dozen or so households each. Then as the second step, we called on the peasants to organize, on the basis of these mutual aid teams and still in accordance with the principles of voluntary [participation] and mutual benefit, small agricultural producers' cooperatives that are semisocialist in nature and characterized by the pooling of landholdings as shares and by unified management. Only later, as the third step, will we call on the peasants to combine further and organize, on the basis of these small semisocialist cooperatives and in accordance with the same principles of voluntary participation and mutual benefit, large agricultural producers' cooperatives that are fully socialist in nature.[31] [These steps] make it possible for the peasants to gradually raise their level of socialist consciousness through their own experience and to gradually change their way of life so as to lessen their feeling of an abrupt change in their way of life. Taking these steps will basically allow us to avoid a drop in crop production during a period of time (say, the [first] one or two years); instead of a drop, it must ensure an increase in production each year, and this can be done.[32] Of the 650,000 existing agricultural producers' cooperatives, more than eighty per cent have increased production, while over ten per cent have not had any increase or decrease in production, and a few per cent have shown a decrease. Things with the two latter categories are not going well, particularly the category with a drop in production, and a great effort must be made to reorganize [them]. Since more than eighty per cent of the cooperatives have increased production (the margin of increase being ten to thirty per cent), while over ten per cent of them, though showing neither increase nor decrease in production in the first year, may increase production in the second year after going through reorganization, and since even the few per cent with a drop in production may increase production or break even through reorganization, the development of cooperativization is on the whole healthy and can basically guarantee an increase in production and avoid any decrease. Moreover, these steps constitute a good course for training cadres; by [carrying out] the steps, management and technical personnel for the cooperatives can be gradually trained in large numbers.

Third, each year a control figure[33] for the growth in agricultural cooperativization must be worked out in light of the actual situation, and the cooperativization work must be checked several times. In this way concrete steps for the annual expansion [of cooperativization] in each province, *xian,* and *xiang* can be decided on according to changes in the circumstances and the quality of [their respective] achievements. In some areas [expansion] can be halted temporarily while reorganization is being carried out; in other areas, expansion and reorganization can be carried out simultaneously. Some members of certain cooperatives may be allowed to withdraw, and in individual cases a cooperative may be allowed to be dissolved temporarily. In some areas new cooperatives should be set up in large numbers, while in others it will suffice to increase the number of peasant households in the existing cooperatives. In every province or *xian,* after establishing a batch of cooperatives, there must be a period of time in which expansion is halted and a reorganization is carried out before proceeding with the establishment of another batch of cooperatives. The idea of not allowing any pause or intermission is wrong. As for the work of inspection of the cooperativization movement, the Party Center and Party committees of every province, autonomous region, municipality, and [special] district must take a firm hold of the work and see that [inspection] is done not only once but several times a year. As soon as a problem crops up, tackle it right away; don't let problems pile up and then try to resolve them all at once. Make criticism in good time; don't get into the practice of making criticism after the fact. For instance, in the first seven months of this year, the Central Committee alone called three conferences, including this one, of comrades in responsible positions from the localities to discuss the question of agricultural cooperativization. Using this method of taking such measures as are suitable to local conditions and of giving timely guidance ensures that we make fewer mistakes and that, when mistakes are made, they will be quickly corrected.

Judging from the conditions described above, can it not be said that the guiding principle of the Party Center on the question of agricultural cooperativization is a correct one and therefore one that ensures the healthy development of the movement? I think we can and should say so; to evaluate this principle as "adventurist advance" is totally incorrect.

IX

Proceeding from the standpoint of the bourgeoisie, the rich peasants, or the well-to-do middle peasants with a spontaneous tendency toward capitalism, some comrades have taken a wrong view on the extremely important question of the alliance between the workers and the peasants. They believe that the cooperativization movement is presently in a very dangerous situation, and they advise us to "get off the horse quickly," [halting our advance] along the road of cooperativization that we are presently taking. They have warned us: "If [you] don't get off the horse quickly, [you] run the risk of disrupting the alliance of the workers and peasants." We believe the very opposite [to be true], that if [we] don't get on the horse quickly, there will be the risk that the alliance of workers and peasants will be disrupted. It appears that there is the difference of only a single word here. One is to get off the horse while the other is to get on it. Yet it indicates the difference between two lines. As everybody knows, we already have a worker-peasant alliance built on the basis of the bourgeois democratic revolution, a revolution that opposed imperialism and feudalism, that took the land from the landlords and distributed it to the peasants to free them from [the bondage of] feudal ownership. But this revolution is now over, and feudal ownership has been abolished. What exists in the rural areas today is capitalist ownership by the rich peasants and individual ownership by peasants as extensive as a vast ocean. It is evident to all that the spontaneous forces of capitalism in the rural areas have been growing steadily in the last several years, new rich peasants are emerging everywhere, and many well-to-do middle peasants are striving to become rich peasants. Because of insufficient means of production, however, many poor peasants are still bogged down in poverty. Some of them are in debt, and others have sold or rented out their land. If this situation is allowed to develop further, polarization in the countryside will become more and more serious every day. Those peasants who lose their land and those who still [live] in poverty will bear a grudge against us, and they will complain that we are not coming to their rescue when they are in peril, not helping them overcome their difficulties. Those well-to-do middle peasants heading in the direction of capitalism will also be dissatisfied with us, for their demands will never be met if we do not intend to take the capitalist road. Can the alliance of the workers and peasants continue to be consolidated under these circumstances? Obviously not. This problem can be solved only on a new basis. This means bringing about step by step the socialist transformation of the whole of agriculture along with the gradual realization of socialist industrialization and of socialist transformation of handicraft and capitalist industry and commerce, that is to say, carrying out cooperativization and eliminating the rich peasant economy system and the individual economy system in the countryside so that all the people in the rural areas will become well-off together. We believe that only in this way can the alliance between the workers and peasants be consolidated. Otherwise, this alliance runs the risk of being disrupted. Those comrades who advise us to "get off the horse" are completely wrong in their thinking.

X

It is inevitable that there will soon be a nationwide high tide of socialist transformation in the countryside. This must be recognized right now. By the spring of 1958, the end of the last year of the First Five-Year Plan and the beginning of the first year of the Second Five-Year Plan, there will be about 250 million people or about 55 million peasant households (taking four and a half persons per household as an average), that is, half of the total rural population, in semisocialist cooperatives. By that time, semisocialist transformation of the agricultural economy in many *xian* and some provinces will have been basically accomplished, and a small number of cooperatives in every part of the country will have developed from being semisocialist into being fully socialist . By 1960, [toward the end of] the first half of the Second Five-Year Plan, we shall have basically completed the semisocialist transformation of [that part of] the agricultural economy that involves the other half of the rural population. By then, the number of cooperatives changing from being semisocialist into being fully socialist will have increased. During the period of the First and Second Five-Year Plans, social reform will remain as the principal [aspect] of the reform in the countryside, and technical transformation will be the secondary [aspect]; the number of large-scale agricultural machines will certainly increase, but not by any large margin. During the period of the Third Five-Year Plan, social reform and technical transformation will proceed simultaneously in the reform of the countryside; there will be an increase each year in the use of large-scale agricultural machines, and in the field of social reform, from 1960 on, semisocialist cooperatives will gradually develop by stages and in batches into fully socialist ones. Not until the socialist transformation of its social and economic system has been completely accomplished and, in the field of technology, machinery is used in all sections and places where operation by machinery is applicable, will the social and economic outlook of China change completely. In light of our country's economic conditions, the period of technological tranformation will be longer than that of social reform. It is estimated that it will take roughly four to five five-year plans, or twenty to twenty-five years, to basically complete the technological transformation of agriculture on a nationwide scale. The whole Party should strive for the fulfillment of this great task.

XI

There must be overall planning, and leadership must be strengthened.

There must be plans for the staged realization of cooperativization in the whole country and throughout every province, [special] district, *xian*, district, and *xiang*. Moreover, plans must be constantly revised in light of the actual conditions of progress in the work. The Party and Youth League organizations at each level of province, [special] district, *xian*, district, and *xiang* must pay serious attention to rural problems and earnestly improve their leadership in rural work. Comrades in major positions of responsibility in the local Party and Youth League organizations at all levels must get a firm grip on the study of the work of agricultural cooperativization and become knowledgeable about it. In short, we must take the initiative, we must not be passive; we must strengthen leadership, we must not abandon it.

XII

In August 1954 (this is no longer news), the Heilongjiang Provincial Committee of the Chinese Communist Party reported:

Along with the formation and expansion of the upsurge of rural cooperativization, mutual aid, and cooperative organizations of various types and the masses of people of various strata in the rural areas have all, to varying degrees, started to move [ahead]. The existing agricultural producers' cooperatives are planning and fermenting [a drive] to expand their membership, and the agricultural producers' mutual aid teams that are the targets for the formation of cooperatives are also planning and fermenting [a drive] to increase the number of their [member] households; even those mutual aid teams lacking the prerequisites [for cooperativization] are anxious to develop further and move up to a higher level. Some [people among the] masses are busy trying to join new cooperatives, others to join existing ones. Those who are not prepared to join cooperatives this year are nevertheless actively preparing to find a slot for themselves in mutual aid teams. The scope of activity is very broad, and a mass movement has already been formed. This is a new and outstanding feature in the great development of agricultural cooperativization. But because some leading comrades in certain *xian* and districts have not been able to keep pace with this new feature and strengthen the leadership in time, certain unhealthy phenomena have begun to arise in a number of *cun* and *tun* (note: in Heilongjiang Province the *cun* is an administrative unit corresponding to the *xiang* in the provinces south of the Great Wall, and the *tun*, which is not an administrative unit, is equivalent to the village in the latter provinces), such as, in the masses' self-motivated search for targets [i.e., people to bring into cooperatives as fellow members], "the strong seek out the strong, ostracizing peasants who are badly-off," "disunity is being fermented through competition to recruit backbone elements and members," "backbone elements are sticking together blindly," and "the rich peasants and those well-to-do peasants with a fairly strong capitalist way of thinking seize the opportunity to organize lower-level mutual aid teams or rich peasant cooperatives," and so on. All this amply demonstrates that, under the conditions in which agricultural cooperativization is undergoing great development, it is no longer enough to think only in terms of and within the confines of establishing new cooperatives when implementing the Party's policy and guiding the movement. It is necessary to think in terms of the entire *cun* (note: that is, the entire *xiang*) and of promoting the agricultural cooperativization movement in its full scope, and to give consideration both to expanding the old cooperatives and to establishing new ones, both to developing the cooperatives and to raising the level of the mutual aid teams, and both to [the work for] this year and to [the work for] the next year, and even the year after. Only in this way can the Party's policy be implemented in its entirety and the agricultural cooperativization movement pushed forward in a healthy manner.

We mentioned here that "some leading comrades in certain *xian* and districts have not been able to keep pace with this new feature and strengthen the leadership in time." Is this the case in Heilongjiang Province only? Is this the case in certain *xian* and districts only? As I see it, it is possible to find in many leading organs across the country people who typify this grave situation in which the leadership lags behind the movement.

The report of the Heilongjiang Provincial [Party] Committee also said:

Xiqin *cun* in Shuangcheng *xian* has carried out overall planning with the *cun* as a [basic] unit by adopting the method of combining leadership with voluntary participation of the masses. This is an innovation in leading the big expansion of cooperativization. Its important effect lies first in the fact that through [such] planning the Party's class line in the countryside has been fully implemented, the unity between the poor and middle peasants has been strengthened, and a vigorous struggle has been launched against the rich peasant tendency. Backbone elements have been properly deployed in the interests of overall cooperativization of agriculture. Relations between the [various] cooperatives and between the cooperatives and the [mutual aid] teams have been readjusted and strengthened so that the agricultural cooperativization movement has advanced in a planned way and with an overall approach. Second, through such planning, the work of developing agricultural cooperativization on a large scale has been allocated through specific assignments to the leadership at the basic level and to the broad masses so that Party branches at the *cun* level have understood how to give guidance, the old cooperatives have understood how to keep on advancing, the new cooperatives have understood how to establish themselves, and the mutual aid teams have understood the direction in which they must go to move to a higher level. Thus the initiative and enthusiasm of the Party branches at the *cun* level and of the broad masses have been further brought into play, and the correct principle of relying on the Party branch and on the experience and wisdom of the masses has been fully carried out. Finally, it is precisely through such planning that it is possible to acquaint [oneself] further with the true situation in the countryside and to carry out the Party's policy in a concrete and comprehensive manner. Hence, it has been possible to avoid impetuosity and adventurist advance as well as conservatism and the [the practice of] letting things drift along on their own, so that the Center's policy of "active leadership and steady advance" has been correctly implemented.

How were the various "unhealthy phenomena" mentioned in the report of the Heilongjiang Provincial [Party] Committee tackled? The provincial [Party] committee's report did not answer this question directly. But a report of the Shuangcheng *xian* [Party] committee was appended to the report of the provincial Party committee, and this report did answer the question. This report said:

As a result of carrying out overall planning by combining the leadership of the Party branch and the voluntary participation of the masses, the deviation of barring the households that are badly off from the cooperatives has been corrected, the problem of excessive concentration of backbone elements in one place has been solved, the phenomenon of competition in recruiting backbone elements and members has disappeared, the relations between the cooperatives and the mutual aid teams have grown closer, the rich and well-to-do peasants have failed in their attempt to organize rich peasant cooperatives or lower-level [mutual aid] teams, and the plan of the Party branch has been basically fulfilled. Two old cooperatives have expanded their membership by forty per cent, the frameworks of six new cooperatives have been set up, and two mutual aid teams have been reorganized. It is estimated that if everything is done well, the whole *cun* will be cooperativized next year (i.e., in 1955). At present, the masses in the entire *cun* are actively engaged in fulfilling this year's plan for expanding agricultural cooperativization and doing a good job of increasing production and ensuring [a good] harvest. The *cun* cadres all share the opinion: "It's lucky we've done it this way; otherwise things would have been in a mess. Not only would things have been in bad shape this year, but next year would have been affected as well."

In my opinion, let us just do things that way.

Overall planning and strengthening of leadership – this is our policy.

Notes

1. For more information on these struggles, see text 1960 Reading Notes, note 9; K. Walker (April-June 1966), pp. 216-243; Kang Chao (1970); *CB*, 884 (July 18, 1969), 663; and Su Xing (1965) (trans. in JPRS, *32414, 32420, 32793*).

2. See R. Levy (1976), pp. 108-122.

3. See K. Walker (April-June 1966), and R. Levy (1976), pp. 122 ff.

4. Mao was referring to the common practice in traditional China for the feet of women of the upper and middle classes to be bound in such a way that their growth is artificially and forcibly stunted and they in fact become misshapen. According to ancient documents such as the *yuefu*

(ballads) of the early Han dynasty (ca. 3rd-2nd century B.C.) the practice began with dancers in ancient times. It was popularized in courtly and nobility circles in the late-tenth century by Li Yu, the ruler of the state of the Southern Tang (reigning 961-976) and since then had become a common characteristic of upper-class women in Chinese society. It is commonly considered by Chinese women in modern times as a mark of the oppressiveness and sexual inequality of the old "feudalistic" society. Though it was romantically described in classical literature (the term *jin lian*, or golden lotus, was coined for the practice) it is generally condemned in modern days even though it was not officially outlawed by the government until the establishment of the PRC.

5. For some indication of what these classifications mean in the early 1950s, see text March 12, 1950, notes 1 and 2. For agricultural producers' cooperatives (APCs) see text Oct. 15, 1953, note 2.

6. See text Aug.12, 1953, note 9.

7. Between 1930 and 1934, land redistribution and low-level mutual aid organization was carried out in the Central Revolutionary Base with Ruijin in Jiangxi Province as its capital. This was aimed at activating the peasants and solving the problem of agricultural labor shortage. It entailed the organization of five to ten rural households into a collective mutual aid unit. The reference to labor exchange teams in Northern Shaanxi and mutual aid in North China, East China, and the Northeast is to the situation during the period of the War of Resistance against Japan.

8. This refers to the formation of twelve-household agricultural producers' cooperatives (then also called collective farms) in Miaodianzi, at No.5 *xiang*, in the Gaoqiao district of Ansai *xian* in early 1944. It entailed the collective concentrated utilization of labor and fertilizers, as well as other technological innovations.

9. The Draft Resolution on Mutual Aid and Cooperativization in Agricultural Production was adopted on December 15, 1951, by the Central Committee of the CPC. Copies were circulated to Party branches at all levels to be implemented on a selective experimental basis. (See Mao's circular to Party units, text Dec. 15, 1951.) On February 15, 1953, these resolutions were partly amended on the basis of experience gained in practical implementation and were adopted officially by the Central Committee. For a translation of this document see T. Chen (1967), pp. 218-221. The document itself was first published in *RMRB* (March 26, 1953), and in *XHYB*, 4 (April, 1953), 118-121. See also *SR*, p. 418, note 2. According to the *Xuanji* source, Mao personally took part in the drafting of this draft resolution. See text Dec. 15, 1951, note 1.

10. Here the *RMRB* version has February instead of March. There appears to be similar confusion in terms of dating in other secondary commentaries as well. See T. Chen (1967), p. 218; and Kang Chao (1970). We believe the *SW*, V, dating of March to be correct. (See previous note.)

11. This refers to the "Resolution on the Development of Agricultural Producers' Cooperatives," December 16, 1953. It was published in *XHYB* (Feb. 1954), 142-147, and in translation in a supplement to *People's China* (April 1, 1954). For a brief discussion of the debate within the CPC over the issue of agricultural cooperativization between 1951 and 1953, see Kang Chao (1970), pp. 16-18. Also see *SR*, p. 418, note 3.

12. See text Oct. 15, 1953, note 2.

13. See text Mar. 19, 1953, note 4.

14. "During the cooperative transformation [editor: i.e., cooperativization] of agriculture, those who were formerly poor peasants but rose to middle peasant status after the agrarian [editor: i.e., land] reform were called new middle peasants. Those who were formerly middle peasants and whose economic status remained unchanged were called old middle peasants." (*SW*, V, p. 207, note 1.)

This differentiation was clarified in considerably greater detail in the September 1964 Revised Draft of the "Provisions of the Central Committee of the Communist Party of China Concerning Certain Specific Policies Regarding the Socialist Education Movement in the Rural Areas." Liu Shaoqi was the main architect of this document and the policies advocated in general in the document were later severely criticized by Mao, although the schema for the classification of the peasantry on the whole was not affected. For a discussion of this last document see R. Baum and F. C. Teiwes (1968).

15. See text Jun.15, 1953, note 2.

16. "At that time, agricultural cooperatives which were well run, middling and poorly run were usually called Class I, Class II and Class III cooperatives respectively." (*SW*, V, p. 207, note 2.) The descriptions of these three types, or classes, of cooperatives suggest that the classification was done with rather impressionistic standards (*SR*, p. 419, note 7). According to an article in the journal *Xuexi* (Study), 12 (1955), 32, these demarcations differed also from place to place.

17. "The three poor peasant households here referred to were those of Wang Yu-kun [Wang Yukun], Wang Hsiao-chi [Wang Xiaoqi] and Wang Hsiao-pang [Wang Xiaopang] in Nanwan-chuang [Nanwanzhuang] village, Anping County *[xian]* of Hopei [Hebei] province. The agricul-tural producers' cooperative they set up was the predecessor of the present Nanwangchuang [Nanwanzhuang] Brigade of the people's commune of the same name." (*SW*, V, p. 207, note 3.) For a slightly more detailed description of the situation see *SR*, pp. 419-420, note 8. See also text Dec. 27, 1955(2), note 9.

18. The "resolute reduction" policy mentioned here and in the next two paragraphs refers to the policy of "halting, reduction, and reorganization" advocated by the faction led by Liu Shaoqi at the Third National Conference on Rural Work in May 1955. From the autumn of 1954 to the spring of 1955, the number of cooperatives grew from about 100,000 to about 650,000, and in the spring of 1955, the Central Committee of the CPC resolved to have the number of cooperatives increased to 1 million before the autumn harvest of 1956. The Liu faction then argued that the establishment of cooperatives had gone beyond the limits of practicability and had gone ahead of the levels of the masses' socialist consciousness and the standard of the cadres' experience. Arbi-trarily they called for, and in certain localities carried out, the reduction of the number of cooper-atives. It was later claimed that in the two months between May and July 1955, over 200,000 cooperatives were disbanded. This policy was not limited to Zhejiang but spread across the coun-try and was conducted in many, though not all, areas after its promulgation by the Third National Conference on Rural Work.

19. We have no concrete data on the dimensions of this "cutback" in 1953 mentioned here by Mao. The formal launching of the cooperativization movement (that is, the establishment of agri-cultural producers' cooperatives [APC's]) did not begin until the end of 1953 and early 1954. However, mutual aid teams were established on a national scale after the promulgation of the first Draft Decision on Mutual Aid and Cooperativization in Agriculture (December 1951). This deci-sion was ratified in finalized form in February 1953. According to *RMSC* (1952), pp. 356-357, many of the mutual aid teams, by becoming year-round mutual aid units, had already transformed themselves into cooperatives of a transitional nature. These were later known as lower-level or elementary APC's. (See text Oct. 15, 1953, note 2.) There is therefore evidence of considerable growth in the establishment of elementary APC's in 1953 which undoubtedly would have elicited significant response. While we do not have concrete or statistical data regarding the form and dimensions of this reaction, we do have some comments about the situation. (See F. Schurmann [1971], pp. 439-440, and Mao's own speech on the subject of cooperativization to the members of the Rural Work Department of the Central Committee of the CPC – text October 15, 1953, and *SW*, V, pp. 133 ff.).

20. See text Feb. 18, 1951, note 8, and text June 30, 1953, source note.

21. This refers to small plots of land that belonged to members of cooperatives and were retained by them in view of their need to grow vegetables and other garden produce not subjected to taxation or planned unified purchasing of the cooperative system. Their existence was affirmed in the "Model Regulations for an Agricultural Producers' Cooperative" of late 1955. In 1958, at the beginning of commune establishment, they were abolished; they were later reinstituted, their total area being limited to 5 per cent of the land within the commune jurisdiction. Since then the issues of the existence, size, roles, and consequences of "private plots" have been a focus of con-siderable struggle.

22. See text June 6, 1950(1), note 11.

23. Mao's reference to the Soviet experience here is quite important as the Soviet Union's experience in coordinating agricultural and industrial development was perceived quite differently by different groups in the leadership. Mao was referring to the Soviet experience in

order to counter the general understanding of that experience held by those coalesced around Liu Shaoqi, Deng Zihui (director of the Party's Rural Work Department), and others, which was in line with the official Soviet position that the Soviet experience demonstrated that agricultural co-operativization must be preceded by the mechanization of the agricultural means of production and that this was the necessary sequence of the two developments. Mao argued to the contrary that the Soviet experience in fact demonstrated that agricultural cooperativization had taken place *before* agricultural mechanization and this was the correct sequence. See Mao's "Reading Notes on the Soviet Textbook on Political Economy" (text 1960 Reading Notes). For more on the relationship between agricultural and industrial development in the Soviet Union during the 1920s and 1930s, see C. Bettelheim (1978).

24. "Commodity grain" refers to grain produced for exchange, not for direct consumption by the producer, that is, the amount of grain that producers could produce above the amount they needed for their own food and seed supply. Thus this amount of commodity grain would be the amount that could be counted on as the basis of food supply for urban areas and poor areas and as a potential basis for international trade.

25. The relationship between heavy and light industry and Mao's concept of each is clarified in his speech "On the Ten Major Relationships" (text April 25, 1956). See also F. Schurmann (1968), p. 80.

26. In 1938, under Stalin's direction, a new history of the Communist Party of the Soviet Union was compiled and published to bring the past into line with the purges within the Party. This resulted in the *Short Course in the History of the CPSU (Bolshevik)*, which was incorporated into Stalin's *Problem of Leninism* but which also appeared in separate form as the *History of the Communist Party of the Soviet Union (Bolshevik), Short Course*.

27. See text Aug. 12, 1953(1), note 22.

28. See text Feb. 18, 1951, note 2.

29. See text June 6, 1950(1), note 7.

30. *Short Course* (see note 26), English translation (International Publishers, 1951 edition), p. 472.

31. See text Oct. 15, 1953, note 2.

32. For an analysis of how Mao's approach to collectivization anticipated yearly increases in production, see J. Gray (1974).

33. See text Oct. 15, 1953, note 6.

Conversation with Security Guards

(Mid-July 1955)

Source: Quoted in "Mao zhuxi guanhuai jingwei zhanshi xue wenhua" (Chairman Mao Cares About the Security Guards' Studying to Become Literate), in *RMRB* (May 23, 1960), 3. Other Chinese Text: *Mao jingwei*, pp. 5-6; also excerpt on p. 20. Available English Translation: *SCMP*, 2271 (June 3, 1960), 2-5.

According to the source, in May 1955 Mao instructed the security guards to train themselves by writing reports about their experiences after they had gone home for vacations. Most of these reports were about their home villages and districts. Mao personally made comments and corrections on these reports. Some of these conversation excerpts reflect Mao's responses. Also, for source information, see text May 1955, source note.

This report isn't badly written; it contains analysis as well as supporting examples. . . .

We must make them study some more cultural matters and some general scientific knowledge; [let them] learn some geography, history, mathematics, physics, and chemistry, so that they can attain the level of a middle-school graduate in three to five years. . . .

You are all good comrades; it is just that your reading and writing [levels] are a little low. If you earnestly raise your literacy level somewhat, you will then be able to master scientific knowledge, do more things for the people, and serve the people better. . . . In our cause we need a great many intellectuals who come from the ranks of the workers and peasants.

Telegram to the Democratic People's Republic of Korea
(August 12, 1955)

Source: *RMRB* (Aug. 15, 1955), 1. Other Chinese Text: *XHYB*, 9 (Sept. 28, 1955), 86. Available English Translation: HNA, *Daily News Release* (Aug. 15, 1955), 1.

Comrade Kim Du Bong, Chairman of the Standing Committee of the Supreme People's Assembly of the Democratic People's Republic of Korea, Comrade Kim Il Sung, Premier of the Democratic People's Republic of Korea,
Comrade Nam Il, Minister of Foreign Affairs of the Democratic People's Republic of Korea:

On the occasion of the tenth anniversary of the liberation of the Korean people, on behalf of the Chinese government and people of the People's Republic of China, we extend to you and, through you, to the government and people of the Democratic People's Republic of Korea, our sincere and warm congratulations.

In the ten years since the great army of the Soviet Union defeated the Japanese militarists, the Korean people, under the leadership of the Korean Workers' Party and the government of the Democratic People's Republic of Korea, have carried out unflagging struggle for the peace, unification, and independence of their homeland. After the Korean Armistice in 1953,[1] the Korean people have also carried out the arduous task of restoring and developing their national economy and have achieved great successes. These achievements of the Korean people have given the greatest inspiration and support to the Chinese people, who are in the midst of their socialist construction.

Since the Korean Armistice, the Korean People's Army and the Chinese People's Volunteers have strictly abided by the agreements of the Korean Armistice, and the two governments of Korea and China have all along worked for a peaceful resolution of the Korean question by the principle of negotiation; but the enemies of peace have seized every opportunity to plot to undermine the Armistice, such that the Korean Armistice is still in a state of instability. Nevertheless, the Korean Armistice agreement cannot be allowed to be undermined, and a peaceful resolution of the Korean question must be actualized.

May the Korean people achieve even greater victories in their struggle for the peace, unification, and independence of their homeland. The Korean people will forever have the deep sympathy and fullest support of the Chinese people and government in this struggle.

May you achieve even greater successes in the cause of strengthening the democratic bases and restoring and developing your national economy.

(Co-signed as Chairman of PRC with Liu Shaoqi as Chairman of Standing Committee of NPC and Zhou Enlai as Premier of State Council and Foreign Minister, dated in Beijing)

Note

1. See text June 30, 1953, note 2.

Telegram to the Republic of Indonesia
(August 15, 1955)

Source: *RMRB* (Aug. 17, 1955), 1. Other Chinese Text: *XHYB*, 9 (Sept. 28, 1955), 68. Available English Translation: HNA, *Daily News Release* (Aug. 17, 1955), 3.

Mr. Sukarno,
President,
The Republic of Indonesia

Your Excellency:

On the occasion of the tenth anniversary of the Republic of Indonesia, I express warm greetings to Your Excellency and the people of your country. May the Indonesian nation prosper, may its people thrive, and may Your Excellency enjoy good health.
(Signed as Chairman of PRC, dated in Beijing)

Telegram to the People's Republic of Romania
(August 21, 1955)

Source: *RMRB* (Aug. 23, 1955), 1. Other Chinese Text: *XHYB*, 9 (Sept. 28, 1955), 67. Available English Translation: HNA, *Daily News Release* (Aug. 23, 1955), 1.

Comrade Petru Groza, Chairman of the Presidium of the Grand National Assembly of the People's Republic of Romania,
Comrade Gheorghe Gheorghiu Dej, Chairman of the Council of Ministers of the People's Republic of Romania,
Comrade Simion Bughici, Minister of Foreign Affairs of the People's Republic of Romania:

On the occasion of the eleventh anniversary of Romania's liberation, on behalf of the government and people of the People's Republic of China, we extend to you and, through you, to the government and people of the People's Republic of Romania our warm and heartfelt congratulations.

With feelings of boundless elation, the government and people of the People's Republic of China have watched the great successes achieved during the past eleven years by the People's Republic of Romania under the leadership of the Romanian Workers' Party in the cause of socialist construction. These successes have added to the strength of the socialist camp for peace and democracy headed by the Soviet Union. May our brothers, the Romanian people, achieve new victories in the cause of consolidating and winning prosperity for their homeland and in defending peace in Europe and throughout the world. May the unbreakable friendship between China and Romania be further consolidated and developed.

(Co-signed as Chairman of PRC with Liu Shaoqi as Chairman of Standing Committee of NPC and Zhou Enlai as Premier of State Council and Foreign Minister, dated in Beijing)

Telegram to the Democratic Republic of Viet Nam
(September 1, 1955)

Source: *RMRB* (Sept. 2, 1955), 1. Other Chinese Text: *XHYB*, 10 (Oct. 28, 1955), 92. Available English Translation: NCNA, *Daily Bulletin* (Sept. 2, 1955), 7.

Comrade Ho Chi Minh, President of the Democratic Republic of Viet Nam,
Comrade Ton Duc Thang, Acting President of the Standing Committee of the National Assembly of the Democratic People's Republic of Viet Nam,
Comrade Pham Van Dong, Vice-Premier and Minister of Foreign Affairs of the Democratic People's Republic of Viet Nam:

On the occasion of the tenth anniversary of the founding of the Democratic Republic of Viet Nam, on behalf of the government and people of the People's Republic of China, we extend to you and, through you, to the government and people of the Democratic Republic of Viet Nam our warm and heartfelt congratulations.

In the last ten years, the Vietnamese people, under the leadership of the Viet Nam Workers' Party and President Ho Chi Minh, have carried out a heroic and arduous struggle in opposing colonial aggression and in striving for peace, unification, independence, and democracy, and have achieved great victories. These victories not only have inspired all peoples struggling for national independence and freedom but have also contributed greatly to the cause of defending peace in Asia and throughout the world. The Chinese people are overjoyed and filled with admiration for this.

In 1954 at the Geneva Conference an agreement was reached on restoring peace to Indochina and actualizing Viet Nam's unification through nationwide elections;[1] however, at present the enemies of peace are still scheming to undermine the implementation of the Geneva Agreement. This is totally impermissible by all those who uphold justice. The Chinese people give all their sympathy and support to the Vietnamese people in their continuous efforts in struggling to actualize the Geneva Agreement thoroughly and to convene a consultative conference between the north and the south in preparation for free elections throughout the country.

May the Vietnamese people achieve even greater victories in the struggle for peace, independence, unification, and democracy!

May you achieve further successes in the tasks of consolidating the democratic political power, healing war wounds, and restoring and developing your national economy!

(Co-signed as Chairman of PRC with Liu Shaoqi as Chairman of Standing Committee of NPC and Zhou Enlai as Premier of State Council and Foreign Minister, dated in Beijing)

Note

1. See text July 23, 1954, note 1.

Telegram to Antonin Zapotocky
(September 1, 1955)

Source: *RMRB* (Sept. 3, 1955), 1. Other Chinese Text: *XHYB*, 10 (Oct. 28, 1955), 80. Available English Translation: HNA, *Daily News Release* (Sept. 3, 1955), 4.

President,
Republic of Czechoslovakia

Dear Comrade Antonin Zapotocky:

On hearing the news of your illness, the Chinese people and myself express to you, with the deepest concern, our earnest good wishes and sincerely hope that your health will soon be restored.

(Signed and dated in Beijing)

Intra-Party Directive on Agricultural Cooperativization
(September 7, 1955)

Source: *Xuanji*, V, pp. 192-194. Available English Translation: *SW*, V, pp. 208-210.

According to the source note in the Xuanji *text (p. 192), this is an internal Party directive that Mao drafted on behalf of the Central Committee of the CPC. When he talks about the League here, Mao is referring to the New Democratic Youth League (NDYL) (see text Feb. 18, 1951, note 8, and text June 30, 1953, source note). However, it is of some significance to note that it was about this time that the proposal was made to change the name of the NDYL to the Communist Youth League. (The proposal was officially made in a resolution at the Third Plenary Session of the Second Central Committee of the NDYL on Sept. 18, 1955.) The rationale for making the change was based on the demarcation between the period of the new democratic revolution and the socialist revolution (i.e., that the former had drawn to a close and the latter had begun). See also text June 30, 1953, note 2. Since the NDYL thus represented the progressive element in this theoretical problem, one can detect beneath the surface a subtle ideological significance in this speech.*

At present, the slogan "Rely on the poor peasants (including all the new middle peasants who were formerly poor peasants) and unite solidly with the middle peasants" is still basically correct. Nevertheless, (1) among the new middle peasants, some well-to-do middle peasants (i.e., upper-middle peasants) have emerged; of these people, except for some who have relatively higher levels of political consciousness, the remainder are still, for the time being, reluctant to join the cooperatives;[1] (2) the lower-middle peasants among the former middle peasants are generally interested in joining the cooperatives because their economic status was not well-off to begin with and in some cases because they unjustly suffered some encroachments during the time of the land reform; they generally have the same economic status as the lower-middle peasants among the new middle peasants.[2] For these two reasons, in places where cooperativization has not yet reached a high tide, and where the well-to-do middle peasants are still lacking in consciousness, it is appropriate for us to first absorb these three sections of people into the cooperatives: (1) the poor peasants; (2) the lower-middle peasants among the new middle peasants; (in the revised edition of Comrade Mao Zedong's report,[3] the middle peasants are divided only into two categories, the upper-middle peasants and the lower-middle peasants, and no mention is made of the middle-middle peasants, so as to avoid hairsplitting and difficulty in making out the differ-

ences. The lower-middle peasants mentioned here in fact include the two categories – the lower-middle peasants and the middle-middle peasants – among
the originally mentioned new middle peasants); and (3) the lower-middle
peasants among the former middle peasants. (Moreover, we should divide
them up according to the levels of their [political] consciousness into different
groups for absorption [into the cooperative], and absorb first of all those
whose level [of consciousness] is higher.) All those well-to-do middle peasants who are for the time being reluctant to join the cooperatives – that is, the
upper-middle peasants among the new as well as the former middle peasants –
should not be dragged in against their will. At the moment, in many places,
the well-to-do middle peasants are being forced to join the cooperatives; the
purpose being to take over their draft animals and farming tools (by fixing too
low a price [for these things] and setting the reimbursement schedule over too
long a period). This in fact is an encroachment on their interests, and a violation of the principle of "uniting solidly with the middle peasants." Yet this
Marxist principle is one that we certainly cannot violate at any time. In all
places where at present the cooperative has just been set up or where it is not
yet in a dominant position, it is very detrimental to the establishment of the
poor and lower-middle peasants' position of leadership for those people
among the well-to-do middle peasants who have a strong capitalist ideology to
be dragged into [the cooperatives], or for them to attempt to worm their way
into the cooperatives themselves to seize the leadership (and this not because
they have real political consciousness), or for attempts to be made to establish
lower stage cooperatives such as those discovered at Shuangcheng *xian* in
Heilongjiang Province.[4] (Of course exceptions have to be made for some
individual well-to-do middle peasants who are just, capable, and who have a
high level of political consciousness.) And [we know that] the establishment
of the poor and lower-middle peasants' position of leadership is a must for all
cooperatives. Some people say that by what we suggest now we seem to have
abandoned the slogan "Rely on the poor peasants, unite solidly with the middle peasants." This is not true. We are not abandoning this slogan; rather, we
are concretizing this slogan in accordance with a new set of conditions, which
means that with regard to those people among the new middle peasants who
have been elevated to becoming well-to-do middle peasants, we no longer
consider them as part of these people on whom we rely; instead, we consider
the lower-middle peasants among the former middle peasants as part of the
people on whom we are to rely. These differentiations are made based on their
economic status and on whether they adopt a positive attitude toward the cooperativization movement. This is to say, the poor peasants and the two sections of lower-middle peasants are comparable to the former poor peasants
and are the ones on whom we seek to rely, while the two sections of upper-
middle peasants, which are comparable to the former middle peasants, are the
people with whom we aim to unite solidly. And at the present moment, one of
the ways to unite with them is not to force them to join the cooperatives and
not to encroach upon their interests.

Regarding the problem of whom we should rely on in the countryside, there are a few more things we must clearly understand. We should first of all rely on the Party members and League members. It is wrong for our cadres in the leadership organs above the district level or cadres sent to direct the work in the countryside not to rely first on the Party and League members in the countryside and to confuse Party and League members with the non-Party and non-League masses. Second, we should rely on some of the more active elements among the non-Party masses; these people ought to make up about five per cent of the population in the countryside. (For instance in a *xiang* with a population of about 2,500, there should be about 125 active elements of this sort.) We should make an effort to train a group of people like these, and at the same time, we should not confuse them with the masses in general. Only in the third place should we rely on the broad masses of the poor peasants in general and of the two sections of lower-middle peasants. Unless we are clear on this problem of which people to rely on and the methods of relying on them, mistakes will be committed in the cooperativization movement.

Notes

1. See text Oct. 15, 1953, note 2.

2. For a summary of the classes in China's countryside, see text Mar. 12, 1950, note 1. New middle peasants are those who were designated as poor peasants during the time of the land reform movement and who subsequently improved their economic status to reach the level of middle peasant in 1955. Old middle peasants are those who had remained in the middle peasant category since the land reform. See text July 31, 1955, note 14.

3. The earliest specific mention of these terms that we can trace in the published works of Mao is found in the report on cooperativization he made to the Conference of Provincial, Municipal, and Autonomous Region Party Secretaries on July 31, 1955 (i.e., text July 31, 1955). It is therefore most likely that this report is what is referred to here, although we are unable to ascertain that there was a "revised edition" of this report.

4. See end of text July 31, 1955.

Telegram to the People's Republic of Bulgaria
(September 7, 1955)

Source: *RMRB* (Sept. 9, 1955), 1. Other Chinese Text: *XHYB*, 10 (Oct. 28, 1955), 79. Available English Translation: HNA, *Daily News Release* (Sept. 9, 1955), 1.

Comrade Georgi Damyanov, Chairman of the Presidium of the National Assembly of the People's Republic of Bulgaria,
Comrade Vulko Chervenkov, Chairman of the Council of Ministers of the People's Republic of Bulgaria,
Comrade Mincho Neichev, Minister of Foreign Affairs of the People's Republic of Bulgaria:

On the occasion of the eleventh anniversary of Bulgaria's liberation from fascist enslavement, on behalf of the government and people of the People's Republic of China we express to you, and, through you, to the government and people of the People's Republic of Bulgaria our sincere congratulations.

The government and people of the People's Republic of China note with great excitement and elation the tremendous achievements in the cause of socialist construction that the People's Republic of Bulgaria, under the leadership of the glorious Communist Party of Bulgaria, has made during the past eleven years. These achievements have enabled the Bulgarian people to achieve a daily prospering and happy life, and has strengthened the forces of the camp for peace, democracy, and socialism headed by the Soviet Union. May our brothers the Bulgarian people achieve even greater victories in their causes of implementing the second five-year plan and safeguarding European and world peace. We are deeply convinced that the fraternal friendship between the two countries of China and Bulgaria is bound to further consolidate and develop with the advance of our two countries' cause of building socialism.

(Co-signed as Chairman of PRC with Liu Shaoqi as Chairman of Standing Committee of NPC and Zhou Enlai as Premier of State Council and Foreign Minister, dated in Beijing)

Inscription for Tokuda Kyuichi
(September 12, 1955)

Source: *RMRB* (Sept. 14, 1955), 1. Other Chinese Text: *RMRB* (Oct. 16, 1955), 4. Available English Translation: HNA, *Daily News Release* (Oct. 16, 1955), 16.

This inscription, written by Mao personally on a memorial banner, was draped over the portrait of Tokuda Kyuichi at a funeral ceremony held by the Communist Party of Japan at Toyoshima Hall, Tokyo, on October 15, 1955. Tokuda was general secretary of the Communist Party of Japan (Nihon Kyosanto).

Immortal glory to Comrade Tokuda Kyuichi.

First Preface to *Upsurge of Socialism in China's Countryside* (September 25, 1955)

Source: *Xuanji*, V, pp. 218-221. Available English Translation: *SW*, V, pp. 235-237.

This is the original, or first, preface that Mao wrote for a collection of reports on co-operativization that would eventually be published under the title Zhongguo nongcun de shehui zhuyi gaochao *(Upsurge of Socialism in China's Countryside). As indicated in this document, the title that was originally contemplated for the book was quite different –* Zenyang ban nongye shengchan hezuoshe *(How to Run Agricultural Producers' Cooperatives) – and, one may surmise, in Mao's opinion, rather bland. Mao evidently took a tremendous personal interest in the preparation and publication of this book, and mentioned it several times in his speeches (particularly in the October 11, 1955, speech; see texts Oct. 11, 1955[1] and [2]) and in his correspondence (see text Sept. 27, 1955). In the course of the editorial work on this book, which took over two months' time, Mao wrote another preface, and the first, i.e., this document here, was subsequently not published with the book itself, or with other collections of material on the subject published at that time or in the years immediately thereafter. For more information on the publication of the book, see texts Dec. 27, 1955(1) and (2).*

The general line of the Chinese Communist Party during the period of transition from capitalism to socialism is to basically accomplish the industrialization of the country, and at the same time basically accomplish the socialist transformation of agriculture, handicraft industries, and capitalist industry and commerce.[1] This period of transition will take approximately eighteen years, that is, three years of rehabilitation plus three five-year plans. In our Party everybody appears to agree on the formulation of this general line and on the specification of its time span, but in reality differences of opinion exist. At present, these differences of opinion find their expression mainly in the issue of the socialist transformation of agriculture, that is, the issue of agricultural cooperativization.

Some people say that in the last few years there seems to have emerged a certain rule in connection with the question of agricultural cooperativization, namely, that expansion is advocated in winter, but when spring comes, some people will oppose [it as being an] adventurist advance.[2] There are reasons for holding this view, for they have witnessed opposition to the so-called adventurist advance several times. For example, there was an expansion in the winter of 1952, only to be followed by a [wave of] opposition to adventurist advance in the spring of 1953; again there was an expansion in the winter of 1954, and again it was followed by a [wave of] opposition to adventurist advance in the spring of 1955. The so-called opposition to adventurist advance did not merely mean halting the expansion but also meant forcibly dissolving (also called "chopping off") batch after batch of cooperatives that were already established, and this caused disaffectation among the cadres and peasant masses.[3] Some peasants were so angry that they refused to eat, or they lay down on their beds and refused to get up, or they stayed away from work for more than a dozen days at a stretch. They said, "It's you who told us to set up [the cooperatives], and it's also you who are telling us to dissolve [them]." Dissolving [the cooperatives] delighted the well-to-do middle peasants but saddened the poor peasants. When the poor peasants in Hubei Province heard the news about halting [the establishment of cooperatives] or dissolving them, they were "chilled from the waist down,"[4] but some middle peasants said, "This is comparable to a pilgrimage to Mulan Hill."[5] (There is a Mulan Hill in Huangpi *xian,* Hubei Province, on which stands Mulan Temple, where the peasants like to pay homage.)

Why do some comrades waver like this, a wavering which, in the eyes of most people, is totally uncalled for? It is because they have been influenced by some of the middle peasants. At the initial stages of cooperativization some of the middle peasants, especially the well-to-do middle peasants among whom there is a severe tendency to lean toward capitalism, held hostile sentiments toward socialist transformation.[6] This has to do with the policy and the method of work that the Party has pursued with respect to the middle peasants in the cooperativization movement. Many middle peasants who have a relatively low economic status but whose political consciousness is relatively high, which means primarily the lower-middle peasants among the new middle peasants, and the lower-middle peasants among the old middle peasants,[7] are willing to join the cooperatives, provided that we pursue a policy that brings mutual benefits to both strata, namely, the poor and the middle peasants, and that does not benefit the poor peasants exclusively while being detrimental to the middle peasants, and also provided that our method of work is good. However, some middle peasants would still prefer to stay out of the cooperatives for the time being even if we carry out such a policy, so as to "be free even if it just for a year or two." This situation is completely understandable, because cooperativization will change the system of the peasants' private ownership of the means of production and the entire mode of management. The change is a very fundamental one for them; it is natural that they should want to give the matter careful consideration, and they may find it difficult to make up their minds for some time. Some of our comrades did not try to solve problems [in the area of] the Party's policy and its method of work; as soon as the well-to-do middle peasants squealed and there were some aberrations in our work, they panicked and went all out against "adventurist advance" and wanted to "chop off" cooperatives at the slightest provocation, as if they were malignant tumors that would be fatal if not promptly cut out. This is completely at odds with how things really are. There are shortcomings in our work, but the movement on the whole is healthy. The broad [masses of] poor and lower-middle peasants welcome the cooperatives. If some of the middle peasants need to wait and see, we should let them do so. What's more, the well-to-do middle peasants, except for those who [are joining] voluntarily, should be given a longer time to wait and see. At the moment, the main short-coming with regard to this question is that in many places the Party leadership has failed to catch up [with the movement]; it has not grasped the leadership of the whole movement in its hands; it does not have a complete plan for each province, each *xian,* each district or each *xiang,* but goes about its work in a disjointed and piecemeal manner; [people in the leadership] lack a spirit of ini-tiative, enthusiasm, happiness, responsiveness, and all-out effort. A big prob-lem has therefore arisen. At the lower levels the movement is very extensive, but at the higher levels it is receiving inadequate attention; this is bound to give rise to some trouble. In the face of these troubles, instead of trying to strengthen the leadership and improve the planning, we have adopted the neg-ative approach of trying to halt the progress of the movement or rushing to "chop off" a number of cooperatives. This is wrong of course and is bound to give rise to more trouble.

We have now compiled a book entitled *How to Run Agricultural Producers' Cooperatives.*[8] A total of over 120 articles are collected in this book which are all factual examples from various provinces, municipalities, and autono-mous regions. The far greater portion of the material is from [the period between] January and August 1955, while a smaller portion is from the second half of 1954. The bulk of the material was selected from the intra-Party publications of the various provinces, municipalities, or autonomous regions; a few articles were selected from newspapers; a few others were reports by lower-level Party committees or comrades engaged in [cooperativization] work to Party committees at higher levels; and one was a transcript of a talk given by the director of a cooperative who had been invited to Beijing.[9] We have only corrected some of the language of the material, and have kept the original contents intact. We have written notes for some of the material. In order to differentiate our notes from the notes written for some of the material by the editors of the original publications, our notes are written under the title of "The Editors of This Volume."[10] We believe that the view-points expressed by all the authors of this material are correct or basically cor-rect. From this material the readers will see the scope and direction of the co-operativization movement throughout the country as well as the prospects for its development. The material shows that the movement is healthy. The places where trouble occurred were all places where the Party committees had failed to provide good leadership. Once the Party committees caught up [with the mass movement] and gave it proper guidance according to the principles laid down by the Center, the problems in these places were immediately solved.

This material is very convincing: it will activate those who even up to now have had a passive attitude toward this movement; it will help those who still do not know how to run a cooperative find a way to run one; what is more, it will make those who have been fond of "chopping off" cooperatives at the slightest whim keep their mouths shut.

Carrying out the socialist transformation of agriculture among several hundred million peasants is a monumental task. Taking the country as a whole, it has not been very long [since the movement started], and our experience is still quite inadequate. In particular we have not yet carried out extensive and effective propaganda work throughout the Party. As a result, many comrades have not paid attention to this question and do not understand the principles, policies, and methods for conducting this movement; thus there is still no unity of will within the Party. The Sixth Plenum of our Party's Central Committee will meet very soon to discuss this problem,[11] and a new resolution on it will be adopted before long. We should carry out extensive and effective propaganda work in accordance with this resolution so as to achieve unity of will within the whole Party. The publication of this book may be of some help to this propaganda work.

Notes

1. See text June 15, 1953, note 1.

2. See text Aug. 12, 1953(1), note 22.

3. See text July 31, 1955, note 18.

4. This colloquial expression means utter disappointment with a sudden unfavorable turn of events.

5. Mulan is a legendary heroine. The story of Hua Mulan from the *yuefu* (ballads) of the Han dynasty (206 B.C.-205 A.D.) tells of a girl who disguised herself as a young man and enlisted in the army as a substitute for her father. She returns home after twelve years of service in the army without ever being discovered. Hua Mulan has been lauded in theatrical works and worshiped in folk religion in China for her courage and filial piety. Mao is probably referring to the sense of futility and disappointment resulting from making an arduous pilgrimage and receiving nothing tangible in return.

6. See text Mar. 12, 1950, notes 1 and 2.

7. See text July 31, 1955, note 14.

8. "The book was renamed *Socialist Upsurge in China's Countryside* when it was published." (Note 1, *SW*, V, p. 241.)

9. This refers to Wang Zhiqi, chief of the Dongchuankou agricultural producers' cooperative in Yintai *xian*, Hebei.

10. It should be noted that in our translation of these comments in this volume (text Dec. 27, 1955(2)), we have given them the general title of "editor's notes."

11. The Sixth Plenum of the Seventh Central Committee of the CPC met on October 4-11, 1955, in Beijing. See K. Lieberthal (1976), p. 73-74.

Letter to Tian Jiaying
(September 27, 1955)

Source: *Shuxin*, pp. 498-499.

See text Mar. 2, 1954, source note.

Comrade Tian Jiaying:

Please send [the enclosed] to the [print-] shop, and have them make corrections accordingly. The title for each province and for each article should be amended as I have indicated on the table of contents. As for the rest, you do not need to send them over for my inspection today.[1]

Please type up eight copies speedily (in addition, one copy should go to Comrade Chen Yun),[2] and the best thing would be if you could have them delivered this afternoon or tonight to the various comrades.

You and Qiaomu,[3] each taking half [of the material], must go through [this material] once thoroughly, and make corrections to the language, including making the titles more lively. Please forward [this instruction] to Qiaomu.

Mao Zedong
September 27
4:00 [p.m.]

Notes

1. This refers to the material in the impending publication *Zhongguo nongcun de shehui zhuyi gaochao* (Upsurge of Socialism in China's Countryside); see text Sept. 25, 1955.

2. According to the source, Chen's position at the time – which is relevant to the matter at hand – was secretary of the secretariat of the Central Committee of the CPC. See text Dec. 18, 1950, note 2.

3. This refers to Hu Qiaomu, who was then Mao's secretary and deputy secretary general of the Central Committee of the CPC. See also text May 22, 1950, note 2.

Letter to Zhou Shizhao
(October 4, 1955)

Source: *Shuxin*, pp. 500-501.

See text Oct. 15, 1949, source note.

My dear Dunyuan:[1]

I received some time ago your gracious letter, and I apologize for being so tardy in responding. I am very grateful to you for sending me a copy in your hand of the works of Cheng Songwan.[2] Please convey my feelings of gratitude also to Mr. Cao Zigu.[3] Concerning [your suggestions about my] writing editorial coments and inscriptions [for the book], I would be happy to write something when I have the time, but at the present moment and in the immediate future I am afraid I will not be able to give this any attention. I am greatly interested when I read your various masterpieces; [so much that] I wrote, in response, a piece of my own. I hope that you will reward me with your kind instruction.

On the banks of the rolling Spring River I tarry for a moment
Then stretch my steps upon the layered mountains.
My yearning eyes are
  blessed with an unfolding vista.
The wind arises over the green islet and chases
  away the billows
While the rain pursues the verdant forests
  up the hillslopes.
My friends, we remain the same as we gather for our tales and laughter
  around the drinking table
'Though the trivial affairs that bother us beyond our borders are indeed saddening.
Let us not lament that time has passed us by so fleetly;
Thirty years have gone, and we are once more met
  at Kexi Terrace.

I hope you have been well of late.

Mao Zedong
October 4, 1955.

Notes

1. See text Oct. 15, 1949, note 1.

2. Cheng Songwan was a poet of the late-Qing period.

3. Cao Zigu (1876-1960, a.k.a. Cao Dianqiu) was, before Liberation, director of the Department of Education of the Hunan provincial government and the chancellor of Hunan University. Since 1949 he was a member of the Standing Committee of the Hunan Political Consultative Council and deputy director of the Hunan Province Historical and Cultural Studies Institute.

Telegram to the German Democratic Republic
(October 6, 1955)

Source: *RMRB* (Oct. 8, 1955), 1. Other Chinese Text: *XHYB*, 11 (Nov. 28, 1955), 86. Available English Translations: HNA, *Daily News Release* (Oct. 8, 1955), 1; FBIS, *Daily Report* (Oct. 10, 1955), AAA 13.

Comrade Wilhelm Pieck, President of the German Democratic Republic,
Comrade Johannes Dieckmann, Chairman of the Presidium of the People's Chamber of the German Democratic Republic,
Comrade Otto Grotewohl, Premier of the German Democratic Republic:

On the occasion of the sixth anniversary of the founding of the German Democratic Republic, on behalf of the government and people of the People's Republic of China, we extend to you and, through you, to the government of the German Democratic Republic and the people of all Germany our warm congratulations.

In the last six years, the German Democratic Republic has achieved significant successes in the areas of consolidating the system of the people's democracy, building socialism, and raising the people's standard of living. The German Democratic Republic has already become a strong bulwark in the fight for the peaceful unification of Germany and an important factor in maintaining peace and security in Europe. The Chinese people totally support the German people in their struggle carried out for peace, unification, and democracy and the efforts made by the Soviet Union for a peaceful resolution of the German question.

May the friendly and cooperative relations between the People's Republic of China and the German Democratic Republic develop and become more consolidated with each passing day! We wish the German Democratic Republic new successes in the cause of economic and cultural construction and in the struggle for the peaceful unification of Germany and the collective security of Europe!

(Co-signed as Chairman of PRC with Liu Shaoqi as Chairman of Standing

Committee of NPC and Zhou Enlai as Premier of State Council and Foreign Minister, dated)

The Debate Over Agricultural Cooperativization
and the Present Class Struggle
(October 11, 1955)

Source: *Xuanji*, V, pp. 195-217. Available English Translation: *SW*, V, pp. 211-234.

This is the concluding speech at the Sixth (Enlarged) Plenum of the Seventh Central Committee of the CPC, held October 4-11, 1955. Another version of this speech appears under the date September 1955, in Wansui *(1969), pp. 12-25 (available English translation:* JPRS, Miscellany, *I, pp. 14-26). The dating of this latter version is obviously incorrect. The two versions differ substantially; whereas the latter seems to be notes on the main items that Mao discussed, the former seems like a more detailed account of his actual words, although it contains certain significant variations from the latter document. Therefore, in order to provide the fullest available text of the relevant portions of the speech and to highlight the meaningful differences between the versions, while using the* Xuanji *version as the base text (simply because it represents a fuller text), we have footnoted all significant differences between the two texts. In addition, paragraphs where the* Xuanji *version is expanded in comparison with the* Wansui *version but in which the meaning is basically the same have been marked with an (E) at the end of the paragraph.*

This conference of ours has been a very great debate. It was a great debate over the question of whether during the period of transition from capitalism to socialism, our Party's general line is entirely correct or not.[1] It was the question of the orientation of policy toward agricultural cooperativization that led to this great debate throughout the whole Party, and the comrades' discussions have focused on this question. But the facets involved in this debate have been many; they have included the work of the agricultural, industrial, communications, transportation, fiscal, financial, trade, cultural, educational, scientific, and public health departments; they have included the transformation of the handicraft industries and of capitalist industry and commerce; they have included the suppression of counterrevolutionaries and also military and foreign affairs. In sum, they have involved all areas of Party, government, military, and civil work. We should have a great debate such as this because our Party as yet has not had a debate of this type since the promulgation of the general line. This debate must unfold in the countryside and in the cities so that all aspects of our work, [including] its speed and quality, can be adjusted to meet the tasks set out in the general line and so that [all aspects of our work] will fit into a comprehensive plan. Now I will express a few opinions on the following questions.

(1) The Relation between Agricultural Cooperativization and the Transformation of Capitalist Industry and Commerce

The question of the relation between agricultural cooperativization and the transformation of capitalist industry and agriculture, that is, the question of the relation between basically completing the socialist transformation of agriculture within a period of approximately three five-year plans [on the one hand] and basically completing the socialist transformation of capitalist industry and commerce within the same period [on the other] is also the question of the relation between agricultural cooperativization and the bourgeoisie.(E)

We believe that only when agriculture is in the process of undergoing a thorough socialist transformation can the alliance between the working class and the peasants be gradually consolidated on a new basis, i.e., on the basis of socialism; then and only then can we completely sever the ties between the urban bourgeoisie and the peasants; then and only then can we isolate the bourgeoisie completely and thus make it easier for us to transform capitalist industry and commerce thoroughly. Our goal in carrying out the socialist transformation of agriculture is to pull out the roots of capitalism over the vast expanse of rural areas.(E)

At present, we still have not completed agricultural cooperativization, and the working class still has not yet formed a solid alliance with the peasantry on a new basis; the alliance between the working class and the peasants is still unstable. The alliance we formed with the peasants in the past on the basis of the land revolution no longer satisfies the peasants.[2] They have become somewhat forgetful of the benefits that they gained in that [struggle]. Now there must be new benefits for them – that is, socialism. At present the peasants have not all prospered together; food grain and industrial raw materials are still very insufficient. In this situation the bourgeoisie may be able to find our faults on this question and attack us. [But] in a few years we will see a completely new situation: the working class and the peasants will have formed a far more consolidated alliance than that of the past on a new basis.(E)

This alliance of the past, which was [based on] opposing the landlords, attacking the local despots, and dividing up the land, was a temporary alliance.[3] It was consolidated for a short while, but then it could not remain consolidated any further. After land reform, the peasants started to polarize. If we don't have anything new for the peasants and cannot help them improve the forces of production, increase their income, and make them prosper together, the poor [peasants] will have no faith in us. They will feel that going along with the Communist Party is meaningless, for, if after the dividing up of the land they are still poor, then why should they want to go along with you? As for those well-off ones, those who have become rich peasants or very well-to-do peasants, they won't trust us either. They feel that the policy of the Communist Party has never been to their taste. The result is that neither [side] has faith [in] us; the poor peasants don't believe [in] us; nor do the rich peasants. Thus the worker-peasant alliance is far from consolidated. If we want to consolidate the worker-peasant alliance, we must lead the peasants onto the socialist road and enable the peasant masses to become prosperous together. The poor peasants must prosper. All the peasants must prosper, and moreover, the level of their prosperity must exceed by far the present level of prosperity of the well-to-do peasants. Once cooperativization is realized, the entire rural population will become increasingly prosperous year by year, and [the production of] commodity grain[4] and industrial raw materials will grow continuously. At that time the bourgeoisie will have nothing more to say and will find itself in a completely isolated position.(E)

At present we have two alliances: one is the alliance with the peasants, the other is an alliance with the national bourgeoisie. These two alliances are both very necessary for us: Comrade Zhou Enlai also discussed this topic.[5] What advantages does the alliance with the national bourgeoisie have [for us]? We can get even more industrial products to exchange for agricultural products. After the October Revolution there was a time when Lenin planned to do just this. Because the state didn't have industrial products to exchange [for grain], the peasants didn't hand over food grain; nor could [the state] simply buy [the grain] with [mere] paper money. Therefore Lenin proposed to allow the proletarian state authority to form an alliance with national capitalism in order to secure more industrial products to cope with spontaneous [capitalist] forces in the countryside.[6] It is also precisely for the purpose of obtaining even more industrial products to satisfy the peasants' needs and to make it easier to change the peasants' reluctance to sell food grain and even some other industrial raw materials that we are now forming an alliance with the bourgeoisie and, for the time being, are implementing the policy of utilizing, restricting, and transforming capitalist enterprises rather than confiscating them.[7] This is using the alliance with the bourgeoisie to overcome the peasants' reluctance to sell [grain and other raw materials]. At the same time, we rely on the alliance with the peasants to obtain food grain and industrial raw materials with which to control the bourgeoisie. The capitalists have no raw materials, [but] the state has raw materials. If they want raw materials then they will have to hand over their industrial products for sale to the state, thus putting into effect state capitalism.[8] If they don't do so, we won't give them raw materials. Either way, we will hold them in check. This will block up the capitalist road the bourgeoisie intends to follow – the road of setting up free markets,[9] freely obtaining raw material, and freely selling industrial products – and moreover it will cause the bourgeoisie to become politically isolated. Here, I am talking about the interaction between these two alliances. Of these two alliances, the alliance with the peasants is the principal [one], the basic [one], the primary [one], while the alliance with the bourgeoisie is temporary and secondary.[10] In an economically backward country such as ours, both of these two alliances are necessary at the moment.(E)

The land reform enabled us to form an alliance with the peasants on the basis of democracy and enabled the peasants to obtain land. For the peasants to obtain land is a matter that has a bourgeois democratic revolutionary nature [since] it only destroys feudal ownership [but] does not destroy either capitalist ownership or individual ownership. That alliance made the bourgeoisie feel isolated for the first time. In 1950, at the Third Plenum of the [Seventh] Central Committee, I said that we shouldn't hit out in all directions [at the same time].[11] At that time many areas throughout the whole country had still not carried out land reform, the peasants still hadn't completely come over to our side. If we had opened fire on the bourgeoisie then, things would not have worked. Once land reform had been carried out and the peasants had completely come over to our side, then we could and would have to carry out the "Three-Anti's" and "Five-Anti's" [campaigns].[12] The cooperativization of agriculture would enable us to consolidate the alliance with the peasants not on the basis of bourgeois democracy but on the basis of proletarian socialism. This then will cause the final isolation of the bourgeoisie, [thus] making it simpler to finally eliminate capitalism. We have absolutely no qualms about doing this! Marxism is fierce in this way; it doesn't have many qualms [in these matters]; it aims to eradicate imperialism, eradicate feudalism, eradicate capitalism, and eradicate small-scale [modes of] production. In these matters, it's better to have fewer qualms. We have some comrades who are too merciful; they are not forceful enough; that is to say, they are not that Marxist. To bring about the eradication of the bourgeoisie and of capitalism in China with its population of six hundred million is a very good undertaking; it is an immensely meaningful and good enterprise. Our goal is to eradicate capitalism, to root it out from the face of the earth, and to turn it into a thing of history. All things that have arisen historically will eventually be eliminated. There is nothing on earth that has not arisen historically; what is born will also die. This thing [called] capitalism has developed historically; hence it will also die; it has a very good place to go; that is, it can go to its [last] "sleep" in the sod.(E)

At present the international environment is conducive to our completing our general task in the period of transition.[13] We must basically complete socialist industrialization and socialist transformation in a period of three five-year plans.[14] We must definitely strive to gain such a length of time for peaceful construction. Three of the fifteen years have already passed, [so] twelve more years [of peace] will do. It seems that this [time] can be gained, [but] we must strive hard for it. We must redouble our efforts in our work in foreign affairs and national defense construction.

During this fifteen year period[15] the international and domestic class struggle may be very tense. We have already seen that it is very tense. We have already achieved a good many victories in the class struggle, and moreover we must continue to win [such] victories in the future. Looking at the domestic class struggle in the last year [we can say that] we have principally accomplished four things: one was carrying out the struggle against idealism; the second was suppressing the counterrevolutionaries; the third was resolving the problem of food grain, and the fourth was resolving the problem of agricultural cooperativization. The struggle over all four of these issues had the nature of a struggle against the bourgeoisie; we dealt the bourgeoisie a severe blow and are continuing to deal them blows that will smash them to bits.

Beginning with the struggle over the question of *Hongloumeng* [Dream of the Red Chamber], and in conjunction, the criticism of *Wenyi bao* [Literary Gazette] and, subsequently, criticizing and repudiating Hu Shi and Liang Shuming, we have already been carrying out [the struggle against idealism] for a year.[16] We must carry out the opposition to idealism in earnest, and we are prepared to carry on [this struggle] for [a period of] three five-year plans. In the struggle against idealism we must build an army of cadres [who uphold] Marxist dialectical materialism so that the broad [masses of] our cadres and people can arm themselves with the basic theories of Marxism. In the suppression of counterrevolutionaries, we are prepared to carry out, during this year and the next, the work of purging the counterrevolutionaries, [taking as the scope of this struggle] the state-run factories, state-run commercial [enterprises], cooperatives, all the various organizations at the *xian*, district and *xiang* levels, and furthermore, including cadres in the military and workers in the factories – generally speaking, a scope that encompasses some twelve million people in all. When we talk about counterrevolutionaries, it seems as though there aren't too many [of them]; if you [just] look you can't see them. If investigation is done, [however,] [you will find that] they are indeed there. At present we have already exposed a bunch of them. [We] have also fought a great battle over the problem of food grain. The bourgeoisie used the grain problem as an excuse to attack us; within the Party there also emerged a spate of rumors, and therefore we launched a criticism [campaign]. Over the issue of agricultural cooperativization we have carried out a good number of struggles. This conference, too, has focused on the discussion of this question. We have inaugurated a tremendous battle over these four issues; we have struck blows at the resistance and the attacks of the bourgeoisie, [and] we have gained the initiative.(E)

The bourgeoisie is afraid that we will launch an attack against it on these issues; in particular, it is afraid of [the campaign for] the suppression of counterrevolutionaries. Our work in suppressing counterrevolutionaries has been done well. In [doing] this work we must pay attention to criteria [because] it would be very dangerous not to have criteria. Only when someone meets the criteria [which define a counterrevolutionary] can that person be called a counterrevolutionary; this means that we want to suppress only true counterrevolutionaries; we don't want to suppress anybody who is not really a counterrevolutionary. We must allow for the possibility that we may turn up phony counterrevolutionaries: it's very difficult to rule out [this possibility]. But [nonetheless] it is our aim that fewer cases of false counterrevolutionaries will be turned up, and none at all if possible. Everything must fit the criteria and must be the real and genuine article; they simply have to be real counterrevolutionaries, and we must not wrong good people. At the same time, it is also possible that we might neglect a few true counterrevolutionaries. You might say that this time we have cleaned up [all the counterrevolutionaries]. Not necessarily; it is very hard to avoid letting a few slip by us. Nevertheless, we must make every possible effort to let as few as possible slip by us.

(2) Summing up the Debate over the Question of Cooperativization

On the issue of agricultural cooperativization, many inventions coming from the masses have broken down a good number of superstitions and have dispelled a good number of incorrect viewpoints.[17] This discussion has resolved many of the questions that a lot of people still hadn't fully understood a few months ago.

The question is first whether it is better to develop [cooperativization] in a big way or in a small way. This is a major question, [and] the debate [on it] has been a very big [one], [but] now it has been resolved. The masses demand development in a big way; the general tasks of the period of transition require that agricultural [development] correspond to industrial [development]; consequently the viewpoint advocating development in a small way is incorrect.(E)

The next question is whether or not [cooperativization] can be developed in those areas that were liberated later, whether or not it can be developed in the mountainous areas, the backward *xiang*, and the disaster areas. This question has now been resolved; development is possible in all these areas.

The third question is whether the minority nationality regions can set up cooperatives or not. By now it has been proven that any place where conditions are ripe can set up cooperatives. There are some areas, such as Tibet and the Daliang and Xiaoliang mountains,[18] where conditions are still not ripe, in which case we cannot as yet go to set up cooperatives [in these places].

The fourth question is whether [in places] without funds, without carts, without oxen, and without the participation of well-to-do middle peasants cooperatives can be set up or not. It has now been proven that they, too, can set up [cooperatives].

The fifth issue concerns the saying, "Cooperatives are easy to set up but hard to consolidate." This superstition has also been broken down. Setting up cooperatives isn't really all that easy on the one hand, [and] on the other hand, consolidating them is not necessarily all that hard. [Those who] insist on saying that cooperatives are easy to set up but hard to consolidate are actually advocating not setting up cooperatives [at all] or [are advocating] that it is best to set up only a minimum.

The sixth question is whether [places] that do not have agricultural machinery can set up cooperatives or not. At present the idea that only when [an area] has [agricultural] machinery can it set up a cooperative is no longer very widespread, although some [people] still persist in this viewpoint. This superstition is also one that can be completely destroyed.[19] (E).

The seventh question is whether all the cooperatives that have been poorly run should be disbanded or not. Naturally there is a small number of cooperatives that simply cannot continue to be run, [and these] can revert back to mutual aid teams. But generally speaking the so-called poorly run cooperatives ought not be disbanded; [all they need is to] undergo reorganization and then they can be turned into well-run cooperatives.[20]

The eighth point concerns the "argument," most likely transmitted to the lower levels by the Rural Work Department of the Central Committee,[21] that "If we don't get off the horse quickly, we will destroy the worker-peasant alliance." The Rural Work Department of the Central Committee has not only been producing rumors, but it has also been producing many [such] "arguments." For the most part I think this sentence is "correct" as long as you change one word; that is, [as long as you] change "off" to "on" then it would be all right. You folks at the Rural Work Department needn't get depressed. I accept as many words as you have given me, with the exception of only the one word that I changed. The difference is in only one word; what we are debating is only one word; you want to get off the horse, I want to get on the horse. "If we don't get on the horse quickly we will destroy the worker-peasant alliance"; the prospects of its destruction are indeed present.[22] (E)

The ninth point concerns the saying that "The cooperatives are to blame for the death of the draft oxen." This interpretation isn't fully in accord with the actual situation. In the main, the deaths of draft oxen are not owing to the cooperatives but owing to flood, to the excessively high price of oxhide, and to insufficient feed; and then there are some draft animals that are old and had to be killed.

The tenth point involves the allegation that "the tense situation in the countryside basically stems from the fact that too many cooperatives have been set up. " This interpretation is wrong. The tense situation in the rural areas this spring arose principally [as a result of] the grain problem. The alleged shortage of grain was, in the main, a fraud; it was the clamoring of the landlords, the rich peasants, and the well-to-do middle peasants. On this matter, we did not have time to do sufficient education among the broad masses of peasants, [and] at the same time our work in the area of food grain had some shortcomings. Last year we didn't find out what actually was the proper amount of grain we should buy and [consequently] purchased seven billion catties in excess of the necessary amount.[23] Now we will readjust and are prepared to buy seven billion catties less. Furthermore, this year's harvest is good. In this way, the situation in the countryside can be ameliorated.

Eleventh, there is also the saying that "the cooperatives can only have three years of superiority." This is pessimistic. In my view the superiority of the cooperatives definitely will not be limited to three years; socialism will continue for quite a long time. When we get to that point in the future, when socialism can no longer represent superiority, then the superiority of communism will supplant it.

Twelfth, should we establish some higher-stage cooperatives in the near future or not?[24] [We] were not very clear on this question in the past, [and now] it has been brought up [at the conference]. We should set up a group of higher-stage cooperatives. As for how many we should establish, [it's up to] you to deliberate.

The thirteenth point concerns the allegation that "junks and animal-powered carts cannot be cooperativized." This is wrong. Today one can see that the millions of laborers in the transportation trades involving junks and animal-powered carts also should be organized into cooperatives.

On the basis of your discussion we have resolved a good many problems; this is the great result of this plenum of the Central Committee.

(3) On the Question of Comprehensive Planning and Strengthening Leadership

Comprehensive planning should include: first, the planning of cooperatives; second, the planning of agricultural production, [and] third, overall economic planning. Overall rural economic planning includes [planning of] sideline occupations, handicraft industries, diversified economic undertakings, synthesized multipurpose economic undertakings, short-distance reclamation of wasteland and resettlement, supply and marketing cooperatives,[25] credit cooperatives,[26] banks, technique-dissemination stations, etc., plus afforestation of barren hills and villages. I think that the barren mountains in the North in particular should be afforested, and it certainly can be done. Do [you] comrades from the North have this courage? Many places in the South also must still be afforested. It would be good if we could see forests everywhere throughout the North and South in a few years. This work is beneficial to agriculture, to industry, to everything.

What other planning is there? There is also the planning of culture and education, which includes eliminating illiteracy,[27] running primary schools, running middle schools that are appropriate to the needs of the countryside, increasing the curriculum related to agriculture in the middle schools a bit, publishing popular reading materials and books that suit the needs of the peasants, developing the rural broadcasting network and movie projection teams, organizing cultural and recreational activities, etc. In addition, there is consolidating and building the Party, consolidating and building the League,[28] work among women, and also the suppression of counterrevolutionaries. All these aspects should be included in the overall planning.

There should be these different types of planning: (1) the planning of the village cooperatives. Every cooperative should have a plan. Even if [a cooperative] is small it should have a plan; [we should] make them learn how to do this kind of thing. (2) Planning on a *xiang* scale. Our country has about 220,000 *xiang* [therefore we should] make 220,000 or so plans for the *xiang*. (3) Planning on a *xian* scale. We hope that each *xian* will draw up a plan. At present some of the *xian* have already worked out excellent plans, and they make really interesting reading. Their thinking is liberated; they fear neither heaven not earth; they are not fettered by any leg-irons or handcuffs; the plans that they have drawn up are quite lively. (4) Planning for provinces (or autonomous regions, or the suburban areas of all municipalities). Among these plans [we must] emphasize the *xiang* and *xian* plans. We must grasp these two links firmly [and] quickly draw up a group [of such plans]. For example, in a province, three or four *xian* plans can be drawn up and published so that all the other localities can follow suit.(E)[29]

The planning of cooperativization should establish different speeds of development for different areas. These areas can be divided into three types. The first type makes up the majority of the areas; the second, a small portion of the areas; and the third makes up another small portion of the areas. For the majority of the areas there should be three waves [of cooperativization], three winter-spring [periods]. The three waves are: this winter and next spring, next winter and the following spring, and the following winter and spring. [These] three winter-spring [periods] are the three waves, with one wave arising before the previous one has fully subsided; between waves we should rest a bit. Between two mountains there is a valley, between two waves a trough.[30] In these areas it will be possible for semisocialist cooperativization to be basically accomplished by the spring of 1958.[31] In the second type of area two winter-spring [periods], two waves, will be enough, for example, in North China, the Northeast, and some suburban areas. Among these areas there are some individual areas that can basically complete cooperativization by spring of next year; that is, only one wave will be enough. The third type of area, that is, those others that make up the minor portion of the areas, will require four, five, or even six winter-spring periods [to basically complete cooperativization]. In this we must still make exceptions of some of the minority nationality areas, such as the Daliang and Xiaoliang mountains, Tibet, and other minority nationality areas where conditions are not ripe, [since cooperativization] cannot be carried out where conditions are not ripe. What do we mean by basically completing semisocialist cooperativization? It means that seventy to eighty per cent of the rural population will have entered semisocialist cooperatives. Within these [guidelines] there is also some margin for maneuver; seventy per cent is all right and so is seventy-five, or eighty, or even a few per cent more – this is what we mean by basically completing semisocialist cooperativization. That little bit that is left over can be taken care of later. Going too slow is no good, [but] neither is going too fast. Going too slow and going too fast are both opportunism. There are two types of opportunism; one is the opportunism of [going too] slow; the other the opportunism of [going too] fast. It is easier for the people to understand if we explain it in this way.(E)

The three levels of provinces (municipalities and autonomous regions), [special] districts, and *xian* must keep up on the conditions of the development in the movement every minute and resolve problems as soon as they arise. We must remember not to allow problems to build up before we make a summary; [that would be] to give belated criticism. In the past, much of our work was done in this way; problems that evolved along the way were not resolved; we let them build up, and then at the last minute we made a summary and a criticism. Some comrades committed this error during the "Three-Anti's" and "Five-Anti's" campaigns. We mustn't indulge in criticism after the event. It is necessary to criticize things [after they occur], but it would be best to criticize [errors] just when they appear. It is no good to indulge in criticizing things [only] after the event and to fail to give guidance in changing circumstances at the moment of change. What is to be done when one encounters an unfavorable situation? [If we encounter] an unfavorable situation we must immediately put on the brakes, or call a halt to things. It's like riding in a car – if you run into danger going down a very steep slope, you immediately brake the car to a halt. The provinces, [special] districts, and *xian* all have the power to put a halt to things. We must pay attention to guarding against "Left" [deviation]. Guarding against "Left" [deviation] is Marxist, not opportunist. Marxism does not advocate "Left" deviation; "Left" opportunism is not Marxism.

From now on, in our work of developing cooperatives, what should the areas of our competition be? Our competition should be in quality and in [meeting] specifications. As for quantity or speed, it will be fine as long as the provisions referred to earlier are met; the emphasis is on competition over quality. What are the criteria for [measuring] quality? They are increasing production and not [allowing] livestock to die. What do we have to do before we can increase production? What do we have to do before we can prevent livestock from being killed? To accomplish these goals we will have to observe the principle of voluntary participation and mutual benefit, make comprehensive plans, and provide flexible leadership. If we follow these few points I think that the quality of the cooperatives will improve so that production can be increased and there will be no loss of livestock. We must at all costs avoid the mistake the Soviet Union made in allowing large numbers of livestock to be slaughtered.[32] The key is in the next two years, during which the next five months are the most important, that is, this winter and next spring. From this November until next March, I ask you all to pay attention to avoiding major disturbances by all possible means and to avoiding any [large] loss of cattle. Since at present we still have very few tractors, oxen are a treasure; they are the primary tools for agricultural production.[33]

In the next five months, the principal cadres at the five levels of the province, the [special] district, the *xian*, the district, and the *xiang*, primarily the [Party] secretaries and deputy secretaries, must by all means probe into the question of cooperatives and become familiar with all aspects of their problems. Is this period too short? I think five months is enough if you make a conscientious effort to probe. Of course it is very important for the comrades at the provincial level to make such a conscientious effort to probe; [but it is] especially [important] for the *xian*, district, and *xiang* cadres, for if they don't probe into the question, and [if] they set up a lot of cooperatives while they themselves don't know anything about them, it would be very dangerous. What should be done if [someone simply] cannot probe into the question even if he keeps at it? In that case [that cadre's] work assignment should be changed. After five months, that is after next March, the Central Committee may well call another meeting like this one. At that time we will have a competition over quality; our speeches should then center on something new rather than repeating the speeches made at this [conference]; that is, we will discuss the problem of comprehensive planning, the problem of administration and management, and the problem of leadership methods. [We] will discuss what methods are good for setting up more and better cooperatives faster. That is, we will talk about the problem of quality.

Leadership methods are very important. If we don't want to make mistakes, we must pay attention to leadership methods and strengthen the leadership. Here are some suggestions on leadership methods; see if they are practicable. This is what we are all doing now, holding several conferences a year, either large ones or small ones, in order to resolve current problems. If a problem arises, one must look for what is universal in particular [cases]. One does not have to catch all the sparrows and dissect them to prove that "although the sparrow is small, it has all the vital organs." Scientists have never done things that way.[34]

Once it is clear about a few cooperatives, one can draw the appropriate conclusions. Aside from the method of calling meetings, there are also the methods of sending telegrams, making telephone calls, and going on inspection tours, all of which are important leadership methods. In addition, each province should select suitable persons to do a good job of running periodicals and to improve periodicals [in order to] exchange experiences rapidly. [There is] another suggestion that I would ask you to try out. I spent eleven days of time and effort reading over 120 reports to which I made corrections and added comments.[35] In doing so I "traveled through all the kingdoms," traveling even more widely than Confucius did; I have even "traveled" to Yunnan and Xinjiang.[36] I wonder if it is possible for each province and autonomous region to publish a book in a year or half a year with each *xian* contributing an article so that the experiences of all the *xian* can be exchanged. This could be helpful to the rapid expansion of the cooperativization movement. Still another method is issuing bulletins. The *xian* [Party] committee should send bulletins to the [special] district [Party] committee, and the [special] district [Party] committee should send bulletins to the provincial [Party] committee or [autonomous] region Party committee, while the provincial and [autonomous] region Party committees should send bulletins to the Central Committee. [The bulletins should] report on how progress is being made in cooperatives and on whatever problems have cropped up. Upon receiving such bulletins, leaders at each level will be in the know about the situation and will have suggestions regarding various leadership methods. Comrades, please think them over.

(4) On Ideological Struggle

Past experience has demonstrated one thing: ideological struggle must be to the point. At present there is a saying that different ideas must cross swords with each other. This is like fighting; you thrust and I parry; the two swords must cross – this is what is called a duel. If different ideas do not cross swords with each other, then [we] will lack clarity and thoroughness, which is not good. At this meeting we have crossed swords ideologically; we have [achieved] clarity and thoroughness. The primary benefit of this method is that it [can] help the majority of comrades to perceive questions clearly, while another benefit is that it [can] help comrades who have made errors to correct their errors.

As for comrades who have committed errors, I think there are only two rules: first, they themselves must want [to continue to] make revolution, and second, other people must also allow them to continue to make revolution. There are also some individuals who themselves do not want to continue making revolution. For example, Chen Duxiu was no longer willing to continue [making revolution]; Zhang Guotao was no longer willing to continue [making revolution]; Gao Gang and Rao Shushi were no longer willing to continue [making revolution], but such people are an extremely small minority.[37] The great majority want to continue [making] revolution. But there is also another rule: one must let others [make] revolution. We should not be like the fake foreign devil in *Ah Q zhengzhuan* [True Story of Ah Q][38] who did not allow Ah Q [to make] revolution; nor should we be like the White-robed Scholar Wang Lun in *Shuihu zhuan* [Water Margin][39] who also did not allow other people [to make] revolution. People who do not allow others [to make] revolution put themselves in a very dangerous position. The White-robed Scholar Wang Lun did not allow others [to make] revolution, and as a result he ended up losing his own life. Gao Gang did not let others [make] revolution, and didn't he lose his life in the end too?

Past experience has proven that the overwhelming majority of people who have committed the error of dogmatism or the error of empiricism can be corrected. Here there must be two rules: on the one hand there must be serious criticism, and on the other there must be an attitude of forbearance. It is no good to do without the latter, for without it relations would become abnormal. Who has not made some mistakes? Regardless of who he is, everyone has made some mistakes, big or small. There are, as a rule, only a very few incorrigible people, such as Chen Duxiu, Zhang Guotao, Gao Gang, Rao Shushi, and also Chen Guang[40] and Dai Jiying.[41] Aside from this extreme minority, the other people can all be saved; they can all correct their errors with the help of comrades. This is the way we should do things; we should have this confidence. Those who have made errors should themselves also have such confidence.

Some comrades in the Rural Work Department of the Central Committee, and principally Comrade Deng Zihui,[42] have made mistakes. The errors that he has made this time are of the nature of a Right deviation and empiricism. Comrade Deng Zihui has made a self-criticism. Although in small-group meetings some comrades feel that his self-criticism was still not thorough [enough], on the other hand, our comrades in the Political Bureau and some other comrades have discussed it a bit and feel that it is basically good. For the moment, the understanding that he has is good enough. In the long revolutionary struggle of the past, Comrade Deng Zihui has done a good amount of work and has achievements [to his credit]; these must be recognized. But he must not consider these achievements to be baggage. On this point he himself has spoken; he said that he flaunted his seniority somewhat. People must be a bit more modest. As long as [Comrade Deng] is modest and willing to accept the help of other comrades, we believe that his errors can be corrected.

In the past Comrade Deng Zihui made a programmatic suggestion that we should rely on merchants (that is, rely on the bourgeoisie) and the "four big freedoms."[43] That was wrong. It was indeed a bourgeois program, a capitalist program, not a proletarian program; it violated the decision of the Second Plenum of the Seventh Central Committee to restrict the bourgeoisie.[44] At present we are using the policy of restriction in dealing with the urban bourgeoisie and the rural bourgeoisie (the rich peasants).[45] Therefore the "four big freedoms," which place no restrictions on hiring laborers, trade, lending money, and renting land, are problematic. I would say there are "four small freedoms." There is a distinction in the degree of magnitude [between my "freedoms" and theirs.] Under [the policy of] restriction, the bourgeoisie has a bit of freedom [in these areas], [but] only a little bit. We must prepare the conditions for abolishing [even] these small freedoms of the bourgeoisie. With regard to the urban bourgeoisie, we call this [the policy of] utilization, restriction, and transformation. We must use [them], but we must restrict that portion [of the bourgeoisie] that is not beneficial to the national economy and the people's livelihood. This type of policy is neither "Left" nor Right. No restriction [of the bourgeoisie] at all would be too Right; extremely rigid restrictions, not allowing them to do anything at all, would be too "Left." Lenin said it would not only be foolish, but moreover suicidal, for a political party to think of completely eliminating capitalism at one stroke when tens of millions of small producers [still] exist.[46] Nevertheless, Comrade Deng Zihui's suggestion was incorrect because he did not mention restriction and was therefore at variance with the formulation of the Central Committee and the formulation of the Second Plenum.

Some comrades have paid almost no attention to Party resolutions and to policies that the Party has advocated over long periods of time. It's as if they have never seen them nor heard of them – I don't know why. For example, the mutual aid and cooperative movement was implemented, for a good number of years, in the central revolutionary base areas, in Yanan, and in each and every base area, yet it's as if [some comrades] hadn't seen them or heard of them.[47] In the winter of 1951 the Central Committee already adopted a resolution on mutual aid and cooperativization in agricultural production,[48] but it likewise passed unnoticed. Up until 1953 they were still not talking about fundamentals, preferring instead to be doing small favors.[49] By saying that they were not talking about fundamentals, I mean that they did not talk about socialism; by saying that they preferred to be doing small favors, I mean that they preferred to do small favors such as the "four big freedoms." That is to say, there were some comrades who completely ignored the Party resolutions and some policies and programs long advocated by the Party; [instead] they did things in their own way. Moreover, they never tried to find out whether problems similar [to this] had been discussed by some other people before, [and if so,] how they were discussed. Some historians even study tortoise shells,[50] inscriptions on bronzes, and stone tablets, as well as other unearthed ancient artifacts, and yet these comrades don't care in the least about things in our recent past; nor do they bother to look into these things. In short, their ears don't hear anything from beyond their own walls; they just write whatever they want and say whatever they want, as for example, they have been talking about such things as those "four big freedoms"; very well, in the end, they have run into a wall.

There are also some comrades who always prefer dispersionism[51] and assert their independence even to the point of setting up their independent kingdoms[52] and who find dictatorship quite to their taste. At first it was for comfort that they set up a kingdom and declared themselves kings. But what was the result? The result was that it made them very uncomfortable; they had to undergo criticism. Isn't there an opera called *Da deng dian* [Grand Pageant of Ascending the Throne]? Look how comfortable Xue Pingguei was when he became king, for at that time there was no such thing as self-criticism.[53] That was not good.

There are some people who never like to discuss things with others. Some comrades always pay lip service to [the principle of] collective leadership, but in fact they are extremely fond of being individual dictators; it's as if they would not have the appearance of being leaders if they were not dictatorial. To be a leader one need not be a dictator; you know that. The bourgeoisie has a bourgeois democracy; it emphasizes class dictatorship. The proletariat and the Communist Party must also have a class dictatorship; it would not be good to carry out the dictatorship of an individual. When there are problems, they should always be discussed with others; they should be resolved by a collective; it is better to pool the wisdom of the majority.

There is still another type of situation that must be discussed. There are some comrades who always bury themselves in their office work and never study problems. Do we do office work? Office work must be done. It is not acceptable not to do office work, but it would be dangerous if one only did office work and did not study problems. If you do not come into contact with cadres, if you do not come into contact with the masses, or if when you do come into contact with them, you are always lecturing them but not discussing things or exchanging ideas with them [by saying], "Do you think my ideas are correct or not? Please tell me your ideas," [if you are like that] you won't be able to sense the political atmosphere; your noses will become very insensitive, and politically, you will catch a cold. Once your nose is stuffed up, you can't sense what climate prevails at a certain time. Today Comrade Chen Yi[54] said that one must be able to grasp a thing as soon as it is budding. When something exists all around you in large numbers and you still don't see it, then [your nose] has become too insensitive. We must pay attention to such situations. This type of attitude of being preoccupied with office work and not paying attention to studying problems, not paying attention to getting in touch with the masses and cadres and not consulting them is very bad.

(5) Certain Other Problems

Most of the questions I will talk about below have been brought up by [other] comrades.

First, on the question of removing well-to-do middle peasants from leadership positions in the cooperatives, we must pay attention to [doing this] step by step and pay attention to [choosing] our method; we should not remove them all in one fell swoop. Although it is not suitable for the well-to-do middle peasants to be leaders, nonetheless they are laborers. We should analyze each case separately, looking at how they have acquitted themselves in their work. There are some people who must be removed [from their posts] because it really will no longer do to let them continue in these posts. But [we] must also make it clear to the masses (for example, the members of the cooperatives) and to the well-to-do middle peasants involved that it is indeed not suitable for these people to continue to be leaders. There is also another condition, which is that only when better people have been prepared as replacements, only when we have trained better people to replace them, can we remove them from their jobs. Some [of the well-to-do middle peasants] may continue at their posts after making self-criticisms and correcting their errors, and some can become deputy leaders or committee members.[55] Naturally, those who have done good work should not be on the list of those who are to be removed [from their posts] even though they are well-to-do middle peasants. We must not treat well-to-do middle peasants like rich peasants; well-to-do middle peasants are not rich peasants. We must not remove them all in one fell swoop. We must be careful in handling this problem, and we must resolve it appropriately. Each province and locality must analyze for itself whether the methods suggested above are feasible or not.(E)

Second, we must explain to people at the Party branches and among the masses that we are not drawing class distinctions all over again at this time when we say that the lower-middle peasants and the upper-middle peasants are two different strata, but rather [we are saying it] because in fact there are differences between each of the strata in terms of their either active or passive attitude toward collectivization. Moreover, there are such differences [of attitude] between individuals within any given stratum as well. For example, [even] among the poor peasants there are some who do not want to join the cooperatives just now. This point can be used to convince the well-to-do middle peasants; we could tell them, "Look! Even among the poor and lower-middle peasants there are some who are relatively passive. They don't want to join [the cooperatives], so we don't want them to join. So you well-to-do middle peasants who don't want to join now don't have to join either." First we should draw [into the cooperatives] the people who are enthusiastic [about joining]; then we should do propaganda among a second group of people so that once they become enthusiastic they will also be drawn in; then we should move on to do propaganda among a third group. We must [draw them in] by stages and batches. In the future, everyone will join the cooperatives. Therefore, it doesn't mean that we are redefining the class distinctions.

Third is the question of landlords and rich peasants entering the cooperatives. [See if it] can be done this way: taking the *xian* and the *xiang* as the units [of analysis] (using the *xian* alone as the unit is insufficient because [even if] a *xian* is basically cooperativized it is still possible that some of its *xiang* don't have cooperatives), if a *xian* and its *xiang* have been basically cooperativized, that is, seventy to eighty per cent of the peasant households have joined cooperatives, then those cooperatives there that have already been consolidated may begin to deal with [the problem of] rich peasants and landlords, in batches and in stages, according to how they have acquitted [themselves individually]. Those who have distinguished themselves favorably all along and who are honest [and] abide by the laws of the state can be designated members of the cooperative. Some can labor together [with the members] in the cooperatives and receive their share of the reward, but they are not to be called members of the cooperatives; in fact, they are probationary members; if they work well, then they can become [full] members of the cooperative; this will give them a good goal to work toward. A third group of people are temporarily not allowed to join the cooperatives; we will have to wait until the future to discuss it again and resolve it on an individual basis. None of the landlords or rich peasants admitted to the cooperatives will be allowed to take on positions of responsibility in them.[56] As for young intellectuals who come from landlord or rich peasant families and who have passed some tests and scrutiny, can they be absorbed and be given the responsibility for work such as teaching people in the villages to become literate? In some places there are very few other intellectuals, and there definitely is this need, so we should let them take on the work of teaching people to become literate under the leadership and supervision of the Party branch and the management committee of the cooperative. At present, among primary school teachers there are still many such people. I don't think it is necessary to insist that young people coming from landlord and rich peasant families, who are only seventeen or eighteen years old, and who have graduated from senior primary school or junior middle school should not be allowed to serve even as teachers to help people become literate. We can use them to wipe out illiteracy, to teach the peasants to read. Please study whether this is possible or not. On the other hand, making them responsible for such work as bookkeeping would be rather dangerous.(E)

Fourth, today I am still not going to talk about the conditions for [setting up] higher-stage cooperatives and the question of the number of higher-stage cooperatives that should be set up. On the question of the conditions [for setting up higher-stage cooperatives], we are still asking everybody to study further, and next year we can talk about it again. [Then] each locality can set up [higher-stage cooperatives] according to their [individual] situations and realities. In short, we can set them up where conditions are ripe, but where conditions are not ripe we cannot set them up. We should set up just a few at first and then gradually increase their numbers.(E)

Fifth, regarding the time for setting up cooperatives, can we give some thought to not necessarily concentrating [the building of cooperatives] in the winter and spring of each year, but also build some during the summer and fall? In fact, there are some places that at present are doing just that. But the point must be made: between two waves [of construction], there must be a period to rest and regroup; after a batch [of cooperatives] have been developed, there must be [a period to] regroup and consolidate, and then there can be another [period of] development. This is like fighting; between two battles there must be a period to rest and regroup. It is completely wrong not to rest and regroup, not to take a break, not to take a breather. In the military there was once the view that no rest and consolidation were needed, that we should not [stop to] take a breath, and what was necessary was to press forward and fight all the way nonstop. This is in fact impossible. People must sleep. If we didn't end today's meeting but continued it forever, everyone including myself would protest. Everyone has to have a big recuperation every day; they must sleep seven to eight hours, or at the least, five to six hours [a day]. That doesn't count all the short rest and regrouping periods in the interim. To talk about doing such a major thing as setting up cooperatives without [time to] rest and regroup is to be extremely naive.

Sixth, "Run cooperatives diligently and frugally"[57] is a very good slogan. This was put forward by the lower levels. [We] must be exactingly economical and oppose waste. At present there is a big [movement] to oppose waste in the cities and in the countryside as well. We must promote running households diligently and frugally, running cooperatives diligently and frugally, and building the country diligently and frugally. Our country must be, first, diligent, and second, frugal; [we] must not be lazy, and [we] must not be extravagant. Laziness leads to decay, [and] that is no good. In order to run cooperatives diligently and frugally, we must raise labor productivity, practice strict economy, reduce production costs, implement economic accounting, and fight against lavishness and waste. Raising productivity and reducing production costs is something that all cooperatives must do. [But] as for economic accounting, this must come about gradually.[58] As the cooperatives are enlarged, it will not do not to have economic accounting, [so we] must gradually learn to do economic accounting.

Seventh, at this conference no one talked about the question of state farms. This was a shortcoming. I hope that the Rural Work Department of the Central Committee and the Ministry of Agriculture will study the question of state farms.[59] In the future, the relative importance of state farms [in agricultural production] will increase year by year.

Eighth, [we] must continue to oppose Han chauvinism.[60] Han chauvinism is a form of bourgeois thought. It is easy for the Han, with so many people, to look down on the minority nationalities and to not help them sincerely; therefore [we] must vigorously oppose Han chauvinism. Naturally, among the minority nationalities, some narrow nationalism will arise, [and] this too must be opposed. But of these two things, the principle one, the one that must be opposed first, is Han chauvinism. As long as the attitudes of the Han comrades are correct, as long as [they] treat the minority nationalities in an honest and just way, as long as their nationalities policy and their standpoint on the relations among nationalities are entirely Marxist and are not bourgeois viewpoints, that is to say, as long as there is no Han chauvinism, the narrow nationalist viewpoints among the minority nationalities will be relatively easy to overcome. At present there is still quite a bit of Han chauvinism [among the Han people]; for example, [it is manifested] in monopolizing the affairs [of the minorities and not letting them do things for themselves], in not showing respect for other peoples' customs and habits, in considering oneself to be always in the right and looking down on others, in talking about how back-ward [other nationalities] are, and so on. At the National Party Conference this March, I already said that it would not do if China had no minority nation-alities. China has dozens of nationalities. The places in which the minority nationalities reside is a vaster area than the areas where the Han reside, and the material wealth hidden there is enormous. It would not do if our national economy did not include the economy of the minority nationalities.

Ninth, on the movement to wipe out illiteracy, I think we'd better get on the move. In some places the campaign to wipe out illiteracy has itself been wiped out. This is no good. In the midst of cooperativization, we must wipe out illiteracy. We must not wipe out the campaign to wipe out illiteracy. [The object] is not to wipe out [the campaign] to wipe out illiteracy, but to [actually] wipe out illiteracy [itself].(E)

Tenth, some people have asked: what do we mean by "Left" and Right devi-ations? As we have said in the past, things move in space and time. Here we are talking primarily about the time [aspect]. If people are out of touch with the actual situation in their observation of the movement of things, and if the [proper] time has not yet arrived but they are looking too far ahead [and think the time has arrived], this is called "Left" deviation; [if they don't look far ahead enough,] it's called a Right deviation. Taking the cooperativization movement for example, we already had, to begin with, these conditions that have already ripened – the enthusiasm of the masses, the widespread existence of mutual aid teams, and the leadership strength of the Party – but some comrades say they are still not [ripe]. The cooperativization movement, this thing, at the present moment (not several years ago but right now) has already [reached the point where it] can develop in a big way, [but] they say that it still cannot [develop in a big way]; all this is a Right deviation. [But] if conditions such as the level of the peasants' consciousness and the leadership strength of the Party were not ripe, [and] one still said that the entire country could be eighty per cent cooperativized within a very short period of time, that would be a "Left" deviation. China has a couple of proverbs that say: "When a mellon is ripe it falls from the stem"[61] and "When water comes, the ditch will be formed."[62] We should do things on the basis of specific conditions and do them so as to achieve our goals in a natural, rather than a forced, manner. Take giving birth to a child, for example. This takes nine months [of child bearing]; it is no good if, after seven months, a doctor presses down and forces the child out. This would be called a "Left" deviation. [But] if it has already been nine months and the child itself wants to come out, but you don't let it come out, this would be called a Right deviation. In short, things move in time; do things when the proper time has come; if you don't it would be a Right deviation; [but] if a certain thing's time hasn't come and you try to force it, that would be a "Left" deviation.

Eleventh, some people have asked: Is there the possibility of a "Left" deviationist error arising? Our answer is: It is utterly possible. If the leadership in any given place – regardless of whether it is the *xiang* Party branch, the district [Party] committee, the *xian* [Party] committee, or the [special] district [Party] committee – does not pay attention to the level of consciousness of the masses, [if it] does not pay attention to the situation [regarding] the development of mutual aid teams, [if it] has neither a program nor any control, or if it does not [establish the cooperatives] by stages and groups, but [rather] has an exclusive fondness for quantity without regard to quality, then serious "Left" deviationist errors will definitely occur. During a time when the masses' enthusiasm is surging forward, with everybody demanding to join the cooperatives, we must anticipate every type of difficulty and all possible unfavorable situations and openly explain them to the masses so that the masses can think [the problems] over thoroughly [for themselves]. If they are not afraid, they can go ahead with it. If they are afraid, they need not go ahead. Naturally we don't want to scare people off.(E)

I anticipate that I am not scaring you off today because we have already been meeting for so many days. At appropriate times it is necessary to put a bit of pressure on peoples' minds and to depress them a little bit lest they get too swell-headed.

We are opposed to incessant anxiety and to innumerable taboos and prohibitions. Is it possible, then, to be utterly without anxiety? Are we going to dispense with every last taboo, every single prohibition? Of course not.(E)

[There are] necessary anxieties, anxieties that we ought to have; is there anybody who does not have anxieties? We should also have the necessary taboos and prohibitions. How can we do without any taboos and prohibitions whatsoever? We absolutely ought to have the necessary anxieties, the necessary taboos and prohibitions, and the necessary pauses, intermissions, applying of brakes, and cut-offs.

There is [also] this method: Whenever people are just about to get arrogant, or whenever their tails are just starting to rise,[63] give them a new task, then they won't become arrogant [because] they won't have time. (For example, at present we are advocating competition in quality; when you come next year you must [be able] to compete in quality, [for] by that time the question of quantity would have become secondary.) We tried out this method in the past. After an army unit had won a victory, when some of the comrades were just discussing [this victory] with great zest with the people around them, when their tails were raised ever so high, we assigned them the new task of fighting a second battle. As soon as you assigned them a new task, they would have to think the problems over immediately, and they would have to do preparatory work. Then their strutting tails would come down and they wouldn't have time to get arrogant.

Twelfth, some comrades have posed [the question] of whether or not it is possible to allow the *xian* level to have ten per cent of the authority [to act with] flexibility?[64] For example, in talking about establishing cooperatives, [this would mean that they] might have ten per cent fewer or ten per cent more [cooperatives]. I think this suggestion can be accepted; it is a good one; [we] must not do things in too rigid a way. Please give this matter further consideration.

Thirteenth, will there be people who [would want to] reverse decisions?[65] The people who want to reverse decisions are quite numerous. They think that the cooperatives will come to nothing and that all we have done [with respect to the cooperatives] will be completely reversed in the future. They [even] say that we are not Marxists, but opportunists. However, as I see it, the trend is unmistakable; this decision cannot be reversed.(E)

Fourteenth, some people have asked: what will the future trend be like? The trend is as follows: within the time period of about three five-year plans, [we will] basically complete socialist industrialization and the socialist transformation of agriculture, of handicraft industries, and of capitalist industry and commerce. As I see it, this is precisely the trend. However, it is possible to go a bit further; as I said at the previous [National] Party Conference,[66] in a period of about fifty to seventy-five years, that is, within the period of ten to fifteen five-year plans, it will be possible to build [our country] into a powerful socialist country.(E)

Within fifty to seventy-five years many serious and complicated conflicts and struggles will definitely occur internationally, domestically, and within the Party. We will definitely encounter many difficulties. In our own experiences, we have gone through any number of conflicts, [both] armed [and] peaceful, [both] bloody [and] bloodless, in our lifetime. Can you say that from now on there will be no more [such conflicts]? There definitely will be, and moreover, they will be many rather than few. Included among them is the possibility of fighting a world war, having atom bombs dropped on our heads, plus the appearance of Beria's, Gao Gang's, Zhang Guotao's and Chen Dixiu's.[67] There are many things that are unforeseeable at present. But as we Marxists see it, it can be affirmed that all difficulties can be overcome and that a strong socialist China will definitely emerge. Is this certain? I think it is. According to Marxism it is certain.(E)

The bourgeoisie has already prepared someone to dig its grave. The grave is already dug; will it not die? In discussing the trend, [we can say that] roughly speaking this is the trend.

Fifteenth, you have had a lot of suggestions for revising the two documents – the resolution and regulations.[68] This is very good. We will collect [these suggestions] and give them some thought. After the resolution has been passed today, it will take only a few days for it to be revised and made public by the Political Bureau. As for the regulations, [though,] we'll have to go a bit slower; [we] should discuss them with the democratic personages and adopt legislative formalities. Perhaps, as with the military conscription law,[69] it must first be discussed by the Standing Committee of the National People's Congress, then sent to the State Council to be published, so as to seek the opinions [of the people]. Then the localities can try out [the regulations] in this way for a period of time, and then next year [the regulations] will again be submitted to the National People's Congress for ratification.(E)

Finally, in passing I would like to say a little about asking you to pay attention to the problem of writing articles. I hope those present will all become "language teachers." The articles you have written have been written quite well, with perhaps the exception of a few shortcomings. You must pay attention to helping others to improve the writing style in their essays. At present some of [our] comrades' essays are still full of empty phrases, but [such essays] are relatively few; the more important shortcoming is the prevalence of the classical style in writing and the excess of a semiclassical, semivernacular flavor [to it]. [When] writing an article one must give emphasis to [its] logic; one must pay attention to the structure of the article or the speech as a whole. The beginning, the middle, and the end must be linked; there must be an internal connection, and [the different parts] must not be mutually conflicting. You must also pay attention to grammar and syntax. Many comrades leave out subjects and objects that should not be left out, or [they] use adverbs in place of verbs or even leave out verbs completely. All of this is ungrammatical. [You] must also pay attention to rhetoric [and] ways in which [the article] could be written a bit more vividly. In all, [writing] logically, grammatically, and with better rhetoric, these are the three things I ask you to pay attention to when you are writing articles.

Notes

1. See Text June 15, 1953, note 1.
2. Mao is referring to the land reform program (see text Feb. 18, 1951, note 2) which became the basis for the class struggle in the countryside in China and for the program to forge an alliance between the workers and peasants nationwide in scope. While it returned the ownership of the land to the peasants, however, it did so on an individual basis. Consequently, because of the greater accessibility of rich peasants to agricultural means of production and better position in the urban-rural exchange, for instance, they continued to have an inherent advantage over poor peasants (see text Mar. 12, 1950, note 1). Moreover, individual production and exchange limited the possibilities for agricultural mechanization and thus for increasing agricultural production and, in turn, intensifying the worker-peasant alliance. Only by moving beyond the bourgeois-democratic land reform into cooperativization, Mao argued, could the gains of the poor peasants and the worker-peasant alliance be consolidated.
3. See text Jan. 17, 1951, note 1.
4. See text July 31, 1955, note 24.
5. A brief transcript of Zhou Enlai's speech at this plenum can be found in *XHYB* (Oct. 16, 1955).
6. "V. I. Lenin, 'The Tax in Kind'" (*SW*, V, p. 233). This is published as "On the Grain

Tax," in *The Collected Works of V. I. Lenin.* See also text 1960 Reading Notes, note 244.

7. See text Aug. 12, 1953, note 14.

8. See text July 9, 1953.

9. The Political Report of the Eighth National Party Congress stated that within the limits of the socialist market and subject to the guidance of the state, free markets should and would be permitted to exist (see Y. Lau [1977], p. 580); this includes a definition of "free markets under the leadership of the state."

Free markets basically took the form of markets in which peasants sold goods to other peasants or to urban residents outside of the state purchase and marketing system. Since prices paid on the free market were frequently higher than those paid by the state, free markets had a tendency to reduce the supply of goods available for state purchase. Hence free markets have been frequently attacked as capitalist practices. Here Mao seems to be referring to the possible emergence of this phenomenon in the industrial sector.

10. Here the *Xuanji* version has omitted the following: ". . . because the bourgeoisie is to be eliminated. In the future several million bourgeoisie will enter the ranks of the proletariat." See *Wansui* (1969), p. 14.

11. See text June 6, 1950.

12. See text Nov. 1951-Mar. 1952, source note.

13. This is similar to the "General Line of the Party" (text Sept. 25, 1955). The "general task" is the term used to describe this "line" in the 1954 Constitution of the PRC.

14. The *Wansui* (1969) version (p. 14) here has "within the next twelve years" and then adds: "Every year we can produce from 18 to 20 million tons of steel; about 73 billion kilowatt hours of electricity; about 280 million tons of raw coal; about 18 million tons of crude oil; about 60,000 metal cutting lathes; 183,000 tractors (equivalent to 15 horsepower each); 208,000 motor vehicles; about 16.8 million tons of cement; about 7.5 million tons of chemical fertilizer. (These levels correspond to the [production] levels of the Soviet Union in 1940; speaking of tractors alone, the output will be about the same as the Soviet Union's in 1954.) Grain production will reach 600 billion catties, an increase of 100 per cent; more than six million tons of cotton, an increase of more than 100 per cent (all compared with 1952 yields). By then the total number of tractors will reach 600,000 and the total acreage under mechanized cultivation will be 61 per cent of the total farmland. With another two five-year plans, when we will have completed the technological transformation of agriculture, the acreage under cultivation will be 100 per cent of the total. To accomplish these tasks we need a period of peaceful construction. Can we get such a period or not? Our comrades in the Ministry of Foreign Affairs, in the International Liason Department, and in the military must strive hard for it before we can get it."

15. Here, the *Wansui* (1969) version (p. 15) reads "five years" instead of "fifteen years."

16. See texts Sept. 16-18, 1953, Oct. 1954(1), Oct. 1954(2), and Oct. 16, 1954.

17. See text June 14, 1954, note 14.

18. This latter region refers to the Yi minority people's autonomous region in Southeast Sichuan.

19. These six issues basically correspond to the list in *Wansui* (1969), although the *Wansui* discussion is only a total of nine lines long. *Xuanji,* V also drops Mao's affirmation that cooperatives can be started in places where the people do not have a high level of literacy and cultural development and with only a small number of cadres while adding the assertion by Mao that they can be started without carts, oxen, or the participation of middle peasants.

20. This paragraph omits Mao's suggestion for dissolving bogus cooperatives which had been set up by rich peasants that appears in *Wansui* (1969), p. 18.

21. On the Rural Work Department's opposition to cooperativization, see text Dec. 6, 1955, note 1, and the latter part of this document itself.

22. See text July 31, 1955, section 9.

23. Here the *Wansui* (1969) version says "six billion."

24. See text Oct. 15, 1953, note 2.

25. The Resolution on the Development of Agricultural Producers' Cooperatives (APC) adopted by the Central Committee on December 16, 1953, stipulated three forms of agricultural

cooperativization, of which the supply and marketing cooperative is one. It performs an auxiliary function in supporting the mutual aid teams and APC and is a commercial organization providing cooperatives and their members with production materials and daily necessities that they do not themselves produce. The operations of these cooperatives are regulated by the "Regulations of the All-China Federation of Supply and Marketing Cooperatives," adopted by the First Congress of the All-China Federation of Cooperatives on July 25, 1954. See text Oct. 15, 1953, note 15.

26. These refer to the savings and loan organizations that were established by peasants responsible for the management of funds owned by individuals and that were not part of the collective's funds. This allowed people with surplus funds to obtain interest through low-interest loans to other needful individuals and collectives. Their operation began in 1951, but became obsolete by 1957, when agricultural cooperativization reached a much higher level than in 1955. (See the "Draft Regulation of Rural Credit Cooperatives" in *Jinrong fagui huibian* [Compendium of Regulations regarding Finance and Fiscal Management], 1949-1952.)

27. See text Dec. 6, 1955, note 4.

28. This refers to the Communist Youth League. See text Feb. 18, 1951, note 8, text June 30, 1953, source note, and text Sept. 7, 1955, source note.

29. In this paragraph Mao is obviously referring to plans that were then being drafted and some of which were described in the book *Zhongguo nongcun de shehui zhuyi gaochao* (Upsurge of Socialism in China's Countryside); the comments that Mao wrote for some of these plans thus subsequently published are presented as text Dec. 27, 1955 (2).

30. For Mao's philosophy of advancing in a wave-like pattern, see text Apr. 1959, note 1.

31. Here the *Wansui* (1969) version (p. 18) omits the word "spring."

32. According to *Ciyu jianshi* (pp. 43-44), when collectivization (i.e., the nationwide establishment of collective farms) took place in the Soviet Union in 1929-30, many CPSU cadres at the local levels violated the principle of "voluntarism" and the directive of the CPSU center that only the basic means of production, not including farmhouses and small livestock, were to be turned over to collective ownership. In response to the "forced collectivization" and in fear of losing their poultry and small livestock, the peasants of the Soviet Union began to kill off the livestock themselves. According to this information, there were only 27 million horses in the Soviet Union in 1931, as compared with 32.1 million in 1928, i.e., before collectivization – (a decrease of 16 per cent). The reduction in other areas were even more remarkable: Cattle (from 60.1 million to 42.5 million, 29 per cent); pigs (22 million to 11.7 million, 47 per cent), sheep (107 million to 68.1 million, 36 per cent).

33. Here the *Wansui* (1969) version includes two paragraphs that were omitted from *Xuanji*, V, dealing with how to avoid the slaughter of cattle and on the need to avoid problems in the next five months in order to allow the longer plan to succeed.

34. Mao is referring to the slogan "dissect a sparrow," which is an applied theory and a work method to acquire knowledge and sum up experiences. Instead of attempting to generalize about a vast number of repetitions of a phenomenon, this work method advocates the in-depth analysis thorough study and investigation of a prototype, and a summing-up experience through such analysis. The slogan is derived from the common saying, "while a sparrow is small, it contains all the vital organs." The origin of the saying cannot be traced.

35. These reports would become the basis of the book *Zhongguo nongcun de shehui zhuyi gaochao;* see note 29.

36. Mao uses here a common saying, *zhou you lie guo*, used first by Sima Qian in *Shi ji* (Historical Records), describing Confucius' travels throughout many of the states during the late Spring and Autumn period (i.e., ca. 590 B.C.) in search of a ruler who would hire him and apply his teachings to the ruling of his principality. This practice was spontaneously adopted by many of Confucius' contemporaries who were philosophers and/or political strategists, and by those of the ensuing generation through the "Warring States period" (475-221 B.C.).

37. See text Aug. 12, 1953, note 23, and text Mar. 31, 1955, note 7.

38. *Ah Q zhengzhuan* (The True Story of Ah Q) is a novelette written by Lu Xun and collected in the anthology *Na han* (Clamor). In this story, the son of a prominent villager, educated in

Japan, returns with affectations of Western mannerisms and dress styles. Liu Xun gives him the sobriquet *jia yang guizi* (the fake foreign devil). When the revolution arrives, the opportunistic "fake foreign devil" assumes the airs of a revolutionary. This impresses Ah Q, the village vagrant, who then "negotiates" with "the fake foreign devil" to join the revolution, but is drummed out of his residence by the latter. "The fake foreign devil" later organizes a looting session, euphemistically called a revolutionary movement. Ah Q is barred from this, but in an attempt to impress others, he imagines and boasts of being a participant of the "revolution." As a result, and since he had no alibi, Ah Q is later arrested and executed for a crime he did not commit. Also see text Apr. 25, 1956, note 42.

39. *Shuihu zhuan* (Water Margin) is a Ming dynasty novel, written by Shi Naien, about a group of "Robin Hood" type social bandits in the Southern Song dynasty. The White-robed Scholar Wang Lun was originally the chief of the Liangshanbo gang. He was, however, a very narrow-minded leader and did not readily take in newcomers. When Chao Gai and Wu Yong arrive with intentions to join his gang, he refuses them and, in an ensuing fight, is killed by Lin Chong, who then sets Chao up as the new leader.

40. Chen Guang was the deputy commander of the 115 Division of the Eighth Route Army during the War of Resistance against Japan. He was doing political work in the Northeast after 1946, and after Liberation, became the deputy commander of the Guangdong Military Region and commander of the Guangzhou Garrison of the PLA. He later became a member of the Jiangsu People's Provisional Government and remained in the position until 1955. In February 1955, being implicated for his association with Gao Gang in the Gao-Rao affair, he was removed from office. For more biographical information on Chen, see *Zhonggong renming lu*, pp. 581-582.

41. Dai Jiying became a member of the Communist Youth League in 1926 and a member of the CPC in the following year. In 1952, he was a member of the Henan provincial committee of the CPC and the secretary of the Kaifeng CPC municipal committee. He was later accused of obstructing the "Three-Anti's" movement in Kaifeng and was removed from his positions of responsibility.

42. Deng Zihui has been a member of the CPC since 1926. From July 1953 to September 1956, he was director of the Rural Work Department of the Central Committee of the CPC. In April 1959 he became a vice-premier of the State Council, and later in that year he headed the Office of Agriculture and Forestry under the State Council. In October 1959 he resumed his position as head of the Rural Work Department of the Central Committee. Mao's criticism of Deng and the Rural Work Department became more severe in the last two months of 1955. See text Dec. 6, 1955. For more biographical information on Deng, see D. Klein and A. Clark, eds. (1971), II, pp. 833-838.

43. See texts Oct. 15, 1953, note 9. Here the *Wansui* (1969) version (p. 21) merely says that the "four big freedoms" and "the consolidation of the New Democratic order" were the program of the bourgeoisie, and does not link them to Deng Zihui.

44. The Second Plenum of the Seventh Central Committee of the CPC was held at Xibaibo in Hebei in March 1949. See text June 6, 1950(2), note 1. The decision was made to effect the transition of the revolution from the countryside to the urban areas, and certain policies to deal with the capitalists were discussed. See K. Lieberthal (1976), pp. 49-50.

45. See text Aug. 12, 1953, note 14. For the manner in which this policy, which up to this point had been largely aimed against the urban capitalists, was made to include the rich peasants, see text 1960 Reading Notes, note 248.

46. "V. I. Lenin, op. cit." (*SW*, V, p. 234). As noted in note 6, this is published under the title "On the Grain Tax," in Lenin, *Collected Works*. The reference to Lenin does not appear in the *Wansui* (1969) version.

47. See text July 31, 1955, note 7.

48. Mao is referring to the Draft Resolutions of the CPC Central Committee on mutual aid and cooperativization in agricultural production, issued on December 15, 1951, and circulated to Party branches at all levels to be carried out on an experimental basis, and finally enacted as a CPC Resolution on February 15, 1953. See *SW*, V, p. 71, and T. Chen (1967), pp. 218-221, for text of these resolutions.

49. Mao is here using an aphorism, *yan bu ji yi, hao xing xiao wei,* derived from the book *Wei Ling gong* in *Lun yu* (Confucius' Analects). See text Nov. 4, 1953, note 4, for more detailed explanations.

50. Mao is using the vulgar descriptions of forms of writing in China. In the third millenia B.C., in the Shang dynasty, the ancient Chinese used tortoise shells and animal bones for purposes of divination and recorded the significance of the oracle on these shells and bones. This is known as *jiagu wen*, or shell and bone writing, and is the earliest form of writing discovered in China so far. Toward the end of the Shang dynasty the Chinese had begun to use bronze utensils, and they carved writing on bronze instruments and vessels. This is known as *jin wen* (metal writing) and also as *zhongding wen* (bell and vessel writing). This became the prevalent form of preserving written records of events in the Zhou dynasty. Later, during the Warring States period, the Chinese began to carve writings on slabs of stone, and, when China was united under the Qin dynasty, the Qin monarch recorded his own exploits on monolithic monuments in many places throughout his empire. The *shike wen* (stone carving writing), as it came to be known, became very common in the Han dynasties. Together, these three forms of writing constitute the most important source of information for the archaeological and anthropological study of ancient China.

51. See text Mar. 19, 1953, note 1, and text Mar. 21, 1955, note 7.

52. This refers to the tendency among some CPC cadres to regard departments and areas of work placed in their charge as their own personal spheres of influence and to manage work within these areas in their own interests, as individuals or as cliques, resisting the leadership of the Center. This is considered to be an acute development of the phenomenon of departmentalism. In the period since the establishment of the PRC in 1949, the most famous incidence of this phenomenon was when Gao Gang (see text Mar. 31, 1955, note 15) administered the affairs of Northeast China, which had been placed under his leadership, in this fashion. The term, however, does not necessarily refer to a geographical area, but can apply to administrative divisions as well. During the Cultural Revolution period, Liu Shaoqi and his group were also later repeatedly accused by Mao of creating independent kingdoms. See also text Apr. 1956, note 16.

53. This is an act from an old Beijing opera, *Hong song lie ma* (The Red-maned Stallion), which tells a story set in the Tang dynasty. The daughter of the prime minister, Wang Yun, balks at her father's wishes and marries a poor man, Xue Pinggui, who later joins the army and, through a strange twist of fate, marries the princess of the state of Western Liang. Xue eventually raises an army against the Tang, captures the Tang capital Changan, declares himself emperor, and wreaks vengeance, with redoubled vindictiveness and arrogance, on his erstwhile detractors.

54. Chen Yi (1900-1972) became a member of the Communist Party soon after his sojourn in France (1919-1921) as a participant of the work-study movement. He was deported from France in 1921. He participated in the Nanchang Uprising in 1927, and then was CPC provincial secretary of Jiangxi in the Jianxi Soviet period. When Mao and Zhu De embarked on the Long March, Chen remained behind in the Central Soviet. During the War of Resistance he commanded the First Division of the New Fourth Army. In the War of Liberation, he commanded the Third Field Army. After Liberation, he was primarily active in the area of foreign affairs; in Feb. 1958, he replaced Zhou Enlai as minister of Foreign Affairs, and in Mar. 1958, he also assumed the position of the director of the Foreign Affairs Office of the State Council, thus making him nominally the number one officer in the area of foreign policy, although in reality Zhou Enlai, as premier, still held the reins of policy. Zhou and Chen worked well together and shared a friendship that went back to the time when they were both in France. Chen was criticized during the Cultural Revolution. For more biographical information on Chen, see D. Klein and A. Clark, eds. (1971), I, pp. 104-113.

55. This sentence does not appear in *Wansui* (1969).

56. *Wansui* (1969), p. 22, says, "for three to five years." In his July 31, 1955, talk "On Agricultural Cooperativization," Mao had called for excluding landlords and rich peasants from the cooperatives. In line with this, the "Model Regulation for the Development of APC's," adopted by the Standing Committee of the NPC on November 9, 1955, stated that "during the first few years, the APC shall not accept former landlords and rich peasants as members." In his December

21, 1955, "Circular Requesting Opinions on the Seventeen Articles on Agricultural Work" Mao called on cadres to study both approaches to the problem. By January 1956, the seventeen points had become forty and were adopted on January 23 by the Political Bureau as the "Draft National Program for Agricultural Development (1956-1967).'' Point Four of the Draft Program stated that "during 1956 attempts should be made to settle the question of admitting to the cooperatives former landlords and rich peasants who have given up exploitation and have asked to join...,'' reflecting the ongoing struggle over this issue. The "Model Regulations for an Advanced [higher-stage] APC," adopted on June 30, 1956, revised the position and permitted former landlords and rich peasants to join as members.

57. Mao is not referring to an already popularized slogan, but rather to an idea that would shortly be brought to the forefront in the articles in *Upsurge of Socialism in China's Countryside* (text Sept. 25, 1955, and texts Dec. 27, 1955[1] and [2]). The second article in *Upsurge* carries this slogan as its title, and Mao's commentary on this article appears as no. 28 of the editorial notes in *SW*, V, p. 267. See text Dec. 27, 1955(2), note 7.

58. The economic accounting system is a system adopted in the PRC in assessing the value of an enterprise in which the unit cost of product, the unit price, the managerial costs of the plant, and the circulation of funds for the development of production are connected in an integrated accounting matrix. Its purpose is "to obtain maximum economic results through the recording, calculating, understanding, and analyzing of labor consumption and disbursement in production." (See *HQ*, 12 [1962], 28; 2 [1959], 5-8.) For a discussion of the struggle over the methods of economic accounting, see S. Andors (1977), pp. 101-103, 108-113, 217-218, and passim.

59. See text Mar. 19, 1953, note 4.

60. See text Mar. 16, 1953, source note.

61. This aphorism, *gua shu ti le*, from the Song dynasty book *Yunji qiqian* (Seven Oracles from the Cloud Chest), denotes that things will take place according to the rules of nature and do not require premeditation or human intervention.

62. This saying, *shui dao qucheng* (literally, when the water arrives the channel will be formed), has the same meaning as that in the preceding note. The aphorism is derived from a poem by the Song dynasty poet Fan Chengda.

63. See text June 14, 1954, note 13.

64. The *Wansui* (1969) version (p. 24), here has "ninety per cent."

65. The term here, *fan an*, translates as reversing of verdicts, in a judicial sense, and generally refers to changing verdicts or decisions that have already been made. In the CPC it is often used to refer to the reversal of decisions on individuals' standing in the Party, especially when Party lines have shifted.

66. See texts Mar. 21, 1955, and Mar. 31, 1955.

67. See text Mar. 31, 1955, note 7, and text Aug. 12, 1953, note 23, for information on Gao, Rao, Chen, and Zhang. Lavrenti Pavlovich Beria (1899-1953), became vice-chairman of the Council of Ministers of the USSR in 1941. He was a member of the Political Bureau of the Communist Party of the Soviet Union (CPSU) from 1939 onward and a member of the Presidium of the Supreme Soviet from 1952 to 1953. He was minister of Internal Affairs of the Soviet Union from March 1953 (i.e., after Stalin's death) to his own purge from the CPSU in July 1953. In December of that year he was sentenced to death.

68. These refer to the "Resolution on Agricultural Cooperativization," adopted on the day this speech was given (October 11, 1955) by the plenum of the Central Committee, and to the "Model Regulations for the Development of Agricultural Producers' Cooperatives," adopted by the Standing Committee of the NPC on November 9, 1955.

69. The Report on the Draft of the National Military Conscription Law was submitted to the Second Session of the First NPC on July 16, 1955, by Peng Dehuai. The law itself was approved by the Congress and promulgated on July 20.

A Speech at the Enlarged Sixth Plenum
of the Seventh Central Committee
[October 11, 1955][1]

Source: *Wansui* (1969), pp. 12-25. Available English Translations: JPRS, *Miscellany*, I, pp. 14-26; *Issues and Studies*, X:7 (April 1974), 103-111.

This is the other version of Mao's concluding speech to the Sixth Plenum of the Seventh Central Committee. See source note of preceding text in this volume for an explanation.

None of the annotations and explanations of terms done for the preceding text will be duplicated here. The reader is advised to use the two translated texts here together and comparatively.

I. This meeting has covered a very wide range [of issues]. It has been a great debate.

This meeting has resolved many problems and has been a very great debate. It has been a great debate over whether the general line of the Party during the period of transition is entirely correct or not. It was the question of the orientation of agricultural cooperativization that touched off this great debate throughout the entire Party involving a very wide range [of issues] – heavy industry, light industry, fiscal matters, finance, trade, communications, culture and education, health, science, suppression of counterrevolutionaries, transformation of the handicraft industries, transformation of capitalist industry and commerce, the Party, the League, trade unions, youth, women, internal affairs, the military, etc. Such a great debate was warranted. No debate of this sort had developed after the promulgation of the general line. We should extend this debate so that it be carried out among the comrades of the [Party] branches in the countryside. We should also extend it so that it can be carried out among the members of the [Party] branches in the cities, so that the tempo and quality in all areas of work will conform with the tasks prescribed by the general line. There should be comprehensive planning in all fields of work.

We will take about three five-year plans to complete the socialist transformation of agriculture. Within the same period, the socialist transformation of capitalist industry and commerce will also be completed. By then, it will be possible for the alliance between industry and agriculture, and between the workers and the peasants, to be consolidated on a new, socialist basis; only then can the ties between the peasants and the bourgeoisie be completely severed; only then can the bourgeoisie be completely isolated; and only then can the sources of capitalism be ultimately rooted out and eliminated over the vast expanse of territory of the countryside.

At present, we have not yet completed agricultural cooperativization, and the workers and the peasants have not yet formed a solid alliance. The worker-peasant alliance that was established in the past on the basis of land reform is currently in a state of instability. The peasants are no longer content with the gains they have made from the land reform. Some of them have already forgotten [such gains]. We have not yet given the peasants new benefits, (the new benefit is simply socialism). The peasants have not yet achieved prosperity together [with everybody else]. Grain and raw material for industries have not yet become plentiful; [therefore] the bourgeoisie is going to find pretexts to attack us.

A few years from now, we will see a new situation. The workers and the peasants will form a more solid alliance on a new basis. The worker-peasant alliance of the past, which was formed on the basis of land reform, was temporary and also unstable. Without changing the relations of production in the countryside, it would be impossible to enhance the agricultural forces of production; nor would it be possible to enable the peasants to attain collective prosperity. The classes would become polarized. Neither the poor nor the rich would have faith in us, and we would be unable to consolidate the worker-peasant alliance. [But as it is,] after a number of years, the landlords and the rich peasants will also gain faith in us. As all the peasants get richer every year and commodity grain increases, an entirely new situation will emerge and the bourgeoisie will be gagged.

We now have two alliances: one is the alliance with the peasants; another is the alliance with the bourgeoisie. Both alliances are necessary under the condition of China's economic backwardness. Our alliance with the bourgeoisie, [in which] we utilize and restrict [their capital] without confiscating it for the time being, is for the purpose of obtaining from them manufactured goods so as to amply provide for the needs of the peasants. Just like us, the peasants must eat and be clothed. With regard to many things (manufactured goods), it is not enough to give them coupons only; they would still hide their grain and not sell it. We are using our alliance with the bourgeoisie to deal with the peasants' mentality of being reluctant to sell [grain]. At the same time, we are using our alliance with the peasants to obtain grain and industrial raw materials, so as to gain control over the bourgeoisie. [We] want them to hand over manufactured goods and be transformed. If you don't hand over manufactured goods, we won't give you the grain and industrial raw materials. In this way, economically we have curbed the bourgeoisie from organizing free markets, and politically we have isolated the bourgeoisie. Without this, they would not admit defeat. This is the mutual relationship between the two transformations.

Of the two alliances, the alliance with the peasants is a basic and permanent one, while the alliance with the bourgeoisie is temporary. This is because the bourgeoisie is going to be eliminated. In the future, the proletarian ranks will be joined by several million people from the bourgeoisie. Nevertheless, the struggle against the bourgeois ideology is a long-term one. Land reform was a democratic revolution that was bourgeois in nature. It broke up the system of feudal ownership but did not break up the system of capitalist ownership or the system of individual ownership. It enabled the peasants to acquire [their portion of] land, enabled the workers and the peasants to form an alliance on the basis of the democratic revolution, and caused the bourgeoisie to feel isolated for the first time. In 1950, at the Third Plenum of the [Seventh] Central Committee, it was pointed out that we should not attack on all sides before land reform was completed.[2] Only after the land reform had been completed, and with the peasants leaning toward our side, were we able to launch the "Three-Anti's" and the "Five-Anti's" [campaigns]. With the completion of agricultural cooperativization, the worker-peasant alliance will be finally consolidated on the basis of socialism. This new worker-peasant alliance will ultimately isolate the bourgeoisie and bring about the extinction of capitalism among the 600 million people of China. Some people are saying that we are too heartless. We would say that toward the bourgeoisie, a Marxist does not have much of a conscience. In this connection, it is better for us to be heartless. Some of our comrades are too kind. We want to bring about the extinction of capitalism on earth, and make the bourgeoisie a thing of the past. This is a very meaningful and a very good thing. Anything that occurs in history is bound to be eliminated. Capitalism is also bound to be eliminated.

The current international environment is favorable to the completion of our overall tasks in the period of transition. In another twelve years, we will be able to have basically completed the building of socialism. We will be able to annually produce 18 to 20 million tons of steel, generate about 73 billion kilowatt hours of electricity, produce 280 million tons of raw coal, about 18 million tons of crude oil, about 60,000 metal-cutting lathes, 183,000 tractors (equivalent to 15 horsepower each), 208,000 motor vehicles, about 16.8 million tons of cement, about 7.5 million tons of chemical fertilizers. (These levels correspond to the [production] levels of the Soviet Union in 1940. For tractors alone, the output will be about the same as that of the Soviet Union in 1954.) Grain production will reach 600 billion catties – an increase of 100 per cent; and [we will produce] over 6 million tons of cotton – an increase in excess of 100 per cent (all compared with 1952 yields). [By then] the total number of tractors will reach 600,000 and the total acreage under mechanized cultivation will be 61 per cent [of the total farmland]. With two more five-year plans, when we will have completed the technological transformation of agriculture, the acreage under mechanical cultivation will be 100 per cent [of the total]. To accomplish these tasks, we need a period of peaceful construction. Can we get such a period or not? Our comrades in the Ministry of Foreign Affairs, in the International Liaison Department, and in the military must strive hard for it before we can get it.

During the current five-year [plan], the class struggle both at home and abroad is very acute. We have already won a very, very big victory in this struggle, and we will gain even more and greater achievements. During the past few years, we have scored victories in four areas: in the opposition to idealism and in the propagation of materialism, in the suppression of counterrevolutionaries, in the [state] unified purchasing and marketing of grain, and in the cooperativization of agriculture. Our victories in these four areas all have an antibourgeois nature, and have dealt very severe blows to the bourgeoisie. In the future, we will continue to deal crushing blows to them. Opposition to idealism must be continued on a long-term basis. [We will] thoroughly suppress idealism and build up the ranks of Marxist materialism in three five-year plans. This year and next, we will be carrying out the suppression of counterrevolutionaries among 11 to 12 million people. The counterrevolutionary elements are not [easily] visible, but they will be identified once investigations are made. Counterrevolutionary elements have been uncovered in both the Organization Department of the Central Committee and the Ministry of Public Security at the Center. Among the 2.2 million people [under investigation] in the entire country, 110,000 counterrevolutionary elements have been uncovered, and there are in addition 50,000 major suspects. In rooting out the counterrevolutionaries, it is necessary to observe standards and criteria. [We] must get at the real ones, so missing a few will be unavoidable (for example, in the rectification [campaign] during the Yanan period, we left out Pan Hannian[3] and Liu Xueying),[4] but we should not leave out too many. On the issue of grain, we have scored a big victory. On the issue of agricultural cooperativization, too, we have scored a victory. On these four issues, we have launched an even greater struggle against the bourgeoisie and have dealt it a blow, causing it to be unable to rear its head; we have seized the initiative; if we had not done so we would have been put on the defensive.

II. This meeting has broken down many erroneous views and smashed a great number of superstitions.

Many speeches made at this meeting have smashed a lot of superstitions and have broken down many erroneous views.

First of all, should there be a big development or a small development? This [meeting] has resolved this question. The masses ask for a big development. In order to be in step with industry, the agricultural sector also demands a big development. To advocate a small development is a mistake.

Can the new [liberated] areas be developed? The new areas can also be developed.

Can mountainous areas be developed? Mountainous areas can also be developed.

Can disaster areas be developed? Disaster areas can also be developed.

Can backward rural areas be developed? Backward rural areas can also be developed.

Can areas occupied by minority nationalities be developed? Except for Tibet and the Daliang and Xiaoliang mountains, areas occupied by minority nationalities can also be developed.

Can we set up cooperatives without funds? Yes, we can.

Can we set up cooperatives without educated [people]? Yes, we can.

Can we set up cooperatives with only a few cadres? Yes, we can.

In the past, some people said: "It is easy to construct but difficult to consolidate." Construction is not necessarily very easy, and consolidation is not necessarily difficult. If you talk about difficulty, maybe it is somewhat difficult; if you say it's easy, everything is easy in some ways. Why do they choose to say that "consolidation is difficult?" It simply means they don't want to set up cooperatives.

[The opinion] that a cooperative cannot be set up without machinery is also not being aired much now.

As for bad cooperatives, third-class, fourth-class, and fifth-class cooperatives,[5] apart from dissolving them, what roads are open to us? Except for particular cooperatives that simply have to be dissolved and fake cooperatives that have been set up by the rich peasants, in which cases it is all right for them to be dissolved, the others need not be dissolved. They can be run well after an overhauling.

The Rural Work Department of the Central Committee does not merely produce rumors. It also produces rationalizations. Some people have said: "If we don't dismount quickly, we will break up the worker-peasant alliance." We will dispute only one word in this sentence. We say: "If we don't mount the horse quickly, we will break up the worker-peasant alliance."

Part of the "blame" for the death of draft oxen must be shouldered by the cooperatives, but the major cause does not lie with them. The reason that [draft] oxen have died has to do with the question of grain, the question of the price of oxhide, the question of the old age of the oxen, and the question of flood and drought.

There was tension in the countryside this spring. Some people said that it stemmed from organizing so many cooperatives. This is not the way to put things in the first place. It was mainly owing to the clamoring of the landlords and the rich peasants, and the clamoring of the well-to-do [middle] peasants. They rushed to buy grain even though they were not short of grain. In part, it was caused by the grain problem, but in part it was just a false appearance. It was not bad to have some clamoring. [As a result,] we got to the bottom of the grain problem. Last year, there was a decrease in output owing to [natural] calamity, and we purchased 6 billion catties in excess of the necessary amount.[6] This year there was an increase in output of 20 billion catties, and we purchased six billion catties less [than last year]. Therefore, in terms of the peasants' [share], there will be an increase of 26 billion catties of grain.

The argument that "the superiority of the cooperative can last for only three years" is also pessimistic. The Soviet Union has been working on socialism for several decades; it still has superiority. As I see it, the superiority of socialism will certainly last at least several decades. After several decades, when socialism loses its superiority, we will be working on communism.

In the next few years, should we organize some higher-stage cooperatives? We should. As for how many should be organized, let each locality deliberate and decide.

Cooperatives can also be set up among [those who work on] junks and animal-drawn carts. We should get the several million laborers [in these trades] organized.

III. Comprehensive planning and the strengthening of leadership.

There should be comprehensive planning. In my essays I talked about planning for the cooperatives. Apart from this, there should be overall economic planning for agricultural production, ([taking also into consideration] sideline occupations, handicrafts, diverse economic undertakings, land reclamation, migration of people over short distances, afforestation of the mountainous areas [the barren mountains in northern China, in particular, need to be afforested; both Beidaihe and Xiangshan[7] are rocky mountains, and even they too can be afforested], supply and marketing cooperatives, credit cooperatives, and technology dissemination stations); [beyond this,] there should also be planning in [the work of] culture and education (including current affairs, elimination of illiteracy, primary education, traditional Chinese medicine, opera, film projection, radio, and publishing), in the rectification and building of the Party, in the rectification and building of the [Youth] League, in the suppression of counterrevolutionaries (the talk given by the secretary of the Jiangjin [special] district [Party] committee in Sichuan is worth a look), in work among women (without women, there would be no sons; we were all born of women; to neglect women is to oppose motherhood, and to oppose motherhood is to be unfilial), and in youth work.

Every cooperative should have its own plan. Every *xiang* should have a plan for the entire *xiang*. Throughout the country there should be 220,000 *xiang* plans. Some people say that we don't need planning for the districts. I think it's better for them to have one, otherwise they won't have any responsibility. Each *xian* should have a plan for the entire *xian*. Each province should first work out one or two *xiang* and *xian* plans and then circulate them and have every place follow their example.

The speed of development: according to the opinion of you people, there are three types of areas. One type [consists of] the majority of the areas; another type is made up of one part of the smaller portion of the areas, and the third type is made up of the other part of the smaller portion of the areas.

1. [In] the majority of areas, there will be three waves in the three winter-spring periods of 1956, 1957, and 1958. Before one wave subsides, another wave will rise. There will be a trough between two waves, [just as] there is a valley between two mountains. There should be an interval. By 1958, semisocialist cooperativization is to be basically accomplished.

2. [In] one part of the smaller portion of the areas (in North China, in the Northeast, and in the suburban areas), there will be two waves, namely, in the two winter-spring periods of 1956 and 1957. In some particular areas, it is also permissible to basically accomplish semisocialist cooperativization with only one wave, that is, in one winter-spring period.

3. [In] the other part of the smaller portion of the areas (except Tibet and the Daliang and Xiaoliang mountains): Four, five, or even six waves are needed.

Semisocialist cooperativization is to be basically accomplished by 1960, but even then it cannot be considered socialism. Because such a long time is [really] required, it cannot be shortened. In a word, don't do it where the conditions are not ripe.

What is meant by basically accomplishing semisocialist cooperativization? It means accomplishing seventy, seventy-five, or eighty per cent [of the transformation].

Being either too slow or too fast is no good, both are called opportunism. There is the opportunism of slowing down; and there is the opportunism of speeding up.

It is necessary to strengthen leadership. [The leadership organs at] the three levels – the province, the [special] district, and the *xian* – must be in command of the development of the movement at all times, and once they see problems they should solve them. As soon as a problem arises, they should go solve it right away and not make belated criticisms. (You can call a meeting even if you only have [people from] half [of the *xian* and special districts] of a province.) Don't indulge in making criticism after the event. It is best to make one's criticism as soon as a problem crops up. Don't wait until problems have piled up before you make your criticism. If things are not going right, put the brakes on immediately. All three levels of [leadership] – province, [special] district, and *xian* – have the power to put on the brakes.

[You] must pay attention to guarding against "Left" [deviations]. It is also a Marxist [principle] to guard against "Left" [deviations]. Marxism does not merely guard against "Right" [deviations]. [If we advance at] the speed mentioned above that's fine. After that it becomes a matter of competing over quality and over [meeting] specifications. The criteria for quality is in having an increase in production, and having no loss of oxen. (I did not say that we don't want pigs to die, but pigs shouldn't die either.) How do we meet the criteria? (1) Carry out the policy of voluntary participation and mutual benefit; (2) comprehensive planning; and (3) flexible leadership. The leadership must grasp these three points well. People have warned us, citing the "leftist" mistakes that the Soviet Union has committed. We should remember and learn from the experiences of the Soviet Union.

The crucial period is the coming two years, and mainly the coming five or six months (from October of this year to March of next year). It is essential that there not be any big problems during these five or six months.

The wave of oxen dying should be considered past. Don't let it happen again. Oxen also need to be clothed, fed, and sheltered. They need someone to look after them, and whether or not a price is set for them when they are turned over to the cooperative, in any case, we don't want the oxen to die. If the Chinese Communist Party is to show its stuff, we must not let the wave of oxen dying occur again from now on. We should create [a situation where] "the three do not cry out": the people don't cry out, the cattle don't cry out, and the pigs don't cry out. When they cry out, there is a chance of their dying.

In the five months ahead, persons in positions of major responsibility in the provinces, [special] districts, *xian* districts, and *xiang,* and above all the secretaries and deputy secretaries, should dig deeply into the [matter of running] cooperatives and become experts. Those who cannot go deeply into it should have their jobs changed, and then we won't ask them to do that any more.

After five months, the Center probably will have to hold another meeting like this one. Each province perhaps should invite the secretaries of a few *xian* [Party] committees to participate. It will amount to an increase of 200 to 300 [representatives] for the entire country. Everybody should prepare a draft for a speech; we must have new [ideas] and speak on new topics such as comprehensive planning and management.

A few suggestions on leadership methods (on how to achieve more, faster, and better results):

1. Hold several meetings a year. Hold both big meetings and small meetings.

2. Solve problems whenever [you] encounter them. Don't let problems pile up. As long as [you] understand a few cooperatives clearly, you can draw conclusions. Catch a sparrow and dissect it. Although the sparrow is small, it has all the vital organs. Chinese sparrows and foreign sparrows are all alike. You don't have to dissect each and every one of them.

3. Send telegrams and make telephone calls.

4. Go on inspection tours. It doesn't matter if you go in a jeep or if you ride in a horse-drawn cart or even if you go on foot.

5. Improve publications. I have read the publications of all the provinces; some are well edited. One shortcoming is that the editors are irresponsible; they publish any article that is contributed without regard for its content. The type used in publications should not be too small, and the lines should not be too close. Don't use the new No. 5 type; use the old No. 5 type, so that it will be easier for people to read. This time, in compiling *Zenyang ban nongye shengchan hezuoshe* [How to Run Agricultural Producers' Cooperatives], the Rural Work Department of the Central Committee read 1,200 essays. I shut myself up for eleven days and read 120 essays. [It was like] making a tour of all the different states,[8] and I wrote introductory comments and the preface. I think that each province and each autonomous region should compile a book every year, with each *xian* contributing an essay, to be published openly. They are labeled "intra-Party secret," but I think there is nothing secret about them at all. Let's ask the People's Publishing House to publish *Zenyang ban nongye shengchan hezuoshe* and send a copy to every one of the democratic personages.

6. Issue brief reports. The *xian* Party committee should submit a brief report to the [special] district [Party] committee every ten days, and the latter [should do the same] to the provincial Party committee; when the situation is tense, it should be done every five days. The content should include whatever problems have developed and whatever progress has been made. The provincial [Party] committee should make a brief report to the Center every half month, or every ten days when the situation is tense. Its content should be

clear and concise; and a few hundred words will do.

IV. Concerning the ideological struggle.

At this meeting we have crossed swords ideologically; this is very good. The experiences of history have proven that ideological struggle must be to the point. In ideology, people should cross swords, with one making a thrust and another making a parry. Without crossing swords, there will be a lack of clarity and thoroughness [in thinking]. When swords are crossed, it will help the majority of comrades to understand the problems clearly, and it will help those comrades who have made mistakes to correct such mistakes.

Historically, there have been two kinds of people who have made mistakes. Those who were willing to correct themselves are one kind, and those who were unwilling to correct themselves are another. We should try to win over those who are willing to correct themselves. As for those comrades who have made mistakes, there are only two requirements [regarding their problem]: one is that they themselves are willing to continue to make revolution, and the other is that others must also allow them to make revolution. Anybody who does not permit other people to make revolution is [creating] a very dangerous [situation]. Wang Lun, the "white-robed scholar," and Old Squire Zhao[9] are people who did not permit others to make revolution. Chen Duxiu, Zhang Guotao, Gao Gang, and Rao Shushi are also people who did not permit others to make revolution. As a result, they themselves ended up being revolted against and overthrown by others. Historically, those who have made the mistakes of empiricism and dogmatism have been for the most part able to correct themselves. One way [to do it] is to correct oneself; another way is to do so with other people's help; one should have the attitude of welcoming criticism. Except for a very few people, such as Chen Duxiu and Dai Jitao[10] and the like, everybody can correct their mistakes.

Some comrades of the Rural Work Department of the Central Committee, primarily Comrade Deng Zihui, have made mistakes. The nature of their mistake is that of a Right empiricist deviation. Comrade Deng Zihui has done a lot of work during the protracted struggle in the past, and he has his achievements. However, one mustn't turn one's accomplishments into a burden. All you need to do is to be a little more modest and not to flaunt your seniority, then you will be able to correct your mistakes.

The "four big freedoms" and "consolidating the order of new democracy" are the programs of the bourgeoisie and run counter to the resolutions of the Second Plenum. Proposing such slogans is an error in program. There should be restrictions on the "four big freedoms"; [they should be] changed into "four small freedoms." After utilizing, restricting, and reforming [these freedoms], we should eventually eliminate them. They cannot be left both unrestricted and unchanged. In order to eliminate them, we must prepare and must have something ready with which to replace them. If we eliminate them without having found something with which to replace them, we will be committing the mistake of "Left" deviation.

Some comrades "never talk about fundamentals but take pleasure in dispensing small favors." Such comrades do not study hard, take no heed of what happens outside their windows, and ignore the Party's resolutions altogether. They don't touch their books; nor do they ask their secretaries to look things up for them.

Some comrades are very fond of excessive decentralization and like to set up independent kingdoms. They love [to practice] dictatorship and don't like to consult other people or exchange opinions. They always lecture people. These comrades cannot sense the political climate. Although certain things are already generally in existence everywhere and in a large quantity, they do not feel them. This amounts to catching a political cold.

V. Concerning certain questions of a specific nature.

1. It is necessary to pay attention to procedure and methods in removing the well-to-do middle peasants from leadership positions in the cooperatives. It is necessary to let them as well as the masses all understand that they are no longer fit to be in such leadership positions. Moreover, it is necessary to have better people with which to replace them. The method of handling [this matter] should be different for different situations, and we should not pull everybody down like a gust of wind. Some of them may be pulled down; some may be demoted to deputy positions or to become committee members. In individual cases where performance has been good, they should be allowed to stay on and should not be removed. Don't treat well-to-do middle peasants as if they were rich peasants. Their attitude toward cooperativization is different from that of the rich peasants. Theirs is an [attitude of] vacillation, whereas the rich peasants' [attitude] is one of opposition. They are laborers, not exploiters.

2. Explain in [Party] branches and among the masses that our division of people into strata, namely, into upper-middle peasants and lower-middle peasants, is not a redefining of class status. [Rather] it is because the upper-middle peasants and lower-middle peasants are different in economic status and political attitudes, and there is also a difference between them in their enthusiasm or lack of enthusiasm toward the cooperatives. Even within one stratum, attitudes of people differ. Therefore it is necessary to induce them to join the cooperatives in stages and in different groups. After a few years when all the peasants have joined the cooperatives, there will no longer be any differentiation between strata.

3. As for the landlords and the rich peasants joining the cooperatives, in the basically cooperativized areas, they can be accepted into the cooperatives in groups, in accordance with their concrete performance. In the past we said that only after over fifty per cent of the entire nation was cooperativized could we absorb [the landlords and rich peasants into the cooperatives]. Now we can absorb them whenever a *xian* has been basically cooperativized. Those among them who are honest may be given the title of members of the cooperative. As for those who are dishonest, some of them will not be given the title of member but will be called only an "probationary member," to undergo reform through labor; financially, [however,] they will also receive compensation for their labor. Some of them will not be admitted into the cooperatives. Without

exception, none of those landlords and rich peasants who have joined the cooperatives will be permitted to assume positions of leadership within three to five years. Can young intellectuals of landlord or rich peasant background be allowed to serve as literacy teachers? I think they can, but let's not draw any conclusion yet. You people should study this some more. But don't let them serve as bookkeepers for the cooperatives. It's a bit dangerous to have them serve as bookkeepers.

4. As for the conditions for [organizing] higher-stage cooperatives, I urge each area to study them according to actual circumstances. When the conditions are ripe, they can be set up.

5. Neither cooperativization nor the "three-fixed" [policy] with regard to grain should be neglected.[11] [The question of] how to arrange the "three-fixed" [policy] with regard to grain [in order to fit] the time for cooperativization should be determined by each area on its own.

6. The military draft in individual areas can be postponed until April of next year. But on the whole it should not be postponed.

7. Cooperatives can be set up in the summer and fall. Don't concentrate all the work in the winter and spring. Nevertheless, between every two waves, there should be a period of rest and regrouping. Even people have to rest once every day. Without rest and regrouping, they won't be able to catch their breath.

8. The slogan of "running the cooperatives diligently and frugally" is very good. As we oppose waste in the cities, so we should also oppose waste in the countryside. Build up your households diligently and frugally, run the cooperatives diligently and frugally, and build the country diligently and frugally. Don't be lazy and don't be extravagant. Raise the productivity of labor, lower costs, practice strict economy, oppose waste, do economic accounting, etc. All cooperatives should carry these things out. But economic accounting should be implemented step by step.

9. Don't carry out the suppression of counterrevolutionaries at the three levels of *xian,* district, and *xiang* before April of next year. Last year we combined the work of setting up the cooperatives with grain production and conscription; this made our work rather crude. This year it should be meticulous. Don't [do things to] make everybody complain.

10. The question of the state farms has not been mentioned at this [meeting]. This is a shortcoming. Next time there should be somebody to speak [on the subject]. The Rural Work Department of the Central Committee should [send people] down [to the basic units] and study the matter a bit. In the future, the proportion of state farms [in the agricultural sector] will become greater and greater.

11. [We should] continuously and rigorously oppose Han chauvinism. Han chauvinism is a bourgeois idea. Of course, we should also oppose narrow nationalism on the part of the minority nationalities, but first we must oppose Han chauvinism. We should help the minority nationalities in a wholehearted and sincere manner. We cannot do without the minority nationalities. They

occupy seventy to eighty per cent of the land where [natural] resources abound. We cannot do without Seypidin and X X X.[12]

12. In the cooperatives, [we] must wipe out illiteracy and not wipe out the [campaign] to eliminate illiteracy.

13. What is meant by "Left" deviation? What is meant by Right deviation? Things move in time and space (especially in time). When people observe things, if it is not in accordance with the actual conditions, it will be "Left" if they see too far ahead, and it will be Right if they fail to see [the things]. For example, not to develop the cooperatives in a big way when the conditions for a big development are ripe is to be Right. To insist that eighty per cent of the entire country [be cooperativized] within a single year next year is to be "Left." There are [two] old sayings in China: "When the mellon is ripe, it falls from the stem." [And,] "When water comes, the ditch will be formed." [Both aphorisms] simply mean that one should attain one's goal in a natural way, not by forcing things.[13] It is just like a woman giving birth to a baby. If the baby is forced out after only seven months [of pregnancy], it is a case of being "Left"; if it is not allowed to come out [even] after nine months, then it is Right.

14. Is it possible that a "Left" deviation will occur? It is entirely possible. If the leadership does not pay attention to the state of development, does not pay attention to the consciousness of the masses, does not do comprehensive planning, and does not do things by stages and by groups; if it favors only quantity without paying attention to quality or does not exercise control, then the mistake of a "Left" deviation will certainly occur, and it will definitely make the people cry out, the cattle cry out, and the pigs cry out. Once they start crying out, they will die – people will die, cattle will die, and pigs will die. This is not "reverse propaganda."[14] [We] must anticipate all unfavorable situations and the various difficulties that could emerge, such as a possible decrease in production, the loss of cattle, etc. [We] should openly tell the masses so that they can be prepared. Naturally, we should not scare the masses either. At appropriate moments, when people's heads are swollen, it is necessary to compress them a little, so that they won't become too swollen.

Should we not worry at all? We should still have the necessary worries, regulations, and commandments. It is not that we don't want them at all. Even Zhu Bajie[15] has to observe three regulations and five commandments. We should have the necessary periods of respite and the applying of brakes, as well as gates.[16] When people are strutting around, we will give them new tasks (for example, there will be competition for quality next year), so that they won't have enough time to become conceited.

15. Can we allow the *xian* level to have a ninety per cent[17] operational flexibility factor? I think we can. But don't draw any conclusion yet. I suggest you people consider the matter.

16. Kerosene is too expensive. Can we reduce the price? Comrade Chen Yun said that this [problem] can be solved.

17. Some people are skeptical about whether or not our decision [on cooper-

ativization] will be reversed in the future. I think that [since] that is the way things are going generally, it will be impossible to reverse the decision.

18. Some people have asked what the general trend will be. In about ten years, that is, by about the time of the Third Five-Year Plan, the construction of socialism will be basically completed. There's another point to this, [and that is that] in about fifty to seventy years, that is, after about ten to fifteen five-year plans, we can hope to catch up with or surpass the United States. Within this period, there are bound to be many serious and complicated conflicts and struggles of varying degrees, both domestically and internationally, both in and outside the Party. There are bound to be many difficulties, such as world wars, the [dropping of] the atom bomb, the emergence of people like Beria, Gao Gang, and Rao Shushi. There are many things that cannot yet be anticipated. But we are Marxists, and all difficulties can be overcome. There is bound to be the emergence of a powerful socialist China. Fifty years from now a Communist China will appear.

19. About the resolutions and [twelve-year] Program [for Agricultural Development]:[18] Once the resolutions have been adopted by this meeting and revised by the Political Bureau, they should be made public very quickly. The Program is equivalent to a second constitution. It has to wait to be made public by the State Council and for opinions [about it] to be solicited before it can be submitted to the National People's Congress for ratification.

20. [You] may take with you all the drafts of the speeches [made here], but don't print them. Each of you should leave behind a [copy of the] revised draft [of your speech]. Turn over the draft you want to exchange to the General Office under the Central Committee before October 25. You can take the sample copy of *Zenyang ban nongye shengchan hezuoshe* home. Nowadays there is too much of the classical style in the essays [people write]. They are half-classical and half-vernacular. *"Yinggai"* ["should"] is written only as *"ying"*; *"bingqie"* ["moreover"] is written only as *"bing"*; *"shihou"* ["when"] is written only as *"shi"*; and *"guanche zhixing"* ["carry out thoroughly"] is written only as *"guanche."* In writing essays one must pay attention to logic (the structure of an essay must have inner coherence and there should be no conflict between what comes before and what comes after) and to grammar and rhetoric (the writing must be compact and the language vivid). [You] should seek help from expert writers.

21. How do we transmit the things [discussed here]? During work discussions, express what you can remember in your own words. The resolutions and the Program must be studied.

22. Pay attention to doing a good job of electing the delegates to the "Eighth Congress."

23. Premier Zhou will make a report to everybody on current affairs.

24. Each unit of the provinces and greater [administrative] regions should each hold a small meeting.

Notes

1. This date is given, not in the *Wansui* (1969) text here, but in the *Xuanji*, V, text, and is the correct date, since the Plenum was held October 4-11, 1955. The date given in *Wansui* (1969) is September 1955.

2. See text Jun. 6, 1950(2).

3. Pan Hannian was a political worker in the Jiangxi Soviet who later went to the Soviet Union. After Liberation, he was a member of the National Committee of the CPPCC, a member of the East China Military and Political Commission, third secretary of the Shanghai Municipal Committee of the CPC, and ultimately a deputy-mayor of Shanghai. He was implicated in the Gao-Rao Affair and was "uncovered" as a counterrevolutionary in 1955, being traced to ties with the Chen Lifu-Chen Guofu clique in the KMT before Liberation. He was arrested and incarcerated in 1955. For the Yanan rectification, see text June 20, 1953, note 9, and text Aug. 12, 1953, note 24.

4. We are unable to identify this person. Neither Pan Hannian nor Liu Xueying was mentioned in the *Xuanji*, V, version here.

5. These classifications were not specifically mentioned in the *Xuanji* version. Mao may be being facetious here, since, while there is a known classification called *san lei she*, or third-class (or category) cooperative, there is to our knowledge no standard definition of fourth- or fifth-class cooperatives. See text July 31, 1955, note 16.

6. Here the *Xuanji* version says "seven billion."

7. Beidaihe is located in the far eastern tip of Hebei Province, near Qinhuangdao (see text Summer 1954, source note). Xiangshan is a suburb of Beijing, about twelve km. northwest of the capital proper and within Beijing Municipality. Neither of these places is mentioned in the *Xuanji* version.

8. See text Oct. 11, 1955(1), note 36.

9. This is a character in Lu Xun's *Ah Q zhengzhuan* who is the "Fake Foreign Devil's" father. See text Oct. 11, 1955(1)

10. In the *Xuanji* version, this reads as Dai Jiying. Dai Jitao was a senior member of the KMT, and his political profile does not seem to fit here. The reference to Dai Jiying appears to be more accurate. See text Oct. 11, 1955(1), note 41.

11. The "three-fixed" policy – of fixing production, purchase, and sale – was implemented in March 1955 and derives from the unified purchasing and supply system of 1953. In this policy, the grain output for each farming household was calculated according to production figures at the *xiang* level before and after the spring plowing of 1955, and fixed through *xiang*-level discussions considering land quality, natural conditions, peasants' labor capacity, management, etc. In fixing purchase, the peasants' surplus grain was calculated by deducting grain consumption (food, seed, and fodder) and public grain (which goes to the collective) from grain output. Eighty-five to ninety per cent of the surplus grain would then be purchased by the state. In turn, the state had fixed sales, or supply, to peasants whose grain output was lower than their grain consumption and public grain quota. See K. Chao (1960), pp. 219-22; and Y. Lau (1977), p. 323.

12. Seypidin (Saifudin) Azizi (b. 1915) was, at the time of the founding of the PRC, vice-chairman of the People's Government of Xinjiang Province, chief commissar of the Nationalities Affairs Commission, and deputy commander of the Xinjiang Military Region. In 1954 he was a delegate to the NPC from the Xinjiang Autonomous Region, and in 1955 chairman of the Xinjiang Committee of the CPPCC and chairman of the People's Council of the Xinjiang Uighur Autonomous Region. For more information on Seypidin, see D. Klein and A. Clark, eds. (1971), II, pp. 742-747. We are unable to locate conclusive evidence to identify X X X. Neither person is mentioned in the *Xuanji* version.

13. See text Oct. 11, 1955(2), notes 61 and 62.

14. For Mao's idea of "reverse propaganda" and use of the term, see texts Sept. 25, 1955, and Dec. 27, 1955(1) and (2), particularly text Dec. 27, 1955(2), note 13, and *SW*, V, p. 276, fn. However, it should be noted that this definition renders Mao's meaning here rather ambiguous.

15. Zhu Bajie is a character (often known as The Pig) in the classical novel *Xiyou ji* (Journey to the West), who is noted for his gluttony, buffoonery, error-proneness, and wanton passions. He is often a foil to Mao's heroic figure in the same novel, Sun Wukong, or the Monkey King.

16. Mao's use of the term *guanzha* appears to refer to the notion of gates where work is temporarily suspended so that people's achievements may be assessed. See text June 23, 1950, note 8.

17. Here we have a major inconsistency between the two versions. The *Xuanji* version reads "ten per cent."

18. This refers to the National Program for Agricultural Development, 1956-1967, which at this time was only in draft. See text Oct. 11, 1955(1), note 56. For more detail, see text Dec. 6, 1955, note 3.

Conversation with Members of the Japanese Diet
(October 15, 1955)

Source: FBIS, *Daily Report* (Oct. 21, 1955), HHH7-8.

We have no Chinese text of this conversation. The FBIS transcript, here reproduced in part as it appeared in the original, represents a release in the Asahi Evening News *(in English, Oct. 21, 1955) of the report of Yasushi Okubo, correspondent for* Asahi shimbun. *Parts of this report (all but the first paragraph here) were based on notes released by Tokio Nakamura, delegate of the Japanese Socialist Party, who was present at the conversation with Mao. It is worth noting that this transcript contains terms and names that, in our opinion, are alien to Mao's usage (e.g., "Formosa" for Taiwan). We are unable to discover whether these problems of substitution occurred in Mr. Nakamura's notes or in the release issued by Mr. Okubo. We have not changed anything in this transcript, in spite of the fact that it contains some grammatical and orthographic errors. The annotations (not those in the text, but those appearing as notes at the end) are ours. A joint statement on Sino-Japanese relations was issued by the Chinese government and the visiting delegation of members of the Japanese diet on October 17, 1955. The chief Chinese signatory was Peng Zhen, in the capacity of general secretary of the Standing Committee of the NPC.*

"Communism arose from war – the Soviet Union after World War One, and many other Communist nations after World War Two. If world war three should start, at least 80 percent of the world will become communized. If you want, I'll make a wager on that. So, there is no reason for us to be fearful of war. Moreover, we have no colonies. We have nothing to lose."

"Conditions have changed in Japan. I did not like Japan before because there were militarists, but now I like Japan because there are no more militarists. I sympathize with Japan because she is being ill-treated by other countries. Our ideologies and social systems differ, but I believe that this is no obstacle to mutual respect and friendly relations between Red China and Japan. What is past is past, and the question is the future.

"Everyone has good and bad points. We have many bad points, and there is need for us to learn many things from Japan. Japan is an industrial nation. China is still an agricultural nation, but I would like to say that Red China is exerting efforts to become an industrialized agricultural nation. Japan is more advanced than my country in industry, economy, and culture, and there is need for the Chinese People's Republic to learn many things from Japan.

"I would like to go to Japan sometime in the future. It would not be for the purpose of creating trouble. I want to go sightseeing in Japan and inform Japan of the friendship of the Chinese people. I would like to go to the United States too, but there is no possibility for the time being. I wonder if Japan and the United States won't invite [1]

"Japan profited from its disaster (war defeat–ASAHI). Japan is in a position of leadership; that is, she is in a position to criticize the United States, France, the Netherlands, Britain and Portugal (for their colonial policies–ASAHI). The day will come when both the United States and Japan will recognize Red China, even if it is one hundred and one years from now. It will take time for the hand of the oppressor (the United States–ASAHI) to be removed from Japan, South Korea, Formosa, and the Philippines. We understand you well. The day will come when the Foreign Office,[2] which recognizes the Government of Generalissimo Chiang Kai-shek, will be criticized. The day will surely come when we will chase the United States out of Formosa.

"Japan believes that Red China is an independent nation, but we are not completely independent. Japan is also semi-independent. This is a common point. The hand of the United States is long and extends over Formosa, the Philippines and South Korea, but this will not continue for long. Asia would be controlled by Asians, not by occidentals."

Notes

1. See text Oct. 1960, note 4.
2. Mao was, of course, referring here to the foreign ministry of the Japanese Government.

Telegram to the USSR
(October 24, 1955)

Source: FBIS, *Daily Report* (Oct. 26, 1955), CC 9-10.

We have no Chinese text of this telegram; the FBIS transcript is produced here. The telegram was addressed to Voroshilov, chairman of the Presidium of the Supreme Soviet of the USSR, Bulganin, chairman of the Council of Ministers of the USSR, and Molotov, first vice-chairman of the Council of Ministers and minister of Foreign Affairs of the USSR. It was signed by Mao, Liu Shaoqi, and Zhou Enlai.

Your congratulations on the occasion of the sixth anniversary of the formation of the Chinese People's Republic have inspired us and the peoples of our country, for which we express our sincere gratitude to you and to the Soviet people.

On the joyful occasion of our national day the Chinese people, taking stock of all their achievements over the past 6 years, cherish a feeling of cordial gratitude to the great Soviet Union for the tremendous help given us in all spheres. Every achievement of the Chinese people is inseparably linked with this help of the great Soviet Union.

On its own initiative the Soviet Union has recently taken a series of steps in the field of foreign policy which has already resulted in a lessening of international tension. The Chinese people and the Chinese Government will give full support to the Soviet Union in all its efforts for the sake of peace.

Long live the bulwark of peace throughout the world, the great Soviet Union.

Letter to Zhang Naiqi
(November 1, 1955)

Source: *Shuxin*, p. 502.

According to the source, Zhang was at the time of this letter minister of Food Administration. For more information on Zhang, see text, Jan. 27, 1957(1), note 50.

Minister Naiqi:

I have received and read both of your letters. I am grateful for your sending me the information on these circumstances and also your opinions. There are bound to be one-sided points of view among the cadres; the problem is to do a good job of helping them to learn that [the attitude of] seeking truth in facts[1] is the [proper] method for making a comprehensive analysis [of things]. I have not yet had time to read the article you enclosed; when I have done that I shall send it back to you.

My best regards.

Mao Zedong
November 1, 1955

Note

1. Here Mao is possibly referring to the problem of peasants joining agricultural producers' cooperatives and thereby, as the plan goes, enhancing their productivity of food grain. See text Mar. 5, 1955, note 1, and text Sept. 25, 1955. For the source and meaning of the phrase *shi shi qiu shi*, translated here as "seeking truth in facts," see text May 15, 1957, note 10.

Telegram to the USSR
(November 6, 1955)

Source: *RMRB* (Nov. 7, 1955), 1. Other Chinese Text: *XHYB*, 12 (Dec. 28, 1955), 118. Available English Translations: HNA, *Daily News Release* (Nov. 7, 1955), 1; FBIS, *Daily Report* (Nov. 7, 1955), AAA 26-27.

Comrade K. E. Voroshilov, Chairman of the Presidium of the Supreme Soviet of the Union of Soviet Socialist Republics,
Comrade N. A. Bulganin, Chairman of the Council of Ministers of the Union of Soviet Socialist Republics,
Comrade V. M. Molotov, First Vice-Chairman of the Council of Ministers and Minister of Foreign Affairs of the Union of Soviet Socialist Republics:

On the occasion of the thirty-eighth anniversary of the great October Socialist Revolution, on behalf of the Chinese people and the Chinese government, we extend to you and, through you, to the great Soviet people and the Soviet government, our warmest congratulations.

With extremely great joy, the Chinese people congratulate our brothers the Soviet people on the brilliant successes they have achieved in the past year in the noble cause of building communism. These successes further strengthened the camp for peace, democracy, and socialism, inspiring the confidence of the people of the various people's democracies[1] in building socialism and of the people of the entire world in their struggle to attain peace and progress.

The great Soviet Union is the strong bulwark of world peace. Over the preceding year, the Soviet government has made a series of great efforts to relax the tension in the international situation and promote international cooperation, and moreover it has achieved significant results. The recent proposals and propositions put forward by the Soviet government concerning European security and the German question, disarmament, and the development of East-West contacts are in accordance with the common interests of the people of the whole world.[2] The Chinese government and the Chinese people completely support these efforts made by the Soviet government.

The brotherly friendship and firm unity between the Chinese and Soviet peoples play an increasingly important role in enhancing the common prosperity of both countries and maintaining peace in the Far East and throughout the world. The overall economic and cultural cooperation between the two countries of China and the Soviet Union and the great assistance given by the Soviet Union to China has immense significance for the cause of building socialism in our country. May the great unbreakable friendship between the Chinese and Soviet peoples develop and become more consolidated with each passing day!

Long live our great ally, the Union of Soviet Socialist Republics!
(Co-signed as Chairman of PRC with Liu Shaoqi as Chairman of Standing Committee of NPC and Zhou Enlai as Premier of State Council and Foreign Minister, dated in Beijing)

Notes

1. See text Sept. 21, 1949, note 4.
2. In July 1955 the USSR proposed the dissolution of both NATO and the Warsaw Treaty Organization in favor of an all-European security system, including the U.S.

Letter to Huang Yanpei
(November 17, 1955)

Source: *Shuxin*, p. 503.

See text Feb. 17, 1951, source note.

Mr. Renzhi:[1]
I have received your letter which was sent to me from the hospital. I am extremely happy that you are completely recovered from your illness. I hope that you will continue to pay attention to taking good care of yourself so that your health may be fully restored.[2] There is marked improvement in the work of reforming the industrial and commercial circles [in our country], which is

very gratifying. It appears to me that, evidently, it is possible to adopt the method of self-criticism in [this work of reforming] the industrial and commercial circles.[3] The recent experience [which emerged through the] discussions of the [All-China] Federation of Industry and Commerce can be propagated.[4] Owing to the fact that I am on the road, I was unable to respond [to your letter] earlier.

I send my respect.

Mao Zedong
November 17, 1955

Notes

1. See text Jul. 15, 1951.
2. See text Nov. 23, 1954.
3. See text Sept. 7, 1953, and text Apr. 25, 1956.
4. The problem of reforming the industrial and commercial enterprises that Mao mentions here entails a combination of several problems and methods contemplated at the time, including the promotion of more joint state-private enterprises and implementing the policy of fixed interest (also known as the ''redemption policy''; see text Jan. 20, 1956, note 11). While we do not know which discussions Mao was referring to here, the movement to speed up this transformation was evidently gathering momentum at this time, and would culminate in the resolution adopted at the second congress of the All-China Federation of Industry and Commerce in December 1956. See text Dec. 8, 1956, and *RMSC* (1957), pp. 541-550.

Remark Made to Li Kaiwen
(November 20, 1955)

Source: *Shengping ziliao*, p. 328, quoted from *Wenhui bao* (July 14, 1957).

Li Kaiwen was an old acquaintance of Mao's from Yanan days. On this occasion Mao, in the company of Li Fuchun and Cai Chang, discussed the matter of centralized state purchasing and marketing and cooperativization in Anhui. Li suggested that there were tendencies toward commandism (see text June 6, 1950[1], note 11) in some cadres' work-styles.

That's really subjective; they don't even study the problem a bit first. These things ought to be planted only if people can afford to do so; if they cannot, then just don't plant them!

Letter to Panchen Gnoertehni
(November 24, 1955)

Source: *Shuxin*, p. 504.

The source uses the full name of Panchen Gnoertehni Choekyi-Gyaltsan. See text Nov. 23, 1949, source note.

Dear Panchen Gnoertehni:

Your letter to me of August 13, 1955, has been received; I thank you greatly. I am very happy to hear that work in your area has improved.[1] I hope that your unity with the people in Lhasa will grow daily and become even more consolidated. I hope that the entire Tibetan region will prosper more and more each year.

In response, and with best wishes for your health!

Mao Zedong
November 24, 1955

Note

1. See text Apr. 6, 1952.

Letter to Zhou Shizhao
(November 24, 1955)

Source: *Shuxin*, p. 505.

See text Oct. 15, 1949, source note.

Dear Dunyuan:[1]

I received your letter quite some time ago already, and I have read your masterpiece and all the enclosed material. I am extremely grateful. I have still

not had the time to comply with your bidding to write those words for you.[2] I
hope that you are not urgently in need of that, and I'd like to let the subject sit
for a while; is that all right with you? Have you gone down [to the country-
side] for a stroll? It is best if you can go down several times a year, and, each
time, for two, three weeks. I went out once recently, and feel that my head is
greatly cleared and refreshed. When you go down don't just look at schools;
you should look at other things as well. Let us talk again some time.

Wishing you the best in your teaching.

> Mao Zedong
> November 24, 1955

Notes

1. See text Oct. 15, 1949, note 1.
2. See text Oct. 4, 1955.

Telegram to the People's Republic of Albania
(November 26, 1955)

Source: *RMRB* (Nov. 29, 1955), 1. Available English Translations: HNA,
Daily News Release (Nov. 29, 1955), 2; FBIS, *Daily Report* (Nov. 29, 1955),
AAA 2-3.

Comrade Haxhi Lleshi, Chairman of the Presidium of the People's Assembly
of the People's Republic of Albania,
Comrade Mehmet Shehu, Chairman of the Council of Ministers of the People's Republic of Albania,
Comrade Behar Shtylla, Minister of Foreign Affairs of the People's Republic
of Albania:

On the occasion of the eleventh anniversary of the Albanian people's liberation, on behalf of the Chinese people and the Chinese government, we extend
to you, and through you, to the heroic Albanian people and government our
warm and heartfelt congratulations.

In the last eleven years, the Albanian people who have a glorious revolutionary tradition have, under the leadership of the Albanian Workers' Party,
already achieved brilliant successes in the areas of consolidating the people's
democratic political power, defending the independence of their homeland,

and creating a prosperous and happy new life. The Chinese people are joyous at the achievements of our brothers, the Albanian people, and moreover hope that the fraternal friendship and unity between the two peoples of China and Albania will be further consolidated and developed in our common cause of building socialism and maintaining world peace.

(Co-signed as Chairman of PRC with Liu Shaoqi as Chairman of Standing Committee of NPC and Zhou Enlai as Premier of State Council and Foreign Minister, dated in Beijing)

Telegram to the Federal People's Republic of Yugoslavia
(November 26, 1955)

Source: *RMRB* (Nov. 29, 1955), 1. Other Chinese Text: *XHYB*, 12 (Dec. 28, 1955), 125. Available English Translations: HNA, *Daily News Release* (Nov. 20, 1955), 2; FBIS, *Daily Report* (Nov. 29, 1955), AAA 8.

Comrade Josip Broz Tito, President and Chairman of the Federal Executive Council of the Federal People's Republic of Yugoslavia,
Comrade Mosa Pijade, President of the Federal Assembly of the Federal People's Republic of Yugoslavia,
Comrade Koca Popovic, State Secretary for Foreign Affairs of the Federal People's Republic of Yugoslavia:

On the occasion of the tenth anniversary of the founding of the Federal People's Republic of Yugoslavia, on behalf of the people and government of the People' Republic of China, we extend warm congratulations to you and, through you, to the heroic Yugoslavian people.

A deep friendship already exists between the two peoples of China and Yugoslavia in the struggle for the independence and liberation of their respective homelands in the past. The friendly cooperation between China and Yugoslavia has made great progress since the establishment of diplomatic relations between the two countries. We believe that this friendship and cooperation will continue to be unceasingly strengthened and developed. May the Yugoslavian people attain further successes in the cause of building socialism and maintaining world peace.

(Co-signed as Chairman of PRC with Liu Shaoqi as Chairman of Standing Committee of NPC and Zhou Enlai as Premier of State Council and Foreign Minister, dated in Beijing)

Reply to Ambassador of the Democratic Republic of Germany
(December 3, 1955)

Source: *RMRB* (Dec. 4, 1955), 1. Available English Translation: HNA, *Daily News Release* (Dec. 4, 1955), 4.

Richard Gyptner became ambassador of the Democratic Republic of Germany to the PRC at this time. The text of this speech provided in the RMRB *source appears, though no definitively, to be an excerpt of a longer speech. Also, the* RMRB *source breaks convention here and does not render Mao's remarks in direct quotation, as it usually does.*

The Democratic Republic of Germany is the first truly peace-loving democratic state in German history. The Democratic Republic of Germany has achieved tremendous success in the struggles of building socialism, striving for the peaceful unification of Germany, and safeguarding European and world peace. The Democratic Republic of Germany has already become a strong bulwark of the forces of peace and democracy in all of Germany and an important factor in maintaining European security and world peace. I am confident that the construction of socialism in the Democratic Republic of Germany and the German people's struggle for the peaceful unification of Germany are bound to attain even greater victories. In this struggle, the German people will continue to receive the full support of the Chinese people. In the last few years, the close cooperation between our two countries in the areas of politics, the economy, and culture has brought about daily increasing consolidation and development in the friendship between our two peoples. This overall cooperation and brotherly friendship are in accord with our two people's common interests and wishes, and also serve to strengthen the force of the camp for peace, democracy, and socialism headed by the Soviet Union.

Telegram to the Republic of Finland
(December 5, 1955)

Source: *RMRB* (Dec. 6, 1955), 1. Other Chinese Text: *XHBYK*, 1 (Jan. 6, 1956), 48. Available English Translation: HNA, *Daily News Release* (Dec. 6, 1955), 1.

President J. K. Paasikivi,
The Republic of Finland

Your Excellency:

On the occasion of the thirty-eighth anniversary of the founding of the Republic of Finland, on behalf of the Chinese people and on my own behalf, I extend warm congratulation to the Finnish people and to Your Excellency. May the Republic of Finland prosper and may the people of Finland be happy. (Signed as Chairman of PRC, dated in Beijing)

Talk on Opposing Right-Deviation and Conservatism
(December 6, 1955)

Source: *Wansui* (1969), pp. 25-27. Available English Translation: JPRS, *Miscellany*, I, pp. 27-29.

This text is cited in K. Lieberthal (1976), pp. 76-77. No other information is available.

By the time Mao made this speech in December 1955, some five months after he had given his major speech on cooperativization (text July 31, 1955), a "high tide of socialism" was, in his view, sweeping the country as targets for cooperativization were rapidly surpassed (see texts Sept. 7, 1955, Sept. 25, 1955, Oct. 11, 1955, Dec. 27, 1955, Dec. 21, 1955). It was on this "high tide" that the "Leap Forward" of 1956 was based.

Although the Leap Forward of 1956 and the Great Leap Forward of 1958 were quite different in contents and goals,[1] the 1956 Leap and Mao's role in it presaged the events in 1958 in numerous ways. In both, Mao played an initiating role against the opposition of many other leaders.[2] During the period leading to the 1956 Leap, Mao introduced many of the ideas that would be incorporated, in revised form, into the latter Great Leap. For instance, work on the "Seventeen Articles on Agricultural Work" (see text Dec. 21, 1955; see also text Oct. 11, 1955 (1), note 55, and text Oct. 11, 1955(2), note 15), which later became the "Forty-Point Program for Agricultural Development"[3] was initiated in November 1955; the slogan "faster, more, and better [results]," which would be incorporated as part of the Great Leap slogan "go all out, aim high, and achieve greater, faster, better, and more economical results in building socialism,"[4] was put forward in this speech, as was the thesis that later became central to the Great Leap, namely, that progress is made only through massive breakthroughs, not by seeking an ever-elusive equilibrium. This document is indicative of Mao's role in initiating the Leap of 1956 and of his incredible optimism at the time, a level of optimism that he returned to at the beginning of the Great Leap in 1958.[5]

To say the "Left" is better than the Right is incorrect; to say the Right is better than the "Left" is also incorrect. Some people are falling behind reality in their thinking; they have no horns on their heads; they do not possess spirit. In the struggle between the two lines they do not carry out criticism, or if they do, their criticism is blunted. They are afraid of criticism and are afraid of losing votes. All these are manifestations of a Right deviation, and it is necessary to oppose them in the Party. The Sixth Plenum [of the Central Committee] criticized the Right-deviationist empiricism of the Rural [Work] Department.[6] That the thinking of the leadership has fallen behind reality is a grave problem. In the transformation of capitalism, in the suppression of counterrevolutionaries, and in the cooperativization [movement], it's all like that. We underestimated our own capacity. In the past, agriculture lagged behind industry. After the Seventeen-Article [Program] came out,[7] agriculture caught up with industry and forced industry to make progress. For instance, it would have been to [our] disadvantage had we allowed the primary-stage [agricultural producers'] cooperatives to remain as they were for three or four years without advancing to the higher stage.[8] It is possible that socialism will be realized in 1959. The idea of the Seventeen Articles is to oppose conservatism. [It involves] overall planning, the strengthening of the leadership, fundamental measures, and advanced experience. Half a year ago, we did not consider these; now we have changed. Tremendous changes and immense productive power have emerged as if a new continent has been discovered. The new continent has been in existence; it's just we did not see it. The socialist transformation of industry and commerce will be ninety per cent completed in 1957. The transformation of handicraft industries must also be accelerated. Our [current] plan is too modest; [we aim at] seventy to eighty per cent transformation in 1957. Originally the nationalization of industry and commerce was planned for 1962; perhaps this can be accomplished ahead of schedule.

After [the stage of] joint state-private ownership [is reached], it is not difficult to transform it to state ownership. Instead of taking the eighteen years [called for in the original plan], cooperativization took ten years. This proves that we have fallen behind reality. The masses have tremendous potential; they can tackle many things. [So] we should oppose Right deviations and conservatism in order to accomplish transformation ahead of schedule. I propose that we achieve our goals in excess of the targets before fifteen years and delete such uncertain expressions as "approximately," "basically," and "about fifteen years." We should strive to achieve what can be achieved [through effort]. For instance, when we put in an order for products we can demand earlier delivery. We should take advantage of this period of cessation of hostilities [with the United States] to speed up the tempo and accomplish our general tasks. This is the idea of the "Eighth Congress."[9] If we can accomplish the general tasks of the period of transition ahead of schedule, things on the battlefield will be easily handled. It is most advantageous to have things done quickly, for then we will be in a better position to fight Taiwan if we have to. But if we don't fulfill our tasks of construction, it will be difficult. We must accelerate and achieve faster, greater, and better [results] in all aspects of our work. We must obtain better results in a shorter period of time. If we undertake things for which there are adequate conditions, if they stem from the masses' demands, and if we accomplish more and better [results], that would mean that we are advancing steadily. In the past we made [some] mistakes in opposing blind and adventurist advance;[10] we dampened the activism of the cadres and the masses. This was wrong. The movement to eliminate illiteracy[11] was swept away by the movement to oppose adventurist advance. The good spirit of uprightness was repressed, and there was an upsurge in evil and sinister influence; both the cadres and the masses lost their drive. By not having been able to notice such a problem at the very earliest opportunity the Center has neglected its duty. The masses say, "One can't go wrong in following the Communist Party." In terms of general orientation, we have not been wrong. But in specific cases, we have made mistakes, and the masses have also made mistakes in following us. There are several ways in which to advance: the best, the mediocre, and the not so good. The more correct and reasonable line is to stand in front the masses and to give them encouragement to go forward, and not to stand behind them and pour cold water on them. If we achieve comparatively great accomplishments in a comparatively short time, we will be advancing steadily, whereas if we do things in the conventional way, spending a longer time but achieving little, we will be following the conservative line. There are two ways to overcome this: overall planning and getting close to the masses. It is not the method of sitting in the office, but rather, getting close to the masses to find out new things, new experiences, [to gather] advanced experiences and popularize them. One does not have to catch many sparrows to know [a sparrow's] insides.[12] If you know that Zhejiang and Anhui can carry out cooperativization quickly, you'll know that the same can be done nationally. Conservatism is not any one individual's problem. Take hold of the advanced [experiences] in order to criticize the backward; discover new productive forces and the potential of the masses. This is a principle of leadership, a method of leadership; only with this can we convince people. It will not do to sit in the office not getting close to the masses and not taking hold of the advanced experiences. Official business has indeed to be trans-acted, but it will not do to limit yourselves to transacting official business alone. Even when you go out [for an inspection], you have to take hold of the advanced; you can't simply engage in some laggardly projects and bring them back with you. People who are in responsible positions should allot seven to ten weeks [a year] as a period for getting close to the masses. The work-style of sitting in the office can only [be used in] dealing with conventional matters. Advanced experience [can be had] only by breaking through convention. In the things of objective reality, breakthroughs are made every day; imbalance is a constant, while equilibrium is only temporary. This is the law of progress. The viewpoint that there can be no further change after equilibrium is achieved is incorrect. On the contrary, it is only when one takes hold of the advanced [elements] in disequilibrium and uses them to bring the rest forward that there can be progess. One should not be afraid of breakthroughs or of the emergence of contradictions. Perpetual peace and tranquility are bound to produce mistakes. There are dialectics only when there are both break-throughs and the attempt to achieve equilibrium. Only in this way can we stir up the activism of the masses and hasten the construction of socialism. We should [build socialism] with faster, more, and better [results], fulfill [this task] in excess of the targets in less than fifteen years, and thus advance stead-ily.[13]

Comparing our country with the Soviet Union: (1) We had more than twenty years experience in the base areas and the practice of the three revolutionary wars. We are extremely rich in experience. By the time of the victory [of 1949] we had already accumulated experience in every area, and we've had Right and Left deviations quite a few times. We quickly formed our state and accomplished our revolutionary tasks ([whereas] in the case of the Soviet Union, it was a newly started business for them; at the time of the October Revolution, they had no army, no government, and few Party members). (2) We have the help of the Soviet Union and other democratic countries. (3) Our population is large and our location is good. Though diligent and able to endure hardship, the peasants will have no future if they do not cooperativ-ize. Chinese peasants are even better than British and American workers; we can therefore step into socialism faster and with greater and better results. We should not always compare ourselves with the Soviet Union. After three five-year plans we shall be able to produce twenty-four million tons of steel. This is faster than the Soviet Union. Right now the two flanks are riding high, and the main body is possibly lagging behind. The two flanks are prone to be conceited, but it is the industrial sector that is most prone to be conceited, especially heavy industry. The Anshan [Iron and Steel Works], for instance, has already become conceited.[14] It is very possible for a nation to become socialized without being industrialized (with the proportion [of industry] less than sixty per cent, the system is not yet established). Can we ask the peasants to wait? This is impossible. The socialization of the peasants does not hinder industrialization. We cannot make them wait. The work at the two flanks has been seriously examined. In addition, we ought to have a serious examination of the problem of industry and [make industry] go through big campaigns according to schedule. We should investigate financial and fiscal matters, trade, and cultural and educational matters as well. The Eighth [Party] Congress should make a summing-up investigation. This is the central problem. We should oppose conservatism, Right deviation, passivity, and arrogance; we should discover advanced experience, change the method of leadership, and achieve faster and better results. We should mobilize the masses to conduct criticism and self-criticism, to overcome conservatism, and to score greater achievements. The whole Party must be prepared, and the entire nation must be prepared.

Notes

1. For a summary of the 1956 Leap, see R. MacFarquhar (1974), pp. 27-32, 86-91.

2. By December 1956 some of the opposition within the Party had been overcome, i.e., the Rural Work Department had been criticized for Right empiricism (see text Oct. 11, 1955[1], notes 21 and 34) and Liu Shaoqi had allegedly taken up self-criticism for moving too slowly on cooperativization. Nonetheless, there was still considerable opposition; see R. MacFarquhar (1974), pp. 27-91. It is important to remember, however, that although both Leaps encountered significant opposition within the Party, it was not necessarily the same individuals who opposed both.

3. The "Forty-Point Program," or "Forty-Article Program," known formally as the "Draft Program for the National Development of Agriculture, 1956-1967," was the result of the process begun with seventeen points in November 1955 (see text Dec. 21, 1955; see also text Oct. 11, 1955[1], note 55, and text Oct. 11, 1955[2], note 15). The Draft Program was submitted by the Political Bureau of the Central Committee of the CPC in January 1956 and adopted by the Supreme State Conference on January 25, 1956 (see Mao's speech, text Jan. 25, 1956). The Program is translated in R. Bowie and J. Fairbank, eds. (1962), pp. 119ff. The Program was part of the 1956 Leap Forward but was shelved in late 1956. It was brought forward again at the time of the Great Leap Forward. See also text Jan. 28, 1958, note 5, concerning the suggested speed-up implementing the "Forty-Point Plan" at that time.

4. For the evolution of this slogan, see text Apr. 25, 1956, note 1.

5. Despite his great optimism at this time and at the beginning of the Great Leap in 1958, Mao was aware that his enthusiasm often led to even more overly enthusiastic reactions throughout society. Although he commented negatively on this (see R. MacFarguhar [1974], p. 329, citing *Wansui* [1969], p. 31, i.e., text Jan. 21, 1956, paragraph 3), Mao tended to keep his criticisms of such overreactions within the Party.

6. See text Oct. 11, 1955(1), especially notes 21 and 34. Here the criticism of Liu Shaoqi for "moving too slowly" on carrying out cooperativization policies was also implied. Liu made a self-criticism at this Plenum.

7. The "Seventeen-Article" program concerning agricultural development in general and about speeding up agricultural cooperativization in particular was drafted after a meeting of the provincial Party secretaries in Tianjin in November 1955. This draft, circulated and discussed in the subsequent two months (see text Dec. 21, 1955) became the forerunner of and basis for the

"Forty-Article Program" (see note 3).

8. See text Oct. 15, 1953, note 2.

9. In late December, shortly after Mao's Second Preface to *Upsurge of Socialism in China's Countryside* (see text Dec. 27, 1955[1]) was published, Zhou Enlai told a conference of intellectuals that the Central Committee had decided to "make opposition to rightist conservative ideology the central question for the Eighth National Party Congress" to be held in September 1956. See R. MacFarquhar (1974), p. 27.

10. See text Aug. 12, 1953(1), note 22. Adventurist advance was, to begin with, a "Left deviation." Here Mao suggests that, because of a tendency, or swing, toward a "Right deviation," mistakes are made in the opposition against "adventurist advance." While this did not in itself justify the original "adventurism" in certain cadres' work-style in the early 1950s, it did mean that the opposition that people such as Liu Shaoqi, whom Mao considered to be "conservative," raised against what they saw to be the manifestations of adventurism in the late 1950s – i.e., the cooperativization movement and later the Great Leap Forward of 1958-59 – had itself to be opposed. Thus in the remainder of the decade, for the most part Mao would employ the term *maojin* (adventurist advance) – usually put in quotation marks – in this reverse positive sense, i.e., as something to be defended rather than criticized. For a more detailed discussion of this, see R. MacFarquhar (1974), pp. 86-91, 122-129.

11. In "On Coalition Government," written in 1945, Mao had set the elimination of illiteracy as a vital task for New China. In June 1950 the GAC issued a directive on spare-time education to decrease illiteracy. In July 1950 Beijing ran a campaign to eliminate illiteracy. In December 1950 the Ministry of Education initiated a nationwide program of worker-peasant spare-time education focused on eliminating illiteracy. In September 1952 the Ministry of Education and the All-China Federation of Trade Unions jointly convened a National Symposium on the Work of Eliminating Illiteracy, which urged its elimination in five to ten years. See Y. Lau (1977), pp. 363-364.

12. See text Oct. 11, 1955(1), note 34.

13. See text Sept. 7, 1953, note 4.

14. See text Dec. 14, 1952, source note.

Letter to Zhai Zuojun
(December 12, 1955)

Source: *Shuxin*, p. 506.

See text Spring 1952, source note.

Comrade Zuojun:

Your letter of December 2 has been received. I am very happy to receive it. I guess you have returned to Taiyuan. I have also received some of your earlier letters, but it seems to me that I may not have received all of them. We are all very well here. I hope that you will do a good job of studying. When next you come to Beijing, please let us know ahead of time ([you may] contact Li Yin-qiao, the commander of my bodyguards, on the telephone), and we should arrange for a meeting.

My regards.

> Mao Zedong
> December 12, 1955

Circular Requesting Opinions on the Seventeen Articles on Agricultural Work

(December 21, 1955)

Source: *Xuanji*, V, pp. 260-263. Available English Translation: *SW*, V, pp. 277-280.

This is a circular drafted by Mao on behalf of the CPC Central Committee and sent to the Shanghai Bureau of the CPC as well as to the various provincial and autonomous region Party committees.

As noted in the opening paragraph of this document and elsewhere in this volume (see text Dec. 6, 1955, note 7, and texts Oct. 11, 1955[1] and [2]), the seventeen articles discussed here were part of a larger process of developing a consensus within the Chinese leadership over the key elements for developing agricultural production. By January 1956, as a result of this process of circulating and discussing these draft articles, the forty-point Draft National Program for Agricultural Development was produced.

This document sheds light on Mao's role in developing that consensus and on his openness to key issues, e.g., whether landlords and rich peasants should be allowed to join the cooperatives, and how fast and in what form cooperativization should proceed. Mao's efforts to initiate discussion and struggle over such critical issues are also apparent in his discussions of the issues surrounding communization in late 1958 and early 1959 (see texts Mar. 15, and 17, 1959).

In November this year, Comrade Mao Zedong had discussions in Hangzhou and Tianjin with the secretaries of the [Party] committees of fourteen provinces and of the Inner Mongolia Autonomous Region, respectively, and together they decided on the Seventeen Articles [on Agriculture].[1] The Central Committee believes that these should be discussed and confirmed at the conference to be convened by the Center on January 10, which will be attended by the secretaries of the various provincial, municipal, and autonomous region Party committees,[2] so that they can be incorporated into the plan for 1956, and their implementation can be begun earnestly. For this purpose, you are asked, immediately upon receiving this telegram, to summon together the various [special] district [Party] committee secretaries and some of the *xian* [Party] committee secretaries under your jurisdiction to study [these points] in detail: (a) whether all [the Seventeen Articles] are, after all, totally practicable or some are impracticable; whether the basis for carrying out each of the articles is adequate; (b) whether there should be any further additions to the Seventeen Articles (as long as they are practicable, additions can be made); and (c) whether you are prepared to incorporate them immediately into your plan for 1956 and to begin to implement them. Please conclude your study of these aforementioned points before January 3, 1956, and prepare your opinions [for discussion at the conference].

The contents of the Seventeen Articles are as follows:

1) The rate of cooperativization of agriculture: The work of establishing primary-stage [agricultural producers'] cooperatives[3] should be fundamentally completed in the second half of 1956. At the level of provinces, municipalities, and autonomous regions (excepting Xinjiang), the target should be to get seventy-five per cent of the peasant households to join the cooperative; at the lower levels, let [this target] be exceeded somewhat and reach about eighty to eighty-five per cent.

We must strive to fundamentally achieve the higher-stage form of cooperativization by 1960.[4] Is it possible to shorten the time by one year and strive to achieve [this goal] fundamentally by 1959? To this end, it is necessary for one or several large-size (over 100 households) higher-stage cooperatives to be established in 1956 in each *xian* or each district under the direct control of the *xian* or, preferably, district [authorities]. Then, in 1957, another group should be established. These two groups [of cooperatives] should make up about twenty-five per cent of the peasant households and should serve as examples. Is this possible? Another [question] concerns the size [of cooperatives] after small cooperatives are transformed [by merging] into big cooperatives. [How big should they be?] Can several cooperatives [be merged to] form a *xiang*, or should each cooperative form a *xiang*, or should a cooperative be made up of several *xiang* – are all three [of these methods] practicable? What is the most suitable figure for the total number of cooperatives in the country? Three hundred thousand, 400,000, or 500,000? The Soviet Union has 100,000 cooperatives; is it more suitable for our country to have 300,000 or 400,000 cooperatives? Also, is it better to have the cooperatives merge first and then raise them to a higher stage [of cooperativization], or is it better to merge the cooperatives and promote the level [of cooperativization] at the same time? Or is it best to promote the level first and then merge the cooperatives? Please study these various points as well.

2) [Regarding the question of] landlords and rich peasants joining the cooperatives,[5] should we, in 1956, handle this according to the suggestion [made by] the provinces of Anhui, Shanxi, and Heilongjiang,[6] that is, allow those who are good to join the cooperative, and allow those who are not good, but

not bad either, to participate in the production in the cooperative without giving them the title of membership, and have bad ones engage in production under the surveillance of the cooperative? In all old cooperatives where there are strong cadres this can be done. There are many advantages to this, but there is one shortcoming, which is that inevitably this will compel those upper-middle peasants who are presently still reluctant to join the cooperative to do so involuntarily, and, moreover, only by allowing them to join the cooperatives first, before the landlords and rich peasants, can we preserve their dignity. Is this advantageous? Or should we postpone it for a year, that is, wait until 1957 to carry out the aforementioned method? Which of these two [methods] is more advantageous? Please study this.

3) The composition of the cooperatives' leadership: Two-thirds should be composed of present-day poor peasants and [members of] the entire [strata of] new lower-middle peasants who were formerly poor peasants; one-third should be made up of the former lower-middle peasants and the two categories of upper-middle peasants – the former [upper-middle peasants] and the new upper-middle peasants.[7]

4) [Regarding] the conditions for increasing production: (a) [We must] carry out several basic measures (the contents [of which] are still to be discussed, and there can be differences from place to place); (b) [We must] propagate advanced experiences. (Every year [we should] collect [information on] typical cases, and each province should publish a volume [based on them].)

5) In 1956, all provinces, [special] districts, *xian,* districts, and *xiang* must produce a comprehensive, long-term plan covering all necessary items, giving emphasis to the plans of the *xian* and *xiang.* The preliminary draft should be done in the first half of the year, and in the second half of the year the draft should be finalized, [although] it can still be revised in the future. The time covered by the plans should be at least three years, preferably seven, [but] can [even] be [as long as] twelve years. We should make haste to get this matter done. Have you already made arrangements for it? For lack of experience, many [of these plans] may be very rough. Still, we must strive to make the plans of a few *xian* and *xiang* relatively realistic so that they can be easily propagated [as models].

6) [There should be] an overall plan for protecting and breeding cattle, horses, mules, donkeys, pigs, sheep, chickens, and ducks. In particular, young animals must be protected. The plan for breeding them is to be discussed; please prepare your opinions.

7) Integrated with the plans for river basins, small-scale water-conservation projects should be built extensively in order to guarantee that within seven years ordinary floods and droughts will be basically eliminated.

8) Within seven years, more than a dozen insect pests and diseases that are harmful to the crops should be basically eliminated.

9) Within twelve years we must basically eliminate wastelands and barren hillsides. Trees should be planted according to specified requirements in all available space, [for instance] beside houses, beside villages, along roads,

beside streams, and on wasteland and barren hills so as to achieve the greening of our country.

10) Within twelve years, ninety per cent of the fertilizer in most areas and 100 per cent in some areas should be provided by the localities and cooperatives themselves.

11) Within twelve years, the average grain yield per *mu* for places north of the Yellow River, the Qinling [Mountains], the Bailongjiang, and the Yellow River ([that part of it] inside Qinghai [Province]) should aim at reaching four hundred catties; [for areas] south of the Yellow River but north of the Huai River it should be five hundred catties, and [for areas] south of the Huai River, the Qinling [Mountains], and the Bailongjiang it should be eight hundred catties.[8] As for the targets for such items as cotton, oils, soy beans, silk, tea, hemp, sugarcane, and fruits, please suggest quotas for future discussion.

12) [We must,] within seven years, basically eliminate some of the diseases that are most severely harmful to people and livestock; for instance, schistosomiasis, filariasis, bubonic plague, encephalitis, rinderpest, and hog cholera. Please study the endemic diseases in each province and autonomous region to see which ones are capable of being basically eliminated within seven years, which may require a longer period before they can be eliminated, and which ones are impossible to eliminate at the present time.

13) Eliminate the four pests, that is, within seven years, basically eliminate rats (and other harmful animals), sparrows (and other harmful birds; but whether or not it is advisable to eliminate crows remains to be studied), flies, and mosquitoes.[9]

14) Within seven years, [we must] basically sweep away illiteracy.[10] Each person must be able to recognize 1,500 to 2,000 characters.

15) Within seven years, [we must] build, according to specified requirements, all types of necessary roads in the provinces, [special] districts, *xian*, districts, and *xiang*. (Some of them are highways, some are roads, others are pathways.)

16) Within seven years, [we must] set up a wired broadcasting network so that every *xiang* and every cooperative can receive broadcasts.

17) Within seven years, [we must] complete a telephone network between the *xiang* and the large-scale cooperatives.

Please study the items mentioned above with comrades concerned and complete your preparation before January 3. The Central Committee may, around January 4, first invite some provincial [Party] committee secretaries to meet and study [these matters] for a few days in order to prepare suggestions for the conference of January 10.

Notes

1. For information on the Tianjin meeting, see K. Lieberthal (1976), pp. 75-76. Lieberthal also states that there is no available data on the Hangzhou meeting.

2. This refers to the Conference on the Question of Intellectuals sponsored by the CPC Central Committee, January 14-20, 1956, in Beijing. See K. Lieberthal (1976), p. 77. Lieberthal also suggests that there is indication that a meeting starting on Dec. 28, 1955, was held prior to this meeting, which may have been devoted to the study of the question of the twelve-year program for agricultural development. There is, however, no available documentation of this earlier meeting.

3. See text Oct. 15, 1953, note 2.

4. See text Oct. 15, 1953, note 2.

5. For more on the issue of landlord and rich peasant membership in the cooperatives, see text Oct. 11, 1955.

6. There is no specific indication of the documents which Mao might have been referring to here. About this time, many CPC provincial committees, including those of the three mentioned here, filed reports on the cooperativization movement in their provinces. These reports usually followed the convening of conferences in the provinces on the work of cooperativization. A rather lengthy set of these reports can be found in Shi Jingtang et al., eds. (1957), II, pp. 859-898. A brief reading of the reports from these three provinces does not reveal any significant connection to Mao's point here. What Mao may have been referring to instead are Heilongjiang provincial Party Committee first secretary Feng Jixin's report to the third meeting of the First People's Representative Conference of Heilongjiang Province on Dec. 1, 1955, and a report compiled by the Rural Work Department of Shanxi Province in early 1954 (in Shi Jingtang et al., eds. [1957], III, pp. 774-785, 659-663, respectively). There is no document from Anhui Province in this collection that is relevant precisely to this point.

7. See text July 31, 1955, note 14.

8. The targets for these three areas were incorporated as article 6 of "The Draft Program for Agricultural Development." They were subsequently referred to as "the three categories of land."

9. Mao's suggestion here was incorporated into article 27 of the "Forty-Article Program," and these became officially known as the *si hai* (four pests). See text Jan. 25, 1956, note 3. Later, a directive drafted by Mao on behalf of the Party Center in March 1960 stated: "Another thing, we need not eliminate any more sparrows; we should put bugs, instead of sparrows, in our slogan, which should read 'Eliminate rats, bugs, flies, and mosquitoes.'" See *SW*, V, p. 280, footnote.

10. See text Dec. 6, 1955, note 11.

Second Preface to *Upsurge of Socialism in China's Countryside* (December 27, 1955)

Source: *Gaochao*, pp. 1-4. Other Chinese Texts: *Xuanji*, V, pp. 221-224; *RMRB* (Jan. 12, 1956), 1; Shi Jingtang et al., eds. (1957), II, pp. 76-78; *Gaizao wenji*, III, pp. 71-73; *Xuexi*, 1 (1956), 1-2. Available English Translations: *Socialist Upsurge*, pp. 1-6; *SW*, V, pp. 238-241.

See texts Sept. 25, 1955, and Dec. 27, 1955 (2).

This is a book of collected materials for people working in the countryside to read. A preface for this book was originally written in September. Three months have since passed and that preface is already outdated, so the only thing to do is to write a new one.

The situation is this. This book has been edited twice – once in September and once again in December. One hundred and twenty-one articles were collected for the first editing. Most of these reflected the situation during the first half of 1955, while a smaller number reflected the situation in the latter half of 1954. At that time [galley] proofs were made of these materials and distributed to comrades in positions of responsibility in provincial, municipal, autonomous region, and [special] district Party committees who were attending the Sixth (Enlarged) Plenum of the Seventh Central Committee of the Communist Party of China, which was being held from October 4 to October 11, 1955. Their opinions were solicited, and they felt that additional material was needed. After the meeting, most of the provinces, municipalities, and autonomous regions sent additional material. Much of this material reflected the situation in the latter half of 1955. This is what necessitated another editing. We deleted 30 of the original 121 articles, leaving 91, and we selected 85 articles from the newly collected material. Together this makes a total of 176 articles, about 900,000 characters, which became this book. All the material collected in this book has been gone over by the several comrades who were responsible for editing it, and some changes have been made in phrasing; they have added notes to explain difficult terms and have prepared a topical index [to it] according to the nature of the problems [that the articles deal with]. In addition, we have written some comments on some of the material, criticizing certain erroneous ideas and making some suggestions. In order to distinguish these from the comments written by the editors of the periodicals in which the material originally appeared, we have used the appellation "Editors of this book" for the comments that we have written. Since some of the comments were written in September and others were written in December, there are some differences in tone between them.

The problem is not simply a matter of the material, but rather [is owing to the fact] that the situation in China underwent a fundamental change during the latter half of 1955. At the present time, late December 1955, more than 60 per cent, that is, over 70 million of China's 110 million peasant households have responded to the call of the Central Committee of the Chinese Communist Party and have joined the semisocialist agricultural producers' cooperatives.[1] In my report of July 31, 1955, regarding the question of agricultural cooperativization,[2] I stated that 16.9 million peasant households had joined cooperatives; in only a few months [since], some 50 million [more] households have joined cooperatives. This is a tremendous event. It indicates to us that only one year, 1956, will be required to basically accomplish semisocialist cooperativization in agriculture. Then, in another three or four years, by 1959 or 1960, we can basically accomplish the transformation of the cooperatives from a semisocialist [character] to a fully socialist [character]. This event indicates to us that we should also strive to accomplish the socialist transformation of China's handicraft industries and capitalist industry and commerce a bit ahead of schedule, and that only then can the needs of agricultural development be met. This event indicates to us that the scale and rate of China's industrialization as well as the scale and rate of its development in the various enterprises in the areas of science, culture, education, public health, and so forth can no longer remain entirely as originally intended but also must be appropriately expanded and accelerated.

Is such a rapid advance in agricultural cooperativization being carried out in a healthy way? Absolutely. Party organizations everywhere are giving overall leadership to this movement. The peasants have joined this movement with such great enthusiasm and in such an orderly fashion. Their enthusiasm for production has never been higher. For the first time the broadest masses can see their own future clearly. By the time three five-year plans are completed, that is, by 1967, the [annual] production of grain and of many other agricultural products will possibly be two to three times higher than the highest annual output prior to the establishment of the People's Republic. Illiteracy can be wiped out in a relatively short time (for example, in seven or eight years).[3] Many of the most serious diseases that are harmful to people, such as schistosomiasis and so forth, for which people in the past have thought there were no treatments, can now be treated. In short, the masses can already see their great future.

The problem that now confronts the whole Party and the people of the entire country is no longer the problem of repudiating rightist conservative thought with regard to the speed of the socialist transformation of agriculture; that problem has already been resolved. Nor is it the problem of the speed of transforming capitalist industry and commerce into fully joint state-private enterprises by entire trades; that problem has also already been resolved. The question of the speed of the socialist transformation of the handicraft industries ought to be discussed a bit during the first half of 1956, [but] this problem, too, can be resolved easily. The current problem is not in these areas but rather lies in other areas. It lies in the areas of agricultural and industrial production (including state, joint state-private, and cooperative owned [enterprises]); handicraft production; the scale and speed of basic construction in industry, communications, and transportation; the coordination between commerce and other sectors of the economy; the coordination between scientific, cultural, educational, and health work; and the various kinds of economic undertakings, etc. In all these areas there is the shortcoming of underestimating the situation. This must be criticized and overcome in all areas so that [our work] will correspond to the development of the entire situation. People's thinking must correspond to the changed situation. Of course, individuals cannot indulge in ungrounded, wild flights of fancy; they cannot exceed the conditions allowed by the objective situation in planning their own actions. They must not force themselves to do what is not actually possible. But the current problem is still that of rightist conservative thought making trouble in many areas and making it impossible for our work in many areas to correspond with the development of the objective situation. The present problem is that many things that, if given the effort, are essentially feasible are considered by many people to be infeasible. Therefore, it is absolutely necessary to unceasingly repudiate the rightist conservative thought that really does exist.

This book is for comrades working in the countryside to read. Can people in the cities read it? Not only can they read it, they ought to read it. This [cooperativization] is a new thing. Just as new things in the cause of socialism occur each day and each hour in the cities, so too do they occur in the countryside. What are the peasants doing? How does what the peasants do relate to the working class, the intellectuals, and all patriotic personages? Reading this material about the countryside will be helpful to understanding these things.

In order to let even more people understand the current situation in the countryside, we plan to choose 44 articles out of the 176, approximately 270,000 characters, and print an abridged edition.[4] This will allow those who cannot read the entire book to stay in touch with the issue.

Notes

1. See text Aug. 12, 1953, note 9, and text Oct. 15, 1953, note 2.
2. See text in this volume under this date.
3. See text Dec. 6, 1955, note 11.
4. Forty-three of the commentaries written by Mao on the articles in this collection were published in *SW*, V, pp. 242-276. For data on the publishing of the abridged version of 44 articles and accompanying commentaries, see text Dec. 27, 1955(2), source note.

Editor's Notes to *Upsurge of Socialism in China's Countryside*
(December 27, 1955)

Source: *Gaochao,* passim. Other Chinese Texts: *Xuanji*, V, pp. 225-259 (excerpts); Shi Jingtang et al., eds. (1957), II, pp. 78-107; *Xuandu* (1965a), pp. 319-326 (excerpts); *Xuandu* (1965b), pp. 159-169 (excerpts). Available English Translations: *Socialist Upsurge,* passim; *SW*, V, pp. 242-276 (excerpts); *SR*, pp. 421-429 (excerpts).

These are editorial comments written by Mao on individual articles contained in the book Zhongguo nongcun de shehui zhuyi gaochao *(hereafter cited as* Gaochao), *edited by the General Office of the Central Committee of the CPC, which describes the experiences of various localities throughout the country during the agricultural cooperativization movement. The main thrust of these articles, and of the book itself, was to support the nationwide cooperativization movement, and by contrast, to condemn the postion taken by some leaders other than Mao himself (especially Liu Shaoqi), who in the spring of 1955 repudiated the cooperativization policy, calling it an "adventurist advance" (see text Aug. 12, 1953[1], note 22, and text Dec. 6, 1955, note 10) and attempting to supplant it with a policy of reversal, calling for the disbanding of cooperatives that had already been established. Mao called this policy a policy of "drastic reduction" (see text Jul. 31, 1955, note 13). The lines of conflict were obviated in Mao's first preface to the book* Gaochao, *which is collected here as text September 25, 1955. Mao's defense of the cooperativization policy is even stronger in the comments that he wrote here for the articles in the book* Gaochao.

The book Gaochao *was originally published in three volumes in 1956 by Renmin chubanshe and contained 176 articles, excluding the preface. Mao wrote comments on 104 of these articles, concentrating on the articles in the early parts and tapering off toward the end. The articles were divided according to provincial locations.*

As indicated by Mao at the end of his second preface to the book Gaochao, *containing 44 of the articles, all of which included Mao's comments, was published separately. This was done in January 1956. An English translation of this abridged version, titled* Socialist Upsurge in China's Countryside, *was published in 1978 by the Foreign Languages Press, Beijing.*

In March 1958, some of Mao's comments here were reprinted for an enlarged meeting of the Political Bureau of the Central Committee of the CPC at Chengdu, and Mao wrote an accompanying explanation for this effort on March 19, 1958. This explanation was published for the first time in 1977 in Xuanji, V. *(See* Xuanji, V, *pp. 225-226,* SW, V, *pp. 242-244, and text Mar. 19, 1958.) Eventually, 43 of the comments in the book* Gaochao *were published in* Xuanji, V, *in 1977. Of these, 30 overlapped with the ones published in the abridged version of 1956. Earlier, in 1965, in the two volumes of* Xuandu, *several of these comments were also published. In* Xuandu *(1965a) there were four comments, all of which were previously published in the abridged version of 1956, and in* Xuandu *(1965b) there were five comments, three of which were published in the abridged version.*

The order in which these comments appeared in the secondary sources does not, in each case, correspond to the order in which they appeared in the original book. We have here reproduced the full 104 comments in the order in which they appeared in Gaochao. *The location of each comment in the original, and where applicable in the secondary sources, follows the text of each comment, indicated by an* *. In these notes the citation* Socialist Upsurge *refers to* Socialist Upsurge in China's Countryside, *the English translation of the abridged version, published in 1978.*

[Editor's Note to] "With the [Party] Secretary Taking Part,
the Entire Party Should Be Engaged in Running Cooperatives"

This article is very well written. It is worthy of being recommended to our readers as the first article of this book. There are still quite a few people everywhere who are like those described in the first part of this article, people who don't understand [the cooperatives] themselves and are afraid of people asking them questions, and so "skirt around the cooperatives." So-called "resolute reduction," the issuing of orders to dissolve large groups of cooperatives in one fell swoop,[1] is also a manifestation of "skirting around the cooperatives." The only difference is that theirs is not a passive evasion; on the contrary; they go as far as to "chop down" (this is their term) many cooperatives in large bunches with one blow, and do it with a very enthusiastic attitude. With knife in hand, they simply skirt around [all] the troublesome problems with a single chop. They say that there is this or that difficulty in running a cooperative; according to them, the difficulties simply defy the imagination. [However,] there are countless examples throughout the country which refute this kind of talk. The experience of Zunhua *xian* in Hebei Province is just one such example. In 1952, none of the people there knew how to run a cooperative. Their way was simply to learn. Their slogan was: "With the [Party] secretary taking part, the entire Party should be engaged in running the cooperatives." That resulted in "going from a [total] lack of understanding to understanding," "going from having [only] a few people knowing how to [run the cooperative] to having most people knowing how [to run the cooperative]," and "going from having the district cadres run the cooperative to having the masses run the cooperative." The tenth district of Zunhua *xian* in Hebei Province is made up of eleven *xiang* and 4,343 households. In the three years from 1952 to 1954, it basically accomplished the semisocialist stage of cooperativization.[2] Eighty-five per cent of all peasant households in the area have joined the cooperatives. Comparing the 1954 output of this district in agriculture, forestry, and animal husbandry with that of 1952, there has been an increase by 76 per cent in food grain [production], 56.4 per cent in timber [output], 62.87 per cent in [the number of] fruit trees, and 463.1 per cent in [the number of] sheep.

We now have reason to put the following question to people: Why can these things be done here and not in other places? If you say that it can't be done, what is your reason for saying so? As I see it, there is only one reason, simply that they don't want to be bothered with it, or, to put it more bluntly, [the reason is simply] Right opportunism. As a result, people just "skirt around the cooperatives," meaning that the secretaries do not take part and the entire Party is not engaged in running the cooperatives, meaning that people go from not understanding to still not understanding, from having [only] a few people knowing how to [run cooperatives] to still having [only] a few people knowing how to [run cooperatives], and from having [only] the district cadres [running cooperatives] to still having [only] the district cadres [running cooperatives]. Otherwise, they simply take up their knives and, whenever they come across a troublesome cooperative, chop it down. As long as people go by this kind of reasoning nothing will be accomplished. We have put forth such slogans as "active leadership, steady advance" and "make comprehensive plans, strengthen leadership," and moreover we approve of the absolutely correct slogan that has been put forward by the comrades of Zunhua *xian*: "With the [Party] secretaries taking part, the entire Party should be engaged in running the cooperatives." Does that mean that there is no "active leadership and steady advance" in Zunhua *xian?* Is there no "comprehensive planning and the strengthening of leadership"? Of course there is. Is this dangerous? Does it constitute "adventurist advance"?[3] The danger is in "skirting around the cooperatives"; this the comrades of Zunhua *xian* have already overcome. The danger is also in using the pretext [that the cooperatives are] "adventurist" in order to "chop [them] down" in large bunches. There is none of this in Zunhua *xian*. How can the claim that "the speed of development of the cooperatives has outstripped the consciousness of the masses and the leadership capabilities of the cadres" be reconciled with the situation in Zunhua *xian?* The masses there actually pressed for cooperativization and the cadres there actually went from not understanding to understanding. Everyone has eyes. Is there anyone who can see danger in [the situation of] Zunhua *xian?* Is it to be considered as some sort of danger that in the last three years, as a result of the gradual realization of cooperativization, there has been an increase of 76 per cent in [the production of] grain, an increase of 56.4 per cent in [the output of] timber, an increase of 62.87 per cent in the number of fruit trees, and a 463.1 per cent increase in the number of sheep? Is this to be considered "adventurist advance"? Is this to be considered "outstripping the consciousness of the masses and the leadership capabilities of the cadres"?

In the cooperativization movement in Zunhua *xian* there is Wang Guofan Cooperative – twenty-three poor peasant households with only a three-quarters share of a donkey.[4] People call it the "paupers' cooperative."[5] Through their own efforts they have, in three years, "wrested from the mountain" a good deal of the means of production.[6] Some visitors are moved to tears. I see this as being the image of our entire country. Can't 600 million paupers become a rich and powerful socialist country in a few decades through their own efforts? The wealth of a society is created by the workers, peasants, and intellectuals who are integrated with labor themselves. As long as these people take hold of their own destiny and have a Marxist-Leninist line, and as long as they do not evade problems but, instead, tackle them with a positive attitude, then any difficulty on earth can be resolved.

Finally, we must thank the anonymous author of this article. With wholehearted enthusiasm and a vivid style, a detailed narrative of the process of cooperativization in one district has been recounted [to us]. This is no small contribution to the cause of cooperativization throughout the entire nation. We hope that each province, each special district, and each *xian* will have one or several articles like this.

* "Shuji dongshou quan dang ban she," originally published in *Tangshan nongminbao* [Tangshan Peasant News], April 30, 1955; collected and reprinted in *Gaochao*, pp. 3-6; *Xuanji*, V, pp. 225-228; *Socialist Upsurge*, pp. 7-10.

* * *

[Editor's Note to] "Running the Cooperatives Industriously and Frugally"[7]

The cooperative introduced here is the so-called "paupers' cooperative" under the leadership of Wang Guofan.[8] Industrious and frugal management should be the guideline for all agricultural producers' cooperatives throughout the country. No, it should be the guideline for all economic undertakings. Be industrious and frugal in running factories, in running stores, in running all state-owned enterprises and cooperative enterprises, and all other undertakings. The principle of industry and frugality should be applied to all things. This is the principle of practicing economy. Practicing economy is one of the fundamental principles of the socialist economy. China is a big country but as yet still very poor, and it will take several decades to make China prosperous. Even after several decades it will still be necessary to apply the principle of industry and frugality, but it is especially in the next few decades, in the period of the next few five-year plans, that we must advocate industry and frugality and pay particular attention to practicing economy. Currently there are many cooperatives that have a kind of bad work-style in which they don't pay attention to practicing economy. This should be corrected quickly. Each province and each *xian* can find some examples of cooperatives being run industriously and frugally. They should publicize these examples and let everyone emulate them. We should commend those [cooperatives] that are run industriously and frugally, whose output is high, and that are well-run in all respects, and we should criticize those cooperatives that are wasteful, whose output is very low, and that are poorly run in all respects.

* Wang Lin, "Qinjian ban she," originally published in *Hebei ribao* [Hebei Daily News], May 4, 1955; collected and reprinted in *Gaochao*, p. 16; *Xuanji*, V, p. 249; *Socialist Upsurge*, pp.67-68; *Xuandu* (1965a), p. 168.

* * *

[Editor's Note to] "The Direction for Five Hundred Million Peasants"

In the past several months this cooperative [consisting of] three poor peasant households has had a great impact on villages throughout the country.[9] Everyone knows that there is this great heroic cooperative in Hebei. It has given the poor peasants courage.

* Li Kai and Qing Shen, "Wu yi nongmin de fangxiang," originally published in *Renmin ribao* [People's Daily], November 28, 1955; collected and reprinted in *Gaochao*, p. 27; *Socialist Upsurge*, p. 121.

* * *

[Editor's Note to] "They Resolutely Chose the Path of Cooperativization"[10]

This is a very interesting story. The birth of a new thing such as socialism must go through an intense struggle with old things before it can come into being. At one time, some people in society may so stubbornly want to follow their old road, and at another time, the very same people may change their attitudes and indicate their approval of new things. In the first half of 1955, the majority of well-to-do middle peasants were still opposed to cooperativization; by the latter half of the year, some of them have already changed their attitude and indicated that they want to join the cooperatives, although for some of them the purpose is to join the cooperatives in order to seize the power of leadership in the cooperatives. Others have shown a great deal of vacillation; they say they wanted to join, but in their hearts, they still do not really want to. A third group still stubbornly wants to wait and see [what the outcome will be]. The rural Party organizations must be patient with this stratum [among the well-to-do peasants] regarding this problem. It is actually beneficial for some of the well-to-do middle peasants to enter the cooperatives a little later since it allows the poor and new lower-middle peasants to establish [their] dominant position in the leadership.

* Shi Shufang, "Tamen jianjue xuanze liao hezuohua de daolu," originally published in *Renmin ribao* [People's Daily], September 20, 1955; collected and reprinted in *Gaochao*, p. 37; *Xuanji*, V, p. 243; *Socialist Upsurge*, pp. 135-136.

* * *

[Editor's Note to] "A Whole Village Is Cooperativized
in a Little Over a Month"

This material is very persuasive. The problem of leading a locality in achieving cooperativization on a sound footing is the problem of the Party's policy and its method of work. As long as the various policies of our Party for dealing with the problem of cooperativization are correct, and as long as the method that our Party uses when it motivates the masses to join the cooperatives is not the method of commandism[11] or oversimplification but rather is the method of reasoning with the masses, making analyses, and completely relying on the consciousness and willingness of the masses, then cooperativization and increased production will certainly not be difficult to achieve. Dongchuankou Village in Xingtai *xian*, Hebei Province, is in an old liberated area.[12] Prior to 1952, all seventy households in the village had joined mutual aid teams; they had a strong Party branch, and they also had, in Wang Zhiqi, a leader who was trusted by the masses; all the conditions [for cooperativization] were ripe. So in 1952, that village established a cooperative in just over a month, thus accomplishing semisocialist cooperativization. What about localities in which conditions are not as good as in this village? For them, then, the question is one of preparing the conditions, and a few months, a year, or even a bit longer will be sufficient [to resolve] this problem. Conditions can be prepared while the [work of implementing cooperativization] is being done. Set up some small cooperatives; this will be preparing the conditions for cooperativizing the whole village, the whole xiang, and the whole district. This article about Dongchuankou Village also gave emphasis to clarifying the problem of how the Party branch [should] carry out its propaganda and educational work among the masses, and how it [should] rely on the consciousness and willingness of the masses in establishing the cooperative. There is [in this article] something called "negative propaganda," which is well worth paying attention to.[13] With regard to the problem of organizing and managing labor, this article portrays the whole circuitous process of change, which resulted in a great achievement – increased production from year to year. Facts prove that this cooperative is on a sound footing. All the cooperatives should use [the standards of] whether or not there are increases in production and the rate of increases in production as the primary criterion by which to judge whether or not they are on a sound footing.

* "Zhi hua yi ge duo yue shijian jiu shi quan cun hezuohua," record of a talk by Comrade Wang Zhiqi, head of the Dongchuankou Agricultural Producers' Cooperative, August 15, 1955; collected and reprinted in Gaochao, pp. 44-45; Xuanji, V. pp. 236-237; Socialist Upsurge, pp. 25-26.

* * *

[Editor's Note to] "A So-called Backward Village
Is Not Necessarily Backward in Every Aspect"[14]

The year 1955 can be said to have been one of breaking down superstition[15] for many people in China. While in the first half of 1955 many people still clung so very tightly to their beliefs about certain things, they could no longer hold on [to these beliefs] in the latter half of the year and had to believe in the new things. They once believed, for example, that the [demand] put forth by the masses for "cooperativization in three years" was nothing more than wishful thinking; that cooperativization could be a bit faster in the north but it couldn't be fast in the south; that cooperatives couldn't be established in backward xiang, in mountainous areas, in minority nationality regions, in areas where several nationalities are integrated, or in areas afflicted by natural disasters; that setting up cooperatives is easy but consolidating them is hard; that the peasants are too poor and have no means of accumulating funds; that the peasants have no education and no bookkeeping can be found; that the more cooperatives there are, the more trouble there will be; that the rate of the development of cooperativization has outstripped the level of the masses' consciousness and the level of the cadres' experience; that the peasants' enthusiasm for production has been lowered because of the Party's policy of unified purchasing and marketing [by the state] and its policy of cooperativization; that if the Communist Party does not quickly back down from [its policy on] cooperativization it will run the risk of destroying the worker-peasant alliance; and that cooperativization will create a great pool of surplus labor power for which there will be no outlet. So forth and so on, we could pick out many more [examples]. In any case, all these [ideas] are superstitions. These superstitions, after being repudiated at the Sixth (Enlarged) Plenum of the Seventh Central Committee of the Communist Party of China in October 1955, were all completely smashed. An upsurge of socialist transformation has now emerged in the countryside throughout the country, and the masses are rejoicing. This is an indelible lesson for all Communists. There was such enormous enthusiasm for socialism lying latent among the masses. Why was this not felt or felt so slightly in many of the leading organs several months ago? Why was the thinking of the leaders and the thinking of the broad masses so different? Taking this as a lesson, how should we deal with similar situations and problems from now on? There is only one answer, that is, we must not become divorced from the masses, and we must be adept at discovering the enthusiasm of the masses in its essence.

* Work team of the Provincial Committee of the CPC of the former province of Jehol, ''Suowei luohou xiangcun bing fei yiqie dou luohou,'' originally published in *Qunzhong ribao* [The Masses' Daily] (Chengde), October 15, 1955; collected and reprinted in *Gaochao*, pp. 56-57; *Xuanji*, V, pp. 228-229; *Socialist Upsurge*, pp. 159-160.

* * *

[Editor's Note to] "We Should Not Set Back the Socialist Enthusiasm of the Cadres and the Masses or Recklessly Dissolve Cooperatives"[16]

Dissolving cooperatives in this way is completely erroneous. The viewpoint of the author of this article is correct.

* Work team of the Hebei Provincial Committee of the CPC, "Bu yingdang cuozhe ganbu he qunzhong de shehui zhuyi jijixing, huluan de jiesan hezuoshe,'' originally published in *Hebei jianshe* [Hebei Reconstructs], no. 290 (March 14, 1955); collected and reprinted in *Gaochao*, p. 63.

* * *

[Editor's Note to] "The Xingtai *xian* Democratic
Women's Federation's Plan for Work Among Women in the
Movement to Develop Agricultural Cooperativization"

This is a very good article. I hope that the Democratic Women's Federations
in all *xian* will do likewise. *Xian* [Party] committees ought to strengthen their
leadership in this area so that the total labor power of women will take its
place at the labor front under the principle of equal work and equal pay. This
demand should be met as soon as possible.

* The Xingtai *xian* Democratic Women's Federation, "Xingtai xian minzhu
funü lianhehui guanyu fazhan nongye hezuohua yundong zhong funü gongzuo
de guihua," November 1955, collected and reprinted in *Gaochao,* p. 66; and,
under a different title, in *Socialist Upsurge,* p. 298.

* * *

[Editor's Note to] "The Experience of Implementing
the Fixed Financial Supply System"[17]

This article is very well written. This is one concrete way of implementing
the principle of running the cooperatives industriously and frugally. All the
cooperatives can follow suit.

* Cai Wutian, "Tuixing 'caiwu baogan' de jingyan," October 1955, collected
and reprinted in *Gaochao,* p. 90.

* * *

[Editor's Note to] "Run the Cooperatives Industriously and
Frugally; Develop Construction in the Mountainous Regions"

This is about Jinxing [Gold Star] Agricultural, Forestry, and Animal Husbandry Producers' Cooperative led by Li Shunda.[18] This cooperative has
been going for three years and has become a big cooperative that encompasses
283 households. The location of this cooperative is a poor area in the Taihang
Mountains.[19] Through everyone's hard work, in three years it has begun to
take on a new look. The utilization rate of its labor power has increased by
110.6 per cent in comparison with the situation prior to the [War of] Resistance against Japan, when [the system of] individual labor was in effect, and
74 per cent when compared with the period of mutual aid teams, before
the cooperative was established.[20] The cooperative's public accumulation
has already increased from 120 *rmb* the first year to more than 11,000
rmb. In 1955, each member of the cooperative received an average of
884 catties of food grain, 77 per cent more than before the War of Resistance [against Japan] and 25.1 per cent more than before the establishment of

the cooperative. This cooperative drew up a five-year plan, and as a result of only three years of implementation, its gross output value has already reached 100.6 per cent of [the entire target set for] the five-year plan. The experience of this cooperative [poses the following question to] us: If areas where the natural conditions are relatively poor can achieve big increases in production, why can't areas where the natural conditions are more favorable do even better?

* Li Lin and Ma Ming, "Qinjian banshe, jianshe shanqu," September 15, 1955; collected and reprinted in *Gaochao,* p. 101; *Xuanji,* V, p. 256, *Socialist Upsurge,* pp. 84-85.

* * *

[Editor's Note to] "The Comprehensive Plan of Pingshun *xian"*

This article is worth reading. It can serve as a reference for every *xian* [Party] committee in guiding the cooperativization movement, in the production drive, and in other work. We hope that for every province there will be a number of such articles that deal with *xian*-wide plans and that describe all aspects of the situation comprehensively.

* Li Lin, secretary of the Pingshun *xian* Committee of the Chinese Communist Party, "Pingshun xian de quanmian guihua," September 20, 1955; collected and reprinted in *Gaochao,* p. 110: *Socialist Upsurge,* p. 373.

* * *

[Editor's Note to] "A Serious Lesson"

Political work is the lifeline of all economic work. This is particularly the case when the economic system of a society is undergoing a fundamental change. The movement for cooperativization in agriculture has been a serious ideological and political struggle from its very inception. No cooperative can be established without going through this kind of struggle. For a brand-new social system to establish itself on the foundation of an old [social] system, it must sweep this foundation clean. Remnants of the old ideology that reflect the old system always linger in people's minds for a long time; they will not readily retreat. After a cooperative is established it must still go through many struggles before it can consolidate itself. Even after it is consolidated it could still collapse if it simply relaxes even once. [For example,] here Sanlousi Cooperative of Xieyu *xian* in Shanxi Province is one cooperative that nearly collapsed because of a relaxation of effort after it was consolidated. Only after the Party organization there criticized [itself for] its own mistakes, undertook to start all over again to educate the masses of the cooperative members in opposing capitalism and strengthening socialism, and revived its political work was it able to overcome this crisis and step onto the road of continuous development. Opposition to the spontaneous tendency toward selfish, self-serving capitalism and advocacy of the socialist spirit in which the principle of uniting the interests of the collective with the interests of the individual is taken as the standard by which all words and deeds are judged is the ideological and political guarantee for the step-by-step transition from a dispersed, small[-scale] peasant economy to a large-scale cooperativized economy. This work is enormous and arduous; it must be done according to the life experiences of the peasants and done in a very concrete and meticulous way. We cannot have a crude attitude or use a simplistic method. [Political work] must be done so that it is linked with economic work; it cannot be done in isolation. We already have considerably rich experience in this type of work on a nationwide scale. Almost every article in this book demonstrates this characteristic.

* Correspondent Yan Guanghong, "Yanzhong de jiaoxun," originally published in *Shanxi ribao* [Shanxi Daily], February 1, 1955; collected and reprinted in *Gaochao*, pp. 123-124; *Xuanji*, V, pp. 243-244; *Socialist Upsurge*, pp. 330-331; *Xuandu* (1956b), pp. 163-164; and, under a different title, *Xuandu* (1965a), p. 325.

* * *

[Editor's Note to] "The Experience of Changzhi Special District in Establishing a Network of Cooperatives"

This method of having networks of cooperatives is very good. All areas should follow suit.

* Rural Work Department of the Changzhi [Special] District Committee of the CPC, "Changzhi zhuanqu jianli hezuowang de jingyan," March 22, 1955; collected and reprinted in *Gaochao*, p. 157.

* * *

[Editor's Note to] "A Popular Evening School for Agricultural Technique"[21]

All *xiang*, or at present at least the majority of *xiang*, should set up evening technical schools like this. Organizations of the Youth League[22] at every level should take care of this matter. The peasants' technical study should be linked up with the elimination of illiteracy. The management of both [tasks] is the responsibility of the Youth League. Teachers for [each of] the evening technical schools can be chosen from the local area. Moreover, [we should] also encourage people to study while they are teaching.

* Jinnan [Southern Shanxi] local work committee of the [New Democratic] Youth League, "Yi ge shou kuanying de nongye jishu yexiao," originally pub-

lished in *Xuexi ziliao* [Study Materials], no. 1 (May 10, 1955); collected and reprinted in *Gaochao*, p. 165; *Socialist Upsurge*, p. 451.

* * *

[Editor's Note to] "We Should Enable Each
Person to Have One *mu* of Irrigated Land"[23]

This article is very useful; it can be used for reference by all *xian*. In its own overall planning each *xian* ought to draw up an appropriate plan for water conservation. The construction of water conservation [projects] is a great undertaking that will guarantee an increase in agricultural production. Small-scale water conservation [projects] are things that all *xian*, districts, *xiang*, and cooperatives can undertake. It is absolutely necessary to draw up a plan that will be carried out stage by stage over a designated number of years and that will guarantee that, apart from extraordinary and irresistible floods and droughts, there will be [a supply of] water in times of drought, and drainage in times of waterlogging. This [task] is completely possible. On the basis of cooperativization, the masses have great strength. Problems of recurrent floods and droughts that we have not been able to solve for several thousand years may now be solved in a few years.

* Fenyang *xian* Committee of the CPC, "Yingdang shi mei ren you yi mu shuidi," October 11, 1955; collected and reprinted in *Gaochao*, p. 206; *Xuanji*, V, p. 251.

* * *

[Editor's Note to] "Relying on Cooperativization to Initiate Large-Scale
Water and Soil Conservation Projects Is Completely Possible"[24]

This is a good article; we hope that everyone will read it. In 1956 every *xian* in the country should draw up a comprehensive plan under the leadership of the *xian* [Party] committee; [these plans] should encompass such items as cooperativization, agriculture, forestry, animal husbandry, sideline occupations, fisheries, industry or handicraft industries, water conservation, fertilizers, farming tools, improvement in the techniques of cultivation, seed improvement, commerce, finance, culture, education, and public health. If it is not possible to be so comprehensive [at first], it would be all right to just take up a few of the major items first. The period incorporated into the plan can be three, five, or even seven years. If we could make estimates up to twelve years [in advance] (that is, the last year of the Third Five-Year Plan), that, of course, would be even better. The provinces ought to urge all special districts, *xian*, districts, and *xiang* to do this; [but] the emphasis should be placed on *xian* and *xiang*. It shouldn't matter even if [the plans are drafted] a bit roughly; they can be revised in 1957 and thus be made concrete and refined; in

1958 they can be revised again and made even more concrete and refined. This water and soil conservation plan of Lishan *xian* can be used as a reference for making similar plans by all the *xian* in the Huang He [Yellow River] basin and by all the mountainous areas.

* Liu Yao, secretary of the Lishan *xian* Committee of the CPC, ''Yikaohezuohua kaizhan da guimo de shui tu baochi gongzuo shi wanquan keneng de,'' November 1, 1955; collected and reprinted in *Gaochao*, pp. 217-218.

* * *

[Editor's Note to] "Look, Daquan Mountain Has Changed!"[25]

I was very glad to have read this good article. With this typical example, the whole of North and Northwest China and all areas that have the problem of water loss and soil erosion can now model the solution of their problem after that [of Daquan Mountain]. Moreover, it will not take a very long time; three years, five years, seven years, or just a bit longer would be enough. It is a matter of overall planning and strengthening leadership. We ask that the secretary of each *xian* Party committee learn from the secretary of the Yanggao *xian* [Party] committee and diligently seek out the advanced experience among the local masses, sum them up, and then propagate them.

* Wang Jin, secretary of the Yangao *xian* Committee of the CPC, ''Kan, Daquanshan bian le yangzi!'' November 1, 1955; collected and reprinted in *Gaochao*, p. 227.

* * *

[Editor's Note to] "A Serious Struggle Must Be Waged Against Such Criminal Behavior as Corruption and Theft"[26]

This article ought to attract the serious attention of all cooperatives. Cooperatives ought to set up control committees responsible for auditing the cooperatives' accounts and carrying out a stern struggle against corruption and theft among the cadres. Party and [Youth] League branches ought to pay earnest attention to this problem.

* Yanbei [Special] District Committee of the CPC, ''Bixu xiang tanwu, daoqie de fanfa xingwei jinxing yansu de douzheng,'' originally published in *Qianjin* [Advance], the Party publication of the Shanxi Provincial Committee of the CPC, no. 195 (June 24, 1955); collected and reprinted in *Gaochao*, p. 242; *Socialist Upsurge*, p. 480.

* * *

[Editor's Note to] "The Ongniot Banner Establishes
Twelve Animal Husbandry Cooperatives
and Gives a Big Boost to Livestock [Production]"[27]

This article is very well written. It can be used by all animal husbandry cooperatives as a reference.

* Office of the Provincial Committee of the CPC of the former province of Jehol, "Wengniute qi jianli liao shier ge chumuye shengchan hezuoshe, shi shengchu da wei fazhan qilai," September 20, 1955; collected and reprinted in *Gaochao*, p. 249; *Socialist Upsurge*, p. 97.

* * *

[Editor's Note to] "A Cooperative That Made the Transition
from the Primary Stage to the Higher Stage"[28]

Consideration should be given to changing cooperatives in which conditions are already ripe from the primary-stage form to the higher-stage form [of cooperativization] so as to allow production and the forces of production to develop a step further. Because the primary-stage cooperatives retain a semi-private system of ownership, at a certain time this semiprivate system of ownership will restrict the development of the forces of production; the people will then demand that this system be changed so that the cooperative can become a collectively managed economic organization with the means of production owned completely by the public. As soon as the forces of production are liberated a step further, production will undergo an even greater development. There are some places where this change can take place fairly quickly, and there are places where it will have to be a bit slower. In general, primary-stage cooperatives that have been under operation for three years or so will basically have these conditions. Party organizations of all provinces, municipalities, and autonomous regions should investigate this matter and make arrangements; in the two years 1956 and 1957, on the condition that the agreement of the masses is secured, some experimental higher-stage cooperatives should be established. Currently, most of the cooperatives that have been established are small-scale cooperatives. When they are turned into higher-stage cooperatives, the agreement of the masses should be sought, and then many small-scale cooperatives should be merged into one large-scale cooperative. If each district can have one or more cooperatives of this type in these [next] two years, and if their superiority over the primary-stage cooperatives is made apparent to the masses, then favorable conditions will be created for the work of merging cooperatives into higher stages in the next few years. This work must be coordinated with the overall planning for the development of production. When people see that large-scale cooperatives and higher-stage cooperatives are more advantageous than small-scale cooperatives and primary-stage cooperatives, when they see that long-range planning will bring them a far higher standard of living both materially and culturally, they will agree to merge cooperatives and advance to higher-stage [cooperatives]. The advance to the higher stage will be quicker in the suburban areas. The experience of this cooperative in Beijing can serve as a reference for cooperatives with similar circumstances.[29]

* Rural Work Department of the Beijing Municipal Committee of the CPC, "Yi ge cong chuji xingshi guodu dao gaoji xingshi de hezuoshe," originally published in *Beijing ribao* [Beijing Daily], October 28, 1955; collected and reprinted in *Gaochao*, pp. 285-286; *Xuanji*, V, p. 258-259; *Socialist Upsurge*, pp. 517-518.

* * *

[Editor's Note to] "How the Baipanyao Agricultural Producers' Cooperative Was Set Up as a Higher-Stage Cooperative"[30]

These are two cooperatives that went directly from being mutual aid teams to being cooperatives of the higher-stage form without going through the primary-stage form [of cooperativization]. In some places where conditions are appropriate this can be done. The situation in Baipanyao is a joyful sight. Some of their experiences can also be learned by primary-stage cooperatives.

* Rural Work Department of the Beijing Municipal Committee of the CPC, "Baipanyao nongye shengchan hezuoshe shi zenyang bancheng gaojishe de," October, 1955; collected and reprinted in *Gaochao*, p. 294; *Socialist Upsurge*, p. 530.

* * *

[Editor's Note to] "The Long-range Plan of Huangantuo Agricultural, Forestry, and Animal Husbandry Producers' Cooperative"[31]

This is a long-range thirteen-year plan and can be used for reference everywhere. The usefulness of this kind of plan is in its long-range targets, which extend peoples' vision beyond the step that they are to take immediately. A plan of this type is only a broad orientation; it still needs [the spelling out of] each five-year plan and annual plan to make it specific. Invariably, after the implementation of several annual plans, the long-range plan will be repeatedly revised.

* Planning work group of the Beijing Municipal Bureau of Agriculture and Forestry, "Huangantuo nong lin mu shengchan hezuoshe de yuanjing guihua," October 1955; collected and reprinted in *Gaochao*, p. 301.

* * *

[Editor's Note to] "The Long-range Plan of the Red Star Collective Farm"[32]

This is a long-range seven-year plan of a large cooperative (they call it a collective farm, which is the same as a cooperative), which is made up of an entire *xiang* of over one thousand households. It can be used as a reference by all localities. Once they take a look at its content, people will know why there must be long-range plans such as this. Humanity's development has taken place over hundreds of thousands of years, but here in China, it is only now that we have achieved conditions under which we can develop our own economy and culture according to plan. Having achieved these conditions, our country will begin to change its appearance year by year. Every five years there will be a comparatively large change, and after stacking up several five-year periods there will be even greater changes.

* Joint planning work group of the Rural Work Department of the Beijing Municipal Committee of the CPC and the Beijing Municipal Bureau of Agriculture, Forestry , and Water Conservation, "Hongxing jiti nongzhuang de yuanjing guihua," originally published in *Beijing ribao,* [Beijing Daily], October 10, 1955; collected and reprinted in *Gaochao*, p. 311; *Xuanji*, V, pp. 249-250; *Socialist Upsurge*, p. 437.

* * *

[Editor's Note to] "Political Work at Zhangguozhuang Cooperative"[33]

The viewpoint of this article is correct. The cooperatives must stress good political work. The basic task of political work is to unceasingly instill socialist thought in the masses of the peasants and to criticize capitalist tendencies.

* Sha Zhun, "Zhangguozhuang hezuoshe de zhengzhi gongzuo," originally published in *Beijing ribao* [Beijing Daily], July 6, 1955; collected and reprinted in *Gaochao,* p. 328; *Xuanji,* V, pp. 244-245.

* * *

[Editor's Note to] "Cooperatives Can Solve
[the Problem of] Production Funds Themselves"[34]

This article reflects a common situation, which is that there is a great potential among the masses of the peasants for the accumulation of agricultural funds. In the course of agricultural cooperativization, the state ought to give the peasants the necessary assistance in the area of funds, for example the poor peasants' fund[35] and other loans that have already been set up. But we should still rely on the peasants to accumulate the major portion and larger amounts of funds themselves. Moreover, it is perfectly feasible. It is a mistake to underestimate the potential of the peasants.

* Office of the Rural Work Department of the Beijing Municipal Committee of the CPC, "Hezuoshe ziji keyi jiejue shengchan zijin," originally published in *Jiaoqu nongcun gongzuo* [Work in Suburban Villages] (Beijing), no. 1 (March 10, 1955); collected and reprinted in *Gaochao*, p. 335.

* * *

[Editor's Note to] "The Laiguangying Model Pig-Raising Cooperative"[36]

This experience is worth being propagated.

* Rural Work Department of the Beijing Municipal Committee of the CPC, "Yang zhu mofan de Laiguangying hezuoshe," October 1955; collected and reprinted in *Gaochao*, p. 340.

* * *

[Editor's Note to] "A Cooperative with a Very Good Work-style"

The leading cadres of this cooperative have a socialist work-style that is worthy of being emulated in every locality.

* **Southern Suburbs Work Team of Tianjin, "Yi ge zuofeng hen hao de hezuoshe,"** originally published in *Shengchan hezuo cankao ziliao* [Reference Materials on Producers' Cooperatives] (Tianjin), no. 4 (March 12, 1955); collected and reprinted in *Gaochao*, p. 349.

* * *

[Editor's Note to] "We Must Wage a Resolute
Struggle Against Capitalist Tendencies"[37]

This situation is worth paying attention to. Capitalist tendencies among the well-to-do peasants are serious. If, during the cooperativization movement and for a very long time thereafter, we were to merely let up a little bit on our political work with the peasants, capitalist tendencies would emerge like a flood.

* Reporter of the *Jin jiao nongcun xiaobao* [Tianjin Suburban Rural News], "Bixu dui ziben zhuyi qingxiang zuo jianjue de douzheng," originally published in *Shengchan hezuo cankao ziliao* [Reference Materials on Producers' Cooperatives] (Tianjin), no. 25 (June 1955); collected and reprinted in *Gaochao*, p. 353; *Xuanji*, V. p. 245.

* * *

[Editor's Note to] "Women Came to the Labor Front"

In order to establish a great socialist society, the mobilization of the broad masses of women to take part in production activities is of the utmost significance. In production we must put into effect equal work and equal pay for men and women. True equality for men and women can only be realized through the process of the socialist transformation of the whole society.

* Zhanzhuangzi *xiang* work team,[38] "Funü zou shang le laodong zhanxian," originally published in *Shengchan hezuo cankao ziliao* [Reference Materials on Producers' Cooperatives] (Tianjin), no. 24 (June 8, 1955); collected and reprinted in *Gaochao*, p. 357; *Xuanji*, V, pp. 246-247.

* * *

[Editor's Note to] "New Situations and New Problems"[39]

This material is useful and is worthy of general attention. This material describes the trends of the various strata in the countryside. The poor peasants are the most active in cooperativization. Many middle peasants want to "take another look"; they like to "stay outside and relax." They primarily want to see whether the cooperatives will give them a square deal if they hand their means of production over to the cooperatives. They can go this way or that. Many well-to-do middle peasants have strong feelings against cooperativization; those with the worst attitude are selling off the means of production, spiriting their funds away or organizing fake cooperatives. In some individual cases they even collude with [former] landlords and rich peasants to do evil things. We hope that the comrades doing rural work everywhere will pay attention to checking and analyzing the trends of the various strata in their own areas and [on that basis] adopt a suitable policy. This material points out the mistaken tendency of paying attention to the cooperatives and overlooking the mutual aid teams and puts forth the view [in favor of] comprehensive planning with due consideration to all factors; this is correct. The method of [setting up] "a network of mutual aid teams and cooperatives" is good; it takes both cooperatives and mutual aid teams into consideration. The cooperatives must truly help the mutual aid teams and individual households solve the thorny problems they have with their current production. The poor peasants' fund must be sent down [to the villages] at once. We must tell the poor peasants who have not yet joined the cooperatives that when they join the cooperatives they can draw on these funds.

* Zhang Dianju, Fu Yanlong, Hao Jingmin, and Sun Rongsheng, "Xin qingkuang he xin wenti," originally published in *Renmin ribao* [Peoples' Daily],

May 22, 1955; collected and reprinted in *Gaochao,* p. 373; *Xuanji,* V, pp. 241-242; *Socialist Upsurge,* pp. 237-238.

* * *

[Editor's Note to] "The Production Plan of District Eleven of Shuangcheng *xian*"

The experience of Shuangcheng *xian* in Heilongjiang Province merits the attention of every locality. That place has become famous for its comprehensive planning of cooperativization and production.

* Work team of the Rural Work Department of the Heilongjiang Provincial Committee of the CPC, "Shuangcheng xian shiyi qu de shengchan guihua," February 1955; collected and reprinted in *Gaochao,* p. 380.

* * *

[Editor's Note to] "Regarding Financial Management"[40]

This experience is useful. All *xian* can manage [their finances] accordingly.

* Lalin *xian* committee of the CPC, "Guanyu caiwu guanli," August 1, 1955; collected and reprinted in *Gaochao,* p. 391.

* * *

[Editor's Note to] "The Experience of Siyi Agricultural Producers' Cooperative of Anguang *xian* in [Establishing] Fixed Production Teams and Carrying Out the Experience of Establishing Labor Contracts and Fixing Production Contracts and Fixing Production Quotas"[41]

The method presented in this article is not perfect, but the article describes the problems of establishing labor contracts and fixing production quotas[42] in a very systematic way, and it can be used as reference for all the localities.

* Rural Work Department of the Anguang *xian* Committee of the CPC, "Anguang xian siyi nongye shengchan hezuoshe guding shengchandui he shixing baogong baochan de jingyan," March 25, 1955; collected and reprinted in *Gaochao,* p. 419.

* * *

[Editor's Note to] "The Autumn Harvest Distribution Proposal"[43]

This article is very well written. It can be used as a reference for all the localities.

* Rural Work Department of the Jilin Provincial Committee of the CPC, "Qiushou fenpei fangan," originally published in *Jilin ribao* [Jilin Daily], October 8, 1955; collected and reprinted in *Gaochao*, p. 426.

* * *

[Editor's Note to] "A Poor Cooperative That Was Ridiculed by Others"[44]

This cooperative led by Liu Yuru is like Wang Guofan Cooperative in Hebei.[45] Both were looked down upon by people because they were poor but, after a bitter struggle, they overcame their difficulties in the end. All provinces have many similar examples; they ought to be given widespread propaganda so as to inspire everyone.

* Rural Work Department of Jin *xian* Committee of the CPC, "Yi ge bei ren jixiao de qiong hezuoshe," December 25, 1954; collected and reprinted in *Gaochao*, p. 437.

* * *

[Editor's Note to] "The Experience of a Bookkeepers' Mutual Aid Network Organized by Bookkeepers from Agricultural Producers' Cooperatives, Supply and Marketing Cooperatives, and Credit Cooperatives"[46]

This article is very good; all localities can follow its example.[47] "There aren't any bookkeepers" is an excuse used by people who oppose the rapid development of cooperativization. The cooperativization of the whole country calls for several million people to be bookkeepers. And where can they be found? Actually, people are available; we can mobilize large numbers of primary school graduates and junior middle school graduates to do this work. The point is that we must rapidly train them and raise their literacy and technical level in the course of their work. With the district as a unit, all bookkeepers from the producers' cooperatives, supply and marketing cooperatives, and credit cooperatives [within the district] can form a bookkeepers' mutual aid network. This would be a good way to raise the literacy and technical level of the bookkeepers. The network of No. 3 District of Zhangwu *xian* has not only helped the bookkeepers raise their literacy and technical levels, but also has done a lot of economic and political work. *Xian* and district Party organizations should pay attention to giving leadership to such work.

* Zhangwu *xian* No. 3 station for popularizing agricultural techniques, "Yi ge you nongye shengchan hezuoshe gongxiao hezuoshe he xinyong hezuoshe de kuaijiyuan zucheng kuaiji huzhu wang de jingyan," originally published in *Nongye shengchan huzhu hezuo cankao ziliao* [Reference Materials on Mutual Aid and Cooperativization in Agricultural Production] (Liaoning),

no. 9 (August 1955); collected and reprinted in *Gaochao*, p. 451; *Xuanji*, V, p. 254.

* * *

[Editor's Note to] "An Agricultural Producers' Cooperative That Increased Production by Sixty-seven Per Cent in Three Years"[48]

This is a very well-run cooperative; much beneficial experience can be derived from it. Qufu *xian* is Confucius' native place. He, our old venerable, ran a school there for many years and educated many talented students; this is a well-known fact. But he didn't pay much attention to the people's economic life. When his student Fan Chi asked him about how to go about agriculture, he not only brushed the question aside and ignored it but also called him a "mean person"[49] behind his back. Now the people of his native place have set up socialist cooperatives. The people had been so poor and destitute for over two thousand years, but after three years of cooperativization both their economic and cultural lives have begun to change in appearance. This proves that this socialism is truly unprecedented. Socialism is I don't know how many times better than Confucius' "classics." I advise people who are interested in going there to see Confucius' Temple and Confucius' Grove[50] that they might as well also visit this cooperative on their way.

* Report of the Qufu *xian* committee of the CPC, "Yi ge zai san nian nei zeng chan baifen zhi liu shi qi de nongye shengchan hezuoshe," November 15, 1955; collected and reprinted in *Gaochao*, p. 475; *Xuanji*, V, p. 257.

* * *

[Editor's Note to] "A Cooperative That Drew Up a Three-Year Production Plan"[51]

This plan is useful. It can be used as reference everywhere. Every cooperative ought to make a production plan that covers a few years, have it discussed many times among the members of the cooperative, revise it, and then implement it.

* Wang Houli, Wang Kexiang, "Yi ge zuo liao san nian shengchan guihua de hezuoshe," originally published in *Dazhong ribao* [The Masses' Daily] (Shandong), November 20, 1955; collected and reprinted in *Gaochao*, p. 483.

* * *

[Editor's Note to] "The Experience of the Youth League Branch of Gaojialiugou Village of Junan *xian* in Setting Up a Class in Work Point Recording"

This experience ought to be widely popularized. Lenin said, "A communist society cannot be established in a country full of illiterates."[52] Our country has so much illiteracy now, but socialist construction cannot wait until illiteracy is eliminated to begin; this has created an acute contradiction. At present there are in our country not only many children who have reached school age but have no schools to enter, but also a large number of children and young people who have already passed that age but have no schools to attend, to say nothing of the adults [in the same situation]. This serious problem must be solved in the process of agricultural cooperativization, and it is only in the process of agricultural cooperativization that it can be solved. After the peasants have organized cooperatives, because of economic necessity, they will urgently demand to be educated. When the peasants have organized cooperatives and have gained collective strength, the situation will have changed completely and they will be able to organize to educate themselves. The first step, to meet the need in recording work points,[53] is to learn the names of people and places in their own villages, the names of tools, and the labels for different sorts of farm work and other necessary vocabulary – about two or three hundred characters. The second step is to learn more advanced characters and vocabulary. These two kinds of textbooks must be compiled. The first type of textbook ought to be compiled by the local intellectuals with the help of the comrades who are guiding the work of cooperativization, and in each case in accordance with the needs of the local cooperatives. Each locale should compile its own book; we cannot use one unified text. This type of textbook needn't be checked [by the authorities]. The second type of textbook also ought to be compiled by the local intellectuals with the help of the comrades who are guiding the work of cooperativization and be based on the affairs and vocabulary of a relatively small area (for example a *xian* or a special district) and, in addition, in part be [based on] affairs and vocabulary pertaining to a province (municipality and autonomous region) and to the nation as a whole. These, too, should only contain a few hundred characters. This type of textbook need not be uniform from place to place either, but it should be examined promptly by educational organizations at the *xian*, the special district, or the provincial (municipal [and] autonomous region) level. After having taken these two steps, a third step ought to be taken; the educational organizations of each province (municipality, and autonomous region) [should] compile a third type of text for general purposes. In the future more advanced textbooks will be continually compiled. The cultural and educational organizations at the Center ought to give this matter appropriate guidance. The Youth League branch of Gaojialiugou Village in Junan *xian* of Shandong Province has done a creative piece of work. Seeing this kind of situation makes one very happy. There are teachers – the primary school graduates of their own *xian*. Progress has been rapid; in two-and-a-half months, over a hundred young people and middle-age people have [all] learned over two hundred characters. They were able to keep records of their own work, and some people became the bookkeepers of the cooperative. This name, work point recording class, is also very good. Such classes should be emulated and established everywhere. Youth League organizations at all levels ought to give leadership to this work, and all Party and government organizations should support it.

* "Junan xian Gaojialiugou cun qingniantuan zhibu chuangban jigong xuexiban de jingyan," originally published in *Huzhu hezuo tongxun* [Mutual Aid and Cooperativization Bulletin (Shandong), no. 6 (January 29, 1955); collected and reprinted in *Gaochao*, p. 507-508; *Xuanji*, V, pp. 255-256; *Socialist Upsurge*, pp. 462-464.

* * *

[Editor's Note to] Resolving the Difficulty of Insufficient Production Funds''[54]

The experience of this cooperative also proves that it is entirely possible to mobilize members of the cooperative to make investments in order to resolve the difficulty of insufficient production funds, provided that [the investments are made] under such conditions that they are appropriate and not excessive, the consciousness of the members of the cooperative has been fully awakened, and allowance has been made for the poorer cooperative members.

* Junan *xian* Committee of the CPC, "Jiejue shengchan zijin buzu de kunnan," originally published in *Huzhu hezuo tongxun* [Mutual Aid and Cooperativization Bulletin] (Shandong), no. 12 (April 24, 1955); collected and reprinted in *Gaochao*, p. 517.

* * *

[Editor's Note to] "The Story of Fanshen Cooperative's Experience of Overturning Its Old Life in One Year's Time"

Hebei has the Wang Guofan cooperative, Liaoning has the Liu Yuru cooperative, and this place has the Kai Mingyi Fanshen cooperative.[55] They were all very impoverished and were jeered at, but after a resolute struggle they have overturned their old lives. There must be many heroic deeds of this kind everywhere. We hope that each province will write articles [about them] and give them wide propaganda.

* Zhang Shirong, "Fanshen hezuoshe yi nian fanshen ji," originally published in *Nongcun gongzuo tongxun* [Rural Work Bulletin] (Anhui), no. 68 (October 20, 1955); collected and reprinted in *Gaochao*, p. 541.

* * *

[Editor's Note to] "Chen Xuemeng, Pacesetter in Cooperativization"

There is a Chen Xuemeng here.[56] In China how can there be less than thousands and thousands of heroes like him? It is a pity that the writers haven't tried to seek them out yet. The people who go down to the countryside to guide the work of cooperativization also see a lot but write little.

* Xiao Kefei, "Hezuohua de daitouren Chen Xuemeng," originally published in *Nongcun gongzuo tongxun* [Rural Work Bulletin] (Anhui), no. 68 (October 20, 1955); collected and reprinted in *Gaochao*, p. 544; *Xuanji*, V, p. 248.

* * *

[Editor's Note to] "Only After
Cooperativization Can Natural Disasters Be Resisted"[57]

This is a lively example of organizing to resist natural calamities. No laboring peasants, no matter what their social strata, can resist natural calamities unless they organize themselves into collective production. The words of Ke Xianfu, a middle peasant of Fanchang *xian*, Anhui, and Ke Baifa, a poor peasant, tell of this truth.

* "Zhiyou hezuohua cai neng dikang tianzai," originally published in *Nongcun gongzuo tongxun* [Rural Work Bulletin] (Anhui), no. 41 (December 8, 1954); collected and reprinted in *Gaochao*, p. 548.

* * *

[Editor's Note to] "A Model [Party] Branch Worthy of Recommendation"[58]

The line followed by this Party branch in its work is correct in all its aspects and is worthy of being recommended to all the comrades doing rural work. This is what is meant by a creative, Marxist spirit and method of work.

* Rural Work Department of the Fengyang *xian* Committee of the CPC, "Yige zhide tuijian de mofan zhibu," originally published in *Nongcun gongzuo tongxun* [Rural Work Bulletin] (Anhui), no. 58 (June 11, 1955); collected and reprinted in *Gaochao*, p. 565.

* * *

[Editor's Note to] "The Lesson of Mistakenly
Dissolving Eighteen Spontaneous Cooperatives"[59]

This is another lesson about the harmful results of recklessly dissolving cooperatives. Here it was "mandatory reorganization"; in Zhejiang it was "drastic reduction"; both were done when some cadres were seized by a feeling of panic and lost control. We hope that this kind of mistake will not be repeated.

* Rural Work Department of the Chu *xian* [Special] District Committee of the CPC, "Cuowu de jiesan shiba ge zifashe de jiaoxun," originally published in *Nongcun gongzuo tongxun* [Rural Work Bulletin] (Anhui), no. 58 (June 11, 1955); collected and reprinted in *Gaochao,* p. 569.

* * *

[Editor's Note to] "Excess Labor Power Finds an Outlet"[60]

This is also a common problem. According to the situation of these two cooperatives, on the basis of the current conditions of production, there is already a surplus of approximately one-third of the total labor power. Two people can now, after cooperativization, do the work that it used to take three people to do; this shows the superiority of socialism. Where will this excess one-third, or even more, of labor power find an outlet? Primarily it will still be in the countryside. Socialism has not only liberated the laborers and the means of production from the old society, but it has also liberated a vast [portion of] nature that the old society was unable to utilize. The masses of the people have unlimited creativity. They can get organized and march on all places and sectors where they can bring their own strength into play; they can march on deepening and expanding production and create an ever increasing number of undertakings for their own well-being. And this still hasn't touched on [the issue of] agricultural mechanization. After mechanization, labor power will be saved in even larger amounts; is there an outlet for it? According to the experiences of some mechanized farms, there is still an outlet because the scope of production will be expanded, [the number of] sectors [of production] will be increased, and the work will become more intensive. So we need not fear that there will be [labor] power without a place to use it.

* Feidong *xian* Committee of the CPC, Shitang District, "Duoyu laodongli zhaodaole chulu," originally published in *Nongcun gongzuo tongxun* [Rural Work Bulletin] (Anhui), no. 58 (June 11, 1955); collected and reprinted in *Gaochao,* p. 578; *Xuanji,* V, p. 253.

* * *

[Editor's Note to] "This *xiang* Became Cooperativized in Only Two Years"[61]

Those people who don't believe that a primary-stage form of cooperativization can be reached within three years as far as individual areas are concerned (the slogan of cooperativization in three years was put forth by the masses; it has been criticized by the opportunists), and those people who don't believe that cooperativization can be carried out in the areas that were liberated later at the same time as in areas that were liberated earlier: Please take a look at this *xiang* in Kunshan *xian* of Jiangsu Province! Here, cooperativization was accomplished not in three years but in two years. This place wasn't an earlier-liberated area but a pure and genuine later-liberated area.[62] This later-liberated area has gone ahead of many earlier-liberated areas. What can you do about it? Can you pull it back? Of course not; the opportunists must admit defeat, that's all. There is a vast reserve of socialist enthusiasm lying latent among the masses. Those people who even in a revolutionary period can do no better than proceed according to routine are unable to see this type of enthusiasm at all. They are blind; they can only see a shroud of darkness ahead of them. They sometimes go as far as to clamor until truth is stood on its head and white is confused with black. Haven't we seen enough of these people? These people who only know how to follow routine and always underestimate the enthusiasm of the people, whenever a new thing emerges they never approve; they [always] oppose it first. Then they admit defeat and do a bit of self-criticism. When a second novel thing emerges, they do the same thing all over again by alternating one attitude with the other. From then on, whenever any new things appear, they will apply the same formula again and again. Such people are always passive; they can never take a step forward at a critical moment; someone else must always give them a sharp cuff on the back before they are willing to take a step forward. When will these people be able to walk by themselves, and moreover walk properly? There is one way to cure this ailment, and that is [for them] to take some time out to go among the masses, to see what the masses are thinking, what they are doing, to find some advanced experiences among them, and to popularize them. This is an effective curative for rightist obstinacy. We suggest that people give this a try.

* Department of production and cooperativization of Kunshan *xian* Committee of the CPC, "Zhege xiang liang nian jiu hezuohua liao," October 14, 1955; collected and reprinted in *Gaochao*, p. 587; *Xuanji*, V, pp. 229-230; *Socialist Upsurge*, pp. 43-44; *Xuandu* (1965a), pp. 319-320.

* * *

[Editor's Note to] "Yitao *xiang*'s Overall Planning"[63]

This *xiang* has done a two-year plan for cooperativization, [which features] measures to increase production, water conservation, the consolidation of the Party and [the Youth] League, and cultural and educational work. All *xiang* throughout the country ought to do likewise. Some people say that planning is hard to do. Why was this *xiang* able to do it? In 1956, all *xian*, districts, and *xiang* throughout the country should make comprehensive plans that should include even a bit more than this plan; for example, [they should include planning for] sideline occupations, commerce, finance, afforestation, and public health. Even if they are a bit rough and do not entirely conform to actual situations, it is still better than not having any at all. If in a province there are one or two *xian*, one or two districts, and one or two *xiang* that have made decent plans, they can immediately be publicized, and other *xian*, districts, and *xiang* can be called upon to follow suit. [Planning] is said to be hard but in fact it isn't that hard.

* Department of production and cooperativization of the Huaiyin [Special] District Committee of the CPC, "Yitao xiang de quanmian guihua," October 22, 1955; collected and reprinted in *Gaochao*, p. 598; *Xuanji*, V, pp. 250-251; *Socialist Upsurge*, p. 393.

* * *

[Editor's Note to] "The Superiority of Large Cooperatives"[64]

This essay is well written and is worth reading. Because they are easy to establish, and so that the cadres and the masses can acquire experience immediately, most of the semisocialist cooperatives currently established are small cooperatives of twenty or thirty households. However, small cooperatives have few people, little land, and little funds; they cannot be run on a large scale and cannot utilize machinery. These small cooperatives still confine the development of the forces of production. They cannot remain [in this condition] too long; they should gradually merge [with other cooperatives]. There are some places where one *xiang* can be a cooperative, there are a few places where a number of *xiang* can form a cooperative, and of course there are many places where one *xiang* can become several cooperatives. Not only can large cooperatives be run in the plains areas but they can also be run in the mountainous areas as well. The *xiang* in Anhui where the Foziling Reservoir is located is completely hilly, with hills stretching for several dozen *li* around, yet a large-scale cooperative combining undertakings in agriculture, forestry, and animal husbandry has been established there. Naturally this type of merger must be done step by step; there must be suitable cadres, and it must have the approval of the masses.

* Xinhailian Municipal Committee of the CPC, "Da she de youyuexing," September 21, 1955; collected and reprinted in *Gaochao*, p. 611; *Xuanji*, V, pp. 257-258; *Socialist Upsurge*, p. 499.

* * *

[Editor's Note to] "Weeding Out Bad People,
Consolidating the Cooperative"[65]

The question this essay addresses has universal significance. It is worthy of everyone's attention.

* Department of production and cooperativization of the Jiangning *xian* committee of the CPC, "Qingchu huairen, gonggu hezuoshe," originally published in *Xinhua ribao* [New China Daily] (Jiangsu), September 10,

1955; collected and reprinted in *Gaochao,* p. 623.

* * *

[Editor's Note to] "Setting the Fixed Norm of Labor Contracts[66]
and Evaluating Work and Alloting Work Points"[67]

This article portrays the circuitous process of change in the organization of labor in one cooperative.[68] It can serve as a reference for all areas.

* "Dinge baogong he pinggong jifen," originally published in *Nongcun gong-zuo* [Rural Work] (Jiangsu), supplement, May 26, 1955; collected and reprinted in *Gaochao,* p. 640.

* * *

[Editor's Note to] "The Higher-Stage Cooperatives Are
the Most Advantageous, and They Are Not Hard to Run"

It makes one happy to read this article. I hope everyone will read it carefully. I hope that in every primary-stage cooperative where the conditions are ripe this article will be read out to the members of the cooperative and will also be discussed, so that they may be mobilized to gladly merge [with other cooperatives] and enter the higher stage [of cooperativization]. These great achievements of Wudongzha Cooperative of Ciqi *xian* of Zhejiang Province should be publicized throughout the country. In the *xiang* in which Wudong-zha Cooperative is located, Qishan *xiang* of Ciqi *xian*, ninety-two per cent of the peasant households have joined eight higher-stage cooperatives. Who says that higher-stage cooperatives are so hard to run?

* Department of Rural Work of the Zhejiang Provincial Committee of the CPC, "Gaojishe liyi zui da er qie bing bu nan ban," October 23, 1955; collected and reprinted in *Gaochao,* p. 651; *Socialist Upsurge,* p. 540.

* * *

[Editor's Note to] "Dengjia *xiang* – A Model of Cooperativization"[69]

This experience ought to be universally publicized. For all *xiang* that have completed land reform, established Party branches, and have had some mutual aid teams, as long as they simply follow the line of Dengjia *xiang* of Zhejiang Province in doing things, then it will be possible for them to bring about a semisocialist cooperativization within the confines of a *xiang* in one or two years in a relatively healthy manner and without too many mistakes and, moreover, raise productivity a step higher. Some comrades feel that cooperativization is very difficult and many mistakes are bound to be made, and therefore they hang back and don't dare to promote cooperativization. This is simply because they have separated themselves from the kind of leadership line of Dengjia *xiang* of Zhejiang Province. And yet this line followed by Dengjia *xiang* of Zhejiang (going deeply at one point, acquiring experience, and applying it everywhere), like the line of No. 10 District of Zunhua *xian* in Hebei or that of Chengxi *xiang* of Fengyang *xian*, Anhui,[70] is none other than the famous Marxist-Leninist line that has already proved so effective in all our Party's work among the masses throughout the country.

* "Hezuohua mofan dengjia xiang," originally published in *Zhejiang nongcun gongzuo tongxun* [Zhejiang Rural Work Bulletin], no. 51 (March 17, 1955); collected and reprinted in *Gaochao*, p. 658; *Socialist Upsurge*, p. 60.

* * *

[Editor's Note to] "The System of Networks of Cooperatives Ought to Be Promoted Throughout the Country"[71]

This article is very good; it is worthy of recommendation. Networks of cooperatives ought to be established everywhere, and they should be made into a system. Currently most of the cooperatives are small and the *xiang* need to establish networks of cooperatives; the districts also ought to have networks of cooperatives. Eventually when there are more medium-sized and large cooperatives [we] ought to emphasize the networks of cooperatives in the districts. We hope that by 1956 each district and each *xiang* will have a network of cooperatives. Naturally in those places where a whole *xiang* is made into only one or two large cooperatives, the *xiang* doesn't have to establish this kind of network.

* Rural Work Department of the Zhejiang Provincial Committee of the CPC, "Hezuowang de zhidu yingdang zai quanguo tuiguang," October 23, 1955; collected and reprinted in *Gaochao*, p. 663; *Socialist Upsurge*, p. 228.

* * *

[Editor's Note to] "Mobilizing Women to Join Production Has Resolved the Problem of Insufficient Labor Power"[72]

Before cooperativization, many places throughout the country had a problem of a surplus of labor power. After cooperativization, many cooperatives felt that labor power was no longer sufficient and that it had become necessary to mobilize the broad masses of women, who had hitherto not participated in work in the fields, to participate on the labor front. This is an important occurrence that many people did not expect. In the past, people always thought that after cooperativization there would be a surplus of labor power. There was already a surplus. With another surplus, what could be done? In many places the practice of cooperativization has rid people of this apprehension; there was not a surplus of labor power; rather there was not enough. After cooperativization, some places experienced a surplus of labor power for a time, [but] that was because [the cooperatives] still hadn't expanded the scale of production and hadn't yet begun diversified operations[73] and had not yet begun to intensify cultivation either. In many areas, once the scale of production was expanded, once operations were expanded into more areas, once the scope of labor was broadened and deepened into Nature, once work was done more intensively, then labor power was felt to be insufficient. Such situations are now only beginning, [but] in the future they will develop year after year. After the mechanization of agriculture, [the situation] will also be the same. Eventually enterprises will emerge that people have never even thought of and that will raise our agricultural production several times, more than a dozen times, or even several dozen times. The development in industrial, communications, and exchange enterprises would be even more unimaginable to people of an earlier period. The same holds true for enterprises in science, culture, education, and health. China's women are a great human resource. This sort of resource must be tapped for the struggle to establish a great socialist country. To mobilize women to participate in labor, the principle of equal work and equal pay for men and women alike must be implemented. The experience of Jiande *xian* of Zhejiang Province can be utilized by all cooperatives [everywhere].

* "Fadong funü touru shengchan jiejue le laodongli buzu de kunnan," originally published in *Zhejiang noncun gongzuo tongxun* [Zhejiang Rural Work Bulletin], no. 60 (May 24, 1955); collected and reprinted in *Gaochao*, p. 674; *Xuanji*, V, pp. 252-253; *Socialist Upsurge*, pp. 311-312.

* * *

[Editor's Note to] "Supply and Marketing Cooperatives and Agricultural Producers' Cooperatives"[74]

This is the only article in this book that discusses this issue; it is worthy of widespread recommendation. The essay is also not badly written. The conclusion of contracts on coordination between supply and marketing cooperatives and agricultural producers' cooperatives should be universally implemented.

* "Gongxiao hezuoshe he nongye shengchan hezuoshe yingdang dingli jiehe hetong," originally published in *Zhejiang nongcun gongzuo tongxun* [Zhejiang Rural Work Bulletin], no. 49 (March 4, 1955); collected and reprinted in *Gaochao*, p. 679.

* * *

[Editor's Note to] "Cooperatives with Wooded Areas Must Quickly Deal with the Problem of Incorporating the Woods into Cooperatives"

This is a common problem. All wooded areas, whether in the mountains or not, ought to quickly tackle, according to the Party's policy, the problem of whether or not the woods should immediately be incorporated into cooperatives and how they should be incorporated. The method of Fengming *xiang* of Longquan *xian*, Zhejiang Province, can serve as a reference for all areas.

* "You cheng pian linmu diqu de hezuoshe bixu xinsu chuli shanlin rushe de wenti," originally published in *Zhejiang nongcun gongzuo tongxun* [Zhejiang Rural Work Bulletin], no. 59 (May 20, 1955); collected and reprinted in *Gaochao*, p. 687.

* * *

[Editor's Note to] "This Place Raised a Lot of Live Hogs"

Raising hogs is an important problem related to fertilizer and meat [supply], and to earning foreign exchange through export. [Consequently] all cooperatives must take the matter of hog raising into their plans. Naturally, each province, special district, *xian*, and district should have its own plan. [The question of] fodder for hogs is easy to solve; certain kinds of green grass, certain kinds of tree leaves, sweet potato vines and leaves, and sweet potatoes are all fodder. Feed concentrates are not necessarily required, and in particular we need not necessarily use a great deal of feed concentrate. Apart from [the hogs that are] raised publicly in the cooperatives, each peasant family should be encouraged to raise one or a few hogs. This goal can be reached bit by bit in a number of years. Some minority nationalities that forbid the raising of hogs and some individual families that are reluctant to raise hogs because of religious custom are naturally not included in [this project]. There must be a system of rewards for the development of the hog raising enterprise; the experience of Shanghua Cooperative of Zhejiang Province can be used as a reference everywhere.

* "Zheli yang liao yi da pi maozhu," originally published in *Zhejiang nongcun gongzuo tongxun* [Zhejiang Rural Bulletin], no. 55 (April 26, 1955); collected and reprinted in *Socialist Upsurge*, p. 695; *Xuanji*, V, pp. 251-252.

* * *

[Editor's Note to] "The Lesson of the Appearance of a 'Middle Peasant Cooperative' and a 'Poor Peasant Cooperative' in Fuan *xian*"[75]

The problem discussed here has universal significance. We must unite with the middle peasants; it would be a mistake not to unite with the middle peasants. But on whom should the working class and the Communist Party rely in the rural areas to unite with the middle peasants and implement the socialist transformation of the entire countryside? Naturally it is only the poor peasants. It was like this in the past during the struggle against the landlords and in carrying out the land reform, and it is the same now in struggling against the rich peasants and other capitalist factors and in implementing the socialist transformation of agriculture. In both of these revolutionary periods the middle peasants wavered in the initial stage. They waited until they could see the general trends clearly, until the revolution was on the verge of victory, and only then did the middle peasants join the revolutionary side. The poor peasants must do work among the middle peasants to unite the middle peasants and bring them to their own side, and broaden the revolution day by day all the way up to the final victory. The cooperative affairs management committees of the agricultural producers' cooperatives today, like the peasant associations of the past,[76] should bring in old lower-middle peasants and some representative new and old upper-middle peasants who have a comparatively high level of [political] consciousness, but not too many of them; about one-third would be appropriate. About two-thirds of the people on the committee should be made up of poor peasants (including those who are currently poor peasants as well as new lower-middle peasants who were originally poor peasants). The primary leading cadres' [positions] in the cooperatives should in general be occupied by the poor peasants (to repeat, this includes those who are currently poor peasants as well as all the new lower-middle peasants who were originally poor peasants) with the exception that the old lower-middle peasants and certain new and old upper-middle peasants whose [political] consciousness is very high and who are indeed fair and capable can still serve [in those positions].[77] We should not see the kind of situation in Fuan *xian* of Fujian Province, in which the cooperative led by poor peasants and that led by middle peasants have expressed different attitudes toward the cause of socialism, as an isolated phenomenon; it has universal significance.

* Louxia *xiang* work team, "Fuan xian fasheng zhongnongshe he pinnongshe de jiaoxun," originally published in *Fujian ribao* [Fujian Daily], August 16, 1955; collected and reprinted in *Gaochao*, p. 701-702; *Xuanji*, V, pp. 240-241; *Socialist Upsurge*, pp. 247-248.

* * *

[Editor's Note to] "A Good Experience of Consolidating a Cooperative"[78]

This is a very good article on the experience of consolidating a cooperative. It is worthy of recommendation. The birth of a new social system is always accompanied by a great uproar and a great outcry. This is simply propagandizing the superiority of the new system and criticizing the backwardness of the old one. Such an earthshaking undertaking as causing the more than 500 million peasants of our country to implement socialist transformation cannot occur under conditions of gentle winds and calm seas. It requires that we Communists carry out our propaganda and educational work with patience, in a lively way, and in a way that they can easily understand, among the broad masses of peasants who carry on their backs the baggage of the old system. Currently this kind of work is going on all over the country, and many comrades engaged in rural work and who excel at propaganda [work] have emerged. The "four comparisons and five calculations"[79] described in this article is a good method by which to explain to the peasants which system is good and which is bad, and one that allows people to understand immediately upon hearing. This kind of method has great persuasive power. It is not like [the method used by] some of those comrades who are no good at doing propaganda and who simply put forth the so-called [slogan] "You either take the road of the Communist Party or take the road of Chiang Kai-shek." That is just using labeling[80] to coerce their audience and not holding in their hands any goods with which to motivate people. But [the method put forward in this article] – taking the experiences of the local peasants and giving them a detailed analysis – that truly has great persuasive power.

* Department of Production Cooperativization of the Longqi [Special] District Committee of the CPC, "Yi ge zhengshe de hao jingyan," originally published in *Nongcun gongzuo tongxun* [Rural Work Bulletin] (Fujian), no. 13 (July 9, 1955); collected and reprinted in *Gaochao*, p. 706; *Xuanji*, V, pp. 245-246; *Socialist Upsurge*, pp. 275-276.

* * *

[Editor's Note to] "The Ill Wind of Opportunism Is Falling, the Righteous Wind of Socialism Is on the Rise"[81]

The nearly ubiquitous Right opportunist elements within the Party who hinder the broad masses of poor and lower-middle peasants from taking the road of cooperativization are in collusion with the forces of capitalism in [our] society. This article is an apt description of this kind of situation. The writer reproaches the opportunists with great indignation and supports the poor suffering peasants. There are some people who, even though they call themselves Communists, show very little interest in the tasks of socialism that must be done now. Not only do they not support the enthusiastic masses but, on the contrary, they pour cold water on the heads of the masses. In China, 1955 has been a year of decisive struggle between socialism and capitalism. This decisive struggle was first manifested at the three conferences called by the Central Committee of the Chinese Communist Party in May, July, and October.[82] In the first half of 1955 the air was filled with smog and poisonous gas and the sky was filled with dark clouds. There was a complete change in the latter half of 1955, a change to a completely different climate. Several tens of millions of peasant households took action and, in response to the call of the Party Center, carried out cooperativization. By the time this editor is writing these lines, more than sixty million peasant households throughout the country have joined cooperatives. This is like a raging wave sweeping away all the monsters and freaks. The face of each individual in society can [now] be seen clearly for what it is. The same is true within the Party. By the end of this year the victory of socialism will have been greatly assured. Naturally there will still be many struggles ahead, and we must still struggle hard.

* Li Yijun, "Jihui zhuyi de xieqi kua xiaqu, shehui zhuyi de zhengqi sheng shanglai," October 7, 1955; collected and reprinted in *Gaochao,* p. 729; *Xuanji,* V, pp. 232-233; *Socialist Upsurge,* pp. 169-170.

* * *

[Editor's Note to] "The Baiyiqiao Vegetable Producers' Cooperative Changes from a Primary-Stage Cooperative into a Higher-Stage Cooperative"[83]

The experience of this cooperative can be used as a reference not only in suburban areas near cities, but in other areas as well.

* Ji Yin, Tao Guizhang, Yang Guosen, "Baiyiqiao sucai shengchan hezuoshe you chujishe zhuandao gaojishe," October 24, 1955; collected and reprinted in *Gaochao,* p. 735.

* * *

[Editor's Note to] "The Enthusiasm of the Workers' Families Is Extremely High in the Cooperativization Movement"[84]

This is also a very interesting article. Even though there are opportunists almost everywhere who want to stem the tide, the tide can never be stemmed. Socialism is advancing victoriously everywhere, putting all stumbling blocks behind it. Society is advancing in this way every day; peoples' thinking is being transformed; it is especially so in the high tide of revolution.

* Wu Qiang, Zhai Guizhao, "Zai hezuohua yundong zhong, gongren jiashu de jijixing feichang gao," October 7, 1955; collected and reprinted in *Gaochao,* p. 748; *Xuanji,* V, p. 233.

* * *

[Editor's Note to] "Zhudi *xiang* Absorbs Many Peasants Who Are Also Peddlers into Agricultural Cooperativization"[85]

The circumstances in this *xiang* also demonstrate that with the development of many diversified [economic] undertakings, surplus labor power will have an outlet. The present small and primary-stage cooperatives are still a fetter on the full utilization of labor power and of all kinds of means of production.

When the time comes to establish large and higher-stage cooperatives, it will be possible to ram through such obstacles, and all the forces of production can take a big step forward. At that time, there will be an even greater necessity for developing diversified [economic] undertakings and many large-scale undertakings that serve both the cities and the countryside. Only in this way can all the forces of production, primarily human resources, be fully utilized.[86]

* Dai Xingming, Wang Shuren, Dong Junming, "Zhudi xiang ba da pi jianying xiaoshangfan de nongmin xiyin dao nongye hezuo zhong lai liao," October 24, 1955; collected and reprinted in *Gaochao,* p. 756.

* * *

[Editor's Note to] "The Experience of the Liziyuan Agricultural Producers' Cooperative of Zhenru District in Economizing on Production Expenses"[87]

This article is also very good. Every socialist economic undertaking must pay attention to making all possible efforts to fully utilize human resources and equipment, to improve labor organization and business management, to raise labor productivity, to economize on all the human and material resources that can be conserved, to implement labor competition and economic accounting, and thus year by year reduce production costs, increase individual income, and increase accumulation. This should also apply to agricultural producers' cooperatives. Much work must be done in this area.

* Dong Quan, Shao Jian and Gui Shihang, "Zhenru qu Liziyuan nongye shengchan hezuoshe jieyue shengchan feiyong de jingyan," October 24, 1955; collected and reprinted in *Gaochao,* p. 768.

* * *

[Editor's Note to] "Who Says Chicken Feathers Can't Go to Heaven?"[88]

This article is very good. It can persuade many people. The Party organization in this location has never wavered on the question of cooperativization. It has resolutely supported the poverty-stricken peasants in their demand for establishing a cooperative, achieved a victory in their competition with the well-to-do middle peasants, changed from a small cooperative to a large cooperative, increased production each year, and realized the cooperativization of the entire village within three years. The well-to-do middle peasants said, "These paupers want to run a cooperative, [but] we haven't ever seen chicken feathers that could fly up to heaven."[89] But the chicken feathers did indeed have the audacity to fly up to heaven. This is the struggle between the two roads – socialism and capitalism. In China the economic strength of the rich peasants is very weak (during the period of land reform the portion of land that they held under semifeudal conditions was confiscated; the great majority of old rich peasants no longer hire labor; and their reputation in society is very bad). The strength of the well-to-do and relatively well-to-do peasants, who make up twenty to thirty per cent of the rural population, however, is fairly great. An important aspect of the struggle between the two roads in China's countryside is manifested in the peaceful competition between the poor peasants and lower-middle peasants on one side and the well-to-do middle peasants on the other. [The outcome] depends on which side will increase production in two or three years; will it be the well-to-do middle peasants who are going it alone or will it be the cooperatives that have been organized by the poor and lower-middle peasants? In the beginning it was only the cooperatives, formed by some of the poor and lower-middle peasants, which were in competition with the well-to-do middle peasants who were going it alone; the great majority of poor and lower-middle peasants were still there watching. It was [a situation in which] both sides were trying to win over the masses. Behind the well-to-do middle peasants stand the landlords and the rich peasants. They support the well-to-do middle peasants, sometimes openly and sometimes secretly. On the side of the cooperatives stands the Communist Party; its [members] should be like the Communists of Nancui *xiang* of Anyang *xian* and support the cooperatives resolutely. Unfortunately, however, not every Party branch in every village is like that. Under these conditions, then, there is confusion. First of all there is the problem of public opinion on the question of whether or not chicken feathers can fly up to heaven. Naturally this is a serious issue. In thousands of years, has anyone ever seen chicken feathers that could fly up to heaven? It seems to be a matter of truth [that it cannot be done]. If the Party does not criticize [this idea], it will lead to the confusion of many poor and lower-middle peasants. Second, with regard to the cadres, and third, with regard to material means such as loans, if they cannot get the support of the Party and the state, the cooperatives will run into very great difficulties. The reason that the well-to-do middle peasants dared to spread [rumors of] ancient adages such as [the one that] chicken feathers can't fly up to heaven was that the cooperatives had not yet become rich cooperatives, and individual, isolated cooperatives had not yet become thousands and tens of thousands of cooperatives. It was because the Party had not yet vigorously propagandized the benefits of cooperativization on a nationwide scale and with great fanfare, and because it had not yet clearly pointed out that the ancient adage "chicken feathers can't fly up to heaven" is no longer true in the age of socialism. The poor will overturn their old lives.[90] The old system will be obliterated. A new system is being born. Chicken feathers will indeed fly up to heaven. In the Soviet Union, they have already flown up to heaven. In China, they are flying up to heaven right now. And they will fly up to heaven all over the world. Many of our local Party organizations have not been able to give their resolute support to the impoverished peasants, but we cannot blame everything on them; the higher levels have not yet struck opportunist thinking a mortal blow, have not yet made a comprehensive plan for cooperativization, and [have not yet] strengthened the leadership of this movement on a nationwide scale. In 1955 we did this work, and in a few months' time the situation was completely different. The broad masses who stood and watched came over, group by group, to stand on the side of cooperativizaiton. The well-to-do middle peasants have also changed their tune. Some are asking to join the cooperatives, and some have already prepared to join the cooperatives. Even the most stubborn no longer dare to argue whether or not chicken feathers can fly up to heaven. The landlords and rich peasants are completely deflated. This also has something to do with the punishment meted out by the People's Government to a group of counterrevolutionaries who had been breaking down public security and wrecking the cause of cooperativization. In short, during the latter half of 1955, a basic change occurred in the balance of class power in our country; socialism soared and capitalism took a plunge. With another year of hard work in 1956, the basis will have been basically put down for the socialist transformation in the period of transition.

* The Cooperativization Campaign Office of the Anyang [Special] District Committee of the CPC, "Shui shuo jimao buneng shang tian," originally published in *Henan ribao* [Henan Daily], November 2, 1955; collected and reprinted in *Gaochao*, p. 777; *Xuanji* V, pp. 230-232; *Socialist Upsurge*, pp. 144-147; *Xuandu* (1955a), pp. 320-322; *Xuandu* (1966b), pp. 165-167.

* * *

[Editor's Note to] "The Experience of Planning Cooperativization in a *xiang*"[91]

This is also a good article; it can be used as a reference everywhere. Where it mentions organizing middle school students and primary school graduates to participate in the work of cooperativization is particularly worthy of close attention. All these intellectuals who can go to the countryside to work should go there happily. The countryside is a vast universe where there is plenty to be done.

* Prepared by the Rural Work Department of the Xuchang [Special] District Committee of the CPC, "Zai yi ge xiang li jinxing hezuohua guihua de jingyan," originally published in the Rural Work Department of Xuchang [Special] District Committee, *Huzhu hezuo* [Mutual Aid and Cooperativization], no. 15 (September 4, 1955); collected and reprinted in *Gaochao*, p. 795; *Xuanji*, V, pp. 247-248; *Socialist Upsurge*, p. 411.

* * *

[Editor's Note to] "Yingyang *xian* Committed an Error in Carelessly Weeding Out Members of the Cooperative"

What is discussed here is not even the dissolution of a whole cooperative, but rather just the weeding out, in some cooperatives, of people who should not have been weeded out. This has already had very bad consequences. The policy of the Henan provincial [Party] committee is correct.

* Rural Work Department of the Henan Provincial Committee of the CPC, "Yingyang xian huluan de qingxi sheyuan fan le cuowu," originally published in *Henan tongxun* [Henan Bulletin], no. 290 (February 11, 1955); collected and reprinted in *Gaochao*, p. 802.

* * *

[Editor's Note to] "The Advisory Group for
Forming Cooperatives in Xuchang [Special] District"

This experience is very good and can be used and can be copied everywhere.

* Rural Work Department of the Xuchang [Special] District Committee of the CPC, "Xuchang diqu de ban she fudaotuan," originally published in *Henan ribao* [Henan Daily], October 30, 1955; collected and reprinted in *Gaochao*, p. 805.

* * *

[Editor's Note to] "The Experience of the Xianggao
Agricultural Producers' Cooperative of Houpai *xiang* in
Xiangyang *xian* Regarding the Feeding and Use of Draft Oxen"

The author has studied this question very enthusiastically. The opinions the peasants recounted are indeed in the peasants' own words. It seems that the author has gone to this *xiang* and studied this problem with the peasants. We hope that the more than two hundred [special] district Party committee secretaries throughout the country will each go down to the countryside to investigate one or more cooperatives and that each will write one or two articles.

* Zhao Xiu, secretary of the Xiangyang [Special] District Committee of the CPC, "Xiangyang xian huopai xiang xianggao nongye shengchan hezuoshe guanyu weiyang he shiyong gengniu de jingyan," originally published in *Hubei nongcun* [Rural Hubei], no. 106 (April 18, 1955); collected and reprinted in *Gaochao*, p. 841.

* * *

[Editor's Note to] "How the Dominant Position in Wutang
Agricultural Producers' Cooperative of Gaoshan *xiang* in
Changsha *xian* Shifted from the Middle Peasants to the Poor Peasants"

This is a common and serious problem. Party committees at all levels and all comrades who have been sent to the countryside to guide the work of cooperativization should give this problem their full attention. The organizations of leadership in the cooperatives must see to it that the dominant position of the current poor peasants and new lower-middle peasants is established in the organizations of leadership [of the cooperatives], with the old lower-middle peasants and both new and old upper-middle peasants acting as an auxiliary force [only]. Only then can the poor peasants and middle peasants be united, the cooperatives consolidated, production developed, and the socialist transformation of the countryside be completed successfully in accordance with the Party's policy. Without this condition, the middle peasants and the poor peasants cannot be united, the cooperatives cannot be consolidated, production cannot be developed, and socialist transformation of the whole countryside cannot be realized. Many comrades do not understand this principle. They think that regarding the question of establishing the dominance of the poor peasants, [this dominance] was necessary during the period of land reform[92] because at that time the poor peasants who made up fifty, sixty, or seventy per cent of the rural population had not yet become middle peasants, whereas the middle peasants were wavering with regard to land reform; therefore it was indeed necessary to establish the dominance of the poor peasants at that time. [But they argue that] now is the period of the socialist transformation of agriculture, that the poor peasants of the past have for the most part risen to the status of middle peasants, and that moreover the old middle peasants own a good deal of the means of production, and without their participation it would be impossible to solve the problem of the shortage of the means of production in the cooperatives. Thus, these comrades feel that we should not now put forth the slogan of relying on the poor peasants and establishing the dominance of the poor peasants. They think that such a slogan will be harmful to cooperativization. We consider such a view to be wrong. If the working class and the Communist Party are to use the socialist spirit and the socialist system to thoroughly transform the system of private ownership of the means of production in small[-scale] peasant holdings in the entire countryside, then it is only by relying on the broad masses of poor peasants who were formerly semiproletarians that the transformation can be achieved relatively smoothly; otherwise it will be very difficult. This is because the rural semiproletariat are not so stubborn in clinging to the system of private ownership of the means of production [vested] in small[-scale] peasant holdings, and they are people who will accept socialist transformation more easily. Most of them have already become new middle peasants, but compared to the old middle peasants, apart from some new well-to-do middle peasants, the majority of them have a relatively higher level of political consciousness, and the bitterness of their lives in the past is still rather easily recalled. In addition, the economic position and political attitude of the lower-middle peasants among the old middle peasants are closer to that of the lower-middle peasants among the new middle peasants, and are not the same as [those of] the upper-middle peasants among either the new or old middle peasants, that is, the well-to-do and relatively well-to-do middle peasants. Therefore, in the process of cooperativization, we must pay attention to these three types of people who will accept socialist transformation relatively easily: (1) the poor peasants who are still in a difficult position, (2) the lower-middle peasants among the new middle peasants, and (3) the lower-middle peasants among the old middle peasants, and we should bring them first of all into the cooperatives by groups and at intervals. Moreover, a number of people from among them who have a relatively high level of [political] consciousness and who have strong organizational abilities should be selected and trained to serve as the backbone of leadership in the cooperatives. We should pay attention to selecting these backbone elements from among the current poor peasants and the new lower-middle peasants. This does not imply that a new drawing of class distinctions[93] is to be made in the rural areas, but rather that this should be taken as a guideline to which Party branches and the comrades who have been sent to the countryside to guide the work should pay attention and grasp in the process of cooperativization. This guideline should be publicly proclaimed to the masses of the peasants. At the same time, we are not saying that the well-to-do middle peasants cannot join the cooperatives. Rather we are saying that we should wait until the socialist consciousness of the well-to-do middle peasants has been raised and until they have expressed a willingness to join the cooperatives and, moreover, to obey the leadership of the poor peasants (including the current poor peasants and all the new middle peasants who were originally poor peasants) before absorbing them into the cooperatives. Don't coerce them into joining the cooperatives before they are willing to join just to obtain the use of their draft oxen and farm tools. Those who are already in the cooperatives and who wish to remain can continue to do so without any changes made. Those who intend to withdraw from the cooperatives but, after some persuasion, are willing to stay, should also be allowed to stay. Cooperatives can be organized even with fewer means of production; the many cooperatives organized by the poor and lower-middle peasants have proven this point. Nor are we saying that not a single well-to-do middle peasant can become a cadre in a cooperative. Those individual well-to-do middle peasants whose socialist consciousness is high, who are fair-minded and capable, and who have the respect of the great majority of the people of the entire cooperative can become cadres. But the dominance of the poor peasants (to say it once again, this includes the current poor peasants, and all the new lower-middle peasants who were originally poor peasants; they make up the majority or the great majority of the rural population) must be established in the cooperatives. In terms of composition, the poor peasants should make up about two-thirds [of the leadership organs], while the middle peasants (which include the old lower-middle peasants and both the new and old upper-middle peasants) can only make up, and should make up, about one-third. As for the policy guiding the cooperatives, we must implement the policy of mutual benefit for both the poor peasants and the middle peasants, and must not damage anyone's interests. It is also in order to achieve this that we must establish the dominance of the poor peasants. In cooperatives where the middle peasants are dominant, they will always squeeze out the poor peasants and harm their interests. The experience of Gaoshan *xiang* of Changsha *xian* of Hunan Province fully demonstrates to us both the necessity and possibility of establishing the dominance of the poor peasants and the subsequent firm unity with the middle peasants as well as the dangers if this is not done. The author of this article completely understands the Party's line. The method is also very correct: First completing the urgent task of increasing production and then establishing the dominant position of the poor peasants in the leadership. As a result the poor peasants are holding their heads high and even the middle peasants are truly and sincerely impressed. The author of this article also tells us about an important matter. That is, for a cooperative in which the situation is chaotic, is it better to have it dissolved? Or is it better to set it in order so that it goes from a state of chaos to a state of health? Can such cooperatives be set in order and consolidated? The author of this article tells us quite persuasively that we ought not to dissolve the "third-class cooperatives"[94] and that we ought to do the work of setting them in order. After such work it is altogether possible for a third-class cooperative to be transformed into a first-class cooperative. There have already been many experiences of this kind throughout the entire country, not only in Gaoshan *xiang* of Changsha *xian*.

* Zhou Jingwen, "Changsha xian gaoshan xiang wutang nongye shengchan hezuoshe shi zenyang cong zhongnong zhan youshi zhuanbian wei pinnong zhan youshi de," originally published in *Huzhu hezuo* [Mutual Aid and Cooperativization], no. 9 (July 26, 1955); collected and reprinted in *Gaochao*, p. 857; *Xuanji*, V, pp. 238-240; *Socialist Upsurge*, pp. 255-259; *Xuandu* (1965a), pp. 322-324; and, under a different title, in *Xuandu* (1965b), pp. 159-162.

* * *

[Editor's Note to] "The Party Branch of Qingfeng *xiang*, Xiangtan *xian*, Helps the Impoverished Members of the Cooperative Resolve Their Difficulties"

The policy of this cooperative is correct. All cooperatives ought to do things this way. Each province ought to point out in its resolutions or directives on the question of cooperativization that all cooperatives have the responsibility to help resolve the difficulties of its members who are widowers, widows, orphans, elderly people who are childless, or who lack labor power (they should incorporate them into the cooperative) and also of cooperative members who have labor power but whose lives are extremely difficult. At present many cooperatives lack the socialist spirit of helping households in difficulty, or even simply shut out the poor peasants. This is completely wrong. At present, the government has already established a poor peasant fund. It can help the poor peasants solve their difficulties of draft oxen and farm tools, but it still cannot solve the difficulty of a lack of the means of livelihood that some households experience during the hiatus period between farming seasons.[95] These [difficulties] can only be resolved by relying on the strength of the broad masses in the cooperatives.

* Gu Jianpeng, "Xiangtan xian qingfeng xiang dang zhibu bangzhu pinku sheyuan jiejue kunnan," originally published in *Hunan nongcun* [Rural Hunan], no. 113 (May 17, 1955); collected and reprinted in *Gaochao*, p. 870; *Xuanji*, V, pp. 242-243.

* * *

[Editor's Note to] "Xiangyin *xian* Solves the Problem of Finding an Outlet for Excess Labor"

The situation in this *xian* also tells us that an outlet for excess labor power can be found in the villages. The [number of] work days for each man and woman in a year can be increased as methods of management are improved and the scope of production expands. It is not, as it is said in this article, that men can put in one hundred or more work days and women a few dozen work days. Rather it can be done so that men put in more than two hundred work days and women one hundred and more work days, or even more. Such numbers [of work days] have already been achieved in some cooperatives elsewhere. Sideline occupations must have a definite market; they cannot be developed blindly; this is correct. Taking the country as a whole, rural sideline occupations in large part serve the countryside, but there must be a not too small portion that serves the cities and export [needs]. Eventually this sector can be expanded. The issue is that the country must have a unified plan so as to eliminate blindness step by step.

* Ren Peiwu, "Xiangyin xian jiejue liao shengyu laodongli de chulu wenti," originally published in *Hunan nongcun* [Rural Hunan], no. 110 (April 3, 1955); collected and reprinted in *Gaochao*, p. 887; *Xuanji*, V, pp. 253-254.

* * *

[Editor's Note to] "A Model Cooperative"[96]

This article is very good. It can be used as a reference everywhere.

* Liu Junxiu, second secretary of the Jiangxi Provincial Committee of the CPC, "Yi ge mofan hezuoshe," originally published in *Nongcun jianshe* [Rural Construction] (Jiangxi), no. 96 (February 10, 1955); collected and reprinted in *Gaochao*, p. 907.

* * *

[Editor's Note to] "A Cooperative Established Its Bylaws"[97]

This is a useful article. It can be used as a reference in establishing bylaws for cooperatives everywhere.

* Work Team of the Seventh District Committee of Nanchang *xian* of the CPC, "Hezuoshe yi ding shezhang," originally published in *Nongcun jianshe* [Rural Construction] (Jiangxi), special edition no. 14 (February 2, 1955); collected and reprinted in *Gaochao*, p. 924.

* * *

[Editor's Note to] "My Experience as a Director of a Large Cooperative"

Do not think that the cooperativization movement can be promoted on a large scale only in old liberated areas,[98] and not in areas that were liberated later. This way of thinking is not in accord with the real situation. Areas that were liberated later can also promote cooperativization on a large scale. In terms of particular *xian*, districts, and *xiang*, the areas that were liberated later can complete cooperativization at the same time as, or even before, the old liberated areas; there are already some examples that prove this. This is completely dependent on whether or not the leadership work of the Party is appropriate, and whether or not fewer mistakes are committed. This article is the record of a talk given by the director of a cooperative in Zhongshan *xian*, Guandong [Province]. What he has said is no worse than what a director of a cooperative in an old liberated area [might say]; in fact some cooperatives' directors in old liberated areas might not be able to match him.

* A talk by Liang Xiangsheng, director of the First Qunzhong [Masses'] Agricultural Producers' Cooperative of Zhongshan *xian*, "Wuo dang da she zhuren di jingyan," recorded by the work team stationed at the cooperative, May 1955, originally published in *Zhongshan xian gonggu nongyeshe jingyan* [The Experience of Zhongshan *xian* in Consolidating Agricultural Cooperatives]; collected and reprinted in *Gaochao*, p. 951; *Socialist Upsurge*, p. 210.

* * *

[Editor's Note to] "The Youth Shock Brigade of the No. 9 Agricultural Producers' Cooperative of Xinping *xiang*, Zhongshan *xian*"[99]

This article is very good. It can be used as a reference everywhere. Young people are the most active and dynamic part of all the social forces. They are the most willing to study and are the least conservative in their thinking, particularly in the socialist era. We hope that Party organizations everywhere will work with the Youth League organizations, paying attention to studying how the energy of the young people in particular can be brought into fullest play; don't treat them the same way that everyone else is treated or ignore their special characteristics. Naturally young people must learn from old people and adults and should strive to engage as much as possible in useful activities with the consent of the old people and adults. Old people and adults have more conservative thinking [than young people], and they often suppress the progressive activities of young people. It is only after the young people are successful that they are convinced. This article describes such a situation very well. Naturally no compromise should be made with conservative thinking. All right then, let's try it and see; if it is successful, then they [the conservatives] will agree.

* Work team of the Central Guangdong Regional Work Committee of the [New Democratic] Youth League, "Zhongshan xian xinping xiang de jiu nongye shengchan hezuoshe de qingnian tujidui," originally published in *Huanan qingnian* [South China Youth], no. 16 (August 25, 1955); collected and reprinted in *Gaochao*, p. 959; *Xuanji*, V, p. 247; *Socialist Upsurge*, pp. 319-320; and, under a different title, in *Xuandu* (1965b), p. 169.

* * *

[Editor's Note to] "Red Flag Agricultural Producers' Cooperative of the First District of Qiongshan *xian* Was Consolidated in the Struggle Against Natural Calamities and Capitalist Thought"

The superiority of having large-scale cooperatives and higher-stage cooperatives is also demonstrated by the experience of Red Flag Cooperative of Hainan Island. This large-scale cooperative had a history of only one year when it made preparations for the transformation to a higher-stage cooperative. Of course this is not to say that every cooperative should follow suit. They must [of course] still see whether or not their own conditions are ripe before making a decision on when it would actually be best to merge [with other] cooperatives and advance to a higher stage. Nevertheless, generally speaking, three years' time will be about right. What is important is to set examples for the peasants to see. When the peasants see the superiority of having large-scale and higher-stage cooperatives over having small-scale cooperatives and lower-stage cooperatives, they will demand the merger of cooperatives and the advancement to higher-stage [cooperatives].

* Qiongshan *xian* Committee of the CPC, "Qiongshan xian di yi qu hongqi nongye shengchan hezuoshe zai tong ziran zaihai he tong ziben zhuyi sixiang zuo douzheng zhong gonggu qilai le," October 10, 1955; collected and reprinted in *Gaochao*, p. 976; *Xuanji*, V, p. 258; *Socialist Upsurge*, p. 342.

[Editor's Note to] "The Agricultural Producers' Cooperative of Bianhai *xiang*, Which Matured in the Struggle Against Natural Calamities"[100]

This piece is written very vivaciously and is worth reading. The Party branch of this *xiang* is a model branch; it has led the masses in carrying out numerous heroic struggles and has [thus] won the support of the masses.

* Wang Xiuping, "Zai he ziran zaihai zuo douzheng zhong chengzhang qilai de bianhai xiang nongye shengchan hezuoshe," originally published in *Huanan ribao* [South China Daily], May 8, 1955; collected and reprinted in *Gaochao*, p. 987.

* * *

[Editor's Note to] "The Experience of Tianmei Village Agricultural Producers' Cooperative of Taishan *xian* in Organizing Production on Reclaimed Land"

This is land reclamation within short distance. Areas with [adequate] conditions can all do likewise. But we must pay attention to the work of water and soil conservation; we absolutely cannot create floods in downstream areas as a result of reclaiming [upstream] land.

* The Department of Cooperativization of the Taishan *xian* Committee of the CPC, "Taishan xian tianmei cun nongye hezuoshe zuzhi kaihuang shengchan de jingyan," originally published in *Yuexi tongxun* [West Guandong Bulletin], no. 90 (September 19, 1955); collected and reprinted in *Gaochao*, p. 996.

* * *

[Editor's Note to] "The Red Star Agricultural Producers' Cooperative of Jiangbu *xiang* of Guangning *xian* Has Developed Diversified Economic Undertakings and Solved a Very Major Problem"

This is a very good experience. It is worthy of being studied and popularized everywhere.

* Jianbu *xiang* work team of Guangning *xian* Committee of the CPC, "Guangning xian jiangbu xiang hongxing nongye shenchan hezuoshe fazhan liao duozhong jingji jiejue liao hen da de wenti," originally published in *Yuezhong tongxun* [Central Guangdong Bulletin], no. 254 (May 18, 1955); collected and reprinted in *Gaochao*, p. 1006.

* * *

[Editor's Note to] "The Experience of Mo Shouquan Agricultural
Producers' Cooperative of Cenqi *xian* in Launching
[the Drive to] Make Rational Proposals'' [101]

This is a creative experience. We hope the readers will pay attention to it.

* Yang Zhiqing, "Cenqi xian mo shouquan nongye shengchan hezuoshe kaizhan helihua jianyi de jingyan," originally published in *Guangxi nongcun*
[Rural Guangxi], no. 134 (February 7, 1955); collected and reprinted in *Gaochao*, p. 1029.

* * *

[Editor's Note to] "Combined Mutual Aid Teams in the Agricultural
Producers' Cooperativization Movement in Sichuan"

This experience is still useful in those areas where the progress of cooperativization has been relatively slow.

* Xinhua News Agency reporter Li Chao, "Sichuan sheng nongye hezuohua
yundong zhong de huzhu lianzu," originally published in *Sichuan ribao*
[Sichuan Daily], November 1, 1955; collected and reprinted in *Gaochao*, p.
1053.

* * *

[Editor's Note to] "The Production Plan for 1955 of Jiefang
[Liberation] Agricultural Producers' Cooperative of Jianyang *xian*"

Among the many production plans we have seen, this one is comparatively
concrete and has clear explanations, enabling people to understand it easily.

* Jianyang work team of the Rural Work Department of the Sichuan Provincial Committee of the CPC, "Jianyang xian jiefang nongye shengchan hezuoshe yijiuwuwu nian de shengchan jihua," February 1955; collected and
reprinted in *Gaochao*, p. 1059.

* * *

[Editor's Note to] "How Xipu and Gucheng *xiang* of
Pi *xian* Dealt With All Kinds of Specific Problems"

This is a very good document. All localities can take this as a reference and
act accordingly.

* Report to the Pi *xian* Party Committee, the Hunjiang [Special] District [Party] Committee, and the Sichuan Provincial [Party] Committee, made by the work team assigned to Xipu and Gucheng *xiang* of Pi *xian* by the Sichuan Provincial Committee of the CPC, "Pi xian xipu he gucheng liang ge xiang shi zenyang chuli ge xiang juti wenti de," April 10, 1955; collected and reprinted in *Gaochao*, p. 1077.

* * *

[Editor's Note to] "The Experience of Nine Agricultural Producers' Cooperatives of Shehong *xiang*, Jianyang *xian*, in Reorganizing Financial Management Work"

This article describes the circumstances in which nine cooperatives violated the principle of running the cooperatives with diligence and frugality and made some other mistakes in financial management. We hope that all cooperatives take this as a warning.

* Shehong *xiang* work team of the Rural Work Department of the Sichuan Provincial Committee of the CPC, "Jianyang xian shehong xiang jiuge nongye shengchan hezuoshe zhengdun caiwu guanli gongzuo de jingyan," October 14, 1955; collected and reprinted in *Gaochao*, p. 1103.

* * *

[Editor's Note to] "How the Collective Agricultural Producers' Cooperative of Tianchi *xiang*, Yibin *xian*, Planned to Breed Draft Oxen"

This article is very good. All other places should act accordingly. Some cooperatives not only ignore the breeding of small livestock, but pay no attention to the small livestock that they have either. This is entirely wrong. A unified arrangement should be made for all livestock, big and small, strong and weak. And moreover, there should be planned breeding of small livestock such as that done in Yibin *xian*.

* Chen Jing, "Yibin xian tianchi xiang jiti nongye shengchan hezuoshe shi zenyang jihua fanzhi gengniu de," originally published in *Nongmin bao* [Peasants' News] (Yibin), July 25, 1955; collected and reprinted in *Gaochao*, p. 1118.

* * *

[Editor's Note to] "Chongxin *xiang* of Fenggang *xian* Developed the Mutual Aid and Cooperativization Movement Under the Leadership of the Party Branch"

The line followed in this place is correct. This *xiang* already has five agricultural producers' cooperatives, seven combined mutual aid teams, three year-round mutual aid teams, fourteen temporary mutual aid teams, [all of which] encompasses 98.4 per cent of the peasant households that should be organized.[102] Before December 1954, the Party branch of this *xiang* had not placed the emphasis of its leadership work on the mutual aid and cooperativization [movement]. The Party members were afraid of the difficulty involved in the work of guiding mutual aid teams. What the [Party] branch relied on was not "having the [Party] secretary take part and all Party [members] engaged in running cooperatives,"[103] but rather [it relied on] the work team (apparently the work teams sent there from above). There are still many rural Party branches all around the country that show this kind of weak, helpless attitude with regard to the question of agricultural cooperativization. Not only [Party] branches, but even some higher-level Party committees may be like this. The problem is precisely on this point. Whether or not the socialist transformation of agriculture in our country will correspond to the speed of the nation's industrialization, whether or not cooperativization will develop in a healthy way, with fewer problems and a guaranteed increase of production, depends on whether or not the emphasis of leadership of the local Party committees at all levels can be quickly and accurately turned to this aspect. The work teams must be sent, but it must be made clear that the purpose of their going is to assist the Party organizations there, not to substitute for them so that they won't do anything themselves but rely solely on the work teams.[104] Since this *xiang* in Guizhou changed its attitude toward work in December 1954, it has achieved great results in just five months. They don't depend on the work teams any longer, but take the initiative themselves, and the Party members are no longer afraid of difficulties. This kind of change first of all depends on the Party committee secretaries at every level, the secretaries of provincial [Party] committees and autonomous region [Party] committees, the secretaries of [special] district [Party] committees and autonomous *zhou* [Party] committees, the secretaries of *xian* and autonomous *xian* [Party] committees, district [Party] committee secretaries and [Party] branch secretaries. They ought to take up the whole task of agricultural cooperativization. If they are afraid of the trouble, or of the difficulties, if they do not personally take part when faced with this great task, but merely pass it down to the rural work departments or to the work teams, if they have this type of attitude, then not only will it be impossible to complete the task, but there will be great chaos as well.

* Liu Yaohua, "Fenggang xian chongxin xiang shi zenyang zai dang zhibu lingdao xia kaizhan huzhu hezuo yundong de," originally published in *Guizhou gongzuo* [Guizhou Work], no. 82 (May 13, 1955); collected and reprinted in *Gaochao*, p. 1125; *Xuanji*, V, 234-235; *Socialist Upsurge*, pp. 222-223.

* * *

[Editor's Note to] "The Political Work in Cooperatives"[105]

This article is very well written. It deserves to be recommended to all Party and [Youth] League *xian* committees, district committees, and *xiang* branches. All cooperatives should follow this example. The author of this article understands the Party's line, and everything he says hits the mark. Also, the writing style is good; it enables people to understand it at a glance. It does not have the air of stereotyped Party writing.[106] Here, we must ask our readers to pay attention. We have many comrades who, when they are writing an essay, just love stereotyped Party writing, which is neither lively nor graphic; it gives people headaches. Neither are they careful about grammar or rhetoric; they like a form of writing that is a cross between the classical and the vernacular. Sometimes they say a lot of nonsense, sometimes they are elliptical and archaic; it's as if they wanted to make the reader suffer. Many of this book's one hundred and seventy articles are heavy with stereotyped Party writing. It was only after several revisions that they were made more readable. Even so, a few are still obscure, clumsy, and hard to understand. They were selected only because their content was important. When will we see less of that stereotyped Party writing that gives people headaches? We ask our comrades who edit the newspapers and periodicals to pay attention to this, to ask the authors to write lively, fluent, and understandable articles. Moreover, they should take the initiative themselves to help the authors in revising [their] articles.

* Propaganda Department of the Suiyang *xian* Committee of the CPC, "Hezuoshe de zhengzhi gongzuo," originally published in *Guizhou gongzuo* [Guizhou Work], no. 61 (November 10, 1954); collected and reprinted in *Gaochao*, p. 1134; *Xuanji*, V, pp. 248-249; *Socialist Upsurge*, pp. 359-360.

* * *

[Editor's Note to] "It Is Necessary to Wage a Resolute
Struggle Against Counterrevolutionary Sabotage Activities"

The problem of counterrevolutionary sabotage of the cooperativization movement is a common one. This is not a local problem [confined to] the Fifth District of Duyun *xian*, Guizhou Province, but we see very little about this problem reflected in similar publications from other provinces. In the process of cooperativization all comrades engaged in rural work must pay attention to this problem of struggling against counterrevolutionary sabotage activities. They must learn from this district in Duyun *xian* and establish, in the cooperatives, security organizations, with Party and [Youth] League members as the backbone. It is absolutely imperative that the Party district committees, under the leadership and supervision of the *xian* [Party] committees, after having studied the situation and publicizing and explaining [the policy] to Party members and nonmembers alike, and after having raised the vigilance of the masses with regard to counterrevolutionary sabotage, should investigate, weed out, and deal with the counterrevolutionaires and other bad elements who have wormed their way into the leading organizations of the cooperatives. However, those who are to be weeded out must be real counterrevolutionaries or truly bad elements; we must not label good people or people with only certain shortcomings as bad people. The actual handling [of the cases] must, in particular, be appropriate and must be approved by the *xian* [authorities].

* Adapted from a draft from the Public Security Bureau of Duyun *xian* dated June 6, "Bixu he fangeming de pohuai huodong zuo jianjue de douzheng," originally published in *Guizhou gongzuo* [Guizhou Work], no. 85 (July 30, 1955); collected and reprinted in *Gaochao*, p. 1142.

* * *

[Editor's Note to] "A Cooperative's Three-Year Production Plan"[107]

This is a good article. It deserves to be read by everyone and can be used by cooperatives everywhere as a reference in making long-term plans. What the author of this article says is very correct: "The entire process of drawing up a production plan is the process of a struggle between progressive thinking and conservative thinking." Conservative thinking is now causing trouble nearly everywhere. In order to overcome this kind of conservative thinking and to allow the forces of production and production itself to take a large step forward, all localities and all cooperatives must draw up long-term plans for themselves.

* Panjiang work team of the Guiding *xian* Committee of the CPC, "Yi ge hezuoshe de san nian shengchan guihua," October 7, 1955; collected and reprinted in *Gaochao,* p. 1146; *Xuanji*, V, p. 250; *Socialist Upsurge*, p. 423.

* * *

[Editor's Note to] "Carry Out Equal Work and
Equal Pay for Men and Women in the Cooperatives"

This is a short article, and easy to read. We urge that all *xiang* and cooperatives generally follow this example.

* "Zai hezuoshe nei shixing nan nü tonggong tongchou," October 1955, originally published in Guizhou Democratic Women's Federation, *Tongbao* [Bulletin], no. 99; collected and reprinted in *Gaochao,* p. 1156.

* * *

[Editor's Note to] "Seasonal Labor Contracts"[108]

The author of this article says that after a joint conference of directors of cooperatives in this *xian* was convened, this cooperative implemented a system of seasonal labor contracts on the basis of occasional work contracts. It can be seen from this that leadership by the *xian* is very important. We hope that the leadership organizations at the *xian* level of the two thousand and more *xian* all over the country will pay close attention to the developing situation in the cooperativization movement throughout the *xian*, that they will identify problems, study ways to solve them, and convene timely conferences of directors of all the cooperatives in the *xian* or of the directors of important cooperatives throughout the *xian*, and make decisions and carry them out quickly. Don't wait until problems pile up and create a lot of confusion before resolving them. Leadership must move in the vanguard of the movement and not lag behind it. Within the scope of a *xian*, the *xian* Party committee should play the main leadership role.

* Work team of the Zhenning *xian* Committee of the CPC, "Jijie baogong," originally published in *Guizhou gongzuo* [Guizhou Work], no. 70 (March 10, 1955); collected and reprinted in *Gaochao*, p. 1159.

* * *

[Editor's Note to] "A Cooperative in Confusion Was Put in Good Order"[109]

This material points out the truth that any cooperative in a state of confusion can be put in good order. Because those who join the cooperatives are all laboring peasants, regardless of the differences of opinion of various strata among them, in the end they can all be straightened out. For a time there really was confusion in some cooperatives; the only reason [for this] was that they didn't get any leadership from the Party, and the Party had not clearly explained its policies and methods to the masses. "We know that it is a good thing to set up a cooperative. But after we set one up, neither the *xian* [Party] committee, the district [Party] committee, nor the [Party] branch will take care of us anymore. Perhaps they felt uneasy about our poor village [because] they couldn't eat well or live well [here], so they never came to our cooperative." There is only this reason and no other reason for such confusion. If [a cooperative] can't get leadership from the Party, naturally there will be confusion. Once leadership is provided, confusion will immediately cease. This material also brings up the issue of whether or not cooperatives can be set up in backward villages. The answer is affirmative. The cooperative that the writer of this article writes about is located in a backward village. Some five per cent of the villages throughout the country are backward; we must set up cooperatives in all [these villages], and in the struggle to set up [these] cooperatives we will wipe out the backwardness of these places.

* Xichou *xian* Committee of the Chinese Communist Party, "Yi ge hunluan de hezuoshe zhengdun hao liao," originally published in *Nongcun gongzuo tongbao* [Rural Work Bulletin] (Yunnan), no. 111 (June 30, 1955); collected and reprinted in *Gaochao*, pp. 1167-1168; *Xuanji*, V, p. 237; *Socialist Upsurge*, pp. 239-240.

* * *

[Editor's Note to] "The Question of Sideline Occupations"[110]

This article's discussion of sideline occupations is relatively comprehensive. Moreover, it discusses sideline occupations in several dozen agricultural producers' cooperatives in one *xian*. The author has given a summary description of subsidiary production in this *xian*. We suggest that each *xian* do a summary of this aspect [of their work].

* Zhang Xinghua, "Fuye wenti," originally published in *Nongcun gongzuo tongbao* [Rural Work Bulletin] (Yunnan), no. 101 (March 11, 1955); collected and reprinted in *Gaochao*, p. 1172.

* * *

[Editor's Note to] "The Question of Draft Oxen in Fumin *xian*"[111]

This article is relatively long, and there are some shortcomings in the writing, but its author has investigated the situation with regard to draft oxen in an entire *xian* with great enthusiasm, and his viewpoint with regard to policy is also correct. Therefore we have included this article.

* Department of Production and Cooperativization of the Fumin *xian* Committee of the CPC, "Fumin xian de gengniu wenti," originally published in *Nongcun gongzuo tongbao* [Rural Work Bulletin] (Yunnan), no. 118 (April 20, 1955); collected and reprinted in *Gaochao*, p. 1186.

* * *

[Editor's Note to] "The Experience of Four Cooperatives
in Wang Mang *cun*,[112] Changan *xian*, in
Organizing a Federated Cooperative"[113]

This experience is useful; all areas can emulate it. Party district committee and *xiang* [Party] branches can draw up plans, first organizing a joint management committee of a federated cooperative for those smaller cooperatives *t* are prepared to merge into a larger cooperative, such as in Wang Mang *cu* Changan *xian*, and then, after a period, they can proceed with a merge

* Rural Work Department of the Shaanxi Provincial Committee of th'

"Changan xian wangmang cun si ge hezuoshe zuzhi lianshe de jingyan," August 1955; collected and reprinted in *Gaochao*, p. 1197; *Socialist Upsurge*, p. 487.

* * *

[Editor's Note to] "A Cooperative Set Up on the Masses' Own Initiative, Against the Wishes of the Leadership"[114]

This is a moving story. We hope that the reader will read it carefully. In particular, we ask those comrades who do not believe that the broad peasant masses have enthusiasm for taking the socialist road and those comrades who are always ready with knife in hand to "chop down" the cooperatives to read the article carefully. At present in the rural areas throughout the country, the socialist factor is increasing daily and hourly; the broad masses of peasants are demanding the organization of cooperatives. A great number of intelligent, able, fair-minded, and enthusiastic leaders have sprung forth from among the masses. This is extremely encouraging. The greatest shortcoming is that Party leadership in many localities has not taken the initiative in keeping up [with the masses]. The present task is to get the local Party committees at every level to take a positive Marxist-Leninist stand, take the task of agricultural cooperativization into their own hands, and lead this movement with enthusiasm and joy, welcoming [the task] and exerting their utmost efforts. They should not reenact the story of Lord Ye, who [professed to] love dragons, [115] by talking about socialism for so many years and then when socialism comes to them, being afraid of it.

* *Shaanxi ribao* [Shaanxi Daily] reporter Chen Taizhi, "Yi ge weibei lingdao yiyuan you qunzhong zidong ban qilai de hezuoshe," originally published in *Shaanxi ribao* [Shaanxi Daily], August 31, 1955; collected and reprinted in *Gaochao*, p. 1204; *Xuanji*, V, p. 234; *Socialist Upsurge*, pp. 179-180.

* * *

[Editor's Note to] "The Party Branch of Yangheba *xiang*, Xixiang *xian*, Correctly Leads the Mutual Aid and Cooperativization Work There"

This article is useful. All rural Party branches in the countryside should do things this way.

According to what is reflected in several localities, it is necessary to establish in the management committee of each agricultural producers' cooperative a deputy position to take charge of political work. All localities can establish one such position, which can, under the leadership of Party branch committees, devote itself exclusively to the task of carrying out political work.

Organizing a *xian*-wide network of mutual aid [teams] and cooperatives or organizing a "federated cooperative committee" such as that of Yangheba *xiang* in Shaanxi appears to be very advantageous.

We must definitely believe in one thing, which is, that with the proper political work, the shortcomings and mistakes made by the laboring people can be overcome and corrected. The reader can see that after political work was done in this *xiang*, those members of the cooperative who had been in the business of peddling pigs stopped doing it, and those members who had been starving the publicly owned oxen soon fattened them.

* "Xixiang xian yangheba xiang dang zhibu zhengque de lingdao liao na li de huzhu hezuo," originally published in *Shaanxi gongzuo* [Shaanxi Work], no. 18 (July 6, 1955); collected and reprinted in *Gaochao*, p. 1223; *Socialist Upsurge*, p. 213.

* * *

[Editor's Note to] "The Three-Year Development Plan of Gaolan *xian*"[116]

This is a very interesting article. Regardless of whether or not conditions in the next few years will permit certain portions of this plan to be put into practice (for example, tractor stations and educational expenditures), and regardless of whether the accounting aspect of this plan is accurate or not, at any rate it counts as a comprehensive plan for the entire *xian*, the general spirit of which is good. The section of it concerning agricultural cooperativization may be quite appropriate to the conditions in Gaolan *xian*. This plan for agricultural cooperativization was established in 1954 and was characterized by great enthusiasm and initiative. At that time the ill-wind of "reducing" and "chopping down" cooperatives had not yet risen, so these local comrades were able to think about things in a positive way. We suggest that within the framework sanctioned by the national and provincial (autonomous region) plans, each *xian* should produce a practicable, comprehensive plan in accordance with the actual local situation and send it to the province (autonomous region) [authorities] for approval and [authorization of] implementation. With regard to this matter of having each *xian* do its own plan, the Rural Work Department of the Gansu Provincial [Party] Committee feels that the outline of the plan can first be distributed by the *xian*-level [authorities] to the districts and *xiang*, and then each district or *xiang*, according to the *xian* plan and local circumstances, can draw up its own plan and report it to the *xian*. Then the *xian* can synthesize [these plans] and decide upon a *xian* plan. We think this is a good idea.

* Gaolan *xian* Committee of the CPC, "Gaolan xian de san nian fazhan jihua," originally published in *Gongzuo ziliao* [Work Materials] (Gansu), no. 140 (December 18, 1954); collected and reprinted in *Gaochao*, pp. 1235-1236.

* * *

[Editor's Note to] "How Yinda *xiang*, Jiuquan *xian*, Launched
a Spare-time Cultural Education [Program] for Peasants"

Not much space in this book is devoted to the discussion of cultural work.
This article can be considered a good one. In order to basically eliminate illiteracy and meet the urgent needs of agricultural cooperativization within seven years, that is, within the Second Five-Year Plan,[117] every locality must make comprehensive arrangements in 1956 and fulfill their plans for the first year.

* Che Hongzhang, Huang Xiande, "Jiuquan xian yinda xiang shi zenyang jinxing nongmin yeyu wenhua jiaoyu de," August 1955, collected and reprinted in *Gaochao*, p. 1262; *Socialist Upsurge*, p. 470.

* * *

[Editor's Note to] "How Guanting Agricultural Producers'
Cooperative of the Fifth District of Minhe *xian*
Solved the Problem of Impurity in Organization"

This article is a bit inadequate in the quality of its writing, and it is insufficient in terms of detailed descriptions of the activities of the impure elements, but its content is very important and deserves to be read. This cooperative appears to be a very large one, but the "*xian* and district Party committees were lax in leadership and the [Party] branches did not intervene." This led to the impure elements worming their way into the cooperative and also to abnormal relations between the poor peasants and the middle peasants. It was only after the *xian* and district Party committees paid attention to [giving it] leadership and relied on the [Party] branch [there] to mobilize the masses that the problem was resolved.

* Hu Junde, secretary of the CPC Committee of the Fifth District of Minhe *xian*, "Minhe xian di wu qu guanting nongye shengchan hezuoshe shi zenyang jiejue zuzhi buchun de wenti de," originally published in *Nongcun gongzuo cankao ziliao* [Agricultural Work Reference Materials] (Qinghai), no. 10 (July 20, 1955); collected and reprinted in *Gaochao*, p. 1274.

* * *

[Editor's Note to] "Change the Abnormal Relations
Between the Poor Peasants and the Middle Peasants and Methodically
Establish the Dominant Position of the Poor and
New Lower-Middle Peasants in the Leadership"[118]

Any place where a situation such as that in Xunhua *xian* of Qinghai Province exists (and there are many instances of this kind of situation) must, through educating the cadres and the masses, methodically achieve a change in this kind of situation.

* Rural Work Department of the Qinghai Provincial Committee of the CPC, "Gaibian pinnong he zhongnong de bu zhengchang guanxi, you buzou de zuodao shi pinnong he xin xia zhongnong zai lingdao shang zhan youshi," June 1, 1955; collected and reprinted in *Gaochao*, p. 1279.

* * *

[Editor's Note to] "The *xiang* and *cun* Cadres Have the Ability to Give Leadership to the Establishment of Cooperatives"[119]

This is a good article. Reading this article informs people that the peasants of the Uighur nationality are very enthusiastic about taking the road of cooperativization. They have already trained the cadres needed to put semisocialist cooperativization into effect. Some people say that cooperativization cannot be carried out among the minority nationalities. This is incorrect. We have already seen that the Mongol, Hui, Uighur, Miao, and Zhuang, and some other minority nationalities have already set up many cooperatives, or [in some cases] people of several nationalities have joined together in setting up cooperatives; moreover, they have done so very successfully. This refutes the erroneous view of those people who look down on the minority nationalities.

* Ye Han, "Xiang cun ganbu you nengli lingdao jianshe," originally published in *Tiannan ribao* [Tiannan Daily] (Xinjiang), October 16, 1955; collected and reprinted in *Gaochao*, p. 1293; *Xuanji*, V, p. 230; *Socialist Upsurge*, p. 190.

Notes

1. See text July 31, 1955, note 18.
2. For an explanation of "semisocialist" cooperativization throughout this document, see text Aug. 12, 1953(1), note 9, and text Oct. 15, 1953, note 2.
3. See text Aug. 12, 1953(1), note 22, and text Dec. 6, 1955, note 10.
4. When the members joined this cooperative, they pooled their resources toward the price, or cost, of a mule. This cost was itself divided into four parts, symbolizing the four legs of the mule. Some were able to contribute 1/6 of "a leg" (i.e., 1/24 or about 4 per cent of the total cost), and others 1/8, and still others only 1/18, and so on. In all, the members came up with funds equivalent to 2.8 "quarters," hence "three legs of a mule." The cooperative then arranged to have the members use the mule for three days out of four, while nonmembers had the use of the animal on the fourth day.
5. This refers to Jianming Agricultural, Forestry, and Animal Husbandry Cooperative in Xipu Village in Zunhua *xian*, Hebei, under the leadership of Wang Guofan. The example of this *qiong bangzi she* (pauper's cooperative) gave rise to the model of the highly praised *qiongbangzi jingshen* (paupers' spirit). Wang Guofan was cited as a "labor model in agriculture," gained nationwide fame, was elected as a standing member of the Hebei Province Revolutionary Committee in February 1967, and as member of the Ninth Central Committee of the CPC in April 1969.

6. "In its early days the Wang Kuo-fan [Wang Guofan] Co-operative was woefully short of means of production. Instead of asking for state loans, the co-operative organized its members to go into the mountains some thirty *li* away to collect firewood which they sold to pay for means of production. So the co-operative members said that they 'made the mountains yield' a substantial amount of the means of production." (*SW*, V, p. 276.)

7. See text Oct.11, 1955(1), note 56.

8. See note 5.

9. This refers to the agricultural producers' cooperative (hereafter in these notes abbreviated as APC) at Nanwangzhuang, Anping *xian*. Mao referred to the three poor peasant households mentioned here, namely, the households of Wang Yukun, Wang Xiaoqi, and Wang Xiaopang in his earlier essay on agricultural cooperativization. See text July 31, 1955, note 17.

10. This article refers to the experience of the APC at Dongwangzhuang, Xinle *xian*, in Hebei Province. It was originally made up of three households of poor peasants and one household of lower-middle peasants, and yet it increased production of grain by over 4,000 *jin*.

11. See text Jun. 6, 1950(1), note 11.

12. See text Jun. 6, 1950(1), note 7.

13. "Here 'reverse [negative] propaganda' means making clear to the masses the difficulties and adversities they may come across in forming cooperatives, in addition to publicizing the advantages and favourable conditions. This was done when the masses were fully aroused and applied in great numbers for co-operative membership, so that they could weigh the matter thoroughly and join of their own free will." (*SW*, V, p. 276.) See also text Oct. 11, 1955(2), note 13.

14. This article refers to the experience of Caoliangzi Village, Chengde *xian*, the former province of Jehol.

15. See text June 14, 1954, note 14.

16. This article refers to the experience of Caozhuang, Shahe *xian*, Hebei Province.

17. This article refers to the experience of Aiguo (Patriotic) APC in Tuqiao *xiang*, Tong *xian*, Hebei Province.

18. This APC is in Xigou Village, Pingshun *xian*, Shanxi Province.

19. The Taihang Mountains straddle the boundary between Shanxi and Hebei and partially between Shanxi and Henan. This poor area that Mao talks about is on the southern rim of this ridge, in southeastern Shanxi.

20. See text Oct. 15, 1953, note 2.

21. This refers to the experience at the APC in Xi Zhang Geng Village at Xieyu *xian*, Shanxi Province.

22. Mao is referring to the New Democratic Youth League, see text Feb. 18, 1951, note 8, and text Jun. 30, 1953, source note.

23. This article refers to the experience of Fenyang *xian*, Shanxi Province. The experiences of collectives in water conservation projects was one of the key factors that led to the creation of larger collective units (that is, communes) that could handle such large scale projects better.

24. This article refers to the experience of Lishan *xian* in western Shanxi.

25. This article refers to the experience of Yanggao *xian* in northeast Shanxi, approximately 35 km. northeast of Datong. Daquan Mountain is located on the Nanyang River, 7 km. south of Yanggao.

26. This article refers to the experience in several *xian* in Yanbei District, which is the section of northern Shanxi surrounding Datong. The article's contents cited deal with corruption especially in Daren *xian*, Shanyin *xian* (particularly with the leader of the APC at Beiluozhuang in Shanyin, Luo Shoufan), and Guangling *xian*.

27. Originally referring to a military-tribal distinction, the *qi* (banner) is a tribal-oriented administrative division of the Mongolian minority nationality and the region that they inhabit. This article refers to the experience of what was, until July 1955, The Ongniot "banner" Mongolian Autonomous Region in Jehol Province. In a geographical rearrangement announced in July 1955, the province of Jehol was officially abolished and the areas originally within its boundaries were later divided among and assimilated by the Inner Mongolia Autonomous Region, Liaoning Province and Hebei Province. Consequently, the Ongniot banner also lost its original status as a

separate autonomous region. However, at the time this article and Mao's comment on it were written, these shifts had not yet been consolidated.

28. See text Oct. 15, 1953, note 12.

29. This refers to Yuanda APC in Dongyancun *xiang*, in the suburbs of Beijing Municipality.

30. Baipanyao *xiang* is situated in the suburbs of Beijing Municipality, and, the article tells us, is primarily a green vegetable producing village. Two APC's were formed here in winter-spring, 1952-53.

31. This cooperative is situated in the hilly region in the western suburbs of Beijing Municipality, where a joint production planning task force was formed in autumn 1954.

32. This refers to Hongxing Collective Farm (*jiti nongzhuang*), a large APC in the southeastern corner of Nanwan District of Beijing Municipality, and includes three *xian* (Yinghai, Yile, Sihai) and more than thirty other smaller villages.

33. Zhangguozhuang *xiang* is in Fengtai District of Beijing Municipality.

34. This article refers to the experience of an APC located at Sanluju *xiang* in Fengtai District of Beijing Municipality.

35. In the early stages of cooperativization, funds were necessary for the accumulation and preparation of means of production such as seeds, fertilizer, etc., and for the "buying over" of draft animals and farm implements previously owned by individuals. Such funds were collected in the form of shares from those peasants who joined the cooperatives. In many cases these were also accounted for as part of the price of animals and tools sold by these peasants to the cooperatives. Many poor peasants, however, were unable to come up with their share of the funds and, therefore, were initially barred from or hesitant to join the cooperatives. The government thereupon established the poor peasant cooperativization loan fund, which provided poor peasants with the necessary funds for the cooperativization of their livelihood. According to *RMSC* (1956), the China People's Bank gave out more than 700 million *rmb* worth of such loans to some 40 million households of poor and lower-middle peasants in that year.

36. This cooperative is located in an eastern suburb of Beijing.

37. This refers to the situation in Wangdingti *cun* in the western suburbs of Tianjin Municipality.

38. This *xiang* is in the eastern suburbs of Tianjin, and the reference is to two cooperatives here, Minsheng APC and Minqiang APC, both established in November 1954.

39. This article refers to the situation in the three villages of Pingfang, Shuangquan, and Wufu in Nahe *xian* in Heilongjiang Province.

40. This refers to Lalin *xian*, Heilongjiang Province.

41. Anguang *xian* is located in northern Jilin Province. The APC here was established in the spring of 1952.

42. See text Oct. 11, 1955(2), note 9.

43. This article refers to the experience of Datun Village in Kouqian District, Rongji *xian*, Jilin Province.

44. This refers to Xiaoguang APC in Jin *xian*, near Jinzhou in southern Liaoning Province, established in February 1954.

45. See note 5.

46. For the definitions of supply and marketing cooperatives and credit cooperatives, see text Oct. 15, 1953, note 11, and text Oct. 11, 1955(1), note 26.

47. This refers to the example of the six villages of Dade, Guanjia, Laihu, Wujiazi, Halagantu, and Fujuchang in Zhangwu *xian*, Liaoning Province.

48. This refers to the experience of Chenjiazhuang APC in No. 3 District, Qufu *xian*, Shandong Province.

49. "*Confucian Analects*, Book XIII, 'Tsu Lu' [Zi Lu]." (*SW*, V, p. 276.) The Chinese term for "mean person" is *xiaoren*, which in the Confucian world-view means a person of petty thoughts and deeds. It is juxtaposed to the *junzi* (often translated as the gentleman or the princely man), which connotes a person of noble thoughts and deeds.

50. Confucius' Temple and Confucius' Grove are both in Qufu *xian*, Shandong Province. The

Grove is in the temple itself and consists of trees that supposedly Confucius planted himself.

51. This refers to the experience of the APC at Louxia Village, Putou *xian*, Qingshan District, Rongcheng *xian*, Shandong Province, established in winter 1952.

52. "V. I. Lenin, 'The Task of the Youth Leagues.'" (*SW*, V, p. 276.) See text Dec. 6, 1955, note 11; see also note 22 here.

53. After cooperativization, within each cooperative, the value of each day of labor contributed by members of the cooperative had to be assessed in order to facilitate the evaluation of work done. The system was known as *ping gong ji fen* (evaluating work and alloting work points). The units of work were known as work points (generally a standard day's work is worth ten work points) and in reality the value of work points in each cooperative had to be different, depending on local conditions, from the value of work points in other places. However, in most cases these were standardized and assigned an average monetary value. Thus, it was often possible that the actual value of work points (based on the net income of the cooperative) came out to be either higher or lower than the assigned estimated value. At this time the work point system was still rather rudimentary in structure. Individuals, households, or labor units were awarded "basic work points" on a completed job. These were accumulated in the unit's account, and deductions could be made for poor work. At year's end, wages were paid accordingly. Later, in the late 1950s, when the transition to people's communes was made, the system became much more elaborate, with such variations as basic work points, bonus work points (for work done above the normal number of hours or days), and subsidy work points. Work points then also became the basis for the distribution of a part of the grain allocated to the individual worker (work point grain, or *gong fen liang*), the other part being *jiben kou liang*, or basic grain ration.

54. This refers to Xinjian APC at Qian Village, Wangjiafang, Fangqian *xiang*, No. 8 District of Junan *xian*, Shandong Province.

55. Fanshen APC in Shihe *xiang*, Tongcheng *xian*, Anhui, was established under the leadership of CPC branch secretaries Zhang Renhuai and Kai Mingyi. For the meaning of the term *fanshen*, see text Feb. 17, 1951, note 6.

56. The article introduces Chen as "a native of Wudian *zhen* [township], Fengyang *xian*, Anhui Province. Fifty-six, poor peasant, family member of a revolutionary martyr, member of the Communist Party. A family of seven, owning 21.5 *mu* of land." He was reputed to have started, beginning in the spring of 1953, over eighty cooperatives, of which he had personal input in fifteen.

57. This refers to the experience of Ge Shiyu APC at Fouhu *xiang*, Oqiao District, Fanchang *xian*, Anhui Province.

58. This refers to the CPC branch at Chengxi *xiang* in Fengyang *xian*, Anhui.

59. The term "spontaneous cooperatives" refers to APC's that were formed by the peasants without prior approval and planning by the leading organs. In some cases, they were not even accorded formal recognition as such by the leading organs in the locality. In others, those that were formed with authorization but that, in the process of formation, demonstrated much greater spontaneous enthusiasm and self-determination on the part of the peasants than anticipated, were ordered by the local authorities to be reorganized. See *Xuexi*, 12 (1955), 13. On the subject of "drastic reduction" or "resolute reduction" mentioned here, see also text July 31, 1955, notes 14 and 18. This article draws on the experience of several *xiang* in Chu *xian*, eastern Anhui.

60. This refers to the Qinghun and Chensi APC's at Luchen *xiang*, Feidong *xian*, Anhui.

61. This refers to Xishu *xiang* in Kunshan *xian*, Jiangsu. Two APC's were established there in the spring of 1954, and by the end of that year there were ten cooperatives there.

62. By *wan jiefang qu* (later liberated area) Mao obviously means *xin jiefang qu* (newly liberated area). See text June 6, 1950(1), note 7.

63. This refers to Yitao *xiang* in Machang District, Muyang *xian*, Jiangsu Province.

64. This refers to the experience of Qianjin APC in Zhaoyang *xiang*, Xinhailian Municipality of Jiangsu Province. Xinhailian Municipality was a new municipality combining the three earlier towns of Xinanzhen, Haizhou, and Lianyungang. Qianjin APC was made up of 578 households.

65. This refers to the experience of the APC at Zhongqian *cun*, Jiangning *xian* of Jiangsu Prov-

ince, which was established in October 1954.

66. The term here, *ding e bao gong,* refers to the allocation of labor contracts by specifying the amount of product to be completed within a certain period of time, based on the determination of a norm with regard to how much and what quality of work can be done on that particular job by an average member of the cooperative in a day, working on a specified area of land, with certain draft animals and farm tools and under certain weather conditions.

67. See note 53.

68. This refers to the experience of No. 1 Qianjin APC in Qianzhou, Jiangsu Province, which was established in 1952.

69. This article refers to the experience of several APC's (of which the first was Guangming APC established in the spring of 1954) in Dengjia *xiang,* Shouchang *xian* of Zhejiang Province.

70. See note 5 and note 56.

71. This article refers to the experience of several APC's in Longnan *xiang* of Yuyao *xian* in eastern Zhejiang.

72. This refers to the experience of Qianhao higher-stage APC in Ankou *xiang,* Jiande *xian,* Zhejiang Province.

73. This term, *duo zhong jingying,* sometimes translated as "multiple undertakings," became a stipulation for the communes' undertaking in the Regulations on the Work of the People's Communes in 1962 (Article 25).

74. This article refers to the experience of the APC's in Xinchuang *xiang,* Pinghu *xian,* Zhejiang. See also text Oct. 15, 1953, note 15.

75. This refers to the experience of Xinfu and Sinkang APC's at Louxia *xiang,* Fuan *xian,* Fujian Province.

76. See text Feb. 17, 1951, note 4.

77. See text July 31, 1955, note 14.

78. This article refers to the experience of Xianfeng APC, Longfeng *xiang,* Huaan *xian,* Fujian.

79. "The four comparisons were to compare and see which was better: (1) the co-operative, the mutual-aid team, or peasants working on their own; (2) socialism or capitalism; (3) a system with exploitation or a system without exploitation, and (4) personal enrichment or prosperity for all. The five calculations referred to the calculations of the superiority of the co-operative with respect to (1) coping with natural disasters, (2) increasing earnings through the promotion of side-lines, (3) increasing work-points for arousing enthusiasm for labour, (4) increasing production as a result of mutually beneficial co-operation by the poor and middle peasants, and (5) overcoming difficulties in production and in livelihood." (*SW,* V, p. 276.)

80. Mao uses the term *da maozi,* which literally translates as "big hats" and which is a common expression in the PRC for forcing a label, usually a political category, on people. A common variation is *kou maozi* (slapping a hat on), and a related term is *zai maozi* (taking off the hat). See text Dec. 8, 1956, note 33. For a specific reference to this "label" mentioned here, see text Mar. 5, 1955.

81. This article refers to the experience of APC's in Xinjing District, a suburb of Shanghai Municipality, and especially to the conditions in Hongnan *xiang* there, contrasting the enthusiasm of the poor peasants and the hesitation of the cadres. For the usage of the term "wind" here, see text Nov. 4, 1953, note 3.

82. Mao is referring, we think, to the Rural Work Conference, held May 1955, the Second Session of the First NPC held July 5-30, 1955, and the Sixth Plenum of the Seventh Central Committee of the CPC, held October 4-11, 1955. See K. Lieberthal (1976), pp. 70-74. A conference of Party secretaries from provincial, municipal, and autonomous region Party committees was also convened on July 31-August 1, 1955, and in fact dealt more specifically with the issue of agricultural cooperativization. However, it was at the meeting of the NPC that the basic principles and the lines of the debate that Mao described were set forth.

83. This is situated at Tangnan *xiang,* Dachang District, in the suburbs of Shanghai Municipality.

84. This refers to the experience of Taixing *xiang* in Wusong District, a northern suburb of

Shanghai Municipality. Here, of 627 agricultural households, there were 447 households from which a total of 529 people were drawn into industrial occupations in the various industrial (primarily steel and textiles) enterprises in Shanghai. Therefore the "workers" in the title connote industrial workers.

85. This refers to a village in the western suburbs of Shanghai Municipality.

86. C. Bettleheim (1978), provides an in-depth analysis of the Soviet experience with respect to surplus labor power in the countryside.

87. This refers to an APC in Diantai *xiang* of Zhenru District, which is a suburb of Shanghai Municipality. This APC was formed in October 1953, and by the end of 1954 it had become a higher-stage APC.

88. This refers to Fuli APC in Nancuizhuang in Anyang *xian*, Henan Province.

89. Mao is extrapolating from a common Henanese saying that "If a chicken feather flies up to heaven, it must be borne on the wind."

90. Mao is using the famous term *fanshen;* see note 55, this document.

91. This refers to the experience of Dalizhuang *xiang*, Jia *xian*, Henan.

92. See text Feb. 18, 1951, note 2.

93. The earlier drawing of class distinctions was done during the period of the land reform. See text Mar. 12, 1950, note 1, and text Feb. 18, 1951, note 2.

94. Third-class cooperatives (*san deng she* or *san lei she*) refers to cooperatives where "the Party leadership was weak and no leading core was formed; where political consciousness was not high and capitalist thinking prevailed; where cadres did not have a democratic style; and where illegal landlords, rich peasants and counterrevolutionary elements were rampant. Because production was not carried out properly and management was run in a disorderly manner, output in some of these cooperatives decreased seriously." *RMRB* (Jan. 5, 1958), quoted in Y. Lau (1977), p. 342. See also text July 31, 1955, note 16.

95. The term Mao used here is *qing huang bu jie* (hiatus between green and yellow), which means a time of shortage of supply, either of products or of energy. See text May 8, 1950, note 2.

96. This refers to Yi Ruisheng APC, which, the article claimed, was one of the most renowned of the APC's in Jiangxi and was located in Hujiafang Village, Nianfeng *xiang*, 50 *li* east of the seat of Pingxian *xian*, Jiangxi Province.

97. This refers to Luoxian APC, Nanqi *xiang*, Nanchang *xian*, Jiangxi Province.

98. See text June 6, 1950(1), note 7.

99. *Tujidui*, or "shock brigade," comes from the military term "*tuji*," meaning "surprise attack." This means to concentrate all forces and, in a rather short period of time, solve relatively more urgent problems. For instance, during harvest seasons, shock teams were established to launch a sudden onslaught in procurement of farm crops. See Y. Lau (1977), p. 433.

100. This *xiang* is located south of Yangjiang *xian*, Guangdong Province.

101. This APC is in Malu *xiang*, Cenqi *xian*, Guangxi Province.

102. Mutual aid teams were originally divided into three categories: (1) temporary, seasonal small mutual aid teams; (2) year-round, fixed mutual aid teams, with 10-30 households, and (3) lower-stage agricultural producers' cooperatives. In the year-round mutual aid teams, work points systems were sometimes employed, sideline production was sometimes carried out, simple production plans and a simple division of labor in technical work were sometimes implemented. Some mutual aid teams even gradually established public ownership over some farm implements and draft animals and accumulated a small amount of public funds. See Y. Lau (1977), p. 165. See also text Oct. 15, 1953, note 2.

103. This slogan was popularized at this time; see the first editorial notes in this document, relating to the article "With the Party Secretary Taking Part, the Entire Party Should Be Engaged in Running Cooperatives."

104. In order to carry out a specific objective, the Party committees, or higher-level Party organizations, would choose a number of cadres to form leadership groups and transfer these groups to lower level-units and localities to expedite and lead the projects or movements to be carried out there. After the particular tasks were completed, these groups, or work teams, would be disbanded, and its members would return to their original units or be assigned new tasks. See Y. Lau

(1977), p. 140.

105. This refers to the example of three APC's (Shenguang APC, Nongyuan APC, and Yangjia-zai APC) in Guangda *xiang*, Suiyang *xian*, Guizhou Province.

106. The term here is *dang bagu*, or "Party eight-legged essays." This alludes to the prescribed form of writing adopted in the imperial examination system from the Ming dynasty down to the nineteenth century. In this form of writing, the essays are divided up into eight standard parts, or "legs": thus the argumentation and extrapolation of the subject became extremely rigid and pre-dictable. It became a major target of criticism in the 1920s during the New Culture Movement. In applying this term to writing generated and circulated within the CPC, Mao is referring not only to the form but also to the substance of the writing, in that such a criticism may apply wherever creativity of thought and expression is replaced by a stereotypical adherence to dogma. Mao began attacking "stereotyped Party writing" during the CPC rectification campaign at Yanan in 1942, and particularly in his three essays "Reform Our Study," "Rectify the Party's Work Style," and "Oppose Stereotyped Party Writing." See *SW*, III, pp. 17-26, 35-68.

107. This refers to the experience of Pingbao APC, Panjiang *xiang*, Guiding *xian*, Guizhou Province.

108. This refers to the experience of No. 1 APC, Maanshan *xiang*, Zhenning *xian*, Guizhou Province.

109. This refers to Dongsheng APC, Guomu *xiang*, Xichou *xian*, Yunnan.

110. This refers to the experience of some 40 APC's in Ma Longquan *xian*, Yunnan Province.

111. This refers to Fumin *xian* in Yunnan Province, some 25 km. northwest of Kunming.

112. The locality mentioned here is named after Wang Mang, an historical figure who seized the throne of the Han dynasty emperor and for a brief period of 15 years established the Xin dynasty (9-25 A.D.) He was traditionally vilified in Chinese history but is considered a progressive ruler in the revisionist historiography of the PRC.

113. This is located in central Shaanxi Province, near Xian Municipality. Xian is the modern name of what was originally called Changan, which was a major capital city of China in Tang and Song times.

114. This refers to the experience of No. 1 APC of Shang Village, Guodu District of Chang-an *xian*, Shaanxi, and that of nearby Yang Village.

115. This story is from Liu Xiang's *Xinxu: Zashi* (early Han dynasty), which tells of a man by the name of Ye Zigao who loved the image of dragons and, wherever he could, carved or painted dragons in his house. This moved the dragon in the heavens to pay him a visit, whereupon Ye was frightened out of his wits and fled.

116. Gaolan *xian*, also known as Shidongsi, is located in central Gansu, 30 km. north of Lan-zhou.

117. The Second Five-Year Plan was projected, at this time, to cover the years 1958-1962.

118. This refers to Xiatan APC, Xunhua *xian*, Qinghai Province.

119. This article refers to the experience of Semen District of Suofu *xian*, Xinjiang Province.

BIBLIOGRAPHY

This bibliography lists material used in this volume of Mao Zedong's works in translation. It is divided into two sections. The first section includes materials which have been used as primary sources, i.e., the sources of the texts we have used in this volume for our translation, as well as the other sources cited in the "Other Chinese Text(s)" and "Available English Translation(s)" segments of the source notes at the front of each document in this volume. This first section is itself divided into two parts: books and serials. The second section consists of secondary references that appear in our annotations and commentaries.

The reader is asked to take note of two things:

☐ **a.** The initial line for each entry in this bibliography corresponds to the way in which the source has been cited in the volume. This is a presentation of the title of the source in full, or, more often, an arbitrary abbreviation of the title, e.g.,

Buyi for Ding Wang, ed. *Mao Zedong xuanji buyi* (Supplement to the *Selected Works of Mao Tse-tung);*

and:

RMRB for *Renmin ribao;*

or

the name of the author followed by the date (year) of the publication of the material, e.g.,

J. Chen (1969) for Chen, Jerome, *Mao.*

☐ **b.** Where a source is listed in section I, it is not repeated in section II, even if it also serves, in these volumes, as a reference source for our annotations.

When the notation: (Red Guard publication) follows an entry in this bibliography, it means that the cited work is a publication of one of many Red Guard groups during the Cultural Revolution period. In some, but not all of these cases, the source provides us with information concerning the original editor/compiler, publisher and/or publishing date of the item, and in such cases this information is presented in this bibliography. Where such information is not available, the notations "N.p." or "N.d." or both will be used. These publications have been collected and published in *Red Guard Publications*, Washington, D.C.: Center for Chinese Research Materials, 20 vols., 1975; Supplement, 8 vols., 1980. This publication information will not be repeated for each of these entries in this bibliography. The reader should also note that a valuable directory of these Red Guard publications is provided in: Lee,

Hong Yung, *A Research Guide to Red Guard Publications, 1966-1969*, Armonk, NY: M. E. Sharpe, 1987.

Some collections of documents on the People's Republic of China have been consulted but not cited in our sources or in this bibliography, notably, for instance, Harold Hinton, ed., *The People's Republic of China, 1949-1979: A Documentary Survey*, 5 volumes, Wilmington, DE: Scholarly Resources, Inc, 1980.

Details concerning United States government documents cited in this bibliography – translations of Chinese documents made by information agencies of the U.S. government, for instance – and listed herein under JPRS (Joint Publications Research Service) and FBIS (Foreign Broadcast Information Service) and various departments of the United States federal government can be found under the appropriate entry, as indicated in this bibliography, in U.S. Superintendent of Documents, *Monthly Catalog of U.S. Government Publications*, Washington, D.C.: United States Government Printing Office. The publication information of this catalog is not repeated under the various relevant entries in this bibliography.

I. PRIMARY SOURCES

a. Books

Buyi

Ding, Wang, ed. *Mao Zedong xuanji buyi* (Supplement to the *Selected Works of Mao Tse-tung*), vol. 3 (1949-1959). Hong Kong: Mingbao Monthly Press, 1971.

CCSD

Jacobs, Dan, and Hans Baerwald, eds. *Chinese Communism, Selected Documents*. New York: Harper and Row, 1963.

J. Chen (1967)

Chen, Jerome. *Mao and the Chinese Revolution*. London: Oxford University Press, 1965.

J. Chen (1967)

Chen, Jerome. *Mao and the Chinese Revolution*. New York: Oxford University Press, 1967.

J. Chen (1969)

Chen, Jerome. *Mao*. Englewood Cliffs, NJ: Prentice Hall, 1969.

J. Chen (1970)

Chen, Jerome, ed. *Mao Papers: Anthology and Bibliography*. London: Oxford University Press, 1970.

Dahai hangxing

Dahai hangxing kao tuoshou (When Sailing on the High Seas, One Needs to Rely on the Helmsman). N.p.: N.d. (Red Guard publication.)

Dang de jianshe

Zhongguo renmin jiefangjun zong zhengzhi bu (The General Political Department of the Chinese People's Liberation Army). *Mao zhuxi lun dang de jianshe* (Chairman Mao on Party-building). N.p.: 1968.

K. Fan (1972)

Fan, K. *Mao Tse-tung and Lin Piao: Post-Revolutionary Writings*. Garden City, NY: Doubleday, 1972.

Gaizao wenji
   Nongye shehui zhuyi gaizao wenji (Collection of Essays on the Socialist Transformation of Agriculture). 3 volumes. Beijing: Caizheng jingji chubanshe, 1965.

Gaochao
   Zhongguo gongchan dang zhongyang bangong shi (General Office of the Central
   Committee of the Communist Party of China), ed. *Zhongguo nongcun de shehui
   zhuyi gaochao* (Upsurge of Socialism in China's Countryside). 3 volumes. Beijing:
   Renmin chubanshe, 1956.

Guanyu nongye hezuohua wenti
   Mao, Zedong. *Guanyu nongye hezuohua wenti* (On the Question of the Cooperativization of Agriculture). Beijing: Renmin chubanshe, 1955.

Hu Feng cailiao
   The Editorial Board of *Renmin ribao* (People's Daily), ed. *Guanyu Hu Feng fan
   geming jituan de cailiao* (Material On Hu Feng's Counterrevolutionary Clique).
   Beijing: Renmin chubanshe, June 1955.

Huiyi Mao zhuxi
   Huiyi Mao zhuxi (Memories of Chairman Mao). Beijing: Renmin wenxue, 1977.

JPRS, *Miscellany,* I and II
   Joint Publications Research Service. *Miscellany of Mao Tse-tung Thought (1949-
   1968), Parts I and II* (JPRS, 61269-1; 61269-2). Arlington, VA: February 1974.

JPRS, 69195
   Joint Publications Research Service. *Translations on People's Republic of China.*
   No. 382. (JPRS no. 69195.) Arlington, VA: October 1977. (See under entry no.
   77-14105, U.S. Superintendent of Documents, Monthly Catalog of U.S. Government Publications, October 1977.)

Jiaoyu geming
   Mao zhuxi lun jiaoyu geming (Chairman Mao on the Revolution in Education). Beijing: Renmin chubanshe, 1967.

Jiaoyu yulu
   Hongdaihui zhandou bu dou-pi-gai bangongshi zhongxuan zu (Central Propaganda
   Group, Office of Struggle, Criticism and Reform, Combat Department, Red Guard
   Congress). *Mao zhuxi jiaoyu yulu* (Chairman Mao's Sayings on Education). N.p.:
   July 1967. (Red Guard publication.)

Kyoto daigaku (1980)
   Nakamura, Kimiyoshi, et al., eds. *Mo Takuto chosaku nempyo* (Chronology of the
   Writings of Mao Zedong). 2 volumes. Kyoto: Kyoto daigaku jimbun kagaku ken-
   kyujo (Institute of Humanistic Sciences, Kyoto University), 1980-81.

Lun qingnian
   Mao Zedong tongzhi lun qingnian he qingnian gongzuo (Comrade Mao Zedong on
   Young People and the Work Among Young People). Beijing: Zhongguo qingnian,
   1961.

Mao guanhuai
   Mao zhuxi guanhuai zuo wuomen (Chairman Mao Is Concerned about Us). Shanghai: Wenhua, 1958.

Mao gushi
   Mao zhuxi de gushi (Stories of Chairman Mao). Hong Kong: Zhaoyang chubanshe,

vol. 1, 1976; vol. 2, 1977.

Mao Hubei

Mao zhuxi zai Hubei (Chairman Mao in Hubei Province). Wuhan: Hubei renmin chubanshe, 1958.

Mao jingwei

The Editorial Board of *Jiefang jun bao* (Liberation Army Daily), ed. *Mao zhuxi guanhuai jingwei zhanshi xue wenhua* (Chairman Mao Is Concerned About Security Guards Learning to Become Literate). Beijing: Jiefang jun wenyi she, July 1960.

Mao liang

Mao zhuxi lun dang nei liang tiao luxian douzheng (Chairman Mao on the Two-line Struggle within the Party). N.p.: 1969.

Mao qunzhong

Mao zhuxi zai qunzhong zhong (Chairman Mao Among the Masses). Beijing: Renmin chubanshe, 1958.

Mao shici

Mao, Zedong, *Mao zhuxi shici sanshiqi shou* (Thirty-seven Poems by Chairman Mao). Second edition. Beijing: Wenwu chubanshe, April 1964.

Mao zai xinzhong

Mao zhuxi yongyuan huo zai wuomen xinzhong (Chairman Mao Will Live Forever in Our Hearts). Beijing: Renmin wenxue, 1977.

Mao Zedong lun caizheng

Zhongguo kexue yuan jingji yanjiusuo caijing muyi yanjiu zu (Financial and Commerce Studies Group, the Institute of Economic Studies, the Chinese Academy of Sciences). *Mao Zedong lun caizheng* (Mao Zedong on Finance). Beijing: Caizheng chubanshe, 1958.

Poems

Wong, Man, trans. and ed. *Poems of Mao Tse-tung*. Hong Kong: Eastern Horizon Press, 1966.

Poems of Mao Tse-tung

Barnstone, Willis, trans. and ed. *The Poems of Mao Tse-tung*. London: Harper and Row, 1972.

L. Pye (1976)

Pye, Lucian. *Mao Tse-tung: The Man in the Leader*. New York: Basic Books, 1976.

Rendai hui di yi ci

Zhonghua renmin gonghe guo di yi jie quanguo renmin daibiao da hui di yi ci huiyi wenjian (Documents of the First Session of the National People's Congress of the People's Republic of China). Beijing: Renmin chubanshe, 1955.

SR

Mao, Zedong. *Selected Readings from the Works of Mao Zedong*. Beijing: Foreign Languages Press, 1971.

SW, I-V

Mao, Zedong. *Selected Works of Mao Tse-tung*. Beijing: Foreign Languages Press, vols. I-IV, 1967; vol. V, 1977.

S. Schram (1969)

Schram, Stuart R. *The Political Thought of Mao Tse-tung*. New York: Praeger, 1969.

S. Schram (1974)
Schram, Stuart R., ed. *Chairman Mao Talks to the People: Talks and Letters, 1956-1971*. New York: Pantheon Books, 1974.

P. Seybolt (1973)
Seybolt, Peter J. *Revolutionary Education in China: Documents and Commentary*. White Plains, NY: International Arts and Sciences Press, 1973.

Shengping ziliao
Huang, Yuchuan, ed. *Mao Zedong shengping ziliao jianbian* (A Brief Compilation of Materials on the Life of Mao Zedong). Hong Kong: Union Research Institute, 1970.

Shici
Mao, Zedong. *Mao zhuxi shici* (The Poems of Chairman Mao). Beijing: Renmin wenxue chubanshe, 1976.

Shuxin
Mao, Zedong. *Mao Zedong shuxin xuanji* (Selections from Mao Zedong's Letters). Beijing: Renmin chubanshe, 1983.

Socialist Upsurge
The General Office of the Central Committee of the Communist Party of China. *Socialist Upsurge in China's Countryside*. Beijing: Foreign Languages Press, 1978.

URI (1976)
Union Research Institute, *Unselected Works of Mao Tse-tung*. Hong Kong: Union Press, 1976.

Wansui (n.d.)
Mao Zedong sixiang wansui (Long Live Mao Zedong Thought). N.p.: N.d. (Red Guard publication.)

Wansui (n.d. 2)
Mao Zedong sixiang wansui (Long Live Mao Zedong Thought). N.p.: N.d. 411 pp. (Red Guard publication).

Wansui (1967a)
Mao Zedong sixiang wansui (Long Live Mao Zedong Thought). N.p.: 1967, 280 pp. (Red Guard publication.)

Wansui (1967b)
Mao Zedong sixiang wansui (Long Live Mao Zedong Thought). N.p.: April 1967, 46 pp. (Red Guard publication.)

Wansui (1967c)
Mao Zedong sixiang wansui (Long Live Mao Zedong Thought). N.p.: April 1967, 38 pp. (Red Guard publication.)

Wansui (1967d)
Mao Zedong sixiang wansui (Long Live Mao Zedong Thought). Beijing: 1967. (Red Guard publication.) (We have only one page of this source; see explanation on p. 378 of this volume.

Wansui (1969)
Mao Zedong sixiang wansui (Long Live Mao Zedong Thought). N.p.: 1969. (Red Guard publication.)

Wenge wenjian
Zhonggong wenhua da geming zhongyao wenjian huibian (A Compilation of Major Documents on the Great Cultural Revolution in Communist China). Taipei: Zhonggong yanjiu zazhi she, 1973.

Wenge wenxuan

Zhonggong zhongyang guanyu wuchan jieji wenhua da geming wenjian xuanbian (Selections from Documents of the Central Committee of the Communist Party of China on the Great Proletarian Cultural Revolution). Yunnan: Department of Education. April 1967.

Wenyi yulu

Shanghai xiju xueyuan "geming lou" chuban xiaozu (Editorial Group of "Geming lou," Shanghai Institute for Operatic Studies). *Mao zhuxi lun wenyi yulu* (The Sayings of Chairman Mao on Literature and Art). Shanghai: N.d. (Red Guard publication.)

Wuge wenjian

Mao zhuxi guanyu wenxue yishu de wuge wenjian (Five Documents by Chairman Mao on Literature and Art). Hong Kong: Sanlian shudian, 1967.

Xuandu A, or *Xuandu* (1965 a)

Mao, Zedong. *Mao Zedong zhuzuo xuandu, jia zhong ben* (Selected Readings from the Writings of Mao Zedong, A). Beijing: Renmin chubanshe, 1965.

Xuandu B. or *Xuandu* (1965 b)

Mao, Zedong. *Mao Zedong zhuzuo xuandu, yi zhong ben* (Selected Readings from the Writings of Mao Zedong, B). Beijing: Renmin chubanshe, 1965.

Xuanji, I-V

Mao, Zedong. *Mao Zedong xuanji* (Selected Works of Mao Zedong). Beijing: Renmin, vols. I-IV, 1969; vol. V, 1977.

Xuexi wenjian

Xuexi wenjian (Documents for Study). Reprints of articles from *Renmin ribao* (People's Daily) and *Xinhua yuebao* (New China Monthly). N.p.: N.d. (Red Guard publication.)

Xuexi wenxuan (1967)

Xuexi wenxuan (Selected Writings for Studying). N.p.: 1967, 415 pp. (Red Guard publication.)

Yijiu wusi nian guojia yusuan

Jingji ziliao bianji weiyuanhui (Editorial Committee for Economic Material). *Yijiu wusi nian guojia yusuan* (The National Budget for 1954). Beijing: Caizheng jingji chubanshe, 1954.

Yulu

Zhongguo renmin jiefang jun zong zhengzhi bu (General Political Department of the Chinese People's Liberation Army), ed. *Mao zhuxi yulu* (The Sayings of Chairman Mao). Guangdong: Xinhua yinshuasuo, 1967.

Yulu (1969)

Mao zhuxi yulu (Sayings of Chairman Mao). Beijing: General Political Department of the People's Liberation Army of the People's Republic of China, 1969.

Zhengxie di si ci

Zhongguo renmin zhengzhi xieshang huiyi di yi jie quanguo weiyuanhui di si ci huiyi wenjian (Documents of the Fourth Session of the First National Committee of the Chinese People's Political Consultative Conference). Beijing: Renmin chubanshe, 1953.

Zhengxie er ci
   Zhongguo renmin zhengzhi xieshang huiyi di yi jie quanguo weiyuanhui di er ci huiyi (The Second Session of the First National Committee of the Chinese People's Political Consultative Conference). Beijing: Xinhua, 1950.

Zhengxie jiniankan
   Zhongguo renmin zhengzhi xieshang huiyi di yi jie quanti huiyi jiniankan (Commemorative Issue of the First Plenary Session of the Chinese People's Political Consultative Conference). Beijing: Xinhua, 1950.

Zhengxie san ci
   Zhongguo renmin zhengzhi xieshang huiyi di yi jie quanguo weiyuanhui di san ci huiyi wenjian (Documents of the Third Session of the First National Committee of the Chinese People's Political Consultative Conference). Beijing: Renmin chubanshe, 1951.

Ziliao xuanbian
   Ziliao xuanbian (Selected Compilation of Materials). N.p.: Jan. 1967. (Red Guard publication.)

Zui weida de youyi
   Mao, Zedong. *Zui weida de youyi* (The Greatest Friendship). Beijing: Renmin chubanshe, 1953.

b. Serials (Newspapers, Periodicals, News Services)

Asahi Evening News
   Asahi Evening News. Daily, Tokyo: Asahi Shimbun.

BR
   Beijing Review. Weekly, Beijing. (Formerly *PR* [*Peking Review*].)

CB
   Current Background. Weekly (approx.), Hong Kong.

CDSP
   Current Digest of Soviet Press. Biweekly, New York.

CLG
   Chinese Law and Government. Quarterly. Armonk, NY (formerly White Plains, NY).

CR
   China Reconstructs. Monthly, Beijing.

Changjiang ribao
   Changjiang ribao (Yangtze River Daily). Hankou.

Chinese Sociology and Anthropology
   Chinese Sociology and Anthropology. Quarterly, Armonk, NY (formerly White Plains, NY).

Dagong bao
   Dagong bao (Dagong Daily). Shanghai.

Dongfang hong
   Dongfang hong (The East Is Red). N.p.: N.d. (Red Guard publication.)

FBIS, *Daily Report*
   Foreign Broadcast Information Service. *Daily Report, Foreign Radio Broadcasts.* Washington, D.C.

GMRB
   Guangming ribao (Guangming Daily). Beijing.

Gongren ribao
   Gongren ribao (Worker's Daily). Beijing.

HNA, *Daily News Release*
   Hsinhua News Agency, *Daily News Release.* Hong Kong.

HQ
   Hongqi (Red Flag). Semimonthly, Beijing.

Henan ribao
   Henan ribao (Henan Daily). Zhengzhou.

Issues and Studies
   Issues and Studies. Monthly, Taipei: Institute of International Relations.

JFJB
   Jiefang jun bao (Liberation Army Daily). Beijing.

Jiefang jun huabao
   Jiefang jun huabao (Liberation Army Pictorial). Semimonthly, Beijing.

Jiefang jun wenyi
   Jiefang jun wenyi (Literature and Arts in the People's Liberation Army). Monthly, Beijing.

Jiefang ribao
   Jiefang ribao (Liberation Daily). Shanghai.

Jinbu ribao
   Jinbu ribao (Progress Daily). Tianjin.

Keji geming (A)
   Hong dai hui zhongguo keda dongfang hong gongshe chedi pipan Liu, Deng, Tao, lianluo zhan keji pigai zu (Science and Technology Criticism and Reform Group, Liaison Station for the Thorough Criticism of Liu Shaoqi, Deng Xiaoping and Tao Zhu, East Is Red Commune at Chinese Science University, Red Guard Congress), ed. *Keji geming* (Revolution in Science and Technology), no. 1. Mao Zhuxi guanyu keji gongzuo de zhishi (Chairman Mao's Directives on the Work in Science and Technology). N.p.: July 1967. (Red Guard publication.)

Keji geming (B)
   Shoudu keji jie geming zaofanpai pipan Liu, Deng, lianluo zhan (Criticize Liu Shaoqi and Deng Xiaoping Station, Revolutionary Rebel Faction of the Science and Technology Circles at the Capital), ed. *Keji geming* (Revolution in Science and Technology), no. 1. N.p. (Beijing?): July 28, 1967. (Red Guard publication.)

Kexue geming
   Zhongguo kexue yuan geming weiyuan hui kexue geming bianzhi bu (Editorial Board of *Revolution in the Sciences*, Chinese Academy of Sciences), ed. *Kexue geming* (Revolution in the Sciences), no. 4. N.p.: September 15, 1967. (Red Guard publication.)

Liang Chen anjian
 Liang Chen anjian zhuankan (Special Issue on the Cases of the Two Chen's), no. 4.
 N.p.: 1968. (Red Guard publication.)

Luxing jia
 Luxing jia (Traveler). Monthly, Beijing. Formerly known as *Luxing zazhi* (Travel
 Magazine).

Meishu fenglei
 Meishu fenglei (Wind and Thunder in the Fine Arts), 3 (August 1967). N.p.: (Red
 Guard publication.)

NCNA, *Daily Bulletin*
 New China News Agency. *Daily Bulletin*. London.

NCNA, *Weekly Bulletin*
 New China News Agency. *Weekly Bulletin*. London.

NCNA, *Supplement*
 New China News Agency. *Supplement*. Irregular publication, London.

PC
 People's China. Semimonthly, Beijing.

PR
 Peking Review. Weekly. Beijing. (Later *BR* [*Beijing Review*].)

Pi Tan zhanbao
 Pi Tan zhanbao (Combat Bulletin for the Criticism of Tan Zhenlin). N.p.: N.d. (Red
 Guard publication.)

Quanwudi
 Quanwudi (Invincible). 2 (February 5, 1967), and 7 (May 4, 1967). N.p. (Red
 Guard publication.)

RMSC
 Renmin shouce (People's Handbook). Annual, Shanghai.

Renmin wenxue
 Renmin wenxue (People's Literature). Monthly, Beijing.

RMRB
 Renmin ribao (People's Daily). Beijing.

SCMM
 Selections from China Mainland Magazines. Weekly, Hong Kong.

SCMP
 Survey of Chinese Mainland Press. Daily (approx.), Hong Kong.

Shijie zhishi
 Shijie zhishi (World Knowledge). Semimonthly, Shanghai-Beijing.

Tianjin ribao
 Tianjin ribao (Tianjin Daily). Tianjin.

Tiyu bao
 Tiyu bao (Sports). Triweekly, Beijing.

Wenhui bao
 Wenhui bao (Literary Compendium Daily). Shanghai.

Wenyi bao
  Wenyi bao (Literary Gazette). Semimonthly, Beijing.

Wenyi hongqi
  Wenyi hongqi (Red Flag in Literature and Art), 5 (May 30, 1967). N.p. (Red Guard publication.)

XHBYK
  Xinhua banyuekan (New China Semimonthly). Beijing.

XHYB
  Xinhua yuebao (New China Monthly). Beijing.

Xian ribao
  Xian ribao (Xian Daily). Xian.

Xin guancha
  Xin guancha (New Observation). Semimonthly, Beijing.

Xin jianshe
  Xin jianshe (New Construction). Semimonthly to October 1950; monthly thereafter, Beijing.

Xin tiyu
  Xin tiyu (New Physical Culture). N.p.: N.d. (Red Guard publication.)

Xinwen zhanbao
  Xinwen zhanbao (Combat Bulletin in Journalism). N.p.: May 23, 1967. (Red Guard publication.)

ZFYJ
  Zhengfa yanjiu (Studies in Government and Law). Beijing: Zhongguo zhengzhi falu xuehui (Chinese Association of Government and Legal Studies) and Institute for Legal Studies, Chinese Academy of Sciences. Quarterly, Beijing.

Zhongguo gongren
  Zhongguo gongren (China's Workers). Semimonthly, Beijing.

Zhongguo qingnian
  Zhongguo qingnian (China Youth). Semimonthly, Beijing.

Zhongguo qingnian bao
  Zhongguo qingnian bao (China Youth Daily). Issued thrice weekly through 1955, daily (except Mondays) thereafter, Beijing.

Zhongguo yuwen
  Zhongguo yuwen (Chinese Language). Monthly, Beijing.

II. REFERENCE SOURCES

G. Alitto (1979)
  Alitto, Guy. *The Last Confucian: Liang Shu-ming and the Chinese Dilemma of Modernity*. Berkeley, CA: University of California Press, 1979.

S. Andors (1977)
  Andors, Stephen. *China's Industrial Revolution: Politics, Planning and Management, 1949 to the Present*. New York: Pantheon, 1977.

R. Baum and F. Teiwes (1968)
  Baum, Richard, and Frederick C. Teiwes. *Ssu-ch'ing: The Socialist Education Movement of 1962-1966*. University of California Center for Chinese Studies Research Monographs, no. 2. Berkeley, CA: University of California Press, 1968.

C. R. Bawden (1968)
Bawden, Charles R. *The Modern History of Mongolia*. New York-Washington: Praeger, 1968.

C. Bettelheim (1976) (1978)
Bettelheim, Charles. *Class Struggle in the USSR*. New York: Monthly Review Press, vol. 1, 1976; vol. 2, 1978.

G. Bocca (1973)
Bocca, Giorgio. *Palmiro Togliatti*. Rome-Bari: Laterza, 1973.

H. Boorman et al., eds. I-IV (1967), (1968), (1970), (1971)
Boorman, Howard, et al., eds. *Biographical Dictionary of Republican China*, vol. 1 (1967), vol. 2 (1968), vol. 3 (1970), vol. 4 (1971). New York and London: Columbia University Press, 1967, 1968, 1970, 1971.

R. Bowie and J. Fairbank, eds. (1962)
Bowie, Robert, and John King Fairbank, eds. *Communist China, 1955-1959: Policy Documents with Analysis*. Cambridge, MA: Harvard University Press (Center for International Affairs Series), 1962.

Z. Brzezinski (1969)
Brzezinski, Zbigniew K. *The Soviet Bloc: Unity and Conflict* (revised and enlarged edition). Cambridge, MA: Harvard University Press, 1969.

R. Butow (1961)
Butow, Robert. *Tojo and the Coming of the War*. Princeton, NJ: Princeton University Press, 1961.

Kang Chao (1970)
Chao, Kang. *Agricultural Production in Communist China, 1949-1965*. Madison, WI: University of Wisconsin Press, 1970.

K. Chao (1960)
Chao, Kuo-chun. *The Agrarian Policy of the Chinese Communist Party, 1921-1959*. New Delhi: Asia Publishing House, 1960.

J. Chen (1965)
Ch'en, Jerome. *Mao and the Chinese Revolution*. London: Oxford University Press, 1965.

T. Chen (1967)
Chen, Theodore H. E. *The Chinese Communist Regime: Documents and Commentary*. New York: Praeger, 1967.

Chow Tse-tsung (1960)
Chow, Tse-tsung, *The May Fourth Movement: Intellectual Revolution in Modern China*. Stanford, CA: Stanford University Press, 1960.

Ciyu jianshi
Mao Zedong xuanji di wu zhuan ciyu jianshi (Brief Explanations of Terms and References in *Mao Zedong xuanji, volume 5*). Hong Kong: Xin zhishi chubanshe, 1977.

Collected Works of V. I. Lenin
Lenin, Vladimir I. *Collected Works of V. I. Lenin*. London: Lawrence & Wishart, 1960-1970.

B. Compton (1966)

Compton, Boyd, trans. and ed. *Mao's China: Party Reform Documents, 1942-1944.* Seattle: University of Washington Press, 1966.

J. Crowley (1970)

Crowley, James, ed. *Modern East Asia: Essays in Interpretation.* New York: Harcourt, Brace and World, 1970.

J. DeFrancis (1972)

DeFrancis, John. *Nationalism and Language Reform in China.* New York: Octagon Books, 1972. (First edition, 1950.)

J. DeFrancis (1984)

DeFrancis, John. *The Chinese Language: Fact and Fantasy.* Honolulu: University of Hawaii Press, 1984.

J. Dreyer (1976)

Dreyer, June. *China's Forty Millions.* Cambridge, MA: Harvard University Press, 1976.

Faling huibian

Zhongyang renmin zhengfu faling huibian (Compendium of Laws and Ordinances of the Central People's Government of the PRC). Beijing: Renmin chubanshe, 1949.

Far Eastern Economic Review

Far Eastern Economic Review. Weekly, Hong Kong.

First Five-Year Plan

First Five-Year Plan for the Development of the National Economy of the People's Republic of China (1953-1957). Beijing: Foreign Languages Press, 1956.

J. Gray (1974)

Gray, Jack. "Mao Tse-tung's Strategy for the Collectivization of Chinese Agriculture: An Important Phase in the Development of Maoism," in de Kadt, Emmanuel, and Gavin William, *Sociology and Development.* London: Tavistock, 1974.

J. Grieder (1970)

Grieder, Jerome. *Hu Shih and the Chinese Renaissance: Liberalism in the Chinese Revolution, 1917-1937.* Cambridge, MA: Harvard University Press, 1970.

E. Hammond (Jan. 1978)

Hammond, Edward. "Marxism and the Mass Line," in *Modern China,* IV: 1 (January 1978), pp. 3-25.

J. Harrison (1972)

Harrison, James P. *The Long March to Power: A History of the Chinese Communist Party, 1921-1972.* New York: Praeger, 1972.

W. Hinton (1966)

Hinton, William. *Fanshen: A Documentary of Revolution in a Chinese Village.* New York: Monthly Review Press, 1966.

T. L. Hsiao (1961)

Hsiao, Tso-liang. *Power Relations Within the Chinese Communist Movement, 1930-1934: A Study of Documents.* 2 volumes. Seattle: University of Washington Press, 1961.

Hu Shi (1953)
Hu, Shi (Hu Shih). *Hu shi wencun* (The Collected Writings of Hu Shi). 4 volumes. Taipei: Yuandong tushu gongsi, 1953.

A. Hummel, ed. (1943)
Hummel, Arthur, ed. *Eminent Chinese of the Ch'ing Period, 1644-1912*. Washington, D.C.: United States Government Printing Office, 1943.

JPRS *32414*
Joint Publications Research Service. *Translation from Ching-chi yen-chiu [Jingji yanjiu]* (Economic Research) [Economic Studies]. No. 7, 1965. (JPRS no. 32414.) Washington, D.C.: December 1965. (See under no. 851, U.S. Superintendent of Documents, *Monthly Catalog of U.S. Government Publications*, December 1965.)

JPRS *32420*
Joint Publications Research Service. *Translations from Ching-chi yen-chiu [Jingji yanjiu]* (Economic Research) [Economic Studies]. No. 8, 1965. (JPRS no. 32420.) Washington, D.C.: December 1965. (See under no. 851, U.S. Superintendent of Documents, *Monthly Catalog of U.S. Government Publications*, December 1965.)

JPRS *32793*
Joint Publications Research Service. *Translation from Ching-chi yen-chiu [Jingji yanjiu]* (Economic Research) [Economic Studies]. No. 9, 1965. (JPRS no. 32793.) Washington, D.C.: January 1966. (See under no. 852, U.S. Superintendent of Documents, *Monthly Catalog of U.S. Government Publications*, January 1966.)

Jinri shijie
Jinri shijie (Today's World). Weekly, and later monthly, Hong Kong.

Jinrong fagui huibian
Jinrong fagui huibian (Compendium of Fiscal Laws and Regulations, 1949-1952). Beijing: Caizheng jingji chubanshe, 1956.

R. Kagan (1974)
Kagan, Richard C. *The Chinese Trotskyist Movement and Chen Tu-hsiu: Culture, Revolution, and Polity*. Doctoral dissertation. Philadelphia: University of Pennsylvania, 1969. Ann Arbor, MI: University Microfilms, 1970, 1972, 1974.

D. Klein and A. Clark, eds. (1971)
Klein, Donald W., and Anne B. Clark, eds. *Biographic Dictionary of Chinese Communism, 1921-1965*, vols. 1 and 2. Cambridge, MA: Harvard University Press, 1971.

Land Reform Law
The Land Reform Law of the People's Republic of China. Beijing: Foreign Languages Press, 1950.

T. C. Lai (1973)
Lai, T. C. *Ch'i Pai Shih*. Seattle and London: University of Washington Press, 1973.

Y. Lau, ed. (1977)
Lau, Yee-fui, et al., eds. *Glossary of Chinese Political Phrases*. Hong Kong: Union Research Institute, 1977.

J. Legge (1933)
Legge, James, trans. and ed. *Ssu shu* (The Four Books). Shanghai: The Chinese Book Company, 1933.

W. Lehman (1975)

Lehman, Winfred, ed. *Language and Linguistics in the People's Republic of China.* Austin, TX, and London: University of Texas Press, 1975.

J. Leung (1982)

Leung, John. *The Chinese Work-Study Movement: The Social and Political Experience of Chinese Students and Student-Workers in France, 1913-1925.* Unpublished doctoral dissertation. Providence, RI: Brown University, 1982.

R. Levy (1976)

Levy, Richard. *The Political-Economic Thought of Mao Tse-tung, 1917-1965.* Unpublished doctoral dissertation. Ann Arbor, MI: University of Michigan, 1976.

J. Lewis (1963)

Lewis, John W. *Leadership in Communist China.* Ithaca, NY: Cornell University Press, 1963.

T. T. Li (1956)

Li, Tieh-tseng. *The Historical Status of Tibet.* New York: King's Crown Press, Columbia University, 1965.

Li Da (1955)

Li, Da, ed. *Hu Shi fandong sixiang pipan* (Criticism of Hu Shi's Reactionary Thought). Hankou: Hubei renmin chubanshe, 1955.

K. Lieberthal (1976)

Lieberthal, Kenneth G. *A Research Guide to Central Party and Government Meetings in China, 1949-1975.* White Plains, NY: International Arts and Sciences Press, 1976.

Li Liming (1977)

Li Liming (Lee Lip-ming). *Zhongguo xiandai liubai zuojia xiao zhuan* (Sketch Biographies of Modern Chinese Writers). Hong Kong: Po Wen Book Co., 1977.

Liu Shaoqi (1968), (1969)

Liu, Shaoqi. *Collected Works of Liu Shao-ch'i.* Hong Kong: Union Press, vols. 1, 3 (1968), vol. 2 (1969).

R. MacFarquhar (1974)

MacFarquhar, Roderick. *The Origins of the Cultural Revolution: Contradictions Among The People, 1956-1957.* London: Oxford University Press for the Royal Institute of International Affairs, 1974.

Y. Maxon (1957)

Maxon, Yale C. *Control of Japanese Foreign Policy: A Study of Civil-Military Rivalry, 1930-1945.* Berkeley, CA: University of California Press, 1957.

Mo Takuto Shu

Mao, Zedong. *Mo Takuto shu* (*Mao Zedong ji*—Collected Writings of Mao Zedong). Supervised by Takeuchi Minoru. 10 volumes. Tokyo: Hokubosha, 1971-72; revised edition, Sososha, 1983; supplement (10 vols.), 1983-86.

L. Petech (1972)

Petech, Luciano. *China and Tibet in the Early XVIIIth Century: History of the Establishment of Chinese Protectorate In Tibet* (T'oung Pao: Monographie I). Leiden: E. J. Brill, 1972.

J. Prybyla (1970)
Prybyla, Jan S. *The Political Economy of Communist China*. Scranton, PA: International Textbook, 1970.

J. Prybyla (1978)
Prybyla, Jan S. *The Chinese Economy: Problems and Policies*. Columbia, SC: University of South Carolina Press, 1978.

T. Rawski (1980)
Rawski, Thomas. *China's Transition to Industrialism*. Ann Arbor, MI: University of Michigan Press, 1980.

H. E. Richardson (1962)
Richardson, Hugh E. *Tibet and Its History*. London-Toronto-Melbourne: Oxford University Press, 1962.

J. Rue (1966)
Rue, John. *Mao Tse-tung in Opposition, 1927-1935* Stanford, CA: Stanford University Press, 1966.

A. J. K. Sanders (1968)
Sanders, Alan J. K. *The People's Republic of Mongolia: A General Reference Guide*. London-New York: Oxford University Press, 1968.

S. Schram (1967)
Schram, Stuart. *Mao Tse-tung*. Baltimore, MD: Penguin Books, 1967.

S. Schram (1973)
Schram, Stuart R. "The Cultural Revolution in Historical Perspective," in S. Schram, ed. *Authority, Participation and Cultural Change in China: Essays by a European Study Group*. Cambridge: Cambridge University Press, 1973.

F. Schurmann (1968)
Schurmann, Franz. *Ideology and Organization in Communist China* (Second edition, enlarged). Berkeley-Los Angeles-London: University of California Press, 1968.

M. Selden (1971)
Selden, Mark. *The Yenan Way in Revolutionary China*. Cambridge, MA: Harvard University Press, 1971.

P. Seybolt and G. Chiang, eds. (1979)
Seybolt, Peter, and Gregory K. K. Chiang, eds. *Language Reform in China: Documents and Commentary*. White Plains, NY: M. E. Sharpe, 1979.

J. Sheridan (1975)
Sheridan, James E. *China in Disintegration: The Republican Era in Chinese History, 1912-1949*. New York: Free Press, 1975.

Shi Jingtang et al., eds. (1957)
Shi Jingtang, Zhang Lin, Zhou Qinghe, Bi Zhongjie, Chen Ping, Li Jinggang, eds. *Zhongguo nongye hezuohua yundong shiliao* (Historical Material on the Cooperativization Movement in Chinese Agriculture). 2 volumes. Beijing: Sanlian shudian, 1959.

Short Course
History of the Communist Party of the Soviet Union (Bolshevik). Moscow: Foreign Languages Publishing House, 1951.

Situ Meitang (1956)

Situ, Meitang (See-to Mee Tong). *Zuguo yu huaqiao* (The Motherland and Overseas Chinese). Hong Kong: Wenhui bao, 1956.

Su Xing (1965)

Su, Xing. "Tugai yilai woguo nongcun shehui zhuyi he ziben zhuyi de liang tiao luxian douzeng" (The Two line Struggle Between Socialism and Capitalism in Our Rural Areas Since Land Reform), in *Jingji yanjiu* (Economic Studies), nos. 7-9, 1965.

U.S. Department of State, *Bulletin*

United States Department of State. *Department of State Bulletin*. Weekly, Washington, D.C.: U.S. Government Printing Office.

F. Wakeman (1966)

Wakeman, Frederic Jr. *Strangers at the Gate: Social Disorder in South China, 1839-1861*. Berkeley, CA: University of California Press, 1966.

N. Wales (1952)

Wales, Nym (Helen Snow). *Red Dust: Autobiographies of Chinese Communists as Told to Nym Wales*. Stanford, CA: Stanford University Press, 1952.

K. Walker (Apr.-Jun. 1966)

Walker, Kenneth. "Collectivisation in Retrospect: The 'Socialist High Tide' of Autumn 1955-Spring 1956," in *China Quarterly*, 26 (April-June 1966), pp. 1-43.

B. Watson (1964)

Watson, Burton, trans. and ed. *Han Fei Tzu: Basic Writings*. New York: Columbia University Press, 1964.

Wen shi zhe

Shandong daxue wenshizhe bianji weiyuanhui (Editorial Committee for *Wen shi zhe*, Shangdong University). *Wen shi zhe* (Literature, History, and Philosophy). Quarterly, Jinan: Shandong Renmin chubanshe.

D. Wilson (1971)

Wilson, Dick. *The Long March, 1935: The Epic of Chinese Communism's Survival*. London: Hamish Hamilton, 1971.

Xianggang shibao

Xianggang shibao (Hong Kong Times). Daily, Hong Kong.

Xuexi

Xuexi (Study). Semimonthly, Beijing.

Xuexi wei renmin fuwu

Tian, Jiaying. *Xuexi wei renmin fuwu* (Learning to Serve the People). Beijing: Xuexi zazhi she, April 1954.

Yu Yingshi (1976)

Yu, Yingshi (Yu Ying-shih). *Li shi yu sixiang* (History and Thought). Taipei: Lianjing chuban shiye gongsi, 1976.

Zhang Chukun et al. (1984)

Zhang, Chukun, et al. *Huiyi Chen Jiageng* (In Memory of Chen Jiageng), Beijing: Wenshi ziliao chubanshe, 1984.

Zhang Guotao (1972)

Zhang Guotao (Chang Kuo-t'ao). *The Rise of the Chinese Communist Party: The Autobiography of Chang Kuo-t'ao*, vol. 2. Lawrence. KA: University of Kansas Press, 1972.

Zheng Zhuyuan (1963)

Zheng, Zhuyuan (Cheng Chu-yuan). *Communist China's Economy, 1949-1962: Structural Changes and Crisis*. South Orange, NJ: Seton Hall University Press, 1963.

Zhiyuanjun yingxiong zhuan

Zhiyuanjun yingxiong zhuan (Biographies of Heroes in the Chinese People's Volunteers). Beijing: Renmin chubanshe, 1956.

Zhonggong renming lu

Guoli zhengzhi daxue guozhi guanxi yanjiu zhongxin zhonggong renming lu bianxiu weiyuanhui (Committee for the Compilation of *Zhonggong renming lu* of the Center for International Relations Studies, National Political University). *Zhonggong renming lu* (Biographies of the Chinese Communist Party). Taipei: Center for International Relations Studies, National Political University, 1967 (first edition), 1978 (revised edition).

Zhou Jingwen (1962)

Zhou, Jingwen. *Feng bao shi nian* (The Storm That Raged for Ten Years) (third edition). Hong Kong: Shidai piping she, 1962.